The History of

WAKE FOREST UNIVERSITY
(1983–2005)

VOLUME 6 | THE HEARN YEARS

The History of

WAKE FOREST UNIVERSITY (1983–2005)

VOLUME 6 | THE HEARN YEARS

Samuel Templeman Gladding

WAKE FOREST UNIVERSITY

WINSTON-SALEM, NORTH CAROLINA

Publisher's Cataloging-in-Publication data

Names: Gladding, Samuel T., author.
Title: History of Wake Forest University Volume 6 / Samuel Templeman Gladding.
Description: First hardcover original edition. | Winston-Salem [North Carolina]:
Library Partners Press, 2016. | Includes index.
Identifiers:| LCCN 201591616.
Subjects: LCSH: Wake Forest University–History–United States. |
Hearn, Thomas K. |
Wake Forest University–Presidents–Biography. |
Education, Higher–North Carolina–Winston-Salem. |.
Classification: LCC LD5721.W523. |

First Edition, Second Printing

Copyright © 2016 by Samuel Templeman Gladding

Book jacket photography courtesy of Ken Bennett, Wake Forest University Photographer

ISBN: 978-1-61846-013-4 (cloth)
ISBN: 978-0-69267-100-9 (paperback)

LCCN 201591616

Produced and Distributed By:

Library Partners Press
ZSR Library
Wake Forest University
1834 Wake Forest Road
Winston-Salem, North Carolina 27106

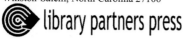

library partners press

a digital publishing imprint

www.librarypartnerspress.org

Manufactured in the United States of America

*To the thousands of Wake Foresters who, through being
"constant and true" to the University's motto,*
Pro Humanitate, *have made the world better,*

*To Claire, my wife, whose patience, support,
kindness, humor, and goodwill encouraged
me to persevere and bring this book into being, and*

*To Tom Hearn, whose spirit and impact still lives at Wake Forest
in ways that influence the University every day and whose
invitation to me to come back to my alma mater positively
changed the course of my life. I will always be grateful!*

CONTENTS

Prologue   xi

1 The Selection, Reactions, a Settling In, and Graylyn, 1983–1984   1

2 Celebration and Reorganization, 1984–1985   21

3 A Bold Move, a Rhodes, and the Comeback, 1985–1986   39

4 The Baptists and the Building, 1986–1987   53

5 A Farewell to Elms and Other Transitions, 1987–1988   71

6 The Presidential Debate, 1988–1989   89

7 Upgrading, Expanding, and Renewing, 1989–1990   107

8 A National Campaign, a New Provost,
the Beck Report, and Cable, 1990–1991   123

9 Starting Over, 1991–1992   139

10 Fifty Years of Women, 1992–1993   157

11 To Dream with One Eye Open, 1993–1994   175

12 A National Nod, Heart Trouble, Basketball,
Plan Approval, and Campaign Success, 1994–1995   191

13 A Pivotal Year of Change, 1995–1996   209

14 The Plan, the Year of the Arts, Prestige, Tragedy,
and the Gates, 1996–1997   229

15 The Year of Religion, Transitions, Construction,
and a New Name, 1997–1998   249

16 Speaking with a Southern Accent:
Culture and Unity, 1998–1999   267

17 A Divinity School, Vienna, Anticipation and
Controversy, 1999–2000   281

18 A Presidential Debate, the Beginning of a
Campaign, and the Z. Smith Reynolds Gift, 2000–2001   305

19 September 11, Reynolda House, and Health
Sciences, 2001–2002   327

20 Transitions, Field Hockey, a Centennial, and
Remembrance, 2002–2003   347

21 Brain Cancer, a Sixth Theme Year, and
Another Field Hockey Title, 2003–2004   367

22 The End and Start of an Era, 2004–2005   387

Epilogue   407

Appendix A   *Faculty and Departments, 1983–2005*   413

Appendix B   *Death of Faculty, Staff, and Trustees, 1984–2005* 565

Appendix C   *Retirees from the Reynolda and Medical
School Campuses, 1984–2005*   573

Appendix D   *Board of Trustees, 1983–2005*   583

Appendix E   *Medallion of Merit, 1984–2005*   588

Appendix F   *Distinguished Alumni Awards, 1983–2005*   590

Appendix G   *Sports Hall of Fame, 1983–1984 to 2004–2005*   593

Appendix H   *Commencement Speakers, 1994–2005*   596

Appendix I   *Baccalaureate Speakers, 1984–2005*   597

Appendix J   *Residential Professors for
Overseas Houses*   599

Appendix K   *Reynolds Research Leaves, 1983–2005*   605

Appendix L   *Average Full-Time Faculty
Salaries during Hearn Years*   615

Appendix M   *Award for Excellence in Advising, 1988–2004*   616

Appendix N   *The Alumni Association/Schoonmaker Faculty Prize for Community Service*   617

Appendix O   *Award for Excellence in Research*   618

Appendix P   *Founders' Day Speakers, 1984–2005*   619

Appendix Q   *Honorary Degrees, 1984–2005*   620

Appendix R   *Jon Reinhardt Award for Excellence in Teaching, 1985–2005*   625

Appendix S   *Reid-Doyle Excellence in Teaching Award, 1983–2005*   626

Appendix T   *The Kulynych Family Omicron Delta Kappa Award Recipients, 1987–2005*   627

Appendix U   *Wake Forest University Graduation and Student Percentages, 1983 and 2005*   628

Appendix V   *Alumni Council Presidents, 1983–2005*   629

Appendix W   *College Board of Visitors Chairs, 1983–2005*   630

Appendix X   *Administrative Personnel, Schools on the Reynolda Campus, 1983–2005*   631

Appendix Y   *Personal Interviews Conducted for the Book*   638

References   639

Index   659

PROLOGUE

Some eras in the life of an institution begin dramatically. Change occurs rapidly and suddenly. Historically stable systems and settings are abruptly uprooted, and disturbance is felt immediately and from then on. At other times, modifications transpire quietly, almost unnoticed, at least initially. They are seen as benign; a few notable personalities come or go, and ways of working shift slightly.

The beginning of what would become the twenty-two-year Hearn administration has been described both ways. Wake Forest University's twelfth president was an unknown outsider to most people in North Carolina, especially to those associated with the institution. Hearn was a forty-five-year-old Vice President at the University of Alabama at Birmingham (UAB). He was swept into the Wake Forest presidency in a flawed search process with a leak to the press. From the beginning, he had to prove himself a man of all seasons, not just some.

The task was challenging. The institution was on the rise. Hearn's predecessors had been visionaries and excellent stewards of the college and the university into which it grew. Faculty and staff were dedicated and caring. Students were smart and engaged. The atmosphere of *Pro Humanitate* was supported by traditions and generations of graduates who literally invested their lives for the good of society. Modesty and friendliness were part of the fabric of the University.

This book does not focus on the man, Thomas K. Hearn Jr., but on Wake Forest University, its people, and its place in the world. As in any story, some characters play a more prominent role than others, and certain events are more notable. Overall, however, the reported challenges, struggles, triumphs, and changes and the people who acted in them affect us now and will influence generations to come. As Gavin Stevens says in William Faulkner's novel *Requiem for a Nun* (1951), "The past is never dead. It's not even past." The present and future of Wake Forest University will continue to be shaped by what took place from 1983–2005.

A Brief History of the Writing of this Book:
A Saga I Could Never Make Up

I never intended to write a history book, let alone a history of my alma mater. I was a history major at Wake Forest and fortunate enough to have classes with Ed Wilson and Bynum Shaw, who wrote the previous two University histories of the Tribble years and the Scales years. However, even though I loved and still love history, most of my professional life has been spent clinically and academically as a mental health counselor. I say "most" because, for a few years, I was more an administrator than a counselor or an academic. I served Wake Forest as Assistant to the President for special projects from 1990–1997 and as Associate Provost from 1998–2007. I thought of myself as merely taking a sabbatical from my chosen full-time profession, and, like Ed Wilson, I continued to teach one class a semester and to write.

Thus I was a bit stunned when Tom Hearn asked me in 2006 to write the book about his years as Wake Forest's President. I had written a couple dozen books by that time, mainly counseling texts and a semi-autobiography. I was not a stranger to writing or to putting together original materials in a coherent and readable way. How hard could such a project be? I had been in the Hearn administration for fifteen of its twenty-two years. Now, nine years later, I know the magnitude of Tom's request. The project was more than I envisioned and maybe even more than any of my predecessors—Paschal, Shaw, and Wilson—thought when they started their journeys to capture an era.

I began by examining President Hearn's papers, specifically his correspondence. He began his presidency at a time when letters were still the most popular means of personal expression, but little did I suspect that he had written or received 3,690 of them. Over a two-year period, I read every one and became new best friends with the archives room staff on the sixth floor in the Z. Smith Reynolds Library. I also began a series of interviews with people who were prominent in the administration and in the Winston-Salem community at the time. The President Emeritus was my first target, and I was able to have three sit-down conversations with Tom before he died in 2008. Carolyn Dow, his assistant, was very helpful in this process, as was Sandra Boyette. I followed up with twenty-one other interviews, some as recent as 2015. I wanted to get as clear a picture as possible of the times and the people.

My next task was to read all of the issues of *Wake Forest Magazine* published during this period, with four to six issues each year. Janet Williamson was a jewel in making sure I had access to each issue, and Alumni Hall became my favorite hangout. In fact, some staff members think I work in their building. Then I went on to all the print volumes of *Window on Wake Forest* to get a snapshot of internal events and concerns. Janet let me take materials home once, on the condition I would treat them as well as I did my wife. I complied.

In the midst of my research, my body decided to have a bit of a breakdown. I will not go into the details, but I learned to love the Wake Forest School of Medicine. Unfortunately, however, medical conditions slowed my research. The good news is that in the midst of these medical complications, I discovered that some of the materials I needed could be found on the Wake Forest website and elsewhere on the Internet.

Working in the archives of the Z. Smith Reynolds Library

Before this discovery, I was on the sixth floor of the library reading the *Old Gold and Black* from 1983 on. Now, I could read the *Old Gold and Black* online either in my office or at home. I read approximately 440 issues of the Wake Forest weekly publication (which covers the campus like the magnolias) and then examined the twenty-two *Howlers* from the period. When I had a question, I emailed former students, staff, and faculty, and most were quick to respond, usually with more information than I had requested. Finally, the process stopped as I gathered everything I needed and put it together during the last half of 2014 and first six months of 2015. More than seventy people assisted me, and I appreciate them all. I have listed them under acknowledgements, but a few stand out.

Susan Faust is first for devoting so much time to this project. Susan tracked down faculty who worked at Wake Forest during this era. She also found or copied photographs of events and people during the Hearn years. We exchanged boxes of Susan Mullally's photographs, which Ed Wilson also stored for over a year, and Susan had great suggestions for materials to include in this book. Next, and on par with Susan, Julie Edelson copyedited each chapter. Her patience and professionalism were simply amazing. I think she turned a sow's ear into a silk purse, and I can only express my deepest thanks to her. Janet Williamson spent literally dozens of hours with me finding materials and setting up my access to them in Alumni Hall. For her sensitivity to my needs and ability to provide what I needed, I am most grateful.

Someone who would probably not take credit but who deserves it is Provost Rogan Kersh. Without his financial and psychological support, I would still be writing. He provided the means to finish this project in a timely way. I also want to thank President Nathan Hatch for authorizing the writing of this book. Bill Kane in the Z. Smith Reynolds Library was excited about the project and provided a way to get from the manuscript to the final form of the book in an efficient and interesting way. His innovative spirit and enthusiasm helped me get over the last hump.

Finally, I want to thank my wife, Claire, for her patience, support, humor, and good will. I spent many nights and weekends writing in a makeshift office in the basement of our house instead of spending time with her. I am not sure I would have been as understanding as she was, especially when I told her I was writing this work as an expression of my love for Wake Forest, and that the reward would be simply in capturing and sharing an era with others.

Structure of the Book

This history is separated into sections that cover each year that Tom Hearn was President of Wake Forest. Within each chapter, I start from the overriding "big" stories of the year—generally, three or four stories, once just two, once five. Then I focus on the stories that reflected or affected academics, administration and staff, athletics, the arts, campus and student life, facilities, finances, and alumni. Finally, I sum up the overall impact of the year. I know some will believe some stories deserve more ink, and some events or people could or should have been left out or added. I accept such criticism.

I believe a history must be filled with stories. I do not just list names and facts but tell as many stories as I can. Some are serious and some, particularly those involving students, are humorous or inspiring. Tying all this material together is a developmental thread: the University's movement from regional to national status. I concentrate on the Reynolda campus and events and people in the undergraduate college. I did not cover happenings in the professional schools, especially the medical school, in great depth for a simple reason: they each warrant a history of their own. I am also following my predecessors, who focused on the college and its advancement. Note that I have been democratic in not using prefixes, such as Dr., and abjured footnotes in favor of simple, in-text references when necessary. Scholars wishing to find more specific information should consult the reference list, where they will find an abundance of sources.

Wake Forest and Me

I transferred to Wake Forest at the end of my sophomore year. I was told by one of my best high school friends, Ed Hallman, who was already enrolled, that "Wake Forest is the next best place to Heaven." Being religious—I intended to be a minister—I thought Ed's recommendation was about as good as it gets. I was not disappointed. The college—still a college in 1965—welcomed and accepted me. The grandfather of my roommate, Jeff Kincheloe, had been roommates with my mother's father, Samuel Templeman, at the University of Richmond at the turn of the twentieth century. I thought our pairing was a positive sign, and I immediately fell in love with the institution. I was treated with respect and fairness. I thought the emphasis on honor, friendship, and service to others was noble. I found the sometimes good-natured rowdiness of the place refreshing and the seriousness of living *Pro Humanitate* inspiring. I liked the rivalry of the Atlantic Coast Conference (ACC) and my interactions with professors and friends. On many nights, I sat quietly on the Quad and soaked up what I considered the air of goodness and kindness that descended from the history of those who preceded me. My experiences at Wake Forest motivated me to be better.

Now, I have been given a chance to give back. I hope you enjoy what I have written and learn from it. The Hearn administration was transformative: an exciting, moving, and turbulent time. So much happened in so many places that only the essence of events and people can be captured in a book. Perhaps a movie would have been more enlightening, but it would have to be a very long movie, and filling in the back stories would be impossible. So page through a time that is gone but will ever remain.

Samuel Templeman Gladding
Winston-Salem, North Carolina
June 30, 2015

Acknowledgments

The individuals listed below helped me in multiple ways. I could not have written this book without their input.

Allman, Martha
Anderson, John P.
Bennett, Ken
Bennett, Stephanie
Bergesen, Glenn
Best, Deborah
Bland, Doug
Boyette, Sandra
Brown, David G.
Bumgarner, Steve
Calhoun, Brian
Carter, Stuart
Corbett, Leon
Cox, Kevin
Diaz, Nancy
Denlinger, Kyle
Dow, Carolyn
Edelson, Julie
Escott, Paul
Fansler, Craig
Faust, Susan
Flowers, Kim
Ford, Mike
Frey, Don
Fulton, Becki
Gerardy, Mary
Geyer, Granice
Gibson, Carole
Gindrich, Cindy
Griffith, Ross
Griffin, Julie
Guastaferro, Tomma
Gung, Donna

Hagy, David
Hale, Toby
Hallman, Ed
Harkey, Melanie
Harriger, Katy
Harris, Catherine
Hatch, Nathan
Hatfield, Weston
Hearn III, Thomas K.
Hearn, Barbara
Hearn, Thomas K., Jr.
Hearn, Laura
Henson, Maria
Hughes, Anita
Hume, Jon
Joyner, Bill
Kairoff, Claudia
Kane, Bill
Kersh, Rogan
King, Kerry
King, Milton
Klein, Scott
Leonard, Bill
Levy, David
Locklair, Dan
Louden, Allan
Maine, Barry
McConnico, Kelly M.
McNally, Minta
Medlin, John
Morgan, Reid
Mulder, Megan
Mullally, Susan

Mullen, Tom
O'Brien, Joanne
Parker, Lynn
Petersen, Rebecca
Phillips, Tom
Poovey, Cherin
Puckett, Jenny
Rowell, Chelice
Shelton, Lillian
Shutt, Steve
Smith, Mike
Street, Becki
Sutton, Lynn
Taylor, Tom
Teague, Marie
Tedford, Beth
Vidrine, Robert
Walker, Cheryl
Wellman, Ron
Wells, Bill
Wells, Byron
West, Ken
Wilkerson, Jack
Williamson, Janet
Wilson, Ed
Wilson, Emily
Wilson, Tylee
Womack, Hu
Wood-Parker, Priscilla
Zanish-Belcher, Tanya
Zick, Ken

CHAPTER ONE
1983–1984

The Selection, Reactions, a Settling In, and Graylyn

Always there is the determination to make our great visions for this school into reality. I have yet to comprehend our special Wake Forest mystique, but this year has been a grand induction.

Thomas K. Hearn Jr., May 21, 1984;
Charge to the Graduates, Wake Forest University Commencement

In the summer of its 149th year, Wake Forest University made a major leadership decision that would transform the institution over the next twenty-two years. The Board of Trustees appointed Thomas K. Hearn Jr. as the University's twelfth president on June 23, 1983. More than two hundred educators were in the applicant pool, but, as an editorial in the *Greensboro Daily News* (June 29, 1983), "New Man for Wake Forest," noted, "Hearn was not among them. His reputation prompted the University to recruit him."

Hearn was forty-five years old, just a few days shy of his forty-sixth birthday in July, and for six years he had served as Senior Vice President of the University of Alabama at Birmingham (UAB)'s College of Arts and Sciences. He had earned high marks as "a forceful administrator" and for "strengthening the liberal arts curricula." He was also praised for his organizational and fundraising abilities, but he was almost unknown in North Carolina academic circles. At Wake Forest, no one knew him except Philosophy Professor Marcus Hester, who went to graduate school with him at Vanderbilt and recommended him to the search committee.

Hearn and former President James Ralph Scales, who had served since 1967, had much in common. Both had strong Baptist backgrounds, were over six feet tall, enjoyed playing tennis, and were not from North Carolina. They had both been senior administrators at public universities before coming to Wake Forest, and they were

Newly appointed President Thomas K. Hearn in front of Wait Chapel

deep, reflective thinkers in their scholastic disciplines. However, their interests and the paths they took personally, academically, and administratively diverged. Scales, the historian, with a quick wit and personal charm, first made his administrative mark as President of Oklahoma Baptist University and next as a Vice President at Oklahoma State University. Hearn was a philosopher, an expert on David Hume, with a scholarly interest in the poet Robert Frost and a love for the pop lyrics of Simon and Garfunkel. A native of the Sand Mountain region of Alabama, after receiving his doctorate from Vanderbilt, he taught for ten years at the College of William and Mary. At that time, sensing a chance to move his family closer to relatives, he accepted an academic position in the newly created UAB Department of Philosophy. He ascended rapidly through the administrative ranks as Chair, Dean, and Senior Vice President. Like Scales, he was ambitious and wanted to be a university president. Unlike Scales, he was an introvert and often initially perceived as somewhat distant.

Coming from an urban university, Hearn practiced a style of interaction that was not familiar to Wake Forest. He was direct, aggressive, and oriented toward the big picture. He spent less time with faculty than his predecessor had and more time with Winston-Salem's major corporate executives. He reasoned that Wake Forest would only prosper if its community prospered. Furthermore, he knew that while Wake Forest was rich in heritage, its endowment was weaker than that of most comparable institutions. By cultivating relationships with the affluent and influential in the Piedmont Triad, he hoped to benefit all.

Reactions to the Appointment

Due to other commitments, Hearn could not officially begin his duties until October 1, but response to his appointment was immediate. Friends and colleagues in Alabama conveyed congratulations tinged with sadness. The first telephone call the new president received was from Bert Shore, Wake Forest College Class of 1937, who lived in Birmingham. Hearn would recount Shore's warm welcome on later occasions: "I don't know you, Hearn, but I love you because I love Wake Forest."

Gerald Johnson, Editor Emeritus of the *Baltimore Sun* and Wake Forest's most famous non-athletic alumnus at the time, simply wished the new president well. Dozens of other letters and notes flooded Hearn's mailbox. Wake Forest Trustees

C.C. Hope and Glenn Orr and past Trustee Chair Leon Rice addressed matters related to the University; those from University of North Carolina President William Friday, Duke President Terry Sanford, North Carolina Baptist State Convention officials, such as Cecil Ray, and other dignitaries and business leaders in North Carolina and Winston-Salem, such as R.J. Reynolds Industries' CEO J. Tylee Wilson, were more formal and broader in scope. Some letters carried requests for jobs and interviews. Perhaps the most interesting came from Mary Garber, sportswriter for the *Winston-Salem Journal*, on June 28, 1983, not only requesting an interview on intercollegiate athletics, but including her set of questions. The same day's mail brought the Reverend Warren Carr's invitation to consider joining the Wake Forest Baptist Church. Hearn, now a practicing Presbyterian, had a Baptist heritage that, Carr recognized, might be revived. Most media and ministers had noted that Hearn would be the first non-Baptist to lead Wake Forest.

Among the many letters from colleagues, associates, and leaders in Alabama were congratulations from UAB President S. Richardson Hill, U.S. Senator Howell Heflin, *Birmingham Post-Herald* editor David W. Brown, and Thomas Bartlett, Chancellor of the University of Alabama. Higdon C. Roberts Jr., a professor in the UAB School of Business, wrote on June 23:

> When you first became Vice President, I was not happy about it. I thought you lacked experience and were naïve, both in internal University politics and the external political system. What I didn't count on was how smart you are and how quickly you could learn. More importantly, I underestimated your integrity and commitment to education.
>
> I am glad I was wrong. I hate like hell to see you go. I think you've become a first-rate academic administrator and I've enjoyed working with you and for you. In addition to this professional respect, I like you as a man.
>
> The very best in your new position.

Tom Hearn answered most of these letters, regardless of their source and, in the process, acknowledged that he felt good about being named to his new position. He mentioned in his return letters, especially to his friends, that his wife, Barbara, was also "very happy" about the move. Of their three children, son Will was in the new undergraduate honors program at UAB; daughter Lindsay was an undergraduate at the University of Texas, Austin; and son Thomas was finishing his MBA/MPH at UAB and, in spring 1984, would do an internship at a hospital in Charlotte.

Inauguration

Although Tom Hearn could not leave his UAB position until October, the Inauguration Committee made extensive plans for the actual event on November 4. The committee was chaired by Bill Joyner (Vice President for Development). Members were Leon Corbett (University Counsel), William H. Flowe Sr. (University Alumni Association President), Ralph S. Fraser (German), Barbara Hearn (for the Hearn family), Robert M. Helm Jr. (Philosophy), C.C. Hope (Chair, Board of Trustees), Beth Norbrey Hopkins (for Reynolda Campus alumni), Richard Janeway (Vice President for

Medical Affairs), Donna I. Lambeth (for the Winston-Salem community), Joanne O'Brien (Student Government President), and Edwin G. Wilson (Provost). Sandra Connor (Director of Foundations Relations) coordinated inauguration preparations.

The Hearns moved their belongings in mid-September, and on October 3, the President wrote to the Board of Trustees, "This is to let you know that the new administration at Wake Forest is in place as of Saturday." The letter went on to recount a hectic schedule of University, alumni, and Baptist State Convention meetings; to praise Ralph and Betty Scales for their hospitality; and to recount toward the end that "at 7 a.m. on Saturday, the student body had black and gold balloons delivered to the house by a clown!" On October 4, Hearn wrote A.C. Reid, a former member of the Philosophy Department, that it was his first working day in the office.

On the official inauguration day, a Friday, the day started out cloudy with light rain, but the sun came out in the early afternoon, and by 2 p.m. the sky was clear. Barbara Hearn commissioned Dan Locklair, then an assistant professor of music, to compose an anthem for the occasion. The result was an anthem for organ, choir, brass, and timpani entitled *The Fabric of Creation*, with words written by Marty Lentz, University editor. The brass fanfare that preceded the ceremony, and the processional and recessional—both for organ and brass—were written by local composer Douglas Borwick. The audience was so impressed by Borwick's recessional that they remained seated and listened to the music even after the academic procession had left the building.

Various constituencies brought President-elect Hearn greetings before the new president spoke. In order, the greetings came from Joanne O'Brien ('84), speaking for the students; Germaine Brée (LLD '69), speaking for the faculty; William H. Flowe Sr. ('41), bringing greetings from the alumni; William Friday (LLD '57), bringing greetings from colleges and universities; Wayne Corpening, speaking on behalf of the City of Winston-Salem; and James B. Hunt (LLD '80), bringing greetings from the State of North Carolina. Hearn then delivered his inaugural address, emphasizing the dual nature of the celebration by saying: "This is both Inauguration and Sesquicentennial, a time to anticipate the future and to honor the past." He quoted President Truman's words at the 1951 groundbreaking ceremony for the new campus, noting that a college is an institution dedicated to the future: "That faith and that hope we reaffirm here today." He singled out the "special Wake Forest character" and "above all ... the character of personal concern we take in each other." He also thanked former President Scales for his contributions

Newly appointed President Thomas K. Hearn and former President James Ralph Scales share the podium at the inauguration of Hearn

and his friendship and advocated for continuing international education, research, and the cultivation of imagination as well as intellect. Approximately one hundred minutes after the ceremony began, President Hearn and President Emeritus Scales emerged from Wait Chapel and led the procession across the Quad to Reynolda Hall. There the faculty assembled on the steps for the first faculty photograph in more than fifty years.

First Impressions

In a front-page article on the new president in the *Old Gold and Black* on September 30, 1983, Hearn told reporter Marjorie Miller he planned to preserve the "things we are doing right." Among those strengths, he saw a "real sense of intellectual and academic community" with "many exciting graduate programs …." He thought the faculty was strong and devoted to academic freedom and that the trustees formed an unusually loyal and committed group. He went on to say: "Everyone seems to agree that there is a special spirit about Wake Forest …. There is really a family feeling about this place." He said he felt fortunate to follow such a "worthy man" as James Ralph Scales.

Hearn indicated in the article that he had been given only one particular mandate by the trustees. The only thing the trustees requested was that a planning effort be initiated. The new president intended to carry out this mandate by creating a new position: Vice President of Planning and Placement. In doing so, he would address concerns from the trustees and also those in a report titled "The Year 2000." In the Year 2000 report, a committee representing faculty and administrators from each of the major academic units had assessed the University's prospects for the millennium and what needed to be done. Thus, without other specific directives, Tom Hearn took his place as Wake Forest's president with imagination, vision, and plenty of new ideas.

A Flawed Presidential Search

No sooner had Hearn been appointed President of Wake Forest than the University began to bubble with criticism, not of the man, but of the search process. While pleased with the selection, Scales said the procedure did not live up to the expectations of several groups that believed they had been promised some role or other in the search. He claimed that he himself did not know what was going on and that the selection committee did not follow a faculty resolution passed in December 1982 to follow the same procedure used in the 1966–1967 search that selected him. He stated that the Chair of the Board of Trustees, C.C. Hope, Vice Chair of the Board of First Union National Bank in Charlotte and Secretary of Commerce for North Carolina, should not have chaired the search committee for a new university president. At the same time, he acknowledged that there were no uniform procedures for selecting college and university administrators.

Assistant Professor of Political Science Don Schoonmaker ('60) also weighed in on the presidential search. He stated that the major defect was a lack of clearly specified guidelines and procedures. A ten-member faculty committee had advised the trustees' search committee, but no written document enumerated the desired qualifications of the next University President, nor how the search should be conducted.

The faculty advisory committee met with the trustee search committee early in the nomination process and again in early May and early June, just before the announcement. It asked to interview the final four candidates: R. Kirby Godsey, President of Mercer University; Jasper D. Memory Jr., Vice Provost of the graduate school at North Carolina State University; William E. Hull, pastor of the First Baptist Church of Shreveport, Louisiana; and Thomas K. Hearn Jr.

The request was not granted because the names of these four candidates were leaked to the press. There was no time to conduct interviews, and the candidates could not afford to have their interest in the position known by their current employers. The faculty advisory committee was made aware of the fourteen applicants whom the trustees had rejected; overall, eighteen were explored in depth. Because Hearn was selected overnight after the leak, both faculty and student advisory groups felt left out and angry.

Sesquicentennial

In his inaugural address, Hearn referred to the 150th anniversary of Wake Forest. The celebration began with the Sesquicentennial Concert on January 29, 1984. The Winston-Salem Symphony, featuring Assistant Professor of Music Louis Goldstein on piano, flute instructor Kathryn Levy, and voice instructor Teresa Radomski as soloists, premiered a commissioned orchestral work, "Phoenix and Again," by Assistant Professor of Music Dan Locklair. The free concert was conceived as a way to give back to the Winston-Salem community for its many years of support.

Members of the LYNKS society carry a banner celebrating Wake Forest's 150th anniversary

On February 3, 1984, the day on which Wake Forest was founded a century and a half earlier, classes were cancelled, and John W. Chandler, president of Williams College and a Wake Forest alumnus, spoke to an audience of students, staff, faculty, and alumni in Wait Chapel on the sesquicentennial theme of "Faith and Reason." Other special events to honor the occasion followed. The most widely attended was a trek back to the old campus on April 15, 1984. More than two thousand students, alumni, faculty, and staff took part in the all-day celebration. President Hearn would later say his sesquicentennial experiences were like enrolling in "History of Wake Forest 101."

Academics

President Hearn addresses the crowd on the old Wake Forest campus in the spring of 1984

One of the first challenges Wake Forest and its new president faced at the beginning of the academic year was the 1983 Law School graduates' disappointing 74 percent passage rate on the bar exam, the lowest of the state's five law schools. Corrective measures were discussed both within and outside

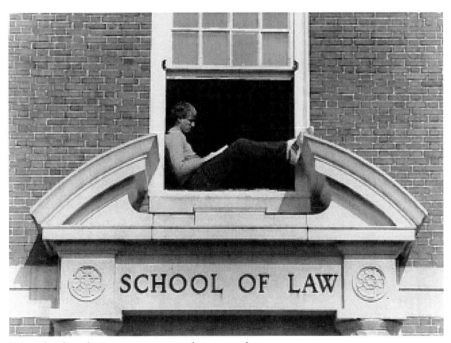

Law school student enjoys a sunny place to study

the University: more financial support to the Law School and addressing difficult academic and personnel questions were at the top of the list. As a first step, Development Officer Julius Corpening ('49), who worked under both Law Dean John Scarlett and Vice President of Development Bill Joyner, was appointed to address the school's critical capital needs.

In December 1983, the Board of Trustees took the following action, as outlined by Hearn to Robert Caldwell, Chair, Board of Trustees' Investment Committee, in a February 10 memo:

> The University should move, over a ten-year span, to provide an endowment of at least $10,000,000 (or its equivalent monetary support), for the School of Law, drawn from all available resources. [As president] it will be my intention to deal with this directive through the regular mechanisms of the budget allocation process rather than by placing restrictions upon endowment. I will make certain that the academic needs of the School of Law are considered as part of the regular process of resource allocation leading to the preparation of the budgets.

The needs of the College were comparatively minor. They mainly revolved around enriching and updating the curriculum. The boldest innovation was adding a Women's Studies minor in the fall of 1983. It consisted of an introductory core course, Humanities 121, and five other courses, at least two in the social sciences and two in the humanities. Other courses would be distributed among three departments to produce a total of twenty-four credits. The required introductory course was taught for the first time in spring semester 1984 by Associate Professor of Art Margaret Supplee Smith and Assistant Professor of Education Linda Nielsen. The minor created two new courses and drew on other courses.

Another change honored the legacy of those who had contributed substantially to the University's good. The annual Wake Forest Dixie Classic Debate Tournament was renamed in honor of Professor of Speech Communication Franklin R. Shirley, the institution's first debate coach (1948–1967). During his tenure, the debate team won the majority of its matches, acquired four national superior ratings, and advanced to the semi-final round of the National Debate Tournament. While still teaching, Shirley served two terms as mayor of Winston-Salem.

As an interdisciplinary academic event, the Wake Forest Tocqueville Forum on Contemporary Public Affairs was supported by the National Endowment for the Humanities (NEH) as a co-sponsor and organizer of the first of four colloquia held across the nation in celebration of the U.S. Constitution's 200th birthday. An array of speakers arrived on campus the week of April 9, starting with NEH Chair William Bennett. A number of panels emphasizing scholarly and public dialogue on the Constitution were held thereafter.

Also in early April 1984, the North Carolina Political Science Association convened on campus. Over two days, April 6–7, panels made up of association members discussed various topics in American, international, and comparative politics; public administration and public policy; women and the law; and the 1984 elections. Professor of Political Science Jack Fleer was the event organizer.

To add to the excitement of the time, albeit in a different way, Davis Field hosted a two-day reenactment of the encampment of eighteenth-century American and British troops on April 6–7. Six regiments participated in the program, which included military, drill, and craft demonstrations. According to the April 12 issue of the *Old Gold and Black*, it brought the "18th century to life."

Most other academic news in the college involved promotions and personnel changes. Rick Heatley was hired as Director of the Office of Educational Planning and Placement, while its former Director and Assistant Dean of the College Toby Hale was promoted to Associate Dean. History Professor Howell Smith became the pre-law advisor, and Patricia Johansson became the foreign study advisor. Among notable faculty achievements and milestones, retired President James Ralph Scales became the University's first Worrell Professor of Anglo-American Studies, and Robert M. Helm ('39), member of the philosophy department since 1940, was appointed the second Worrell Professor of Philosophy. Biology Professor Ronald V. Dimock became President-Elect of the North Carolina Academy of Science.

Administration and Staff

Few changes were made to senior administration upon Hearn's arrival. Hearn was aware that former President Scales had assembled a competent team, and he was not anxious to cause disruptions. In fact, as Hearn recalled some years later, his first call was to Provost Ed Wilson, asking him to stay. Hearn knew Wilson had a comprehensive, long-term knowledge of the institution and realized what a valuable ally and confidant Wilson could be. Wilson graciously agreed to stay on.

Next, Hearn sought someone to fill the new position of Vice President of Planning and Administration. On October 6, he wrote to John Anderson, a civil engineer by training and Dean and Director of UAB Special Studies and Continuing Education, to inform him that UAB President S. Richardson Hill had nominated him for the Wake Forest position. Hearn encouraged him to apply by the October 21 deadline. On November 18, Anderson accepted the offer extended eight days earlier to start January 1, 1984.

At the beginning of 1984, the president's inner circle was composed of:

- Provost Edwin G. Wilson;
- John G. Willard, Vice President and Treasurer;
- Richard Janeway, Vice President for Health Affairs and Dean of the Bowman Gray School of Medicine;
- Bill Joyner, Vice President for Development, who was promoted to Vice President for University Relations in March;
- Vice President for Administration and Planning John P. Anderson;
- University Counsel Leon Corbett, who was appointed University Secretary on June 1, while remaining Secretary of the Board of Trustees;

John Anderson

- Henry Stroupe, Dean of the Graduate School;
- Director of Athletics Gene Hooks;
- John D. Scarlett, Dean of the Law School;
- Robert W. Shively, Dean of the Babcock School; and
- Director of Communications Russell Brantley.

One other administrative action taken at this time had an immediate and long-term impact on both the University and the wider community. Hearn founded "Leadership Winston-Salem," patterned on the Leadership Birmingham program in which he had been heavily involved before coming to Wake Forest. In a letter to Albert Butler on February 8, Hearn wrote: "I need your good name and influence to recruit a Board strong enough to ensure the financial viability of the program, and to guarantee that our first class of participants is outstanding." Enlisting trustees and city corporate leaders, Butler, along with J. Tylee Wilson and John G. Medlin, recruited new leaders to assess opportunities and resources and to establish new networks to meet community needs. The first Executive Director, Deborah Martin, was hired on May 14, her salary paid through the Chamber of Commerce. Leadership Winston-Salem, a connection between the University and the community, became a reality.

In early January, John Anderson announced the promotion of Lu Leake from Dean of Women to Assistant Vice President for Administration and Planning. He appointed former Dean of Men Mark Reece to Dean of Students. Both positions were new, and the earlier deanships were eliminated, their duties assigned to the Dean of Students position, which Anderson oversaw.

Effective March 1, the following administrative changes took place:

President Hearn and Reynolda Campus Vice Presidents, 1984. Seated from left to right: Dick Janeway, Tom Hearn, and Ed Wilson; standing from left to right: Bill Joyner, Leon Corbett, John Anderson, and John Willard

- Ross Griffith became Planning Analyst and Director of Space Management in the Office of the Vice President for Administration and Planning. His former duties in the area of affirmative action and equal opportunity were transferred to the Office of the University Counsel.

Mark Reece and Lu Leake

- The Office of the Director of Denominational Relations was transferred to the Office of Development, now called the Office of University Relations.
- Chaplain Ed Christman started reporting to the Vice President of Administration and Planning, who now oversaw Student Life activities.

In other events, two administrators were recognized by extramural organizations in 1984:

- Margaret R. Perry, Registrar, was elected President of the Southern Association of Collegiate Registrars and Admissions Officers.
- Rich T. (Dick) Clay, Director of Wake Forest University Stores, was elected President of the College Stores Association of North Carolina.

Athletics

The 1983–1984 athletic teams had their usual ups and downs. Most had average years with about equal numbers of wins and losses. Outstanding performers included Laird Dunlop, who finished third in the ACC tennis championships; Brenda Corrie, who captured second place as the women's tennis team placed third in the ACC tournament; and Kevin Bunn, who set a new ACC career homerun mark with thirteen round-trips. The men's golf team finished second in the ACC tournament, with Jerry Haas capturing an individual second-place finish.

Beyond individual recognition, three teams stood out: the men's basketball team and the men's and women's track teams. The men's basketball team had to play most of its ACC games in the Greensboro Coliseum because the Winston-Salem Memorial Coliseum was deteriorating. While the distance from campus was inconvenient for fans, the team did quite well. On February 8, Carl Tacy became only the second Wake Forest basketball coach to win two hundred games. Later in the season, he led the team to the NCAA Tournament, where the Deacons defeated DePaul 73–71 in overtime on March 23. The victory ended the career of Hall of Fame Coach Ray Meyer and resulted in what was described as the "greatest Quad roll in Wake Forest history." The win sent Wake to the regional finals, where the Deacons lost to Houston but ended the season with a record-setting twenty-three

The elm trees on the upper quad were decorated in toilet paper after Wake Forest defeated DePaul 73-71

wins. After the season, the team was honored both on campus and by Winston-Salem Mayor Wayne Corpening, who officially declared Wednesday, April 11, "Demon Deacon Basketball Day."

At the end of the track season, the men's and women's track teams had set and broken twelve school records, with nine by the women. Among the outstanding athletes for departing Head Coach Ramsay Thomas were first-year students Karen Dunn, Maria Merritt, a Reynolds Scholar, and Mike Palmer; sophomore Kim Lanane; junior Becky Corts; and senior David Crowe. Although both teams came in sixth in the ACC meet, the performance was the men's best in a decade; in all earlier meets, they had finished last. The ACC meet was only the women's second. The teams also qualified two runners for the U.S. TAC Junior Nationals during the June Olympic Trials in Los Angeles.

An unofficial athletic team, the Equestrian Club co-hosted Winston-Salem's first intercollegiate horse show on March 1 at the Cozy Fox Farm. Co-sponsors were Duke, University of North Carolina, and Salem College. The twelve-member team placed fourth out of the ten teams competing. Marianna Schafer won first place in her jumping class, and Kaye Shearin placed second in her beginning walk-trot-canter class.

Notable changes in the department of athletics included:

- Amy Geitner ('81) was named Women's Golf Coach, replacing Marge Crisp;
- Phil Warshauer resigned as Sports Information Director to enter private business, while David Van Pelt took over duties as Sports Promotion Director;

- Assistant Football Coach Dennis Haglan was named Assistant Athletic Director, replacing Jon LeCrone; and
- Charlie Patterson, former Vice Chancellor of Development at UNC-Greensboro (UNCG), became Wake Forest's first Assistant Athletic Director for Development on May 1. He supervised all athletic fundraising, particularly endowments and large capital gifts.

The Arts

The University Theatre presented Mary Chase's play *Harvey*, Shakespeare's *As You Like It*, A.R. Gurney's *The Dining Room*, Paul Osborn's *Mornings at Seven*, a dinner theater (co-sponsored by the College Union), and Gilbert and Sullivan's opera *The Mikado*.

The men's basketball team defeats DePaul in the NCAA Tournament

The Wake Forest Equestrian Club, spring 1984

Shakespeare's As You Like It *was performed in the Scales Fine Arts Center*

The Artists Series, directed by David Levy (Music), presented violinist Shlomo Mintz, soprano Roberta Peters, pianist Aldo Ciccolini, the Concert Royal, the New Baroque Dance Company, the Kalichstein-Laredo-Robinson Trio, and the Canadian Brass.

Campus and Student Life

According to Carolyn Dow, President Hearn's administrative assistant, who came with him from UAB, one of Hearn's first actions was to take both the student government president and the *Old Gold and Black* editor to lunch. Hearn worked with student leaders and secured their opinions on everything. He depended on them for candid feedback and wanted them to become more involved in the life of the institution. Many of the student leaders that year were women: Joanne O'Brien, President of the Student Government Association; Stephanie Houser, President of the College Union; Laura Walker, Editor of the *Old Gold and Black*; and Carolyn Smith, Editor-in-Chief of *The Howler*.

Students were concerned about the University's restrictive visitation policy. It changed on March 19, when open visitation was extended to weeknights and weekend hours in both men's and women's residence halls. Student party hours were extended in February.

Student Government President Joanne O'Brien

The new administration also sought to ease the stress of final exams in the spring semester. In a May 7 memo to John Anderson, Hearn instructed him "to make extra [study] places available during the exam period" and to have food services make a special effort "to stay open extra hours during exams."

Other matters were not as easy to address. For instance, in a February 13 memorandum to the Executive Committee of the Board of Trustees concerning alcohol consumption, Hearn advised planning a drug and alcohol education program as well as adopting honest, reasonable, and enforceable safety practices. The Board's Student Life Committee and faculty were charged with these responsibilities. Meanwhile, Hearn had to answer letters from a number of Baptist ministers and others when the *Old Gold and Black* began accepting advertisements for alcohol products. To these critics, he pointed out that campus newspaper editors enjoyed the same freedoms as other editors. In a February 23 letter to Guy C. Rogers, Chair of the Evangelism Committee of the North Carolina Baptist General Board, he commented that Wake Forest did not "sponsor or endorse any product or service advertised in our publications."

The Wake Forest student body remained predominantly white and middle class. Herman Eure (Ph.D., '74), Director of the Office of Minority Affairs and Assistant Professor of Biology, reported in the March 30 issue of the *Old Gold and Black* that "Blacks currently compose about 3.8 percent of the undergraduate student population."

In a noteworthy scholarly event, Edward K. (Ted) Bilich was named a Truman Scholar, and the first four Reynolds scholars, Jeanette Sorrell, Brian Rollfinke, Laura Novatny, and Rogan Kersh, returned to campus from productive summers conducting research both abroad and elsewhere in the United States.

WAKE radio celebrated its official kick-off as a completely student-run campus station on Monday, March 26, from 3 to 5 p.m. Promotions Director Shari Hubbard organized the festivities and told the *Old Gold and Black* in a March 23 interview that she hoped to have WAKE playing from dorm windows around the Quad and a large speaker in front of Reynolda Hall.

> WAKE will be on the air weekdays from 7 a.m. to 2 a.m. The morning hours will feature approximately 50 percent new music. The remaining time will be filled with requests and DJs' choices of mainstream such as the Rolling Stones, Genesis, and [other bands] but in the evening, DJs are free to program whatever they please, from funk to punk.

An underground newspaper, *Tunnels*, appeared on campus, too. It stated that it aimed to encourage "free thought" among students. It lasted only a year.

Lisa Birnbach, author of *The Official College Preppy Handbook*, gave the opening College Union lecture on September 13 in Wait Chapel. Bob Hope performed before a sellout crowd of 32,000 people after the Wake Forest/Western Carolina football game on September 17. Over Parents' Weekend, the Dallas Cowboy cheerleaders performed before 28,000 spectators during halftime of the Wake Forest–North Carolina State football game on October 1; the previous evening, fifteen of the cheerleaders performed in a variety show at Reynolds Auditorium, with proceeds going to the University's athletic fund. Doc Severinsen and Xebron also performed on October 30 in Wait Chapel.

Facilities and Finances

Improvements to facilities and finances had been, and continued to be, a major concern for the

Herman Eure

administration. A priority for the University, though, was the restoration of Graylyn and its use. Funds for restoring the home of the Grays had been raised in the last three years of the Scales administration, but virtually no action had been taken to refurbish the property to its condition before the fire of 1980. The delay had to do with a debate as to how Graylyn would be or could be used and how much it would cost to maintain it. The winner of the debate was John Anderson, who had the idea that Graylyn could make money for the University as a conference center and not lose money as a dorm or mental health facility, as it had been used before. Thus, with funds from the sale of ten acres on the back of the estate, which raised a million dollars, and the money raised over the previous three years, Anderson's plan was put into motion and the project was finished after Gordon Gray signed off on it. (Gray not only signed off for the use of the property but was generously benevolent in giving $750,000 to fit the manor house with air conditioning.)

While open house celebrations at Graylyn for Wake Forest students and the Winston-Salem community took place on November 30 and December 1, student access to the grounds was limited by Director Albert Ginchereau because of a series of break-ins and other mischief.

Ginchereau's edict was controversial, but it was not the only controversy surrounding Graylyn. In October, before the restoration was completed, the University ended eighteen years of uninterrupted use of Graylyn by the Winston-Salem Symphony for its *Music at Sunset* concerts. The University paid the Arts Council the amortized value of the Rudolph Shell and scheduled its removal for February 1, but some in the community did not understand. Hearn wrote explanatory letters to L.M. Baker Jr., President of the Arts Council; Milton Rhodes, Executive Director of the Arts Council; George Lautemann, President of the Winston-Salem Symphony Association; and others: "It was important for everyone to understand that the use of Graylyn as a dormitory and its grounds as public park was a temporary expedient. Such use was incompatible with the terms under which the estate was donated to the

Bob Hope

University." He was more specific in a letter to Mr. L. Donald Long Jr. on November 17: "Developments following the fire of [June 22] 1980 made it feasible for the University to create a continuing education and conference center," and "the Gray family and others made substantial gifts" for the restoration. "A specific gift was made for the landscaping and that gift requires that the grounds be protected from automobiles and excessive crowds." The March 1980 agreement for Arts Council use of Graylyn

Graylyn International Conference Center

was terminated and settled officially on February 6, when the University gave the Arts Council a check for $145,000.

In a letter of March 12 to Mrs. Gordon (Connie) Gray of Washington, D.C., Hearn reported on the first month of operation of the Graylyn Conference Center. Wake Forest was the primary user, and he mentioned a gala May 5 tea dance at which the many contributors to Graylyn, especially the Gray family, would be recognized and honored. The official dedication of Graylyn Conference Center was held on May 5. The $6 million project was not part of the Sesquicentennial Campaign.

Another important dedication occurred earlier on October 14, when the Coy C. Carpenter Library on the Bowman Gray campus was dedicated. Carpenter was primarily responsible for the Medical School's move to Winston-Salem and its development into a major teaching center.

On the Reynolda campus, the Office of Residence Life reinstated room inspections, known as "facilities assessments," in fall 1983. They took place in late November and early April. The head resident of each dorm recorded maintenance needs and generated initial work orders for problems, such as room repairs. High-resistance appliances, including hotplates, toasters, toaster ovens, popcorn poppers, and immersion-type hotpots, were removed if found during the assessments, and their owners were fined $25 and given low priority for future housing.

In new construction, the Board of Trustees announced in early March that a $3 million coeducational residence hall would be built to house 226 students, mostly women. Construction was to begin in May and be completed by August 1985. At the time, the male/female ratio at Wake Forest was three to two (60 percent men, 40 percent women). In the summer of 1984, a $2.2 million renovation to the men's residence halls started with Poteat and Davis. Remodeling included new prototype suites.

In another action, a plan was made to build an attractive and clearly visible front entrance to the University, which had been under discussion since the move to Winston-Salem. The institutional planning committee now recommended building a brick wall that was 40 feet long, 44 inches high, and flanked on both sides by 4 × 4 × 10 ft columns at the Silas Creek Parkway entrance (the plan was later modified). In an almost parallel action, the Forsyth County Board of Commissioners acted favorably on the Silas Creek Parkway extension proposal on January 24, clearing the way for the North Carolina Board of Transportation to approve funding for engineering and environmental studies to divert traffic away from the center of campus. In addition to all of the discussion and plans, the University submitted a proposal for a new physics building to the Olin Foundation in March 1984.

On the financial front, Wake Forest was featured in the March issue of *Money Magazine* as one of the nation's "Ten Top Colleges at Bargain Prices." The article said the University was strong in business, English, history, biology—and basketball. Among other assets, it mentioned Reynolds Professor Maya Angelou and the four Reynolds Scholarships available each year.

The trustees set tuition for 1984–1985 at $5,500 for the College and the Graduate School; $6,150 for the Law School; and $7,150 for the Babcock School. The College Fund raised a record-setting $1,053,827 in 1983–1984.

Summing Up the Year

The academic year of 1983–1984 was marked by the presidential transition from James Ralph Scales to Thomas K. Hearn Jr. It was not a radical change for senior university officials; a Vice President of Planning, John Anderson, was added and other top administrators remained. The more significant shift, however, was in the way that Wake Forest was administered. The casual atmosphere of the Scales years gave way to more structured, formal processes, and questions about the conduct of the search for a new president remained.

Corrective measures were taken to strengthen the law school, a women's studies minor was created, and plans were drawn up for a new, primarily women's, residence hall. Graylyn Conference Center was opened, and the concert shell that had welcomed *Music at Sunset* guests to the estate for eighteen years was removed. The offices of Dean of Men and Dean of Women were abolished and replaced with an office for Dean of Students. Restrictive inter-visitation policies were revised and became more liberal. Student-run WAKE radio debuted, and the University was noted in national publications for excellent quality at a bargain price.

The men's basketball program set a record for most wins in a season, including an NCAA tournament win over DePaul University and Hall of Fame coach Ray Meyer. The success of the team boosted the spirits of Deacon fans both on and off campus.

Overall, the University functioned well during the year with honors gleaned by students, faculty, and administrators. The celebration of the Sesquicentennial and a trek to the old campus created a feeling of optimism for the future and quickly baptized the new president in the rich traditions and history of a place and its people, a condensed set of experiences that most beginning executives acquire only gradually, if at all. New roles and responsibilities in the administration signaled some of the future direction that the University would take, such as an emphasis on planning, but there were no major initial changes, and a good sentiment prevailed as the past was honored and aspirations nourished. The main question that lingered was, once the activities of newness and renewal settled, how would the Hearn years differ in style and substance from the Scales era?

CHAPTER TWO
1984–1985

Celebration and Reorganization

This was ... my sophomore year—the time when the newness is over and one settles down. The Sesquicentennial Celebration concluded with a stunning sound and light show in this spot.... This year may have had a less dramatic conclusion, but we have continued to go about our business, which is celebrating the life of the mind. That celebration—of the life of the mind—is what Wake Forest calls upon you to translate into productive, useful lives—lives which exhibit our guiding purpose: Pro Humanitate.
Thomas K. Hearn Jr., May 20, 1985;
Charge to the Graduates, Wake Forest University Commencement

The 1984–1985 academic year marked the 150th anniversary of the founding of Wake Forest University. The University had survived the Civil War, which closed it temporarily, World War I, and World War II. It had weathered "The Removal" to a new campus in Winston-Salem, 110 miles from its origin. The Cold War, the Civil Rights movement, and Vietnam protests changed the focus of the faculty and student body. To commemorate and celebrate its longevity, endeavors, and the impact of its graduates and friends, the University began its Sesquicentennial Campaign in 1983, which continued into the fall of 1984. Wayne Calloway ('59), Pepsico Chief Financial Officer, was the General Chair; Tylee Wilson, Chief Executive Officer of R.J. Reynolds Industries, was the Primary Gifts Chair; and Kay Lord ('64), Frank Lord ('63), and Steve Kelley ('68) chaired the Alumni Committee for the campaign. Its goal was to raise $17.5 million.

One of the highlights was the production of a spectacular eighty-minute sound and light show, the first presented at an American university, from Sunday, August 19 through Sunday, August 26, 1984. It was originally scheduled for May 15–19, but

Jim Dodding

it was postponed due to technical difficulties. The musical score *Visions and Dreams* was written and directed by Jim Dodding, an extraordinary British director whose deep and abiding relationship with the University was based on friendships with Provost Ed Wilson and such theatre faculty as Harold Tedford and Donald Wolfe, as well as the artistic freedom and openness to his creative talents the University afforded him. The cast included the voices of faculty and students from both the old and new campus, with Ed Wilson, the common link, narrating. Admission for faculty and staff, who were given first priority, was $3.00 per person. Everyone else was charged $5.00. At each presentation, there were approximately one thousand seats on risers; one night during orientation was reserved for first-year students, and another for returning upper classes.

Ed Wilson has described this event in detail in volume 5 of *The History of Wake Forest*, so it will not be reiterated here. As Wilson points out, no effort was spared to highlight the events and people that built Wake Forest. In tandem, Emily Herring Wilson published *Pro Humanitate: The Sesquicentennial Story*, a pamphlet relating the stories of prominent Wake Forest personalities who made a difference at the University and in society.

The end of the first full year of the Hearn administration was also a moment for assessment. On the surface, everything seemed to be working well. In a letter to Katharine R. Pawson, Secretary and Treasurer of the Charles A. Frueauff Foundation in New York City, Hearn wrote:

The Sesquicentennial Sound and Light Show in front of Wait Chapel

This year 3,209 students are enrolled in the undergraduate college. 1,816 of them are out-of-state students, and of that total approximately 33 percent receive some form of financial aid. We have begun construction of a new dormitory, built primarily to relieve some crowded housing, and expect our total number of students to increase by approximately 64. Our tuition for the current year is $5,550, and room and board plans average about $2,300.

On the national level he penned:

This year *Money Magazine* cited a Wake Forest education

as one of the top ten academic bargains in the country. *U.S. News and World Report*, based on a survey of college and university presidents, ranked Wake Forest as one of the best small comprehensive universities in the nation. Our student/faculty ratio is 14 to 1, and the average S.A.T. score in the 1984 freshman class is 1126. Approximately 30 to 40 percent of our alumni attend graduate or professional schools .... Eighty-four percent of the faculty hold earned PhD's .... [T]his year our alumni won the CASE/U.S. Steel Award for sustained performance in annual giving.

Indeed, the College Fund goal for the year was $1,250,000.

In another letter focused on the present, Hearn wrote to Nancy Susan Reynolds in Greenwich, Connecticut, on October 25 to acknowledge her gift to Z. Smith Reynolds Library: "Your generosity has enabled us to increase the general collection to its present level of over 649,000 volumes. We spend more per student than any university in the Southeast on our collection." He wrote to her again six days later to elaborate on financial matters, noting that the $17 million Sesquicentennial fundraising campaign was the largest in University history and had gone $5 million above goal, "and we are continuing to receive significant gifts."

Nonetheless, several problems had to be addressed: finances, diversity, space, and the governance relationship between the University and the North Carolina Baptist State Convention.

Finances

If Wake Forest's prestige in the academic world was growing, such progress cost money. The University was highly dependent on tuition, and when an 8 percent increase ($450) to $6,000 was announced for the 1985–1986 academic year, reaction was immediate, including a student protest. Tuition at the University of North Carolina at Chapel Hill at the time was just over $700. An *Old Gold and Black* headline claimed that tuition was being raised to improve the University's image. The fact that Wake Forest was listed by *Money Magazine* as a bargain along with nine other schools, including New College of the University of South Florida, Millsaps College, and Trinity University, brought mixed reviews. "These are not the types of universities Wake Forest compares itself to," some professors said. Many were less kind in their assessment of the tuition hike and what it was meant to do.

Hearn replied to the criticism in a letter to faculty summarized in an *Old Gold and Black* article. A study was being conducted; no decision had been made. "The Year 2000 Report was the document which first interested the Board of Trustees in long-range planning," Hearn noted. "It contained the recommendation that the so-called tuition gap between Wake Forest and the other institutions with which we are usually compared be studied." Compiled by faculty senate committees and adopted several months before Hearn became President, the Year 2000 Report contained the following recommendation: "The University should consider the implications of the tuition differential that exists between Wake Forest and its peer group of excellent colleges and universities, particularly when considering the ongoing needs of the University."

In a January 11 letter to Charles M. Davis of Louisburg, North Carolina, Hearn wrote: "Tuition is almost 70 percent of the academic budget. If we require additional resources for academic development, tuition must reflect that decision." In 1983–1984, the average salary for a professor at Wake Forest was $38,000. Professors at Duke University earned $45,000; North Carolina State University, $40,000; University of North Carolina, $42,500; and University of Virginia, $45,000. A first-year assistant professor at Wake Forest made $2,000 less than a first-year public school teacher in Forsyth County, according to an *Old Gold and Black* editorial. To retain its present faculty and to recruit new professors, Wake Forest had to charge more tuition.

Another financial concern was the endowment. For many years, monies returned from University departments at the end of the fiscal year were deposited in the endowment. Treasurer John Willard pursued this conservative strategy aggressively. Hearn objected, however, to the way it was carried out because it was not overtly stated. In fact, it was not a policy at all. In a January 21 memo to Willard, Hearn stated: "I am concerned … about the necessity that we continue to make substantial additions to the endowment …. I do not want … for endowment development to receive a kind of 'hidden' priority …. This is something that should be discussed with the Investment Committee at one of its upcoming meetings when we have a plan to propose."

Another financial change addressed faculty raises. Hearn recommended in a memo to his vice presidents and deans on January 15 that "some proportion of the total salary pool increase allowed each unit … be allocated to individuals on the basis of merit." Until this time, raises were usually across-the-board for all faculty members, regardless of productivity.

Diversity

Tuition was not the only controversy of 1984–1985. A March 26 memo to Bill Starling, Director of Admissions, instructed him to "consider policy changes which will redirect some existing scholarship funds to make our minority program more reasonably competitive." The president had been approached by a delegation of black faculty who advised him that talented black students might go elsewhere if they did not receive a more attractive financial package. Hearn wanted a more representative student body.

Space

Space was at a premium. Academic departments, such as economics, were housed in Z. Smith Reynolds Library. Student organizations were confined to the second and third floors of Reynolda Hall and often several groups shared an office. Even the Dean of the College and the Provost were housed together. There simply was no room to expand any student, faculty, or staff organization.

Baptist Governance

In January 1981, the University entered into a "covenant relationship" with the Baptist Convention of North Carolina and ceased to be its agency. Before the covenant, the Convention both nominated and elected Wake Forest trustees; afterward, the University nominated trustees, and the Convention elected them. Hearn had become aware that fundamentalism was dominating the more moderate wing of the Baptist church, and this change had important consequences for the University, especially with regard to its financial resources.

In a letter to his predecessor James Ralph Scales on July 2, Hearn wrote: "The Southern Baptists apparently just went crazy in Kansas City." He was referring to a strongly worded resolution against women in the pastorate adopted by the Southern Baptist Convention at its annual meeting. "What the implications of these developments may be for North Carolina Baptists are difficult to predict," he wondered, "especially for a novice in Baptist politics such as myself. They cannot be good, however, and there are already some indications that the committee structures with which we have to deal will be more rigid."

On October 30, Hearn wrote to William W. Leathers, III, Pastor, First Baptist Church, Rockingham, North Carolina:

> The basic problem … is the unstable and unpredictable political environment of the Convention. We have received a specific warning that certain [Baptist] churches and certain industries will be unacceptable to the nominations committee. The fundamentalist group has been strengthened on that committee and elsewhere in the denomination. Wake Forest cannot … take these developments lightly. If our basic mission and our freedom to pursue this mission be challenged, then we must resist. We must remain faithful to that heritage of independence and constant direction toward educational excellence, which has always been the hallmark of Wake Forest.

In another letter to Scales on December 3, Hearn stated that at the November North Carolina Baptist State Convention in Asheville, he "did not explicitly affirm our [Wake Forest's] desire to continue the covenant in its present form."

His readiness for a new relationship was evident in a May 15 letter to W. Henry Crouch, Pastor, Providence Baptist Church, Charlotte, North Carolina: "What we do for the churches and Baptist people and the character of our campus and academic programs is what gives substance to our religious heritage …. [W]e must take whatever steps are necessary to protect Wake Forest from those in the Convention who would compromise the bright future you see for us." A week later, on May 23, he wrote to L. Glenn Orr Jr., Vice Chair, Southern National Bank of North Carolina in Lumberton: "I am afraid . . . that there are fundamental differences between the interests of Wake Forest and those of some members of the Baptist State Convention now in positions of authority."

Clearly, a storm was brewing. When controversies with Wake Forest had arisen before, the Convention had prevailed. The new president was aware, however, that the covenant relationship his predecessor had signed a few years earlier was valid for a five-year term. He was determined to see it changed in the University's favor or the fraternal relationship would have to end.

Academics

The biggest academic story of 1984–1985 concerned the law school, which was floundering. Running on tradition in a cramped facility, it focused primarily on educating North Carolina attorneys. It needed new direction. Thus the 440 Plan was developed to align it with the University as a whole and to expand its horizons. The plan had four main goals:

1. To reduce the student body from 500 to 440 over the next five years to promote a closer community, especially closer interaction between professors and students;
2. To follow the University's lead and concentrate more of its efforts on becoming recognized as one of the outstanding regional law schools in the country, while making every effort "to preserve and nurture the loyalty, affection, and support of an unusually committed alumni body which is largely centered in North Carolina";
3. To "design and implement an integrated business-oriented specialty area" over the next few years and to continue developing the JD/MBA program; and
4. To develop and integrate an academic support program to accomplish the following objectives:
   a. To recruit promising students, diverse in background and interests, from a wide geographical area, mainly east of the Mississippi but maintaining a solid North Carolina base;
   b. To teach first-year students in "small classes of approximately 42" beginning in fall 1985;
   c. To provide faculty who combined academic and law practice experience;
   d. To provide a clinical educational experience concentrating on substantive trial experience and extensive criminal and civic practice;
   e. To engage in an aggressive placement program;
   f. To provide students with extensive opportunities for orientation and training in computer-assisted legal research and instruction as well as law office management; and
   g. To expand the Continuing Education program throughout the eastern United States "in limited, carefully selected areas and topics."

To publicize these changes, a new administrative position was created on February 1, 1985. Law Professor James Taylor ('47) became Associate Dean of External Affairs, with responsibility for admissions, placement, public relations, continuing legal education, and clinical education. His colleague Ken Zick became Associate Dean of Internal Affairs to oversee academic matters.

As a result of the 440 Plan, the law faculty revised evaluation standards for promotion and tenure decisions, emphasizing teaching, scholarship, and service.

Law school governance procedures were also revised to redefine areas of responsibility shared by the faculty and the administration. The plan and the process to achieve a regionally recognized School of Law were radical in the best sense of the word. They were in harmony with the ambitions and strategies of the undergraduate college and the institution as a whole.

Apart from the Law School, the Babcock Graduate School of Management was accredited by the Association to Advance Collegiate Schools of Business (AASCB). President Hearn sent a congratulatory memo to faculty and staff shortly after the official letter arrived on April 22. Outside of accreditation, the Babcock Foundation gave the Babcock School $500,000, which the school used to create Babcock fellow scholarships and to endow an international travel fund. In addition, the Winston-Salem Foundation awarded the Graduate School a $21,600 grant "to establish a masters of arts in liberal studies program." Throughout the year, the undergraduate faculty discussed whether the pass/fail option was working properly; specifically, were students who took the option working as hard as those taking the class for a letter grade? No unified decision was reached.

The Tocqueville Forum featured speakers such as George Ball, Paul Warnke, Vladimir Bukovsky, and Edward Luttwak. Although not household names, these scholars were stimulating and lived up to the Tocqueville goal of bringing fine scholars to American campuses. Forum Director Robert Utley and Assistant Director Patricia Gray were praised by the *Old Gold and Black* and by faculty.

On the University level, the Experimental College resurfaced. It offered eight short, noncredit courses in such areas as ceramics, photography, sign language, and cardiopulmonary resuscitation (CPR). The main objective was for students to have fun.

On a departmental level, on May 9 the Department of Political Science named its new seminar room (A302 Tribble Hall) in honor of Professor C.H. Richards, who was its first chair and had taught at Wake Forest for thirty-three years. Similarly, the Department of Religion gave a banquet in honor of the ninety-second birthday (July 23, 1984) of Professor Owen F. Herring ('13, MA '14) and named the department's seminar room on the third floor of Wingate Hall for him.

Individual Recognitions

On an individual level, Deborah Best ('70, MA '72) was one of five psychologists, thirty-five years old or younger, chosen by U.S. psychology department chairs to present a paper at the 23rd International Congress of Psychology in Acapulco, Mexico, in September 1984. She had shown herself prepared to present original, unpublished work of high quality. Best's research focused on sex stereotyping in various cultures.

Deborah Fanelli (Art) received a $5,000 visual artists fellowship from the National Endowment for the Arts. Other grant recipients for the year were Richard T. Williams ('68, Physics) for $25,230 from the William and Flora Hewlett Foundation; Richard D. Carmichael ('64; Mathematics) for $29,692 from the National Science Foundation; David J. Johns (Mathematics) for $8,850 from the National Science Foundation; Robert L. Utley Jr. ('71, Humanities) for $41,630 from the Smith Richardson Foundation; and Claire H. Hammond (Economics) for $17,924 from the Department of Housing and Urban Development. Hammond also won a national award, the Irving Fisher

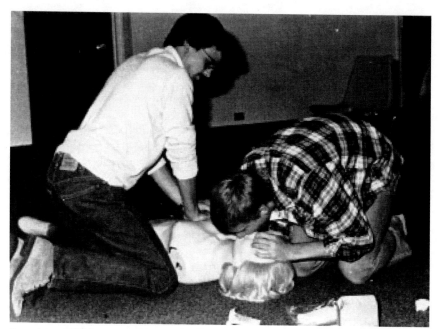

Practicing CPR in an experimental college class

Deborah Best

Award, for her dissertation, *The Benefits of Subsidized Housing Programs.*

Dudley Shapere, a professor at the University of Maryland, was named Reynolds Professor of History and Philosophy of Science, and his wife, Hannah M. Hardgrave, became Adjunct Professor of Philosophy. Physicist Richard T. Williams ('68) was also named a Reynolds Professor. When named, he was head of the ultraviolet technology section of the optical probes branch at the Naval Research Laboratory in Washington, D.C.

Catherine T. Harris (Sociology) won the Excellence in Teaching Award given on Founders' Day; James Ralph Scales (former President and Worrell Professor of Anglo-American Studies) received the Ecumenical Institute's Cuthbert E. Allen Award; and Andrew Ettin (English) published a well-received book, *Literature and the Pastoral* (Yale University Press).

Administration and Staff

The administration adopted a new logo for Wake Forest in the summer of 1984. Designed by the R.J. Reynolds graphics department, it was meant to encompass the different parts of the University but instead sowed discord. First, various constituencies were upset that the administration had made the decision without consulting more faculty members. Second, many were concerned that the logo had dropped the University seal. The logo was also criticized as "stiff, lifeless, and blocky."

Wake Forest University seal

Hearn and other administrators responded that the University seal would appear as a watermark on all new stationary and as the University's signature on official documents such as diplomas. Still, Ralph Wood, Associate Professor of Religion, criticized the new logo: "Without the seal, we do not declare the school's antiquity. We lose our strong humanistic commitment and we give up our overt Christian tradition." History Professor David Smiley wrote a protest sonnet, "The Seal," that read, in part:

> The symbol was once the seal of the fact.
> What made the school special was her impact
> On the mind, and on the faith that she backed.
> The letters will now display a new head.
> The tradition of tradition is dead.

In an *Old Gold and Black* editorial titled "The Great Seal Caper," a student weighed in: "The administration seems to have made a mistake by not consulting with more faculty members. Granted, a stationery change doesn't usually result in a lot of controversy, but someone should have anticipated that dropping the seal might upset the faculty." The next week, a longer editorial argued that "the only valid argument against the new stationery logo is that it is not as attractive as the former letterhead." The author pointed out that the University still had the seal, but, further, "our religious/liberal arts tradition does not depend on the seal for its existence. Whether or not the seal appears on the official stationery has nothing to do with the vivacity of Wake Forest's tradition."

Much more propitiously, the administration invited two of the most powerful men of the century to speak on campus to students, faculty, and staff. Holocaust survivor Elie Wiesel, professor, author, and 1986 Nobel Peace Prize winner, spoke on Founders' Day in February, and a few weeks later former President Jimmy Carter delivered the annual Irving E. Carlyle lecture.

Individual Recognitions, Promotions and Transitions

Administrative recognitions, promotions, and transitions during the year included the installation of

Wake Forest logo

David Smiley

Richard Janeway as Chair of the Association of American Medical Colleges, the highest office in academic medicine, on October 30. In a less prestigious but significant accomplishment, Richard (Dick) Clay, Director of the Wake Forest University Bookstore, received the Outstanding Manager Award for 1985 from the National Association of College Stores.

A flurry of internal promotions and hires included the promotion of Gerald W. Esch, Chair of Biology, to Dean of the Graduate School on August 1, succeeding Henry S. Stroupe ('35, MA '37), who retired that summer. Leon Corbett ('59, JD '61), former Associate General Counsel, became University Counsel and Secretary to the Board of Trustees.

In other appointments, Provost Ed Wilson selected Political Science Professor Richard Sears to coordinate the Office of International Studies, a project made possible by a $497,000 gift from the Pew Memorial Trust of Philadelphia. Wake Forest was one of only fifteen schools nationally sponsored to participate in the Liberal Arts Enrichment Program, which encouraged study of non-Western cultures with grants to faculty for summer and year-long leaves.

Henry S. Stroupe

New additions to the administration included Laura C. Ford ('70), who became the University's first Associate Provost, and Ernest Wade, who succeeded Biology Professor Herman Eure (PhD '74) as Minority Affairs Director. Alan S. Cameron became the University's first Coordinator of Substance Abuse Services, and Brian M. Austin, Director of the University Counseling Center, was appointed to the new position of Assistant Vice President for Student Affairs.

On March 25, the first meeting of the administrative council was held. The group was established to meet periodically with the president and executive council to discuss administrative policies.

Weston P. Hatfield ('41) was reelected Chair of the Board of Trustees, and J. Tylee Wilson (LLD '84) became Chair of the College Board of Visitors.

Athletics

It was a good year for Deacon sports in both the short and long terms. In football, Wake Forest was undisputed champion of North Carolina's Big Four with wins over UNC, NC State, and Duke. However, the overall team record was six wins and five losses.

In women's sports, the basketball team had a winning regular season record at 14–12, its first since 1972–1973. The cross country team topped a seven-team field at the UNC-Charlotte Invitational, winning their first meet in their seven-year history. Later, they took twelfth place at the District III meet to conclude their best season.

A long-term benefit for the Athletic Department was seeded in June 1985 when the City of Winston-Salem passed a bond referendum to build a new coliseum by a margin of 4 to 1. Memorial Coliseum was in poor shape, and four of the men's basketball team's seven home ACC games had to be played in Greensboro, with attendant inconvenience and loss of fan support. When the new coliseum was built, the Deacons could play all of their games in Winston-Salem again. Wake Forest also took a step forward in publicizing its revenue-generating teams by entering into a new multiyear agreement with Brookmont Communications of Nashville, Tennessee. The company would broadcast mainly football and basketball games via satellite, a switchover from phone-line transmission, and promised to bring Wake Forest sports to more markets, particularly Charlotte and Raleigh.

In the Athletic Department, Cook Griffin ('65) was named new Executive Director of the Deacon Club. He was the husband of Julie Davis ('69). The previous director, Bob Bartholomew ('57), a Wake Forest Hall of Fame football player, was killed in an automobile accident on April 19. In another change, Jim Leighton, the men's tennis coach, retired. He had served since 1963, compiling a record of 277 wins to 172 losses, and had been named ACC Coach of the Year in 1981. He was deeply admired, respected, and loved. As former player Ken West ('70) wrote in a personal letter:

> Jim Leighton was the Best Man in my wedding in 1973 but he was also the Best Man in my life. For so many of us, Coach and his insightful, talented wife, Betty, provided a home and unconditional love when we most needed support. Coach was inducted into the NCAA and Wake Forest Halls of Fame for his astonishing tennis excellence still seen in his ground-breaking book *Inside Tennis*. Each day players would arrive early for practice or stay late to improve techniques, and also to hear Coach's wisdom, to listen to his stories and to leave feeling more special than when we arrived.

Men's golf coach Jesse Haddock celebrated his twenty-fifth year at the helm, having produced fifty-one All-Americans, two NCAA team championships, four NCAA individual champions, seventeen ACC championships, and nineteen individual medalists.

Gil McGregor ('71) became the athletic program's Academic Advisor and Placement Director. He succeeded Bill Faircloth ('64), who became a full-time Assistant Athletic Director.

In a bizarre and frightening incident, Warren B. Brooks of Clemmons, a former industrial engineer with the City of Winston-Salem, threatened the life of basketball

Los Angeles Guitar Quartet

guard Tyrone "Muggsy" Bogues in a call to the secretary of the Winston-Salem Board of Aldermen on January 15, 1985. He was indicted by a Forsyth County grand jury on an extortion charge, arrested, freed on a $10,000 bond on January 17, and later sentenced to serve time in prison.

The Arts

The University Theater produced four plays: Philip King's *See How They Run*, Anton Checkhov's *The Cherry Orchard*, Tennessee Williams's *Cat on a Hot Tin Roof*, and *The Wake Forest Passion Play*. In addition, the College Union and University Theatre teamed up to present the Broadway musical review *Tintypes* by Mary Kyte, Mel Marvin, and Gary Pearle at a dinner theater. Another musical drama, *The Cotton Patch Gospel*, by Tom Key and Russell Treyz, with songs by Harry Chapin, was presented by the national touring company of Dallas Theatre Three. Actors from the Royal Shakespeare Company gave two performances of *Twelfth Night* during a week-long campus residency, and alumnus John Chappel ('61) performed his *Mark Twain on Stage*, based on Twain's own words, as a university commencement program.

The Artist Series schedule for the year included performances by the Los Angeles Guitar Quartet, The English Concert, Los Angeles Philharmonic Orchestra, Greg Smith Singers, and pianist Ursula Oppens. A chamber music series co-sponsored by the University and Reynolda House featured the Albegg Trio, Kodaly Quartet, Folger Consort, pianist Carlos Rodriguez, and the Budapest Brass Quintet.

Other performances included Music Professor Louis Goldstein on piano, Chuck Mangione on jazz flugelhorn and trumpet, folk singer and actress Odetta, folk singer Mike Cross, modern dancer Sharon Kinney, the Ruth Mitchell Dance Theatre, Jamaican poet and comedienne Louise Bennett, the improvisational comedy troupe Second City, and comedian Steven Wright.

In another arts-related activity, Barbara Hearn founded the Friends of the Arts (FoA). Members made a commitment to attend at least one theatre production, concert, dance program, and art exhibit and, at some time, to "help with a reception at the Scales Fine Arts Center in conjunction with a performance."

Campus and Student Life

A few changes marked student life during 1984–1985. For instance, the homecoming dance was held on campus in the athletic center; Student Services offices moved to 111 Davis House, directly below Wachovia Bank and the Sundry Shop on the upper quad; and with support and funding from student government, Public Safety Director Alton M. Hill implemented the first on-campus Crimestoppers program in the nation. As always, a host of extracurricular activities such as dating, rush, working on pub row, participation in athletics, studying, and serious discussions (on matters from academic honor to sexual orientation) filled students' lives as well as the pages of the *Old Gold and Black*. High-profile student leaders included College Union President Angie Patterson, Student Government President Brent Wood, *Old Gold and Black* Editor Kerry King, and *Howler* Editor Anna Draughn.

The University's first Senior Class Campaign was organized and publicized by the Student Alumni Council (SAC), and during February more than a hundred SAC members solicited pledges from their classmates payable one to three years after graduation.

The Association of Wake Forest Black Alumni (AWFUBA) initiated an Adopt-A-Freshman project in January, in which each participating Association member was assigned to an incoming first-year black student. President Beth Hopkins stated that the program was one way the AWFUBA hoped to strengthen ties between minority alumni and the University.

One bizarre exception to a positive campus atmosphere was the appearance of Brother Jed Smock and Sisters Cindy and Beth Smock on the quad on a mild Monday in early November. Their purpose was evangelism, and their methods included screaming at students to stop their sinning. They also distributed Smock's pamphlet, "On Christian Perfection," which sparked considerable anger and agitation among surrounding students. Cindy Smock, a former disco dancer, condemned rock and roll, including songs by "John Lennon, Janis Joplin, Jim Morrison," so students in Davis House responded by blaring music from their windows. Other students performed the wave cheer in response to such outrageous comments as "God is a Republican" and women's only purposes are "to make babies and to be obedient to their husbands." While Director of Public Safety Alton Hill had given the trio permission to be on campus, no campus group sponsored them. At the end of the day, Dean of Students Mark Reece shook his head and simply said, "I couldn't understand why students just didn't walk away."

Apart from this strange incident, student life progressed on a number of fronts. A new co-ed residence hall (now Collins) was under construction near the existing women's residence halls behind Bostwick and Johnson, while sixty female undergraduates, mostly sophomores, were housed in two faculty apartment buildings. Extensive renovation of the men's residence halls on the quad continued.

A new visitation agreement, extending hours, was overwhelmingly supported by students and faculty. John Anderson, who was the opening convocation speaker on September 11, was instrumental in visitation activities, eager to involve students in making decisions that affected their lives. Students who worked with him were enthusiastic in his praise. After the visitation policy was revised, the *Old Gold and Black* was effusive, calling Anderson "a beacon for students," a sobriquet that prompted a great deal of kidding from colleagues.

George H.W. Bush, the Republican candidate for president, made a campaign stop on campus on Monday, September 10, 1984. Sponsored by the College Republicans, he spoke before a crowd of 3,000 assembled on the Magnolia Court behind Reynolda Hall and was featured in the *Winston-Salem Journal* the next day with the Demon Deacon. The cheerleaders and the band performed at the rally; Bill Morgan, Vice President of the College Democrats, and three law students protested to Vice President Anderson, who assured them that the University had not endorsed any candidate, and the matter slowly died down. Governor Jim Hunt, Democratic candidate for the U.S. Senate, delivered a political address in Brendle Recital Hall a few weeks later.

From 3,900 applications, (an increase of 20 percent over the previous year), 1,500 students were accepted to the entering class of 800, according to Thomas O. Phillips ('74, MA '78), Assistant Director of Admissions. Outstanding students were awarded a total of thirty-three Carswell, forty-one Hankins, eleven Poteat, and four Reynolds scholarships. The first O.W. Wilson scholar was Kimberly Page from Clifton Park, New York, who also held a Carswell scholarship. SAT scores for Reynolds scholars averaged in the mid-1400s and in the 1300s for Carswell scholars. Overall, the University committed more than $6 million in academic, need-based, athletic, and other scholarships, work programs, loans, and institutional aid to over one third of its 3,100 undergraduates.

An additional $250,000 scholarship program for minorities was set up. Beginning in fall 1985, three scholarships of $2,000 each were designated to be awarded each year, without regard to financial need, to minority students who showed exceptional academic promise and leadership potential. These scholarships were established with undesignated funds raised during the Sesquicentennial Campaign. As for Carswell scholars, the Committee on Scholarships and Student Aid assigned each recipient a faculty sponsor, who "encouraged and advised the development of the scholar's academic and leadership potential."

Individual Student Achievements

Among notable student activities and achievements, senior Lewis McMillan cycled 3,700 miles over the summer via the Bikecentennial TransAmerica Trail. Rebecca May Almon, a senior psychology major, became a student trustee. The Leadership Excellence Application and Development (LEAD) course began with the selection of twenty first- and second-year students. The international club was revitalized, and Sigma Nu was chartered as the newest fraternity on campus. Mike Ford, director of the College Union, and students across campus advocated for building a Student Center.

A Wellness Resource Center, engaging physical, emotional, spiritual, social, intellectual, and occupational dimensions of life, was set up in the lobby of New Dorm (Luter) and open from 4 to 6 p.m. on Mondays, Wednesdays, and Thursdays. Bookmarks printed with "Wellness Tips" were distributed on campus. Later in the spring, the University held its first Wellness Fair, HEALTHFEST '85. Winston-Salem community organizations and Wake Forest faculty and staff set up booths, demonstrations, and exhibitions relevant to the theme.

Deke, the Delta Kappa Epsilon canine mascot, was crowned Homecoming King. Granice Geyer was crowned Homecoming Queen. WFDD, located on the second floor of Reynolda Hall, was on the air eighteen hours a day and provided a limited number of assistantships and work-study opportunities for students. It provided the background music for channel 2, a cable channel operated by the Forsyth County

Board of Education. WAKE radio entered its second year of operation and struggled financially. Nevertheless, the station sponsored a community service event in the spring entitled "Spring into Action," in which students from the University, Salem, and Winston-Salem State donated two hours each to collecting trash, participating in a softball game with members of a local orphanage, or painting or doing yardwork to improve the community. As usual, a large number of students participated in Springfest as well, which was held at Davis Field on a Friday, Saturday, and Sunday in mid-April. The event, sponsored by the College Union, featured everything from movies to folk art and included a reggae band and a Happy Hour.

One down note in an otherwise upbeat year was a report from Toby Hale, Associate Dean of the College, that each year, Wake Forest lost 12 percent of its student body as a result of transfer to other schools, drop-out, and academic failure. Increasing retention would require much more work. Another report stated: "Ten percent of all freshmen leave, with a small group leaving at Christmas break and a larger group leaving after the spring semester." Of an incoming freshmen class, 75–80 percent would graduate from Wake Forest, according to Hale. Nationwide, the rate was about 50 percent.

Facilities, Finances, and Alumni

In April, the University converted Lovette House at the corner of Reynolda and Polo Roads for commercial rental. The property had housed approximately twenty-five French and Spanish students *George H.W. Bush; Jim Hunt* since Graylyn's renovation required the original language houses to move. The timing of the decision disturbed students. New houses were purchased: 1020 Polo Road for the French House and 1210 Polo Road for the Spanish House.

On campus, the University opened a new microcomputer center in Reynolda Hall, room 9-A, in late November. The center allowed full-time Wake Forest students, employees, and staff to purchase a personal computer at a discount. Three personal computer brands were available: IBM, Wang, and Apple Macintosh.

A formal garden near the entrance of the president's home honoring Betty Scales was planned and planted by Barbara Hearn and Physical Plant Director Pete Moore.

Deke - Homecoming King dog; Granice Geyer - Homecoming Queen

Alumni

The generosity of alumni giving was acknowledged nationally:

> The University's alumni giving program was chosen the best in the country among major private universities for the four-year period beginning in 1979. The competition, sponsored by the Council for Advancement and Support of Education (CASE) and the United States Steel Foundation, had been held for the last twenty-five years.... The 'sustained performance giving award' won by the University was based on the percentage of alumni who participated in the annual giving program over the last four years, the average gift per alumnus, total giving, and the overall quality of the program.... The average gift from University alumni during the four years was $167. It was the highest in North Carolina and was above the national average of $103. Thirty-one percent of alumni participated in the annual giving program. The national average was 19 percent.

George E. Brooks ('71) of Charlotte was installed as the new President of the Alumni Association during the 1984 homecoming banquet. He had been National Chair of the College Fund in 1983–1984 and led the campaign past the $1 million mark for the first time. In addition, the Alumni in Admissions (AIA) program, started in 1983, expanded and recruited alumni in different parts of the country to help admissions personnel recruit and enroll the best students from those areas.

Barbara Hearn and Betty Scales

The University awarded Distinguished Service Citations to Arthur D. Gore ('49), photographer/poet; James E. Peters ('33), who signed up over 20,000 eye donors; and William Raymond Cowan ('54, MD '57), Director of the Armed Forces Institute of Pathology, the most demanding and prestigious post in military pathology. Gene Overby, a college dropout and the longtime voice of Wake Forest athletics, became an honorary alumnus, and the Johnson-McMillan-Memory-McNeil clan from eastern North Carolina received the first Distinguished Wake Forest Family Award.

On an individual achievement level, Trustee D. Wayne Calloway ('59) was promoted to President and CEO of PepsiCo.

Summing up the Year

The academic year 1984–1985 buzzed with activities: the Sesquicentennial celebration, reorganization of the Law School, controversy over a new University logo, a relaxed inter-visitation policy that gave students more independence, and a considerable tuition hike that sparked a student protest. Alumni were singled out for their generous giving. Wake Forest and those who worked within it were honored and recognized for excellence in many areas by national groups and periodicals.

Headlines from the October 26, 1984, edition of *Old Gold and Black* reflected collective sentiment about the new president: "Hearn passes first anniversary; reactions vary." On the positive side, the president was seen as thoughtful and organized, and as a planner; on the negative side, he was seen as bureaucratic, authoritarian, invisible to the faculty, and dismissive of their opinions. In a November editorial from the campus newspaper titled, "Report Card," a student summary of the administration's first year was given. It read: "Judging from the present as we must, we think Hearn's first year as president will go down in Wake Forest history as an outstanding one in which a slumbering giant awoke and took great steps toward realizing its full potential." Future plans would focus on increasing diversity in the student body, dealing with the Baptist State Convention, and making the University more financially secure, but in 1984 and 1985 only faint hints of those directions were present.

CHAPTER THREE
1985–1986

A Bold Move, a Rhodes, and the Comeback

If education consists in the speaking of many languages, we must have the rudiments of a common grammar and vocabulary if the university is to be a university, rather than a modern tower of Babel.

Thomas K. Hearn Jr., May 19, 1986;
Charge to the Graduates, Wake Forest University Commencement

The 1985–1986 academic year at Wake Forest was marked by three exciting events: the University's daring preliminary move away from the Baptist State Convention, the award of a Rhodes scholarship to an undergraduate, and the comeback of the men's golf team to win the NCAA national championship.

A Bold Initial Move: University Governance and the Baptist State Convention

At the beginning of the year, the University's longtime struggle with the Baptist State Convention of North Carolina was coming to a head. It had simmered since President Tribble had attempted to loosen the Covenant, in effect since the days of Wake Forest President William Poteat in the 1920s, which gave the Baptist State Convention the right to select all College trustees. In return, the Convention allocated a portion of its yearly budget to University support. President Hearn thought the time had come to end this practice, and negotiations started out optimistically. In a September 26 letter to the Board of Trustees, he reported that the Convention's General Board had unanimously approved the recommendations for an amendment of the Covenant at its September 24 meeting. The amendment would give the University trustees the power to elect one-third of their members, and it was supported by Convention leadership.

During the annual meeting in November, however, delegates from the Baptist churches attending the meeting voted down the recommendation by a narrow margin. Soon afterward, Wake Forest trustees held a special meeting and took what might best be described as a radical but necessary action. They voted on December 6 to elect their successors without seeking approval from the Baptist State Convention of North Carolina. Furthermore, they voted to increase the number of trustees from thirty-six to forty and stated, "Trustees will elect their successors." J. Robert Philpott of Lexington chaired the trustee committee that proposed the new arrangement. It sent shockwaves through the Baptist and educational worlds of North Carolina and Baptist institutions of higher learning elsewhere.

The letters announcing the trustees' decision were signed by Weston P. Hatfield ('41), the Board's retiring chair, and Joseph Branch ('38), the new chair, who was also Chief Justice of the Supreme Court of North Carolina. The letters were sent by couriers to Convention officials immediately following the early December trustee meeting.

Soon afterward, Hearn explained the action to several correspondents. He wrote to the Reverend Lamar J. Brooks of the Winter Park Baptist Church in Wilmington, North Carolina, on December 16: "I assume you are aware that the Convention played little or no role in the election of Wake Forest trustees until 1927. We certainly were a Baptist institution for all those years when we had a distinction between governance and our services to the Baptists. We have, therefore, a history upon which to establish this new covenant." However, in a letter to Claude A. McNeill Jr. on December 18, the president lamented: "We were . . . disappointed that the proposals to revise the covenant failed. That left Wake Forest in a procedural dilemma with respect to the critical matter of the election of trustees. It distresses me that *our* action is described as 'unilateral.'" On December 19, to William F. Bondurant, Executive Director of the Mary Reynolds Babcock Foundation, Hearn wrote: "No doubt the recent decision by the Board of Trustees to be a fully self-perpetuating Board will have a great impact on the future of Wake Forest."

In a letter on January 2, 1986, to Reverend Carl R. Elledge of Pleasant Grove Baptist Church, Ronda, North Carolina, President Hearn discussed the tension between Wake Forest and the Convention: "What constitutes our religious commitment and our fidelity to our Baptist heritage is what we do on the campus and in programs and services we render." He wrote Mr. Rex N. Gribble of the Charlotte Machine Company on February 5: "The Baptist State Convention with which Wake Forest has dealt for so long is no more. It is now a divided and divisive forum involved in an essentially political struggle. That constitutes our basic problem. We must

Weston Hatfield   *Joseph Branch*

distinguish, therefore, our desire to be of service to our Baptist constituency from a governance relationship with the Convention which meets just three days a year."

By April 24, the situation began to turn around. In a letter to Wake Forest Trustee Russell W. Meyer Jr. of Cessna Aircraft Company in Wichita, Hearn wrote: "There have been positive developments in our negotiations with the Baptist State Convention in recent days. I am fairly confident now that there will be some resolution acceptable to Wake Forest."

The Rhodes

The initiation of a proposed new covenant with the Baptist State Convention was not the only major news story of the academic year. Just as exciting, but with much less tension attached, was the selection of senior Richard Chapman for one of the oldest, most prestigious scholarships in the world. Every year, more than 80 college students, 32 of them from the United States, are chosen as Rhodes Scholars to study for degrees at Oxford University. As far back as the 1920s, Wake Forest students had been counted among the recipients, but beginning in January 1986 a new era of scholastic achievement began. Chapman was a Carswell Scholar, a math major with a 4.0 grade point average, and an avid cyclist. He conducted research both in physics and on the Italian painter Giovanni Bellini as a result of a semester in Wake Forest's Venice program. He later reported to Tom Phillips that the experience altered his perspective more than any other in his life. He credited Associate Professor of History James P. Barefield, who directed the Venice program he had attended, with an instrumental role in his award.

Chapman's award was the first in a stream of prominent scholarship honors awarded to Wake Forest students. From 1984 to 2005, Wake Forest students garnered nine Rhodes, nine Truman, nine Rotary, seventeen Fulbright, and a goodly number of Luce, Beinecke, Mellon, Javits, Goldwater, and Cooke awards. This steady achievement was unprecedented in University history and may be attributed to three factors. First, in the 1980s the University began to attract many more well-prepared and high-achieving students. Second, professors like Barefield in History and Katy Harriger in Political Science, as well as Tom Phillips in Admissions, became more directly involved in identifying exceptional candidates in their sophomore and junior years and providing them with model writing and interviewing sessions. Susan Faust, administrative assistant in the Provost's Office, also did an excellent job of preparing Truman, Rotary, and other scholarship nominees for interviews. Third, Reynolds and Carswell Scholars started taking greater advantage of summer grant opportunities offered by both scholarship programs to find the intensive and atypical summer experiences that would speed their intellectual and social maturity.

James P. Barefield

An Unbelievable Golf Championship

On May 31, the Wake Forest men's golf team under Coach Jesse Haddock capped a great year. Playing on its home course, Bermuda Run Country Club, the team rallied from sixteen strokes down to win its third NCAA Golf Championship on the final day of the tournament, beating the heavily favored Oklahoma State University team by four strokes. Chris Kite, Billy Andrade, and Len Mattiace finished in the top twenty. "I've been in sports all of my life and golf twenty-five years," Haddock said after the victory, "but I have never seen anything like this." Rounding out the team were Tim Straub and Barry Fabyan.

Complementing the men's victory, although less dramatically, the impressive women's golf team under Coach Mary Beth McGirr won the ACC Tournament Championship. Brenda Corrie won top honors in individual competition.

Academics

Richard Groves, new pastor of the Wake Forest Baptist Church, was the speaker at the Opening Convocation on September 3. Betty Ford, wife of former President Gerald Ford, was the Founders' Day convocation speaker on February 4. The Jon Reinhardt Award for Distinguished Teaching was established and slated to be given for the first time at the Opening Convocation in fall 1986.

In another noteworthy milestone, Wake Forest University Press marked its tenth anniversary in May 1986. Established by English Professor Dillon Johnston, the press was (and still is) the premier publisher of Irish poetry in the United States.

1986 Men's NCAA national championship team

Individual Recognitions

Faculty recognition during 1985–1986 included Dan Locklair, who received the Hinda Hongiman Composer's Cup from the North Carolina Federation of Music Clubs in recognition of his composition *Flutes*, a suite of inventions for soloists. In August, his *Phoenix Fanfare and Processional* was played at the new student convocation.

In the book publishing realm, Doyle Fosso (English) published a collection of poetry, *Parabola Rosa* (Stuart Wright). James C. O'Flaherty (German), Timothy E. Sellner (German), and Robert M. Helm ('39, Philosophy) edited the book *Studies in Nietzsche and the Judeo-Christian Tradition* (University of North Carolina Press). Terisio Pignatti (Art History) published two books: *Five*

Co-captains of 1986 Wake Forest golf team: Chris Kite and Billy Andrade

Centuries of Italian Painting: 1300–1800 and *Drawings from Venice.* G. McLeod Bryan ('41, MA '44, Religion) published a text on another outstanding Wake Forest minister, W.W. Finlator ('34, HDD '73). The book was titled *Dissenter in the Baptist Southland: Fifty Years in the Career of William Wallace Finlator* (Mercer University Press). Dillon Johnson (Wake Forest Irish Press) also published a new work: *Irish Poetry after Joyce* (University of Notre Dame Press and Dolmen Press).

Sally J. Schumacher (Medical School) was elected president of the American Association of Sex Educators, Counselors, and Therapists (AASECT). Rhoda Bryan Billings (JD '66) was appointed by Governor James Martin to the North Carolina Supreme Court, taking the oath of office on September 4. She was only the second woman justice in the 166-year history of the court. A member of the Wake Forest law faculty since 1973, Billings became a full professor in 1977. Her specialty was constitutional law and evidence.

To recognize exemplary faculty teaching, alumnus Wilbur S. Doyle of Martinsville, Virginia, gave $25,000 in honor of Philosophy Professor A.C. Reid, his favorite

Dan Locklair

Rhoda Bryan Billings

professor at Wake Forest. The money went to establish the Reid-Doyle prize for Excellence in Teaching. The first recipients of the award were presented at Founders' Day to Carole L. Browne (Biology) and Saguiv A. Hadari (Political Science). An additional first-time award presented at Founders' Day was the Excellence in Research Award. It was presented to Associate Professors Deborah L. Best ('70, MA '72, Psychology) and W. Jack Rejeski (Health and Sports Science).

Two more Reynolds Professors were named: Maya Angelou, Professor of American Studies; and John Wood, Professor of Economics. In addition, K.A.N. Luther of the Babcock Graduate School of Management received a Fulbright grant to conduct research in Japan for a year, and Education Professor Joe Milner was appointed to the Standing Committee on Teacher Preparation and Certification of the National Council of Teachers of English. He received a $50,000 grant from the North Carolina Department of Public Instruction as well.

A number of other faculty received research grants of more than $10,000 each, including Dudley Shapere (Philosophy & History of Science) for $18,000 from the National Science Foundation, Wayne Silver (Biology) for $24,071 from the National Science Foundation and for $95,750 from the National Institute of Neurological and Communicative Disorders and Strokes, Mordecai Jaffe (Biology) for $30,000 from the National Science Foundation, Raymond E. Kuhn (Biology) for $348,000 from the National Institutes of Health and for $33,220 from Disease Detection International Incorporated of California.

Furthermore, in other large grant actions, Natalie A. Holzwarth (Physics) received $21,500 from the National Science Foundation; George M. Holzwarth (Physics) $10,000 from Research Corporation and $15,000 from the North Carolina Biotechnology Center; Richard T. Williams ('68, Physics) $22,000 from AMP, Inc., and $30,000 from Martin Marietta Energy Systems, Inc.; J. Ned Woodall (Anthropology) $4,200 from the Department of the Army and $59,853 from the Corps of Engineers; Robert L. Utley ('71) $100,000 from the National Endowment for the Humanities and $20,000 from the North Carolina Humanities Committee; Charles F. Jackels (Chemistry) $22,809 from NASA; Deborah L. Best ('70, MA '72, Psychology) and Rosalind M. Vaz (Pediatrics) $45,256 from the Bowman Gray School of Medicine Venture Grant; and Linda B. Robertson (Anthropology) $18,023 from the Institute of Museum Services.

Administration and Staff

As the University's chief administrator, President Hearn indicated in his second annual report that of the three primary aspects of University planning—academic, financial, and physical—he was most concerned about academic and student space, i.e., the physical aspect. To coordinate efforts and to unify information distribution, he set up the Academic Council. Composed of deans and vice presidents, this Council met the first Friday of each month in the Board Room of Reynolda Hall.

In personnel matters, Associate Provost Laura Ford, Director of Human Services Jim Ferrell, and Director of Planning Ross Griffith prepared an early retirement study for the Reynolda campus. The study looked at positive ways to allow long-serving individuals to retire early for any number of reasons. New faculty could be recruited earlier and resources within a department and the College as a whole could be redistributed.

Personal Achievements, Promotions, and Recognitions

Thomas P. Gilsenan was appointed on June 30 as the Director and General Manager of Graylyn Conference Center after Albert P. Ginchereau resigned.

G. William Joyner ('66), Vice President for University Relations, received the General Baptist Foundation's annual award for excellence.

One of the most significant promotions was the naming of Julius Corpening ('49), Director of Development and Estate Planning since 1978, to Assistant Vice President for Development. This new position reported to Vice President of University Relations Bill Joyner. Bob Mills ('71, MBA '80) was also appointed to a new position. From Director of Alumni Activities, he became Assistant Vice President and Director of Alumni Activities in January 1986. Mike Ford ('72) was promoted to Associate Dean for Student Development. Replacing Ford as Director of the College Union was Mary T. Beil, who had previously worked at Hiram College. At the medical school, Richard Janeway was named Executive Dean and Chief Executive Officer, and Fairfield Goodale became Dean. Outside the University, Margaret Perry, University Registrar, became editor of *SACRO Journal*, a new publication of the Southern Association of Collegiate Registrars.

Athletics

Basketball dominated the early athletic news in 1985–1986 with an unexpected announcement: on July 15, Carl Tacy resigned as men's basketball coach. In thirteen seasons, he had compiled a record of 222 victories and 149 defeats. He led the Deacons to six postseason tournaments and five 20-win seasons, including four consecutive 20-win seasons from 1980 to 1984. The suddenness of his resignation sent Athletic Director Gene Hooks scrambling to assemble a committee to find a replacement.

On August 3, Bob Staak, Head Coach of Xavier University in Cincinnati since 1979, was named the seventeenth coach of the Wake Forest men's basketball program. He was the sixth new coach in the past fifty-one years and came to Wake Forest with winning credentials. Unfortunately, the sudden transition was compounded by numerous player injuries, and the Deacons had eight wins and twenty-one losses overall, while their 0–14 record in the ACC was the

Margaret Perry

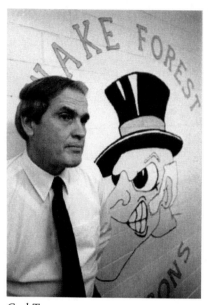

Carl Tacy

worst conference record in the team's history. The most unique aspect of the team was that 6'8" Alan Dickens, a Carswell Scholar, went out for the basketball team and made it after the ranks of the team were depleted.

In February 1986, George Kennedy resigned after six years as men's soccer coach. He was replaced by Walter Chyzowych, a U.S. Olympic and World Cup team coach. At the same time, Athletic Director Gene Hooks announced that the University would increase its soccer scholarships to the maximum of eleven permitted by the NCAA and upgrade its facilities.

The football team compiled a 4–7 season, which was not particularly noteworthy, but a Tucker Mitchell column in the *Winston-Salem Journal* discussing the Wake Forest football budget and program priorities caused considerable public relations fallout. In response, the President set up an athletic policy review. In a February 24 memo to John Anderson, Hearn stated: "I am asking you to convene a group to review the five-year outlook for athletics with Dr. Hooks in preparation for a broad review of this by the Executive Council . . . . Among other things, I would like your group to consider the desirability of maintaining separate residence halls for athletes." Leon Corbett, Ed Wilson, and Bill Joyner were on the review committee. In an April 28 memo, Hearn also instructed Hooks to give him a complete report on the graduation rates for scholarship athletes and to "put it in some sort of context so that I can determine what our trend lines seem to be." In addition, the President proposed strengthening the overall SAT requirement for the ACC, and in a May 12 letter to Dr. Bruce Poulton, Chancellor of North Carolina State University, he wrote: "Wake Forest proposes that the 700 SAT score be a requirement for any athletic aid in the ACC."

Nationally, Hearn began to get involved in the NCAA after its convention in New Orleans. He was especially interested in Proposition 48, which dealt with the minimum academic requirements for students recruited for athletic scholarships. In a February 6 letter to David Cross in Greensboro, he wrote: "Proposition 48 will strengthen the academic standards of all athletes. This should improve the competitive situation for schools like Wake Forest."

In other areas, Karen Dunn and Jennifer Rioux earned All-American honors in women's cross country, and former men's tennis coach Jim Leighton was inducted posthumously into the Collegiate Tennis Hall of Fame on May 23, 1986.

Walter Chyzowych

The Arts

President Hearn's wife Barbara formed Arts at Wake Forest (AAWF) in fall 1984, and by fall 1985 the group had 160 members representing a cross-section of the Winston-Salem and University communities. The group's purpose was twofold: to link the fine arts communities and to promote student awareness of the fine arts on campus.

In music, the year's Artists Series featured performances by pianist Yefim Bronfman, Cuban violinist Rubén González, cellist Janos Starker, the Gewandhaus Orchestra of Leipzig, and baritone Richard Stillwell.

The University Theatre produced four plays: Jean Giraudoux's *The Madwoman of Chaillot*, William Shakespeare's *Macbeth*, Wendy Wasserstein's *Isn't It Romantic?*, and Charles Chilton's *Oh, What a Lovely War*.

Shirley Anders, staff assistant to Vice President John Anderson, received a North Carolina Arts Council fellowship and the Devins Award for a first book of poems from the University of Missouri Press, which published her collection, *The Bus Home*.

In March 1986, WFDD, Wake Forest's NPR radio station, started broadcasting at 100,000 watts, in stereo, eighteen hours a day, 365 days a year. It reached approximately thirty thousand Triad adults each week with National Public Radio programming and classical music.

Campus Life and Students

Wake Forest received a record 5,000 applications for the 850 places in the fall 1986 freshman class, a 9 percent increase over 1984 and a 30 percent increase over the previous two years. Minority enrollment remained low at 3.3 percent, or only 99 out of the overall 3,350 undergraduates. Most minority students were African American.

The major offices for student affairs—the Assistant Vice President, Dean of Students, and three Associate Deans—continued to be located in a suite of offices in Davis Residence Hall, yet student life seemed to flourish.

Emerson (Em) Thompson III was President of the Student Government Association; Mary Elizabeth Sutton and Mary Ellen Lloyd were editors of *The Student*, Jenny Kletzin was Editor-in-Chief of *The Howler*, Jim Snyder was Editor-in-Chief of the *Old Gold and Black*, Mark Hall was President of the Student Union (formerly the College Union), and the student trustee until January 1987 was Linda Colwell.

In Greek life, a new fraternity, Chi Psi, was established.

The only discontent students expressed during the year was over the 10 percent tuition increase to $6,600 for 1986–1987. After the trustees passed the hike in February 1986, sophomore Scott Schneider organized a protest, and fifty students rallied outside the Magnolia Room on a Thursday night when the trustees were meeting for dinner.

Facilities, Finances, and Alumni

While Graylyn Conference Center was named Executive Retreat of the Year by *Hideaway Report* in December 1985, elm bark beetles and Dutch elm disease were the

Students waiting to buy books outside the bookstore

major concerns for facilities on the Reynolda Campus. Jennifer Young summed up the situation on the Quad well: "Eleven of the original forty-two elms have died and two or three others are badly diseased." The damage was due to Dutch elm beetles sucking out the sap and infecting the trees with a fungus. President Hearn appointed an advisory committee, chaired by Biology Professor Nina Allen, and in an October 24 memo asked the committee "to recommend the best course of action to follow with regard to the Quadrangle elm trees, which are falling victim to Dutch elm disease." On November 27, the committee report recommended the best possible care for the remaining elms and the planting of eleven white ash on the Quad in the spring. It was hoped that the white ash, which look much like elms and grow quickly, would blend in, and the appearance of the stately trees, which had graced the campus since 1956, would not be lost. Associated with the maintenance of the Quad, Ed Stoltz retired as Superintendent of Grounds after twenty-three years of service, just shy of the elms' thirty years.

In connection with University upkeep, the President reiterated his intentions to renovate and rebuild. His passion is reflected in a February 14 letter to Mr. and Mrs. Claude S. Abernethy Jr. of Concord, North Carolina:

> When I was hired as President in 1983, the Trustees gave me only one mandate—to institute a planning process which would enable Wake Forest to take advantage of its distinctive strengths and guide it to greater national prominence. . . . Financial and program plans for the next decade are developing and building needs are being identified. A new master plan for the campus is to be drawn for consideration by the Board of Trustees next fall. . . . Beginning now, much of our effort will go toward a major capital campaign for the Reynolda campus. . . .

In fact, the public campaign for the Reynolda campus did not begin until 1990 due to a $40 million campaign under way at the Medical Center.

> The 1990 campaign for the Reynolda campus will concentrate on facilities. . . . [A] shortage of space is being felt in student extracurricular programs and most academic departments and schools. Our last two campaigns were devoted to human resources: scholarships for students, professorships, and academic support. The Scales Fine Arts Center was the only new space added, and it is a highly specialized facility.

Hearn identified the need for a University center, a general classroom building, more space for the science departments, additions to the Z. Smith Reynolds Library, and new or more space for the undergraduate and graduate business programs. He also had a funding source in mind:

> Wake Forest parents represent our most important opportunity for new support. The building projects will be attractive to our parents, especially those of undergraduates. Our research shows that both the interest and the giving potential of our parents are considerable. About 24 percent have annual incomes of $100,000 or more. Moreover, between now and the campaign's conclusion in 1995, another 10,000 parent couples will be added to the 4,500 currently on our rolls.

Besides these future plans, the University continued receiving significant external support. William F. Carl, co-founder and director of the Golden Corral Corporation and a member of the Babcock Board of Visitors, gave a multi-million dollar gift in support of the Babcock School, which at the time enrolled approximately 275 students in its resident and weekend executive MBA programs. Other Babcock donors included a matching gift of $500,000 over five years from the Mary Reynolds Babcock Foundation, and $50,000 from the Broyhill Family Foundation to endow a lecture series that exposed business students to industry leaders.

In other acts of philanthropy, the Z. Smith Reynolds Foundation awarded the University a grant that "includes $1 million to endow additional Reynolds scholarships, $500,000 to be added to the Reynolds professorships endowment, $600,000 for additional minority scholarships, and $130,000 per year to increase the Foundation's annual operating contract from $620,000 to $750,000." Wake Forest was able to award four more Reynolds scholarships beginning with the 1986 freshman class, for a total of twenty. In another generous act, Egbert L. Davis Jr. created the Eleanor Layfield Davis Art Scholarship for undergraduate students in memory of his wife. According to *Wake Forest University Magazine*, "Total giving to Wake Forest for 1985–1986 topped the $20 million mark, an $8 million increase over 1984–1985. These figures place Wake Forest among the five best schools in the South in voluntary support."

In addition, the Charles A. Dana Foundation of New York awarded the University $300,000 to fund four junior-level, tenure-track faculty positions. According to Dean Thomas E. Mullen, the Dana Faculty Fellows would teach in the departments of computer science, chemistry, Romance languages, and history. Likewise, the Andrew W. Mellon Foundation awarded the University $300,000 to develop fresh combinations of teaching and learning to strengthen academic programs at the University.

Nevertheless, undergraduate tuition was set to increase 10 percent for 1986–1987. Hearn met with students to explain the steep rise, noting that less than 60 percent of their educational costs came from tuition. The costs of salaries, maintenance, and replacements had been deferred in years past, so "part of the increase is simply delayed reaction to past inflation."

The Hawthorne Campus was also experiencing a successful financial campaign. In an April 24 letter to J. Tylee Wilson, CEO of RJR Nabisco, President Hearn wrote: "I want to thank you for your company's decision to contribute $4.5 million to the Equation for Progress campaign at Bowman Gray. This is not only the largest gift you have ever made, it is also the largest the medical school has ever received." As a

Reynolds Scholars – First row: David Everman ('89), Lisa Knott ('89), Donna Bowman ('88), David Dixon ('87), Mike Davis ('87); second row: Rogan Kersh ('86), Jeannette Johnson ('88), Janice Telfer ('88), John David Fugate ('89)

prelude to events a number of years away, Hearn continued: "We are also grateful for your interest in seeing the name changed"—that is, from Bowman Gray School of Medicine. "Some measure of the importance of that change was the fact that the name 'Wake Forest' did not appear in the [*Winston-Salem*] *Journal* account of the gift. Indeed, from that story one would conclude that the gift was made to the medical center rather than to the University."

In addition to the RJR Nabisco gift, two Greensboro physicians, James Taylor Brooks and his wife, Jean Bailey Brooks (MD '44), pledged $1 million to the Bowman Gray School of Medicine to provide salary support for young men and women with excellent potential who desired careers in full-time academic medicine.

In a tragic event that produced an altruistic result, Hiram A. "Bif" Meyers III, a first-year student from Roswell, Georgia, died on September 22 while playing football with friends on the campus. In response, a scholarship in his name was established by his parents and friends.

To protect intellectual property, the University Inventions and Patent Policy was adopted. It promotes the application of research advances to the practical needs of the marketplace and established an important role for the University Patent Advisory Committee.

Alumni

Alex Sink ('70) succeeded George Brooks ('71) as 1985–1986 President of Wake Forest's National Alumni Association. In 1984–1985, College Fund National Chair Pete Davis ('40) and his wife Nancy had issued a million-dollar challenge for matching funds that was met in 1985–1986.

Mary Elizabeth Heim ('80) was named a Luce Scholar for 1985–1986. She was one of fifteen young Americans of outstanding promise sent to East and Southeast Asia to develop a deeper understanding of this area of the world. John Ruffin Knight ('78) also won a 1984–1985 Luce Scholarship.

Friends and family of Joel A. Weston ('59, MBA '73) established a scholarship in his name at the Babcock Graduate School of Management.

Summing Up the Year

The 1985–1986 academic year marked the beginning of the end of the University's relationship with the Baptist State Convention of North Carolina. It also started a string of academic achievements, including the award of prestigious scholarships such as the Rhodes. An improbable victory by a determined men's golf team in a dramatic fashion brought pride, satisfaction, and delight to a community frustrated by the performance of many other major athletic teams.

Administrators were brought in or promoted. Faculty achieved recognition, and two more were singled out for endowed Reynolds professorships. Students engaged in activities that expressed their feelings and beliefs and expanded their social networks. Behind all of these activities was a plan to transform the look of the campus by constructing new facilities and creating a planned community.

As the academic year came to a close, the sad news came that Harold Wayland Tribble (1899–1986) had died on June 17 at the age of 86. He was responsible for building the Wake Forest campus in Winston-Salem. Now, it seemed the institution he had shepherded into a new age and a different location would be expanded and transformed physically and academically in ways that would have been impossible for the tenth President to ever have imagined.

CHAPTER FOUR
1986–1987

The Baptists and the Building

This quadrangle was green with new spring, and I was here for an early and almost solitary Sunday walk. As I entered, I was aware of the pitched chirping of birds. Looking up, I saw that the quad had been invaded by a flock of goldfinches. By the scores—or the hundreds—they flew like golden bullets through the trees or hung like nugget ornaments on every branch. The quad was magical. I was captivated and captured. The goldfinches stayed and I stayed. . . . The watch on my arm warned me. I knew this poetic conflict between duty and desire. I stayed until duty could no longer be deferred, and rushed off. . . . Because I lack the poet's muse, my art is but to tell the story. My message is in the telling. Each must appropriate a meaning.

Thomas K. Hearn Jr., May 18, 1987;
Charge to the Graduates, Wake Forest University Commencement

The major event in 1986, and arguably the seminal event of the Hearn years, was the University's formal break with the Baptist Convention of North Carolina. On Tuesday, November 11, 1986, more than 81 percent of delegates at the annual meeting of the Convention voted for the break (2689 to 249).

Under the approved plan, Wake Forest was free to choose its trustees without input or interference from the Convention, which had wielded veto power over the nominations since 1923, maintaining that two-thirds of the Board of Trustees had to be North Carolina Baptists. This change allowed the University to select a more diverse group, and many alumni, formerly ineligible because of geography or creed, could serve on the governing board. In exchange for its autonomy, Wake Forest would no longer receive money directly from the Convention, losing $500,000 a year from an annual budget of $163 million at the time.

Messengers from the North Carolina Baptist State Convention voting

In a November 14 front-page story, the *Old Gold and Black* quoted President Hearn: "We're moving forward with a feeling of friendship in a new relationship." An editorial on the split in the same issue noted that the Convention had been a mentor more than a "financial partner." For the first time in 152 years, the University was without its identity as a Baptist institution of higher education.

During the process, Tom Hearn had kept Wayne Calloway, Chair of the Board of Trustees, informed. In a September 9 letter, Hearn was filled with optimism: "The leadership of the Baptist State Convention has now gone on record as supporting the proposals which will result in our complete institutional autonomy." On October 2, he wrote, "The General Board of the Baptist State Convention has endorsed our proposals by 103 to 9. This is the last stop before the Convention. This is *it* for me. No more negotiation—whatever the outcome."

The break was the result of a negotiation that lasted nearly a year and was conducted by covenant committees from the University and the Convention. Robert Philpott of Lexington was chairman of the Trustee committee, and the Reverend Jim Langford of Ahoskie headed the Convention group. Hearn praised the efforts of Joseph Branch ('38, JD) of Raleigh, the current Chair of the Trustees, and Weston P. Hatfield ('41) of Winston-Salem, the 1985 chair. He said Convention leaders, particularly President Bill Poe ('47), had been strong supporters of the disaffiliation.

Hearn was not open with everyone about his determination to leave the Baptist State Convention of North Carolina for a number of reasons. First, his vision was not universally shared. For instance, in regard to conversations with his predecessor, James Ralph Scales, Hearn told his close friend and ally Leon Corbett, "I became guarded" about sharing this plan to become a private institution. "I talked to him

[Scales] the day that the Baptist decision was made and called him and said it had happened. He said he didn't like it."

By spring 1987, Hearn was more upbeat. In an April 23 letter to Joseph Branch, he praised several members of his staff—Russell Brantley, Bill Joyner, Leon Corbett, and John Anderson—for working with him throughout the process. "This group conferred at every point of decision, and endlessly explored options, tactics and strategy. . . . I regard this as the most important development at Wake Forest since the 'removal.' It has removed the last obstacle which might have prevented the achievement of Wake Forest's full potential."

In a note titled "What It Means," Brantley laid out the crucial points:

- The relationship between the University and the Convention is now fraternal and voluntary, and the Convention no longer has any voice in the governance of the University.
- University Trustees will elect their own successors and will determine the procedures for election.
- The University will continue an expanded program of scholarships for North Carolina Baptist students and will continue to provide existing services for Baptists.
- The Convention will not distribute funds to the University under the Cooperative Program, but individual churches may contribute directly to the University.

"Existing services for Baptists," Brantley wrote, included and would continue to include tuition concessions for ministerial students and children of Baptist pastors, maintaining the Baptist Historical Collection in the Z. Smith Reynolds Library, a pastors' school, and a number of seminars, workshops, and lectures.

Overall, the new agreement allowed Wake Forest to answer only to itself in forging a future. It would never again have to think of how its actions—from faculty writing books to hosting official guests—would "play with the Baptists." Baptist ministers' letters to the administration and visits to campus would no longer carry the weight they had previously. Their recommendations on such matters as the role of women in the church would not be perceived, received, or responded to as before. While some on campus lamented the passing of a long and often beneficial relationship, most did not. The politics and polity of the two entities had moved miles apart over the years. Indeed, joy at the new freedom was probably the overriding emotion of the day among the campus community, alumni, friends, and supporters. Even those who were not fans of Wake Forest seemed pleased with the results.

As if the split with the Baptists were not enough, more good news—almost shocking in its magnitude—came less than three months later on January 15, 1987. RJR Nabisco donated its corporate headquarters building to the University. At the time, it was the largest corporate gift ever made to an educational institution. Although the University's space problems had been discussed before the gift was made, the actual notification came in a fairly brief phone call to President Hearn from F. Ross

Johnson, RJR Nabisco CEO since the 1985 merger of the two companies. Johnson and his family were not happy with their recent move. The *Winston-Salem Journal* reported that Johnson's wife Susan considered the city "bucolic." Johnson summarily uprooted RJR Nabisco headquarters to Atlanta and realized the corporation would no longer need the 519,000 square-foot building, which had been completed in 1977 at a cost of $40 million. Rather than leave it vacant and pay taxes on it, he offered it and its surrounding land to Wake Forest because, he said, of "its proximity to the University and the company's desire to see Wake Forest continue to grow." Ownership would transfer to Wake Forest in March, but RJR Nabisco continued to use it until the move to Atlanta in September. The company made the gift without any stipulations or restrictions regarding its use.

In his April 23 letter to Branch, Hearn celebrated: "This gift—with hard work and luck—promises to accelerate our development by as much as a decade." First, however, John Anderson, in charge of administrative planning, and Leon Corbett, Secretary to the University and the trustees, were tasked to determine the best use of the property. While that was not yet clear, the gift would keep on giving in perpetuity.

Other news from the year paled somewhat in comparison to these two landmarks, but events in the areas of academics, administration, athletics, the arts, student life, facilities, finances, and alumni quietly and significantly shaped the University as it approached the end of the 1980s.

Academics

President Hearn standing in front of former RJ Reynolds Headquarters Building

After the break with the Baptist State Convention, the Poteat Scholarship program was initiated by the University. Poteat scholarships were designated for highly admissible students who were active members of a church that was a member of the Baptist State Convention of North Carolina and who were expected to make a significant contribution to their church and community upon their graduation.

The scholarship was named for William Louis Poteat, an 1877 alumnus and Wake Forest's seventh President from 1905–1927. Poteat, who also served as President of the Baptist State Convention, was a widely respected biologist who believed in the teaching of evolution and articulated Wake Forest's role as a school where faith and reason could co-exist. . . . It was a gesture to the Convention that would indicate Wake Forest's genuine desire to foster the best of Baptist tradition and to educate the finest of Baptist students.

In the fall of 1986, the Graduate Council approved a new degree, the Master of Arts in Liberal Studies (MALS). Nancy Cotton, a professor in the English department, was selected to direct the initiative. With her broad liberal arts interests and knowledge of the University, Cotton was ideally suited to cultivate a cross-disciplinary faculty and to recruit students to pursue the degree. The *Old Gold and Black* editorialized that it would attract older students and help reduce the homogeneity of the student body.

In another important degree-related initiative, the Babcock School of Management was authorized to offer an evening MBA program. John Anderson was responsible for supervising the renovations of Amos Cottage on the Graylyn Estate for this program with the aim of maximizing space gains by this expenditure. Administrators hoped that an evening program would attract nontraditional students who had several years' work experience but would be more likely to hold professional positions than positions in general management. Rather than managers and executives *per se*, the target student base would be lawyers, accountants, actuaries, art directors, designers, journalists, even medical doctors. Students would have to take nine core courses that corresponded to the common body of knowledge prescribed by the national accrediting body and choose three electives in marketing, finance, human resource management, or operations, which would constitute their individual concentration. They were also required to take two electives outside the area of concentration.

While offered off campus, the program would bring in tuition dollars and, hopefully, other kinds of support for the University from those earning their MBA degrees. The program would also enhance Wake Forest's connection to local businesses. The program was launched in January 1987, with Business Professor Peter Peacock as director. Amos Cottage was renamed Management House.

At their September 15 meeting, college faculty overwhelmingly approved establishment of a major in computer science to begin in the spring semester. At the November meeting, faculty approved a minor in Russian and, in February, a new twenty-credit-hour minor in international studies.

On Founders' Day in February, Alumni Association President Earle A. Connelly ('48) announced the creation of the Alumni Scholarship Program. The amount of the award was not specified, but the scholarships were to be supported by the College Fund. The initial scholarships would go to first-year students entering in fall of 1988, with an eventual goal of providing eighty such awards annually, or twenty per class. In a related initiative on the faculty side, Paul H. Broyhill announced that the Broyhill Family Foundation was establishing the Broyhill Chair of Leadership and Management Development at the Babcock Graduate School of Management, with an endowment exceeding $1 million.

A number of faculty members received awards and accolades in addition to those just mentioned. Teresa Radomski, soprano in the Department of Music, appeared with guitarist John Patykula in a recital of Spanish music in June 1987 at the Weill Recital Hall in Carnegie Hall.

Robert A. Browne (Biology) received three grants totaling almost $100,000 from the Fulbright Program, the Whitehall Foundation, and the National Geographic Society to study the important role of brine shrimp evolution in aquaculture, or water farming. He conducted his research at the University of Ghent, Belgium. His departmental colleague, Raymond Kuhn, received a five-year, $883,138 MERIT award from the National Institutes of Health to investigate Chagas disease, a tropical disease prevalent in Central and South America caused by a single-celled parasite that can devastate the heart muscle, the esophagus, and the large intestine.

Stan Thomas in the Mathematics and Computer Science Department was one of ten educators in the United States chosen to receive a ten-week summer fellowship to conduct research at the Kennedy Space Center in Merritt Island, Florida.

On July 31, 1986, Governor Jim Martin appointed former Law Professor Rhoda Billings to replace retiring North Carolina Chief Justice Joseph Branch. Billings had been appointed Associate Justice by Martin in the previous year. On November 4, however, she lost the election to serve out the remaining four years of Branch's eight-year term and returned to teaching law at the University in January 1987.

Internally, Dean of the College Tom Mullen reported that 80 percent of the full-time faculty was tenured, as compared with 60 to 65 percent at most universities. He attributed the difference to "different tenure practices" at other institutions. Concerned about workload, President Hearn wrote to Provost Wilson on February 3, asking him to find a way to compensate department chairs.

Bynum Shaw ('51, English) became the first recipient of the Jon Reinhardt Award for Distinguished Teaching. Professor of German and Russian William Hamilton led thirty-five students and others interested in Russia and the Russian language on a tour of the Soviet Union over spring break, the third since 1985.

On November 20, the Z. Smith Reynolds Library announced the acquisition of its millionth volume. The Museum of Man moved to a space behind the German House at the start of the spring semester and officially opened on May 18, 1987. Since moving out of Reynolda Village, it had been without a home for eighteen months, with its artifacts stored in the basement of Tribble Hall and other buildings.

Administration and Staff

Russell Brantley retired on January 1, 1987. He came to Wake Forest College from the *Durham Morning Herald* in 1953 and had been the institution's primary spokesperson for thirty-four years. He was known for being frank and factual and not shy in voicing his opinions, even if they were unpopular or controversial. For these qualities and his keen ability to delineate and address the University's major concerns, Brantley was not only valued but beloved. Although stepping out of his daily role in the News Bureau, he agreed to stay as a consultant to the President, a role he first filled in the Scales administration. Sandra Connor, Assistant Director of Development, became Director of Public Information and Assistant to the President on February 27.

The year also saw promotions. On January 1, University Counsel Leon H. Corbett Jr. ('59, JD '61) became Vice President for Legal Affairs while retaining the title and functions of Secretary to the University. Robert T. Baker was promoted to

Assistant Director of Development while retaining his previous title as Director of Corporate Relations. James Bullock ('85) was promoted from Assistant Director of Alumni Activities to Law Development Officer. Allen H. (Chip) Patterson ('72) joined the Wake Forest development office as Director of Planned Giving, and James G. (Jim) Welsh Jr. ('87) became the new Assistant Director of Alumni Activities.

Dennis Gregory, a graduate of the University of Virginia, was appointed Director of Residence Life and Housing, replacing Ed Cunnings, who resigned. Gregory was the first person to hold this position since the two offices were combined on July 1, 1986.

Billy Hamilton

The administration continued to be focused on planning. On July 2, President Hearn sent a memo to Provost Wilson, stating that he "would like to have an outline of our faculty recruitment plans for the coming year as best we can project them." Later that month, he sent a second memo requesting the involvement of the Provost and Vice President Joyner in "the planning of meetings of the professional schools' Board of Visitors, alumni conferences, and other activities." In addition to these requests, the President met with the faculty on September 30 in Brendle Recital Hall to report on the state of the University and the progress to date in the long-range planning process. Both in his private memos and at public meetings, Hearn was diligent in fulfilling his promise to the trustees that he would plan for the future of Wake Forest.

Hearn also sought to honor the University's history. He wrote Vice President Joyner on January 19 about having a portrait of James Ralph Scales painted by an artist of national reputation. He estimated that "it will cost between $25,000 and $30,000." However, instead of taking the money out of tuition dollars or a contingency fund, he instructed Joyner to try to find a donor "who might not otherwise be a candidate for gifts to WFU." A year later, the portrait hung with previous portraits of Wake Forest presidents in the second-floor corridor of Reynolda Hall, near the administrative offices of the President and Vice President.

Athletics

Football, basketball, women's cross-country, and field hockey dominated athletics news for the year. Contract extension negotiations between the University and Head Football Coach Al Groh broke down during the late fall and early winter months of 1986. As a result, Groh left Wake Forest. After six years, his overall record against all opponents was 26 wins and 40 losses (.394) with a record against ACC schools of 8 wins and 30 losses (.211). As Hearn explained in a January 21 letter to Jack K. Miller of Winston-Salem, "the pressing point from the University's perspective . . . was our

Russell Brantley

request to know by the beginning of recruitment and planning for spring football that Coach Groh would in fact honor the contract [offered to him] as binding." In a surprise move, Bill Dooley was hired that very day as the new head football coach, within a week of Al Groh's departure. Dooley, who had had previous winning records at the University of North Carolina and Virginia Tech, with an overall record of 132–91–3, became the thirtieth head football coach in Wake Forest history.

Television's *P.M. Magazine* featured a video of the "Deacon Rap" recorded by thirteen Wake Forest football players right before the 1986 season. The chorus went as follows:

We're the Deacs. You know our name.
All this rap is part of our game.
Hustlin' keeps us lean and mean,
A Black and Gold fightin' machine.
It's the Deacon rap and before we're through,
You're gonna be a Wake Watcher, too.

Bill Dooley

The catchy number appeared on MTV, ESPN, and CNN and was noted in newspapers in Atlanta and Charleston. Solo rappers were A.J. Greene, Paul Kiser, Tim Morrison, Jamie Harris, and Darryl McGill.

On the basketball front, negotiations between the City of Winston-Salem and the University for a new coliseum were successful. In a December 8 letter to Deacon Club members, President Hearn wrote: "The University has agreed to contribute nearly $5 million toward construction costs of the Coliseum. We need your help to meet that commitment." Members responded by contributing to The Advantage Drive, and the President wrote to Joseph Branch on April 23: "Ground will be broken this week on the new coliseum. Our approved participation ($5 million) is being secured by a Deacon Club effort which now stands above $4.2 million. The coliseum will be owned and operated by the city and be decorated as a Wake Forest home court. We pay rent and they have the operating costs."

Approximately 3,900 seats in the new coliseum were reserved for Wake Forest students: 153 courtside seats, 744 seats in the lower arena, and 1,698 in the upper level. Student enthusiasm had dwindled, however, under new basketball Head Coach Bob Staak, who had failed to win a single ACC game (0–14) the previous season. The Deacon Spirit, a group of "spirited students" who arrived thirty minutes before each home game except those played over Christmas break and during exams, and sat behind the Deacon bench, disbanded before the 1986 season began. It had formed under former Coach Carl Tacy with the understanding that students would cheer on the team with the cheerleaders in a positive manner and stay until the *alma mater* and fight song had been played. Between 400 and 600 students signed up in the 1985–1986 season, but by the end of most games, only around 50 were still in the stands, and they often did not wear the T-shirts or use the shakers provided them. With the break-up of the Deacon Spirit group, student seating did not change, and in a positive development, students continued to sit behind the bench.

They had much to cheer for, as Muggsy Bogues, the 5'3" sparkplug who had helped lead the United States to the gold medal in the Goodwill Games the previous summer, handled the basketball like a magician. The All-ACC player could not turn the Deacons around, however, and Wake Forest suffered through a second losing season under Coach Staak, finally breaking a twenty-four-game ACC losing streak by beating Maryland 69–58 on February 2. Bogues's jersey (#14) was retired at the end of the season, and he went on to play for fourteen seasons in the National Basketball Association, with one of the teams for which he played being the Charlotte Hornets.

In women's cross-country, Francie Goodridge's squad was ranked nineteenth nationally by *Harrier* magazine. This was the first Deacon squad outside of football, basketball, and men's golf to be ranked nationally. The team was anchored by two All-American runners, Jennifer Rioux and Karen Dunn, female athlete of the year in 1985 and the first Deacon woman to be named a Division I All-American. The team finished second in the ACC Championships behind Clemson.

The field hockey team, with a 16–2 win-loss record, beat Appalachian State in a 2–1 shootout to claim the Big South championship.

A victim of Wake Forest's emphasis on achieving excellence on and off the field was the volleyball team. It was terminated in March of 1987 because it was not seen as competitive.

Muggsy Bogues

During the 1986–1987 academic year, the Athletic Department received constant criticism, regardless of wins or losses or positive publicity. Letters suggesting that the University deemphasize athletics steadily flowed into the President's Office. President Hearn made time to answer them, although he would often send the same letter. On August 15, he wrote to Fred Craven of Concord:

. . . we are justly proud of our record. Wake Forest is one of only sixteen schools (called 'The Sweet 16' in an article in the *Philadelphia Inquirer*) which have never had a sanction or a reprimand from the NCAA. In addition, we have had the only mandatory drug testing program in the Atlantic Coast Conference for the past two years. What other schools are doing now in response to crises [in athletics], we have been doing based on the simple belief that it was good and prudent policy.

Chip Rives, a junior football player, along with mentor and co-founder Robert Egleston ('78), started Santa's Helpers, a charity to provide toys to underprivileged children. Rives had read a story in *Parade* magazine about a project that delivered gifts to underprivileged children. As a result he convinced some of his fellow athletes and other students to donate money to buy non-violent toys. Then, dressed as Santa and his helpers, Rives and his companions delivered the toys they had bought.

The Pruitt Center was completed in the summer of 1986, named in honor of Mark C. Pruitt ('86), who was killed in a water-skiing accident in the summer of 1985. It housed new football offices and meeting rooms that adjoined the Indoor Athletic Complex and was state-of-the-art, with separate offices for coaches, a staff conference room, and a modern learning/education center for all student athletes called DEACS (Deacons' Educational Assistance and Counseling Services). When the facility became operational in mid-July 1986, University academic/athletics counselor Gilbert McGregor ('71) took delight in showing it off. Students made good use of it.

Besides being concerned about winning athletic teams in the ACC, students showed their sense of humor about sports, especially basketball, as revealed in an *Old Gold and Black article* on the names of intramural basketball teams. Names included the Potato Teams (We Love Our Spuds, The Couch Potatoes, and Potato Tuberworms), the We're-No-Good-and-We-Know-Its (Have Nots, Has Beens, Brick Boys, The Handicapped Hoops, The Clueless Crew, and Aaaahhghh), the We're-Awesome-and-We-Know-Its (Phi Samba Jamma, Jabba Jammers, Dunkensteins, and Lords of the

Rim), the Rock 'n' Roll Band Teams (The Mangoes, Captain and His Midnights, Lance and the Romantics, and Dave Clark 8), and the World Affairs Teams (Hazardous Waste, The Plowshares, Infectious Disease, and Oliver North and the Fifth Amendment).

The Arts

The Artists Series received a financial boost as Marion Secrest endowed it in honor of her late husband Willis, who practiced dentistry in Winston-Salem from 1925–1965. The renamed Secrest Artists Series of Wake Forest University brought in pianist Philippe Biaconi; guitarist Christopher Parkening; violinist Elmar Oliviera; the Czech Philharmonic; and the King's Singers, an a cappella ensemble named after King's College, Cambridge, where the group came together.

The University Theatre produced performances of Jerome Lawrence and Robert Edwin Lee's *Inherit the Wind*, Richard Brinsley Sheridan's *The Rivals*, Ugo Betti's *The Queen and the Rebels*, and William Shakespeare's *A Midsummer Night's Dream*.

Campus and Student Life

In 1986–1987, students were generally content and did well academically. According to the Registrar's Office, the most popular major was business, with more than 110 students, followed by economics and biology. Classical languages, Greek and Latin, had the fewest majors. Maria Merritt, a Reynolds Scholar and biology major

Chip Rives as Wake Forest football fullback

Chip Rives as Santa Claus with his helpers

from Franklin, Virginia, became Wake Forest's second consecutive Rhodes Scholar, following Richard Chapman.

Some of the major student leaders this year were Steve LaMastra, Student Government President; Ronald H. Hart II, Editor-in-Chief of the *Old Gold and Black*; Tricia Daisley, President of the Student Union; and Jenny A. Kletzin, Editor-in-Chief of *The Howler*.

Increased visitation hours were welcome and celebrated

In intercollegiate scholastic activities, a team of seniors from the School of Business and Accountancy—Billy Hinshaw, Christy Kokulis, Majorie Buff, and Shannan Spence—won the national championship in the Intercollegiate Business Competition. The team competed against eighteen other schools in a six-week computerized business-simulation game, with the final round at Emory University. Their win solidified Wake Forest's record of winning the competition more times than any other school since the games started in 1966. Wake Forest teams won the national championship in 1976, 1980, 1983, and 1987. No other team had won more than twice.

The Wake Forest Moot Court Team—Scott Lovejoy, Donna Sisson, and Karen Williams—also won national honors,

defeating the University of Kansas at the thirty-seventh
annual National Moot Court competition. Lovejoy and Williams were first and second, respectively, in the best oralist
competition for oral advocacy skills.

On the social scene, a new policy, the first major
change in hours since spring 1984, increased inter-visitation by twenty-nine hours per week in all campus dormitories. The new hours extended visitation from noon
to 1 a.m. on weekdays and 10 a.m. to 1 a.m. on weekends.

On September 1, 1986, the legal drinking age in
North Carolina and nationally changed to 21, and a new
on-campus Student Alcoholic Beverage Policy prohibited the use or possession of alcohol by those under 21.
President Hearn sought other preventive measures, and
in a July 24 memo to John Anderson, who had oversight
of student life at the time, asked for a review of substance abuse programs at Wake Forest. He wished to "be
involved in this matter personally." Hearn made no secret
that his father had abused alcohol, and he did not want

*The change in the NC
drinking law was noted
everywhere*

substance abuse taking a toll on the University. As a result, the Office of the Dean of
Students was directed to conduct an Alcohol Policy Education-Orientation Program
at the beginning of each academic year. Two members from all residential and social
student organizations were required to attend, and each Greek organization had to be
represented by its president, social chairman, and two party monitors.

In communication matters, residents of South, Huffman, and Efird residence
halls returned to campus to find that their hall phones had been removed over the
summer. The expanded administration needed sixty-four extensions, but the maximum had been met until new lines could be installed.

A new computerized registration system was offered for the first time in the
spring of 1987. The Registrar's Office and most students praised the system for its
speed and efficiency. Margaret Perry, the Registrar, said that the process went exceptionally well for a "first-time run." Students seemed "especially positive toward the
decrease in time spent standing in line."

On September 1, Student Government President LaMastra formed the Student
Government President's Select Commission on Race Relations, a ten-person committee that operated through April 1, 1987. In a February 13 article in the *Old Gold
and Black*, the committee reported that only 114 students, or 3 percent of the student
body, were black compared to 3,300 white students. The number of black students
applying to Wake Forest had fallen off from 114 in fall 1986 to 83 in fall 1987. Out
of fifty-six administrators, only one, Ernie Wade, was black; of 229 full-time professors, six were black. Following the commission's report, President Hearn appointed
a faculty committee to examine race relations. Chaired by Provost Edwin Wilson, its
members were John Anderson (Vice President Adminstration); Ernest Wade, Director of Minority Affairs; Beth Hopkins (Legal Department); Margaret Supplee Smith
(Art); Eddie Easley (Calloway School of Business and Accountancy); Susan McCaffrey (History); and Don Schoonmaker (Political Science). Outside of racial matters,

the Student Legislature passed a bill in the spring semester condemning the "harassment of homosexuals." Student Government also sponsored an informal discussion of other campus concerns for students, faculty, and staff called "The President Answers" from 11 a.m. to noon on Thursdays in the main lounge of Reynolda Hall. Overall, the President and students got along well.

The Student Union (which had formerly been the College Union) sponsored two competitions: the College Bowl and qualifying tournaments in ping pong, pool, backgammon, bridge, chess, bowling, and the board game Othello. Winners went on to regional competitions. In the spring of 1987, the Wake Alternative Break began. Instead of going home or to the beach, students spent their spring break helping others less fortunate than themselves.

Before spring came, fifteen inches of snow fell on January 23, 1987. Maintaining its long-standing policy, classes at the University were not officially cancelled (however, some did not meet). Only one-quarter of food service workers reported, and the Snack Bar and Magnolia Room were closed. Students took trays from "the Pit," the main dining hall in Reynolda Hall, for sledding, and Chuck Hess, the Food Services Director, became concerned that there were not enough trays for use by patrons.

Facilities, Finances, and Alumni

Adequate space, traffic, and beautification were the top three physical campus concerns of 1986–1987. Student space was especially scarce, and in a January 28 memo

Computerized registration eliminated congestion in Reynolda Hall like this

to the vice presidents, President Hearn stated, "We are preparing to move ahead with architectural, planning and construction matters regarding the University Center on an accelerated schedule." In an April 23 letter to Joseph Branch, Hearn stated that "current plans call for construction to begin in 1988." The building was projected to cost $8 million and was under the supervision of John Anderson because of his engineering background and seemingly boundless energy. In the fall, Cliff Benson ('64 and Wake Forest parent and trustee) had pledged $1 million. In January, Wayne Calloway ('59), Chair and CEO of PepsiCo, Inc., announced a $1 million gift for the construction of the center, and Joseph Luter and his wife gave $1 million to Wake Forest—$500,000 for the University Center, $100,000 for the Joel Coliseum, and $400,000 for the men's and women's athletic programs.

President Hearn answers student questions

In another physical matter, Silas Creek Parkway's direct route through the campus as a north/south artery had become a major headache. Traffic was congested and pedestrians crossing the circumference roads, especially to the Scales Fine Arts Center, were endangered. Further, on October 13, 1986, President Hearn wrote to Mayor Wayne Corpening, enclosing an article from a recent *Old Gold and Black* "dealing with a chronic institutional problem on this campus—vandalism. A large measure of our vandalism results from juveniles who find themselves here as a result of our current traffic patterns. This is yet another reason why our concern about the Silas Creek Parkway matter is so intense." The President suggested a Silas Creek bypass behind the AT&T building. Otherwise, he thought Wake Forest would deteriorate as a campus and an asset to the Winston-Salem community. Reid Morgan, Assistant University Counsel, said that the proposed Silas Creek Parkway extension to North Point Boulevard could be completed by 1993. It would reduce the traffic flowing through the campus, which was estimated at between 12,500 and 17,500 cars per day.

Trees were another dominant concern, especially the forty-two elm trees on the main quad between Wait Chapel and Reynolda Hall. At thirty years old, they provided a magnificent canopy, but they were dying from a fungus known as Dutch Elm Disease. Nina Allen (Biology) chaired a committee appointed by the President to address the problem. The committee began work in September to develop a landscape plan that would become a part of the University's Master Campus Plan for new building and development compiled by the Capital Planning Committee and updated every five years.

In financial matters, the Pro Humanitate Society was established as a club for donors who agreed to give the University $50,000 over a ten-year period. The President's Club, for donors who agreed to give $10,000 over a ten-year period, reached an

Trustee Wayne Calloway and Student Government President
Steve LaMastra celebrate over a cup of Pepsi

all-time high membership of 762. The College Fund increased by 23 percent to a new record of $1.49 million, surpassing the 1986–1987 goal of $1.35 million. In a July 23, 1987, letter to Joseph Branch, President Hearn stated: "Total University fundraising last year reached $22 million excluding the RJR-Nabisco gift. This includes $13 million for the Reynolda Campus and $9 million at Bowman Gray. This is, of course, the best year in our history, but totals this year are ahead again."

On the other hand, trustees raised tuition 9.9 percent, a $650 increase, at their January 24 meeting. Tuition was set at $7,250 for the 1987–1988 school year, and overall expenses for on-campus students were estimated to be approximately $11,000. Tuition for the Graduate School was the same, and tuition for the Law School was $8,200; for the Babcock Graduate School of Management, tuition was $9,300; and for the School of Medicine, $10,500. Hearn defended the sharp hike in tuition by stating that much of it would be used to increase salaries for instructors and assistant professors; overall, salaries constituted about two-thirds of the University's annual budget.

The December 8 issue of *People* magazine cited Wake Forest as one of ten "value-packed schools," describing it as "one of the most heavily endowed coed universities in America" and having particularly strong departments of history, English, and business.

The University's commitment to the Winston-Salem community was underscored when Don Meredith and Dinah Shore visited the campus on Wednesday, September 24, to kick off the United Way campaign. President Hearn chaired the campaign for Winston-Salem/Forsyth County.

Alumni

In alumni affairs, H. Dean Propst ('56), Chancellor of the University System of Georgia, and Jan McQuere McDonagh ('64), Associate Professor of Pathology at Harvard Medical School and known internationally for her research on blood disease, were awarded the Distinguished Service Citation by the Alumni Association on October 3.

C.C. Hope Jr. ('43) was sworn in as a member of the Federal Deposit Insurance Corporation's Board of Directors.

Earle A. Connelly ('48) of Troy, North Carolina, became President of the University's Alumni Association for 1986–1987.

Summing Up the Year

The year 1986–1987 was one of the zeniths for this administration. The formal end to the connection with the North Carolina Baptist State Convention was profound and freed Wake Forest to grow in many dimensions as an institution of higher education. The gift of the RJR Nabisco corporate headquarters building was also a major acquisition and opened possibilities that were not expected to accrue for at least another decade.

Two new degree offerings, the evening MBA and the Master of Arts in Liberal Studies, attracted more regional students and attention to Wake Forest. The hiring of Bill Dooley as the new Head Football Coach signaled to alumni and rivals alike that the University intended to be competitive in a sport where it had seen little success. The success of women's teams in cross-country and field hockey was another indicator that the Deacons were striving for victory in all their athletic endeavors. Successful negotiations with the City of Winston-Salem over the building of a new coliseum held out hope for a reversal of basketball fortunes and a return to home games in Winston-Salem after several years of playing ACC games at the Greensboro Coliseum.

Planning continued to emphasize both physical facilities, such as the new student center and a Silas Creek bypass, and faculty recruitment and growth. Although students were not aware of it, the consolidation of residence life and housing, as well as President Hearn's interests in preventing substance abuse, would have direct and positive impacts in future years. Finally, Maria Merritt's Rhodes scholarship was continuing evidence in support of Wake Forest's reputation for academic excellence. The University was poised for future growth, both qualitatively and quantitatively. It was independent!

A Farewell to Elms and Other Transitions

In May we will stand with dozens of new trees that will be growing daily to fulfill their identity. In the morning sun, the delicate beauty of the young saplings will hint at future majesty. Drawing strength from the roots we have put down at Wake Forest, let us strive to fulfill our human potential with the same steadfastness of spirit that can be seen in the growth of a young tree. The disappointment that follows a loss is overcome by the joy of new life and thrill of creation. It is our duty to those who came before us and who created the beauty we see today, to maintain the traditions of our University, including the quadrangle. Wake Forest is the garden of our sapling years: each of us is then transplanted to a life where our potential is actualized, where we can reflect the glory of our creation as purely, strongly and beautifully as a mature tree.

Claire Ball at the ceremony preceding the Thanksgiving removal of the elm trees on the Quad; quoted by Thomas K. Hearn Jr., May 16, 1988; Charge to the Graduates, Wake Forest University Commencement

After a transformative year in which Wake Forest became an independent institution of higher education, the 1987–1988 academic year could be characterized as an in-between year, albeit one marked by recognitions, transitions, expectations, and loss. In October 1987, *U.S. News & World Report* brought out its first national rankings of colleges and universities. The criteria were not always clear, but the public impact was; the issue sold briskly as applicants read about their potential choices. Wake Forest was ranked "best comprehensive institution" in the Southern and Border-State Comprehensive Institutions category. It would hold that position for eight consecutive years before the magazine reclassified it from regional to national ranking in 1995. As President Hearn would say later: "We retired after eight years still undefeated." Perhaps more prestigious, the *Wall Street Journal*

Scott DuBois, Mike Smith, and Beth Dawson were responsible for bringing the 1988 Presidential Debate to Wake Forest

included Wake Forest in its list of the sixteen best bargains for higher education in the nation, based on a tuition under $8,000 and admissions standards among the highest 4 percent. In any case, applications were on the rise. In a March 23 letter to William B. Sansom in Knoxville, Tennessee, Hearn wrote, "Applications are up 50 percent in the last four years," and up 15 percent over the previous year. For the 900 spaces in the first-year class of 1988, there were 6,000 applications.

A second significant recognition was the announcement in May of 1988 that Wake Forest had been chosen to host the first presidential debate on September 25, 1988. The staging of the event would cast an unprecedented national spotlight on the University. The idea was generated by three students who were members of the Young Republicans: Mike Smith, Scott DuBois, and Beth Dawson. Smith, who was Vice President of Student Government, had helped coordinate the campus visit of New York Governor Mario Cuomo the year before and had enjoyed the experience so much that he wanted to do more. When he learned that the Commission on Presidential Debates was looking for venues, he persuaded his two friends to join him in proposing Wake Forest.

The students shared their ambition with Director of Public Affairs Sandra Connor. She phoned alumnus Al Hunt, a prominent Washington, D.C., journalist, who knew Janet Brown, executive director of the newly formed Commission on Presidential Debates. He arranged for Ms. Connor and Mr. Smith to meet with her in April 1987, and she advised them on making a formal proposal. Starting in the summer of 1987, Smith worked tirelessly to raise awareness of Wake Forest's desire to host the debates. Through Norman Chambliss, the parent of two Wake Forest alumni, Smith was invited to a reception for George H.W. Bush in eastern North Carolina and while there asked Bush to pick Wake Forest as one of the debate sites. Finally, with the help of Ms. Connor, the student trio assembled an application packet, and Smith made a videotape about the University. They assured the commission that, if selected, Wake Forest would implement an intense voter education program in the area. On October 26, 1987, President Hearn submitted a support letter to the Commission, and Wake Forest was selected.

Amidst the joy, there was a sad transition. The elm trees on the main quad between Wait Chapel and Reynolda Hall were cut down. They had graced the campus with their stately beauty and capacious shade since 1956. Grounds crews had made a stubborn effort to save them, but sixteen of the original trees had succumbed to Dutch elm disease. On November 23, a memorial service was held in front of Wait Chapel. The President as well as members of the student body spoke. When everyone returned after Thanksgiving break, the quad was bare; two elms were left standing in front of Wait Chapel. Autumn purple ash saplings were planted in their place, and the quad looked rather as it had when students first arrived in the fall of 1956 and the elms were saplings. With the help of J. Smith Young ('39), President of Dixie Furniture of Lexington, wood from the plaza elms was salvaged, dried in a kiln, and made into mementos.

At commencement, President Hearn's charge to the graduating class was entitled Trees of '88 Are Symbolic. He reminded graduates of the fleeting nature of trees and life.

> These elms, like all gifts of beauty and love, were for a season. Our task, the human task, is to accept with gratitude the legacy of beauty, truth, and goodness others have created for us, while we turn to the task of creating new monuments of mind, heart, and hand. We plant for those who in future years will sit beneath the shelter of these young trees, as our forebears gave the elms in promise for us whom they did not know. Thus did they and do we now fulfill our motto: *Pro Humanitate.* . . . These new trees are a symbol of . . . commencing, and it is well therefore that you graduates are placed among these sapling ashes—all of you and the trees portending growth and opportunity.

Other internal matters ranged from the quiet announcement that the Z. Smith Reynolds Library's collection had passed one million volumes to the disclosure in a January 13 memo from the President to faculty, staff, and University friends

Elm trees cut down

New ash trees waiting to be planted

Bynum Shaw

that a committee had been appointed to study the feasibility of establishing a divinity school. This committee was chaired by Vice President John Anderson and included Provost Ed Wilson, Religion Professors Carlton Mitchell and Charles Talbert, soon-to-be Vice President Ken Zick, and Richard Groves, minister of the on-campus Wake Forest Baptist Church. Associate Vice President Lu Leake was the staff officer.

Journalism Professor Bynum Shaw ('51) published *The History of Wake Forest College, Volume 4.* It covers the years 1943–1967, including World War II, the admission of women, the offer by the Z. Smith Reynolds Foundation to move the College, the end of the Thurman D. Kitchen presidency, and the inauguration and, later, retirement of Harold Wayland Tribble as president.

Academics

The Opening Convocation speaker on September 8 was Gardner Calvin Taylor, described by *Ebony* and the *Harvard Divinity School Bulletin* as "one of the greatest preachers in American history." He was awarded an honorary degree. His sponsor was Maya Angelou. In the spring semester, former North Carolina Supreme Court Chief Justice and alumnus Joseph Branch ('38) was the featured speaker for the Founders' Day Convocation. As part of the occasion, faculty were recognized. Katy Harriger (Political Science) received the Reid-Doyle Prize for Excellence in Teaching, and Marcellus Waddill (Mathematics) received the Omicron Delta Kappa Award for Contributions to Student Life. Three Awards for Excellence in Research went to Robert Browne (Biology), James Hans (English), and Willie Pearson (Sociology). The Medallion of Merit, the University's highest honor, was presented to Richard Myers in the Department of Surgery at the Bowman Gray School of Medicine.

An ad hoc committee, formed in response to several allegations of sexism, racism, and sexual abuse in the spring of 1986, issued a report to the faculty and the University in September on the social and academic responsibilities of students. The committee was appointed by Provost Wilson and chaired by Margaret Supplee Smith (Art). After polling undergraduates and faculty, the committee found that, although Wake Forest is "unusually blessed with a fine group of students," it "nurtures a homogeneous majority culture that does not have much tolerance for difference, whether that minority culture be black, female, gay, or serious students." It went on: "[S]tudents mostly come from affluent, privileged homes and the faculty and administration are secure and comfortable, perhaps even complacent. If we want our academic community to be intellectually lively, socially responsible, and spiritually open, it is up to all of us, trustees and administration, faculty and students to make it so."

In a related event, the Women's Issues Group signed a statement on February 17 supporting the gay and lesbian community at the University in response to concerns about homophobia on campus. The group also formed committees offering support for gays and lesbians. The group decided to take this action at its January 28 meeting, after discussing racism, sexism, and homophobia, according to Mary DeShazer (English), who served as Director of the Women's Studies Program. The statement read: "I support the gay and lesbian student community on the Wake Forest University campus. I affirm the right of individual differences and I acknowledge my belief that equality is the mutual acceptance of differences."

To promote the hiring of young faculty with children, a faculty group, headed by Becky Myers (Dance) and Claire Hammond (Economics), promoted the idea of a day-care program.

In other matters, the faculty unanimously passed a resolution on March 14 to abolish the campus-wide visitation policy and to allow almost unrestricted visitation. It also established a 50–50 male-to-female ratio as a basis for admissions. Paul Kaplan (Art) headed the committee that formed the resolution and presented it at the faculty meeting.

The Alumni Association formally announced the creation of an Alumni Scholarship program, which would later be called the Presidential Scholarship Program. It aimed to attract students who excelled in the arts, public speaking, creative writing, entrepreneurial activities, service to others, or a specific intellectual pursuit. President Hearn wrote David Rader of Morganton on July 8, 1987: "We anticipate offering thirteen scholarships valued at $3,000 per year, with the number of scholarships increasing to twenty in subsequent years." Actually, ten were offered initially. The purpose was "to increase the diversity of the student body and enrich the Wake Forest undergraduate experience."

In an effort to promote community and to eliminate student problems related to alcohol abuse, the President sent out a memo to faculty on March 4, urging them to have social contact with students "from our academic programs." While Hearn's urging was sincere, no new or program-wide initiatives resulted.

Faculty were active and honored in their own domains. Maya Angelou, Reynolds Professor of American Studies, was one of five recipients of the 1987 North Carolina Award, the state's highest recognition, at a ceremony in Raleigh on November 6. She was the first Wake Forest faculty member to be so distinguished, although poet Archie Ammons ('49) won in 1986.

Cyclone Covey (History) published *The Gulf of the Past*, addressing Henry James's assertion that "fiction is history." Margaret Supplee Smith (Art) coordinated a project on North Carolina women's history for the North Carolina Museum of History. Alumnus and future Trustee K. Wayne Smith was appointed a University Professor, teaching courses in the Calloway School of Business and Accountancy and the Political Science Department; English Professor Mary DeShazer became the first full-time coordinator of the Women's Studies Program; and Dijon Program Director Mary Francis Robinson epitomized heroism by wading waist-deep in the Gardon River in southern France on October 30, 1987, to rescue a drowning woman. In another humane act, Sociology Professor Emeritus Clarence H. Patrick and his wife, Adele, gave $10,000 to establish a fund for sociology lectures. Patrick had chaired the department from 1948–1964.

Allen Easley, Professor Emeritus of Religion, turned 95, a milestone noted by many. He had been awarded the Medallion of Merit in 1972, and although no longer active in the classroom, he was a deeply beloved and respected figure, regularly seen on campus. The University would later name a campus street in his honor. At the birthday celebration in April, John William Angell was named the first John Allen Easley Professor of Religion.

Finally, a report on Reynolda Campus faculty salaries noted that they had increased for all ranks an average of 34 percent over the last five years. The average increase at the instructor level was 46.6 percent; for assistant professors, 40.6 percent; associate professors, 34.9 percent; and professors, 31.2 percent. Still, an *Old Gold and Black* editorial noted that instructor and assistant professor salaries were considerably lower than those at comparable institutions, and if starting salaries were too low, Wake Forest would not attract top-quality entry-level faculty for the coming years.

Maya Angelou

Administration and Staff

Turnover at the two Reynolda campus professional schools, Law and Business, and reorganization of other administrative offices marked major transitions during the year. Dean John Scarlett of the Law School announced his retirement in March 1988. He had been Dean since 1979 and now planned to retire in June 1989. Under his leadership, the student/faculty ratio improved from 31.5:1 to 17:1; the national average for law school class sizes at the time was 25:1. In addition, the Law School reduced its dependence on tuition by 18 percent and was in the forefront in classroom use of electronic technology. The Moot Court teams won the national championship in 1987, and two teams would finish in the final sixteen in Dallas in 1989. A joint program developed with the Babcock Graduate School of Management led to a combined law and business degree (JD/MBA). A search committee headed by Ken Zick was appointed to find Scarlett's replacement.

Robert W. Shively, Dean of the Babcock Graduate School of Management, also submitted his resignation, effective June 30, 1988. President Hearn selected Tom

Alan Easley

William Angel

Taylor to bring the Wake Forest business programs under unified leadership. Taylor had been Dean of the undergraduate School of Business and Accountancy since 1980. However, before Taylor could combine the two schools, he was forced to resign due to health problems. Paul A. Dierks became Acting Dean of the Babcock School, and Provost Wilson was named chair of the selection committee for the next dean.

Tom Taylor

On June 6, 1988, President Hearn announced other administrative reorganizations. Vice President John Willard became Financial Resources Manager, responsible for real estate and the University's endowment operations. John Anderson became Vice President for Administration and Budget, assuming responsibility for Reynolda campus operations, including the physical plant, personnel, and budget. In addition, a new Vice President for Student Life and Instructional Resources was established and a Division of Student Life was created that initially included the Center for Psychological Services, the Placement and Career Development Office, and the University Health Service. Ken Zick, who had held similar responsibilities at the Law School, was appointed in this role. He would supervise student services, University libraries, and Reynolda campus grants and contracts.

Harold Holmes was named Director of Career Placement and Planning (CPP), replacing N. Rick Heatley; Julius H. Corpening was named Assistant Vice President for University Relations; Robert T. Baker was promoted to Director of Development; Lu Leake replaced Percival Perry as Dean of the Summer School; and supervision of WFDD, the University-operated public radio station, was assigned to Sandra Connor. In addition, Robert Prince, a former special agent with the FBI, was named to head the University's reorganized Security Office in March, with Alton M. Hill, the former Director of Public Safety, as his assistant.

With the steady increase in the quantity and quality of admissions since 1983, a Management Oversight Committee on Admissions was appointed to insure that the policies and procedures of the Admissions Office were coordinated with the University's comprehensive institutional objectives. The committee was composed of John Anderson, Bill Joyner, Ed Wilson, and Sandra Connor.

President Hearn turned fifty and was appointed to the NCAA President's Commission in June 1988. He also became Chair of Winston-Salem Business, Inc., a private nonprofit development corporation he had helped create to attract new business to the area. Before tackling either responsibility, he and his wife spent two summer months in Vienna, courtesy of the Board of Trustees as thanks for his five years of service as President.

Ken Zick

Harold Holmes

Athletics

The University's athletic teams had considerable success in 1987–1988. The football team ended the season with 7 wins and 4 losses (4–3 and third place in the ACC). It was only the seventh winning season in thirty-five years, and Bill Dooley was the only Deacon coach to have a winning season in his first year since Wake Forest joined the ACC in 1953. The Associated Press named him ACC Coach of the Year. The Deacons scored Big Four victories over in-state rivals North Carolina (22–14), North Carolina State (21–3), and Duke (30–27).

On the individual level, Chip Rives, a member of the football team, was the only college student honored among the eight Sportsmen of the Year by *Sports Illustrated* in its December 21, 1987 issue. He was lauded for the Santa's Helper program he had started as a junior. He and his teammates raised about $2,000 the previous year and loaded his VW "Magic Bus" to deliver presents to approximately thirty-five families and 125 children. Rives dressed as Santa Claus to distribute the toys.

The Demon Deacon and the Duke Blue Devil engage in off-the-field sparring

Dot Casey was Wake Forest's first Director of Womens' Athletics

The marching band introduced a new fight song at the beginning of the football season, "When the Quad is Rolled Up Yonder." Frank Johnson, a 1987 Wake Forest graduate living in Winston-Salem, wrote the verse, and Marching Band Director Martin Province and Advisor Barbara Trautwein worked with the band on the arrangement during the summer. The words were sung to the tune of "When the Roll is Called Up Yonder."

When the Tar Heels have been booted, and The Pack shall howl no more,
And the Devils are as blue as what they wear,

Barbara Trautwein

Frank Johnson

Then the fans of Wake shall gather up and
hear the tolling bells,
When the quad is rolled up yonder, we'll be
there.
Refrain: When the Quad—is rolled up
yon-der,
When the Quad—is rolled up yon-der,
When the Quad—is rolled up yon-der,
When the Quad is rolled up yonder, we'll be
there.

The song referred to the tradition of "rolling the
quad," or draping the trees in toilet tissue when
athletic teams, especially football and basketball, won.

The men's basketball team tallied a record of
11 wins and 18 losses. The highlight of an otherwise
disappointing season was an exciting win over North Carolina, 83–80, on January 28, the first
victory over the Tar Heels since January 21, 1982. The women's basketball team, nationally
ranked twenty-third by *USA Today*, ended the season with a 23–8 record overall and a 9–5
record in the ACC, both school records. Coach Joseph C. Sanchez was named both ACC and
NCAA District Coach of the Year.

Francie Goodridge, Coach of the women's cross country team, saw her Harriers
take second place in the ACC. At one point during the season, the team was ranked
seventh in the nation. In addition, Women's Tennis Coach Dede Allen was named
the ACC Coach of the Year for the 1987 season after her squad finished with a 21–11
record and a second place standing in the ACC tournament. Furthermore, the field
hockey team captured the Deep South Field Hockey Championship for the second
straight year by defeating Pfeiffer in the championship game 1–0.

Director of Women's Athletics Dot Casey retired after thirty-nine years. She
joined the faculty in 1949 as a physical education instructor, became a coach, and
spent her last thirteen years as Director of Women's Athletics. At her retirement, the
budget for women's athletics at Wake Forest was $900,000, with programs in tennis,
basketball, field hockey, golf, indoor track, and cross-country. In baseball, George
Greer became Head Coach of the Deacon 9, replacing Marvin Crater.

The Arts

The University Theatre produced George Bernard Shaw's *You Never Can Tell*, Tennessee Williams's *A Streetcar Named Desire*, Jean Anouilh's *Antigone*, and Gilbert and
Sullivan's *Pirates of Penzance*.

The Secrest Artists Series featured performances by violinist Kyoko Takezawa, the
Canadian Brass, the Colorado Quartet with Anton Kuerti on piano, Marcel Marceau,
and the Philharmonic Orchestra of Monte Carlo.

The Student Union brought in comedian Rich Hall; jazz-classical harpist
Harvey Griffin; keyboardist Ira Stein and oboist Russell Walder; Barry Drake, who

Pirates of Penzance

lectured on the roots of rock and roll; a Beatlemania show; and the Chinese Magic Revue.

"Brazilian Printmakers" was the opening exhibit in the University gallery. It was composed of forty-six lithographs brought to the United States by David Faber (Art).

Campus and Student Life

Gloria Cabada ('88) won the Brockriede Top Speaker Trophy at the forty-second annual National Debate Tournament held from March 23–25 at Weber State University in Ogden, Utah. Cabada became only the second woman in forty-two years to win the honor, beating out 148 competitors as the nation's top college debater. At the end of the season, the overall squad was ranked ninth nationally, up from fortieth the previous year. Alan Coverstone, Ted Tyson, Judd Kimball, and Gloria Cabada were coached by Ross Smith and Director of Debate Allan Louden.

Some of the major student leaders for the year were John Jackman, Editor-in-Chief of *The Howler*; Will Knetch, Student Government President; Leane Doggett, President of the Student Union; and Joni L James, Editor of the *Old Gold and Black*. The second annual Presidents' Leadership Conference was held at Camp Caraway. Hosted by President Hearn and Student Government President Will Knetch, it focused on group relationships and self-government at Wake Forest.

As a result of a Management Committee suggestion to the Admissions Office, the Harbinger Corps was initiated at the beginning of the year to make student recruitment more standardized. It was composed of students who volunteered to show visitors around the campus, a task previously performed by members of the Alpha Phi

Gloria Cabada

Omega service fraternity. Admissions staff trained the volunteers and assigned specific times for them to lead tours. The Student Union sponsored a bus trip to old Wake Forest in April 1988 to make sure all students had the opportunity to become acquainted with the University's history.

A Harbinger Corps member leads a campus tour

To help students achieve a healthy lifestyle, Cashin Hunt was hired to fill the newly created position of lifestyle coordinator. She worked with Mike Ford, Associate Dean of Students, and Mary Ann Taylor, Director of Student Health.

To increase diversity, the University adopted a recruitment plan to increase black enrollment in the undergraduate school to 10 percent and black faculty appointments to a total of 18 by 1992. The plan, approved by the University's executive council on April 26, would be presented to the Board of Trustees for approval in the fall. Recruitment goals were based on the recommendations of an ad hoc committee of faculty and administrators formed in April 1987. In April 1988, there were 126 black students and six black faculty on campus.

A third microcomputer lab for students opened in Wingate Hall 103 in January 1988. Across from the Chaplain's Office, the lab housed fourteen Zenith microcomputers, which were IBM-compatible, and a letter-quality printer. The two other microcomputer labs at the time were in Poteat and Luter residence halls and featured Apple Macintosh computers that were not compatible with the Wingate lab computers. As for studying, a Z. Smith Reynolds library survey found that 55 percent of students polled spent zero to five hours in the library each week; another 34 percent spent up to fifteen hours per week there.

Most undergraduates received on-campus housing in a process that presented far fewer problems than in previous years. Alternate Estates, a residence life and housing program implemented in fall 1987, allowed students to paint their rooms, to design graphics or murals, and to decorate common areas, such as lounges and halls. It also encouraged the use of lofted beds to open more floor space in the rooms.

A student works on his assignment in the computer lab

While delivery of the 1986–1987 edition of *The Howler* was delayed until the spring of 1988, the 1987–1988 edition came out on time and was mailed to seniors in August. The University also produced an admissions videotape and a video yearbook. They were both shot at the same time, but the yearbook highlighted the year's events, while the admissions video provided more general information. The video yearbook, which cost $28 for a thirty-minute VHS cassette, was not meant to compete with *The Howler*. The admissions video was distributed free to anyone.

During a Student Union-sponsored '60s week in late September, participants could make a wearable tie-dye T-shirt for $2.50 on the Quad. A more substantive event took place in the spring semester. To help students think on a higher moral level, University Chaplain Ed Christman and Learning Assistance Program Director Roger Pearman launched Gray Matters. It was a program designed to prompt upper-class student leaders to reflect on ethical principles that might guide their responses to campus concerns. It aimed to complement the Leadership Excellence Application Development (LEAD) program for freshmen and sophomores supervised by Associate Dean of Students Mike Ford and Director of Student Activities Mary Beil.

Greek Life

Although not tied to and occurring before the Gray Matters program, a significant action to promote better student relations occurred on December 4, when the Tau chapter of Kappa Alpha fraternity voted to stop using the Confederate flag and uniform as a symbol of its chapter and publicly apologized to the Wake Forest community for having used these symbols. The decision was noted as a positive but belated step in a January 15 *Old Gold and Black* editorial.

In other Greek life news, Delta Sigma Theta became Wake Forest's first black sorority in the spring of 1988. In addition, four students sought approval from all necessary student and faculty committees to form a chapter of Delta Delta Delta National Sorority. Tension arose between the Intersociety Council and Tri-Delta Sorority organizers due to misunderstandings and lack of communication, but the Tri-Delta proposal was approved by the Student Government Legislature in April 1988, and the pioneer group acquired housing for fall 1988.

Facilities, Finances, and Alumni

In September, the F.W. Olin Foundation of New York announced it was making a grant of $3,719,625 to Wake Forest to build and equip a new physics building. It was the University's second largest single foundation grant and the only one dedicated to the construction of an entire building since the 1956 move to Winston-Salem. Ground was broken on March 31, and construction started in April. The 31,375 square-foot building was completed by the fall semester of 1989. It freed 16,037 square feet of classroom and laboratory space in Salem Hall for sole occupancy by the Department of Chemistry.

On April 12, another groundbreaking ceremony was held, this time for the University Center, which was named for Clifton L. Benson Sr., thanks to a lead gift from his son. Tylee Wilson, the CEO of RJR Nabisco, also committed half a million dollars.

The building would take two years to complete. In March, the trustees authorized the construction of facilities near the water tower for the School of Law and Babcock Graduate School of Management.

In October 1987, the 300-student residence hall completed in 1970 and known as the "New Dorm" was dedicated as the Joseph W. Luter Jr. Residence Hall. Joseph W. Luter III ('62), Chair of Smithfield Foods, Inc., made a $1 million gift to Wake Forest in late February 1987.

A new baseball facility, Gene Hooks Stadium, was dedicated on April 23 in a ceremony prior to the Wake Forest–Virginia baseball game. Located on the southeastern part of the campus near the Physical Plant, it had dressing rooms, an indoor batting cage, a press box, and permanent seating for 2,500 spectators.

A less positive change was the reduction in window service at the campus post office because of budget cuts to the United States Postal Service. The February 16 decision meant the post office window was open from 9:30 a.m. to 1:30 p.m. It had formerly been open from 9:30 a.m. to 12:30 p.m., closed for lunch, and then reopened from 1:30 to 3:30 p.m.

Off campus, AT&T's Lexington Road plant closed, and President Hearn became concerned about AT&T's Reynolda Road facility, which contributed substantially to the University's financial well-being. On January 29, he charged Vice Presidents Willard, Anderson, and Corbett to study converting the facility to other purposes to prevent any loss of income. Although assured by AT&T executives that the lease would be renewed when it expired in 1990, Hearn wanted to be proactive.

The R.J. Reynolds Tobacco Company announced in July that its Planters + Life Savers division would relocate to Winston-Salem and lease space in its former World Headquarters building, which it had given to the University the previous year. Vice President John Anderson said Planters + Life Savers would rent enough space to cover Wake Forest's operating costs for the entire building.

A five-year campus beautification plan began, targeting improvements to the main quad, the Magnolia Quad, the grounds around the Scales Fine Arts Building, and courtyards in the north campus residence halls. It was originally scheduled to begin in the 1988–1989 academic year, but President Hearn approved its launch in 1987.

In a more significant and comprehensive drive, the Capital Planning Committee, chaired by Vice President John Anderson, developed a five-year plan and a long-range plan, which the Board of Trustees approved on April 1 with an allocation of $54.9 million. Among the thirteen new projects were the new university center and physics building; new athletic facilities, including a baseball stadium, a tennis center, and a golf complex; the professional center for law and business; a new façade and addition to the Z. Smith Reynolds Library; and renovations to Carswell, Babcock, Salem, and Reynolda Halls. Approximately $275,000 had been used this year toward residence hall renovation, and at least that much was to be used for renovations in each of the next six years, according to Dennis Gregory, Director of Residence Life and Housing. This formal long-range planning was in response once again to the "Year 2000 Report," which had informally proposed objectives for the millennium.

In another money matter, even though Wake Forest had been ranked among the nation's top twenty institutions in fundraising by the Council for Aid to Education, President Hearn in a March 17 memo asked Vice Presidents Anderson, Corbett, and

Joyner, together with Director of Public Information Sandra Connor, to reduce their budgets in amounts ranging from $5,000 to $20,000 to balance the overall 1988–1989 budget. The Z. Smith Reynolds Library halted acquisition of books halfway through the year because it ran out of money; however, an infusion of $150,000 from the administration in mid-January 1988 allowed the library to resume book and periodical purchases.

The first issue of *Window on Wake Forest* (volume 1, number 1), a publication for faculty and staff, came out in December 1987.

The Wake Forest Board of Trustees elected Herbert Brenner, President of the Brenner Iron and Metal Company, as its first Jewish member. His term started January 1, 1988. The Trustees also voted unanimously to increase tuition 9.6 percent for the 1988–1989 school year, with undergraduates and graduate students paying $7,950 in base tuition, an increase of $700. Students in the School of Law would pay $8,950, an increase of $750. President Hearn stated the primary reasons for the increases were the need to increase junior faculty salaries and financial aid. Tuition had increased a total of 32.5 percent since the fall of 1985, when tuition was $6,000 per year.

Alumni

James R. Gadd ('71) of Charlotte became President-Elect of the 35,000-member National Alumni Association in July 1987. He succeeded W. Prentiss Baker III ('65). Bob Mills ('71, MBA '80) coordinated the first-ever gathering of all Wake Forest alumni groups at The Homestead in July 1987, following the pattern of summer meetings established by the College Alumni Council.

Three Distinguished Service Citations were presented to alumni during Homecoming weekend, November 6–8. Honored were Bert L. Shore ('37, humanitarian service), Evelyn Patricia Foote ('52, public service), and Lawrence David Hopkins ('72, MD '77, medicine).

Summing Up the Year

From October 1987 on, the *U.S. News & World Report* ranking system would influence the way outsiders viewed Wake Forest. As time went by, it gave prospective students and their parents a concrete, if not totally accurate, source to consult in deciding whether the University was right for them. In most years thereafter, application numbers increased. Likewise, the groundwork completed to host the presidential debate brought Wake Forest to the attention of many who barely knew of it, and surprised others who thought they knew it. Because of the debate, recognition of the Wake Forest name increased, as did the University's prestige.

Subtle and overt transformations in the University's administration included the development of new leaders and the rewarding of seasoned veterans with more demanding, higher-status appointments. Faculty gained wider recognition through publications and grants, and salary increases occurred. In an attempt to enrich the institution in multiple ways, the alumni association worked toward the awarding of scholarships that would make Wake Forest more diverse. The award from the Olin Foundation of a major grant for a new physics building and the naming and rededication of campus landmarks marked significant change and growth.

Perhaps the removal of the elms on the upper quad symbolized the main story of the year. Wake Forest was changing in many ways; things that had seemed permanent, like the elms, made way for innovations and advancement—new trees; comprehensive plans; new, more diverse students, faculty, and staff; and the hard work of students, like Mike Smith, to bring a national event to campus. The change of the University was seeded in the press and in other recognitions. It bled over into the perceptions of those who loved Wake Forest for what it was and those who began to consider it as an academic home. Anticipation of what could be and what would be increased with the breaking of ground for construction, renovations, and relocations.

CHAPTER SIX
1988–1989

The Presidential Debate

The Henny Pennys of this world are certain at each crisis that our sky is falling. Our problems are unsolvable. The apocalypse is at hand. Yet the human record unfolds. We live to fight our woes on other fields on other days. The impossible becomes possible. The imagined becomes real. The hoped for becomes actual. Today you enter that ultimately serious race, the human race. It is yours now not to study, but to run. As you run, do not stop for lunch in a fox's den or heed those doomsayers whose message is that the race is over and lost. Prophets of such feather might turn out to be no more than a bunch of chickens!

Thomas K. Hearn Jr., May 15, 1989;
Charge to the Graduates, Wake Forest University Commencement

Wake Forest gained new prestige in the fall of 1988 with its staging of a presidential debate in Wait Chapel on September 25. As previously mentioned, hosting the event was initially proposed by three members of the class of 1989, Michael Smith, Beth Dawson, and Scott Dubois, who all belonged to the Young Republicans, but the effort was apolitical. It was also the first presidential debate produced by the nonprofit, nonpartisan Commission on Presidential Debates; the next would take place in Pauley Pavilion at University of California Los Angeles (UCLA) on October 13. Governor James Martin called the Wake Forest debate "the largest media and public affairs event in North Carolina's history." Before an international television audience of sixty-five million viewers, candidates George H.W. Bush and Michael Dukakis focused on foreign and domestic policy.

When Wake Forest applied to host the debate, President Hearn called a meeting of Winston-Salem business leaders at Graylyn to raise the $2 million necessary to produce it. Support from corporate sponsors was enthusiastic. USAir Group, Inc.;

One of the Presidential Debate T-shirts of 1988

RJ Reynolds Tobacco Company; Wachovia Bank and Trust Company; Sarah Lee Corporation; Shelco, Inc.; Flow Motors; and the Winston-Salem Foundation were among the largest contributors.

Sandra Connor, Director of Public Information, was coordinator of debate preparations. She and her staff worked long and hard to see that necessary changes to Wait Chapel were made, such as having it recarpeted and having a new heating and air conditioning system installed. Every day, orders from Commission or production staff came, and many were changed from what had been conveyed previously. Connor's team was highly flexible as well as extremely dedicated. It recruited a volunteer brigade to engage students, faculty, and staff in communications with key individuals involved in the debate and to quickly accommodate minute-to-minute changes. About 600 students were able to work with Commission staff, national news media, and campus administration.

For example, two days before the debate, "the Pit," the main dining hall in Reynolda Hall, had to be transformed into a media filing center for 2,000 national press writers and technicians. Thus Connor and her team worked with Student Life staff to deliver "breakfast in bed" to students in the residence halls and sponsored picnics on the Quad. Meanwhile, the Phillip Morris Tobacco Company located free beer and cigarettes for reporters and technicians in the usual site of the salad bar, and whether accidentally or deliberately, Leslie Stahl and the CBS news team commandeered this area for interviews and a post-debate report.

Sandra Connor

Anchor booths for each of the major networks were set up in the Wait Chapel balcony, and the Connor team arranged closed-circuit television broadcast in Brendle Recital Hall and other locations so that students could view the deliberations. The Commission initially distributed only fifty tickets to Wake Forest for the event: thirteen for undergraduates, nine for graduate and professional school students, ten for faculty, four for staff, and three for the student organizers of the event. The rest went to members of the two political parties involved. During fall registration, students, faculty, and staff signed up to win nontransferable tickets to attend, and on that night, the lucky recipients came early to claim their seats. However, at 6:30 p.m. in front of Reynolda Hall, a Commission staff member began passing out unclaimed press passes.

Mary Dalton (Speech Communication and Theatre Arts) accompanied him and was able to secure press credentials for about a dozen of her students. The largest block of student tickets was released right before the debate began when an unidentified Secret Service agent came out on three separate occasions and selected students at random from behind the police lines at Huffman House. According to several Huffman residents, she approached students and touched or shook their hands. The students were then allowed to cross the line and enter the chapel. Altogether, about 150 to 200 students managed to get into Wait Chapel before the debate began, according to Student Government President Mike Smith.

Other students came to the Quad to watch the many dignitaries from both parties arrive. Both Governor Martin and former Governor Jim Hunt were there. Some students set up a game of croquet, and several officials, including Senator Alan Simpson (R-Wyoming) and Transportation Secretary Elizabeth Dole, stopped to hit a few shots before proceeding into the chapel.

President Hearn and the three student leaders who initiated the event welcomed the crowd and left to watch the debate on closed-circuit television. Because seating for faculty and students was so limited, the Trustees also forfeited their seats. Nonetheless, the atmosphere on campus was described as "magical," with physical and metaphorical transformations everywhere.

Academics

While the presidential debate dominated the year's news, other noteworthy events occurred. Religion Professor Emeritus Allen Easley published *These Things I Remember: An Autobiography Written for My Family and Friends*. Other books published by

George H.W. Bush with Wake Forest students, Vice Presidents, and President Hearn

Allan Louden

Wake Forest professors in 1988 included *Isabella Leonarda: Select Compositions* edited by Stewart Carter, *Poona in the Eighteenth Century* by Balkrishna Gokhale, *Dos Passos: The Critical Heritage* by Barry Maine, *Emily Dickinson: Personae and Performance* by Elizabeth Phillips, *Fitness Motivation: Preventing Participant Dropout* co-authored by Jack Rejeski, and *The Comedy of Redemption: Christian Faith and the Comic Vision in Four American Novelists* by Ralph Wood.

Outside of publishing, Allan Louden (Communication) received the National Debate Coach of the Year Award. Tom Taylor remained Dean of the Calloway School but was freed, as described in Chapter 5, from duties as Dean of the Babcock School due to his health. Peter Kairoff (Music) gave what the November 18 issue of the *Old Gold and Black* described as "an enchanting and emotionally charged performance" in his debut in Brendle Recital Hall. He had been recruited from UCLA by the Department of Music in the fall to strengthen its performance faculty.

Tokai University School of Medicine and Bowman Gray School of Medicine signed an affiliation agreement in Winston-Salem during September.

Roone Arledge, President of ABC News, whose father graduated from Wake Forest, gave the Opening Convocation speech on September 8 and received an honorary degree. The Founders' Day Convocation speaker on February 16 was former Head Basketball Coach (1958–1965) Horace A. "Bones" McKinney.

Wake Forest's third Rhodes Scholar in four years was Scott Pretorius of New Philadelphia, Ohio. Scott was also an O.W. Wilson Scholar, with a double major in chemistry and English. The award was announced in January 1989.

The first Upperclass Alumni Scholarships were offered to students with extraordinary talent in music, drama, visual arts, dance, writing for publication, public

speaking, entrepreneur-
ship, community service,
and leadership. Later, as
the Presidential Scholar-
ships, these awards would
be offered only to incom-
ing first-year students.

The Saguiv A. Hadari
Research Award, in mem-
ory of a former assistant
professor of political science who died of cancer
in June 1988, was estab-
lished in November. The
leave that accompanied it

"Bones" McKinney

was given annually to a junior faculty member in a tenure-track position.

Carl Harris (Classical Languages) was the recipient of the first award for Excellence in Advising. Anne Boyle (English) received the Reid-Doyle Prize for Excellence
in Teaching. Gillian R. Overing (English) and Huw M.L. Davies (Chemistry) received
the Award for Excellence in Research. J. Howell Smith (History) received the Omicron Delta Kappa Award for Contribution to Student Life. The Medallion of Merit,
the University's highest award for distinguished service, was presented to Harold M.
Barrow, Professor Emeritus of Physical Education.

The *Public Accounting Report*, a biweekly newsletter, ranked the Calloway School
of Business and Accountancy twentieth in the nation on the basis of a poll of department chairs and faculty members.

The 1989–1990 budget increased undergraduate faculty salaries by an average of 7.5 percent. The University Senate held a faculty forum on the University's
future.

Administration and Staff

In April, the Board of Trustees approved a change in the criteria for selecting its
members: "The board approves the opening of membership to any and all persons
committed to the historical Christian character, Baptist heritage, and North Carolina
roots of Wake Forest University." This change opened board membership to any
qualified individual, regardless of religious denomination or place of residence.

Michael McKinley, an assistant news editor of the *Old Gold and Black*, wrote an
article in the October 13 issue that stated: "If the Hearn administration had to be
described in one word, the word would be 'enhancement.'" He noted that "during
Hearn's tenure, average SATs have risen and the number of applicants has increased
by more than 43 percent" Furthermore, "six months after graduation, 97 percent of
all students are either starting a job or in graduate school." The cost of tuition had
risen from $5,050 in 1983 to $7,950 in 1988–1989, an increase of 57 percent in just
six years. The number of out-of-state students had surpassed the number of North
Carolinians for years, and in 1988–1989, 7.5 percent of the first-year class was black,

President Hearn transformed Wake Forest from a regional into a national university

although the percentage of blacks in the United States at the time was 12 percent. McKinley quoted Hearn's assertion that Wake Forest was now a national university.

In another area, however, an era was ending. Provost Ed Wilson had decided to change administrative roles after twenty-one years as Provost and nine years as Dean. A search began for a Vice President of Academic Affairs. The search committee was headed by John Anderson and included Tom Mullen (Dean of the College), Tom Taylor (Dean of the Calloway School of Business and Accountancy), Paul Dierks (Dean of the Babcock Graduate School of Management), Harold Holmes (Dean of Student Services), Nancy Cotton (Dean of the Graduate School), Tom Roberts (Law), Carole Browne (Biology), Paul Ribisl (Health and Sports Sciences), Michael Hazen (Speech Communication and Theatre), Doug Maynard (Medical School), Sandra Connor (Vice President for Public Affairs), and Student Government President Mike Smith. Reid Morgan represented staff on the committee.

Mark Reece

In October, Mark H. Reece ('49), Dean of Students, retired after thirty-two years of service. He started at Wake Forest as Associate Director of Alumni Affairs. In 1958, he was named Director of Student Affairs and, in 1963, Dean of Men. He became Dean of Students in 1984 and was responsible for the student handbook, freshman orientation, judicial system activities, and fraternity and society/sorority affairs. In recognition of his involvement in helping students buy original art for the University collection, the collection of this art was named in his honor.

Margaret Perry received the Distinguished Service Citation at the annual meeting of the Southern Association of College Registrars and Admissions in recognition of her success in establishing and editing the association's journal.

In preparation for what President Hearn called "second-generation planning," the Executive Council held a retreat at the Isleworth Golf and

Country Club in Windermere, Florida, from September 12–14. Hearn began working with Charlie Rogers of PepsiCo, who specialized in institutional organization and preparation.

Hearn also began putting a new administrative team in place. A memo to faculty, staff, and students on September 26 stated that, effective October 1, Sandra Connor would be promoted to Vice President for Public Affairs. Leon Corbett would become Executive Secretary/Office of the President, rather than Secretary of the University, but retain his title of Vice President for Legal Affairs. Former Associate Counsel Reid Morgan would become University Counsel. In August, other promotions had been announced: John P. Anderson became Vice President for Administration and Budget; John G. Willard, Vice President for Financial Resource Management, with oversight of the University's $290 million endowment; Kenneth A. Zick, Vice President for Student Life and Instructional Resources; and Harold R. Holmes, Dean of Student Services. Robert Baker became Director of Development, and Julius H. Corpening became Assistant Vice President for University Relations. Julie Barber Cole replaced Kimberly Waller as the Director of Research and Sponsored Programs, and Donna Hamilton joined the legal office as a staff counsel.

Elsewhere, Ross Griffith ('65) was promoted to Assistant Vice President for Administration and Planning and Director of Institutional Research, taking over this office from Ben M. Seelbinder (Mathematics), who retired in June 1988. In February 1989, Robert D. Mills (BA '71, MBA '80) was named Assistant Vice President and Director of the Capital Campaign scheduled for public kickoff in early 1991. Kay Lord ('64) was promoted to serve as the new Associate Director of Alumni Activities, and James Bullock ('85) was named Director of Capital Support to work on major gift development for the capital campaign. James Welsh ('87) became the new Director of Alumni and Student Programs, and William C. Currin ('60), a former minister and businessman, was named Director of the Office of Career Planning and Placement.

Two other announcements were issued at this time. On December 20, John McKinnon, President of Sara Lee Corporation, was selected to be Dean of the Babcock Graduate School of Management beginning July 1. A native of Lumberton who had lived in Winston-Salem from 1965–1983, he was the former President of Sara Lee Food Services. Second, Robert K. Walsh, former Dean of the University of Arkansas at Little Rock School of Law and a specialist in litigation for an Arkansas law firm, accepted an appointment as the Dean of the School of Law in April, with a July 1 starting date. Walsh was a 1967 graduate of Harvard Law School and past Chair of the American Bar Association Accreditation Committee. The School of Law, established in 1894, had twenty-two faculty members

William Currin

Robert Walsh

and 464 students when Walsh was appointed. He replaced John D. Scarlett, who retired after ten years.

President Hearn wrote Len B. Preslar Jr., President of North Carolina Baptist Hospitals, Inc., to support the development of the J. Paul Sticht Center on Aging on the campus of the Bowman Gray School of Medicine/ North Carolina Baptist Hospital Medical Center. In addition, Hearn announced that he would serve as Chair of Winston-Salem Business, Inc., an organization formed to recruit new business and industry to the area.

President Hearn formed a university committee chaired by Ed Wilson and composed of Leon Corbett, John Anderson, Bill Joyner, Carlton Mitchell, and Dewey Hobbs to implement a trustees' resolution regarding a School of Divinity. The committee reported on May 17 that a divinity school should be approved on the condition that sufficient funds were available; specifically, resources equivalent to the income from a $15 million endowment must be secured. The school's annual budget would be $1 million, and it would have about 135 students.

Wake Forest Magazine, published five times a year and edited by Jeanne P. Whitman, received an Award of Excellence in the periodicals improvement category of the District III Competition of CASE (Council for the Advancement and Support of Education). *Window on Wake Forest*, the monthly newsletter for University employees edited by Cherin Poovey, received a Special Merit Award in the newsletter competition. CASE District III included colleges, universities and academies in the Southeast.

Finally, a literacy program for staff members was added to the University's fringe benefits. The program aimed to offer classes with broad appeal to employees interested in career development and educational self-improvement. They were taught on the Reynolda campus during working hours by faculty from Forsyth Technical Community College.

Athletics

The football team finished a second winning season with a record of 6–4–1. A bid to the Independence Bowl was not extended, however, because the Deacons tied, rather than beat, Appalachian State in the final game. Wake Forest had more success earlier in the season as it hosted the one hundredth anniversary of the first football game between the Demon Deacons and the University of North Carolina Tar Heels on October 8. The Deacons won 42–24. Before the season began, in July, seven football players—Chris Smith, Marvin Mitchell, Ricky Brown, Steve Brown, Brian Johnson, Rodney Mullins, and Ernie Purnsley—formed a group called Deacons Against Drugs.

It was the first group of its kind in the ACC and an immediate hit in the Winston-Salem community. Members visited youth centers and schools to talk about the dangers of drugs and alcohol. Mike Elkins, senior quarterback, was given top honors at the twenty-sixth Men's All-Sports Banquet. He received the Arnold Palmer Award, the highest honor given to a male athlete at Wake Forest. Three Deacons were drafted into the National Football League: Elkins, linebacker David Braxton, and defensive back A.J. Greene.

At their spring meeting, the Board of Trustees voted to phase out the practice of housing student-athletes exclusively in Palmer and Piccolo residence halls over a two-year period. The move was in line with reforms to intercollegiate athletics being considered by the ACC, the Knight Commission, and the NCAA. President Hearn supported another reform, Proposition 42, which required high school athletes to have a 2.0 average in eleven academic courses and an overall SAT score of 700 to qualify for a college athletic scholarship. It also eliminated the concept of partial qualifiers, or those who had one but not both of these qualifications. Hearn wrote to basketball commentator Dick Vitale at ESPN on January 20 to tell him that his stand on Proposition 42 was "most lamentable." Vitale felt that this proposed change would disadvantage student-athletes who had potential but had not achieved academically. Proposition 42, Hearn stated, aimed to "improve academic performance and motivation."

In the midst of the debate, Hearn was selected by the ACC to represent the conference on the NCAA Presidents' Commission. Almost simultaneously, Provost Ed Wilson was appointed to succeed Jack Sawyer as Wake Forest's faculty representative to the ACC in August 1988. Sawyer had served for twenty-eight years. In another athletic personnel matter, Gilbert McGregor ('71), Academic and Placement Director for the Athletic Department since 1984, left Wake Forest at the beginning of the fall semester to take a position as a color commentator for the 34-radio network of the Charlotte Hornets. Under McGregror, the academic success and graduation rates of student-athletes had increased.

Outside of basketball, the Varsity Tennis Courts were renamed the James H. Leighton Tennis Stadium on April 9. Leighton coached from 1962–1984.

Head Coach Walter S. Chyzowych's soccer team was invited to its first NCAA tournament. It received one of eight at-large bids in the twenty-four team field. The team was ranked in the top twenty for the first time in the program's history and finished the season with an overall record of 11–5–4 and an ACC record of 4–2–2. Unfortunately, it lost in the opening round to North Carolina, 2–0.

Wake Forest qualified for the NCAA Men's Cross Country Championship for the first time in school history by placing fourth at the District III Championships on November

Steve Brown

Liz Becker

12 at Furman University. In its fourth year under Coach John Goodridge, the team finished fourteenth out of twenty-two teams in the November 21 NCAA meet in Des Moines, Iowa. Steve Brown, a rising sophomore and 110-meter high hurdler, was invited to the United States Olympic Trials and the World Junior Track and Field Championships in July, where he won a silver medal. Bill Babcock won the ACC Championship in the 5,000-meter race with a time of 12:27.

Liz Becker won the ACC championship in the women's 3,000-meter event. She was the first Demon Deacon woman to earn an individual championship. Two months later, she was told she had a brain tumor. Fortunately, it was benign, and after it was surgically removed she began running again. In 1990, she received the first NCAA Division I-A Award for Courage. When she returned to competition, she earned all-conference honors in cross country.

Former Wake Forest center fielder Billy Masse was selected to compete on the U.S. Olympic Baseball team for the Olympics slated to be held in Seoul, Korea.

Dianne Dailey began her first year as Head Coach of the women's golf team and Women's Athletic Director. Before coming to Wake Forest, she had spent eight years on the Ladies Professional Golf Association (LPGA) Tour and served as Assistant Academic Dean at Salem College. Dailey replaced Dot Casey, who retired after fourteen years as Women's Athletic Director, and Mary Beth McGirr, who had been a part-time women's golf coach for the past three years.

The Deacon Spirits, an organization for die-hard Demon Deacon basketball fans, was resurrected after a two-year hiatus by Carey Clarke, Jeff Prince, Brian Prince, Mimi Hunt, and Steven Bullock. To be a member, students were required to attend all but one home game and be in their seats fifteen minutes before tip-off. They were allowed to be late twice. In return, the Spirits had reserved courtside seating for all home games and initially attracted 116 students.

The women's basketball team finished the season with a 23–8 record and advanced into the NCAA tournament for the first time since it had been established as a varsity sport in 1971. However, the 1988–1989 men's basketball team finished with a 13–15 record, and Head Coach Robert Staak resigned on March 29 after four years and a record of 45 wins and 69 losses overall, and an ACC record of 8 wins and 48 losses. Clouding his resignation was a question from the NCAA over the recruitment of forward Anthony Tucker, although it never resulted in a charge. Staak was replaced by David Odom on April 8. A former assistant to Carl Tacy and, more recently, Terry Holland at the University of Virginia, Odom would hold this position until the completion of the 2001 season. During his tenure, he compiled a record of 240 wins to 132 losses, won two ACC titles, captured the NIT championship in 2000, and took the Deacons to postseason play eleven times. In 1996, Wake Forest advanced to the round of the Elite Eight in the NCAA men's basketball tournament.

The men's golf team won the ACC Championship for the eighteenth time under Coach Jesse Haddock on April 16, beating runner-up Georgia Tech by four strokes. Tim Straub won the individual title at an even par 216 at the Northgreen Country Club in Rocky Mount, North Carolina. Earlier in the academic year, on October 9, the Jesse I. Haddock Golf Center and Robert P. Caldwell Golf Complex were dedicated. These facilities were located adjacent to the football practice fields and the Palmer and Piccolo residence halls.

Dianne Dailey

Gene Overby, sports director for WSJS-WTQR and the voice of the Deacons on the Wake Forest Sports Network, died of cancer on March 30. He had been inducted into the University's Sports Hall of Fame the previous year on October 29, 1988.

Bill Hottinger, Chair of Department of Health and Sport Science, and Herman Presseren, Emeritus Professor of Education, competed in the North Carolina Senior Games and won thirteen medals between them in track and field, archery, and swimming.

The Arts

The Secrest Artists Series, directed by Music Professor George Trautwein, featured performances by the Amsterdam Guitar Trio; the medieval liturgical play *Daniel and the Lions*; the Guarneri String Quartet; and the Baltimore Symphony with soloist James Galway and actor Alan Arkin.

The University Theatre began its season with William Inge's *Bus Stop* (1955) and included productions of Ben Hecht and Charles MacArthur's *The Front Page* (1928), Henrick Ibsen's *A Doll's House* (1879), and the musical *Man of La Mancha* (1965) with book by Dale Wasserman, lyrics by Joe Darion, and music by Mitch Leigh.

Bruce Hornsby and the Range sold out Wait Chapel in the fall. George Winston and Kenny G did the same in late February and April, respectively. All of these musical events were sponsored by the Student Union. An "All Nighter Party" in January and a dinner theatre event in February were also sponsored by the Student Union.

Campus and Student Life

A new visitation policy, which included privacy hours during the week and twenty-four-hour visitation on weekends, was initiated at the beginning of the academic year. The Student Life Committee had approved the new hours in the spring semester of 1988. Under the policy, students were allowed to visit people of the opposite sex Monday through Thursday from 10 a.m. to 2 a.m. and anytime on weekends. Satellite housing, including student apartments, townhouses, theme housing, and Henley Drive houses, had no visitation rules. Parties still had to end at 1 a.m., but the new regulations did not apply to parties in leased lounges. A student who broke the rules three times would lose a housing point; under the previous policy, a housing point was lost after the first violation. Visitation hours for the two years prior were 12 p.m. to 1 a.m. Monday through Friday and 10 a.m. until 1 a.m. on Saturday and Sunday. From 1984–1986, visitation was allowed from 5 p.m. to 9 p.m. Monday through Thursday, 12 p.m. to 1 a.m. Friday and Saturday, and 12 p.m. to 12 a.m. on Sunday.

In a conscientious effort to increase diversity, Admissions Director Bill Starling informed President Hearn in a July 12 memo that fifty-four minority students were expected to enroll in the fall, a 46 percent increase over the previous year's thirty-seven minority enrollees. In actuality, enrollment of minority students in the freshman class almost doubled—forty-six nonathletes and nineteen student-athletes—for a total of sixty-five students, according to Ernest Wade, Director of Minority Affairs. Wade attributed the increase to the efforts of Gloria Cooper, Coordinator for Minority Recruitment since 1987. She said freshman class enrollment was 7.4 percent minority.

By February, Law School applications were up from 766 to 1,138, and early decision applications to the College had increased 43 percent.

A new keycard security system was put in place on October 13 in every south campus residence hall, as well as Huffman House and Efird House on the north campus. The cards enabled residents to open the front doors of their own halls, which locked automatically from 2 a.m. to 7 a.m. The system was installed to keep out intruders who were entering through exit doors that had been propped open by students. An alarm would now sound if the doors were open for more than fifteen seconds.

In the fall semester, nineteen rooms in the residence halls were converted into triples; only two had originally been study rooms. According to Dennis Gregory, Director of Residence Life and Housing, the need for more beds was occasioned by a

new policy that let children of faculty live on campus instead of attending as day students, a decrease in student attrition over the summer, and the fact that only thirty students decided to live off campus, as opposed to 120 the year before.

A fire in a room on the fourth floor of the Pi Kappa Alpha suite in Kitchin House broke out at 3 a.m. on Sunday morning, February 12, and did about $30,000 in damages. No one was hurt, but other rooms in the suite and below it suffered extensive smoke and water damage. A new student lab, consisting of fifteen Apple MacIntosh computers, was set up in the tunnel between the Johnson and Bostwick dorms. The lab, which opened in January, was similar to labs in Luter and Poteat.

Two students, Marjorie Sharon Klein and Henry Franklin Perritt III, died unexpectedly over the summer. Klein, 19, a junior history major who was active in intramurals and the Fideles

Keycard technology helped to make the campus safer

Society, died suddenly on May 11 of a congenital heart defect. Perritt, a 19-year-old sophomore active in Army Reserve Officer Training Corps (ROTC) and the *Old Gold and Black*, was electrocuted and killed instantly in an accident at his home on July 20. The *Old Gold and Black* plaque honoring the Most Outstanding Freshmen was renamed for Perritt, and a ROTC memorial scholarship was set up in his honor.

In an attempt to achieve better communication with students, President Hearn started the Presidential Aides program in August 1988. Administered by Carolyn Dow, Assistant to the President, the sixteen aides—three sophomores, four juniors, five seniors, and four adjuncts (the presidents of the student government, student union, student alumni council, and the editor-in-chief of the *Old Gold and Black*)— were responsible for serving as hosts at convocations and presidential receptions, as well as meeting with alumni and visitors and attending monthly lunch meetings with the president. A positive attitude toward Wake Forest and a 2.5 grade point average were required to be considered for selection as an aide.

Administrators, students, and faculty leaders met at Camp Caraway for the third Presidents' Leadership Conference. Wayne Smith, a member of the Board of Visitors, was the keynote speaker.

The Volunteer Service Corps started with Henry Cooper ('53) as its part-time coordinator. His father had been a history professor at Wake Forest, and his two sons were alumni. He was persuaded to come out of retirement by Dean Mark Reece and Chaplain Ed Christman. He saw himself as a broker, matching students with volunteer activities.

The merit-based Graylyn Scholarship was first awarded in fall 1988. It was offered each year on the basis of Graylyn Conference Center profits and had a value equal to a Reynolds Scholarship.

Student organizations raised an unprecedented $41,684 for the Brian Piccolo Cancer Fund; Kappa Sigma was the top fundraiser, contributing $6,500. Seniors Lillian Booe and Stan Perry co-chaired the drive.

Students Against Apartheid (SAA) held a rally attended by about seventy students, faculty, administrators, and community members in November. McLeod Bryan (Religion) was the featured speaker. The group pushed for divestment of funds that Wake Forest had invested in South Africa. About seventy-five SAA members rallied again in front of Wait Chapel on April 21 to hear a variety of speakers call for divestment. Chief among them was Robert Griffiths, Professor of Political Science, and Reverend John Mendez

Carolyn Dow

Henry Cooper

of Emmanuel EMC Church in Winston-Salem.

Four students, Sarah Meadows, Sonya Bourn, Virginia DuPre, and Ingrid Kincaid, started a campus chapter of Students Against Drunk Driving (SADD), which was the first collegiate chapter of this organization in North Carolina. Meadows, DuPre, Kincaid, and A.J. Kindel created Safe Rides of Wake Forest to reduce the incidence of drunk driving by providing education and alternatives. Health Educator Cashin Hunt, who was involved in much of the University's alcohol education, became the group's faculty advisor.

A new organization, Students Against Multiple Sclerosis (SAMS), started in November. It aimed to increase student awareness of the disease and to collect money for research. Kevin Dopke was the founder.

Reflecting President Hearn's belief that Wake Forest had a responsibility to train leaders for the next generation, the Student Life Office held a "best practices" conference on leadership development for undergraduate students on January 5–6. Major

Students Against Apartheid rally

student leaders for the year were Mike Smith, Student Government President; Chad Kilebrew, *Old Gold and Black* Editor; Vivian Roebuck, *Howler* Editor; and Tricia Bannister, Student Union President. In addition, Steve Perricone, a sophomore, was chosen on September 23 to serve a two-year term on the Wake Forest Board of Trustees, representing the student body.

Facilities, Finances, and Alumni

Facilities

In an extraordinary contribution, Mrs. Dewitt Chatham Hanes, widow of Ralph P. Hanes, the founder of Hanes Dye and Finishing Company, offered the Ralph Hanes House to the University as the new President's House on December 8, 1988. Located on 14.7 acres off of Robinhood Road, the house was designed by Julian Peabody of Boston and well-suited to the extensive entertaining expected of University Presidents. According to the *Winston-Salem Journal*, the Forsyth County Tax Office valued the house at $500,000 and the surrounding land at $400,000. Ralph Hanes and his family moved in on October 29, 1929, the day the stock market crashed. The gardens were designed by Ellen Shipman and featured in the September 1988 issue of *House and Garden*.

Stipulations for the University receiving the house included occupancy by the President of Wake Forest University, maintenance of the gardens surrounding the house, and a prohibition of future development of the property. Mrs. Hanes lived in the house through the spring of 1989. The Hearns moved in over the Thanksgiving break, even though renovations were unfinished. The former President's House was then renovated as the Welcome Center for the Admissions Department, with personnel moving into the house before the fall semester of 1990. Reynolda Hall became less congested as a result, as the Dean of the College moved into the former Admissions Office space (Suite 104), and the Provost's Office took over the offices previously shared with the Dean (Suite 204). The surprise gift and its consequences were a serendipitous windfall in a whirlwind of dreams, plans, and realizations.

The University completed negotiations for the transfer of property to the State of North Carolina to create an extension of Silas Creek Parkway. It also gave property to the Boy Scouts of America for a new headquarters on the other side of the Silas Creek right-of-way. In an agreement with the City of Winston-Salem, Wake Forest regained control of campus roads once the extension was finished.

In a July 8 memo, President Hearn thanked the Campus Landscape Committee, composed of John Anderson, Lu Leake, Pete Moore, and Jim Coffey, for developing a long-range beautification plan. In February, the Quad's inner row of ash trees was moved to create an outer row on the advice of Hunter Reynolds Jewell, the firm that Wake Forest employed to suggest a comprehensive landscape plan for the campus. The move would provide shade for the sidewalk while maintaining consistency in tree variety, according to Lu Leake, Assistant Vice President for Administration and Planning.

The power plant on the Reynolda campus was renamed the Royce R. Weatherly Central Heating Plant. Weatherly came to Wake Forest in 1947 as Assistant Superintendent of the steam plant, and in 1956 he was promoted to Assistant Superintendent of Buildings. He served as Superintendent of Buildings from 1974 until his retirement in 1981. The ceremony took place on April 29.

Thirty graduate students had to vacate the last large graduate student apartment complex when it was converted into undergraduate housing for the fall of 1989.

Operation of the Reynolda Station branch of the U.S. Post Office was turned over from the U.S. Postal Service to the University on May 26. On June 24, the prefix for all Reynolda campus phone numbers changed from 761 or 750 to 758.

Finances

Trustee Vic Flow ('52) and his son Don (MBA '83) committed $2 million to the construction of the Professional Center for Business and Law, and world-renowned architect Cesar Pelli was engaged to design it. At the same time, the President and the Development Office continued soliciting funds for Benson University Center. By the end of the year, the Benson Center was only $1.5 million away from being fully funded at $12 million.

The international accounting firm of Price Waterhouse and Company gave the University a grant of $125,000 to endow a faculty fellowship in the undergraduate Calloway School of Business and Accountancy.

The thirteenth annual College Telethon raised $453,202. Trustee J. Tylee Wilson offered a $500,000 challenge to match dollar-for-dollar new gifts and increases of $50 or more to the College Fund. This money was allocated for the construction of the Benson Center. Of the 15,000 alumni contacted, 5,113 pledged.

The University received a $2 million grant from the Z. Smith Reynolds Foundation to improve faculty salaries and fringe benefits, to fund projects designed to improve the quality of teaching and research, to aid in the recruitment of new faculty, and to endow ten named professorships. Faculty selected for these positions became Wake Forest Professors.

In February 1989, the trustees voted to increase undergraduate tuition by 10.7 percent for the 1989–1990 school year, an increase of $850, for a total cost of $8,800. According to Vice President John Anderson, most of the funds were to go to faculty salaries and financial aid. For example, the University allocated $6.3 million for undergraduate financial aid, more than doubling the 1985–1986 allocation.

Alumni

The Alumni Council chose A. Doyle Early ('65, JD '67) of High Point as President-Elect of the Alumni Association. It also sponsored a new faculty award, the Alumni Association Faculty Prize for Community Service. Nominations for the first award were solicited from faculty, staff, and students in March. The nominee had to be a member of the teaching faculty. The winner, Mathematics Professor Ivey Gentry, was announced in mid-April and honored at the council's summer planning conference in late July.

Raymond Benjamin Farrow III ('86, Political Science) was one of fifteen scholars nationwide to be named a winner in the 1989 Luce Scholars competition. The scholarship allowed him to spend ten months in Asia on an internship program.

Summing Up the Year

The most outstanding event of the year was the presidential debate in Wait Chapel between candidates George H.W. Bush and Michael Dukakis. It was the first in a series of three debates and attracted a television audience of millions, many of whom had never heard of Wake Forest University. The selection of Wake Forest as a debate site was initiated by students, led by Miles Smith, and its production involved more than 600 campus volunteers. Sandra Connor, Director of Public Information, and her team of volunteers coordinated the preparations masterfully. President Hearn's involvement was crucial in gathering business leaders to support the event financially. It was a triumph for the University, Winston-Salem, and North Carolina.

Other notable events included the retirement of Mark Reece after thirty-two years of service and the announced retirement of Provost Ed Wilson. New deans were welcomed, including Bob Walsh to the Law School and John McKinnon to the Babcock Graduate School of Management. Scholastically, Wake Forest's third Rhodes Scholar recipient in four years, Scott Pretorius, enhanced the University's academic reputation. In athletics, the men's golf team's eighteenth ACC Championship stood out, along with winning records for the football team, the women's basketball team, the soccer team, and the men's track team. The resignation of men's basketball coach Bob Staak and the appointment of Dave Odom promised positive change.

The gift of the historic Ralph Hanes House by Mrs. Dewitt Chatham Hanes not only provided new, spacious quarters for the President but freed the former President's House on campus for other uses. The opening of the criteria for trustee membership was also quite significant. While the increase in minority enrollment was a step in the right direction, the 10.8 percent increase in tuition was problematic for many students.

The Ralph Hanes House became the new President's House

A storm blew down the commencement tent in 1989

The academic year ended for most on the third Monday in May with Ben Bradlee, Executive Editor of the *Washington Post*, addressing graduates as the University's 146th commencement speaker. Rain and wind knocked down the commencement tent the night before graduation, but the program proceeded on schedule and included the first MALS student to graduate from the University, Jean Cooper. Metaphorically, the winds of positive change were blowing in the direction of the University as it continued to gain recognition on a number of academic, athletic, and professional fronts.

CHAPTER SEVEN
1989–1990

Upgrading, Expanding, and Renewing

There are no closed societies. Freedom rides on the technologies of information over whatever barriers are erected. The people of all nations have seen your blue jeans and heard your rock music. These are the rhythms of freedom, and the garments of a new era. As St. Paul said, 'The old order has passed away. Behold! All things have become new.' Commencement is a time of beginning. Yours is now the world to make anew—in gratitude for what has been, and in hope for what, with your labor, may become.

Thomas K. Hearn Jr., May 21, 1990;
Charge to the Graduates, Wake Forest University Commencement

Until the beginning of the 1989–1990 academic year, the Hearn administration had primarily focused outward on such matters as terminating the covenant relationship with the Baptist State Convention of North Carolina and hosting a presidential debate. Internally, three new top administrative positions had been created: John Anderson moved from the University of Alabama, Birmingham (UAB) to become Vice President for Administration and Planning in January 1984; Sandra Connor, former Director of Public Information, became Vice President for University Relations in August 1988; and Ken Zick, who had held a number of positions in the Law School, became Vice President for Student Life in August 1988. Only Anderson's appointment was truly new in infusing an outsider into the Wake Forest culture; Connor and Zick were recruited from the ranks as Hearn recognized their competence and expertise. These positions represented a consolidation and reorganization of a formerly ad hoc structure.

Attention now turned to further upgrading and renewing the campus. New construction on campus was launched with the official March 31, 1988, ground-breaking for the $3 million Olin Physics building, dedicated on October 5, 1989, only 18 months later. It comprised 31,375 square feet and doubled the space that the Physics

Department had in Salem Hall. The first-floor lecture hall was named in honor of Professor George P. "Jack" Williams, longtime department chair.

In addition to Olin, a new soccer stadium was finished in November 1989. It would eventually be called Kentner Stadium and was used as both a soccer field and a football practice field. It had a 3,500-seat bleacher section and artificial turf.

Plans for more buildings—many more—were under way. Just a few hundred yards from Olin, the $13.5 million Benson University Center was going up fast. The "topping out" ceremony, traditionally held when the highest beam is secured in place, occurred July 31, right before the start of the school year, and occupation of the 100,000 square-foot student center was scheduled for August 1990.

Between Olin and Benson, the Z. Smith Reynolds Library was scheduled for a $7 million expansion that included a 54,000 square-foot addition along with renovation of its front façade and new landscaping. At Commencement on May 21, President Hearn announced that the new wing would be completed by August 1991 and named after Edwin Graves Wilson. This popular decision caught Provost Wilson completely off guard.

Winston Hall, home to the Biology and Psychology Departments, was scheduled for a 24,000 square foot expansion by fall semester of 1990. Salem Hall would also be renovated to better accommodate the Department of Chemistry, with a completion date set for the summer of 1991. On March 15, however, Salem Hall had to be padlocked when physical plant workers were exposed to asbestos in a ground-floor ceiling. Chemistry classes were temporarily moved, and the building was not reopened until May after asbestos abatement.

Spring 1990 saw the ground-breaking for a Professional Center for Law and

Management, a 175,000 square foot project with an estimated cost of $26.5 million. Completion was scheduled for spring of 1992. It would become the largest building on campus and was designed by Cesar Pelli and Associates, winners of the American Institute of Architects' 1989 Architectural Firm Award. Distinct wings for each school were drawn in the plans, along with shared space, including a four-level library. Some in the campus community called it "The Palace." Regardless, it was beautifully designed.

In addition, a multiyear plan was drafted with the goal of making the University's landscape one of the prettiest and most efficient in the country. John Anderson worked with the professionals in Buildings and Grounds, especially Jim Coffey, to devise this plan, and President Hearn took it "on the road" when he visited alumni clubs. His enthusiasm was high.

Jim Coffey

At Graylyn, the Mews Renovation was completed in January of 1990, doubling the Conference Center's guest capacity. *Corporate Meetings and Incentives* magazine named Graylyn one of the top ten conference centers in the United States for the second straight year. Across town, at the Bowman Gray School of Medicine/Baptist Hospital Medical Center, an eleven-story clinical sciences building was completed in early 1990 and formed the new main entrance.

Expansion of space and the building or renewal of existing structures seemed to be the theme in 1989–1990. In an interview in the October 19 *Old Gold and Black*, President Hearn stated unequivocally that Wake Forest had become a nationally respected university, and the only question was what that status meant for its academic and intellectual development. He said that the emphasis, although not immediately apparent, was shifting from the construction or expansion of new structures to building and strengthening the faculty.

Academics

Three new Reynolds Professors were announced during the spring semester, effective July 1, 1990: Robert J. Plemmons ('61) in the Department of Mathematics and Computer Science, who was recruited from North Carolina State University; Paul Escott in History, who had been a distinguished Civil War scholar-teacher at UNC-Charlotte and was the son-in-law of Carlton Mitchell in the Department of Religion; and Terisio Pignatti in the Art Department, a distinguished scholar of Italian art history. In addition, Allen Mandelbaum, poet and celebrated translator of Dante and Virgil, joined the college faculty as Kenan Professor of Humanities.

Allen Mandelbaum could be very student friendly and engaging

Arthur Ashe's Opening Convocation speech was captivating

At the beginning of the academic year, tennis star Arthur Ashe was the Opening Convocation speaker on September 5. In his remarks, he urged the audience, especially students, to place academics above athletics. Anne S. Tillett, former Chair of the Department of Romance Languages, was presented the Jon Reinhardt Award for Distinguished Teaching during the Convocation.

The School of Law sponsored a forum on the twenty-fifth anniversary of the passage of the Civil Rights Act of July 1964. Entitled "Twenty-Five Years of the Civil Rights Act: History and Promise," it was organized by Law Professors Suzanne Reynolds and Charles Rose and held in Carswell Hall on November 9–10. The Berlin Wall fell in November 1989, and a colloquium entitled "Springtime of the Nations: Revolution in Eastern Europe" was held in March 1990.

The Association of Women Faculty and Administrators celebrated its first year. Founded by Mary DeShazer (English) on the Reynolda Campus and Mariana Morris (Physiology) at the Medical School, the group had a membership of 135 women and was open to all interested female faculty and administrators. Bill Joyner recommended that Women's Studies be included in the special needs category of the capital campaign set to begin in 1991. The number of black faculty on campus increased to fourteen, twice as many as in 1987, now making up 4.4 percent of the total faculty, while blacks represented 8.8 percent of the student body.

On March 7, 1990, the University Senate sent a letter to President Hearn requesting the establishment of a committee of students, administrators, and faculty to assess environmental and conservation problems on campus and to make recommendations for their remediation. A few years later, an interdisciplinary environmental studies minor grew out of this initiative. The faculty approved a Russian language major, which would be offered for the first time in fall 1990. The Art Department marked its twentieth year with a gallery show featuring works by eighteen alumni of the department from 1980–1987.

White House Chief of Staff John Sununu was the speaker for Founders' Day. He received the honorary degree Doctor of Law. Rhoda Billings was his sponsor and invested him with the Wake Forest hood. Ed Wilson (English) received the Omicron Delta Kappa Award for Contributions to Student Life; Steve Boyd (Religion) received the Reid-Doyle Prize for Excellence in Teaching; Mark Leary (Psychology) received the Excellence in Research Award; Sarah Watts (History) received the first Sears-Roebuck Foundation Teaching Excellence and Campus Leadership Award (in the only year it was given); and Ken Middaugh (Babcock School) received the Graduate

John Sununu

School and the first Sara Lee award for Excellence in Teaching, Research, Service, and Program Development.

Other faculty achievements included contributions to the *Encyclopedia of Southern Culture* by David Smiley (History) and E. Pendleton Banks (Anthropology). George Trautwein (Orchestra and Director of the Secrest Artists Series) was awarded a Fulbright Scholar grant to teach Western music and study Indian classical music at the Kala Academy in Goa, India.

During the year, Wake Forest's overseas academic influence expanded. An agreement between Wake Forest and Tokai University would send Wake Forest undergraduate students to Tokai starting in the spring of 1991 and bring Japanese high school students to Wake Forest for a cultural immersion experience in January/February of each year. The Bowman Gray School of Medicine already had an exchange program for student physicians from each campus. Hearn visited both Tokai University and Moscow State University in November 1989 and arranged for another new exchange program with Moscow State for up to two students from each institution every semester. The first exchange began in the fall of 1990; David Bain, from Gainesville, Florida, and Ann Meador of Lynchburg, Virginia, were the first participants.

The summer term revealed the need for additional revenue. Lu Leake, Dean of the Summer School, reported record enrollments during the summer of 1989, with 851 students in the first session and 726 in the second. An additional thirty-seven groups met on campus during the summer for a total of 5,500 "resident" visitors to the University. Enrollment in the summer term of 1990 was slightly higher, as more Wake Forest students took the Summer Management Program initiated by the Calloway School of Business and Accountancy. This eight-credit program was designed as an introduction to the field for nonbusiness majors. Classes were held from 8 a.m. to 12 p.m. during the first session, with approximately twenty-five students in each class.

The Eric Rust Collection of 3,200 books, valued at $48,000, was donated to the Z. Smith Reynolds Library.

Administration and Staff

President Hearn received accolades along with new responsibilities during the year. On October 31, Tokai University awarded to him an Honorary Doctor of Arts degree. The Winston-Salem Urban League recognized his leadership and service to the community with its 1989 Corporate Leadership Award, citing his contributions to the academic, civic, and corporate sectors. In April 1990, he became a distinguished alumnus of Birmingham-Southern College and was elected to the board of First Wachovia. He also agreed to serve as the Atlantic Coast Conference representative on the Knight Commission for Intercollegiate Athletics, which focused on academic reform. On March 15, he appeared on ABC's *Prime Time Live* and stated that the emphasis on winning was undermining college athletics and the true purpose of a university, which was educating students. On campus, the President led thirteen students in a discussion of John Garner's *On Leadership*, sponsored by the President's Aides.

At the School of Medicine, Richard Janeway was named Executive Vice President for Health Affairs, and Russell Armistead ('80), former Associate Dean for Administrative Services, became Vice President for Health Services Administration.

On the Reynolda campus, Miles Foy was named Academic Associate Dean of the School of Law, succeeding Arthur R. Gaudio, who became Dean of the School of Law at the University of Wyoming. Rhoda K. Channing came from the O'Neill Library of Boston College to direct the Z. Smith Reynolds Library. She replaced Merrill

Merrill Berthrong

Rhoda Channing

Berthrong, who had worked at the library since 1964 and under whose leadership it grew from a regional institution with only 180,000 volumes to a national resource with more than one million volumes.

In other appointments, W. Robert Spinks, former chief fundraising officer for the Southeastern Theological Seminary, was appointed Development Director for the Divinity School on September 1, 1989. Kerry King ('85) joined the University Relations Department as a staff writer. He had been Editor-in-Chief of the *Old Gold and Black* and a reporter for *The Courier-Tribune* in Asheboro. Joanne O'Brien ('84), who served as Student Government President in her senior year, was named Director of Foundation Relations in August 1989, and Brian Eckert ('76) became Director of the Office of Public Affairs in January 1990.

Weston P. Hatfield ('41) and D. Wayne Calloway ('59) were elected Chair and Vice Chair, respectively, of the University Board of Trustees at the fall 1989 meeting. Henry B. Stokes ('38), Director of Denominational Relations since 1977, retired on June 1, 1990.

Athletics

The most exciting news in athletics was the opening of Lawrence Joel Veterans Memorial Coliseum on August 28, 1989. On November 11, "The Joel," as it was called, became the home of Wake Forest basketball. The Deacon men responded with an 82–74 win over Statiba of the Soviet Union in an exhibition game. The 240,000 square foot, 15,000-seat structure (14,300 seats for basketball games) had been a long time coming and a major off-campus emphasis of the Hearn administration. The Board of Trustees pledged an outright gift of $3 million for construction and an additional $1 million for certain items that the University would provide and operate. The total cost of the new construction was $24 million: $20.05 million for the coliseum and $3.95 million for a nearby annex. The Lady Deacons had their third winning season in as many years under Basketball Coach Joe Sanchez.

Enthusiasm about the coliseum made the 1989 football season more bearable. The Deacons suffered their worst record under Coach Bill Dooley, with 2 wins, 8 losses, and 1 tie. On a more positive note, a new football locker room was named for Douglas Clyde "Peahead" Walker, the "winningest" coach in Deacon football history. In addition, the football practice complex was named for Robert Lewis "Doc" Martin, the athletic trainer from 1958 to1980, in a dedication ceremony on November 4, 1989. Furthermore, senior Ricky Proehl gained a recordbreaking 2,949 yards as a receiver to end his career and place him as the top yard gainer as a receiver in Wake Forest football history.

Seana Arnold made University history when she became the first cross country athlete to win an individual ACC title as the 1989 women's individual champion. She also entered the NCAA women's cross country championship as an individual entrant and placed sixth, running the 5,000-meter course in 16:48, and becoming only the second All-American in Wake Forest women's cross country history. (Karen Dunn was the first in 1985.)

The men's cross country team, once ranked sixth nationally, ended its most successful season ever with a third-place finish behind Iowa State and Oregon in the

Seana Arnold   *Ricky Proehl*

NCAA Cross Country Championship in Annapolis, Maryland, under Head Coach John Goodridge. They also won the 1989 ACC championship and the NCAA District III title. Ben Schoonover and Jon Hume were named Wake Forest's first All-Americans in men's cross country.

The men's soccer team under Walt Chyzowych won the ACC championship over Duke in a 5–3 shootout, the first ACC championship in the team's ten-year history. In another impressive athletic achievement, the field hockey team won the Deep South Association tournament under Coach Barbara Bradley. It was the third time in four years that the Deacons won the title. With the opening of a new golf complex on campus near the baseball stadium, Jack Lewis ('70) was appointed assistant coach for the men's golf team.

To keep the quality of the Wake Forest athletics program high, President Hearn instructed Gene Hooks and Doug Bland on April 25, 1990, to prepare academic progress reports on student-athletes by sport each semester. Hearn also established an Athletic Oversight Committee, chaired by John Anderson and composed of Bill Joyner, Sandra Connor, Ed Wilson, and Gene Hooks. The committee was charged with ensuring that no recruit was admitted who could not reasonably be expected to graduate.

C. Hunter Moricle (BS '36, MD '37) was honored as the sole surviving founding father of the Deacon Club on November 10. The A.C. Hunter Moricle Athletic/Academic Excellence Scholarship Fund was established, and the conference room in the new Deacon Club offices was named for him and displayed his photograph.

The Arts

The Theater Department produced four Mainstage productions during the 1989–1990 academic year, none of which had been staged before at Wake Forest. The season began with *The Foreigner*, a contemporary comedy by Larry Shue, followed by *Harlequinade* and *The Browning Version*, two one-act plays by Terence Rattigan

The 1989 cross country team was outstanding

described by theater manager John Friedenberg as "powerful and farcical." In the second semester, *The Prime of Miss Jean Brodie* by Jay Presson Allen was followed by George Farquhar's 1707 comedy *The Beaux' Stratagem*, directed by Jim Dodding.

The Secrest Artists Series featured performances by eighteen-year-old Japanese violinist Midori, Dutch soprano Elly Ameling, clarinet soloist Richard Stoltzman with the National Arts Centre Orchestra of Canada, Spanish pianist Alicia de Larrocha, and the AMAN Folk Ensemble, founded at the University of California, Los Angeles, to preserve and perform music, song, and dance reflecting the multicultural heritage of the United States.

Campus and Student Life

Only 31 percent of a record 6,173 applicants to Wake Forest in fall 1989 were accepted. In addition, average SAT scores for entering freshmen topped 1,200 for the first time. The 50 percent growth in applicants since 1985 may be attributed to the publicity that accompanied the presidential debate. Regardless, the entering class was stronger, and the Admissions Department suspended personal interviews for applicants. *USA Today* ranked Wake Forest twenty-sixth among fifty-two colleges that accepted fewer than half of their applicants.

New and returning students were greeted by tropical storm Hugo, which caused some minor power outages and heavy rain, but classes went on as usual. Hugo had diminished from a deadly hurricane that caused widespread damage and death in North and South Carolina on September 22 to more of a wind and rain storm. After

The 1989 men's soccer team won the ACC championship

the storm passed, student organizations collected canned goods and money for victims of its earlier fury.

Tim Bell, a senior business major, was found guilty of lying by the Honor Council in December in an open trial that drew a great deal of media attention. The Council concluded that Bell did not tell his professors, John Litcher and Steve Ewing, where he was, despite his promise to do so. He was on a university-sponsored trip to Beijing when Tiananmen Square erupted in June. In an editorial, the *Old Gold and Black* took the Honor Council to task for violating Bell's rights. Later, the guilty finding was dropped.

The University changed its policy of randomly checking student IDs in the gym after a black third-year law student, John McLemore, refused to show a security guard his photo identification and was arrested and removed from Reynolds gym. McLemore said the guard's actions were discriminatory, and Leon Corbett, University Legal Counsel, agreed, although he determined the bias was not intentional. Following the incident, security guards were required to receive additional training in procedures and racial sensitivity. In addition, all student IDs were checked at the door instead of randomly after arrival.

The National Association for the Advancement of Colored People (NAACP) received a campus charter as a student organization. The initial membership was approximately fifty, and Stephanie Spellers was elected President.

The Student Union brought to campus performances by Jay Leno, a Backstage History of Saturday Night Live with Doug Hill, hypnotist Tom DeLuca, comedian Rondell Sheridan, and the Indigo Girls. It was awarded the first National Excellence in Programming Award by the National Association of Campus Activities (NACA), according to Mark Hall, the group's advisor, and Mary Beil, Student Union Director.

More than one hundred students and faculty rallied in front of Wait Chapel at 10 p.m. on February 12 to celebrate the release of Nelson Mandela, the seventy-one-year-old anti-apartheid leader of South Africa. The group sang, listened to speakers, and shouted slogans. Another act of joy and altruism occurred when ten students spent Spring Break building houses in Coahoma, Mississippi, as part of a Habitat for Humanity college challenge.

The Brian Piccolo Leadership Luncheon was treated to special guests: former President Gerald Ford and Betty Ford. The former First Lady was the featured speaker. The fund raised over $45,000 during the fall.

An underground newspaper, *Cream Cheese*, was published for the first time on November 10. The student editor remained anonymous but said the name was chosen because "the student body was pasteurized." The paper folded after a year. Late in the spring, two anonymous women posted 375 signs of a character they labeled "Cynical Man" with such captions as "Have a Nice Day" or "Have a Dark Day." When questioned by *Old Gold and Black* reporter Mike McKinley, the two said it was a way of saying "ha" to Wake Forest.

USA Today named senior Ed Clark and junior Bob Esther to its sixty-student All-USA College Academic Team in January 1990. Esther was named to the second team and Clark to the third.

A chapter of Sigma Tau Delta, the national English honor society, was started on campus.

In November 1989, the Z. Smith Reynolds Foundation announced it was extending its 1985 grant at the original amount of $150,000 annually to continue the University's minority scholarship program for two more years, through the spring of 1992. Securing permanent endowment for the program became one of the priorities of the Heritage and Promise capital campaign that would begin in 1991. Wake Forest had increased the percentage of black students in the freshman class from 4.2 percent in 1987–1988 to 7.4 percent in 1988–1989 to 8.6 percent in 1989–1990. The goal envisioned by the University and supported by the trustees was 10 percent minority enrollment by 1995.

The Poteat Scholarship increased in value to $3,000 and was renewable. The merit-based scholarship was awarded to North Carolina Baptist students, one for each of the eleven congressional districts and three for the state at large, for a total of fourteen. Patrick Auld, a sophomore, was one of ninety-two students nationwide to be awarded a Truman Scholarship. He was the first Wake Forest student to receive one since 1984. The award carried a stipend of up to $7,000 a year for the last two years of undergraduate study and up to two years of graduate study.

High-profile student leaders for the year were Aaron Christensen, Student Government President; Paul B. Sidone, Editor-in-Chief of *The Howler*; and Jonathan Jordan and later Alan Pringle, Editor-in-Chief of the *Old Gold and Black*. The reason there were two editors of the *Old Gold and Black* during the year was because Jonathan Jordan ran for a seat in the thirty-ninth district of the North Carolina House of Representatives. He lost and resigned his editorship after the election in order to study and catch up on his academic work, and Alan Pringle took up the post.

Students launched Project Pumpkin in the fall of 1989. Sponsored by the University's Volunteer Service Corps (VSC), a handful of students served on the steering committee and about 125 worked to provide a safe haven for Halloween fun. Children associated with various Winston-Salem social welfare agencies visited the campus from 3:30 p.m. to 5:30 p.m. on Monday, October 30. The idea was not unique to the VSC; Jon Hume, a senior math major, had a similar idea he called Wake-Oween. Winston-Salem children between the ages of five and ten years were invited to trick-or-treat on campus from 6 p.m. to 9 p.m. on Tuesday, October 31.

North Campus residents provided treats, and South Campus residents constructed a haunted house. The Residence Life Association and resident advisors were the hosts, the Resident Student Association bought candy, and Baptist Hospital provided plastic trick-or-treat bags and x-rayed the candy. The athletic department financed the screen-printing of 200 T-shirts that Hume persuaded Hanes Dye and Finishing Company to donate. After Hume graduated, Wake-Oween was discontinued, and Project Pumpkin became very popular.

On April 28, more than 500 students, faculty, and staff participated in the ten-mile March of Dimes Teamwalk Piedmont, Wake Forest's first, raising more than $8,000. The student steering committee was chaired by John Jordan. Kay Lord (Alumni Activities) and Dale Martin (Business) coordinated staff and faculty participation.

Vice President Ken Zick was instructed by President Hearn to review the school's judicial system, which the Southern Association of Colleges and Schools (SACS) reported was "rather complex." Hearn told Zick that the University Ethics Committee's review of the Honor Code noted that "the Honor System needs a greater perception of fairness and even-handedness among students."

A campus pub, officially known as the "University Clubroom," opened on September 22 in the Magnolia Room, operating on Fridays from 3 p.m. to 12:30 a.m. and Saturdays from 6 p.m. to 12:30 a.m. for ten weekends during the fall semester. It was described as a place where students who wanted to remain on campus could enjoy a private, subdued, sophisticated, and conveniently located facility with other University community members and their guests. Ironically, at almost exactly the same time, the University Counseling Center formed a weekly Adult Children of Alcoholics (ACOA) support group, led by counselors Amanda Zabel and Craig Arey.

During the fall semester, a photographer from *Playboy* came to campus to gather material for a feature in the May issue, "Girls of the ACC." A student protest at the Holiday Inn was broken up by city police twenty minutes after it began because the group did not have a parade permit. Graduate student Eve Johnson was the lone Wake Forest representative in the issue.

Project Pumpkin

The James B. Hunt Young Citizens Awards were initiated in August 1989 with leftover campaign funds from Hunt's run for governor. The awards recognized outstanding citizenship among high school students, some of whom might eventually come to Wake Forest.

Scott Kyles, a white student, pledged the predominantly black Alpha Phi Alpha fraternity because he was not satisfied with the white fraternities on campus. In doing so, he became the first white pledge in Alpha Phi Alpha's ten-year history at Wake Forest. The Pi Beta chapter of Alpha Kappa Alpha, the oldest black sorority for women in the nation, received its own campus charter. Overall, 196 men and 145 women accepted bids from Greek organizations at the start of the spring semester.

Facilities, Finances, and Alumni

Facilities

About 300 directional and identification markers were placed around the campus during 1989–1990 in the second phase of the beautification plan that began with the replacement of the diseased elms. Lu Leake, who was responsible for the project, chose the color scheme, off-white and light brown, because the school colors, old gold and black, were unsuitable for the purpose. The signs used numbers to identify buildings and letters to identify parking lots. The numbers and letters corresponded with those on a newly designed map, which was distributed to visitors at the Welcome Center. Students and the *Old Gold and Black* criticized the $175,000 price tag, and some of the signs were stolen or damaged. The Delta Kappa Epsilon (DKE) spring pledge class constructed a sign outside the DKE house that resembled the formal signs but cost $30, approximately $270 less than signs purchased through the beautification plan.

The Environmentally Concerned Organization of Students (ECOS), formed from the Student Union's Outing Club, put out aluminum and paper recycling bins in the fall semester of 1989 but discontinued the effort. Student Government under President Aaron Christensen formed a Recycling Task Force in the spring semester and tried recycling aluminum cans in Davis and South Halls for two weeks in hopes that the campus would adopt the program thereafter. Chair Bo Martin believed that few other universities were recycling. Regardless, after celebrating its twentieth Earth Day on April 22, the University placed the first permanent recycling bins all over campus and launched a consciousness raising effort.

Residents on Polo Road, near the campus, expressed concern over Wake Forest buying a number of houses in the neighborhood. They complained that the University had complete freedom to do whatever it wished with the houses without the approval of zoning boards, unlike all other homeowners. For example, twenty-two students could live in a Wake Forest house, while only six unrelated people could live in a similar private dwelling.

Brenner Children's Hospital, opened in 1986 within North Carolina Baptist Hospital, officially moved into its own wing with a dedication ceremony on July 12, 1989. It served children from newborns to eighteen years of age and included an adolescent care unit.

Mr. Destiny, a film featuring James Belushi, was shot in the former RJR World Headquarters building (which Wake Forest received as a gift from RJR in 1987), among other places in Winston-Salem, including the Ernie Shore baseball field. Filming occurred on April 6–8 and required 1,200 extras, some of them students, who wore clothes from the early 1970s.

The street that ran in front of the residence halls on the south side of campus was named for N.Y. Gulley, the first Dean of the Law School. In traffic news, Ann M. Knox was named supervisor of the new Department of Parking Management, which was responsible for vehicle registration and decals, requests for reserved parking, special permits, traffic citations, matters related to parking violations, and appointment schedules for the Traffic Appeals Board. During the fall semester, 10,032 parking tickets were issued, resulting in revenue of $151,791. A total of 3,751 students registered cars with the University, including 2,788 undergraduates. The number of parking spaces on campus designated for students was 2,901. The cost of registering a car for the year was $60.

Finances

Public radio station WFDD raised $326,800, 10 percent above its goal of $300,000, in its fall Tower and Studio Fund Drive to replace its radio tower on Miller Street, which was destroyed by a May 5, 1989, tornado, and to construct new quarters. WFDD had been located in Reynolda Hall for thirty-three years. Weatherly House, formerly the German House, was renovated and expanded to accommodate its needs by architect Ed Bouldin, who designed the Olin Physical Laboratory and the adaptive reconstruction of Graylyn and Reynolda Village. WFDD began transmitting at 20,000 watts from a tower in Midway, North Carolina.

In other fundraising efforts, almost $20 million was given to the Reynolda Campus during 1989–1990. The College Fund had its best year, raising $1,615,000, and exceeding its goal by over $15,000. Over 10,000 alumni, parents, and friends contributed. The previous high for the College Fund had been in 1987. The College Fund Telethon alone raised $503,842. Sonja H. Murray ('86, MBA '88) served as national chair. Harold Holmes led the University's United Way Campaign, which also exceeded it goals. He was assisted by Jim Ferrell, Director of Human Resources.

Members of the Davis family established the Egbert L. Davis Jr. Scholarship for undergraduates, and the Holding Foundation of Raleigh created the Robert P. Holding Scholarship in memory of Mr. Holding, who was a member of the Wake Forest class of 1916. The University also received $2.3 million from the estate of Julius Calvin Brown of Madison, North Carolina, to support the Law School and undergraduate scholarships. It was the largest estate gift the University had ever received. In addition, juniors and seniors competed for Upperclass Alumni Scholarships in dance, music, art, entrepreneurship, theater, leadership, writing for publication, public speaking, and community service. The newly created scholarship would later be offered only to entering students.

For the first time, the University endowment exceeded $275 million. The Reynolda Campus endowment exceeded $200 million, according to Vice President John Willard. Tuition increased from $8,900 in 1989–1990 to $9,700 for the 1990–1991 academic year.

Summing Up the Year

The completion of the Olin Physical Laboratory and Kentner Stadium in the fall set the stage for major construction projects that would dominate the Reynolda campus for the next five years as social, academic, residential, and athletic space expanded. The opening of the Lawrence Joel Coliseum, just off campus, was also a welcomed sign for Deacons everywhere as it signaled the University's continued competition in the ACC. These physical projects, while important, were the harbingers of what would be. Following them were Benson Center, the Wilson Wing of the Z. Smith Reynolds Library, a major addition to Winston Hall, the renovation of Salem Hall, the groundbreaking for the Worrell Professional Center, as well as new buildings and renovations on the Hawthorne campus. The sound of jackhammers and the sight of scaffolding created an air of excitement in the Wake Forest community and in Winston-Salem. The University was growing more than it had since the campuses first opened on the knolls of Reynolda and Hawthorne Hills.

Administratively, there was not a lot of action. Academics, on the other hand, were infused with the addition of high-powered, high-profiled professors, new student scholarships, and a greater international emphasis through two novel exchange programs. The year witnessed three ACC championships, two in track and one in men's soccer. The women's basketball team also had a stellar season. The increased, upgraded space on campus promised important future initiatives. What could not be seen was what else might happen that would propel the University forward even more and change its dynamics forever.

CHAPTER EIGHT
1990–1991

A National Campaign, a New Provost, the Beck Report, and Cable

What has been our motto and our ideal since 1834 is now required to become fact rather than principle. . . . Never have this institution's seal and promise been so apt for a generation of its graduates. The ultimate test of your education at Wake Forest will be its adequacy to this remarkable challenge. May Pro Humanitate not be a token on the seal of your diploma on your home or office wall, but a guide to your life as the nation and world turn to your generation for new initiative and leadership.

Thomas K. Hearn Jr., May 21, 1991;
Charge to the Graduates, Wake Forest University Commencement

Until 1990–1991, Wake Forest had engaged in only two capital campaigns and had had only one provost. It had run a squeaky-clean athletic program and its students had been active on and off campus in a number of ways and in a number of movements. The first two of those characteristics were about to change. The third and fourth were altered slightly as the faculty took a more active part in helping the University continue to have an athletic program with integrity, and the introduction of cable into the residence halls altered the way some students interacted with their peers and the outside world.

In Wake Forest's first capital campaign, President Harold Tribble in the 1940s and 1950s raised funds to construct the new campus. It was an exhausting and draining experience for nearly everyone involved, especially Tribble. When he retired in 1967, he could truly say: "I am tired. I am very tired." The second national campaign the University ran was a smashing success and a joyful experience tied to its 150th anniversary. It was, however, modest. Starting a few years before the marker date of 1984, when Wake Forest celebrated its sesquicentennial, the $17 million goal was surpassed by more than $5 million. Still, compared to most major universities, the

$22.5 million yield from the effort was limited, especially considering the needs of the institution.

The kickoff of *Heritage and Promise: The Campaign for Wake Forest* on April 4, 1991, marked a significant change in campaign drives and goals. Unlike past fundraising efforts, it first targeted Forsyth County and North Carolina and reached half of its goal even before it went public in 1992. The approach was multifaceted: of the $150 million goal, $89.7 million was sought for the endowment, $40 million for operating support, and $20.3 million to complete the campus building program. A July 1990 article in *Wake Forest University Magazine* itemized Reynolda campus aims even further: "Endowment is needed in three areas: $39.3 million for faculty support to enable the University to attract, retain, and reward outstanding teachers and scholars; $37.4 million for student aid to increase the diversity of the student body and maintain a need-blind admissions policy; and $13 million for support for new programs and curricular enhancement."

Wayne Calloway, John Medlin, and Arnold Palmer were the campaign's designated leaders, but professional staffers were hired to carry out day-to-day operations. Faculty and administrative personnel from the Reynolda campus demonstrated their support for the initiative by committing almost $1.5 million in gifts and pledges. Professor of Psychology Deborah Best ('70, MA '72), a Double Deacon with considerable passion for the institution, headed this on-campus effort in which 71 percent, or 711 of the 1,005 employees who returned their pledge cards, made pledges or gifts averaging $2,020.

Ed Wilson stepped up into a new role as Vice President for Special Projects as the campaign began. Known respectfully and affectionately as "Mr. Wake Forest," he was the ideal advocate for the active phase of the campaign. Wilson was a bridge between generations. He treasured the old campus and was friends with many of those who had studied there. Named a "Super Prof" by *Esquire Magazine* in 1966, he taught generations of students on the new campus after "The Removal," the rather portentous

Ed Wilson

term for the transport of the campus from the town of Wake Forest to the city of Winston-Salem. His courses on the Romantic poets and Blake, Yeats, and Thomas were legendary. Students eagerly enrolled in them, loved them, and related to Wilson with genuine warmth. His continuing presence in the classroom after he became Dean and Provost gave him a singular familiarity with Reynolda campus graduates. Now, he moved out of Reynolda Hall and away from the daily grind of administrative work into an office on the second floor of Z. Smith Reynolds Library to take up his new duties: securing Wake Forest's financial future.

The search committee to replace Wilson as Provost was chaired by John Anderson. The committee first met in 1988, and its first choice in the spring of 1989 was John William Elrod, Vice President for Academic Affairs at Washington and

Lee University and the brother-in-law of Joseph Milner, Chair of the Department of Education. Elrod decided to stay at Washington and Lee, however, where he eventually became its President. When the search was reopened, David G. Brown, Chancellor of the University of North Carolina at Asheville (UNCA) rose to the top of the list. He was offered the Provost position, and a news conference announcing his acceptance was held on June 4, 1990. Tall and lanky, the fifty-four-year-old was a creative, affable, high-energy administrator. A graduate with honors in Economics from Denison University in Ohio, Brown received his master's and doctoral degrees in Economics from Princeton and taught at the University of North Carolina at Chapel Hill from 1961 to 1966. He came with a wealth of experience in academic administration. He had

David G. Brown

been Provost and Vice President for Academic Affairs at Drake University, Executive Vice President for Academic Affairs at Miami University in Ohio, and President of Transylvania College, Kentucky, before serving as Chancellor of UNCA for six years.

The Beck Report, named for the Chair of the Ad Hoc Committee on Athletics and Academics, Robert C. Beck (Psychology), was presented to the faculty in May 1991. It contained thirty-seven recommendations, encompassing four areas of concern: admissions and recruiting; academic monitoring; support services; and other. For almost a year, the committee had studied ways to improve the academic performance of student-athletes. Its members, John Earle (Sociology), Herman Eure (Biology), Michael Hazen (Communications and Theatre Arts), and James Kuzmanovich (Mathematics and Computer Science), recommended raising admissions standards for student-athletes, increasing the academic requirements for enrolled student-athletes, and improving athletes' relations with the general student body. The report also recommended that the Minority Affairs Office work more closely with student-athletes and that minorities be better represented throughout the Athletics Department in such positions as coaching, administration, and academic support. The report was readily accepted and praised on campus generally and in an editorial in the *Old Gold and Black* the following fall.

Finally, in the area of student interaction and contentment, during the summer of 1990 the University installed 1,600 cable connections, one in every residence hall room, so students could choose from thirty-four television stations, including

Robert Beck

CNN, ESPN, HBO, MTV, and Channel 2. CampusVision, a part of the television plan, was operated by the Student Union and the Benson University Center, and it broadcast campus announcements. WAKE Radio, the student-run alternative radio station, provided the sound behind CampusVision from 9 a.m. to 3 a.m. each day. The cost for cable, $35 a semester, was included in room rates. Students without cable-ready TV sets could buy a converter box for $35. While many students came from families that had extensive cable offerings, prior student generations had not had such temptations during their academic residency at Wake Forest. The installation of cable did not seem to affect student grades or retention, but watching television by oneself or with friends increased because of the variety of channels available.

Academics

One of the main highlights of academic offerings during the year was a symposium, *The Minds of the South: W.J. Cash Revisited*. It attracted more than five hundred people from twenty-two states and received significant national press coverage in the *Washington Post*, the *New York Times*, and on NPR's "All Things Considered." W.J. Cash was a Wake Forest alumnus ('22), *Old Gold and Black* editor, and an award-winning journalist. Held on the fiftieth anniversary of the publication of his widely acclaimed book, *The Mind of the South*, the symposium assessed regional progress since his time. Speakers included Hodding Carter III, Assistant Secretary of State in the Carter administration; C. Vann Woodward, Sterling Professor of History Emeritus at Yale; Gerald L. Baliles, former Governor of Virginia; John Hope Franklin, James B. Duke Professor of History Emeritus at Duke; and Bruce Clayton, author of the biography *W. J. Cash: A Life*. The symposium was organized by Paul Escott (History).

In a year that addressed race relations from many points of view, the Faculty Senate passed a resolution stating that the administration should plan an appropriate celebration of Martin Luther King Jr.'s birthday. President Hearn charged Biology Professor Carole Browne, the Senate's President, with forming a committee to carry out the resolution in September.

W. J. Cash

Hearn also congratulated Catherine T. Harris (Sociology) for her work as Chair of the Orientation Committee in a September 4 letter, citing "the splendid way you organized and implemented the orientation" for the Class of 1994. Harris typically ended the dinner held for first- and second-year lower-division advisors with the exhortation: "Now let's get out there and advise!" A few days later on September 6, the President wrote to Joseph Milner (Education), praising "his outstanding leadership in the North Carolina writing project and its related international activities." Co-directed by faculty from local universities and K–12 schools, the Writing Project offered high-quality professional development programs in writing pedagogy both nationally and abroad. Milner also received a

Dana Award for Pioneering Achievement in Education from the Charles A. Dana Foundation in New York.

Elsewhere on the Reynolda campus, the Computer Science Department began in July 1990 to consider offering a master's degree. Also, in August, Mathematics Professors Marcellus Waddill, Frederic Howard, and Elmer Hayashi hosted the Fourth International Conference on Fibonacci Numbers and Their Applications. Waddill later received the Alumni Association's Faculty Prize for Community Service in May 1991.

Professor Harold Tedford in the Department of Speech Communication and Theatre Arts offered a special two-credit course in London for fourteen days (December 28–January 12). Students attended ten plays and visited historic sites.

In the Physics Department, George (Jack) Williams Jr. stepped down as Chair, and William Kerr attended a conference in the Soviet Union on nonlinearity and disorder. In the Department of Health and Exercise Science, Peter H. Brubaker (MA '86), a specialist in research on heart transplants, was named the new Director of the Cardiac Rehabilitation Program on August 1, 1990.

In Religion, William Angell was appointed interim director of the Ecumenical Institute. Ralph C. Wood, an expert on religion and literature, especially the work of Flannery O'Connor, was appointed John Allen Easley Professor of Religion, and Fred L. Horton Jr., an Episcopal priest, was appointed John Thomas Albritton Professor of the Bible in January 1991.

Charles H. "Hank" Kennedy (Political Science) was awarded a Fulbright Award to teach and to conduct research at the University of Dhaka in Bangladesh. Ross Smith, debate coach since 1984, was named Coach of the Year by the National Debate Tournament.

Charles R. "Chuck" Kennedy Jr. (Babcock School) examined the risks in international business in *Managing the International Business Environment*, and Dolly A. McPherson (English) published *Order Out of Chaos: The Autobiographical Works of Maya Angelou*. Allen Mandelbaum (Humanities) opened the University's Writers Reading series in the Ring Theatre with a selection from his five volumes of original poetry and verse translations.

At the August 23 freshman convocation, Carl C. Moses (Political Science) received the award for excellence in advising. John Medlin, Chair, President, and Chief Executive Officer of First Wachovia, was the opening Convocation speaker on September 11 and was awarded an honorary Doctor of Law degree. During the convocation, Carl Everest, Professor of Classical Languages from 1956 to 1989, was given the Jon Reinhardt Award for Distinguished Teaching. Afterward, a groundbreaking ceremony was held at the site of the new professional center for law and management.

Tom Taylor, Dean of the Calloway School of Business and Accountancy, was named Hylton Professor of Accounting. Paul Dierks resigned as Associate Dean of the Babcock School to return to teaching, and on January 18 John McKinnon appointed Jim Ptaszynski to take Dierks's position, effective June 30, 1991. Peter R. Peacock, an Associate Professor in the Babcock School, received the Sara Lee Excellence Award.

Marion Benfield (LLB '59), a national authority on commercial law, was named the first Wake Forest Distinguished Chair in Law, while Miles Foy, winner of several teaching awards, was appointed Associate Dean of the School of Law.

The Center for Research and Development in Law-related Education (CRADLE), established at Wake Forest in 1983 and designated by the Commission on the Bicentennial of the United States Constitution as a repository for teacher-developed lesson plans and materials on the Constitution and the Bill of Rights, received several external grants. Its goal was to encourage and support teachers who wished to study, develop, and implement innovative and creative approaches to citizenship and law-related education.

At the Medical School, the National Cancer Institute designated the Bowman Gray Cancer Center comprehensive and awarded it $4.4 million for prevention research. Only twenty-one centers nationally were recognized as comprehensive, and Wake Forest was one of three in North Carolina, along with Duke and UNC-Chapel Hill. In another name change, the Department of Clinics became WFU Physicians.

Finally, Robert Esther, a senior history major from St. Louis, Missouri, who planned to become a doctor, was awarded a Rhodes scholarship in January 1991. He was the fourth Wake Forest student to win the honor since 1986, putting the University in front of the University of North Carolina and Duke with three each as home to the most Rhodes recipients in the South.

Administration and Staff

In addition to the transition in the Provost's Office, the Office of the Dean of the Graduate School witnessed change. English Professor Nancy Cotton, Assistant Dean of the Graduate School, who had directed the Master of Arts in Liberal Studies program since 1986, was appointed Acting Dean when Gerald Esch (Biology) stepped down. Cotton was a champion of interdisciplinary studies and knew the campus and its faculty well. She continued to direct the MALS program. Both she and Esch were honored by the Graduate School on October 29, 1990, at a reception in the Benson University Center.

In another transition, Harold Sims "Pete" Moore retired as Director of the Physical Plant Department on May 31, 1991. At the Founders' Day Convocation, he was honored for his role "in shaping the 'woods and pastures' which would become Wake Forest's new campus." Later, the physical plant was named for Moore. He served for thirty-seven years, during which time building space grew from about 1.2 million square feet to about two million square feet. He was replaced by Monroe C. Whitt, an expert in the mechanics of building. Mary Ann Taylor, alumna of both Wake Forest College ('56) and the Bowman Gray School of Medicine ('60), retired as Director of University Health Services on June 30. She had served as Director for thirteen years and in other capacities as a student health provider for thirty years. On Founders' Day, she was cited for her care and healing of thousands of students.

In addition, Natascha Romeo became the new health educator for the Reynolda Campus, replacing Cashin Hunt. Her job was taken out of Health Services, and she was given an office in the Benson University Center. Larry Henson (MBA '90) was promoted to Assistant Vice President for Data Services from his former position as

Pete Moore   *Mary Ann Taylor*

Computer Center Director. He was now responsible for microcomputers, academic and administrative computing, and telecommunications. Bob Baker was promoted to Assistant Vice President and Director of Development.

Assistant to the President for Special Projects was a new position created in the President's Office. It was designed to help the President with daily and long-range tasks that he did not have time to address. Hearn chose Sam Gladding ('67, MA '71), who was teaching at the University of Alabama at Birmingham, and although the two men had not known each other before the appointment, rumor had it that Gladding was part of what was sometimes called the "Birmingham Mafia"—a group composed of Hearn, John Anderson, Carolyn Dow, Executive Assistant to the President, and Tom Gilsenan, Director of Graylyn Conference Center—all of whom had worked at UAB before coming to Wake Forest. Gladding's job placed him in a new office carved out of the Board of Trustees meeting room in the President's Suite in Reynolda Hall.

In an academic initiative, Provost Brown wrote Hearn on November 1 about approaching the Mary Reynolds Babcock Foundation about what he called the "spires of excellence" initiative. Brown thought the Reynolda Campus should cultivate three or four areas for which it would receive particular notice. He compared these areas of excellence to the spires on the Wait Chapel steeple.

Jim Ferrell (Human Resources) and Beth Hopkins (Legal Department) studied sexual harassment on campus, along with the Affirmative Action Committee. A new Race Relations Commission was set up in August 1990 with Harold Holmes (Student Services) and Sam Gladding (President's Office) as Co-Chairs. It was a follow-up to the 1986–1987 Student Government President's Select Commission on Race Relations and the President's Commission on Race Relations.

Campus crisis protocols were drafted, and a Crisis Response Team composed of John Anderson, Sandra Boyette, Dave Brown, Leon Corbett, Reid Morgan, Bob Prince, and Ken Zick was set up in September 1990. Julie Cole, Director of Research and Sponsored Programs, published a new research magazine, *Horizons*, in October 1990.

The Women's Network held its first meeting on March 27. According to Helen Etters, one of its founders, it aimed to help secretaries, administrative assistants, and other female staff members get to know and support each other and to socialize from time to time. It had about seventy members.

Finally, in the area of recognition, President Hearn received the Tree of Life Award from the Jewish National Fund on October 16. The humanitarian award recognized his outstanding community involvement, dedication to American–Israeli friendship, and devotion to peace and security. The President also received an honorary degree from Tokai University. Furthermore, he was featured in the cover article of the October 1990 "Southerners" section in *Southern Living*. The magazine, published in Birmingham, Alabama, noted Hearn's success and personality.

Athletics

Don Schoonmaker ('60, Political Science) made a motion in February that was approved by the undergraduate faculty without dissent: "That this faculty commend President Hearn for his reform efforts within the National Collegiate Athletic Association (NCAA) and that we encourage him to persist in those reform efforts at home as well as in the national arena." As a part of his role on the Knight Foundation Commission on Intercollegiate Athletics, Hearn had advocated for Proposition 48, which stipulated that student-athletes must meet minimum high school grades and standardized test scores in order to participate in college sports.

While supporting higher academic standards for student-athletes and winning the praise of the faculty for it, Hearn did not support measures to enlarge the ACC. In a July 23 letter to its commissioner, Eugene F. Corrigan, he stated: "I hope that our conference will be cautious about the question of expansion." Schools under discussion as possible future members were Florida State, the University of Miami, Rutgers, and West Virginia. In a memo to ACC Presidents and Chancellors on July 25, the President wrote, "I hope television will not lead us into decisions which, on the merits, we would not otherwise make." Nonetheless, in September, the ACC invited Florida State to become its ninth member in the first change since Georgia Tech joined in 1979.

The Athletics Department rolled out a new Demon Deacon logo because a committee had found that the old logo scared many preschoolers. The new logo was immediately and intensely criticized by students and alumni, and within a year, the old Demon Deacon reappeared as the official logo of the University. Larry Gallo assumed the role of Associate Athletic Director. He had been Assistant Athletic Director for Facilities and Assistant Baseball Coach.

The football team went 3–8 with victories over Army, Vanderbilt, and Appalachian State. Head Coach Bill Dooley earned his 150th win during the season. All-ACC honors went to John Henry Mills and Anthony Williams.

Two Deacon baseball players, Warren Sawkiw and Paul Reinisch, were selected in the Major League annual draft by the Detroit Tigers. Sawkiw was chosen in the twentieth round and Reinisch in the thirty-first.

The men's soccer team received a preseason ranking of sixth in the nation, but in the NCAA tournament it lost in the first round to the University of North Carolina. Neil Covone, the most valuable player in the 1989 ACC Men's Soccer Tournament, played on the United States World Cup Team during the summer before returning to Wake Forest for the fall 1990 soccer season. Rodney Rogers was named ACC Rookie basketball player of the year for the 1990–1991 season (over Grant Hill), and Dave Odom was named ACC and District III Basketball Coach of the Year by the United States Basketball Writers Association. The team went 19–11 overall, 8–6 in the ACC, and advanced to the second round of the NCAA Tournament. The highlight of the year was the Deacons' victory (86–77) over eventual NCAA champion Duke at the Joel Coliseum in February.

The men's cross country team won its second ACC Championship by six points over N.C. State. John Goodridge was the coach, and Ben Schoonover, Stuart Burnham, and Kyle Armentrout were named All-ACC for finishing in the top ten. The final cross country poll of the season ranked Wake Forest sixteenth in the nation. The women's cross country team was plagued with injuries, but Mary Powell earned All-ACC status for the second year in a row.

The Department of Athletics sponsored a speech by Lonise Bias, mother of Len Bias, in Wait Chapel. She challenged students to be responsible and offered what she described as a "message of hope." Her son was a first-team All-American basketball forward at the University of Maryland who died from a cocaine overdose.

The Arts

The University Theatre produced Thornton Wilder's *Our Town*, Peter Shaffer's *Amadeus*, Neil Barlett's *The Misanthrope*, and Gilbert and Sullivan's *Iolanthe*, which was directed by Jim Dodding.

The Secrest Artists Series featured the Summit Brass, a fourteen-member ensemble of brass players from American symphony orchestras; the Tallis Scholars, a mixed vocal ensemble who performed sacred music from the Renaissance; Chicago Pro Musica, an octet of woodwind, brass, and string players; the Kavafian Sisters, who performed violin duets; and the New World Symphony, which prepared highly gifted graduates of distinguished music programs for leadership roles in orchestras and ensembles around the world.

Dave Odom

In an unusual performance due to the fact that he was a student-athlete and virtually no student-athletes majored in music, fifth-year senior Dale Backus, a punter on the Wake Forest football team since 1986, gave his senior piano recital on December 1.

The Student Union sponsored a three-day program on 1960s and 1970s rock 'n' roll, featuring musical historian Barry Drake. It also sponsored guitarist Kier, doing musical impressions and comedy; Tom Deluca, who blended comedy with hypnosis; Sue Kolinsky, a comedian; Paula Larke, an actress/storyteller; the acoustical duo Disappear Fear; comedian David Naster; political comedian Mark Russell; jazz singer Jane Powell; the Duke's Men of Yale University, an a capella group; and Dan Butterworth and His Marionettes.

Campus and Student Life

At the beginning of the 1990–1991 academic year, Wake Forest enjoyed a 14:1 student-to-faculty ratio, with 3,500 undergraduates, 100 graduate students, 460 law students, 440 enrollees in the Babcock School of Management, and 420 students at the Bowman Gray School of Medicine. The college attracted over six applications for every place in the freshman class, although the number of applicants in fall 1990 was down to 5,400.

Although the installation of cable was a welcome addition to campus life, the University Clubroom closed after a one-year trial period. Held in the Magnolia Room on weekends, it was not economically sustainable. The idea for the creation of Shorty's, a café in the Benson University Center, began in 1988 as part of a Student Government initiative. Ken Zick, Vice President for Student life and Instructional Resources, saw the need for a place where social events could consistently be held throughout the year. "Shorty's was created through an initiative of Student Government . . . after experimentation with social events in the Magnolia Room. That experiment demonstrated the need to offer a separate place with regular hours. A student committee with administrative representation created the original design for Shorty's," Zick said.

In an unexpected move, Rhoda Channing, head of the Z. Smith Reynolds Library, had to lay off 58 of 208 student workers and cut the hours of those remaining on February 27. The reason was that the new addition and renovations to the library required asbestos abatement and moving books to accommodate construction. The usual jobs for students were reduced because of limited access to some areas.

Elaine Massey served as Student Government President while Paul B. Sidone was Editor-in-Chief

Rodney Rogers

of *The Howler* again and Jeff Dimock was President of the Student Union. Mike McKinley was Editor-in-Chief of the *Old Gold and Black*, which won first place for overall excellence and in the "Special Sections" division in the North Carolina Intercollegiate Press Association Contest.

On September 17, the bells of Wait Chapel rang for 203 seconds to celebrate the 203rd anniversary of the signing of the Declaration of Independence as part of a national celebration called *Bells across America*.

A campus-wide recycling program for aluminum, plastic, and glass was put in place in late October. Recycling bins were placed in groups of three in two locations on each floor of each residence hall and in the Benson University Center, Reynolda Hall, and classroom buildings.

At the Homecoming football game with Army, ROTC cadets and other students collected books to send to men and women participating in Operation Desert Shield in Saudi Arabia, launched on August 7, 1990. Doug Bland, Director of Academic Counseling in the Athletic Department, suggested the idea upon learning that the troops had very little reading material.

A student candlelight vigil for peace, led by senior Rosalind Tedford and junior Scott Stubbs, was held on the Quad in front of Reynolda Hall on Tuesday night, January 22. More than one hundred students participated, although some who thought the event was an antiwar protest interrupted briefly. The vigils continued on Tuesday nights until February 26, when Saddam Hussein accepted the United Nations peace resolutions. In addition, during Operation Desert Storm, a banner was hung in Benson University Center with the names of seventy-seven men and women connected to Wake Forest as friends or family members serving in the military.

Hannah Britton, President of Students Against Apartheid (SAA), spent the summer living with host families in South Africa and traveling around the country for a firsthand look. Alton Pollard (Religion) also spent the summer in South Africa. In February, the SAA held a campus-wide boycott of PepsiCo, including a one-day boycott of the Pizza Hut in the Benson University Center, as a protest against Pepsi's continued ties with South Africa.

The University observed its first official Martin Luther King Jr. holiday on Monday, January 21, 1991. Ernie Wade, Director of Minority Affairs, chaired the Celebration Committee. In a candlelight

Recycling was started by students at Wake Forest in the fall of 1990

procession the night before the holiday, students, staff, and faculty marched from the Benson University Center to the front steps of Wait Chapel, where King spoke in 1962. The next day, Edward Reynolds ('64), the University's first black graduate, gave the keynote address in Wait Chapel, emphasizing that while race relations had come a long way since the 1960s, they still had a long way to go. Unfortunately, a little over a month later, he was proven right. Racial tensions rose on campus during Sigma Chi's Derby Days in March, when a member dressed as "Fat Albert" in blackface. The fraternity later co-sponsored a race relations event with the Black Student Alliance to make amends for its insensitive act.

B.A.R.tenders (Building Alcohol Responsibility), a committee of seven students and one administrator, developed an alcohol awareness program called Greeks Associated for Responsible Drinking. During the second semester, 456 students (251 women and 205 men) participated in rush.

The Environmentally Concerned Organization of Students (ECOS) planted a dogwood tree on the Quad in front of Reynolda Hall to commemorate Earth Day. It was the only campus event honoring Earth Day, according to the group's Co-President Greg Galaida.

Paul Escott (History) substituted for *New York Times* columnist Tom Wicker as the main speaker for Founders' Day, February 7, when Wicker could not appear. During the day's events it was announced that the Z. Smith Reynolds Foundation was making a three-part gift of $2 million for minority scholarships, which would be renamed in honor of Joseph G. Gordon, Associate Professor Emeritus of Radiology at the School of Medicine and a member of the Foundation's board. The Foundation also added $500,000 to the Nancy Susan Reynolds Scholarship program and provided an additional $250,000 annually in perpetuity for undergraduate teaching and research.

Facilities, Finances, and Alumni

After almost two years of construction, the Benson University Center, a 110,000 square foot facility, opened on September 29. At an earlier ceremony, Clifford

Ed Reynolds   *Ernie Wade*

Benson Jr. and President Hearn both made speeches, and Weston Hatfield, Chair of the Board of Trustees, recognized donors and special guests. The cost of the building, including furniture and equipment, came to $13 million. A total of seventy-three contributors donated more than $12 million, according to Bob Baker, Director of Development. Watson and Frances Pugh of Raleigh gave $300,000 to lend their name to the Center's 285-seat auditorium. An underground sprinkler system was installed on the Magnolia Quad next to the new structure soon after its completion.

WFDD moved into its new home in Weatherly House, east of the campus stadium, during May 1991. An 1,100-square-foot wing had been added on to the facility, increasing the total square footage to about 3,000, nearly double that of the station's previous quarters in Reynolda Hall. The new quarters had "an acoustically pure performance studio that would permit programming of live performances by area musicians."

In a November 6 memo, President Hearn informed Carlos Holder (Controller) that "asbestos abatement costs and projected costs" for the library renovation would "be over one million dollars for the three-year period from 1988–1989 to 1990–1991," and that the new entrance would cost approximately $250,000.

The estate of Wade M. Gallant Jr. ('52, JD '55) made a $2.5 million gift toward the establishment of the Professional Center. Before he died in 1988, Gallant, a prominent Winston-Salem attorney, had arranged for the bequest. In addition, Eugene Worrell ('40) and Anne Worrell pledged $5 million for the new Professional Center, the largest gift made at one time by an alumnus in Wake Forest's history

Benson University Center dedication

to date. When completed, the Worrell Professional Center was 170,000 square feet. The Worrells had also donated a house in London (1976), an endowed chair in Anglo-American Studies (1982), and the Robert Goldberg Award in Trial Advocacy, an annual cash prize given in memory of a student at the School of Law who was killed in World War II. Groundbreaking for the Worrell Center took place on September 11, 1990.

In a brief memo to President Hearn on April 15, 1991, Dean Robert Walsh noted that 44 percent of the School of Law's alumni made donations to the school during the 1989–1990 academic year. Wake Forest tied for third place with Harvard and Yale in the Association of American Law Schools' national ranking of alumni contributions for the year.

The College Fund raised $520,687 over the twenty-one nights from October 21 to November 20, 1990. The newly announced Divinity School raised over $1 million. Also, the Mary Reynolds Babcock Foundation donated $1 million to the University to reinforce and expand the teaching of ethics, leadership, and civic responsibility, and the United Way Reynolda campus campaign raised more than $100,000 for the first time.

In their January 31 to February 1 meeting, the trustees raised tuition 11.3 percent to $10,800 for 1991–1992 from the 1990–1991 figure of $9,700, and housing fees increased 5 percent.

Doyle Early ('65, JD '67) of High Point was re-elected President of the Alumni Council.

Summing Up the Year

The 1990–1991 academic year was a time of dedication, transition, celebration, examination, and innovation. Dedication was shown in the Heritage and Promise Campaign, which officially kicked off on November 1 on the front patio of the Benson University Center with free food from Pizza Hut and speeches by President Hearn and scholarship students Bob Esther and Stephanie Spellers. Though modest by many measures, the five-year campaign, which went national on April 4, 1991, was the first attempt to tap resources beyond tuition and the traditional constituency systematically. Its goal was to enable the University to construct needed buildings, to meet the financial needs of its students, to better reward and recruit its faculty, and to deepen its endowment. Half of the $150 million goal had been reached when the campaign was announced publicly, yet administrators, alumni, and friends still had much to do to make the campaign a success.

The academic transition from the steady, reliable administrative skill of Ed Wilson to David G. Brown was major. Brown differed from Wilson in style and substance. It became evident early on that a period of adjustment would be needed for University personnel and Brown to get to know each other.

Celebration was most tangible in the awarding of another Rhodes scholarship. Wake Forest continued to be the leading institution of higher education in the South in terms of producing Rhodes Scholars.

Examination extended from race relations to athletics. Robert Beck (Psychology) and his committee studied the athletic department and made recommendations to the faculty about the University's involvement in sports. Promoting racial harmony and increasing diversity remained goals of the utmost importance, even while difficult to achieve. Yet another race relations committee was set up.

Finally, innovation was evident in the creation of more student organizations, rallies against apartheid and calls for divestment from South Africa, and the unique symposium *The Minds of the South*. For most students, "the shock of the new" took two forms: cable television access in the dorms and large-percentage tuition increases.

Overall, the University sailed into the uncharted waters of bettering itself financially, academically, socially, athletically, and morally with contagious optimism and purpose. It was asking for support externally and internally on a scale and in ways it never had before.

President Hearn with Anne and Gene Worrell

CHAPTER NINE
1991–1992

Starting Over

Not all questions have answers, and no important question has an easy answer. In the knowing of our ignorance, there is the wisdom of Socrates. If we have taught you well, your days will contain moments of contemplation about nature and nature's god, human nature and its destiny, and even the structure of the cosmos itself. The nature of education is not so much to know as to be a seeker after truth.

Thomas K. Hearn Jr., May 18, 1992;
Charge to the Graduates, Wake Forest University Commencement

At the beginning of the 1991–1992 academic year, Tom Hearn realized he wanted to get a fresh look at Wake Forest, as well as a fresh start. He had been at the University for eight years, long enough to see two full student classes matriculate and graduate. His new personal theme, "Starting Over," was more than lip service. He sent a three-page letter to students that the *Old Gold and Black* described as "a more personal and reflective message from a man who is a mystery to many students." He explained that once or twice a year he spent time alone reviewing planning processes and "looking over what I have been doing and what the primary problems and opportunities of the school seem to be." In the past, he had always found "a dragon to slay . . . something that was there that had to be done that was over and above the normal, day-to-day routine life of the institution." Wake Forest had broken with the Baptist State Convention of North Carolina; the space problem had been ameliorated under his watch with the construction of Olin Physical Laboratory in 1988 and the Benson University Center in 1990; and he had helped to revise problematic policies with the NCAA. Now, he wanted to "know the things that the students like about Wake Forest, and they think are going well here, the services that are provided well" and "what things they think we need to improve and work harder to affect." He was determined to become a student again, learning what the University was and what it needed.

He was most concerned about leadership and planning and that the University stay in touch with its heritage. "What I need is to let the community talk to me about its problems and opportunities so that I will be able to better understand what my priorities and those of the University should be in this next period." To become more in touch with faculty and staff, he visited every department and school on the Reynolda Campus, including the Department of Athletics and Reynolda Village, as well as the Bowman Gray School of Medicine.

The visits were not always pleasant. The President got an earful of complaints and wishes. Several professors expressed the view that their ranks were being neglected while the administration grew. An *Old Gold and Black* article reported that the number of director-level positions in the undergraduate administration had almost doubled over the past ten years, while undergraduate faculty positions had increased just 25 percent, and the student body, 11 percent. According to the 1981–1982 *College Bulletin*, seventy-three executives worked for the administration in 1981, ten of them also faculty. In fall 1991, 134 people held positions of director or above; seventeen of them were faculty. The Departments of Student Life/Services, Planning and Administration, Admissions and Financial Aid, Public Affairs, and University Relations/Development had seen the largest growth.

Donald Schoonmaker ('60, Political Science) expressed concern that Wake Forest was becoming too corporate, turning into a small research university where teaching had less value. His argument and the focus on the growth of the administration was countered by Controller Carlos Holder, who noted that in both 1981 and 1991, about 2 percent of the budget was allocated for administration salaries.

Nevertheless, Hearn realized he was seen as aloof at times. Those who felt disenfranchised had seized on events of the last academic year, particularly his divorce, and spread outrageous rumors about his personal life. The President had to reestablish

Tom and Laura Hearn

contact with University personnel and to repair his reputation. His marriage to Laura Walters Stephens on February 1 in Birmingham, Alabama, seemed to spark good feelings toward the President. Stephens was beautiful, gracious, and naturally outgoing, with a radiant smile that generated genuine warmth. Her presence on and off campus was welcomed.

However, the year turned on a number of events beyond the President. The first was the official dedication of the $7.3 million Wilson Wing of the Z. Smith Reynolds Library on February 6 as part of the annual Founders' Day celebration. The six-story addition to the back of the library increased stack and study space for students. The groundbreaking had been held in 1990, and the building was completed in the fall of 1991. The wing was named for Provost Emeritus Edwin G. Wilson ('43), who had touched the lives of literally thousands of students both in and outside the classroom. He was the guest speaker at the Founders' Day Convocation in Wait Chapel before the dedication. In his remarks, which he titled "To Honor the Legacy," Wilson emphasized the special character of Wake Forest. It exemplified the marriage of goodness and intelligence spoken of by former President William Louis Poteat nearly seventy years earlier. "For me," Wilson said, "in 1939, coming to Wake Forest, registering, and going to my first classes were, in the immortal words of Humphrey Bogart in *Casablanca*, the 'start of a beautiful friendship.'" A portrait of Wilson, commissioned to Ray Goodbred, an artist from Charleston, South Carolina, was hung at the entrance to the wing.

In addition to Wilson, faculty honored during Founders' Day included Dilip K. Kondepudi (Chemistry), who received the Award for Excellence in Research; Charles R. Kennedy Jr. (Babcock), who received the Sara Lee Excellence Award; and Elizabeth Phillips (English), who received the Medallion of Merit, the University's highest award. Prior to the convocation, Weston Hatfield ('41), a life trustee, presented Hearn with the Presidential Chain of Office, an onyx and gold-plated string of medallions bearing the University seal and the name of each past President, joined by clusters of magnolia blossoms. The chain was designed by Susan Squires Stewart of Winston-Salem.

Beginning with the dedication of the Wilson Wing, Wake Forest designated 1992 as the "Year of the Library." There was much to celebrate. The Z. Smith Reynolds collection had reached a total of 1,126,595 volumes with 18,174 current serials. Hours were extended due to student demand; the stacks were open until midnight Monday through

A portrait of Edwin G. Wilson was placed at the entrance to the Wilson Wing of the Z. Smith Reynolds Library

The Wilson Wing of the Z. Smith Reynolds Library—interior and exterior views

Thursday, and the library remained open for study until 2 a.m. on those days. It still closed at 6 p.m. on Friday, was open from 10 a.m. to 6 p.m. on Saturday, and Sunday hours were from 1 p.m. until midnight. The front entrance and the circulation desk were moved from the fourth to the second floor to make the library more accessible to people with disabilities. In another convenient change, the online catalog was completed, allowing the Wake Forest community to access library resources from their personal computers.

Wake Forest officially celebrated the Martin Luther King Jr. holiday again on January 22. The night before, a candlelit procession of more than one hundred students, faculty, and staff silently marched, as in the previous year, from the Benson Center to the steps of Wait Chapel, where organizers of the event, Deidra Jones and Susan Chorley, spoke briefly about the importance of remembering King. The next day, the Reverend Sam Mann, the white pastor of St. Mark's, a predominantly black church in Kansas City, Missouri, preached in Wait Chapel.

Harold T. P. Hayes ('48), former editor, Esquire magazine (1963–1973)

Academics

One of the academic highlights of the year was a major symposium sponsored by the Z. Smith Reynolds Library and the Publications Board on April 9–10 honoring the late Harold T. P. Hayes ('48), Editor of *Esquire* magazine from 1963 to 1973. "At *Esquire*, Hayes oversaw the development of 'New Journalism,'" which was personified by authors Tom Wolfe, Gay Talese, Joan Didion, and Norman Mailer. Sharon Snow, curator of the Hayes papers for the Rare Books Department, organized the symposium. Hayes had died of cancer in 1989.

Maya Angelou (Humanities) brought excitement to the campus in March when she invited Coretta Scott King to speak to her class on Martin Luther King Jr. and charismatic leadership. Benson 401 was packed with students, far beyond those in the class, who came to hear Ms. King's talk, in which she compared her husband with other civil rights leaders of the 1960s. On August 27, Angelou had been the Opening Convocation speaker. This convocation was held weeks earlier than the traditional date, before classes were in full swing, and at 4 p.m. in hopes of improving student attendance. During the ceremony, John Andronica (Classical Languages) received the Award for Excellence in Advising. Later in the fall, Angelou's play, *Sisters*, was performed in the Ring Theatre.

Shigeyoshi Matsumae, founder of the Tokai University Educational System, died, and his son, Tatsuro Matsumae, became president and board chairman, continuing the relationship with Wake Forest. Vice President for Health Affairs Richard Janeway represented the University at the memorial service of the elder Matsumae.

Don Schoonmaker ('60, Political Science) died on May 20. He had joined the faculty in 1966. The award for Faculty Service was renamed the Schoonmaker Award for Faculty Service in his honor.

Robert Hedin, poet-in-residence for the past twelve years, ended his term. He was responsible for the Writers Reading Series and the Mary Arden Festival.

In an October 8 memo, President Hearn instructed Provost Brown to reintroduce a faculty hiring form that had not been used in recent years. By the end of the academic year, Brown reported to Hearn that 87 percent of the faculty held a PhD or another terminal degree and that the average age of faculty members was forty-seven.

In regard to academic departments, the Wake Forest Board of Trustees approved a plan for the Department of Speech Communication and Theatre Arts to be divided. The Department of Communication focused on communication science, rhetoric, and television, radio, and film studies. The Department of Theatre and Dance would include all dance, drama, and other theatre-related classes, as well as the University Theatre. The change would become effective August 1. In their October 10 meeting, the Board of Trustees also approved a new interdisciplinary doctoral program in molecular genetics. The program involved thirty-five faculty members from eight departments, most on the medical campus.

Individual faculty from a variety of departments achieved wide recognition. Harold Barrow (Physical Education), who retired from the faculty in 1977, was inducted into the Missouri Basketball Hall of Fame on June 27, 1992. In addition to teaching, he coached the Deacon freshmen basketball squad under Coach Murray Greason from 1948–1956.

Gerry Esch (Biology) and John Williams (Psychology) were named to Wake Forest professorships, supported by the Z. Smith Reynolds Foundation. Ralph Wood was appointed John Allen Easley Professor of Religion,

Don Schoonmaker

Ed Hendricks

and in the same department, Alton Pollard III received both the Reid-Doyle Prize for Excellence in Teaching and the Omicron Delta Kappa Award for Contributions to Student Life at the Founders' Day Convocation. Dale Martin was named the first Babcock School of Business and Accountancy Price Waterhouse Fellow.

Dolly McPherson (English) was awarded the Distinguished Literary Critics Award by the Middle Atlantic Writers Association for her paper, "Bearing Witness to the Legacy of My Past," which was presented at the association's annual conference.

Charles "Chuck" F. Longino, a prolific social gerontologist, joined the Wake Forest faculty as a Professor of Sociology in the fall semester of 1991. A few years later, Longino would start a new tradition at Wake Forest: the Late Night Breakfast. The breakfast was served just as the exam period began at the end of each semester. Hours were from 9 p.m. to midnight in "The Pit." Faculty and staff served the breakfast and carried students' trays for them. It was a way to show students that the faculty and staff cared about them during the highest points of stress in the academic year.

Mike Hazen (Communication) spent the fall of 1991 in Japan as Director of Wake Forest's inaugural exchange of students with Tokai University. Eleven students from Tokai came to Wake Forest and stayed in the Japanese House during the spring. These students attended an American Studies course designed specifically for them and taught by David Smiley (History Emeritus) and Lee Potter (English Emeritus).

Ed Hendricks (History) taught a two-credit course on the history of Wake Forest using Bynum Shaw's *The History of Wake Forest College, Volume IV 1943–1967* as his main text. The course enrolled more than 120 students and met in DeTamble Auditorium.

In the professional schools, the School of Law, in conjunction with the Bowman Gray School of Medicine, opened a legal clinic for indigent older adults in August. The clinic, located in the Piedmont Building on the Hawthorne Campus, was part of the J. Paul Sticht Center on Aging and was staffed by a professor and second- and third-year law students. Older patients at Bowman Gray/Baptist Hospital Medical Center and others referred by social service agencies were given free assistance identifying and managing legal problems. The project was made possible by an $87,000 grant to the School of Law by the U.S. Department of Education.

Administration and Staff

There was a great deal of activity among administrators during 1991–1992. Among the most important of these was the appointment of Gordon Melson, Professor of Chemistry at Virginia Commonwealth University, as the new Dean of the Graduate School. David Brown and Richard Janeway of the Medical School made the announcement jointly because the Graduate School spanned the campuses.

Dana J. Johnson was appointed to become Dean of the School of Business and Accountancy on July 1, replacing Dean Thomas C. Taylor, who became the first Dean of this school in 1980. Taylor returned to teaching and became the first Delmer P. Hylton Professor of Accountancy. Before coming to Wake Forest, Johnson was a Visiting Professor of Business Administration at the University of Virginia and taught at Virginia Tech. Within the Babcock School of Management, Chuck Kennedy Jr. was named Director of the Flow Institute for International Studies.

Gordon Melson

Gloria Cooper was appointed Director of Affirmative Action/Equal Opportunity in January. Cecil D. Price ('78, MD '82) became Director of Student Health Services on August 1, succeeding Mary Ann Taylor ('56, MD '60), who retired June 30. Dirk Faude ('83) became Head of the Information Technology Center in the Z. Smith Reynolds Library in January, and Kevin Cox was promoted to Assistant Director of Media Relations.

Regina Lawson also received a promotion. She became the Director of University Security. She had been Assistant Director of the twenty-four-member force since 1989. With her elevation in status, she became one of only thirty-five women directors or chiefs of campus police forces nationwide. She succeeded Robert G. Prince, who retired in the spring. Prince had joined the University in March 1988 after serving for twenty years as an FBI special agent and five years with Piedmont Airlines corporate security.

Dana J. Johnson

The Volunteer Service Corps received a $122,000 grant from the Winston-Salem Foundation, allowing it to hire a full-time professional coordinator, establish its own office, and cover three years of operating expenses.

Ross Griffith ('65) and Susan Hunter in the Office of Institutional Research published the first edition of the *Fact Book* in May. It compiled general information about the University and data on students, faculty, staff, facilities, and finances for each year.

Provost Brown initiated the Spires of Excellence program, a strategy to cluster academic resources in four areas—individualized instruction, worldview, aging, and civic responsibility—to achieve national

Regina Lawson

prominence. It was supported by one-time developmental grants totaling $675,000 from the Z. Smith Reynolds and Andrew W. Mellon Foundations. Any student or faculty member was eligible to draw on its resources.

In an October 24 memo, President Hearn asked Brown and Ken Zick to develop a policy for academic departments to express clear priorities in purchasing books for the Z. Smith Reynolds Library. In a November 4 memo, he instructed John Anderson to "conduct a series of cost efficiency studies" for Reynolda Campus Vice Presidents. "These efforts well done may prevent our experiencing actual retrenchment in the future."

In a November 7 letter to Trustees D. Wayne Calloway and William B. Greene, Hearn stated, "we are freezing non-personnel administrative expenses for the second time in three years. . . . The primary cost associated with this 'plus 10 percent' tuition increase is a 9 percent increase in faculty compensation." The effort aimed to raise average faculty salaries to equal those of "the top quartile of the institutions in our category as measured by the national American Association of University Professors rankings. This is an essential step in our efforts to rebuild our faculty as we experience numerous retirements during this period. . . . We can no longer afford to undercompensate faculty."

Hearn set up a patent policy committee in May, chaired by Graduate Dean Melson. An Oversight Committee co-chaired by Rhoda Channing, Director of the Z. Smith Reynolds Library, and Ernest Wade, Director of Minority Affairs, was formed in April to administer implementation of the fall 1991 President's Commission on Race Relations report, which had made thirty-nine recommendations in seven areas. In a related event involving student organizations, including Student Government, a race relations forum was held, featuring Carey Casey, National Director of the Fellowship of Christian Athletes.

In the community, President Hearn became Chair of the Piedmont Triad Development Corporation, and Charles Moyer was elected President of the Southern Finance Association for 1992–1993.

Athletics

President Hearn responded to numerous letters about deemphasizing football during the year by stating that Wake Forest planned to remain in the Atlantic Coast Conference. The University had spent more than $4 million on football facilities and improvements over the previous five years and had the same number of coaches and football scholarships as other Division I schools. Hearn noted that, "outside of football, Wake Forest did extremely well in sports."

Tensions arose between Athletic Director Gene Hooks and Head Football Coach Bill Dooley when a secret internal investigation, conducted by Hooks to determine what changes would turn the football program around after three losing seasons, became public knowledge. In response, President Hearn formed a self-study committee, tasked to investigate the long-range prospects for Wake Forest sports. Meanwhile, Dooley was asked to serve as Head Coach of the East squad in the East-West Shrine Football Classic in Palo Alto, and senior defensive tackle Marvin Mitchell was chosen to play for the East.

Head Golf Coach Jesse Haddock, sixty-five years old, retired in the spring after thirty-two seasons, two national Coach of the Year citations, fifteen ACC team championships, three NCAA team titles, seventeen individual ACC champions, three individual national medalists, and thirty players named All-American sixty-five times. At a banquet at the Stouffer Winston Plaza Hotel on April 20, President Hearn called Coach Haddock a "legend" and his former players and many friends his "legacy." The Board of Trustees gave Haddock the title "Golf Coach Emeritus."

Jesse Haddock

In women's sports, Joe Sanchez resigned as the women's basketball coach after seven years and a winning record of 109–93. The team had achieved a record of .500 or better for five seasons, including four straight from 1988 to 1991. In other athletic news, Gene Hooks informed President Hearn in January that cost prohibited starting a women's soccer program in 1992–1993. Women's Golf Coach Diane Dailey was elected President of the National Golf Coaches Association, and Field Hockey Coach Barbara Bradley, twice named Deep South Coach of the Year, retired at the end of the 1991 season after eleven years. She was replaced by Jennifer Averill. At the same time, the field hockey program moved from the Deep South Conference to the ACC, facing the four schools with field hockey teams: North Carolina, Virginia, Maryland, and Duke. Diane McKeon, a member of the women's tennis team, received the University's award for most outstanding female athlete.

In men's basketball, Rodney Rogers played on the U.S. national team that won a gold medal at the World University Games held in Sheffield, England, July 15–24. He averaged 12.3 points and 4.5 rebounds during the six games. Later in the year, he received the Arnold Palmer Award as the most outstanding male athlete at Wake Forest. On December 31, Coach Dave Odom "redshirted" guard Randolph Childress, who had a torn left anterior cruciate ligament that needed continued rehabilitation. Derrick McQueen received the Murray Greason Award, given to a basketball player who exhibits outstanding leadership on the court. Former basketball star Charlie Davis administered Athletes Care, which involved 126 student-athletes in helping at-risk children in the Winston-Salem/Forsyth County School System.

The Wake Forest men's basketball team beat Duke on February 23. Fans mobbed the floor of the Joel Memorial Coliseum and did mudslides across the Quad after the Demon Deacons came from behind in the last five minutes to stun the Blue Devils 72–68.

The men's soccer team lost a 1–0 overtime heartbreaker to Furman in the first round of the NCAA tournament in late November. They outshot the Paladins 21–10 to no avail.

The Arts

In the March 1992 issue of *Wake Forest Magazine*, Bynum Shaw ('48) described how two rival groups—the Dramatics Club and the Little Theatre—came together in fall

April 1992 Passion Play

1942 to form what would become the Wake Forest Theatre, which was now celebrating its fiftieth anniversary. Director Harold Tedford attributed its longevity to the fact that the campus became coeducational: the theatre and drama clubs were good places for young men and women to meet.

The department staged four main plays during the year: Eric Graczyk's *Come Back to the 5 and Dime, Jimmy Dean, Jimmy Dean*; William Shakespeare's *Twelfth Night or What You Will*; Dylan Thomas's *Under Milkwood*; and Craig Lucas's *Reckless*. In addition, a "Promenade Passion Play," featuring sixty students and faculty, was performed outdoors on April 12–14. Directed by Visiting Lecturer in Theatre Arts Jim Dodding, the play and the audience moved from place to place, without a stage or seats.

The Secrest Artists Series brought another stellar season to campus: Wynton Marsalis, jazz trumpeter; Chanticleer, a twelve-voice male ensemble; L. Subramaniam, an Indian violinist; the Royal Liverpool Orchestra; and Igor Kipnis, a classical harpsichordist.

At WFDD, Cleve Callison was Station Manager. Its main programming was classical music.

Campus and Student Life

More than 5,500 students applied for the 820 seats in the freshmen class, a 2.5 percent increase in applications over the previous year. With 437 men and 423 women, the class had the closest male-to-female ratio in University history. Approximately 37 percent of undergraduates enrolled in fall 1991 were North Carolina residents, in contrast to about 74 percent of the student body in 1951. The University enrolled students from thirty countries, including six students from Spain and five from Canada. During their time at Wake Forest, 24 percent of graduating seniors received degree credits from study abroad.

Freshmen entering Wake Forest in the fall had a new option: substance-free housing. About 300 students applied to participate and agreed to abstain from alcohol, tobacco products, and illegal drugs. Only forty-five applicants were chosen, and these students lived in the basement of Johnson Residence Hall. Special programming included educational series on healthy lifestyles as well as substance-free social activities.

Applications to the School of Law were up 17 percent from the previous year with 2,189 applicants for the 160 spaces in the first-year class. Applicants for the full-time program of the Babcock School of Management were up 8 percent, while the Graduate School received 412 applications, down slightly from 441 in the previous year.

Super Start Sunday, held on August 25, marked the beginning of the new school year. At 6:30 p.m. on the Magnolia Court, free Frisbees were given to the first 750 students to arrive. The featured performer of the night was Kier, a singer and vocal impressionist. The event was sponsored by the Student Union, Benson University Center, and ARA campus dining services. The Student Union sponsored a number of other entertainers during the year, including juggler Mark Nizer, comedian Dennis Miller, hypnotist Tom DeLuca, the rock group Disappear Fear, screenwriter Richard Price, and filmmaker Jonathan Demme.

Four of the top student leaders for the year were David Upchurch, President of the Student Government; Marian J. House, Editor-in-Chief of *The Howler*; Jane Ballbach, President of the Student Union; and Rocky Lantz, Editor of the *Old Gold and Black.*

To increase the interactions among students, faculty, and staff, a Student Government committee chaired by Matt Smith organized Project *Pro Humanitate* to raise $30,000–$35,000 and construct a house for Habitat for Humanity. The idea originated at the President's Leadership Conference. The house would be built on campus in the spring and then relocated. Various fundraisers were held throughout the year; in the most dramatic event, students spent the night in cardboard boxes on the Quad in mid-February. Despite energy and effort, the project sputtered along, but on February 2, with just a week left to raise the remaining $7,000 of the goal, thirty of the original planners and volunteers went door-to-door in the residence halls and raised the sum in two hours. Construction of the house started the next week, with volunteers working two-hour shifts. The house was moved to its final site on April 27 with interior work remaining. According to Smith, Project *Pro Humanitate* met its three goals: to build a house, to bring the campus together, and to promote the value of service.

Another major event of the year was a March 22 visit to the old campus. Seniors Christine Ruiz, Betsy Brakefield, and Charles Lambert organized the trek to enable participants to learn more about Wake Forest history, traditions, and values. Buses carried 300 participants for the 8:30 a.m. to 5 p.m. excursion. After attending services at the Wake Forest Baptist Church and eating a catered lunch, groups of ten toured with a guide, including some of the students in Ed Hendricks's history of Wake Forest class. It was the fifth trip to the old campus; previous trips were made in 1971, 1975, 1979, and 1984.

Trek of '92 button

An interesting and relationship-building adventure was Operation Dorm Storm. Fourteen administrators, seven from Facilities, spent the night of January 22 in students' dorm rooms all over campus. The event, also referred to as "a slumber party," was organized by the Student Government Student Relations Committee to help students and administrators understand each other's points of view.

After twenty-two years, the Delta Kappa Epsilon fraternity ("the Dekes") was recognized by the University when its charter was approved by Student Government, the Office of Student Life, and the faculty. Recognition mandated regulation of their parties, including rush, but it gave the brothers a representative in the Interfraternity Council for the first time.

A series of three bomb threats for Salem and Winston Halls were phoned in during April. No bombs were found, and no one was ever apprehended.

Senior J. Matthew Smith won $100 in the Volunteer Service Corps logo contest. Edward Brown, a senior Physics major, received an honorable mention in *USA Today*'s selection of an academic team.

Junior Stephanie Spellers was awarded one of fourteen Beinecke Memorial Scholarships for studies in the humanities. The Beinecke carried a monetary award for Spellers's senior year plus $30,000 for her first three years of graduate school.

The Resident Student Association won the 1991 Dan Wooten Award for outstanding accomplishments in residence area programming and leadership. The *Old Gold and Black* earned first place for overall excellence at the North Carolina Intercollegiate Press Association conference.

Controversial issues among students included President Hearn's salary, which he refused to divulge, given Wake Forest policy against divulging the salary of any employee, and the more than 600 parking tickets issued in a span of less than two weeks (September 1–12), at an average of more than fifty tickets a day. Students also rallied to protest the denial of tenure to Assistant Professor of German and Russian Michael Gilbert in late April. A crowd of about one hundred students and faculty stood below President Hearn's office chanting "Give Gilbert tenure." Eric Surface, a senior, organized the rally and later met with the President. At another time, fifty protestors marched into Reynolda Hall, where Provost Brown met with eight of them to discuss the matter. Ultimately, President Hearn upheld the Board of Trustees' decision to deny Gilbert tenure after meeting over the summer with all parties concerned.

Nine students in a seminar on video yearbooks taught by Mary Dalton (Speech Communication) decided to produce one to add to the regular print yearbook. At the end of the year, they produced an hour-long documentary with segments on major University events.

More than 200 students registered for Rush on August 28. Pledge night was September 20, where 83 out of 140 men received bids and 93 out of 144 women.

A chapter of the Golden Key National Honor Society was established on campus, with junior Chris Lucy, who also was the Demon Deacon during the athletic season, as President. Alan Cameron of the University Counseling Center started a chapter of Alcoholics Anonymous that met weekly in the Benson Center and was open to students, faculty, and staff. A chapter of Americans for Democratic Action, a national, liberal, multi-issue, political association, was formed and chartered on September 20, with junior Michael Peil as founder.

Five new theme houses were approved for the academic year, including houses for African American Women's Studies, fitness, fine arts, and two for the Wesley Foundation. Existing theme houses included the International House, French House, German House, Russian House, Italian House, and Wake Radio House. Huffman House had been designated an academic theme house since 1983.

A cross-campus shuttle service for students was started on October 26, providing transportation from 8 p.m. to 1 a.m., Sunday through Thursday, in response to security problems. In one serious incident, Nathan Farmer, manager of the Benson Center food court, fought off two armed attackers on September 9 as he was leaving work shortly after 3 a.m. The attack was the fourth assault on students, professors, and campus workers since classes began August 22. The student-run shuttle made twelve campus stops each half hour.

Another safety program, SAFE Rides, began its fourth year, operating on Thursday, Friday, and Saturday nights, with more than one hundred volunteers. It had its own headquarters in the lobby of Luter Residence Hall. The program was unique in that it was not affiliated with national groups, such as Students Against Driving Drunk. It was lauded for its work in the September 12 edition of the *Old Gold and Black*.

A day-student lounge, Room 216 in Benson University Center, opened at the end of October. It had a refrigerator, bulletin board, couches, study tables, a local access phone, and lockers. Sophomore Ramsey Dow was instrumental in repurposing the existing study lounge for day students, according to Mary Beil, Director of the Benson Center.

Chi Rho

In the fall, Scott Kyles ('92) and Clark Pinyan ('93) identified a need for a campus-based music ministry. They created a Christian mens' a cappella ensemble called Chi Rho. They derived the name from the first two letters in the Greek spelling of Christ, and the group's symbol came from the University seal.

David Upchurch, Student Government President, and other leaders organized and implemented the first ACC Student Government Leadership Conference from November 22 to 24. Besides Upchurch, the leadership included Rod Webb, Treasurer; Jull Weiskopf, Secretary; and Chris Baugher, Speaker of the House. ACC Commissioner Eugene F. Corrigan was the keynote speaker. The conference aimed to disseminate ideas about leadership.

On November 9, a new game room in the Benson University Center was renamed and dedicated as Shorty's in honor of Millard L. "Shorty" Joyner, who ran a student hangout with a grill and game room near the old campus, at 212 White Street. The Half-Century Club and the Class of 1941 undertook the project to rename and furnish the room.

For the first time, rising juniors and seniors had the opportunity to register in the spring for fall courses in their major. Registrar Margaret Perry and her office

A tunnel on the south side of campus

developed the preregistration method through a joint effort with the Student Government Legislature. Rising juniors and seniors could also select a course outside of their major by submitting a "mini-registration form." The Black Student Alliance began publishing a once-a-month, campus-wide newspaper, the *Lifted Voice*. It was similar in format to the *Greek Forum*, featuring stories of potential interest to the whole campus but especially to black students.

A "Best of Wake Forest" survey was conducted by the *Old Gold and Black* and reported by Kristin Bargeron. It listed hot spots frequented by Wake students, hints about how to park illegally on campus, study areas, and to-die-for meals. Some of the highlights included the best overseas program—Casa Artom in Venice; the best place for quiet study—the Z. Smith Reynolds Library, especially the new Wilson Wing atrium and the stacks on the eighth floor; the best place for social study—the third floor of Benson University Center; favorite Wake Forest sports memory—the basketball team's thrilling victory over number 1-ranked Duke on February 23; and the best way to break the rules at Wake—tunneling.

Facilities, Finances, and Alumni

Silas Creek Parkway was extended to bypass the University, but the opening was delayed from August 2 to early in the fall semester. Wake Forest wanted to redirect 17,000 cars a day away from the campus. On July 15, before the academic year began, in the interest of safety the original Wake Forest Road was rerouted to pass in front of Olin Physical Laboratory, the Z. Smith Reynolds Library, and the area between Davis Field and Scales Fine Arts Center. The former route, cutting straight up toward Reynolda Hall, was graded and seeded as part of the landscape plan, and speed bumps were added to the new road to slow traffic. At the October Board of Trustees meeting, Vice President John Anderson reported that campus traffic had been reduced to 2,000 cars daily.

In another effort to prevent through-campus traffic from Silas Creek Parkway to Polo Road, the University permanently closed the entrance at the end of Faculty Drive beside the Student Apartments on Monday, September 29. The closing coincided with the opening of the Silas Creek Parkway extension, which crossed Reynolda Road and ran into North Point Boulevard.

In addition to changes in the campus road system, ARA food services, under new Director Scott Ownby, who insisted on being called either Scott or "the food dude," installed a Taco Bell kiosk in the Benson Center food court. Wake Forest was only the second college in the nation to have a Taco Bell. The kiosk was open until midnight every night. A "To Go" area was also created in the food court. It was a small room beside the deli that sold Ben & Jerry's ice cream, candy, and prepared sandwiches.

In the Pit, cash registers and drink stations were moved, and a pasta bar and an area called Leghorns, which served fresh fried chicken, were added. In other innovations, it offered "100 Percent Satisfaction Guaranteed Money Back" on food students did not like and a new policy that let students pay a one-time, $15 administration fee to carry over their meal money from year-to-year, instead of just between semesters. In an attempt to reduce paper cup consumption, ARA began selling reusable 20-ounce plastic cups with the Deacon's head on one side and the Wake Forest logo on the other.

Plain white "courtesy cups" for water were free, but if students used any of the 8-, 12-, 16-, 20-, or 32-ounce cups for water, they were charged five or ten cents.

On August 26, a campus-wide program to recycle white office paper began. It complemented the campus-wide aluminum can recycling program already in place. Cardboard boxes, marked with a recycling logo and the word "paper" were placed at various locations in each administrative building in close proximity to major work areas. The program was expanded on November 19 to collect newspapers, with sites in residence halls, Student and Faculty Apartments, and the Babcock School of Management. President Hearn reported in a letter to Lauren Davis of Winston-Salem on September 4 that Wake Forest spent $4,000–$5,000 each year on recycling. "Students at Wake Forest voted approximately three years ago to stop using Styrofoam cups, so you will not find this material in our facilities."

In an illustrated book, *The Campus as a Work of Art*, Thomas A. Gaines featured Wake Forest as one of the most beautiful colleges in the nation. Gaines described the campus as "a successful meld of hills, hollies and magnolias. Its plan takes into account the eye's need for spatial diversity by placing differently-scaled quads at various levels." Brian Eckert, Director of Media Relations, attributed the University's beauty to strict adherence to many architectural principles. Apart from the Athletic Center and Palmer and Piccolo residence halls, the campus maintained a central axis, from the historic R. J. Reynolds building in downtown Winston-Salem to Wait Chapel with Pilot Mountain directly behind it.

The Wake Forest Area Property Owners Association was formed in September. Julian Burroughs Jr. (Speech Communication) was its chair. As one of his first acts, he sent a letter to President Hearn on September 19 informing him that seventy-two out of one hundred homes adjoining the campus were association members: "New traffic arrangements and easement created a sense of urgency among property owners and prompted the formation of the Association."

President Hearn wrote a memo on August 27 thanking Physical Facilities staff for assisting students and their families arriving for the opening of school. A desire to retrieve some historical artifacts from the old campus was brought up shortly afterwards. In a September 20 memo, Bob Spinks (Development) told the President that the arch stone had been lost, and the college seals in the floor of the rotunda of the administration building and on the front of the seminary chapel could not be removed.

Reynolda House Museum of American Art reopened to the public on April 1 after fifteen months of renovations, many of which, such as new security and climate control systems, were behind the walls.

The Bowman Gray School of Medicine broke ground on April 4 for the Center for Research on Human Nutrition and Chronic Disease Prevention. Effective July 1, 1992, the telephone exchange prefix for the School of Medicine and Baptist Hospital Medical Center changed from 748 to 716.

In their April meeting, the Board of Trustees approved a 6 percent increase in the Reynolda Campus budget for 1992–1993 to a total of $103.4 million. It was the smallest increase in fourteen years. The total University budget was $321.2 million. To keep it low, the board placed a freeze on all administrative and student service units.

The trustees also raised tuition 11.1 percent to $12,000 for the next academic year. Significant increases in student financial aid and faculty salaries were the

primary reasons, according to Vice President John
Anderson, who explained that despite the increase,
tuition was only about 72 percent of the actual cost
of a Wake Forest education. Raises for faculty would
bring Wake Forest salaries closer to those of the top
20 percent of colleges and universities of similar
size. Approximately 65 percent of students required
financial aid, and more funds were needed there, too.
To show that tuition money would be used for these
two main purposes, Anderson set an administrative
austerity program in place to hold costs down.

Doyle Early

The 1991–1992 College Fund, directed by Sonja
K. Murray, exceeded its goal of $1.59 million on June
23. The donor base increased by more than 500 alumni
parents and friends. The United Way campus campaign again raised more than $100,000 during the fall
of 1991.

In alumni news, Doyle Early ('65, JD '67) stepped
down as President of the Alumni Council. He was the
only alumnus to serve two terms. He was succeeded
by Lou Bissette ('65). Penelope Niven (MA '62) wrote
Carl Sandburg: A Biography, which received superb
reviews.

Summing Up the Year

Penny Niven (MA '62)

The 1991–1992 academic year marked the eighth year
that Thomas K. Hearn Jr. had been President of Wake
Forest. He decided to try to "start over" by visiting each academic and administrative department during which "spirited" exchanges were frank, especially with the
faculty, who complained that the administration was too big and too corporate, and
all-too-often ignored their input. While overt and covert acrimony grew during the
fall, it seemed to die down after the President married Laura Walters Stephens in the
spring.

Other activities dominated the campus imagination. The most notable event
was the dedication of the Wilson Wing of the Z. Smith Reynolds Library. The six-
story addition, named for Provost Emeritus Edwin Wilson, was officially opened after
Founders' Day, with an address by Wilson. A trek to the old campus in March, the
dedication of a game room in Benson in honor of Shorty Joyner from the town of
Wake Forest, and a victory over Duke in men's basketball were also memorable.

Other highlights included a symposium on *Esquire* editor Harold T. P. Hayes
('48), the rerouting of city and campus roads to reduce external traffic, the visit of
Coretta Scott King as a guest of Maya Angelou, and the Habitat for Humanity house,
organized by students and built by the campus community. The beauty of the campus was nationally recognized; a cross-campus shuttle service, the forming of the
Christian a capella group, Chi Rho, the separation of the Departments of Speech

Communication and Theatre Arts, and new deans in the Graduate School and the School of Business and Accounting signaled positive changes.

The academic year ended for most students and faculty with Wake Forest's 149th Commencement on the third Monday in May, with popular novelist Tom Clancy as the speaker. Clancy addressed 739 bachelor degree recipients and 493 recipients of masters, doctoral, and professional degrees. His address was not a mystery but was more like the straightforward, action-packed year the University had just experienced.

CHAPTER TEN
1992–1993

Fifty Years of Women

We can sing each other's songs and tell each other's stories. Despite differences in culture, language, race, sex, and politics, there is a universal humanity, and there is in our commonality the hope for human community here and around the world.

Thomas K. Hearn Jr., May 17, 1993;
Charge to the Graduates, Wake Forest University Commencement

Women's achievements were highlighted as the University celebrated the fiftieth anniversary of coeducation, or "Fifty Years of Women at Wake Forest," during the 1992–1993 academic year. At the Opening Convocation on August 25, Maria Henson ('82) spoke. She had just received the Pulitzer Prize for her editorials on domestic violence in Kentucky's *Lexington Herald-Leader*, and she urged students to strive to create change. That evening, at a banquet in the Magnolia Room, she was named the University's first "Woman of the Year." Earlier in the day, a panel discussion titled "Stirring the Pot," moderated by Garnette "Dee" Hughes LeRoy ('57), featured women from all five decades of coeducation: Beth Perry Upchurch ('43), the first official female student; Harriet Smith Hardy ('51); Martha Swain Wood ('65); Almena Lowe Mozon ('76); and Julie Myers O'Brien ('81).

The March 26–27 Germaine Brée Symposium on Women in Teaching and Research also paid tribute to the University's pioneering female faculty and administrators, who presented their research in various areas of interest, including women's health, as well as their reading and writing from women's perspectives. Biographer Penelope Niven (MA '62) gave the keynote address on "Women in the Shadows, or When a Woman Writes a Man's Life, What Does She Say about His Wife?" Mirroring the increase in female students, the number of female faculty in the college increased gradually, from 48 of 225 (21 percent) in 1986–1987 to 62 of 270 (23 percent) in 1990–1991.

Maria Henson at the Lexington Herald-Leader

The experiences of two pioneering female students were also noted. Evabelle Simmons, the first and, for more than half a century, only female graduate of Wake Forest College, was tutored by faculty and completed the requirements for a degree in 1888. However, the trustees refused to grant her a diploma until 1890, when they reversed their decision. The first black female student, Patricia Smith-Deering of Winston-Salem, arrived on campus as a day student in 1962, the same year that Ed Reynolds, a black student from Ghana, was allowed to attend. In a lecture on February 11, she described the stress she endured, especially when she was allowed to live on campus in her second year; she acknowledged, however, that even if her education was white-centered, Wake Forest opened new doors for her in employment and life.

The Policy Group on Rape Education, Prevention, and Response (PREPAR) sponsored a Rape Awareness Week February 20–26. Coordinated by Charlita Cardwell, events included "Tie a Yellow Ribbon on the Quad" to recognize campus rape victims and "Speak Out" in Wait Chapel to raise awareness about rape.

Maya Angelou

Off campus, Maya Angelou read her poem "On the Pulse of Morning" at the inauguration of Bill Clinton on January 20. It dealt with the timeless unity in nature of how the similarities between us all are greater than the differences. It picked up the messages of healing and renewal that Clinton stressed in his inaugural speech. Susan Faust, Assistant to the Vice President for Special Projects, organized a bus trip to Washington for twenty-seven students. They left cam-

Susan Faust

pus at 2 a.m. on Wednesday morning, attended the inauguration speeches, the parade, and a North Carolina inauguration reception before returning on Thursday morning.

Academics

Mexican author and diplomat Carlos Fuentes delivered the opening address for an early October symposium titled *1492–1992: Worlds Transformed*, in observance of the quincentennial of Columbus's voyage to the Americas. Other prominent speakers included Francis Moore Lappé (*Diet for a Small Planet*), Paul Martin DuBois, co-founders of the Center for Living Democracy, and Native American activist Vernon Bellecourt. The symposium and related educational events, such as panel discussions and musical performances, were organized by William Meyers (History), Sarah Watts (History), and Patricia Dixon (Music).

During Black History Month in February, Ernest Green, one of the Little Rock Nine, who helped desegregate Southern schools, spoke on campus about his experiences.

A resolution to add sexual orientation to the University's antidiscrimination statement was passed 84–16 by the College faculty in April. Drafted by Mary DeShazer (English; Office of Women's Studies) and Perry Patterson (Economics), it was co-sponsored by another fifty faculty members and applied to both faculty and students. Hearn wrote the Wake Forest community on May 3 that "acts of harassment would not be tolerated toward members of the community who have publicly expressed their views regarding homosexuality." While "few in number," he noted, such acts were "disturbing. . . . The overriding principle is the respect required among members of the Wake Forest community whether we agree or disagree with the positions others express."

The Wake Forest Debate Squad, coached by Ross Smith (Speech Communication), was ranked among the top five teams by the National Debate Association. Senior Mark Grant and junior Rick Fledderman reached the final four in the National Debate Tournament.

For the sixth consecutive year, *U.S. News & World Report* ranked Wake Forest the best Southern regional university in its annual "America's Best Colleges" list, making Wake Forest the only institution to rank first in its category every year since the report began. The Babcock Graduate School of Management was ranked among the top fifty graduate schools of business in the nation.

Thirty new faculty members began teaching at the University in the fall, and in the spring former Governor Jim Martin became an adjunct professor, addressing Political Science and History classes during his twenty days of teaching each semester. Kate Daniels joined the English faculty as poet-in-residence.

Rhoda Channing, Director of the Z. Smith Reynolds Library, announced three new technological services to help what she described as a "generation of MTV students" enhance their learning. The new Microcomputer Lab featured ten Macintosh LC II computers with color monitors; the Information Technology Service offered graphics production and other multimedia services used in instruction, research, and presentations; and the Media Center had videocassette recorders and monitors available for viewing videotapes related to academic assignments. All three services were located on the second floor of the Wilson Wing.

Dudley Shapere, Reynolds Professor of the Philosophy and History of Science, gave three lectures on "Links in the Understanding of Nature: Two Recent Discoveries." He spoke to the University community on the origin of the universe and the development of life. The lectures were closely followed and reported in the *Old Gold and Black*.

The Master of Arts in Liberal Studies (MALS) program celebrated its fifth anniversary on September 24 with a reception and dinner. MALS classes were first offered in the summer of 1987. The program had twelve alumni, and 423 students were currently enrolled.

The Academic Planning Committee passed a proposal to allow a double minor beginning in the 1993–1994 academic year. Approximately 30 percent of the student body had a major and a minor, fewer than 10 percent had a double major, and about 60 percent had one major. Associate Dean of the College Billy Hamilton expressed the concern of many faculty that the double minor would lock students into a pattern of choosing courses purely to meet requirements. They would specialize rather than explore new areas.

Katy Harriger (Political Science) testified before the Senate Subcommittee on Oversight of Government Management, deliberating the reauthorization of the Ethics in Government Act of 1978. Specifically, she was asked to discuss the appointment of an independent counsel to investigate alleged criminal activity of the federal government. Her book, *Independent Justice* (1991), was the only comprehensive, in-depth review of the role of the independent counsel.

In addition, Harriger and Jack Fleer (Political Science) offered a unique summer course, "Leadership in a Democratic Society." It included two days at the Center for Creative Leadership in Greensboro, a one-day outdoor challenge course, two weeks of mentoring with community leaders, and living in a theme house.

Katy Harriger

Correspondent Charlayne Hunter-Gault of the MacNeil/Lehrer Report was the Founders' Day Convocation speaker. Peter Weigl (Biology) received the Outstanding Advising Award. Fred Horton (Religion) received the seventh annual Jon Reinhardt Award for Distinguished Teaching. Claudia N. Thomas (English) was awarded the Reid-Doyle Prize for Excellence in Teaching. John R. Earle (Sociology) received the University's Alumni Association Faculty Prize for Community Service. James Fishbein (Chemistry) received the Award for Excellence in Research. Babcock Graduate School of Management faculty Robert E. Lamy, James G. Ptaszynski, and Gary L. Shoesmith were honored with Sara Lee Excellence Awards. David Shores (Law) received the Joseph Branch Award for Excellence in Teaching.

J. Tylee Wilson, former Chair of RJR Nabisco, established the J. Tylee Wilson Chair in Business Ethics in the Department of Communication with a gift of $1.9 million in October.

On January 11, President Hearn met with David Brown, Ed Wilson, and Tom Mullen to review faculty and departmental performance over the last ten years and to look ahead to the next ten. As a follow-up in May, Hearn reviewed each faculty member on probationary status. This practice would continue due to problems in the tenure-evaluation process.

E. Pendleton Banks (Anthropology) spent five weeks during the summer in Mongolia conducting research sponsored by the United Nations Educational, Scientific and Cultural Organization (UNESCO) and the Mongolian government. Jack Wilkerson (School of Business and Accountancy) was awarded a Price Waterhouse Fellowship for Teaching Excellence. John Moorhouse, Professor of Economics, won the 1993 Kenan Enterprise Award, recognizing liberal arts college and university faculty whose significant teaching and research furthered understanding and appreciation of the system of private enterprise found in the United States. Moorhouse was nominated by Provost Brown.

Ten of Ed Wilson's former students published a volume of scholarly essays in his honor entitled *English Romanticism: Preludes and Postulates*. It was presented to him on May 16. The project was conceived and developed by two who were longtime faculty members: Donald Schoonmaker ('60), Professor of Political Science, and David Hadley ('60), Professor of History. Unfortunately, Schoonmaker died before the book was published.

Bynum Shaw ('48, Journalism) and his wife, Charlotte, established The Hummingbird Press, a nonprofit enterprise aimed at giving talented young writers a publishing opportunity.

Enrollment in the School of Law was approximately 450, while 500 were enrolled in the Babcock School of Management's three programs when they moved into the Worrell Professional Center. The Center's completion marked the end of a five-year, $65 million building program. It increased classroom, laboratory, library, and student activity space by 45 percent without increasing the number of students. The Office of University Relations completed fundraising for it on July 27, 1992, although the public announcement came later.

The new Divinity School had commitments of $3 million by the end of the 1992–1993 academic year thanks to a $750,000 gift by Charles C. R. Council ('36) and Frances Council. In their February meeting, the trustees continued pursuit of

C.C Hope

an anchor gift, although only $2.4 million of the required $5 million had been pledged by the 1992 deadline. The Divinity School had been approved in April 1989 contingent upon securing income equivalent to $15 million in endowment.

A five-year MD/MBA degree program began in the fall. It was one of only eight in the nation and was offered through the School of Medicine and the Babcock Graduate School of Management. It was expected to enroll no more than five students a year.

Administration and Staff

In January, Vice President John Anderson initiated Total Quality Management (TQM) on campus as a means of cutting costs and streamlining processes. Physical facilities and all of the offices and departments under him participated, as did some staff of the Z. Smith Reynolds Library and Student Life. This philosophy asked units to analyze their work processes to solve problems and smooth implementation.

In late September, Robin Roy Ganzert ('87, MBA '91), chief accountant in the Controller's Office, and two students, Allen Ramsey and Jason Conley, appeared on "The MacNeil/Lehrer News Hour" to give their views on the presidential race between George Bush and Bill Clinton. Initially interviewed by Charlene Hunter-Gault, Ganzert and Conley were invited back, along with seven other people nationwide, to watch the presidential debates and give their views following each.

In President Hearn's stead, Sam Gladding became the University's representative on the Executive Committee of the North Carolina Association of Independent Colleges and Universities. However, Hearn showed up in person for many other meetings and events, and he spoke at the fiftieth anniversary of Tokai University in Tokyo. He also chaired the Piedmont Triad Development Corporation.

C.C. Hope ('43) died on March 1 at the age of 73. He had directed the Federal Deposit Insurance Corporation since 1986, chaired the Wake Forest Board of Trustees, and led the search committee that hired President Hearn.

The Knight Commission concluded its hard work in reforming athletics. President Hearn wrote letters of appreciation to Theodore M. Hesburgh at the University of Notre Dame and William C. Friday at the University of North Carolina-Chapel Hill. He also worked with D. Wayne Calloway, CEO of PepsiCo, to bring a PepsiCo facility to Winston-Salem. North Carolina Governor Jim Hunt was also involved. A deal was signed on February 22 and announced at a March 15 press conference. Pepsi committed to bring 1,000 jobs to the area.

According to data for 1988–1989 from the American Association of University Professors (the most recent available), Wake Forest spent 22 cents on academic and nonacademic administration for every dollar it spent on instruction. The national average that year was 55 cents. In contrast, University of North Carolina-Chapel Hill spent 27 cents and Duke 44 cents. American Association of University Professors President Mark Leary (Psychology) said, "The data clearly indicate that Wake Forest does not suffer from 'administrative bloat.'" The number of faculty increased from 271 to 317 between fall 1985 and fall 1991, a 17 percent increase. Between 1987–1988 and 1991–1992, the total Reynolda Campus payroll grew 48.4 percent, from $20,494,059 to $30,404,004. In 1987–1988, faculty salaries totaled $15,347,321, or 74.9 percent of total payroll, and in 1991–1992, the figure was $22,553,387, or 74.2 percent.

Hearn addressed the faculty on October 13 in Brendle Recital Hall: "Wake Forest is strong and distinctive and should stride confidently on its own path toward the bright future that awaits it." To realize its promise, however, it "should thoroughly evaluate its instructional programs and reinstitute its planning efforts, focusing not on facilities or external relations but on educational and academic policy issues." He recited a litany of institutional strengths: financial stability, "tremendous" trustee leadership, high national rankings, strong applicant pools in all schools, good student outcomes and morale, solid public and political ties, a beautiful campus, a well-established medical research base, strong institutional themes of leadership, ethics, and public service, and a solid base in international education. The University was national: a college in size but a university in scope; secular, not religious. "The time has come to realize that in accepting our hybrid, heterodox, unorthodox character, we can be second to none, and that in our special mission we can be of special value to the world."

Athletics

On May 28, Gene Hooks, who had served as Wake Forest's Athletic Director since 1964, informed President Hearn that he wished to retire "when a successor was named" to become Executive Director of the newly created NCAA Division I-A Athletic Directors Association. He hoped the announcement could be made before the 1992 football season to leave plenty of time to choose a new Director. His retirement left big shoes to fill. During his twenty-eight years as Director, Hooks had built a reputation as an innovator in promotions. He had been an All-American baseball player for the Deacons in 1949 and 1950 and served as head baseball coach from 1957 to 1959. His major accomplishments, however, were focused on maintaining a sound financial basis for the athletic program (e.g., revenues increased more than ten-fold), with a commitment to integrity and the welfare of student-athletes. Under Hooks, the Deacons won twenty ACC titles (fourteen in men's golf, one in women's golf, one in football, two in men's cross country, one in soccer, and one in baseball) and three national championships in men's golf. His leadership in the ACC produced the conference's revenue-pooling policy that made it possible for small, private universities like Wake Forest to remain competitive in the conference and the NCAA's Division I.

Hooks also saw the construction of some of the finest practice and competition sites in the country, including the 31,500-seat Groves Stadium, which opened in 1968. He took the lead in spurring the University to contribute $5 million

Gene Hooks

to build the Lawrence Joel Veterans Memorial Coliseum, which opened in 1989; Wake Forest's involvement encouraged the citizens of Winston-Salem to pass the coliseum bonds after two earlier referenda had failed. Between the building of Groves Stadium and the Joel Coliseum, Wake Forest built or renovated the indoor tennis courts near Groves Stadium; an athletic center for practice, training, and study; new football offices in the Pruitt Football Wing of the Athletic Center; Kentner Stadium; Spry Stadium; Leighton Tennis Stadium; the Caldwell Golf Complex; a cross country course; practice fields; varsity locker rooms; and a sports medicine clinic. In acknowledging just part of Hooks's legacy, President Hearn wrote to J. Brent Mudd of Raleigh on October 7, "in the last four years, the University has spent over $15 million on improving its athletic facilities." In recognition and appreciation of Hooks's accomplishments, the modern baseball stadium that replaced the campus baseball field in 1988 was named for him.

Hearn honored Hooks's wish about a timeline for his replacement and on June 3 appointed Ed Wilson to chair a search committee for a new Director of Athletics. Ben Sutton recommended Ron Wellman, Athletic Director at Illinois State University and former baseball coach at Northwestern University. Wellman had visited Wake Forest twice, once as the Northwestern coach and again as Athletic Director when the Redbirds played the Deacons in football in September 1988. On both

Ron Wellman became the new Athletic Director in the Fall of 1992

Jim Caldwell

occasions, he had been captivated by the beauty of the campus and impressed by the quality of the students. Still, he was surprised when Tom Hearn called him on a Sunday night and offered him the job. A press conference on October 13 announced Wellman's appointment and his October 26 start date. In an interview years later, President Hearn said, "I was extremely involved in Ron's selection, and he was an outstanding choice."

In accepting Wake Forest's offer, Wellman initially came to campus alone; his wife and three adolescent daughters had known he was in the running but never thought he would get the position. Wellman faced bigger obstacles, however, than living by himself. The first challenge was hiring a new football coach. Bill Dooley, 58, had coached Wake Forest for six years (1987–1992) and announced his wish to retire at the end of the 1992 season. Perhaps inspired by this decision, Dooley had an excellent season, winning six straight games and capping the season with a 39–35 victory over Oregon in the Poulin/Weed Eater Independence Bowl in Shreveport, Louisiana. The bowl victory was the first for the Deacons in forty-six years. Three of Wake Forest's eight winning seasons after moving to Winston-Salem were under Dooley, and he was named ACC Coach of the Year after leading the Deacons to an 8–4 record and the Independence Bowl victory. Dooley's overall record at Wake Forest was twenty-nine wins and thirty-six losses with two ties, for a winning percentage of .448, and fourteen wins and twenty-nine losses in the ACC, for a winning percentage of .326. In one impressive win over Clemson, the first since 1976, more than 1,000 fans tore down both goalposts and the play clocks and uprooted pieces of turf in Groves Stadium. The only downside to the Independence Bowl was a conflict for the marching band, which had been scheduled to perform in the London Holiday Parade but had to cancel to play at the bowl game.

Jim Caldwell, 38, who had served as an assistant coach at Penn State University for seven years, was hired as head coach to replace Dooley in late December. With the announcement of his appointment on January 2, he became the first black coach ever to head a major college football program in the South and one of three black head football coaches in Division I-A.

In basketball, Rodney Rogers was named an All-American and was ACC Player of the Year for 1993. His accomplishments on the court were outstanding. Over his career, he led the Deacons to three straight NCAA tournament appearances (a school first), including the Round of Sixteen in 1992–1993. He had been ACC Rookie of the Year and National Freshman of the Year. On April 26, he announced that he would enter the National Basketball Association draft rather than play his senior season.

The men's basketball team upset No. 3 North Carolina, 88–62, in Winston-Salem, and ESPN's Dick Vitale named Randolph Childress as Pizza Hut's Player of the Week after his 27-point performance. Two weeks later, the team rode into the Associated Press top ten after a 98–86 win over Duke in Durham. They finished with a 20–12 final record, the best since 1984, and advanced to the Sweet 16 in the NCAA Tournament.

On July 2, 1992, Hearn sent Athletic Department staff his editorial from the June 24 *NCAA News*, "Kick foul language out of the games," and instructed them that foul language by coaches or student-athletes would not be tolerated. On March 24, 1993, Hearn wrote TV basketball commentator Billy Packer ('62) about such "abominable phrases" used by sports broadcasters as "totally awesome." He called them "another kind of obscenity," without respect for "the canons of discourse."

Tracy Conner

Hearn also sent a memo to the Deacon Club in September stating that Wake Forest had no intention of deemphasizing athletics in spite of a spotty record. He did acknowledge challenges that needed immediate attention; for example, Kentner Stadium's artificial surface had become unusable, according to men's Head Soccer Coach Walt Chyzowych. It was still used when Wake Forest hosted the ACC field hockey championship in early November. The Lady Deacons lost 2–1 to Virginia in the first round and finished their first season of ACC play with a 3–12–3 record.

In other events, Charlie Davis, along with a group of Deacon athletes and Wake Forest employees, refurbished the home of Vernie Mae Shaw through Operation Paintbrush in October. Marge Crisp and Dot Casey were recognized as the first women inducted into the

Students tore down the goalposts after Wake Forest beat Clemson in the fall of 1992

Wake Forest Sports Hall of Fame on January 9. Mac McDonald, the voice of Demon Deacon radio broadcasts, was named North Carolina Sportscaster of the Year.

Freshman Tracy Conner won the ACC Rookie of the Year Award in women's basketball. She averaged more than 20 points a game and was in the top ten nationally in rebounding. She also received the Marge Crisp Award as Wake Forest's top female athlete.

In fall 1992, Wake Forest was one of five schools with nine teams ranked in the top twenty-five by national polls—the others were Arizona, Stanford, Florida State, and Virginia. Wake Forest was the only one without a nationally ranked football team, although by the end of the season, the Deacons gridiron team cracked the Associated Press poll at No. 25, their first national ranking since 1979. Seniors Mike McCrary, Ben Coleman, and John Henry Mills were drafted by the National Football League, while Maurice Miller and George Coghill signed as free agents.

Stephanie Neill was the 1992–1993 winner of the prestigious Edith Cummings Munson Award

Stephanie Neill

to the All-American women's golfer with the highest grade-point average. Neill, a junior from Charlotte, was a business major with a 3.68 cumulative GPA.

At the ACC Outdoor Track meet, held at Florida State, both men and women came away with the highest point totals in school history. The men dominated the middle- and long-distance events and performed well in the field events. Earlier in the year, the cross country team had qualified to make its fourth appearance in five years in the NCAA championship by tying for third in the NCAA District III Championships. The women did well in all events, and in early November the cross country team won the NCAA District III Championship in Greenville, South Carolina, their first in Wake Forest history.

The Arts

And Still I Rise, a musical written and directed by Reynolds Professor Maya Angelou, had its world premiere at the Arts Council Theatre on September 3. The title came from Angelou's poem by the same name.

Sweet Honey in the Rock, an all-female, Grammy-winning, a cappella quintet, with a sixth member signing for the hearing impaired, sang gospel, jazz, and blues in Wait Chapel in September. Founder Bernice Johnson Reagon, a veteran of the Civil Rights Movement, crafted the performance to communicate religious, social, and political messages.

The Secrest Artists Series began the new season with a performance of the New Sousa Band, which aimed to reproduce the look, sound, and *espirit de corps* of the John Philip Sousa original. It was followed by the Mozartean Players, who specialized in the works of Haydn, Mozart, and Beethoven. In December, the Waverly Consort enacted the Christmas story, both singing and playing reproductions of medieval instruments. The Russian chamber ensemble Moscow Virtuosi performed in February, and a month later pianist Ruth Laredo performed "Homage to Rachmaninoff."

The Wake Forest Theatre presented *Dark of the Moon*, a 1945 Appalachian drama by Howard Richardson and William Berney, in October and Tennessee Williams's *Night of the Iguana* in November. In the spring, it produced *Accidental Death of an Anarchist*, by Nobel-prize winner Dario Fo, and *The Boy Friend*, a 1954 musical by Sandy Wilson. In late January, Broadway actor Bruce Kuhn performed the text of *The Gospel of Luke* in the Ring Theater.

The Battle of Gettysburg cyclorama was displayed in the Scales Fine Arts Center from August through September. The painting by Paul Philippoteaux depicts Pickett's Charge and was rescued by Winston-Salem artist Joe King, who gave it to the University.

Campus and Student Life

Wake Forest entered the 1992–1993 academic year with an official student/faculty ratio of 13:1, an undergraduate enrollment of 3,650, and a total enrollment, including the medical school, of 5,679. Overall, 1,188 undergraduates were from North Carolina; about 64 percent hailed from the South, compared with 71.5 percent in 1988. Applications for first-year admission increased to 5,567, which was 319 more than in

1991–1992; 75 percent of the 904 students accepted scored between 1150 and 1350 on the SAT, and 69 percent were in the top 10 percent of their high school class. Incoming students represented forty states and six foreign countries; 51 percent were men, and 49 percent women. A historic high of more than 200 students studied abroad. Ninety-four men and eighty-four women received bids from fraternities, societies, and sororities during fall rush; in the spring semester, 329 students pledged (172 men and 157 women).

President Hearn wrote Franklin D. Robinson Jr. of Charlotte on July 27 that since 1987, Wake Forest had "dedicated itself to having an enrollment of 10 percent of its students from nonmajority cultures." While this goal was not realized at the start of the academic year, the plan did increase minority enrollment, and the Office of Minority Affairs expanded its programming to accommodate the needs of Asian American, Native American, and Hispanic students. It also moved from Benson 317 to Benson 346.

Five high-profile student leaders for the year were Jay Woodruff, Editor-in-Chief of the *Old Gold and Black*; Zeke Creech, Student Government President; Steve Braskamp, President of the Student Union; Brent Williamson, Editor-in-Chief of *The Howler*; and sophomore Todd Turner, who was appointed to a one-year term as the student representative to the Board of Trustees.

Substance-free housing was offered for the second year in a row. More than 300 entering students took advantage of it on all four floors of Johnson, two floors of Bostwick, and two suites for men in Taylor Residence Halls. In the previous year's trial run, only forty-five students lived substance-free on one floor of Johnson, according to Dennis Gregory, Director of Residence Life and Housing. These students were given the option to continue living substance-free for a second year, but this time in Piccolo Residence Hall.

The Student Life Committee changed the Student Alcoholic Beverage Policy to allow students and their guests, if at least twenty-one years old, to drink beer or unfortified wines in suites and hallway lounges in residence halls. The change was made because members of Greek organizations, who leased lounges, had the freedom to drink alcohol there. On February 5, the Board of Trustees passed a resolution instructing Residence Life and Housing to reconfigure space in residence halls to provide all Greek organizations with a lounge. While the 848 Greek women had 1,500 square feet, or 11 percent, of the total lounge space, the 751 men had 12,000 square feet, or 88.9 percent. Director Gregory stated that at least ten new lounge areas for women would be needed to rectify the disparity.

The security shuttle was restored in early October. Students wishing to use it simply called 5911 for pick-up. This system was more efficient than the previous year's dispatch, which traced a half-hour route across campus. As before, the shuttle ran in the evenings only, when risk of an assault was felt to be greatest.

ARA food services assumed control of the Sundry Shop, which allowed students to use their meal cards to purchase items. In conjunction, ARA added Dunkin' Donuts to the Food Court and cafeteria, replacing Krispy Kreme products, and students bought more donuts. Apart from ARA, Camel City Dry Cleaning opened a store next to the barber shop in the basement of Taylor House and offered a 25 percent discount to anyone affiliated with Wake Forest. Alas, the dry cleaner did not have enough business to continue a second year, so they hung it up. However, the barber shop continued to flourish under the direction of Lloyd Howard.

Student Government President Zeke Creech was mainly interested in student relations, especially race relations. However, Creech formed a task force to examine parking policy when Parking Management issued 3,087 decals, although the campus had only 2,739 parking spaces.

WAKE Radio celebrated its first decade on air. It was created in 1982, when the University's public radio station, WFDD, increased its broadcasting power and eliminated student shows. At first, WAKE Radio was a Student Union committee located in a former game room in the basement of Reynolda Hall. Now it resided in Benson 512 and had converted its broadcasting from AM to FM cable.

The *Old Gold and Black* received a first-place award for excellence and seventeen other awards from the North Carolina Intercollegiate Press Association. A text-only edition was made available on the Internet through Wake Forest's Gopher server, known as Deacons Online. The first issue for the year provided new arrivals with some interesting Wake Forest slang, including *Tommy K*, a nickname for President Hearn; *scoping*, the cool, analytical process of determining the perfect date for the night; and *tunneling*, the illegal act of crawling through dark, intensely hot maintenance tunnels under the campus. In fact, the tunnels between Bostwick and Johnson and Luter and Babcock residence halls were closed in the late fall due to concerns about security and asbestos contamination.

In its December 3 preholiday issue, the *Old Gold and Black* listed the top ten gifts students wanted for Christmas. In order, they were: 1) sleep, 2) clothes, 3) a Bowl win, 4) money, 5) a car, 6) good grades, 7) a ski trip, 8) a CD player, 9) a job, and 10) a VCR. Sleep was the only wish likely to be gratified with some immediacy. *The Howler* for 1991–1992 did not arrive on campus until October 26. Editor-in-chief Marian House's plan to make the yearbook "seamless" instead of divided into sections caused some delays.

Another non-University newspaper circulated on campus and became controversial. It was the *Wake Forest Critic*. Financed by an outside group and edited by junior John Meroney, it was published about once a month by the Wake Forest Critic Society, an offshoot of the Carolina Critic Society, which founded a newspaper in 1989. The University asked that its name be deleted from the masthead because its presence erroneously implied a University affiliation. *Critic* stories often contained personal opinions, attacks on individuals, and inaccurate information. After charges of lying were brought against Meroney in an incident involving the Black Student Association resulted in several mistrials, the *Critic* continued to publish but University judicial policies were more rigorously defined. These reforms streamlined the judicial system from a patchwork of informal and inconsistent procedures to a more uniform body of definitive guidelines designed to determine the truth.

Since their inception in 1988, Presidential Scholarships had been awarded to first-year students, but this year they were eliminated for upperclassman because those who were qualified and had not had an opportunity to apply had graduated. Outside of the Presidential Scholarships, Alexander Crowell, a senior, received a

Goldwater Scholarship, a national award to college juniors and seniors planning careers in mathematics or the natural sciences.

Betsy Greer became coordinator of the Volunteer Service Corps after former part-time coordinator Henry Cooper ('53) left the position in spring 1992. The Volunteer Service Corps was launched in 1989, when Dean of Students Mark Reece asked Cooper, retired from his day-care business in Charlotte, to move to Winston-Salem. Initially, Cooper worked with students who had violated the honor code and were sentenced to community service. Working with Chaplain Ed Christman, however, Cooper wanted to increase community service on campus. They met with a handful of interested students and started a steering committee. Their first open meeting attracted 150 students, and when Cooper left, more than 700 students were involved.

A number of major humanitarian projects to help others took place over the year. Nearly 700 underprivileged children and 400 Wake Forest students participated in Project Pumpkin's fourth year of operation on October 29. In the late spring, members of Visiting Assistant Professor of Art David Helm's class—Scott Smith, Matt Smith, and Phoebe Hillman—designed a memorial arch ("The Thin Blue Line") to commemorate Winston-Salem city police who died in the line of duty.

In other student activities, Dorm Storm 2, which aimed to improve relations between students and faculty, was held on March 16. It was a follow-up to the previous year's Operation Dorm Storm. Faculty and administrators were invited to spend the night in a residence hall and to experience campus life after 5 p.m.

The Student Government Recycling Committee introduced a pilot program for glass recycling in Babcock, Luter, Taylor, and Davis residence halls. It augmented the aluminum, white paper, and newspaper recycling programs established in 1991. The glass had to be separated into bins marked for clear, brown, or green glass. Any glass of the wrong color prevented the entire bin from being recycled.

The 1993 Storm of the Century, which pounded the east coast with heavy snow and gale-force winds, hit the campus during the second week of March. It crippled traffic, and many students were stranded either on campus or at home for several days after Spring Break officially ended. Nonetheless, the University did not call off classes. In an email, Provost Brown assured parents that professors would work with students on any work missed due to the weather.

Facilities, Finances, and Alumni

Facilities

Workers renovated the outside of Wait Chapel from September to November, removing old paint, replacing rotten wood, and repainting the new wood on the bell tower. The renovations were the first in forty years. Elsewhere, ground lights were installed on the side of the Scales Fine Arts Center closest to Davis Field.

Before the Worrell Professional Center for Law and Management was completed, water leaked in when a campus-wide power outage on November 30 caused the City of Winston-Salem water tower on University Parkway to overflow.

Associate Supreme Court Justice Sandra Day O'Connor

The center sustained little damage, but cars parked nearby were flooded. Later in the semester, sprinklers were installed to maintain the grass. On December 17, more than 150 faculty, staff, students, and alumni of the MBA evening program attended a party bidding farewell to Management House, the former Amos Cottage at Graylyn. Evening MBA students started classes at the Worrell Professional Center on January 4.

President Hearn first suggested housing the Schools of Law and Management together in 1986, and on April 3, 1993, the Worrell Professional Center was dedicated with the two sharing the same building. More than 200 faculty and students assembled in the courtyard of the $25.6 million facility. The ceremony capped two days of festivities that included speeches by world-famous architect Cesar Pelli, the designer; Apple Computer, Inc., CEO and chief technology officer John Sculley; and U.S. Supreme Court Associate Justice Sandra Day O'Connor. Hearn wrote to Julius Corpening on April 20, "acknowledging the time and hard work you invested in raising over $15 million of private funding for the Center."

The trustees passed a resolution on October 2 renaming the Family Practice Building at the Medical School as Manson Meads Hall after the Vice President Emeritus of Health Affairs. In 1992, the Bowman Gray School of Medicine and North Carolina Baptist Hospital celebrated fifty years of partnership.

Graylyn Conference Center received its fourth Paragon Award from *Corporate Meetings and Incentives* magazine in January. It had won in 1988, 1989, and 1991. The award was based on a readers' poll that measured the quality of services at ten conference centers. Reynolda House Museum of American Art celebrated its twenty-fifth anniversary in October 1992.

Finances

In January 1993, renovation of Babcock and Carswell Halls began with lead gifts from the Cannon Foundation and the Arthur Vining Davis Foundation. The Annenberg Foundation donated $250,000 for the renovation of Carswell Hall and the establishment of a scholarship in honor of Arnold Palmer ('51). AT&T donated $145,000 in computer equipment to upgrade the Departments of Physics and Chemistry. In new construction, a $2.8 million, ninety-six-bed student residence initially known as North Hall, later named Martin Hall (after Zeno Martin Sr., a member of the Wake Forest College Class of 1926), was begun in May. It was located between the soccer practice fields and Student Apartments on Polo Road and slated for completion in August 1994.

The J. Smith Young Athletic-Academic Excellence Fund was established in honor of the President and CEO of Lexington Furniture Industries by his wife, Helen, and his sons, Jay and Jeff. The scholarship recognized the accomplishments of student-athletes off the field or court. A former student-athlete in basketball, Young was a life

President Hearn with Philip and Charlotte Hanes outside of Middleton House

member of the Board of Trustees and former President of the Alumni Association and the Deacon Club when the $1 million contribution was made.

In a surprise move, Winston-Salem businessman R. Philip Hanes Jr. and his wife, Charlotte, signed a life estate agreement in January that gave the University their 1820s plantation-style Middleton House, their art collection, and twenty-six acres adjoining the Wake Forest President's House. The size of the gift was not disclosed, but the county tax office assessed the house and land at $2.1 million.

The University's endowment in June 1992 was $240,000,000, according to John Willard, Vice President for Financial Resources and University Treasurer, while the overall Reynolda Campus budget increased from $54,318,000 to $60,191,000, or 10.8 percent.

In February, the *Chronicle of Higher Education* ranked Wake Forest's endowment the fortieth largest in the country. At the same time, the Board of Trustees approved an 8.3 percent increase in tuition for 1993–1994. The hike of almost a thousand dollars to $12,996 a year was part of a five-year plan to raise faculty salaries to a level comparable to those at similar institutions. It included a 12.3 percent boost in financial aid, which had increased from $2,390,000 in 1985–1986 to $10,040,000 in 1992–1993. Financial aid for minority students had risen from $194,000 in 1987–1988 to $732,000 in 1988–1989 to $808,000 in 1992–1993. The College Fund, used exclusively for daily operating expenses, reported on June 30 that in its 1992–1993 drive, 9,150 alumni, parents, and friends had contributed $1,838,971.

Summing Up the Year

The 1992–1993 Year of the Woman celebrated fifty years of coeducation at Wake Forest. It was kicked off with an address by Pulitzer-prize winning journalist Maria Henson at the Opening Convocation. Other forums and programs related to women and education followed on and off campus. An outstanding woman, Reynolds Professor of American Studies Maya Angelou, read her poem, "The Pulse of Morning," at the presidential inauguration of Bill Clinton. The year also marked the quincentennial of Columbus's voyage to the Americas, and a three-day symposium brought Carlos Fuentes and many other internationally acclaimed intellectuals and artists to campus to discuss its meaning and ramifications.

Another major highlight was the dedication of the Worrell Professional Center for Law and Management on April 3, with visits and speeches by Associate Supreme Court Justice Sandra Day O'Connor, world-famous architect and Worrell Center designer Cesar Pelli; and Apple CEO and chief technology officer John Sculley. For the sixth consecutive year, the University was ranked best in the region by *U.S. News & World Report*. In March, the 1993 Storm of the Century, which stranded some students on campus and at home as Spring Break ended, disrupted the usual academic rhythm of the University, yet classes were not cancelled.

A new, full-time coordinator of the Volunteer Service Corps was hired, and the Office of Minority Affairs expanded its programming to accommodate the needs of Asian American, Native American, and Hispanic students. In athletics, the Deacons football team beat Oregon 38–35 in the Independence Bowl, and the men's basketball team defeated both Duke and North Carolina and advanced to the Sweet 16 of the NCAA Tournament.

On the third Monday in May, the 150th commencement speaker for Wake Forest was Father Hesburgh, President of the University of Notre Dame. Temperatures soared to the high 90s during the ceremony, and 8,500 bottles of water were distributed as students, families, and faculty celebrated a marker event in the University's history and in personal histories as well.

CHAPTER ELEVEN
1993–1994

To Dream with One Eye Open

No person's circle is self-contained and individual. No one is self-made. We are not, any of us, merely single persons. We live many lives. Our circles are not one. They are many.
The circles of our lives yield stories told in both tragedy and comedy. Not all our endings are happy, but some are wonderful indeed. Live in that spirit, and the circle of your life will be blessed and a blessing.

Thomas K. Hearn Jr., May 16, 1994;
Charge to the Graduates, Wake Forest University

In the tenth year of his administration, President Hearn issued a report, *To Dream with One Eye Open*, a title inspired by philosopher George Santayana. The report focused on the importance to Wake Forest of its Judeo-Christian/Baptist heritage, tradition of democracy, and commitment to liberal education while forging a new voluntary and fraternal relationship with the Baptist State Convention of North Carolina. Wake Forest had become a national institution, a college in size but a university in scope. Its small student body promoted strong, highly productive student/ faculty interactions. Physically, a $65 million building program had increased the Reynolda Campus space by more than one-third. Total investments had grown from $170 million in 1983 to $550 million, and the endowment was the fortieth largest in the country. At the Medical School, total space had more than doubled, and applications had risen nearly 50 percent. It ranked among the top thirty-five medical schools in funding awarded by the National Institutes of Health.

For the seventh consecutive year, *U.S. News & World Report* named Wake Forest the top regional university in the South in the "America's Best Colleges" issue, awarding the University top marks in academic reputation, student selectivity, financial resources, and faculty resources. For the fourth consecutive year, *Money* magazine ranked the University one of the nation's hundred best buys; for the first time, *Barron's* ranked Wake Forest under the heading "Most Selective." In January 1994, *Barron's* ranked the Babcock School of Management the tenth best business school in the nation.

In an even more prestigious recognition of Wake Forest's growing academic reputation, the Oak Ridge Associated Universities (ORAU) elected the University to full membership in its eighty-two-member consortium. Besides managing and operating the Oak Ridge Institute for Science and Education for the U.S. Department of Energy, ORAU works to provide and develop capabilities critical to the nation's infrastructure, especially in the areas of energy, education, health, and the environment.

Hearn was recognized for his service by the trustees and by the Alumni Councils during their summer meeting in Williamsburg, Virginia. Five Winston-Salem corporations contributed $300,000 to establish the Thomas K. Hearn Jr. Fund for Civic Responsibility. Amid all of the celebration, however, the President maintained that his top priority for the future was to enhance institutional values. He stated that Wake Forest had been made strong "by a morally informed conception of education—that education is not just a matter of the mind, but of those values that are summarized by our motto *Pro Humanitate*." A Wake Forest education concerned personal as well as intellectual development. "Personal integrity and intellectual integrity must be our most important goals."

Another noteworthy story that year concerned the colonization of local women's societies. In early October, ten national sororities held forums with question-and-answer sessions and audiovisual aids; then members of the six local societies voted by secret ballot for the organization with which they wished to affiliate. Over the course of a marathon weekend in October, Delphi, Fidele, Lynks, S.O.P.H., Strings, and Thymes were transformed into chapters of the sororities they chose by mutual agreement. Delphi became Delta Gamma; Fidele became Chi Omega; Lynks became Kappa Delta; S.O.P.H. became Kappa Kappa Gamma; Strings became Pi Beta Phi; and Thymes became Kappa Alpha Theta. The Intersociety Council was renamed the Panhellenic Council.

The new chapters held formal rites from November through January, inviting former members to become sorority affiliates. The process of colonization lasted a year. It had been prompted by a tougher state law on social host liability and the sense that the society system deprived members of the professional, scholastic, and programmatic opportunities available to national Greek organization members. Wake Forest's first society, Strings, was founded in 1946 by undergraduates Huldah Lineberry and Edith Rawls in a secret candlelight ceremony in a residence hall laundry room. It and two more—S.O.P.H. in 1956 and Fidele in 1961—stayed underground until late 1963, when the faculty approved a petition recognizing the societies on a three-year trial basis. They became permanent in 1967.

Before the transitions became final, nearly five hundred society members gathered for a celebratory party in the Benson Center. Dressed in white for the impending pledge, they milled around, hugging and congratulating each other. Members of Wake Forest's four existing sorority chapters—Alpha Delta, Delta Delta Delta, Alpha Kappa Alpha, and Delta Sigma Theta—sang their anthems to welcome their new sisters.

Mary Gerardy (top), Ken Zick (center, left), and Joanne O'Brien (center, right) helped Wake Forest societies transition to become national sororities

Ken Zick, Mary Gerardy (advisor to the new women's Panhellenic organizations), and Joanne O'Brien ('84), Director of Foundation Relations, had advised the societies on a voluntary basis for the past three years, putting in long hours planning the colonization process and assuaging any residual anxieties. The result was a win-win for all involved.

Academics

On Saturday, October 2, more than two hundred faculty met to discuss University priorities at a retreat sponsored by the program planning committee, which Provost Brown organized in the spring of 1993 to consider the academic direction of Wake Forest College for the next decade. The retreat lasted nine hours and addressed the committee's white paper, released to all faculty on September 15. During the meeting, the teacher-scholar ideal was proposed as the defining philosophy for Wake Forest faculty, and the twenty-seven needs and opportunities outlined by the committee were discussed. The committee had asked each academic department about its concerns in a spring 1993 survey. Two ideas were almost immediately eliminated because of negative feedback: increasing nontenure-track faculty positions and class sizes.

In March 1994, Provost Brown released an interim draft of the planning committee's findings to faculty, Student Government, and the Provost's Student Advisory Committee. The committee was chaired by Brown and was composed of John Anderson (Administration), Williams Connor (Sociology), Gloria Cooper (Human Resources), Huw M.L. Davies (Chemistry), Paul Escott (History), Frederick Harris (Babcock), Cheryl Leggon (Sociology), Dale Martin (Business and Accountancy), Wilson Parker (Law), Teresa Radomski (Music), Paul Ribisl (HSS), Matthews Rush (Undergraduate Student), Ian Taplin (Sociology), Claudia Thomas (English), and Robert Upchurch (Graduate Student). The committee held three open forums in April to discuss the report's forty recommendations.

In another academic matter that was more universal in scope but applied to Wake Forest, an amendment to the Age Discrimination Act of 1986 stated that the 1993–1994 academic year would be the last when tenured professors were forced to retire at seventy years of age. Provost Brown felt that the new option would have little impact on the University because most faculty retired around that age. In fact, most of the thirty-five faculty who joined the University in the fall were replacing faculty who had retired, resigned, or were on leave.

In specific faculty news, two returning faculty in the School of Business and Accountancy, Umit Akinc and John S. Dinkleberg, became endowed professors. Akinc received the first Thomas H. Davis Professorship, and Dinkleberg was named to the first Benson-Pruitt Professorship. In addition, Wayne King was appointed to teach journalism, filling the shoes of Bynum Shaw, who retired in the spring of 1993 after teaching at Wake Forest since 1965.

Starting on October 13, the Provost's Office revived the interdepartmental scholars' breakfasts initiated in 1991–1992 by Julie Cole, Director of Research and Sponsored Programs. The breakfasts were hosted by Provost Brown and organized by Associate Provost Laura Ford ('70). Associate Professor of Chemistry Mark Welker was the initial speaker. The talks were designed to inform faculty about successful funded research projects on campus, strategies and services to secure external support, and potential collaborations.

At the new student convocation when freshmen first arrived, they were greeted by the President, Deans, and representatives of the parents' council in Wait Chapel. During that ceremony Herman Eure (Biology) and Lu Leake (Vice President) both received Awards for Excellence in Advising. At the Fall Convocation on September 30, Arthur Schlesinger, the Pulitzer Prize–winning historian, was the featured speaker. He addressed the topic of diversity. After Schlesinger spoke, as was tradition, outstanding faculty were recognized for their work with students and in the community. Elmer K. Hayashi (Mathematics) received the Jon Reinhardt Award for Distinguished Teaching, while the Faculty Award for Community Service was given posthumously to Donald O. Schoonmaker, a professor of Political Science who had died the previous spring of cancer at age fifty-five. Schoonmaker's widow, Meyressa Schoonmaker, was informed that the Award for Community Service would be renamed in honor of her late husband. In a surprise announcement near the end of the convocation, Student Government President Jill Weiskopf caught President Hearn off guard by reading a resolution that three of the Upperclass Leadership Scholarships be renamed the Thomas K. Hearn Jr. Scholarships for Excellence in Leadership and Service.

Clifton R. Wharton Jr., former Deputy Secretary of State, was the featured speaker at the Founders' Day Convocation in February 1994. Germaine Brée (Romance Languages) received the Medallion of Merit; Simone M. Caron (History) received the Omicron Delta Kappa Award for Contributions to Student Life. Deborah Best (Psychology) won the 1994 Schoonmaker Faculty Prize for Community Service; Allin F. Cottrell (Economics) received the Award for Excellence in Research; and Page Laughlin (Art) received the Reid-Doyle Prize for Excellence in Teaching. Ralph Peeples (Law) received the Joseph Branch Excellence in Teaching Award. Rhoda Billings (Law) received the Jurist Excellence in Teaching Award. In an award outside of Founders' Day, Katy J. Harriger (Political Science) became the first recipient of a Zachary T. Smith Professorship.

Faculty also won other external recognitions. Robert H. Evans (Education) was awarded a Fulbright Scholar grant to lecture and to conduct research at the University of Kiel in Germany; Alan R. Palmiter (Law) received a Fulbright as well. Mark Welker (Chemistry) was selected for a Camille and Henry Dreyfus Teacher-Scholar Award in 1994. This unrestricted grant of $75,000 supported outstanding young faculty who demonstrated leadership in original scholarly research and excellence in, and dedication to, undergraduate education in the chemical sciences.

The *New York Times* featured the research of Mark Leary (Psychology) in an article on what motivates people to do things that jeopardize their health. Margaret Supplee Smith (Art) opened an exhibit in Raleigh entitled "North Carolina Women

Mark Welker

Making History" in May 1994. Kenan Professor of Humanities Allen Mandelbaum was honored at an Italian Cultural Institute symposium in New York in November 1993, with President Hearn in attendance. The Sara Lee Corporation chose Maya Angelou, also in Humanities, to receive its Forerunner Award, for "women whose outstanding achievements make a difference in society." A $25,000 donation was made in her name to Spellman College and the Children's Defense Fund. Angelou also published *Wouldn't Take Nothing for My Journey Now*, a book-length reflection on spirituality, and delivered a thirty-minute presentation on the theme of hunger and homelessness as part of the second annual "Share Our Strength Writer's Harvest," a literary benefit to alleviate hunger and poverty.

The Law School celebrated its centennial in 1994. As part of many celebrations, Ed Hendricks (History) wrote a history of the school. The Bowman Gray School of Medicine was ranked thirty-sixth among U.S. medical schools in funds received from the National Institutes of Health, and the first two students in the new MD/MBA program enrolled for classes in the Babcock Graduate School of Management. Executive Vice President for Health Affairs Richard Janeway and others from the Bowman Gray School of Medicine, School of Law, and Babcock Graduate School of Management participated in discussions on health care with political pundit William F. Buckley. The interdepartmental coalition taped four episodes of Buckley's television show, "Firing Line," in January, but they were not aired until April.

Administration and Staff

Under a new policy, starting in January 1994, applicants selected for employment had to present themselves for drug testing no more than twenty-four hours after the offer was extended. All offers for regular, nonfaculty employees were conditional until the test was passed, according to James L. Ferrell, Director of Human Resources.

On a happier note, University staff held their first arts and crafts fair in Benson University Center on November 10. The idea for "Life after Five" originated with Margaret Perry (Registrar), who worked with Gloria Cooper, Director of Equal Employment Opportunities, to make it happen. They hoped to help staff get to know one another better and to appreciate their interests and skills apart from their work for the University. Gloria Cooper also worked with Natascha Romeo (Health Educator) to organize a wellness fair for all Reynolda Campus employees. It was held in the Benson University Center in late March.

The Women's Interest Network (WIN) sponsored its second annual women's awareness week in March to raise campus consciousness about relevant concerns. In an unusual fundraiser, the Museum of Anthropology held a dinner called "Culture Choc," where all of the dishes, including entrees, beverages, and desserts, contained chocolate. Chef Don McMillian of Simple Elegance Catering created the menu.

On November 4, President Hearn asked members of the Executive Committee to file a sealed memorandum with the legal office, sharing their advice on how to maintain their duties if they were disabled or died suddenly.

James N. Thompson was promoted to Dean from Associate Dean of the Bowman Gray School of Medicine effective July 1, 1994. Mary Gerardy was promoted to Assistant Vice President of the Division of Student Life, and Paul Orser was promoted to Director of the Benson University Center. Later, in January, he was reappointed by Dean Mullen to serve as an Associate Dean of the College and Dean of Freshmen after Catherine Harris (Sociology), former chair of the first-year orientation program, returned to full-time teaching. Jim Coffey (Facilities) was recognized in the *Winston-Salem Journal* in November as a community volunteer for transforming the grounds of the Children's Center for the Physically Handicapped.

University Security was transferred to Ken Zick from Leon Corbett. It meant that University Police would now be part of the Division of Student Life. Two offices formerly under John Anderson, the Office of Institutional Research and the Registrar's Office, were transferred to the Provost's Office under Dave Brown. Bob Mills became Assistant Vice President of University Relations, primarily responsible for coordinating major gifts, and James Bullock, formerly the Director of the Capital Campaign, became Associate Director of Development, with special responsibility for donations to the School of Law and the Babcock Graduate School of Management.

Robert Spinks was chosen interim director of the Ecumenical Institute. Kenneth W. Overholt was named the new Deputy Director of University Security. Kerry M. King, a staff writer in the capital campaign office since 1989, was named Director of University Relations Communications.

Governor Jim Hunt appointed President Hearn to serve on the seventeen-member North Carolina Standards and Accountability Commission, charged with developing more rigorous high school graduation requirements. Hearn had been visiting public schools to learn more about local primary and secondary education.

On July 20, 1993, President Hearn announced that John Willard, Vice President for Financial Resources and Treasurer, and Ed Wilson, Vice President for Special Projects and Professor of English, would complete their administrative duties on January 1, 1994, and retire. They would not be replaced, and their duties would be reassigned. Willard remained a consultant on endowment matters, and Wilson directed the London program in the spring. At the ages of seventy and sixty-two, respectively, Wilson and Willard had served Wake Forest for a combined total of more than seventy-five years. Willard built the endowment from $15 million to $400 million. He had managed Reynolda Center, the former AT&T building on Reynolda Road, the University Corporate Center, and the former RJR World Headquarters Building.

Thomas E. Mullen, Dean of the College since 1968, announced that he would leave the position on August 15, 1994, to teach history full-time. Ed Wilson was appointed to chair the committee to identify a successor, but in December 1993 Mullen was persuaded to continue his duties until summer 1995 because Wilson was scheduled to leave for the Worrell House in January 1994.

Carlos Holder ('69, MBA '83), Controller and Assistant Treasurer, resigned in January 1994 to become Chief Financial Officer at Guilford College in Greensboro, North Carolina. Thomas J. Gilsenan, former Manager and Director of the Graylyn Conference Center, was named as his successor. Monroe Whitt resigned as Director of Facilities Management following a public incident between him and his former girlfriend in April.

University Editor David Fyten and his staff received the CASE Grand Gold and Improvement awards for their work in 1994. At the Babcock School, there were three recipients of the Sara Lee Excellence Award for extraordinary service in information technology, including: Barry L. Dombro, Director of Information Service; Robert A. Herbert, managing librarian for the Worrell Professional Center; Allen Helms and Stephan Wininger, network administrators and audiovisual specialists.

Athletics

The men's cross country team under Coach John R. Goodridge won the ACC championship and the NCAA district championship in November 1993, finishing twentieth overall in the NCAA championships. The women's golf team, coached by Diane Daley, also won the ACC championship, finishing six strokes ahead of second-place North Carolina. Stephanie Neill placed second overall on the individual leader scoreboard.

The football team under new coach Jim Caldwell completed a record of two wins and nine losses. Home losses were made a bit more bearable by a new scoreboard with graphics and animation. Senior John Leach set an ACC single-game record, rushing 329 yards against Maryland, although the Deacons lost 33–32. However, the Deacons defeated Clemson in Death Valley 20–16 in Coach Caldwell's first ACC and road victory. It was the first time in thirty-two years that Wake Forest had beaten Clemson on its home turf and the first back-to-back wins over the Tigers since the 1946–1947 season.

In another bright spot, nineteen of twenty football players who entered the school in 1989 graduated in the spring of 1994 for a 95 percent graduation rate, earning the team one of the three College Football Association Academic Achievement Awards for the year.

Shotput specialist Andy Bloom, a junior, led the men's track team to a sixth-place finish at the ACC championships. His throw of 60 feet and one-half inch was five inches better than his nearest competitor. The team scored a total of 60.7 points, the most ever scored by a Deacon men's track team in the Indoor Championships.

President Hearn held a planning subcommittee for the NCAA Committee on Integrity and Intercollegiate Athletics at Graylyn September 15–16. Rushworth M. Kidder (Institute for Global Ethics), Norman Sprinthal (North Carolina State University), Wilford Bailey (Auburn University), Ted Tow (NCAA Associate Executive Director), Gene Hooks (Executive Director of the Division I-A Athletic Directors' Association), and Dianne Dailey (Director of Women's Athletics/Golf Coach) attended. Gene Hooks ('50), Win Headley ('71, MA '75), and Jim Flick ('52) were inducted into the Wake Forest Sports Hall of Fame.

Wake Forest began a self-study that led to NCAA certification of the Department of Athletics in the fall of 1993. Ed Wilson and Sandra Boyette were chair and co-chair, respectively, of a certification steering committee composed of representatives of the University's various constituencies.

On June 21, 1994, the NCAA announced it was placing the men's basketball program on one year's probation for "improper activities" in the recruiting of a foreign student-athlete who enrolled at, but never played for, Wake Forest. The NCAA found rule violations in the activities of a "representative of the University's athletic interests," who helped recruit center Makhtar Ndiaye in 1992 and 1993. Head Basketball Coach Dave Odom had asked James Davies, a native of Liberia living in Greensboro, to assist as an interpreter in telephone discussions with Ndiaye and his family in Dakar, Senegal. Following the initial contact, Davies maintained a relationship with Ndiaye, who enrolled at Oak Hill Academy in Virginia as a high school senior. Davies made financial arrangements and provided Ndiaye with meals, lodging, transportation, and clothing, even though Odom had told him that NCAA rules forbade maintaining contact. Ndiaye signed with the Deacons in November 1992 and enrolled at the University in fall 1993.

Wake Forest reported possible violations in connection with Davies's activities to the NCAA in a September 1993 self-report. The University revoked Ndiaye's eligibility and asked the NCAA to restore it, but instead, the NCAA declared Ndiaye ineligible to play for Wake Forest. He transferred to Michigan and was immediately eligible to play. It was the first time that the NCAA had penalized a Deacon program.

Nonetheless, the men's basketball team had a successful year. Its win/loss record was 21–12, and Dave Odom scored his first ACC Tournament win, beating Georgia Tech 74–49. He was named ACC Coach of the Year.

The first Wake Forest Student-Athlete Academic Excellence Banquet was held at the end of March. It honored more than 160 students for combining academic and athletic performance during the spring and fall semesters. Everyone invited had achieved Dean's List honors while participating in a varsity sport. Sportscaster Dan Rath of WXII-TV was the emcee. Golfer Stephanie Neill and cross country runner Stuart Burnham were the Athletes of the Year.

The Arts

The theatre season began with a 1983 comedy by Christopher Durang, *Baby with the Bathwater*, in the Ring Theatre. The first Mainstage production was Brecht and Weill's *The Threepenny Opera* (1928), followed by David Mamet's Hollywood satire, *Speed the Plow* (1988). In the second semester, Mainstage productions included *The Heiress*, a 1947 play by Ruth and Augustus Goetz based on the Henry James novel *Washington Square*, and *The Country Wife* (1665), a comedy by William Wycherley.

The Secrest Artists Series featured the Paul Winter Consort; the Chamber Music Society of Lincoln Center; Apollo's Fire, also called the Cleveland Baroque Orchestra; the Bolshoi Symphony Orchestra; and the Tamburitzans of Duquesne University, who performed mainly Eastern European folk music and dance.

The Student Union featured Thomas Wright in "An Evening with Gershwin"; George Winston, who describes his music as "rural folk piano"; the Minnesota Gospel Sound; the musical/comedy group Scared Weird Little Guys; and The Lemonheads, an alternative rock band. It also sponsored a mystery dinner theater in March: *The Case of the Term Paper Murders*. Comedienne Margaret Cho, a frequent guest on the Arsenio Hall Show, performed in the Benson University Center on October 21 as part of Homecoming activities, and on November 9, stand-up comedian Carrot Top performed in Wait Chapel.

Campus and Student Life

The 1993 entering class was composed of 897 freshmen chosen from 5,664 applicants. Classes began with a total enrollment of 5,624, including 3,500 undergraduates, of whom fifty-three came from thirty countries abroad. There were also 354 minority students, 271 who were African American. Forty first-year students were selected to participate in a new pre-orientation program called Power Up!, which provided three days of instruction on the use of computers. The program was directed by Rhoda Channing, Director of the Z. Smith Reynolds Library. During orientation, all new students played "Get a Clue," a scavenger hunt that led to fourteen stations where participants learned about Wake Forest traditions, met key members of the community, and discovered clues to campus life.

During the academic year, about 17 percent of all students participated in student government; over 30 percent participated in intercollegiate athletics; and approximately 81 percent performed some kind of volunteer service. Among seniors in the Class of 1994, 15 percent had an overall A average, while only 2 percent had an average of C or below.

In extracurricular activities, Taco Bell gave the University $30,000 to purchase and maintain an oversized van that would transport students in the Volunteer Service Corps (VSC) to their projects and to leadership conferences. About 750 students, almost a fourth of the undergraduate student body, participated in VSC activities to serve thirty community programs and agencies, including Habitat for Humanity, Big Brothers/Big Sisters, the Children's Home, Crisis Control Ministry, the Battered Women's Shelter, and literacy programs. The VSC received the Governor's Award for Outstanding Volunteer Service in ceremonies on October 18 in Raleigh. In addition to work in the Winston-Salem community, sixty students participated in Wake Forest's second alternative Spring Break experience in March, working to help community groups in Illinois, South Dakota, New Orleans, and South Carolina.

Jessica Davey, who co-chaired the VSC, was singled out for her work both on campus and abroad. She spent the summer of 1993 working with Mother Teresa in Calcutta and received the *Pro Humanitate* Award at Opening Convocation along with the Governor's Award for Outstanding Volunteer Service. In addition to Davey, alumnus Chip Rives ('87, MBA '89), alumnus Manlin Chee (JD '78), and Associate Professor of Religion Alton Pollard received *Pro Humanitate* Awards for service to mankind.

Carolyn Frantz, a philosophy major and cellist from Lafayette, Louisiana, was named a Rhodes Scholar in December. She was the fifth in eight consecutive years. Loraine V. Fuller was selected as a 1994 Truman Scholar.

For the first time, the fall break was eliminated, and the Thanksgiving holiday lengthened to a whole week. The Easter holiday (both Good Friday and Easter Monday) was also eliminated. The change continued through the 1994–1995 academic year before the fall break was reinstituted, Thanksgiving shrank back to three days, and Good Friday was observed as an official University holiday.

In an effort to create more Greek lounge space, the Office of Residence Life and Housing moved from the basement of Davis House into two offices in the Benson

University Center over winter break. Two more lounges were built at the back of Luter Residence Hall, each attached to a basement wing. At the end of the spring semester, sororities were assured they would all get lounge space by fall 1994, although only one would be on the Quad. In addition, three of the black Greek organizations, which had shared a small lounge in Kitchen House, were given separate lounges. An unusually large number of students—247 men and 348 women—participated in rush during the spring semester, perhaps because there had been no fall rush.

Gamma Phi Chapter of Pi Kappa Alpha Fraternity had its charter revoked by the Student Life Committee in December. The charter was reinstated during February, but the fraternity was placed on strict probation and had to give up its lounge and housing block.

The Princeton Review Student Access Guide: The Best 286 Colleges ranked Wake Forest 92 overall out of 100, 92 on quality of life, and 93 on academics, based on more than one hundred randomly selected student responses to seventy multiple choice questions. The only weak areas reported were the homogeneous student body and gay discrimination.

The Gay, Lesbian, and Bisexual Issues Awareness Group (GALBA) sponsored its first Gay Pride Rally in Carswell Hall on November 8. The event featured speeches by Tanya Domi from the National Gay and Lesbian Task Force Policy Institute, senior J. Ken Stuckey, and sophomore Chris Cooper, who helped organize the event.

The Alliance for Racial and Cultural Harmony (ARCH) evolved from the Student Government's race relations committee and became a separate organization.

The Resident Student Association and Division of Student Life sponsored a series of AIDS awareness activities titled "A Time to Act." Among them, the AIDS memorial quilt was displayed.

The most visible student leaders on campus were Jill Weiskoff, Student Government President; Michael Peil, Editor-in-Chief of the *Old Gold and Black*; Rebecca Gentry, President of the Student Union; D. Brent Williamson, Editor of *The Howler*; and Todd Turner, the student representative on the Board of Trustees.

WAKE Radio began broadcasting a spoof on modern-day soap operas called "Desire under the Mags." Created by freshman Craig Joseph, it aired on Monday nights from midnight to 1 a.m. The sixteen actors and a sound technician introduced the campus to such characters as The Tramp, The Hero, The Villain, The Lover, and the Long-Lost Daughter. The plot revolved around the actions and interactions of two families: the Reynolds clan, who were filthy rich, and the Benson family, who were not even on the social registrar.

In shenanigans at Davis House, three chickens were found in a shower at 7:30 a.m. in mid-October and taken to a nearby farm. On Friday, February 17, students flushed fifty toilets at once to see what would happen: a water main exploded, and many of their rooms flooded three to four inches deep. Physical Facilities responded to the incident and fixed the pipe, but because it was a Friday, students affected by what they described as the "Flood of '94" had to endure the consequences for the weekend or move to unoccupied faculty apartments until Residence Life and Housing could clean up the mess on Monday.

On a serious note, juniors Phil Archer and Joy Goodwin revived the Philomathesian Society for students who, according to Archer, were interested in expressing

Phil Archer and Joy Goodwin

their artistic, philosophical, and political concerns through enjoyable and enlightening activities. The society hosted a film series featuring works of Charlie Chaplain and Woody Allen, among others, and weekly meetings where professors would read and speak on various concerns. Ed Wilson (English), who belonged to the Philomathesians on the old campus, served as the faculty sponsor.

Sophomores Stacey Leaman and Lori Honeycutt organized a chapter of Amnesty International on campus. The group sponsored letter-writing campaigns and programs to promote human rights, especially for those imprisoned for their political beliefs.

The Environmentally Concerned Organization of Students (ECOS) started its fifth year with a variety of activities, such as letter-writing campaigns, field trips to recycling plants, and an environment-education program for fifth graders. On campus, ECOS worked to make students more aware of environmental concerns. Founded in 1989 to improve recycling, the group's faculty sponsor was Robert Browne (Biology).

In concert with ECOS, Student Government's recycling committee, chaired by Tanya Burgos, announced in January that recycling facilities, previously available only on the South Campus, had been expanded to the North Campus. Taylor, Davis, Poteat, and Kitchin Houses were now equipped with sixty-five-gallon bins for glass, plastic, and paper products. To accelerate campus recycling, Jerome McDaniel from the Physical Plant was named the new recycling coordinator in January. He worked with faculty, administration, and staff to implement and expand the recycling effort at Wake Forest. In a related environmentally friendly act, the live Benson Center Christmas tree was planted on Davis Field by Grounds Superintendent Jim Coffey and his staff.

The Critic, now billing itself as "an independent journal *at* Wake Forest," rather than "an independent journal *of* Wake Forest," lost two editors in the first semester: junior Wayne Tarrant resigned on October 14, and junior Emily Cummins resigned on November 3. Senior J. Drew Squires became Editor, but after he graduated, the next appointed Editors, Craig Kidd and Geoffrey Michael, resigned before the end of the school year because of what they described as caustic and extreme methods used by those who controlled the paper, such as personal attacks on administrators and faculty they did not like.

The Worrell House in London was robbed during the fall semester while students were on midterm break. The perpetrators held captive two women who had returned early, but the students were not hurt and immediately called the Hampstead police. David Hadley (History), Director of the London program, once again tightened security. Over time, the house had been burglarized four times.

Cherie Van Der Sluys played the carillon at noon, when Israel and the Palestine Liberation Organization (PLO) signed a peace settlement on September 13.

The Office of Admissions offered a three-week program, Leadership for the 21st Century: Global Concerns, Business Realities, Ethical Responsibilities, in the summer of 1993 for thirty high school students. Martha Allman was the Director. In the fall the Division of Student Life launched an advanced leadership course, Lead II, for twenty upperclass students. Developed by staff members Mike Ford, Mary Gerardy, and Mark Hall, the students evaluated current leadership theories and applied what they learned to a leadership project.

In June of 1994, Wake Forest was one of twenty-five universities invited by the Lilly Endowment to Colorado to attend a workshop on the liberal arts. Representing the University were Tom Mullen (Dean), Carole Browne (Biology), Barry Maine (English), and Teresa Radomski (Music). While at the workshop, they prepared a report on the intellectual and cultural climate of Wake Forest. Their document, known as the Lilly Report, offered eleven recommendations for improving the campus climate and strengthening the University. Some of its proposals included postponing freshman rush, expanding opportunities to engage in intellectual discussions, stricter enforcement of the alcohol policy, and the incorporation of community service as a component of some courses. Unfortunately, during the workshop, Dean Mullen suffered

Lilly Group from left to right: Tom Mullen, Carole Browne, Teresa Radomski, Barry Maine

a heart attack, and the recommendations of the committee were delayed in being presented to the College faculty. While no immediate action was taken on any of the recommendations when they were presented to the faculty, many of the report's proposals were later adopted by the University, e.g., community service as a part of some courses and expanded opportunities to engage in intellectual discussions.

Facilities, Finances, and Alumni

Facilities

Carswell Hall was renovated after the Law School moved to Worrell Center. The departments of Economics, Sociology, Speech Communications and Theater Arts, and East Asian Languages and Literature all moved in, as did the International Studies program. With the Department of Economics moving from the eighth level, the Z. Smith Reynolds Library gained space for special collections and emeritus faculty offices. In its new home in Carswell, the Economics Department named a study room the J. Van Wagstaff Reading Room in honor of its founder and longtime chair, who retired in 1992 after twenty-eight years of teaching.

In another move, the Departments of Mathematics and Computer Science and the School of Business and Accountancy spread out to fill Babcock Hall after the Babcock Graduate School of Management moved into Worrell Professional Center. BB&T made a $150,000 commitment to renovations. As part of the agreement, the first floor of the building was designated the BB&T Level.

The two side-by-side courtrooms in Worrell Center were named for attorneys Allen A. Bailey (JD '50) of Charlotte and James R. Van Camp (JD '65) of Southern Pines. Both were founding members and former Presidents of the North Carolina Academy of Trial Lawyers.

During winter break, the academic computing system was hacked. The perpetrators, two college students and a high school student, were later caught. The winter break allowed the first testing of a voicemail system to notify University personnel and students of class cancellations.

A group portrait, "Women of Letters," featuring the faces of thirty-two female writers painted by Anne Kesler Shields, was loaned to the Z. Smith Reynolds Library and displayed above the circulation desk. It featured two Wake Forest women: Isabel Zuber, a Z. Smith Reynolds Library circulation librarian, and Emily Herring Wilson (MA '62).

Area Code 910 split off from 919 on November 14, requiring the University to reprint stationary and other materials.

Finances

In financial matters, the C. C. Hope Chair of Banking and Law was endowed by gifts of $300,000 from First Union National Bank and $50,000 from the North Carolina Banker's Association. Clifford H. Clarke ('62) made a $5 million pledge to Wake Forest to expand its international study opportunities. The pledge put the Heritage and Promise Campaign over its $150 million goal three years after it began.

Charles R. Tatum ('36) and Francis Tatum Council donated $750,000 to the University. It was first used in the Poteat scholarship program and later transferred to the Divinity School. William A. Collins ('61) and his wife, Sue, donated a rather large sum to Wake Forest, establishing a $2.1 million trust to provide scholarships for students from Virginia. In recognition of this gift, South Residence Hall, built in 1985 and housing 220 students, was renamed Collins Hall and dedicated on March 31. A portrait of William Collins was hung and bolted to the wall in the front hall after having "toured the building" for a week, when several mischievous first-year students thought the portrait would be interested in "a bird's eye view of the elevator, the study lounge, and the first-floor women's bathroom."

William Collins

The Guy T. and Clara Carswell scholarship program turned twenty-five years old. For many years, it was not just the first but the only need-blind merit scholarship program at Wake Forest and had dispersed some $5.25 million in 2,300 awards to 729 students. A reunion of Carswell scholars was held in late March and included a College Bowl competition between alumni and current scholars as well as a Raft Debate in which three professors, hypothetically standing on a raft, each described why his or her discipline was the most important.

Wake Forest was one of only nine private comprehensive institutions out of 149 eligible institutions named to the 1993 Circle of Excellence in Educational Fund Raising by the Council for the Advancement and Support of Education (CASE). Total giving to Wake Forest was $22 million in 1989–1990; $27 million in 1990–1991; and $28 million in 1991–1992.

The administration proposed a $25 million bond issue plan to the Board of Trustees. Of the total, $12 million would be used to up-fit and repair endowment real estate, which was required for recent lease changes, and $13 million would be used to renovate Tribble Hall and residence halls on the North Campus. When the proposed projects were finished, the Reynolda Campus would have $30 million worth of bond indebtedness, and the Bowman Gray Campus $102 million. Federal policies allowed universities to have up to $150 million in bonds. As of December 31, the market value of the endowment stood at $410 million, and Heritage and Promise Campaign pledges stood at just over $142 million. Faculty support and student financial aid were the campaign's main priorities.

Tuition for 1994–1995 was set at $13,850, a 6.5 percent increase. It was the smallest increase since 1976. Tuition had risen 11.1 percent in 1992 and 8.3 percent in 1993. John Anderson said an 8 percent increase in student financial aid and a 5.5 percent overall increase in faculty salaries were the largest factors in determining the tuition increase. The fee for an official transcript was raised to $4.

Alumni

Alex Sink ('70), Nicholas Bragg ('58), and Ed Wilson ('43) were honored by the alumni association at Homecoming 1993. They were given Distinguished Alumni Awards, while Horace Kornegay ('47, LLB '49) of Greensboro received the Law Alumni Award.

The total number of degrees Wake Forest had granted through 1993 was 44,265. Of the 32,850 living Wake Forest alumni in 1993, about 15,000 lived in North Carolina.

Summing Up the Year

The academic year 1993–1994 was noteworthy on many levels. First, it marked the tenth anniversary of Tom Hearn's presidency. By University standards of the time, ten years was not a particularly long tenure, but the milestone was acknowledged in several ways. The President's ten-year report, *To Dream with One Eye Open*, a title referencing philosopher George Santayana, considered how Wake Forest was faring physically, financially, and academically and indicated that it was much stronger than it had been when he arrived. Student Government named scholarships after him, and the alumni association honored him with a special fund for ethics and civic responsibility underwritten by Winston-Salem corporations.

The year also marked transitions for people, buildings, and organizations. The colonization of societies into sororities was a lengthy, carefully planned, and ultimately beneficial process. Ed Wilson (Vice President for Special Projects) and John Willard (Vice President for Financial Responsibilities and Treasurer) both announced their retirement from those positions as of January 1994. Tom Mullen (Dean of the College) also announced his retirement, which was postponed until 1995, and Paul Orser became the first Dean of Freshmen. Carswell Hall and Babcock Hall were renovated for new tenants when the Law School and the Babcock Graduate School of Business moved to Worrell Center.

Oak Ridge Associated Universities (ORAU) elected Wake Forest to full membership, and the *Princeton Review* and *U.S. News & World Report* both gave the University high marks. The Philomathesian Society was revived, and WAKE Radio produced a soap opera. Carolyn Frantz won a Rhodes scholarship, and Taco Bell strengthened the Volunteer Service Corps by donating an oversized van.

Athletically, Wake Forest excelled in the Olympic sports as the men's cross country team won the ACC championship and the NCAA district championship, and the women's golf team won the ACC championship.

Overall, the events of the year lived on in memories and actions as the social structure and physical structure of the University changed, and the academic reputation of Wake Forest increased.

CHAPTER TWELVE
1994–1995

A National Nod, Heart Trouble, Basketball, Plan Approval, and Campaign Success

In talking about his heart surgery: "A health problem reorders and verifies priorities."
Thomas K. Hearn Jr., May 15, 1995;
Charge the Graduates, Wake Forest University Commencement

Five major stories competed for attention at Wake Forest during 1994–1995. The importance of each, like other stories, was judged differently by various constituencies. In chronological order: the University was reclassified by the media from regional to national status; President Hearn underwent heart surgery; the men's basketball's team won the ACC championship; the Board of Trustees approved the Plan for the Class of 2000; and the Heritage and Promise Campaign ended on a high note.

Although not the biggest story of the year within the University, one of the best was that *U.S. News & World Report*'s annual college guide reclassified Wake Forest from the leading regional university in the South to the "first tier" among national universities. After topping the regional category for eight consecutive years, in the fall of 1994, Wake Forest was placed among institutions ranked twenty-sixth to fifty-seventh based on an average SAT score of 1250 for entering first-year students, a 42 percent acceptance rate, and a 37 percent alumni giving rate. The University was at last recognized by its peers and the media as a top-flight national institution. *U.S. News & World Report* was not the only publication to highlight the national status of Wake Forest. *Money* magazine ranked the University the fourteenth best buy among the nation's 3,600 colleges and universities. In addition, *Barron's Profiles of American Colleges* named Wake Forest to its "most competitive" list, comprising only thirty-nine colleges and universities nationally, and just eight of them in the South. Furthermore, President Hearn reported in October that Wake Forest was in

191

The Deacons celebrate their ACC men's basketball championship

the top four universities in the nation on the basis of academic program spending per student ($41,766).

Attention also focused on the President's health as the year went on. He underwent cardiac surgery on February 16 for a leaking mitral valve, which was discovered during a routine physical. The problem was caught before any permanent damage was done, but the valve could be corrected only by surgery. His doctors advised him not to schedule any appointments until after the first of April, and he complied. In his absence, senior administrators cooperated, and the semester progressed as usual. The President returned to a part-time schedule in early April and by May had resumed an almost normal schedule.

In athletics, Wake Forest men's basketball won the Atlantic Coast Conference title on March 12. Led by the dynamic duo of Randolph Childress and Tim Duncan, the team defeated the University of North Carolina in overtime 82–80 in the Deacons' first ACC men's basketball championship in thirty-three years. The team's winning percentage of .813 was the highest since the 1927 team went 22–3 (.880), and it also tied a school record for the highest national ranking of third, last achieved in 1981. The team won twelve straight games, again, the longest winning streak since 1981. Overall, it had the most wins (26–6) in Wake Forest history and the first win over the UNC Tarheels (79–70) in the Dean Smith Center. It also set a new home attendance record of 11,959 per game. Based on winning the ACC tournament and earning a share of the regular season championship, the team entered the NCAA tournament as the number 1 seed in the east. Its fifth straight NCAA tournament appearance was the longest streak in school history. Unfortunately, the Deacons were eliminated from the tournament in the Sweet Sixteen by Oklahoma State, 71–66.

By the end of the season, Coach David Odom had led the Deacons to 104 wins since 1991, the best five-year record in school history. He earned his hundredth win on January 25: 66–60 over Clemson. Randolph Childress, who set an ACC tournament record with 107 points over three days, was selected to the first-team All-ACC for the second consecutive year, and the Associated Press picked him as a second-team All-American. He also broke through as one of the top five performers in Wake Forest basketball history: second in scoring, fifth in assists and steals. Childress received the 1995 Arnold Palmer Award at the Academic Excellence Banquet. He had arrived at Wake Forest in fall 1990 from Clinton, Maryland, as one sixth of Odom's first recruiting class, which included Rodney Rogers, Trelonnie Owens, Marc Blucas, Stan King, and Robert Doggett.

Randolph Childress

As a by-product of the success of the men's basketball team, there was a virtual flood of fans buying T-shirts, sweatshirts, hats, shorts, and bumper stickers. According to David Dyer, Acting Director of the Deacon Shop, more than 50,000 people visited the week after the Deacons won the championship. To accommodate the crowds, bookstore employees were enlisted to help out.

The Plan for the Class of 2000, targeting students entering in 1996, was a long time in the making and went through many revisions. In early 1993, a sixteen-member Program Planning Committee was appointed. This task force of faculty, students, and administrators was charged with charting the University's academic course through the year 2002. It gathered information and opinions from a consulting panel of administrators and students and from 200 faculty questionnaires, an all-day faculty retreat, eighty-two hearings, several open forums, two visits to other universities, and special sessions with a host of key University bodies and constituents. It also sought reaction to 500 copies of a white paper and a thousand copies of an interim report issued in January 1994.

The plan was multidimensional, but the most exciting and highly publicized aspect was providing students with IBM laptop computers and extending Internet access into every classroom and residence hall room. The final report, released in January 1995, made thirty-six recommendations, of which two—the computer proposal and a proposal to offer interdisciplinary first-year seminars—generated the most debate and ultimately the most publicity. Overall, four concepts were emphasized:

- personalizing the professor-student relationship;
- helping students form their aspirations and intellectual habits in their critical first year through an improved campus intellectual climate, small classes, and mentoring opportunities;
- strengthening existing programs instead of establishing new ones; and
- aggressively pursuing new resources to enable Wake Forest to remain competitive with the nation's best liberal arts programs.

The plan was funded by $1 million in annual administrative savings, a one-time transfer of $19.2 million in funds functioning as endowment for front-end capital and other costs, and a special tuition increase of $3,000. An additional $5 million in financial aid would be provided to maintain the University's need-blind admissions policy. Tuition for first-year students in 1996–1997 was set at $18,500, up from $14,750 in 1995–1996.

Provisions of the plan included:

1. Every first-year student would receive an IBM notebook computer with a standard software load. The computer would be replaced with a new model after two years, and graduating students would keep their computers.
2. Forty new, full-time faculty positions would be added by the year 2002.
3. The student/faculty ratio would be reduced 8 percent, from 13:1 to slightly more than 11:1.
4. More than one hundred new upper-level classes and an American Ethnic Studies minor would be offered.
5. The University would create 150 new upperclass merit scholarships and 175 study-abroad scholarships.
6. The library would receive more funding.
7. The faculty leave program would be expanded.

On March 27, the faculty approved the plan by an almost three-to-one margin (140 to 56). The first-year seminar proposal was approved separately by a vote of 106 to 10 on April 3, and on April 19, these actions were unanimously approved by the Board of Trustees. Prior to the trustees' vote on April 18, about 150 students, organized by sophomore John Whitmire, gathered outside Wait Chapel before a capital campaign celebration convocation featuring Arnold Palmer as the principal speaker. Their purpose was to protest the imminent adoption of the plan. They objected primarily to the computer proposal, the $3,000 tuition increase, and the lack of student voice on the Program Planning Committee. Sam McGee and Doug Carriker spoke out against the plan because they believed it had not been fully discussed with students. After everyone attending the convocation had entered the chapel, the protesters sang the alma mater, put their signs in the balcony where they could be viewed from the stage, and quietly left.

The final major story of the year was the Heritage and Promise Campaign. It came to a successful end, as noted in the previous paragraph, on April 18 at a convocation where Arnold Palmer ('51, LLD '70) spoke, and the ACC Championship men's basketball team signed autographs on the Quad afterwards. The road to the $150 million campaign began in November 1990 with a fund drive targeting faculty and staff, about 70 percent of whom contributed a total of $2 million. Deborah Best ('70, MA '72), Chair of the Department of Psychology, led the campus campaign. About 60 percent of alumni made gifts in forty-three regional drives. The Trustees gave $33 million, and by the time the campaign went public in April 1991, more than half of the goal was in hand.

More than $41 million in endowed student support was committed, $4 million over the goal for that area. More than $52 million was raised toward the $40 million goal for operating support, and $32 million was given toward the $20 million building goal. The $11 million received toward the $13 million goal for endowed professorships was short of its target, but twenty-four endowed positions were created during the campaign. In addition, $21.3 million was contributed toward the $39 million sought for endowed faculty support. Seemingly indefatigable, Provost Emeritus Ed Wilson ('43) travelled to thirty-nine regional sites during the campaign. Overall, $171 million was raised, putting the campaign $21 million over its target.

Academics

On the academic side of things, a major event happened in the School of Business and Accountancy. The School changed its name to honor D. Wayne Calloway ('59, LLD '88), Chair and Chief Executive Officer of PepsiCo, Inc., since 1986. From now on the school would be called the Wayne Calloway School of Business and Accountancy. In addition, Babcock Hall, home of the business school and the Mathematics and Computer Science Departments, was renamed Calloway Hall. The honors were announced during the Founders' Day Convocation on February 14, at which Senator Dale Bumpers spoke. Calloway was tri-chair of the Heritage and Promise campaign, a generous supporter of the University, and had been on the Board of Trustees since 1990, serving as Chair from 1991–1994.

On another part of campus, the School of Law began the year-long theme, "Celebrating a Century of Legal Education (1894–1994)," commemorating its longevity. During the year there were barbeques, speeches, and a film festival. There were even reenactments of important legal cases, such as *The Z. Smith Reynolds Foundation v. The Trustees of Wake Forest College* in 1946, the results of which cleared the way for Wake Forest to move to Winston-Salem. *U.S. News & World Report* ranked the Law School thirty-sixth among the nation's 176 accredited schools, and a flawless accreditation report from the American Bar Association in July found "no significant weaknesses in the present program." Overall the school's admissions standards ranked in the top 15 percent of all law schools in the country. The first-year class of 164 students came from seventy-six colleges and universities in twenty-eight states. Women and minorities, respectively, made up 37 and 11 percent of the class. Dean Robert K. Walsh noted that North Carolinians regularly composed between 35 and 40 percent of the school's classes and that 55 to 60 percent of recent graduates had remained in the state to practice. The school's Fall Convocation was held in conjunction with the University's Opening Convocation on October 25, with U.S. Supreme Court Chief Justice William Rehnquist as the main speaker.

In the College, the English Department faculty were singled out by the *Old Gold and Black* as among the most prolific writers at Wake Forest. Scott Klein, Phillip Kuberski, Claudia Thomas, Mary DeShazer, Gillian Overing, Andrew

Wayne Calloway

Ettin, and James Hans had published eleven books in the previous two years. In addition, Robert Lovett, Dolly McPherson, Gail Sigal, and Kate Daniels had published books in the 1990s.

Kathy Kron, Steve Gatesy, Gloria Muday, and Dave Anderson, junior members of the Biology Department, received research grants from the National Science Foundation (NSF). It was the first time in the department's history that four faculty had won NSF grants concurrently. Overall, in the last six months of 1994, the amount of externally funded research on the Reynolda Campus increased 74 percent over the same period in the previous year. The dollar amount was $1.5 million.

Fred Howard (Mathematics) ended his term as Editor of *Fibonacci Quarterly*. David Waddill, a New York investment manager, made a $350,000 gift to establish the Marcellus Waddill Excellence in Teaching Award in honor of his father, who joined the Mathematics Department in 1962. The award's purpose was to recognize two recipients annually who were exemplary as teachers, one on the elementary level (K–6) and another on the secondary level (7–12). Each would receive a $20,000 "no-strings-attached" cash award. It was given for the first time during Founders' Day.

William K. Meyers (History) was awarded a Fulbright grant to study problems confronting Peru, Argentina, and Brazil. As part of a group of twelve scholars, he toured the three countries, meeting with government representatives and other officials in and out of the political system. Perry Patterson (Economics) served as an adviser with the United States Agency for International Development to the National Bank of Ukraine. Helga Welsh (Political Science) oversaw German national and state elections during October. Maya Angelou (Humanities) recited a poem at the United Nations' fiftieth anniversary celebration in June, and C. David Bowen (Music) became Director of the Wake Forest Marching Band.

Marcellus Waddill, his wife, Shirley, and son David Waddill

Catherine T. Harris (Sociology) received the Award for Excellence in Advising at the new-student convocation. Robert Brehme (Physics) received the Jon Reinhardt Award for Distinguished Teaching during fall convocation. Suzanne Reynolds (Law) received the Joseph Branch Excellence in Teaching Award. Anne Boyle (English) received the Omicron Delta Kappa Award for her contributions to student life; Simone Caron (History) won the Reid-Doyle Prize for Excellence in Teaching; Dale Dagenbach

(Psychology) won the Award for Excellence in Research; and Thomas E. Mullen (Dean of the College) received the Medallion of Merit. Michael J. Hyde, a distinguished professor at Northwestern University, was named the first J. Tylee Wilson Professor of Business Ethics in the Department of Communication.

On August 29, in a letter to Bill L. Atchley, President of the University of the Pacific, President Hearn affirmed that the normal teaching load for faculty at Wake Forest was three courses each during the fall and spring semesters (or six courses during the academic year), but he acknowledged that concessions were granted as needed on a case-by-case basis.

The Graduate Counseling Program was reaccredited by the Council for the Accreditation of Counseling and Related Educational Programs (CACREP) for seven years, or until June 30, 2002, the longest possible period for reaccreditation. The Physician Assistant Program celebrated its twenty-fifth anniversary in September, and a five-year program leading to a master's degree in accounting was instituted to meet the increased professional standards for Certified Public Accountant (CPA) candidates. A new Urban Studies minor requiring at least 20 credits was initiated in the fall, with Don Frey (Economics) as coordinator. It was the eighth interdisciplinary minor offered at the University.

Administration and Staff

President Hearn was granted a six-week study leave for summer 1995. He went to France from mid-June to mid-July and then spent a couple of weeks in August at the beach, although he was available as needed.

At their April meeting, the Trustees added a supplemental statement on sexual orientation to existing University anti-discrimination language. In related actions, Gloria Cooper (Director EEO/Training Officer) and Dean-Elect Paul Escott visited department chairs to discuss the recruitment of female and minority faculty in spring 1995.

During the summer of 1994, John McKinnon announced his retirement as Dean of the Babcock School. Dean since 1989, in his last year, McKinnon recommended the opening of an evening MBA in Charlotte starting in the fall of 1995. President Hearn approved the plan and notified the Board of Trustees on January 25. Under McKinnon, applications for full-time admission to the Babcock School increased 52 percent; the average GMAT score rose more than sixty points from 540 to 600; and the Babcock School achieved its first national ranking. The entering class of the Babcock Graduate School of Management's full-time program also had the highest average GMAT score in the school's history, 660. On May 15, Gary Costley, fifty-one years old, was appointed Professor of Management and Dean of the Babcock School. He had been Executive Vice President of cereal giant the Kellogg Company and Chair of Kellogg USA.

Walter Harrelson, former Dean of the Divinity Schools at Vanderbilt University and the University of Chicago, became a University Professor at Wake Forest on July 1 and was given a two-year appointment to structure a Divinity School program that would be both Baptist and ecumenical. His hiring was facilitated by a gift of $300,000 from the E. Rhodes and Leona B. Carpenter Foundation.

Bill Sides became Director of Facilities Management. Joanna Iwata was appointed the new director of the Benson University Center in January. Max Floyd was hired to direct intramural and club sports, and David DeVries was hired as a consultant to help President Hearn in a management review of Reynolda Vice Presidents.

Associate Provost Laura C. Ford published her first book, *Liberal Education and the Cannon* (Camden House). In another artistic and creative endeavor, a portrait of John Willard painted by Anne Kesler Shields was hung on the second floor of Reynolda Hall.

President Hearn wrote a memo to Sandra Boyette and the staff of Public Affairs on January 3 congratulating them on winning the Grand Award in the Total Publications category in the District III competition of the Council for the Advancement and Support of Education (CASE).

The Women's Network, an issues-oriented staff advocacy group, celebrated its fourth year in January.

Athletics

Soccer Coach Walt Chyzowych died on September 2 of a heart attack while playing tennis. He was fifty-seven and had been Head Soccer Coach at Wake Forest since 1986. He led the team to its first ACC title in 1989 and to four invitations to the NCAA tournament. On September 3, the team was scheduled to open its 1994 season at home in the Wake Forest Soccer Classic and elected to play in Chyzowych's honor. Jay Vidovich was named interim and then head coach in November.

The women's soccer team, coached by Chris Turner, began its inaugural season playing at home against the University of Virginia. Its first victory came against Lenoir-Rhyne, 1–0, at home on Polo Field in overtime, as freshman Amanda Lewis scored the game-winning goal.

The Athletics Department announced a five-year plan to expand facilities and increase scholarship support for women's varsity teams in October. It also ended a twenty-year agreement with WSJS-AM and reached a new agreement on July 1, 1995, with WFXF-FM (100.3 FM), which became the new flagship station broadcasting University sports, particularly football and basketball. The 100,000-watt signal from "The Fox" reached thirty-two counties in North Carolina and southern Virginia.

The women's golf team, led by sophomore Laura Philo, who captured the individual championship title, won the ACC Championship and was ranked third in the nation, the highest ever for the women's program and its second straight top-ten finish. Coach Diane Dailey was named ACC Coach of the Year.

Italian officials announced in December that Wake Forest and the Lawrence Joel Coliseum

Andy Bloom

would be the primary training sites for Italy's team in the 1996 Summer Olympics in Atlanta. As many as 250 Italian athletes, coaches, and staff would live at the University from late June to early July 1996.

The football team improved its record over the previous season by one game with three wins and eight losses. In better news, Head Coach John Goodridge earned his fourth ACC Coach of the Year award after guiding the men's cross country team to the ACC Championship for the second year in a row in the fall. The Quad was rolled in their honor. Andy Bloom set a new tournament record in the discus with a throw of 208 feet 3 inches in the ACC track and field championship in April. He also won the shot put with a throw of 60 feet 10.75 inches. ACC coaches named Bloom the men's top conference performer in track and field.

In outdoor track and field events, Warren Sherman was selected as a First Team All-American.

Lew Gerrard (women's tennis) was also named ACC Coach of the Year. During the season, the team was ranked fourth nationally. The women's cross country team, coached by Francie Goodridge, captured the District III championship and went on to compete in the NCAA Championship.

In another milestone event, baseball coach George Greer became the winningest coach in Wake Forest baseball history with a three-game sweep of Maryland in late April. His record improved to 270–187–2.

The Arts

The Mainstage Theatre produced four dramas during the year: Neil Simon's *Lost in Yonkers*, Steven Dietz's *Dracula*, Caryl Churchill's *Top Girls*, and William Shakespeare's *The Tempest.* The Ring Theatre gave performances of Neil Simon's *The Star-Spangled Girl*, Tom Griffin's *The Boys Next Door*, Murray Schisgal's *A Need for Brussels Sprouts*, and Neil Simon's *A Visitor from Forest Hills.*

The Department of Romance Languages sponsored performances of Cuban playwright Jose Triana's *La Noche de los Asesinos* (*The Night of the Assassins*) during September and October as well as instruction in Afro-Cuban dance by Juanita Baro. Both were highlights of a month-long program, Perspectives on Latin American Culture.

The Secrest Artists Series featured performances by jazz violinist Stephane Grappelli, the Handel and Haydn Society, Orpheus Chamber Orchestra, Kronos Quartet, and pianist Mihai Ungureanu.

Leah Dumar ('81) opened a multimedia art exhibit, "Ruination," in the Scales Fine Arts Center in early September. A slide show and lecture considered pictures from the fifteenth century to present-day photography. A three-day festival, *Say Things and Gather About,* celebrating the award-winning poetry of A. R. Ammons ('49) was held in April.

By the 1993-1994 season, George Greer had won over 200 games as the Deacons' baseball coach

A. R. Ammons

In October, the Student Union presented a concert by the rock band Widespread Panic in Wait Chapel. WAKE Radio and the local nightclub Ziggy's teamed up to present the Dave Matthews Band in the same venue later in the year.

Campus and Student Life

Over the Hearn decade, applications for admission increased 72 percent; 5,923 applications were submitted for the 942 spots in the 1994–1995 freshman class, whereas 3,400 were submitted in 1984. In addition, over 90 percent of the entering class had graduated in the top 20 percent of their high school class. The rise in applications was partly attributed to the success of the men's basketball team. Martha Allman, Associate Director of Admissions, said that the large first-year class would not increase the total student body due to lower enrollment at the upperclass levels. Black students made up 6 percent of new students as part of the 10 percent of minority students in the class. North Carolinians accounted for 26 percent of the class, and overall forty states and foreign countries were represented. The total tally of new students was surpassed only slightly by the post-presidential debate surge of 1989; 205 students chose substance-free housing and moved into Johnson and Piccolo residence halls. Jessica Davey and Volunteer Service Director Betsy Greer began SPARC (Students Promoting Action and Responsibility in the Community), recruiting students to serve in homeless shelters, to build a house for Habitat for Humanity, and to work with handicapped children and older adults.

Three of the most influential student leaders for the year were Steve Bumgarner, Student Government President; Connie Marks, Editor-in-Chief of *The Howler*; and Brian J. Uzwiak, Editor-in-Chief for the *Old Gold and Black*.

Both first-year and upperclass students encountered a new experience in managing their expenses. In the past, students on a prepaid meal plan used a meal card. Now, their ID card worked as a debit card using "Deacon Dollars." Students could charge their meals with the Deacon Dining Club card and set up a separate account, Deacon Dollars, for use at the college bookstore, Deacon Shop, telecommunications, microcomputer center, Health Services, campus police, and student union. ARA managed Deacon Dining, and the University managed Deacon Dollars. For the first time, staff and faculty could also use the debit card.

To welcome new students and familiarize them with some professors and staff at Wake Forest, Dean of Freshman Paul Orser organized a speakers' series called Freshman Evenings. It began in late September with Maya Angelou, who was followed later in the first semester by such luminaries as President Hearn, Provost Emeritus Ed Wilson, and Chaplain Ed Christman.

A new policy blocked outside groups from using the Quad to spread their messages, relegating them to Davis Field instead after students complained about a University of Alabama chapter of Chi Alpha whose members were preaching and singing their Christian message on the Quad on March 27–28.

Paul Orser

Among upperclassmen, the top majors during the 1994–1995 academic year were English, history, business, biology, economics, and speech communication. Regardless of major, registration statistics for fall 1994 found that Wake Forest students did not particularly care for early morning or late afternoon classes. The number of sections and enrollments peaked at 10 a.m. on Monday, Wednesday, and Friday and at 2 p.m. on Tuesday and Thursday, sloping off to lows of fifteen sections and 339 students at 8 a.m. Friday and one section with fifty-nine students at 5 p.m. Friday. Students did like and use the computer labs set up by the University. There were seven microcomputer labs available for general student use and located in multiple campus buildings, such as Reynolda Hall. All of them had both Macintosh and IBM-compatible computers.

A short in a 5,000-volt electrical main between Davis residence hall and Benson University Center caused an explosion at 4:55 p.m. on February 8, and electrical service to Davis was completely cut off. More than 300 students had to find temporary housing for the night, with some sleeping in Benson. Crews from Salem Electric stayed on campus all night to restore power. According to Bill Sides, Director of Facilities Management, the switching equipment in the Davis mechanical room was only lightly damaged, and power was restored to all affected areas much sooner than expected.

In a November 9 memo, President Hearn asked Vice President Zick to do more to address eating disorders among students.

During the last week of school, two female Luter residents were abducted from campus at gun point, driven off to an automatic teller machine, and forced to withdraw $300 for the kidnappers.

The Alliance for Racial and Cultural Harmony (ARCH) continued to improve race relations on campus. The student group sponsored an ARCH week with relevant programs every night. Still, an incident in January stirred up a lot of anger, when several black students were pepper-sprayed at the end of a "Pit Jam." As a consequence, black fraternity parties were relocated from the Pit to Reynolds Gym and renamed Gym Jams.

A new Race Relations Committee, co-chaired by Sam Gladding and Harold Holmes, was formed during the year, composed of three administrators, three faculty, and two students in addition to, and chosen by, Student Government President Steve Bumgarner. In a September 21 memo, President Hearn charged, "The committee will meet each semester to monitor activities related to progress in sustaining a healthy climate for campus race relations." Members included Head Football Coach Jim Caldwell, Edward Easley (Calloway), Charles Richman (Psychology), and Loraine Stewart (Education).

The Publication Board amended its by-laws and admitted WAKE Radio, WAKE TV, and *The Philomathesian* as provisional members. In early December WAKE TV aired a variety show, its first, that was available on campus cable. An editorial in the December 8

Andrew Frey (right) with wax statue of
Albert Einstein (left)

Old Gold and Black praised WAKE TV and the recent *Philomathesian* for their educational and entertainment value to the campus.

Under Brian J. Uzwiak, the *Old Gold and Black* began to publish an electronic edition, as opposed to its previous text-only edition, on the Internet. The paper won a Pacemaker Award for 1994–1995 from the Associated Collegiate Press and College Media Advisors as one of the premiere nondaily college newspapers in the country.

The Philomathesian Society started the year with about twenty members and a literary magazine, *The Philomathesian*, funded by Vice President Ken Zick and edited by senior Joy Goodwin. The society was founded on May 3, 1834, but died following the move to the Reynolda Campus. Goodwin and Phil Archer managed to revive it in 1993, and the Euzelian Society, its old campus rival, was resurrected in the spring of 1995. The Euzelians had a more scientific emphasis and attracted about the same number of members.

The *Wake Forest Critic* reappeared briefly with Brad Collins as Editor and David Broyles (Political Science) as its Advisor. As in previous years, it specialized more in personal opinions and individual attacks on administrators than news, and after this year, it disappeared (and was not missed).

Jessica Davey and Mother Teresa

The Gospel Choir celebrated its twenty-fifth anniversary. The Senior Class Campaign shattered its $40,000 goal, collecting $50,500 in cash and pledges for the University. Seniors Russ Hubbard and Jen Jackson, along with junior Erik Lisher, the finance chair, reestablished Project *Pro Humanitate* to raise funds to construct a house for Habitat for Humanity. The project sponsored a number of events to raise the $45,000 needed to build the house, including a "homeless night," when students slept in cardboard boxes on the Magnolia Court.

Freshman Andrew Frey, a Reynolds scholar and son of Economics Professor Don Frey, was one of five students chosen for the U.S. Physics Team in the 25th International Physics Olympiad in July 1994. He came in fifteen out of 229 young physicists from around the world, receiving a gold medal in the theoretical part of the exam and a bronze medal for his overall performance. The U.S. team ranked third behind China and Germany.

Megan E. Reif, a junior from Wyoming, was selected as a 1995 Truman Scholar, one of only seventy nationwide. The honor came with $30,000 to enable her to attend any graduate school in the country in pursuit of a career in public service.

Senior Jennifer Jones and several family members biked from Greensboro to Washington, D.C., over spring break from April 12 to April 16, to raise money for the American Cancer Society in memory of her father, who had recently died. They raised over $25,000.

Four Wake Forest students interned at the White House during summer 1994: Leah Adamson, Wykesha Tripp, Dolly Lynn Pressley, and Zoe Poulson. Nikki Finger, a senior, became the Wake Forest Marching Band's first black drum major.

Jessica Davey was named one of the nation's top ten college women for 1994 by *Glamour* magazine and was featured in their October issue. A religion and sociology major, she spent ten weeks in summer 1993 caring for the poor in India as a volunteer with Mother Teresa's Missionaries of Charity and led a group of ten Wake Forest students to Calcutta over the winter break in 1993–1994, with Cecil Price, Director of Student Health Service, as the faculty/staff advisor. They worked at three homes run by Mother Teresa's religious order, bathing patients, comforting the dying, cleaning hospital wards, and caring for children.

Wake Forest debaters won the nation's highest college award in spring 1995. Adrienne Brovero, a senior from the Bronx, New York, and John Hughes, a junior from Whitefish, Montana, received Wake Forest's first Copeland Award, which honors the team with the best record in the nation. During the regular season, Brovero and Hughes won seventy out of ninety-one rounds and nineteen out of twenty-three rounds against the top sixteen teams. They finished first in three major tournaments and tied for first in a fourth competition

Debate squad, 1994–1995

before finishing third at the national tournament. The debate squad as a whole finished the 1994–1995 season ranked number one in the nation.

From 1988 to 1993, 236 Wake Forest men applied to medical school; 159 were accepted and 77 rejected, a success rate of 67.3 percent. Of the 100 women who applied, 65 were accepted, a 65 percent success rate.

The Alpha Nu chapter of Sigma Pi won four of the top five prizes awarded by Sigma Pi Fraternity International, including the Grand Council Award for excellence in overall chapter operations, the Most Improved Chapter Award, the Chapter Efficiency Award, and the Lyle H. Smith Outstanding Chapter Director Award. In contrast, the Sigma Phi Epsilon fraternity was placed on probation for the academic year in early September for hazing. The Student Life Committee required all Greek organizations to complete pledge activities within eight weeks during spring 1995; sororities were already compliant, but some fraternities were taking up to fourteen weeks. The committee further required that, all pledge activities be completed in six weeks for spring 1996. Lambda Chi Alpha, a substance-free fraternity, officially started a colony on campus. Substance-free housing for upperclassmen was confined to Piccolo residence hall.

Facilities, Finances, and Alumni

Facilities

QualChoice, a health maintenance product originating at the Medical School, became the University's new medical plan, replacing BlueCross/BlueShield in October. It had 231 primary care doctors; of the ninety-nine in Forsyth County, forty-seven became part of what was to be called Wake Forest University Physicians. The changeover was controversial because consumers were limited to physicians in the program. According to Jim Ferrell, Director of Human Resources, however, QualChoice offered cost-saving benefits.

Wake Forest won the 1993 Honor Award of the Professional Grounds Management Society, and photos of the University were featured in the May/June 1994 issue of the *Grounds Management Forum*. President Hearn wrote Jim Coffey, Superintendent of Grounds, a letter of congratulations on July 12.

The Medical School leased a Cessna Citation jet for University use.

The stoplight on Wake Forest Road between Taylor and Davis residence halls was deactivated in April. It had been in place for fifteen years, made necessary by the large number of cars using the campus as a shortcut before the main road was rerouted.

The rededication of Casa Artom took place on October 25 in honor of Bianca Artom and her husband Camillo. Mrs. Artom had died on February 5, 1994, and her photograph was hung in the house before the ceremony. She had taught in the Romance Languages Department for sixteen years before retiring in 1990. The Artom's son George attended the ceremony with a number of Venice residents.

Poteat and Huffman residence halls were renovated over the summer with new key-card entry and central air-conditioning systems. A new residence hall with ninety-two beds, situated near Polo Road and to be renamed Martin Hall, received its first upperclass occupants in fall 1994.

A Subway sandwich shop was opened during the fall semester in the Pit. President Steve Bumgarner and the Student Government Legislature proposed a renovation for Shorty's that was accepted by the administration but not funded. Bob Mills was appointed to raise funds for the project.

The number of vehicles registered on the Reynolda Campus for the academic year was 3,956, while the number of parking spaces was 3,399, or 557 spaces short. The number of parking tickets issued was 6,000. The University Police opened an office in Davis House in October, offering around-the-clock services for anyone on campus, regardless of the circumstance.

The card catalogs in Z. Smith Reynolds Library were replaced by the Dynix Online Library System during the summer of 1995. The card catalogs had been closed for several years and now were physically removed from the atrium on the fourth floor and replaced with seating for thirty-two visitors.

Jim Cogdill, a professional space consultant, joined Facilities Management. His duties included designing better plans for use of the University's many buildings.

The University expanded its recycling program, placing 118 thirty-two-gallon bins on every floor of residence halls to comply with a new state law that prohibited dumping aluminum cans in landfills, according to Jerome McDaniel, the campus recycling coordinator.

Finances

The Council for Advancement and Support of Education once again named Wake Forest to its Circle of Excellence for overall fundraising performance based on the past three years of giving. Total giving to the University, including the Bowman Gray School of Medicine and the Department of Athletics, was $27 million in 1990–1991, $29 million in 1991–1992, and $30 million in 1992–1993. By June 30, 1995, 44 percent of Wake Forest alumni had contributed to the current operations and capital purposes fund. Their giving for the 1994–1995 year increased by $520,000, while overall giving increased by $2.7 million.

Julie B. Cole (Research and Sponsored Programs) reported that external support for faculty projects had increased $762,929 over the past fiscal year to total $3,906,301.

Lowe's Foods gave $100,000 to the Calloway School of Business and Accountancy to fund scholarships and a business competition for students. The Kutteh family gave $170,000 for two new scholarships, and the law firm of Petree Stockton provided for three full scholarships for minority students in the School of Law.

Joseph M. Bryan left $500,000 to Wake Forest to support the men's and women's golf teams upon his death on April 26, 1995.

A $1million plan for improvements to Reynolda Gardens was announced in the summer of 1995. Almost one-third of this amount came from a $300,000 grant from the Z. Smith Reynolds Foundation. Wake Forest committed the equivalent of another $1 million in new endowment to hire staff to better maintain buildings and plantings and to provide educational programming. It would be the first major project in the gardens since 1981, when the greenhouse was renovated. The goal for the campaign was $4.2 million. As of March, it had not been reached, but University officials wanted to get the improvements under way as soon as possible. Funds that came in after the work began were to be used to create an endowment once the improvements were made.

Vice President John Anderson proposed a tuition increase of 6.5 percent for fiscal year 1995–1996, for a total tuition of $14,750, or $900 above the fiscal year 1994–1995 tuition. The increase would provide faculty salary pool increases of 4.25 percent. Salary pools for staff and administrators would increase 3.25 percent, and all other expenditures would increase 2.25 percent. In addition to announcing salary increases for faculty and staff, President Hearn's total compensation package for 1993–1994 was released in November. It was $379,385: $202,288 in salary, $138,119 in benefits, and allowances of $38,978. Vice President Richard Janeway of the Medical School had a total compensation package of $467,500.

Alumni

Among alumni, Murray Greason ('59, JD '62) and Edward Reynolds ('64) received Distinguished Alumni Awards during Homecoming. Wayne Calloway ('59) accepted the nomination to Chair the Board of Trustees, replacing John Medlin. Stephen Coles ('77), a Lexington, North Carolina, attorney, was installed as President of the Alumni Association. Richard Burr ('76) was elected to represent North Carolina's fifth district in Congress.

On April 26, President Hearn sent a letter to alumni and friends of the University outlining the major benefits of the Plan for the Class of 2000 to students, faculty, and staff.

Summing Up the Year

Of the many events in the 1994–1995 academic year, two had lasting effects: the completion of the Heritage and Promise campaign and the public elevation of Wake Forest from a regional to a national university. The campaign began in 1991 and was the largest Wake Forest had ever attempted. Its goal of $150 million was ambitious but achievable; in the end, $171 million was raised. Its national scope came at the same time as the University's reclassification by *U.S. News & World Report* from the number-one regional university in the South to the "first tier" of national universities (institutions ranked twenty-sixth to fifty-seventh). In addition, Wake Forest was ranked the fourteenth "best buy" among the nation's 3,600 colleges and universities by *Money* magazine, and *Barron's Profiles of American Colleges* named Wake Forest one of only thirty-nine colleges and universities, and one of just eight in the South, it deemed "most competitive."

The men's basketball team's victory in overtime against archrival University of North Carolina to win the ACC Championship was perhaps the most satisfying event of the year. It had been thirty-three years since the Deacons had won the championship. Fans were elated, and prospective students were excited. The University gained further prestige from the victory and the team's entry into the NCAA Men's Basketball Tournament. (The University also sold thousands of dollars of merchandise related to the basketball team's success.)

Academically and professionally, the law school celebrated its one hundredth anniversary and its proud tradition. In the undergraduate arena, the adoption of the Plan for the Class of 2000 was the most significant event in the academic life of the College. The plan operated on many levels, but the most publicly and internally interesting feature was the distribution of IBM laptop computers to all students and faculty beginning with the class entering in 1996. It would be accompanied by a $3,000 tuition increase for new students. First-year seminars that every freshman must take and pass would also be introduced in the fall of 1996. Each required seminar enrolled fifteen to nineteen students and aimed to promote "intense intellectual interchange, both written and oral" on wide-ranging topics and "opposing viewpoints."

Finally, the President's heart condition absorbed attention during the spring of the year. President Hearn had to undergo bypass surgery in February for a leaking mitral valve and did not return to campus until April. In his absence, the University ran smoothly as senior members of the administration stepped up to the challenge.

Overall, 1994–1995 was a busy and productive year for the University. Its status and recognition increased and its plans for the future firmed up. New spaces were occupied and older spaces were renovated. Students achieved remarkable success on many levels, academically, athletically, and altruistically. The faculty and administration were also quite productive. While not all was idyllic and ideal, the University as an entity seldom had a better year, and the prospectives for upcoming endeavors looked bright.

CHAPTER THIRTEEN
1995–1996

A Pivotal Year of Change

"Pro Humanitate is the motto given you this day with your diploma. Ed Wilson said during our recent trek to old Wake Forest: 'At our (Wake Forest's) best, we reached not outward for what the world might give us but inward for what we might find within ourselves to give the world.'"

Thomas K. Hearn Jr., May 20, 1996;
Charge to the Graduates, Wake Forest University Commencement

In the 1995–1996 academic year, several events stand out. The Deanship of the College was transferred from Tom Mullen to Paul Escott, and leadership of the Divinity School from Walter Harrelson to Bill Leonard. The construction of gates at the entrances to campus was recommended, and in a major boost to morale, the men's basketball team won its second consecutive ACC championship.

Paul Escott, Reynolds Professor of History and author of four books on the Civil War, was selected Dean of the College in February 1995, replacing Tom Mullen, who returned to teaching in the History Department after twenty-seven years in administration. The three other finalists for the Dean's position were Nancy Cotton (English), Margaret Supplee Smith (Art), and David Weaver (Anthropology). Escott's official start date was July 1, when the academic year also began. He had been at the University since 1988 and was named a Reynolds Professor in 1990. He was seen as knowledgeable, even-tempered, fair-minded, and forward-thinking with high academic standards.

Walter Harrelson's term for planning the Divinity School, which was only two years, ended on June 30, 1996. On May 21, Bill J. Leonard, fifty years old, was appointed the school's first Dean, starting July 1. A noted Baptist scholar like Harrelson, Leonard had written widely on American religion and Baptist studies and had

Paul Escott

Bill Leonard

taught at Southern Baptist Theological Seminary from 1975 to 1991. He came to Wake Forest from Samford University in Birmingham, Alabama, where he had been Chair of Religion and Philosophy since 1992. He arrived to find he had an office, an administrative assistant, a development officer, a Board of Visitors, and a huge challenge—to transform the plans for the Divinity School into a reality. While $11 million in endowment had been raised, $15 million were needed, and in addition to fundraising and teaching in the Department of Religion for the next three years, Leonard had to hire a faculty, recruit an incoming class of students, and integrate the new school into the University fabric. He approached all of these tasks with energy, optimism, and efficiency, demonstrating a strong, creative deanship. He was the perfect fit for the position.

On March 1, the Perimeter Access Control Committee submitted a report recommending that gatehouses be built at all three campus street entrances to monitor late-night traffic. It also recommended hiring three additional police officers and substantially upgrading outdoor lighting. The committee of ten faculty, students, and administrators was formed after two female students were abducted from campus in spring 1995, and the armed robbery of five male students on campus in January 1996 punctuated its deliberation. A small group of students assembled outside the Benson University Center during the spring meeting of the Board of Trustees to protest the building of gatehouses, but to no avail.

On March 10, the men's basketball team, under Head Coach Dave Odom, won the ACC championship, defeating Georgia Tech 75–74 and becoming the first team in fourteen years to win consecutive ACC titles. Tim Duncan was named the most valuable player of the tournament as well as National College Basketball Player of the Year. While Randolph Childress had been the hero of the previous year's ACC championship, Duncan clearly was seen as the leader of the 1996 team. He poured in 27 points, took down 21 rebounds, and had six assists and four blocked shots. He also forced the Yellow Jackets's Stephon Marbury to alter the angle of his potentially game-winning shot with three seconds left and thus preserve the win for the Deacons.

Duncan was not the Lone Ranger in the defeat of Georgia Tech. Rusty LaRue stepped up his game, adding 14 points and taking over at point guard after Tony

Some students protested building gates at the entrances of the campus

Tim Duncan

Rutland was forced to leave the game with a sprained knee with 14 minutes left. Ricky Peral added 10 points, and Jerry Braswell added two free throws in the waning moments. Thus the Deacons prevailed as a team, withstanding a blistering Georgia Tech comeback in the final minutes of the game. As with the year before, Wake Forest fans rushed the court.

The 1996 men's basketball team worked well together

Academics

U.S. News & World Report ranked Wake Forest thirty-first in its 1996 list of the best national universities. It ranked the Calloway School of Business and Accountancy twenty-fifth nationally among undergraduate business programs, while *Money* magazine ranked Wake Forest twenty-fifth in its annual list of best college buys.

The President informed the Trustees that the Southern Association of Colleges and Schools (SACS) was beginning Wake Forest's reaccreditation process, with Ellen Kirkman (Mathematics) and Ross Griffith (Institutional Research) co-chairing the effort. A review team led by Rich Morrill, President of the University of Richmond, would evaluate Wake Forest programs and make a site visit in spring 1997.

Dean Escott raised questions about undergraduate education, two of which created some controversy. In a letter to the faculty, he expressed his concern about students' high grades and reminded them what each grade meant. He also noted that the percentage of students graduating with honors was increasing faster than the quality of the student body seemed to warrant; 70 percent of the senior class was projected to graduate with honors. Students were upset when some faculty interpreted Escott's letter as policy to give fewer high grades. To clear the air, Escott and Psychology Professor Deborah Best ('70, MA '72) held a forum with students. Although no conclusions were reached, the ideas of raising the requirement for honors and implementing a system of pluses and minuses were discussed.

In another academic debate, the Dean proposed that more classes be offered at 8 a.m. to help students meet their requirements. He said that 92 percent of classes were offered between 9 a.m. and 3 p.m. and that more classes at an earlier hour would alleviate some scheduling problems. In the spring semester of 1996, fifty-nine classes were offered at 8 a.m., fifteen more than in spring 1995, and 858 students enrolled in them compared to 645 students the year earlier, an increase of 33 percent.

In September 1995, a Commission on the Status of Women at Wake Forest, chaired by Lu Leake, was created by Provost Brown and asked "to examine the existing climate and conditions for women students, staff, and faculty at Wake Forest." Specifically, it was charged to:

1. assess the ways in which Wake Forest programs and policies encourage and discourage the development and service of women; and
2. recommend feasible and fundable ways in which the development and service of women can be further encouraged.

Luminaries who visited the campus for special occasions were numerous during 1995–1996. Julius L. Chambers, Chancellor of North Carolina Central University, was the speaker at the Opening Convocation. Former President Gerald R. Ford headlined a national two-day symposium on presidential disability and the 25th Amendment in November, and North Carolina Governor James B. Hunt was the speaker for Founders' Day on February 15, which kicked off a two-day symposium called Cyberspace and Civil Society.

Initial first-year seminars were offered in the spring semester of 1996 as a trial run for the fall. The ten classes examined such subjects as economics, philosophy, and World War II. Also in spring 1996, on a voice vote of the faculty, the arts, which had been in Division I with literature, were moved into Division V and designated the Division of Fine Arts. With the move came a mandate that required all students to take at least one course in the arts to graduate. Previously, students could graduate without taking a course in the arts, although 80 percent did so to satisfy Division I requirements. The Division V course requirement that students take a course in the fine arts was not implemented until fall 1996.

In February, the College faculty approved a Latin American Studies minor and an American Ethnic Studies minor. They were slated to begin in the fall. The College faculty also abolished a rule requiring all students to enroll in eight credits of divisional courses each semester until all of their requirements were completed. The rule had been in effect for five years, and students, especially accounting and pre-med majors, found it difficult to fulfill. Instead, students were encouraged to complete their divisional requirements as early as possible, with consultation from their advisers.

Julie B. Cole, director of Research and Sponsored Programs, reported that external awards for faculty research and creative activities in 1994–1995 totaled $3,906,301, an increase of $762,929 over the previous year.

More than 21,000 people visited the Museum of Anthropology during 1995–1996, the highest number since it moved to the Reynolda Campus in 1987. Wake Forest University Press, a leading publisher of Irish poetry in America, celebrated its twentieth anniversary in October.

Z. Smith Reynolds Library and Worrell Professional Center held a contest to name the library's online catalogs. The name chosen from 200 entries was OWL (Online Wake Libraries). *Window on Wake Forest* went completely online with the October 1995 issue.

Many faculty achieved individual recognition. In the History department, James Barefield became the ninth recipient of a Wake Forest Professorship in August, and William K. Meyers received the Omicron Delta Kappa Award for contributions to student life. Katy Harriger (Political Science) was named a William C. Friday Fellow for Human Relations, one of twenty-five emerging leaders recognized by the state of North Carolina. In Music, Dan Locklair was named the 1996 American Guild of Organists Composer of the Year in recognition of his significant contributions to symphonic and concert music, and Peter Kairoff (Music) gave a series of well-received piano concerts in Brazil. James A. Martin Jr. (Interdisciplinary Studies) received the National Faculty Award from the Association of Graduate Liberal Studies Programs. Betsy Hoppe was promoted to Assistant Dean and Director of Information Technology at the Calloway School of Business and Accountancy. Phil Falkenberg (Sociology) and Larry West (German and Russian) were co-winners of the Award for Excellence in Advising. James T. Powell (Classical Languages) received the Reid-Doyle Prize for Excellence in Teaching. Terry Blumenthal (Psychology) received the Award for Excellence in Research; and Ron Wright (Law) received the Joseph Branch Excellence in Teaching Award from the Law School. The University's highest recognition, though, went to administrators Lu Leake and Mark Reece, who were presented with the Medallion of Merit.

Among emeritus professors, Richard C. Barnett (History) received the Donald O. Schoonmaker Faculty Award for Community Service. Ralph S. Fraser (German and Russian) received the Jon Reinhardt Award for Distinguished Teaching, and Harold M. Barrow (Health and Sports Science) received the Hetherington Award, the highest award bestowed by the National Academy of Kinesiology.

Maya Angelou (Humanities) campaigned for Marion Berry as mayor of Washington, D.C., and participated in the Million Man March. President Hearn defended her from outside letters of criticism in November and called her a "caring and dedicated professor." He also defended her from critics who objected to children reading her autobiography, *I Know Why the Caged Bird Sings.*

Sam Gladding (President's Office) served as interim chair of the Department of Religion. He helped the department calm down its rhetoric, settle interpersonal conflicts, and find a new permanent chair: Charles Kimball, an Oklahoma Baptist with a specialty in Islam. Charles Talbert resigned from the department to take an endowed chair at Baylor University. President Hearn wrote Talbert a letter on April 16 thanking him for his service. Because there was a perception that Talbert was being forced out by other members of the Department of Religion, the President also wrote to Princeton Theological Seminary students, who were Wake Forest graduates, informing them that Talbert's decision caught the University by surprise. He said that Talbert felt a calling to go to Baylor after thirty-three years at Wake Forest. He also informed them on May 7 that Charles Kimball would become the new department chair.

Graduate Dean Gordon Melson wrote a memo on May 8 informing the President, Provost, and Executive Vice President for Health Affairs that the Graduate School of Arts and Sciences had approved an MD/PhD program. Students would begin matriculating in the fall of 1997.

In 1995, the endowed professors on the Reynolda Campus were as follows: Z. Smith Reynolds Professors

Charles Talbert

Maya Angelou (American Studies), Paul Escott (History), Terisio Pignatti (Art), Robert Plemmons ('61; Mathematics and Computer Science), Dudley Shapere (Philosophy and History of Science), Richard Williams ('68; Physics), and John Wood (Economics). Wake Forest Professors were James Barefield (History), Gerald Esch (Biology), Kathleen Glenn (Romance Languages), Roger Hegstrom (Chemistry), Willie Hinze (Chemistry),

Charles Kimball

Raymond Kuhn (Biology), Charles Longino (Sociology), Charles Talbert (Religion), and John Williams (Psychology). Two more Wake Forest Professors were added in April, Patricia Cunningham (Education), and Mark R. Leary (Psychology). John C. Moorhouse (Economics) was appointed the first Archie B. Carroll Jr. Professor of Ethical Leadership.

Administration and Staff

The Office of Minority Affairs became the Office of Multicultural Affairs with Barbee Myers-Oakes, an assistant professor in the Department of Health and Sports Sciences replacing former Director Ernie Wade in August 1995. A few months later, she was appointed the permanent director. During the academic year, 430 minority students were on campus.

The Resident Student Association won School of the Year Award at the 1996 conference of the North Carolina Association of Residence Halls. The award was based on having the widest campus involvement, quality leadership, and best programs.

The President instructed John Anderson on December 21 to designate "$130,000 from next year's surplus in the Residence Life and Housing budget in order to provide up to 25 room-and-board awards for entering Reserve Office Training Corps

ROTC cadets at drill

(ROTC) scholarship winners." He expected a report regarding outcomes no later than June 1, 1997. The initiative was aimed at maintaining the viability of the ROTC program in an era of military retrenchment.

The Traffic Commission recommended eliminating reserved parking for senior administrators behind Reynolda Hall. Conveyed to the President by Ken Zick on June 5, the change was implemented immediately.

In order to use available space and staff more effectively, the Student Health Center started requiring students in nonemergency situations to make appointments.

Gloria Cooper Agard, Assistant Director of the Department of Human Resources, announced a program to recognize employees with five or more years of service.

To ease tensions and to coordinate efforts at the highest level, President Hearn instructed Vice Presidents John Anderson and Leon Corbett on November 29 to meet on a bi-weekly basis instead of exchanging e-mails. His memo stated, "We have too much at stake for there to be failures of communication between the legal and financial functions." In an unrelated event, Anderson turned over his planning duties to Vice President Sandra Boyette (Public Affairs).

Two prominent leaders resigned. Dana Johnson accepted a position as Dean of the College of Business and Economics at the University of Delaware effective July 15, 1996. She sent a letter of resignation to the President on May 23 announcing her decision. She had been Dean of the Calloway School of Business and Accountancy for four years (1992–1996), and under her leadership, it was ranked the twenty-fifth best undergraduate business program in the country.

Richard Janeway, Executive Vice President for Health Affairs for the past twenty-five years, announced on June 21 that he would step down on July 1, 1997, to become the University's first Distinguished Professor of Healthcare Management. He was sixty-three years old and had come to the Bowman Gray School of Medicine in 1963 as a National Institutes of Health (NIH) fellow in neurology. He joined the faculty in 1966 and became Dean in 1971. He was named Vice President of Health Affairs in 1983 and Executive Vice President in 1990. With 9,254 employees, the medical center ranked as the largest employer in Forsyth County.

Richard Janeway

Others received new administrative appointments. Claudia Thomas (English) became the fifth Associate Dean of the College, joining Toby Hale, Billy Hamilton, Patricia Johansson, and Paul Orser in January 1996. Clay Hipp (Calloway) also assumed a new position as adviser to students charged with judicial infractions. He replaced Paul Orser, who had held the position for four years.

Harvey L. Lineberry II was appointed Assistant Director of Human Resources. He assumed his new duties on March 11. Previously, he had managed the department's information system for employment, benefits, and wage/salary administration.

Meda Barnes was promoted to Director of Alumni Outreach. Her new duties included responsibility for all ninety-one alumni clubs across the country.

Mary Piette Lai was named director of the Charlotte MBA program of the Babcock Graduate School of Management. She was responsible for managing the admissions process and daily operations. She had been an account representative with Roadway Package System, Inc., in Charlotte and a sales representative with Parke-Davis in Milwaukee.

Louis R. Morrell, a former consultant to the University, was appointed Vice President and Treasurer in August. He had held a similar position at Rollins College in Winter Park, Florida. Irene A. Comito, Assistant to the Vice President and Treasurer for the past ten years, was promoted to Assistant Treasurer. Her new duties included assisting the Treasurer in managing the University's financial assets with specific responsibility for the investment of short-term operating funds.

Kimberly S. Griffing ('92) and Wayne Thompson were hired as media relations officers in the News Bureau. Before taking the position, Griffing was an award-winning reporter with *The Winchester Star* in Winchester, Virginia, and Thompson was a public relations specialist at the Bowman Gray School of Medicine for six years, during which he won numerous awards.

In summer 1995, President Hearn accepted an appointment from Governor Hunt to chair a twenty-five-member commission to draft a master plan for North Carolina public transportation in the next century.

In a health-related event, Chaplain Ed Christman had quadruple bypass surgery.

Athletics

Wake Forest football fans suffered through one of the worst seasons in Deacon gridiron history. The 1995 team's record was one win and ten defeats. Aside from football, 1995–1996 was a successful year; six Wake Forest teams were ranked in the top 25 of their sport in the fall of 1995: women's golf (5th), men's golf (9th), women's tennis (9th), field hockey (10th), women's cross-country (13th), and men's cross-country (25th).

Despite the basketball team's success, some tension was reported in the extension of Coach Dave Odom's contract. John Feinstein, a *Winston-Salem Journal* sports writer, penned a negative column on President Hearn, describing him as playing "mind games" with Odom. A settlement was reached, however, and a press conference on April 9, 1996, announced the extension of the contract without providing details. Odom had compiled a record of 142–72. The President wrote Feinstein on May 1 inviting him over for lunch and signing the letter "Snobbishly and haughtily yours."

In other basketball news, Tim Duncan decided to return for his senior year. A consensus All-American and the ACC Player of the Year, Duncan was the unanimous choice as the outstanding player of the ACC Tournament, and for the second consecutive year he was named national Defensive Player of the Year.

Spry Stadium

Construction of a new campus soccer stadium and practice complex on Polo Field began in February. The new stadium was named in honor of W. Dennie Spry, a retired partner in the Winston-Salem law firm of Allman, Spry, Leggett, and Crumpler. The University received a significant gift from Spry's son, Bill, a long-time Deacon Club member and a major supporter of the soccer programs. The new stadium was planned with a seating capacity of 3,000.

On June 28, ground was broken for a new, $8 million Bridger Field House at Groves Stadium after the old Bridger Field House had been torn down. The new facility featured not only locker and training rooms, but also banquet and meeting rooms, office space, and the Sports Hall of Fame. Construction would soon begin on a new indoor tennis center adjacent to the field house, slated for completion in January 1996. The 64,000-square-foot facility would feature eight tennis courts, locker rooms, and a training room.

Mary Jones, an assistant coach at Florida, was hired in July 1995 to be the first head coach of the revived women's volleyball program, which became Wake Forest's eighteenth varsity team in August 1996.

Wake Forest served as the host institution for the 1995 NCAA Division I Field Hockey Championship. The University also hosted the Olympic Torch as runners carried the flame through the campus on June 24. Students, faculty, administrators, and Winston-Salem residents lined the streets.

Many students were recognized for individual achievements in their athletic specialty. In track and field, senior Andy Bloom won the ACC shot put and discus titles for the second year in a row in April. He went on to capture the national shot put and discus titles at the NCAA Championships in June. Trina Bindel won the women's heptathlon at the ACC track and field championship in spring 1996 for the second consecutive year.

Bill Armstrong (football), Jim Simons (collegiate golfer of the year in 1971), and Brick Smith (baseball) were inducted into the Wake Forest Sports Hall of Fame on January 13.

Mac McDonald, "the Voice of the Demon Deacons," was voted North Carolina Sportscaster of the Year by the state's members of the National Sportscasters and Sportswriters Association.

Rusty LaRue was written up in a March 21 *New York Times* article, "Wake Forest's 'Daddy' Balances His Priorities." Selected to the GTE Academic All-American District Basketball Team, LaRue became the first ACC athlete since 1954 to play football, basketball, and baseball in the same season. He was a computer science major with a 3.2 grade point average, and since the summer before his freshman year he had been involved in research funded by the National Science Foundation. Robert Plemmons ('61, Mathematics and Computer Science) was LaRue's mentor. Plemmons had been an ace on the Deacon baseball team and played minor league ball in the Baltimore Orioles system for four years after graduating. LaRue racked up nearly 5,000 yards passing, setting five NCAA records, including fifty-five pass completions in a single game, and three ACC records against Duke in the fall of 1995. He received the 1996 Arnold Palmer Award as the top male athlete at the University. Trina Bindel won the Marge Crisp Award as the top female athlete of 1996.

In baseball, Ross Atkins ('95), Mark Melito ('95), Kyle Wagner ('95), and senior Bobby Rodgers were all taken in the amateur baseball draft during the summer.

The Arts

The Secrest Artists Series featured performances by the classical piano duo the Paratore Brothers; guitarist Sharon Isbin; violinist Itzhak Perlman; the Guarneri and Orion Quartets; and the early music ensemble Baltimore Consort.

The University Theatre produced four plays on its Mainstage. During the fall semester, it presented the Michael Frayn comedy *Noises Off* and *Big River*, a musical based on Mark Twain's *The Adventures of Huckleberry Finn*, written by William Hauptman, with music and lyrics by Roger Miller. In the spring semester, it produced *Our Country's Good*, a 1988 play about Australian prisoners by Timberlake Wertenbaker, adapted from a novel by Thomas Keneally and directed by Jim Dodding, as well as an updated 1894 French comedy, *Hotel Paradiso*.

The Ring Theatre produced A. R. Gurney's 1986 comedy *The Perfect Party* and Tennessee Williams's *The Glass Menagerie*. A student group, Lilting Banshees Comedy Troupe, presented *In Search of a Corner*, a show spoofing all aspects of campus life. The Banshees held regular shows each semester.

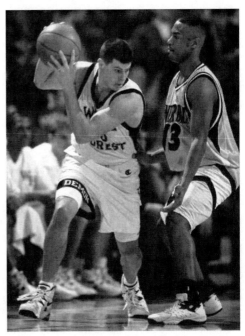

Campus and Student Life

The entering undergraduate class totaled 967—511 men and 456 women—chosen from a record 6,637 applicants. While 31 percent were from North Carolina, forty-two states and eight different countries were represented; fifty-six students were from such places as Kenya, Russia, Singapore, Colombia, Denmark, and Japan. Black students made up 9 percent of the class, and 13 percent of students identified themselves as minorities. Since the endowment of the Gordon Scholarship program in 1990, the number of African American students had

Rusty LaRue played three varsity sports: football, basketball, and baseball

more than doubled. In 1966, 40 percent of students were Baptists; in fall 1995, Baptist representation had dropped to 16 percent.

High-profile student leaders for the year were Evan Peverley, Student Government President; Lori Shores, Editor of *The Howler*; and Brian Uzwiak, Editor-in-Chief of the *Old Gold and Black*. Sophomore Joy Vermillion was elected to a one-year term as a Student Trustee.

One hundred first-year students came to campus a week early to participate in a pilot ThinkPad program administered by Rhoda Channing (Library). Each had already purchased an IBM ThinkPad, and the program continued throughout the academic year. In the spring, fifteen faculty launched a pilot program focusing on first-year seminars with students in Collins Residence Hall.

On August 1, President Hearn wrote a two-page memo to incoming students and their families on the subject of alcohol abuse. "New measures to combat student alcohol abuse, including stiffer penalties and parental notification," were implemented in fall 1995, designed to curb binge drinking. "The new measures include parental notification and mandatory private treatment at the student's expense for first-time violations of the student conduct code involving intoxication or underage possession or consumption. A second such offense could result in suspension or expulsion." In a spring 1995 survey, 72 percent of students said they had drunk alcohol at least once in the previous thirty days, and 44 percent said they had "binged" during the previous two weeks. A shocking 36 percent admitted to some form of public misconduct as a result of binge drinking or using illegal drugs, including fighting, driving while intoxicated, and worse. Another 30 percent reported a serious personal problem, such as considering or attempting suicide, sustaining physical injury, or performing poorly on a test or project. The new measures were clearly needed.

A new, multifunctional ID card that consolidated the meal plan card, the photo ID card, and the key card that most students carried was issued in August to incoming and returning students. The new cards had new ID numbers instead of the student's social security number.

About sixty students lived in theme houses in 1995–1996. Theme houses were established in the early 1980s, according to Connie Carson, Director of the Office of Residence Life and Housing, when language students banded together to live in a house on Polo Road. Six new houses were the Nia House, which served black women who agreed to design programming to address the cultural and academic needs of all black students, the Wake Radio House, the German House, the Health and Wellness House, the Wellness and Nutrition House, and the Fine Arts House.

Two reading days were added to the beginning of the spring semester exam schedule to keep both semesters the same length. Reading days had been scheduled before, but not two days before the start of exams. The most frequently checked-out books at Z. Smith Reynolds Library in 1995–1996 were *The Wall* by Jean-Paul Sartre; Shakespeare plays; *The Stranger* and *The Fall* by Albert Camus; and *I Know Why the Caged Bird Sings* by Maya Angelou. Of the 1,756 videos available to students, faculty, and staff, the five most popular were *Scent of a Woman, Four Weddings and a Funeral, Reservoir Dogs, Sleepless in Seattle,* and *Speed*. The four top-selling items at the campus bookstore were 1996 ACC Championship T-shirts, Demon Deacon screensavers, "Wait's Dream" postcards, and foam mattress pads.

The Student Union brought comedy to campus, including the Fettucini Brothers, Pat McCurdy, and Frank King. It also sponsored a game of Assassin during mid-April. Fifty-eight students started the game with concealed weapons (water guns). At the end of the week, only five were "alive." It was hose or be hosed.

In its seventh year, Project Pumpkin moved from the lower to the upper quad. At a Halloween concert, which would become a Wake Forest tradition, each section of the University orchestra entered Brendle Recital Hall in coordinated costumes at 11:45 p.m. When the chimes rang at midnight, the musicians struck up the Bach Toccata and Fugue in D Minor while conductor David Hagy, in a nebulous black costume, morphed into various characters, such as Darth Vader. With the help of other faculty, staff, and students who were not in the orchestra, Hagy had planned a scenario to take place in their midst, surprising them while they played. These scenarios included a variety of characters who might not be related, such as Sherman and Peabody going through the "wayback machine" and encountering the Flintstones, the Jetsons, and the Wizard of Oz. Meanwhile, other students planned "tricks" that the participants in the scenario knew nothing about, interrupting the process of the concert. Each trick had to eventually bring the music back to the point where the trick was interpolated, so the concert could continue. At 1:00 a.m. almost all the characters were dead, and the conductor either triumphed or was killed.

More quietly, the annual Christmas Lovefeast in Wait Chapel marked its thirtieth anniversary. It was a Moravian tradition, with candles, sweet buns, coffee, and hymns. The event was one of the most well-attended traditions on the campus.

David Hagy

Moravian Lovefeast crowd holds candles and sings "Joy to the World" at the end of the evening's service

In other actions, Wake Forest announced plans to celebrate theme years for the foreseeable future. The Year of the Arts was chosen for 1996–1997. Sandra Boyette (Public Affairs) and Jim Dodding (Theatre) were co-chairs.

The varsity debate squad finished the 1995–1996 season ranked first in the nation for the second year in a row. Daveed Gartenstein-Ross and Chris Cooper won the American Debate Association (ADA) Varsity Championship, and first-year students Nicole Runyan and Kristin Langwell defeated a team from the University of Michigan to win the Novice Nationals Tournament. It was the first time Wake Forest had won the ADA national varsity or novice tournaments, even though teams had made the semi-finals, Coach Ross Smith said. The path to the finals was especially sweet for the young women, who defeated a current boyfriend and three ex-boyfriends on teams along the way. Later in the year, the fiftieth annual National Debate Tournament was held on campus,

George McGovern

with a keynote address delivered by former U.S. Senator and presidential candidate George McGovern.

A team of Babcock MBA students claimed second place and the $1,000 prize in the 1996 KPMG Peat Marwick/George Washington University MBA Case Competition. Members were Bethany Beatty of Tallahassee, Florida; Kristen Helms of Media, Pennsylvania; Dave Lee of Parkersburg, West Virginia; and Nick McKoy of Nyack, New York.

Andrew Frey ('97), Joseph Gagnon ('99), and Hunter Tart ('96) were one of 393 teams representing 235 colleges and universities in nine countries that participated in February's Consortium for Mathematics and its Applications (COMAP) Mathematical Contest in Modeling. They were singled out as one of four teams proposing an outstanding solution to the problem of detecting a silent submarine. Their faculty advisers were Edward F. Allen and Stephen B. Robinson, both Assistant Professors in the Mathematics and Computer Science Department.

WAKE TV started taping and broadcasting the bi-monthly meetings of Student Government legislation. At least one member of the group stated that he planned to dress better for meetings.

The Student was renamed *Three to Four Ounces* after novelist Don DeLillo's estimate of the weight of the human soul, and it continued to publish poetry, prose, art, and photography. An independently funded, student-run editorial magazine, *The Wake Forest Review*, debuted in March. Its co-editors, Geoffrey Michael and Jennifer Loughrey, said it was designed to spark debate about national and student concerns, and articles in the first issue addressed social security, campus crime, and grade inflation.

WILD (Winston-Salem into the Lives of Deacons) sent ninety students to seventeen community sites to do volunteer work on a Saturday in late April. They participated in planting flowers and trees and other beautification and library projects. WILD was sponsored by the Volunteer Service Corps. In another area, a Japanese Culture Society formed to heighten campus awareness of Japanese culture.

Beth Stroupe, a junior, received three national awards for chemistry research. One was for her project in the laboratory of Bruce King (Chemistry) on the potential pharmaceutical use of nitrosothiols as a nitric oxide delivery system to improve muscle contraction, immune response, and memory. The second was the 1996 Undergraduate Award for Excellence in Chemistry from Iota Sigma Pi, a national honor society for women in chemistry. She also received one of only six travel awards from the Organic Section of the American Chemical Society granted nationwide. In addition to her outstanding achievements in chemistry,

The Student changed its name to *Three to Four Ounces*

Will Garin created a set of chain-link figures called "Link"

Stroupe was a flutist in the University's wind ensemble and a Presidential Scholar in the Arts.

Sam O. Kerlin received a Beinecke Scholarship for 1996. It provided over $30,000 for graduate studies in the arts, humanities, and social sciences.

Will Garin, a senior, sculptured three figures out of 1,200 pounds of steel chain. The work, "Link," was the first student sculpture the University bought for its art collection. It was displayed on a grassy slope between Tribble Hall and the Benson University Center.

In Greek Life, the Alpha Delta Pi sorority disbanded. The few remaining members were seniors and simply wanted to enjoy their year and not have to worry about rush and other projects. The Delta Nu chapter of Sigma Chi was presented the Legion of Honor Award by the Sigma Chi Foundation in recognition of its scholarship program. The Alpha Upsilon Delta chapter of Chi Psi received the John Lister Goodbody Trophy from the Chi Psi Educational Trust for academic achievement.

In sad news, a memorial service was held in Davis Chapel for rising senior Paul S. Mory IV, who died on March 29 of complications resulting from a car accident in Winston-Salem in August.

Facilities, Finances, and Alumni

Facilities

The Perritt Flag Plaza was dedicated in a ceremony on April 25. Located on the Benson University Center traffic circle, the plaza features walkways, landscaping, a flagpole, and a memorial plaque. It was funded by H. Franklin Perritt Jr. and his wife, Suzanne, of Jacksonville, Florida, in honor of their son, H. Franklin III, who died in 1988, his first year at Wake Forest.

Renovations totaling $12 million were made to the campus over the summer of 1995, $4 million of which went to Taylor, Davis, and Efird residence halls for data wiring, key-access systems, new ceilings and air conditioning, and improved ventilation and lighting systems in the bathrooms. The second most costly renovation, totaling $3 million, was to the Athletic Center. Indoor tennis courts were removed to add a second floor for coaching staff office space. New lockers and weight rooms were added as well. New cooking equipment was added to the Pit, and space was remodeled to make way for a Kentucky Fried Chicken franchise. Other projects included Groves Stadium, two chemistry labs in Salem Hall, wiring to convert DeTamble Auditorium to a multimedia classroom, and the construction of lounge space in several residence halls. Twenty-five wireless connectors to the campus network were installed, and ThinkPads with special wireless adapters were able to connect to the network and to each other at any access point.

In October, the Trustees approved a plan to build a 3,000-square-foot coffeehouse/pub on campus by fall 1997. The result would be the student-run Coffee Grounds in the lobby of Taylor Residence Hall. In the academic arena, Psychology Chair Deborah L. Best ('70, MA '72) reported another emerging space problem: although the department had more than 250 majors, its space in Winston Hall had not changed since 1962, and some classes had to be held in Wingate Hall.

The bookstore and Deacon Shop expanded, and a new Village Deacon Shop was created in Reynolda Village, offering the community an opportunity to buy Wake Forest merchandise without having to find parking on campus. A mobile Deacon Shop, sporting the head of the Demon Deacon mascot on the front of the trailer, made appearances at athletic events. The bookstore added computers and software merchandise to its inventory, in addition to renting videos and books on tape. It also started a student book club whereby members would receive a 10 percent discount on the eleventh book they purchased, excluding textbooks and books by University professors.

More than 8,500 daffodil, crocus, and tulip bulbs were planted in fall 1995 on the Reynolda Campus, at Reynolda Village, and along the pathway linking the two; in spring 1996, the campus boasted over 100,000 blooms. Using landscape architect Thomas Sears's original 1913 plans for Reynolda Gardens, the University replaced old plants and trees, restored greenhouses and other structures, and repaired walks and walls. A major ice storm on February 2–3, however, downed more than 200 trees on campus and in outlying wooded areas. The power was out for over twenty-four hours, and President Hearn described it as "the blackout of 1996."

Finances

On September 14, 1995, President Hearn sent a memo to the Board of Trustees announcing that Wake Forest's endowment had passed the $500 million mark. Later in the year, the Board of Trustees approved a total operating budget of $453 million for fiscal year 1996 (the 1996–1997 academic year), which included $304.4 million for the Hawthorne campus and $148.6 million for the Reynolda Campus. The Hawthorne campus budget was 7.7 percent higher than the previous year's, while the Reynolda Campus budget rose by 12.7 percent. The total budget increase was 9.3 percent. The Trustees set tuition for 1996–1997 at $18,500 for new students and $15,500 for returning students.

President Hearn announced on March 30 that the University would assume financial responsibility for structural maintenance of the Calvin Jones House on the old campus during a program in Binkley Chapel at the Old Campus Reunion. Susan Brinkley, President of the Wake Forest Birthplace Society, wrote to thank Hearn for his support and for putting a new roof on the birthplace.

In other financial developments, Arthur Andersen & Company pledged $150,000 to the Calloway School to give students access to cutting-edge research technology in accounting. The Davis family of Winston-Salem, including Life Trustees Egbert L. Davis Jr. ('33), Thomas H. Davis (LLD '84), and their sister Pauline Davis Perry, made a $1 million challenge grant in memory of their mother, Annie Pearl Shore Davis, in January. The family would give $1, up to a total of $1 million, for every $2 raised by the University in support of the Divinity School.

Durham resident Roy O. Rodwell Jr. and his daughters Nancy ('92) and Rebecca Rodwell pledged $250,000 to endow the Roy O. Rodwell Sr. ('10) Scholarship Fund. The scholarship gave preference to undergraduate students from thirty-seven designated counties in eastern North Carolina. Elton Manning ('37) of Raleigh established a $2 million scholarship fund, and Porter B. Byrum committed money from his unitrust to the Byrum Law Scholarships and to the Athletics Department. Altogether, gifts to the Reynolda Campus exceeded $25 million in 1995–1996.

Alumni

Bynum Shaw wrote President Hearn on April 22 that 1996 was the fiftieth anniversary of the relationship between Wake Forest and the Z. Smith Reynolds Foundation. It began with the Foundation's offer of annual financial support to help the college relocate to Winston-Salem.

In other alumni news, Stephanie Neill ('95) became the first winner of the Dinah Shore Award for college women's golf. The award required an average round of 77 or better, play in at least half of the school's matches, a 3.2 grade-point average, and demonstrated ability in leadership and community service. After receiving the honor, Neill was featured on the front page of *USA Today*. She was also selected as an All-American for the fourth time and made the NCAA Women's All-Scholar Academic Team.

Summing Up the Year

Unbeknownst to most, including the top administrators who were involved, the 1995–1996 academic year was pivotal, marking innovation and turnover. The college had a new Dean, Paul Escott, and a new Dean-Designate for the Divinity School, Bill Leonard, who would put together a new professional school and integrate it into the fabric of the University. The Plan for the Class of 2000 was in its infancy, with ten first-year seminars offered in the spring, less than a year after the Trustees approved the University's pioneering launch into the world of computer technology. By the next fall, student, professor, and administrator relationships would never be quite the same again because of the new technology.

At the same time as the Plan for the Class of 2000 was beginning, the Trustees approved gates and gatehouses to keep the campus safer. The move was controversial and drew protests by students, but incidents of violence, especially attacks by outsiders on students, made it a wise and necessary decision.

Success was evident everywhere, but most of all in the men's basketball win over Georgia Tech. The ACC Championship and participation in the NCAA tournament gave Wake Forest pride and confidence. Performances by Andy Bloom in the shot put and discus and by Trina Bindel in the women's heptathlon made the year even brighter, and Rusty LaRue, the quintessential student-athlete, performed remarkably on the field, the court, and the classroom. Matching athletic achievement was the construction of Bridger Field House and Spry Stadium.

In a sad change, seventy-six-year-old James Ralph Scales died on March 12 at North Carolina Baptist Hospital. A memorial service was held on March 18 at 2 p.m. in Wait Chapel. He served as President of Wake Forest from 1967–1983. President Hearn wrote an editorial in praise of his predecessor in the March 21 edition of the *Old Gold and Black*, "Scales Improved University."

A total of 1,241 undergraduate and graduate students received their diplomas during commencement ceremonies on the third weekend of May. They were leaving a University that was changing rapidly and entering a world that was doing the same. Their achievements, as a group, were strong. What they were probably most unprepared for was recognizing their alma mater, especially at the college level, at later reunions of their classes.

CHAPTER FOURTEEN
1996–1997

The Plan, the Year of the Arts, Prestige, Tragedy, and the Gates

In talking about the tragedy of student and other deaths during the year: "It has been a year of lamentation. What did we learn that we must recall even on this day when the door of hope is open wide? These truths, often shielded from the young, are at all times for all people. Life is infinitely precious, and our grasp on it is but frail. Death is ever present and powerful. Love is strong, and the grief we saw and felt is testimony to the intensity of the love lost. Life does not mete out justice according to merit. Life's blessings are not given or gotten according to our just desserts.

Thomas K. Hearn Jr., May 19, 1997;
Charge to the Graduates, Wake Forest University Commencement

The Plan for the Class of 2000 began implementation in 1996–1997 with the first class that would graduate under it. It was a huge, multidimensional undertaking, but the most publicized part was the technology initiative. All first-year students were given an IBM ThinkPad 365XD laptop computer, and the infrastructure to support computer-aided education was in place.

In addition, first-year seminars (FYS) were now basic requirements for graduation. The sixty-three classes covering fifty-eight topics, with about fifteen students in each, were scheduled for the fall and spring. President Hearn and Sam Gladding (President's Office) co-taught Leadership in American Life, designed to provide insights into practical leadership and to instill the ideal of ethical leadership. President Hearn wanted to demonstrate his personal interest in first-year seminars and instructional technology: "What better way than to teach the former using the latter?" he said, when asked why he was co-teaching the course. Provost David G. Brown taught The Economist's Way of Thinking completely without paper, relying on LotusNotes groupware for class discussions and to review individual and team student writings.

Other provisions of the plan included adding more faculty positions, increasing financial aid, creating new opportunities for students to assist in faculty research, and continuing to upgrade facilities, with the overall goal of reinforcing Wake Forest's long commitment to individualized instruction, small classes, and mentoring by senior faculty. A more community-oriented element was the development each year of a series of events, including a major symposium, around a common theme as a focus of campus intellectual and social life. The first theme year, the Year of the Arts, was dedicated to the memory of the late James Ralph Scales, Wake Forest President from 1967–1983, and many of the major events took place in the Scales Fine Arts Center. The primary organizer was Jim Dodding (Theatre). The Coca-Cola Foundation underwrote the year and contributed $25,000 to support the year's activities.

Opera legend Beverly Sills, chair of the board of Lincoln Center for the Performing Arts, was the Opening Convocation speaker on September 24. Her address, "The State of the Arts," expressed optimism that the arts would prevail as long as individuals were concerned about them. Four days later, the Winston-Salem Piedmont Triad Symphony premiered *Since Dawn*, a tone poem for narrator, chorus, and orchestra by Wake Forest composer-in-residence Dan Locklair. Reynolds Professor of American Studies Maya Angelou narrated her 1992 presidential inauguration poem.

James Earl Jones

On February 25, critically acclaimed actor James Earl Jones, the voice of King Mufasa and Darth Vader, was the Founders' Day Convocation speaker. His 1993 autobiography, *James Earl Jones: Voices and Silences*, was co-authored by Penelope Niven (MA '62).

In musical celebrations, Marilyn Keiser, a world-renowned organist from Indiana University, performed on October 11 to mark the fortieth anniversary of Wait Chapel's organ. On November 20, Mussorgsky's suite *Pictures at an Exhibition* highlighted a fall concert by the University Orchestra in Brendle Recital Hall. Directed by David Hagy, the orchestra also performed Haydn's *Symphony No. 100*. Wake Forest hosted "Joy's Legacy: Beethoven's *Ninth Symphony*," a March 1–2 festival that included a performance of the symphony, a scholarly symposium, and faculty/student recital. Organizer David Levy (Music) had recently published *Beethoven: The Ninth Symphony*. Under Levy's direction the Wake

Beverly Sills

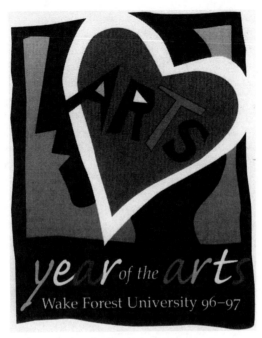

Year of the Arts logo

Forest Orchestra joined with the Winston-Salem Symphony, the Wake Forest Concerto Choir, and Winston-Salem Chorale to perform Beethoven's Ninth Symphony.

A special art exhibit, "Works from Alumni Collections: Color Function Painting and William Hogarth Prints," was shown in the University Fine Arts Gallery from August through October. In mid-November, twenty-five fourth-graders from Sherwood Forest Elementary School took part in a printmaking workshop led by David Faber (Art). Each student made a one-of-a-kind multicolored monotype print.

The University was ranked 25th among "America's Best Colleges" for 1997 by *U.S. News & World Report*, its highest ranking in this national annual college guide. Wake Forest received high marks for student selectivity, student retention rates, and financial resources. Its small classes and high graduation rates were also recognized. *Money* magazine placed Wake Forest among its one hundred best college buys.

The debate team received more accolades, winning first place at the 51st National Debate Tournament (team of Brian Prestes and Daveed Gartenstein-Ross), defeating a team from the University of Georgia. The debate team had previously come in third in 1993 (team of Mark Grant and Rick Fledderman); third in 1994 (team of Marcia Tiersky and Adrienne Brovero); and third in 1995 (team of John Hughes and Adrienne Brovero).

Tragedy struck during the year with the untimely deaths of four students. Maia Witzl of Arlington, Texas, and Julie Hansen of Rockville, Maryland, both nineteen years old and Chi Omega sisters, were killed by a drunken driver, Thomas Richard Jones, on September 4. Jones was not only drunk at the time but had a series of traffic offenses, including driving while impaired. The accident occurred a few blocks from the University as the women were returning from an off-campus party. President Hearn immediately wrote Governor Jim Hunt about this matter and stated that Wake Forest would do all in its power to help get drunken drivers off the road.

Within a week of the accident, about twenty students representing major campus organizations formed Student Action for Eliminating Reckless Drivers, or Safe Rds. They found allies in the Office of Crime Control and Public Safety in Raleigh, and by February the group had organized a Governor's Summit on campus to discuss possible changes to driving-while-impaired laws. Governor Jim Hunt, Lieutenant Governor Dennis Wicker (JD '78), and Secretary for Public Safety Richard Moore spoke to students. Safe Rds. and members of Chi Omega spent the rest of the semester drumming up support, and in April 1997, just before final exams, about 150 students rode buses to the state capital to participate in the Rally in Raleigh, knocking on doors in the state legislature building. They also held a press conference at which President Hearn and the Chancellors of the University of North Carolina at Chapel Hill and North Carolina State University spoke.

In August, less than a year after the accident, Governor Hunt signed into law the bill for which students had lobbied. Repeat offenders could lose their cars, spend more time in jail, and be forced to enroll in a treatment program. Licenses would be revoked for thirty days instead of ten for those charged with driving while impaired, and testimony about the results of roadside sobriety tests or the odor of alcohol would be allowed as evidence that a driver under age twenty-one had been drinking.

No less tragic were the deaths of Matthew Alexander and Graham Gould. Alexander, a rising senior from Florence, South Carolina, was attending Wake Forest on an ROTC scholarship and was on his way to study in Dijon, France, when he and 230 other passengers were killed in the crash of TWA flight 800 over the Long Island

Wake Forest students, left to right, Elizabeth Laney, Laura Acton, Fiona Penney, and Jennifer Steinberg meet in Raleigh with Richard Moore ('82, JD '86), state secretary of crime control and public safety

Sound on July 17. On July 22, ROTC officials laid a wreath at the Perritt Flag Plaza outside Benson University Center in his honor, and about twenty Wake Forest students joined over four hundred friends and relatives at the Florence Baptist Temple on July 26 for his funeral. A campus memorial service was held on September 12, and a five-kilometer race in his honor followed in April, the proceeds of which helped furnish a new classroom named for him. Gould, a sophomore from Sanford, North Carolina, was killed in a car wreck in his hometown just days before the start of the school year.

Gates and gatehouses at the University Parkway and Reynolda Road entrances to Wake Forest greeted new and returning students for the fall semester of 1996. They became operational from 10 p.m. to 6 a.m. on September 9. The University changed its initial plans to build a gatehouse at the Polo

New gatehouses at the entrances of the University made the campus safer

Road entrance because underground utility lines would have caused construction problems. Instead, a wrought-iron gate was constructed to block the Polo Road entrance during the hours when the gatehouses were operating. Altogether, the gates cost between $370,000 and $385,000. Built during the summer, they were part of a security enhancement plan the University announced in March 1996. The plan also called for hiring more police officers and installing additional lights across campus. It was prompted by a number of incidents in recent years, including the 1995 abduction and robbery of two students who were quickly released unharmed. To heighten protection, Wake Forest police issued car decals and tags to members of the University community. If cars did not have a decal or tag they were stopped, and drivers were asked their name and destination. Wake Forest police could then issue them a short-term visitor pass, which expired within twenty-four hours or a designated time frame, or turn them away.

Academics

For the first and last time, a ceremony on December 8 in Brendle Recital Hall recognized fall semester graduates. The ceremony included remarks by Provost Brown and special music by senior Margaret Elizabeth Stroupe and University accompanist Ann Listokin. Dean Paul Escott invited the graduates to attend the May 19 commencement as well.

Associate Dean of the College Claudia Thomas (English) led a committee in the first complete review of the undergraduate curriculum since the 1970s. The process was spurred by the implementation of first-year seminars in the Plan for the Class of 2000. Additional members included Stewart Carter (Music), Rhoda Channing

Claudia Thomas

(Z. Smith Reynolds Library), Natalie Holzwarth (Physics), Paul Juras (Business and Accountancy), Paige Laughlin (Art), Michael Lawler (Economics), Barry Maine (English), Gloria Muday (Biology), Anthony Parent (History), Kurt Shaw (Russian), David Weaver (Anthropology), and Ralph Wood (Religion). Sophomores Ashley Edmonson and Jerome Butler also served.

Apart from this review, the Anthropology Department graduate program was suspended because of gender problems, faculty relations and productivity, and portions of its curriculum. Associate Dean Toby Hale became Acting Chair for 1996–1997 after David Weaver resigned in the spring of 1996. Problems came to light during an annual review that started in September 1995, including the high attrition rate among graduate students, especially women. The Museum of Anthropology was shifted to the permanent supervision of the Dean's Office, and in summer 1997 Carole Browne (Biology) was appointed liaison to the Dean to guide the department in its transitional year, 1997–1998.

Ralph Wood (Easley Professor of Religion) resigned from the University after twenty-six years to take a faculty position at Samford University in Birmingham, Alabama. He was a popular teacher and a well-respected, published scholar whose specialty was theology and literature.

In other news, College faculty voted in favor of implementing a plus/minus system for grades at its April 1997 meeting. The new method would start in fall 1998 and affect current freshmen and sophomores. Two new minors, environmental studies and American ethnic studies, were available to students for the first time. The environmental studies program was coordinated by John Litcher (Education), and American ethnic studies by Earl Smith (Sociology).

On February 5, the NBC Nightly News with Tom Brokaw featured a story on the grocery chain Food Lion. It was taped at the School of Law and featured comments by Law Professor David Logan. On February 12, a special edition of ABC's Nightline, anchored by Ted Koppel, focused on investigative reporting and newsgathering methods and was broadcast live from Wait Chapel. Members of the Wake Forest community participated in the town-hall format. In a recent court case, Food Lion had been awarded $5.5 million in damages by ABC for fraudulent reporting.

Wake Forest University Press, the major publisher of Irish poetry in North America, hosted a "coming of age" party on March 18 to celebrate its twenty-first anniversary. Casa Artom celebrated twenty-five years of welcoming students to Venice for study. Z. Smith Reynolds Library won the Information Management Award of the North Carolina Chapter of the Special Libraries Association (NC/SLA). Library Director Rhoda K. Channing accepted the award for its "support of libraries and information science and the information needs of its community."

Many faculty were recognized for their achievements during the academic year. Jack Rejeski (Health and Exercise Science) was among the experts who contributed to the newly released Surgeon General's report on physical fitness and health. The report stressed that such activities as walking and gardening helped to prevent disease and to improve mental health. In his work for the report, Rejeski focused on the link between exercise and quality of life.

Leah McCoy (Education) and Beth Boyd (Academic Computing Specialist) developed "telementoring" workshops to connect students from Paisley Math and Science Academy with prominent women scientists, engineers, mathematicians, and computer scientists. The Internet, primarily e-mail, was used to encourage seventh- and eighth-grade girls to consider careers in math and science. The workshops were made possible by a grant from the North Carolina Association for Educational Communications and Technology.

In other faculty news, Charles Longino Jr. (Sociology) was named a master teacher by the Association for Gerontology in Higher Education. Jennifer Burg (Mathematics and Computer Science) became the first Director of the Computer-Enhanced Learning Initiative (CELI) to help faculty find innovative and effective ways to use computer technology in teaching. Randy Rogan (Communication), an expert in hostage negotiations, was consulted by Winston-Salem law enforcement when a man took a hostage at a day-care center. Gary Shoesmith (Babcock Graduate School of Management), director of the Center for Economic Studies, published articles in the school's periodical *Quarterly Review* that gained notice in academic circles.

In addition, retired Mathematics Professor Ivey Gentry received the University's highest honor, the Medallion of Merit, while J. Kline Harrison (Calloway School) received the Omicron Delta Kappa Award for Contributions to Student Life, and Gloria Muday (Biology) was given the Award for Excellence in Research. Helga Welsh (Political Science) received the Excellence in Teaching Award.

David Anderson (Biology), in research supported by the National Science Foundation, found a curious irony in the lives of masked boobies, a seabird on Isla Espanola, the most southeastern island in the Galapagos. If the first egg hatches, the parents encourage the killing of the second offspring because to thrive, they could only raise one chick. Unlike many birds, the masked boobies have a poor hatching rate and lay two eggs in the hopes one will survive.

Christy Buchanan (Psychology) published a book with colleagues at Stanford, *Adolescents after Divorce*. It studied 365 post-divorce families to discover what factors predict better or worse adjustment for children following a divorce.

Christy Buchanan

Music by Dan Locklair, composer-in-residence, "Ere long we shall see. . . ," premiered at the 1996 Centennial Convention of the American Guild of Organists (AGO) in New York City on July 9. Archie (A. R.) Ammons ('49), poet-in-residence for the spring semester and a National Book Award winner, taught an advanced poetry workshop for undergraduates and gave several readings.

Beginning July 1, four professors with long and distinguished records of teaching and scholarship became Wake Forest Professors, endowed positions supported by a gift from the Z. Smith Reynolds Foundation: John Baxley (Mathematics), Deborah Best (Psychology), Willie Pearson Jr. (Sociology), and W. Jack Rejeski Jr. (Health and Exercise Science). Michael J. Hyde was named University Distinguished Chair in Communication Ethics and Professor of Communication. Earl Smith, who had been Dean of Social Sciences at Pacific Lutheran University, was named Rubin Professor of American Ethnic Studies.

At the Calloway School of Business and Accountancy, Professor Umit Akinc was appointed Thomas H. Davis Chair in October in recognition of his academic contributions to the field. In November, Associate Professor J. Kline Harrison was awarded the Benson-Pruitt Professorship for a three-year term in recognition of his outstanding scholarly contributions linking business education with the latest practices and controversies, and Assistant Professor G. Page West III was awarded the 1996–1997 T. B. Rose Fellowship in Business on the basis of his innovative teaching—for example, his in-class use of the Business Strategy Game. Dale R. Martin, coordinator of the accounting program, was awarded the Price Waterhouse Professorship for Academic Excellence.

Susan Borwick (Music) became Director of the Women's Studies Program, succeeding Mary DeShazer (English) in January 1997. DeShazer founded the program and had served as its Director for ten years.

John Pickel, an accomplished digital artist and photographer, joined the Department of Art.

Administration and Staff

Bill Joyner, Vice President for University Relations for twenty-seven years, took early retirement in September. During his tenure, Wake Forest raised more than $475 million in charitable contributions. Gifts to the Reynolda Campus schools grew from $3.4 million in 1970 to a record $25 million in 1995–1996. In addition, alumni giving increased from 17 percent to 45 percent, one of the highest figures for any private university in the country. Joyner graduated from Wake Forest in 1966, returned as Director of Alumni Affairs in 1969, was named Vice President for Development in

1977, and Vice President for University Relations in 1984. Wake Forest won numerous honors for fundraising under him. His replacement was Sandra C. Boyette, Vice President for Public Affairs since 1988. She had been Interim Vice President for University Relations but was appointed permanently on May 8, 1997. In her new capacity, she directed University fundraising, alumni relations, publications, special events, and media relations.

Bill Joyner

In addition to Joyner, Gary E. Costley, Dean of the Babcock Graduate School of Management, resigned to become Chair, President, and CEO of the Minnesota-based Multifoods Corporation in March 1997. Kay Doenges Lord ('64), Assistant Vice President and Director of Alumni Activities, also resigned after twelve years in the alumni office on April 23. Minta Aycock McNally ('74), Director of the Office of University Relations, was named to succeed her.

Lu Leake, Associate Vice President of Administration and Planning, retired in the summer of 1997 after thirty-three years of service in a variety of roles, including Dean of Women and Assistant Vice President for Planning. Before departing, she received the first Woman of the Year Award from the Friends of Women's Studies for her service as Dean of Women and her work as Chair of the Commission on the Status of Women. She was named an honorary alumna, and the foyer outside of the Magnolia Room in Reynolda Hall was named for her.

Jack E. Wilkerson Jr. was appointed Acting Dean of the Calloway School of Business and Accountancy in August 1996 following the resignation of Dana Johnson, and he became permanent Dean on July 1, 1997. His position was announced at a news conference at the end of May. Wilkerson joined Wake Forest in 1989 and coordinated the accounting program, chaired a committee that developed a five-year program for undergraduates to earn a master's degree in accounting, and chaired the University's Student Life Committee. Johnson, who served as Dean from 1992 until summer 1996, left Wake Forest to take a similar position at the University of Delaware.

Lu Leake in the foyer in Reynolda Hall named for her

Jack Wilkerson

At the Babcock Graduate School of Management, Charlie Moyer, who joined the faculty in 1988 as the Integon Chair of Finance, was named interim Dean following Gary Costley's departure, and on March 20, President Hearn announced Moyer's full appointment. At the time, the school had 657 students and 3,200 alumni. It offered full-time, evening, and executive MBA programs in Winston-Salem and an MBA program in Charlotte, as well as joint degree programs with the School of Law and the Bowman Gray School of Medicine.

At the School of Medicine, Jim Thompson became Vice President and Dean, and Richard Dean became interim Vice President for Health Affairs in June 1997.

On the Reynolda Campus, Jeryl Prescott (English) was appointed to a temporary part-time position as an Associate Dean of the College when Patricia Johansson decided to reduce her hours as she approached retirement. Prescott became a full-time Associate Dean in fall 1997.

In the Office of Information Systems, Jay L. Dominick became Assistant Vice President and Chief Information Officer; E. O'Neal Robinson was named Director; and Anne Yandell was named Assistant Director for Projects.

Linda Ward became station manager at WFDD in April, replacing Cleve Callison, who left to become station manager of WMUB at Miami University of Ohio. Joshua Else and Melissa N. Combes joined the University Relations staff.

Maureen Carpenter (MBA '95) succeeded Thomas Gilsenan as University Controller in May. The former controller for Champion Products promptly renamed the office Financial and Accounting Services and reorganized it into three areas: 1) financial services (accounts payable, accounts receivable, and payroll); 2) financial reporting and budgeting (including general accounting); and 3) grant and endowment accounting (encompassing cash management and insurance).

In August 1996, the Commission on the Status of Women recommended more training for supervisors to increase the number of women in top administrative posts; hiring more women in tenure-track positions; conducting a definitive study of day-care needs and costs; fostering a climate in and out of the classroom that would lead to more equitable intellectual and social conditions for women students; appointing a committee to monitor the implementation of these recommendations; reallocating funds as necessary to implement them; and securing the active support of the President, provost, Vice Presidents, and Deans to improve conditions for female faculty, staff, and students. In June 1997, the commission issued a final report based on sixteen months of research and interviews with about three hundred students, faculty, staff, and administrators. It included most of the recommendations of the August 1996 document.

The administration responded in August of 1997, and Claudia Thomas chaired a ten-member oversight committee that drafted detailed protocols to address:

1. sexual assault (better education and reporting procedures);
2. campus safety (keycard access to classroom buildings);
3. insufficient numbers and status of women on the faculty (hiring and promoting more women);
4. sexism and "chilly" climate (more education for employees on sexism and sexual harassment);
5. salary inequity (monitor faculty salaries, explore a merit-based salary policy);
6. inflexible tenure clock (resetting the tenure clock from five to eight years);
7. lack of a child-care facility; and
8. paid maternity leave.

With regard to all employees, the University held its first Employee Recognition Day in April.

The Office of Public Affairs won twelve awards in the 1996 District III communications competition of the Council for the Advancement and Support of Education (CASE), the most by any college or university among the nine participating southeastern states. Especially noteworthy were awards for excellence in media placements, periodicals, and publications to promote the Year of the Arts and a special merit award for the University's homepage on the Internet. In the spring, the office won six medals in the national Circle of Excellence program.

Paul Brown, news director at WFDD, received a first-place award for radio enterprise reporting from the Associated Press for the story "R. J. Reynolds Tobacco Workers," which aired on National Public Radio (NPR) "Morning Edition" and on member station WFDD. Reported and produced by Brown, the story profiled tobacco workers and the stresses under which they lived as the tobacco industry experienced increased governmental scrutiny and attacks.

Athletics

Charlene Curtis, formerly an assistant coach at the University of Connecticut, was named Head Women's Basketball Coach in June 1997. She was Wake Forest's first African American female coach and came with outstanding credentials. She replaced Karen Freeman, who resigned to join the WNBA's Charlotte Sting as an assistant coach.

Jeff Zinn replaced Ian Crookenden as Men's Tennis Coach, and Chris Turner resigned as Women's Soccer Coach after three years with a record of 31–26–3. He was replaced by Tony da Luz, who had successfully coached the women's soccer team at the University of San Diego. Stan Cotton became the new "Voice of the Deacs," after Mac McDonald resigned to take a similar job at the University of Virginia.

The football team did not do well but won two more games than in the previous season for a record of 3–8. The highlight of the season came

Stan Cotton

early, when the Deacons started out 2–0, beat Northwestern University, and were described by *Sports Illustrated* the week afterward as an up-and-coming team.

In the summer of 1996, the Italian Olympic teams trained at Wake Forest prior to the competitions in Atlanta. The campus was chosen for its excellent athletic venues and because the heat and humidity in Winston-Salem were similar to Atlanta's.

Volleyball became Wake Forest's eighteenth varsity sport. The University now had nine men's and nine women's athletic teams competing in the ACC.

More than 900 students packed Brendle Recital Hall in early October to sign up for one of the 700 spots available to Screamin' Demons at basketball games. The turnout surprised everyone but pleased Head Basketball Coach Dave Odom. In response, the Athletics Department increased the seating to 750 but stringently enforced the rules: Screamin' Demons could not miss more than one game in the fall semester or two games in the spring semester.

The men's basketball team had a 24–7 record, 11–5 in the ACC. Duke defeated Wake Forest 73–68 on February 5 for the first time since 1993. The team was again invited to the NCAA Tournament but lost in the second round. Center Tim Duncan, forward and three-year starter Ricky Peral, and forward and two-year starter Sean Allen all graduated. Duncan's jersey was retired at the last regular game of the season in Joel Coliseum, where the first and second rounds of the NCAA 1997 Division I Men's Basketball Championship were played on March 13 and 15.

Campus Stadium, home of the field hockey and track and field teams, was named for Touchdown 2000 donor Jeffrey W. Kentner ('78), a real estate developer in Greensboro. The stadium was completed in 1990 at a cost of $3.5 million and had seating for nearly 4,000 spectators. W. Dennie Spry Soccer Stadium, on the edge of campus near Polo Road, opened on September 22. It had seating for 3,000 and featured a fully lit playing field and two practice fields. The University began charging for soccer and volleyball matches, $4 for adults and $2 for students, except for Wake

Screamin' Demons

Kentner Stadium

Forest students. Patrons could also buy an All-Sports Card, which was good for soccer, volleyball, women's basketball, and baseball.

In a bit of trivia, the Almanac section of the December issue of the *Wake Forest
University Magazine* reported: "The Wake Forest football team uses more than 140
footballs during a single season . . . other Wake Forest teams use: 48 basketballs (24
per team); 50 volleyballs; 60 soccer balls; 12 dozen (144) field hockey balls; 114 dozen
(1,368) baseballs; 96 dozen (1,152) golf balls (women); 3,240 tennis balls."

The Arts

As part of Writers Harvest, a nationwide benefit for hunger relief, professors and
students read poetry and prose on Thursday night, November 14, in Scales Fine Arts
Center. The reading was arranged by Wake Forest poet-in-residence Jane Mead and
raised money for the Food Bank of Northwest North Carolina.

Actor Alec Baldwin performed opposite Wake Forest graduate Tess Malis Kincaid ('86) in A. R. Gurney's romance, *Love Letters*, in Wait Chapel on April 8. Baldwin also taught a master class while on campus.

The Wake Forest theatre department, with the help of playwright Romulus
Linney, hosted a Festival of New Plays in February to showcase dramas written or
directed by Wake Forest students, alumni, and faculty. The theatre staged Linney's
Holy Ghosts, Arthur Miller's *The Crucible*, Arthur Laurent's *West Side Story*, Harold
Pinter's *The Dumbwaiter*, and Beth Henley's *Am I Blue.*

As a part of Year of the Arts celebrations, pianist Kerry Grow, soprano Nicole
Blackmer, flutist Kimberly McClintic, guitarist Seth Brodsky, and soprano Jennifer
Boone performed in a special concert on October 27 to highlight outstanding student

performers selected by the music faculty. University Professor Louis Goldstein performed avant-garde piano works by contemporary composer John Cage in a concert on November 5; on November 21, pianists Barbara Rowan and Francis Whang,
known as the Janus Duo, performed nineteenth-century, early twentieth-century, and
more contemporary music in Brendle Recital Hall.

The Klezmer Conservatory Band opened the Secrest Artists Series in October,
performing both traditional and contemporary Yiddish music. The series also featured performances by an a cappella ensemble, Paul Hillier's Theatre of Voices,
featuring carols from various traditions; England's Hanover Band with Nathalie
Stutzmann; and the Wind Soloists of the Chamber Orchestra of Europe.

The Alvin Ailey Repertory Ensemble performed a two-hour dance recital in
Brendle auditorium on February 24.

Color prints by the Englishman who defined a genre, William Hogarth (1697–
1764), inaugurated the Year of the Arts in the Scales Fine Arts Center gallery. "Snip-
er's Nest: Art that Has Lived with Lucy R. Lippard" opened in February. Representing
more than one hundred artists, including Marcel Duchamp, Eva Hess, Robert
Rauschenberg, Alex Katz, Nancy Spero, and Judy Chicago, the collection provided
a visual record of the New York art scene from the 1960s to the 1980s. Most of the
pieces were gifts to Lippard, a New York art critic and champion of women's art, who
spoke at the opening.

Campus and Student Life

Nearly 950 freshmen moved into Collins, Bostwick, Johnson, Taylor, Kitchen,
Palmer, and Piccolo residence halls on Wednesday, August 20. They were chosen
from a record number of applicants, 6,782; forty-two freshmen were valedictori-
ans, and 70 percent were ranked in the top 10 percent of their high school classes.
They were from forty-one states and six foreign countries, and 9 percent were African American. Student volunteers and Wake Forest employees helped them move
into their rooms, while tents with vendors selling milk crates, refrigerators, and other
college basics were set up between Bostwick and Johnson Halls. Approximately 140
first-year students and some upperclass students lived in the substance-free housing
available in Johnson Residence Hall; because of the upperclass students in Johnson,
about three dozen first-year women were housed in Kitchen Residence Hall. Altogether, 2,992 out of 3,500 students lived on campus.

The Babcock School welcomed 111 new full-time MBA students, fifty-eight in
the executive program, forty-two in the evening program, and thirty-nine in the
Charlotte MBA program. The Law School welcomed 161 first-year students.

Upperclass students returned to campus to find a new computer help desk in
Reynolda Hall, new printers in every residence hall, and computer-savvy advisors
in first-year student halls. Prompted by student suggestions and survey results, the
new center expanded on the services offered the previous year in Z. Smith Reynolds Library. Trained support consultants answered calls, and streamlined telephone
menu choices replaced voice messages and call-backs for service. For the first time,
quiet hours went into effect from 10 p.m. to 8 a.m on weekdays and 2 a.m. to 12 p.m.
on Saturdays and Sundays in the residence halls.

Student Government presented its first State of the University address featuring its President, Tina Schippers, and President Hearn. About three hundred people, mostly students, attended. They commented favorably about Hearn, who was very engaged with them. In the *Old Gold and Black,* Karen Hillenbrand was Editor-in-Chief.

Marie Joyner with granddaughter and great-granddaughter

The grand opening of a new Shorty's, the campus coffee bar and lounge, took place on February 16. On hand for the occasion were ninety-five-year-old Marie Joyner, widow of Millard "Shorty" Joyner; his granddaughter, Diane Coghill; and his great granddaughter, Brianna Coghill. A seldom-used game room in the Benson University Center was renovated, and the new Shorty's had a modern pub atmosphere, seating for about a hundred people, and a small stage. It served three different kinds of beer, as well as Starbucks coffee and pastries. Two pool tables filled a back room. Old photographs and theater posters lined the walls, and sealed into the top of each table were photographic collages of students dating from the 1930s to the early 1990s. Display cases held changing exhibits of memorabilia. A large-screen television and smaller ones scattered around the room were donated by Roddey Player ('84), Vice President of Queen City TV and Appliance in Charlotte, and his parents, Woody and Frances Player. Much of the equipment behind the bar was donated by Jay Kegerreis ('70).

George D. Kuh, an outside consultant who specialized in evaluating the intellectual atmospheres of college campuses, was invited to the University to assess Wake Forest's scholarly climate. After meeting with a group of faculty, students, and administrators at a retreat in Montreat, North Carolina, and talking with other groups on campus, Kuh issued his report, "The Climate for Undergraduate Learning at Wake Forest University." He concluded that Wake Forest students did not relate their classroom experiences to out-of-class activities. Furthermore, he debunked the term "Work Forest," finding that half of students spent less than thirty hours a week on school work, class time included, while only 10 percent of respondents said they studied at least fifty hours a week. Kuh also found that minority students had a more negative view of their university experiences than others, and women as a group took advantage of resources more than men and were more engaged in active learning and cooperation with their peers. The undergraduate ethic, "work hard, play hard," resulted in studying from Sunday night to sometime on Thursday and then relaxing for the better part of the next three days. Some used this pattern to justify heavy alcohol use to relieve stress and promote socialization.

Fifteen students spent a weekend in mid-September helping the University's birthplace in the town of Wake Forest recover from Hurricane Fran. The trip was organized by Joy Vermillion, a junior and former resident of the town. Susan Brinkley, an alumna and president of the Wake Forest Birthplace Society, Inc., coordinated the visit and clean-up efforts.

The initial Festival of Light was held during the first week of December in Benson University Center. Student groups performed holiday songs, readings, and skits. Outside of the University, Chi Rho, the men's a cappella Christian chorus, traveled to Washington, D.C., to perform two forty-minute sets at a Christmas party for White House staff and cabinet members on December 15. Back on campus, the twentieth annual Christopher Giles and Lucille S. Harris Competitions in Musical Performance were held in Brendle Recital Hall on February 22. A special commemorative program containing a history of the competitions was published to mark the occasion.

SPARC (Students Promoting Action and Responsibility in the Community) expanded to become a pre-orientation program to introduce the needs and opportunities for service in the Winston-Salem community to new students.

The University's Quiz Bowl team, coached by graduate student Bobby Shepard and Robert Whaples (Economics), was ranked eleventh nationally by the Academic Competition Foundation Rankings. Apart from the Quiz Bowl team, two members of the debate team, Justin Green and Brian Prestes, won the University of Kentucky Thoroughbred Round Robin competition on October 3–4. The tournament extended invitations to the nation's top nine debate teams.

In other debate news, senior Brian Prestes of Worcester, Massachusetts, and junior Daveed Gartenstein-Ross of Ashland, Oregon, went on to win first place in National Debate Tournament, defeating a team from the University of Georgia. Allan Louden and Ross Smith (Communication) were Debate Director and Head Coach, respectively. The tournament was held March 21–24 in Lynchburg, Virginia. The two best players on the Georgia team, Paul Barsness and Daniel Davis, had wanted to attend Wake Forest but, according to Allan Louden, were unable to afford the tuition.

In November 1996, a team of law students—Rebecca Bartholomew, Sean Cole, and John Spargur—won the forty-seventh National Moot Court regional competition in Richmond, Virginia, and advanced to the national finals. The competition featured twenty-two teams, including Duke and the University of Virginia. Spargur also won the award for best oralist. The team's advisor was Charles Rose Jr. (Law).

Charlotte Anne Opal of Falls Church, Virginia, was selected as a Rhodes Scholar in December 1996. An economics major with minors in math and international studies, Opal was also a Nancy Susan Reynolds Scholar and participated in the gospel choir, played viola and oboe in the orchestra, and competed on the lacrosse team. She was the sixth Wake Forest student to be named a Rhodes Scholar in ten years and the ninth in Wake Forest history.

Beth Stroupe, a senior chemistry major, won a fellowship for predoctoral studies in chemistry awarded by the National Science Foundation. Over 5,100 undergraduates applied, and of the 850 awarded in thirteen fields, only fifty-seven went to chemistry majors.

In a non-academic endeavor, Mary Alice Manning, a senior, made ten swings and distributed them across campus. They were made of rope and cedar with words— thoughts on age, transition, responsibility, freedom, and play—burned into the seats.

Manning's idea stemmed from her observations about the contrast between a successful college experience and the carefree existence of a child on a swing. University arborist Wayne Cameron assisted in hanging the swings.

Tycely Williams won the Miss Forsyth County beauty pageant, and on campus Kappa Delta sorority held its first Mr. Wake Forest contest. Various groups nominated contestants and paid a $40 entry fee, all of which went to Kappa Delta national and local philanthropies. Contestants were judged on the basis of their appearance in formal wear and swimwear, talent, and a question round.

Daveed Gartenstein-Ross and Brian Prestes won the National Debate Tournament

Facilities, Finances, and Alumni

During the summer of 1996, a number of classrooms were renovated to accommodate high-speed computer wiring and multimedia upgrades in Tribble Hall, Olin Physical Laboratory, Salem Hall, and Carswell Hall. Tribble was renovated top-to-bottom, including repainting, reflooring, new furnishings, and multimedia upgrades to twenty-eight classrooms. Air conditioning systems, computer wiring, and new flooring were installed in Johnson, Bostwick, and Kitchen residence halls, which were also repainted. Altogether, more than $10 million was spent in renovation and construction projects. The Board of Trustees also approved $1 million to install new smoke detectors in every residence hall.

In April, a new chiller plant was added to the campus landscape. Located near the football practice field, it had two 600-ton chiller units and an emergency generator for the power plant and facilities management. On May 15, construction began on a 70,000-square-foot Information Systems Building that would house the IS department, military science (ROTC) classrooms and offices, a food court, and a bookstore. Construction of a 72,000-square-foot residence hall designed to offer townhouse-style living to 194 students began slightly later in the summer of 1997, along with renovations to Wait Chapel and Wingate Hall. The following fall, students were inconvenienced by this construction: the band's practice field was paved over, student paths to campus were cut off, and a parking lot near Student Apartments was fenced off and turned into a construction site.

A brick-and-concrete stage for special events was built at the northern end of the Magnolia Courtyard on the site routinely used by the Student Union and other student organizations for concerts and outdoor activities. On another positive note, the campus gained more than one hundred new parking spaces by expanding Lot W off Wingate Road and Lot Q behind the Scales Fine Arts Center, and by adding gravel spaces behind Worrell Professional Center. New lots near the Palmer and Piccolo

A lone swing in the morning mist

residence halls and the new soccer stadium added another 240 spaces.

In fall 1996, WFDD began broadcasting Deacon football and basketball games, bumping the Metropolitan Opera, to the dismay of its fans. Although some listeners protested the change, $215,518 was pledged in the WFDD autumn drive, beating the $200,000 goal.

The Student Union set up a new stereo surround system in Pugh Auditorium and brought the band "They Might Be Giants" to campus in late October. In early November, it sponsored three performances in Wait Chapel: the singers Tuck and Patti, the Turtle Island String Quartet, and pianist Philip Aaberg. It also offered a short course in contra dancing, a type of folk dancing much like square dancing.

Facilities management set up the HALL extension, which students could call for such problems as a stopped-up drain, a burned out light, or an infestation of ants. A raccoon in one of the buildings required a call to the Humane Society, according to Joel Rogers, the line manager. In addition to HALL, smoke detectors, sprinkler systems, brighter lights, and emergency call boxes topped with blue lights were installed to assure safety in residence halls and around campus.

On June 15, the area code for northwest North Carolina changed, and the University had to update materials with the new area code, 336. On July 1, the University's prefix was changed from 759 to 758, making it the sole user of the 758 prefix. The final four digits of Wake Forest telephone numbers did not change.

The clinical sciences building at the Bowman Gray School of Medicine/Baptist Hospital Medical Center was named in honor of Richard Janeway, who served as Dean and Executive Vice President of Health Affairs for twenty-six years. Janeway took a sabbatical during 1997–1998 and then became a University Professor and Executive Vice President of Health Affairs Emeritus. On the medical campus, Meads Hall was named after former Dean Manson Meads, and Carpenter Library was named after the first dean, Coy Carpenter, who relocated the medical school to Winston-Salem from Wake Forest, North Carolina, and affiliated it with North Carolina Baptist Hospital in 1941.

The Information Systems Support Center in Reynolda Hall extended its weekend hours to meet increased demand. The new Saturday hours were 8:30 a.m. to 5 p.m., rather than from noon to 5 p.m. The center was also open 4 p.m. to midnight on Sunday. The center replaced the more limited service that had been available in Room 203 of Z. Smith Reynolds Library on weekends and made the room a computer lab.

A power surge in the Scales Fine Arts Center in mid-October resulted in electrical damage to Tribble and Reynolda Halls and cut off power to six other buildings. Faulty wiring was the cause.

In financial matters, the F. M. Kirby Foundation gave $1.25 million to the Wayne Calloway School of Business and Accountancy. It was the largest cash gift ever received by the school and was used to endow a named chair in business ethics. The 1996–1997 College Fund drive exceeded its $2.2 million goal, raising $2,270,000 in unrestricted support. The first fundraising drive for the Poteat Scholarship program raised $40,000, $20,000 of which came from the Baptist State Convention of North Carolina. Twenty Poteat scholarships were awarded each year

Elton Manning ('37) committed $2 million to fund undergraduate need-based scholarships. Friends and colleagues of Barry Dodson, a Mooresville resident and familiar figure in NASCAR, gave more than $40,000 to establish athletic scholarships at Wake Forest in honor of his children, Trey and Tia, who were killed in 1994. The scholarship honoring Trey was for baseball or basketball, and the scholarship honoring Tia was the first for cheerleading.

The Z. Smith Reynolds Foundation increased its gift to Wake Forest by $200,000 a year to fund the Zachary T. Smith (LLD '89) Leadership Scholarships. Supporting one hundred North Carolina students of modest means, they were originally called North Carolina Leadership Scholarships. The program was phased in at twenty-five scholarships a year and was not fully funded until 2000. Each scholarship was worth up to $2,600 a year and was renewable for four years. In making this gift, the foundation increased its annual contribution to the University to $1.2 million a year.

In April, the Board of Trustees approved a total operating budget of $473 million for fiscal year 1997 (July 1, 1997, to June 30, 1998). Of the total, $164 million was earmarked for the Reynolda Campus and $309 million for the Hawthorne campus.

At the hospital, the J. Paul Sticht Center on Aging and Rehabilitation opened on April 14. The $37.8 million facility offered acute care for older adults as well as rehabilitation, geriatric psychiatry, and transitional care.

The Governor's Crime Commission awarded University police a two-year grant of $68,202 to upgrade its computer system. A multi-user system, including software and six personal computers, was purchased.

Summing Up the Year

Implementation of the Plan for the Class of 2000 began in fall 1996. All first-year students were given an IBM ThinkPad 365XD laptop computer and enrolled in required seminars limited to fifteen students. Faculty positions were added; financial aid was increased; new opportunities for students to assist faculty research were created; and facilities continued to be upgraded, especially those involving technology.

The Year of the Arts, the first of six theme years sponsored during the Hearn era, brought such luminaries as Beverly Sills, James Earl Jones, and Alec Baldwin to campus. A symposium on Beethoven was held, and the world premiere of *Since Dawn*, a tone poem for narrator, chorus, and orchestra, composed by Dan Locklair and inspired by Maya Angelou's poem for Bill Clinton's inauguration, was held as well.

More writers, musicians, actors, and artists visited and performed on campus than can be adequately covered in this chapter.

Wake Forest tied for twenty-fifth place nationally in the year's *U.S. News & World Report* rankings, the highest to date. *Money* magazine placed Wake Forest among the one hundred best college buys.

The death of four students saddened the campus. Two—Maia Witzl and Julie Hansen, both 19 and Chi Omega sisters—were killed just blocks from campus by a drunken driver at the start of the school year. In April, 150 students rode buses to participate in the Rally in Raleigh, spending the day knocking on doors in the state legislature and lobbying for legislation to keep habitual drunken-driving offenders off the roads. Most were members of a group called Safe Rds (Student Action for Eliminating Reckless Drivers). Their efforts were successful; almost a year after the young women were killed, new laws were enacted.

The fifth big story of the year was the construction of gates and gatehouses at the University's entrances. Although controversial, they were a reaction to the violence and vandalism coming onto campus from outside; an open campus, especially at night, was too dangerous. If anything, the University community seemed invigorated by meeting its challenges. Wake Forest emerged from the year stronger, safer, and more appreciative of the arts and technology.

CHAPTER FIFTEEN
1997–1998

The Year of Religion, Transitions, Construction, and a New Name

"The central questions of your life are largely yours to answer. More than any other thing, your aspirations will determine what you become. Fickle fate can certainly mark us for good or ill, but people largely live the scripts of their own writing. The ambitions you form and the diligence with which you pursue them will define the substance of your life. Success is not enough. A well-ordered life must be crowned by goodness and happiness."

Thomas K. Hearn Jr., May 18, 1998;
Charge to the Graduates, Wake Forest University Commencement

Wake Forest designated 1997–1998 "The Year of Religion in American Life." Events began on September 4, when Rabbi Harold Kushner, author of *When Bad Things Happen to Good People*, delivered the opening convocation speech. On October 16, Arun Gandhi, grandson of Mahatma Gandhi, asked the campus, "The twenty-first century is coming, but where are we going?" His emphasis was on harmony and nonviolence. He was followed by Bill Moyers, Emmy award-winning journalist, author, and commentator, who gave a speech, "Religion in America: Reflections of a Long-time Observer and Participant," at fall convocation on November 19. The year featured special classes on religious themes, symposia on religion in public life and in the media, a national conference on religion in higher education sponsored by the Lilly Endowment, a film series, guest speakers, religious leaders in residence, and a performance by whirling dervishes. *The Book of Days*, 300- to 400-word personal meditations on matters of faith and life by students, staff, and faculty, was published in late September. An idea of Mary Gerardy, Assistant Vice President of Student Life, and Ed Christman, University Chaplain, and produced by the Year of Religion Steering Committee, it had an entry for every day the University was in session from August 24 to December 19. Gerardy printed a new *Book of Days* for the spring semester.

Frederick Buechner's *The Sacred Journey* was chosen as required reading for first-year students. The News Service hosted a conference for religion reporters in coordination with Poynter Institute of Florida. Bill Leonard (Divinity) and Charles Kimball (Religion) co-chaired the year and its activities.

The University's upper administration experienced losses, gains, and temporary replacements. In a press conference on November 21, Provost David G. Brown announced that, having served as Provost for seven years, he was taking on a new challenge. Starting July 1, he would become Vice President and Dean of the International Center for Computer-Enhanced Learning (ICCEL), a joint initiative by Wake Forest and IBM to promote effective use of technology in academia. The center would sponsor a number of programs as well as custom briefing and consulting services to other educational institutions on both the technological and pedagogical aspects of educational technologies.

Instead of searching for a new Provost immediately, President Hearn announced that Brown's duties would be split. Ed Wilson, Wake Forest's only provost up to Brown's appointment, became Senior Vice President, charged with academic administration of the college, the Law School, the Calloway School of Business, the Babcock School of Management, the Graduate School, and the fledgling Divinity School. Sam Gladding, who had been Assistant to the President for Special Projects since 1990, become Associate Provost and would oversee the academic support offices, specifically Undergraduate Admissions, Financial Aid, Research and Sponsored Programs, Institutional Research, the Registrar, the Secrest Artists Series, and International Studies, in cooperation with Dean of the College Paul Escott. Wilson and Gladding were to work together as necessary. They served on the President's cabinet but did not report to each other.

Wilson's Responsibilities	Gladding's Responsibilities
Academics	Academic Support
Wake Forest College	Undergraduate Admissions
Law School	Financial Aid
Calloway School of Business & Accountancy	Research & Sponsored Programs
Babcock Graduate School of Management	Institutional Research
Graduate School	Registrar
Divinity School	Secrest Artists Series
	International Studies (with Dean Escott)

Prior to the new Provost's office arrangement, Steve Brooks, Director of Financial Aid, resigned to become Executive Director of the North Carolina State Education Assistance Authority. He was replaced by Tom Phillips ('74) during the summer of

1997 until William Wells ('74), Assistant Director of Student Aid for Federal Programs at the University of North Carolina–Chapel Hill, was selected from a strong applicant pool to become permanent director. He accepted the offer on November 14, 1997, and started his duties on January 2, 1998.

ICCEL logo

Two major projects dominated the campus during the year. One was the 70,000-square-foot Information Systems building north of Worrell Professional Center, which would eventually house information systems, a small bookstore, ROTC, ICCEL, and a cafeteria. Construction began on May 15, and one of its lobbies was dedicated to AMP, an international communications and cabling products company, which donated $500,000. On the Magnolia Court between Carswell and Calloway Halls, an 80,000-square-foot classroom building would house the foreign language departments and psychology. It was named for William B. Greene Jr. of the Bank of Tennessee, who generously donated funds.

After fifty-six years, the Bowman Gray School of Medicine became the Wake Forest University School of Medicine. The change, announced in October 1997, was one of a host of nomenclatural and structural changes. Henceforth, the Medical Center would be known as the Wake Forest University–Baptist Medical Center, and the medical school campus would be called the Bowman Gray Campus. The changes were widely attributed to a tobacco controversy, but it was more a matter of unifying Wake Forest. President Hearn apologized to Lyons Gray in an October 13 letter for the storm surrounding the naming. Thomas A. Gray was especially upset, and on November 7 he wrote to the President: "Just so unforgivable as what you did, is how you did it. Our family is still reeling from

Ed Wilson and Sam Gladding

Bill Wells

the initial newspaper accounts, in which you . . . professed universal family approval for your proposal. Nothing could be further from the truth." On November 12, Hearn replied: "I accept the charge of a blunder, a serious one. For that I accept full responsibility." He denied ill intent, however, and elaborated:

We cannot function in this marketplace with multiple labels and confusing identifiers. . . . Having altered the name of the Medical Center, we had little choice but to align the school name accordingly. I believe we serve our legacy best by insuring the survival—and continuing excellence—of the school. . . . We are committed . . . to a continuing public acknowledgment of the Bowman Gray name and legacy.

Academics

Money magazine placed Wake Forest twelfth in a list of "costly but worth it" schools that included Harvard, Yale, and Stanford, and ninety-sixth nationally among "college best buys." *U.S. News & World Report* ranked Wake Forest twenty-eighth among national universities in its annual college guide for 1998, released in August 1997, tied with Brandeis and University of California Los Angeles (UCLA). It ranked the Medical Center among the top forty hospitals in the nation in nine specialties: neurology (21st), cancer (22nd), geriatrics (22nd), cardiology (23rd), orthopedics (27th), rheumatology (31st), otolaryngology (34th), urology (35th), and gynecology (36th).

Wake Forest developed a new website, http://www.wfu.edu. Faculty used ThinkPads in the classroom as spectrometers in general chemistry courses; placed low-resolution videos of physics principles demonstrations on a website; arranged videoconferences with the chief academic adviser for the Globe Theatre in London; and developed an annotated, online guide, with links, to websites with Holocaust-related research and curricular information. The October issue of *Beyond Computing* cited the University as one of ten winners of its second annual Partnership Awards, recognizing their successful alignment of information technology operations with their primary missions.

The Teaching and Learning Center (TLC), a faculty initiative, opened October 3 in Room 330 of Z. Smith Reynolds Library. It offered a variety of resources, including workshops, a reference library, one-on-one evaluation and counseling, a newsletter, and a web page. The idea grew from a faculty teaching-assessment seminar in fall 1994 that had continued informally. Provost Brown approved the center proposal, and it was governed by a board of thirty-one members representing faculty in sixteen departments and the Calloway School. Director Katy Harriger (Political Science) was in the center Mondays, Wednesdays, and Fridays, and a work-study student filled in on Tuesday and Thursday mornings.

The public program in Wait Chapel honoring Martin Luther King Jr. on January 15 featured an address by the Reverend John Thomas Porter, a pastor of the Sixth Avenue Baptist Church in Birmingham, Alabama, and long-time associate of the late civil rights activist. Tony Campolo spoke on Founders' Day, January 22. A Baptist minister, sociology professor, prolific writer, and producer of his own weekly cable television show, Campolo served as President Bill Clinton's spiritual adviser and the Year of Religion's resident scholar during January. After Campolo spoke, David J. Anderson (Biology) and Paul Anderson (Physics) received awards for Excellence in Research; Katy J. Harriger (Political Science) received the Kulynych Family Omicron Delta Kappa Award for Contribution to Student Life; Michele S. Ware (English) was awarded the Reid-Doyle Prize for Excellence in Teaching; and Law School Professor Carol Anderson was presented the Joseph Branch Excellence in Teaching Award. Henry Stroupe (History), former Dean of the Graduate School, was presented the Medallion of Merit.

The undergraduate faculty approved a new humanities minor, to be offered beginning in fall 1998. Chair Charles Kimball took all eleven members of the Religion department on a two-week trip to Israel in June 1998. They visited biblical, historical, and archeological sites, as well as Palestinian refugee camps and Jewish settlements, and met with religious and political leaders. The trip promoted bonding within the group.

Three accounting students in the Calloway School earned the highest scores of all candidates taking the Certified Public Accountant (CPA) exam in North Carolina in May 1998. Wayne Smith Jr. was the Gold Medal winner for the highest score in the state. Calloway accountancy students ranked first in North Carolina and second in the nation in passing the Certified Public Account exam on the first try based on the May 1997 exam, the most recent available. Of the thirty-three students who took the exam during the summer of 1997, almost 80 percent passed all four parts the first time, according to the National Association of State Boards of Accountancy (NASBA).

The Theatre department sponsored an "endow a chair" program, which offered patrons a chance to "purchase" one of the new theatre seats in the Scales Fine Arts Center for $1,000. By the start of the academic year, fifty-five of the 341 seats had been endowed.

A seminar room in the Anthropology department's lab building was dedicated to founder and first chair, E. Pendleton Banks, and featured his portrait. Banks had a forty-year career at the University, retired in 1994, and died in 1995.

E. Pendleton Banks

Individual faculty achieved wide recognition. Dan Locklair (Music) received an award from the American Society of Composers, Authors, and Publishers (ASCAP), and in April his *Concerto Grosso* was performed by the Helsinki Philharmonic Orchestra in Finland. The Buffalo Philharmonic Orchestra performed his *HUES (for Orchestra): Three Brief Tone Poems*. On both occasions, Locklair gave preconcert talks.

Debate coach Ross Smith (Communication) was named the 1997 National Debate Coach of the Year.

Thomas Gossett's 1963 best-seller, *Race: The History of Ideas in America*, which had gone out of print in 1983, was reissued in July 1997 by Oxford University Press as part of its Race and American Culture Series. The work was considered a classic, analyzing the development of racism in a number of disciplines, and was praised for both its scholarship and readability.

David Anderson (Biology) received a $200,000 grant from the National Science Foundation to support the University's albatross project. Under the grant, two species of albatross were tracked by satellite as they flew over the northern Pacific from their nests on Tern Island, a part of Hawaii. The study focused on how food supply affects productivity in a declining albatross population. School children and others interested in the project were able to subscribe to a website and track individual birds.

Administration and Staff

President Hearn was appointed to serve on a statewide commission, Transit 2001. Dave Brown, in his new position as Vice President for Special Programs, worked to market ICCEL, the joint consulting services of Wake Forest and IBM, to other colleges and universities looking for assistance in taking greater advantage of information technology. Brown kept the title of Provost until June 1998 and the Vice President title through 2001.

Sandra Boyette became Vice President for University Advancement in August 1997. Part of her responsibilities included overseeing official University correspondence. President Hearn asked her in an August 21 memo to chair a committee to see that "our communications with admitted first-year students be as timely, accurate, and attractively presented as those publications and audiovisuals in the admissions communication. From all accounts, random mailings, not well planned, are going to our admitted students between April 1 and mid-August. I want this practice to cease." In the same office, Kevin Cox was named Assistant Vice President, and Cheryl Walker was promoted to Associate Director of Media Relations. Robert Mills ('71) was promoted to Associate Vice President for University Advancement, and Kriss Dinkins ('85) was named Assistant Director of Development.

Lloyd Whitehead was named Director of Electronic Communication, responsible for maintaining the institutional home page and subsidiary pages. Chi-Chi Messick was appointed Director of Development at WFDD, while Paul Brown was named Program Director. Brown had served as News Director since 1994, when he launched the station's regional news department.

Minta Aycock McNally ('74) was named Assistant Vice President to manage the Office of Alumni Activities and Volunteer Programs. James R. Bullock ('85, MBA '95), who was also named an Assistant Vice President, became Director of the Office of Major Gifts and Annual Support. In the Divinity School, former Student Government President L. Wade Stokes ('83) was appointed Director of Development, and Scott Hudgins was hired as Director of Student Recruitment. Joshua Else ('93) became Director of the College Fund and annual support for the Reynolda Campus. Bobby Finch ('93) was named Director of Alumni and Development for the School of Law.

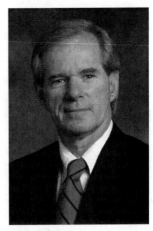

Richard Dean

Lillian Shelton became Director of the Secrest Artists Series. She had been coordinator of the series for twelve years and was named Director after the retirement of George Trautwein (Music). Willie Hughes, who had taken care of former President James Ralph Scales and Elizabeth Randel Scales until their respective deaths, retired from Facilities Management.

Like faculty, administrators were recognized for their achievements. President Hearn wrote Dean Jim Thompson of the Medical School on December 12: "I am delighted to learn of our success in securing a National Center of Excellence in Women's Health. Given the level of the competition, and the limited number of awards, this is further evidence of the quality and growing stature of the Wake Forest University School of Medicine." In a January 29 memo, Hearn informed the entire Wake Forest community that Richard Dean had been permanently appointed Senior Vice President for Health Affairs and Director of Wake Forest University–Baptist Medical Center (WFUBMC).

The Office of University Advancement won four awards in the 1997 District III competition of the Council for the Advancement and Support of Education (CASE). Wayne Thompson, a media relations officer in the news bureau, won Awards of Excellence for feature writing and for the website for the Year of Religion in American Life, which he created with Samantha Hand, Art Director of the University Editor's Office. Its newsletters also won Awards of Merit.

Buck Bayliff was elected President of the Association of College and University Telecommications Administrations for 1997–1998. Connie Lawson, Director of Mail Services, received the 1997 national Industry Excellence Award for Colleges and Universities from the U.S. Postal Service.

Athletics

The most exciting news in athletics was that the baseball team won the ACC championship and secured a bid to the NCAA Tournament, both for the first time in twenty-one years.

The football team had its best record so far under Head Coach Jim Caldwell, completing the season with five wins and six losses—a great improvement over the previous year.

On January 5, President Hearn wrote John Swofford, Commissioner of the Atlantic Coast Conference (ACC), about binge drinking. He asked that the ACC "continue to support the alcohol initiatives of the ACC schools . . . to fight the battle

The 1998 ACC baseball champions

against alcohol abuse on our campuses." He noted that the ACC had made grants to Wake Forest of $2,500 and $10,000 in 1995–1996 and 1996–1997 for this purpose.

A new student-led group, the Freakin' Deacons, was organized during basketball season to encourage fans, especially older fans who sat on their hands, to cheer more at home games. The group of twenty-six members was more controversial than the 600-member Screamin' Demons, an established group supported by the Athletics Department, because some of its cheers and the signs it displayed contained profanity.

The volleyball team got its first ACC win in eleven years, after having been suspended from 1987 to 1995. It defeated North Carolina State 3–2 on October 10 to break a losing streak of twenty-four games, dating back three years. Supporting the team was the Volley Band, a group of twelve saxophonists who split off from their regular gig in the marching band to enhance the atmosphere at volleyball matches.

The women's soccer team won an at-large bid to the NCAA Tournament but lost to University of North Carolina in the first round.

In a belated recognition of a brilliant individual basketball career, Simpson O. "Skip" Brown's jersey (#15) was retired in February 1998. Brown played for the Deacons from 1973 to 1977, during which time he scored more than 2,000 points and had almost 600 assists. He was selected twice to the first All-ACC conference team, was selected as an All-American, and was drafted by the Boston Celtics. In March, the men's basketball team was invited to the National Invitation Tournament (NIT), where they were defeated in the second round by Vanderbilt, 72–68.

Jerry Haas ('85), a second-team All-ACC, All-American, and 1985 Walker Cup Team member for the United States, replaced Jack Lewis ('70) as the men's golf coach. Lewis, who resigned in July 1997 to pursue a career playing on the Senior PGA tour, had coached for six years and led the Deacons to six straight NCAA championship appearances in as many seasons, including a second-place finish in the spring of 1997.

Janelle Kraus won the individual women's title at the ACC cross country championship in Tallahassee, Florida, on November 3. She and Kelly Brady earned All-ACC honors. The women's team placed second overall, defeating the University of North Carolina team for the second time in two weeks. Nolan Swanson became the fourth men's cross country All-American in Wake Forest history on November 24.

The Arts

The Theatre Department staged *You Can't Take It With You* by George S. Kaufman and Moss Hart, Shakespeare's *Much Ado About Nothing,* John Guare's *Six Degrees of Separation,* and Molière's *Tartuffe.* Harold Pinter's *The Caretaker* was performed in the Ring Theatre in January, and its three-member cast featured Jim Dodding. Dodding also produced and directed *A Promenade Passion Play,* enacting episodes in Christ's life, outdoors at various campus locations on April 5–7.

Nolan Swanson

The Secrest Artists Series started the year with Da Camera of Houston performing *Marcel Proust's Paris,* which combined readings from *In Search of Lost Time* with songs by Reynaldo Hahn and chamber music by Faure and Franck. It was followed by the Netherland Chamber Choir, the Nexus Percussion Ensemble, the Orpheus Chamber Orchestra with Richard Good, the Aulos Ensemble with Julianne Baird performing early music on original instruments, and sitar virtuoso Ravi Shankar.

A new woodwind quintet, Opus 5, composed of Kathryn Levy, flute; Steven L. Jones, oboe; Linda Julian, clarinet; Jonathan Julian, bassoon; and Robert Campbell, French horn, played in Brendle Recital Hall in September. Peter Kairoff, piano, joined the group for one number. Mark Kroll, one of the world's leading harpsichordists, performed on March 29 in Brendle Recital Hall.

The Student Union brought comedian Adam Sandler, of *Saturday Night Live,* and the singing duo Indigo Girls to perform in Wait Chapel on October 13 and 20, respectively, earning high praise in an *Old Gold and Black* editorial of October 16.

Campus and Student Life

The first-year class of 1997–1998 numbered 975, the largest in Wake Forest history. Demographically, 12 percent was minority, 9 percent black, and the number of men and women was almost

Mark Kroll, one of the world's leading harpsichordists

equal: 490 women and 485 men. The class was chosen from a pool of 6,841 applicants. Prospective students and their parents made a total of 7,541 visits to campus in 1997, up 8.8 percent from 1996 and up 49.1 percent since 1992. In addition, 163 students entered the Law School.

During the academic year, the University gradually provided IBM ThinkPad computers to all members of the Classes of 2000 and 2001, who also received a Lexmark 20230 color inkjet printer or a $120 credit at the bookstore if they did not want the printer. Unlike the ThinkPads, the printer would not be updated every two years. The idea was to reduce the number of network laser printers.

The University overhauled its judicial system in the fall of 1995 after the Harriger Report, named after study chair Katy Harriger (Political Science), identified several problems:

Those who had the most experience with the judicial system had the least confidence in it.

- Some students questioned the system's legitimacy, saying that representation on the governing bodies had become a popularity contest.
- Delays in handling the case load were resulting in inconsistencies; for example, the Judicial Board was hearing cases technically under the jurisdiction of the Honor Council.

James Powell (Classical Languages) and Robert Lovett (English) guided reforms, which were ratified by the Judicial Council and in a student referendum, and implemented in fall 1998. They included:

- A seven-member central deliberative body called the Honor and Ethics Council (HEC) would adjudicate all honor and conduct cases not heard administratively. The council comprised four students, two faculty members, and one administrator.
- An Election Committee would screen applications from interested students meeting minimum specified criteria and present a slate of candidates for election to the HEC.
- A Board of Investigators and Advisors (BIA) would investigate all cases to be heard by the HEC and advise the accused during all phases of the investigation, serving as his or her representative at the hearing.
- A Judicial Council was charged by the University with the power to "establish and direct the undergraduate judicial system so as to insure justice and due process to all members of the undergraduate academic community." It also served as the appeals body for cases handled by the HEC.

On August 7, 1997, Governor Jim Hunt signed the Safe Roads Act in response to President Hearn and Chi Omega's campaign against drunken drivers after the fall 1996 accident that killed two sorority members. President Hearn attended the ceremony and gave the signature pen to Julie Griffin for the Chi Omega chapter archives. Laura Acton, President of Chi Omega, was also in the audience and wrote to President Hearn on August 19: "I was extremely proud and pleased to see you standing on stage next to Governor Jim Hunt. Knowing that your determination was part of the driving force behind this legislation being passed was very comforting as a student. . . . Thank you for everything you have done this year."

First-year student Alexander Gedicks died of meningococcemia, a bacterial infection, on November 13. More than 400 people, including Gedicks's parents and three sisters, attended a memorial service for him in Wait Chapel on November 16. Student Health Services offered students who had been in close contact with him the antibiotic Cipro, first in Johnson Residence Hall, where Gedicks lived, and later in Benson University Center.

Gregory Wilson, a sophomore, died in his hometown of Fort Wayne, Indiana, over the winter break on January 6. A memorial service was held in Wait Chapel on January 20. Wilson was the eighth Wake Forest student to die within two years.

The thirteen students enrolled in instructor Ralph W. Black's Studies in American Literature class staged a Moby Dick Marathon on Saturday, October 25, under a canopy in front of Wait Chapel. President Hearn started the reading at 10 a.m., and then class members took turns reading chapters, concluding shortly before 6:00 a.m. Sunday, about four hours earlier than expected.

Babcock Residence Hall and Taylor House both became coed, leaving no single-sex housing on campus. The responsibility for party management switched from the Office of Student Development to the Office of Residence Life and Housing. Students complained that prices in the Sundry Shop were higher than elsewhere in Winston-Salem and objected to the stricter enforcement of the alcohol policy by Residence Life and Housing. They were upset that the University collected $500,000 in student parking fines and registrations without adding new parking for them.

Julie Griffin, athletic development officer and adviser to Chi Omega, experienced a range of emotions at the Raleigh event on Safe Roads

Laura Acton ('98), president of Chi Omega who was active in Safe Roads and was instrumental in lobbying for the tougher law, meets the press at the bill-signing ceremony in Raleigh in August

Although Wake Forest was included in the John Templeton Foundation's 1997–1998 Honor Roll for Character-Building Colleges, *Playboy* came to Winston-Salem in April to recruit female students to appear in an October feature, Women of the ACC. A similar recruitment had last occurred in 1989. Fourteen Wake Forest women showed up for the initial interview; three had never seen the magazine.

At its annual meeting in November, the Baptist State Convention of North Carolina passed a resolution expressing "displeasure" with alcohol sales at Shorty's and calling for a re-evaluation of the convention's relationship with Wake Forest.

The Student Life Committee (SLC) reported in October that the campus environment for gay and lesbian students was "tough." At best, it was unsupportive; at worst, hostile. The University Trustees had passed an amended antidiscrimination policy in April 1997, including protection against discrimination based on sexual orientation. The SLC found, however, that not all Wake Forest publications documented the policy. In addition to including the Trustee amendment in University publications, the SLC recommended:

1. discussion of sexuality in community-building dialogues, starting with orientation;
2. construction of a website containing realistic scientific information on sexual orientation, such as the one produced by the American Psychological Association;
3. a statement about the climate for gays and lesbians at Wake Forest;
4. a list of student and faculty role models with diverse sexual orientations; and
5. a list of individuals and organizations on campus whom gay and lesbian students could seek out, if needed.

Vice President Ken Zick assured Perry Patterson (Economics), the faculty adviser for the Gay and Lesbian Association, that the proposed website would be finished by the end of the academic year and that he and his staff in Student Life would work to improve the campus atmosphere. Physically disabled students also raised campus consciousness about their problems; stairs were especially problematic.

Meanwhile, GALA (Gay and Lesbian Awareness) held its first Pride Week in April. Members blanketed the campus with chalk messages and flyers, sponsored speakers, and hosted other events to introduce their needs to the campus community.

The marching band was left without a practice field due to the construction of Polo Residence Hall. At first, it practiced on Poteat field, but this location was also used for intramural sports, so the band finally moved to Davis field, which sloped downward but provided more exposure to fellow students.

The state conference of Amnesty International was held in the Benson University Center on February 20–21. The theme was "cultural relativism." Before the group visited campus, first-year law student Ed Shlikas went on a hunger strike in early January and sued the University for $125 million in punitive and compensatory damages because he felt professors treated first-year law students without the appropriate courtesy and respect. After three weeks, he was escorted off campus on January 27 and given a trespassing warning not to return because he was no longer a student in the law school.

Scott Plumridge was elected Student Government President. Danielle Deaver was Editor of *The Old Gold and Black*; DeAnna Lewis was Editor-in-Chief of *The Howler*; and Lauren Hunt was chosen as the Student Trustee.

By the fall semester, twenty-five of 112 student organizations had created websites. The range of organizations varied and included Greek organizations, religious groups, and ROTC. One new organization that became strong and then essential was founded by Jessica Murray. She came to campus in the fall of 1996 as an Emergency Medical Technician with the goal of establishing a

Wake Forest Emergency Response Team logo

campus Emergency Medical Technician unit. She worked with Cecil Price, Sylvia Bell, and Ken Zick to complete the process; she recruited members, and the group became a recognized student organization with ongoing funding through the Student Government. The Wake Forest Emergency Response Team went into operation in February 1998 and was on call from 5 p.m. to 8 a.m. Monday through Friday and around the clock on Saturdays and Sundays.

Amy Basset, Karen Click, Lauren Furgurson, and Erin Lutz formed a new a cappella group, the Demon Divas. After auditions, the group grew to fifteen. It focused on pop music and paralleled the male a cappella group Temporary Reprieve, established during the previous academic year.

The Honduras Outreach Program and Exchanges (HOPE) launched its first mission, a service trip, with twelve students and Professor Clay Hipp (Calloway) over the winter break. Seniors Jessica Kent and Robert Hamilton developed the plan, and Kent became the student leader. The team worked on a construction project in the Agalta valley.

In October, WAKE Radio began broadcasting on AM 1610 and could be heard within a five-mile radius of campus. Station manager Amy Dotson said that with the upgrade from cable FM, WAKE Radio would now be one of the

Demon Divas

premier college stations in North Carolina. The upgrade was made possible when Vice President John Anderson approved the entire capital expenditure requested by the station, $40,000, during the summer.

Three first-year students, Michele Alesia Johnson, Sarah Holland Rackley, and Dan Durand, were selected from a national pool of eight thousand nominees as Tandy Scholars. They all demonstrated outstanding achievement in mathematics, science, and computer science. Only Harvard, MIT, Stanford, and Princeton had more students chosen for the scholarship.

Junior Jennifer Bumgarner was among a distinguished group of seventy-six undergraduates nationwide elected as a 1998 Truman Scholar. The merit-based $30,000 scholarships are awarded to college students who plan to pursue careers in government or other public service and wish to attend graduate or professional school to prepare.

Two seniors won $73,500 awards from the National Science Foundation for graduate studies. Andrew Frey, a physics major, and Shannon Poe-Kennedy, an anthropology and political science major, were among 766 students nationwide winning prestigious Graduate Research Fellowships. Poe-Kennedy also received an Andrew V. Mellon Scholarship in the Humanities, worth $14,000 plus tuition and mandated fees for the first year of her PhD work. She was the first Wake Forest student to receive the award in eight years.

In Greek life, the Gamma Omicron chapter of Theta Chi celebrated its fiftieth anniversary at Wake Forest, while the Zeta Tau chapter of Delta Gamma sorority decided to close because of low membership. On September 29, twenty-two-year-old Amanda Lee Edwards, a member of Delta Gamma sorority, was awarded her diploma from Wake Forest just a few hours before she died from leukemia. She had left the University the preceding spring, just a few hours shy of graduation. Flags were lowered to half-mast in her honor, and a memorial service was held in Wait Chapel on October 26. Isabel Newton, who met Edwards while studying abroad in Venice, organized a bone-marrow drive in her memory. Held on April 26, the campus raised $17,300 to offset the $75 cost of screening, bloodtyping, and listing 308 volunteers in the National Bone Marrow Registry (NBMR).

The Sigma Pi chapter of Tau Kappa Epsilon fraternity also voluntarily closed at the beginning of the fall semester. The chapter was down to its last four members, all seniors, who did not have time to plan rush and chapter functions. Tau Kappa Epsilon had forty-four members when it was chartered in 1990 but lacked lounge space and exposure on campus. According to Mike Ford, Director of Student Development, it was the first voluntary fraternity closure in University history.

In nonvoluntary action, the Delta Gamma charter of Kappa Sigma fraternity was suspended through the 1999–2000 academic year. The announcement was made November 13 and required the fraternity to immediately cease all operations and activities, to forfeit its chapter lounge in Davis House immediately, and to give up block housing privileges at the conclusion of the academic year. It was found guilty of several group responsibilities, including hazing during the fall pledge process. After the University's action, the fraternity's national organization revoked its charter.

On the positive side, 358 women and 280 men participated in sorority and fraternity rush during the spring semester.

Spirit Walk

Facilities, Finances, and Alumni

The Spirit Walk between Benson and Tribble was constructed in August. About 1,500 alumni, students, faculty, and staff paid $50 to personalize bricks with names and memories. On December 2, a tree was planted outside Tribble Hall and dedicated to Grace O'Neil, the former manager of the Magnolia Room. A ceremony, attended by about forty people, was held along with the planting. President Hearn delivered the invocation, followed by remarks by family and friends and the singing of "Amazing Grace." O'Neil, who died the previous March, was one of a handful of nonfaculty memorialized by the University. Unfortunately, the Quad's ash trees were afflicted with a mysterious disease, and three were removed during the 1998 semester break.

Worrell House in London celebrated its twentieth year on July 4, 1997. It had been used by more than one thousand students. Victor I. Flow ('52) and his wife, Roddy, bought a 7,200-square-foot, 1890s villa in northwestern Vienna (Gustav Tschermakgasse 20) and gave it to Wake Forest as the third residential study-abroad house. While the gift was made in April, the Flow House would not open to students until the fall, after repairs and upgrades were completed.

Just off campus, an electrical substation was built on University Parkway. Its appearance and proximity to homes was controversial, and in response President Hearn wrote to Mrs. Virginia Sams on December 2 that Wake Forest "considered a number of alternatives before deciding to build the electrical substation on University Parkway." He told her that the University had modified the original design to make the site as attractive as possible and to leave as many trees as possible. He explained that "in order to ensure a consistent power source to the University we had little choice but to make the decision we did."

The Faculty Senate sent a petition to President Hearn on November 2, commending him and his administration for "the significant enhancements they have made to the physical environment over the past fifteen years. . . . We think the time has come to reevaluate campus building and parking needs. . . . We ask that plans for the development of the wooded area behind the football practice fields and the Palmer-Piccolo Residence Hall be reconsidered in the broader context of a new long-range planning process that obtains input from all sectors of the University community." The Senate wanted to minimize the consumption of natural areas and open space.

Many campus buildings received safety and cosmetic improvements over the summer. Student apartments got a dramatic face lift, with a new brick facade and the removal of exterior balconies. New kitchens and central air conditioning were added to each unit. Luter Residence Hall also added air conditioning and a sprinkler system. Most North Campus residence halls gained smoke detectors that were connected to the University Police dispatch center. Extensive summer and early fall renovations at Wait Chapel included asbestos abatement, ceiling plastering, a new lighting system, repainting, carpeting, and refurbished seating. The project was scheduled to conclude in summer 1998 with acoustical improvements.

The indoor tennis center next to Groves Stadium, featuring eight courts, was opened to the public in October. At Groves Stadium, Bridger Field House opened in the north endzone in September. The 60,000-square-foot facility was made possible by an $8 million fund drive. It featured locker rooms and the Boyette media room on the ground floor; the Norm Snead banquet room, which could accommodate up to four hundred guests, and the Bill Barnes sports lounge on the second floor; and offices and meeting rooms for the Deacon Club and sports marketing staff on the third floor. New trophy cases and a Hall of Fame exhibition area were developed on the ground floor along with a ticket office.

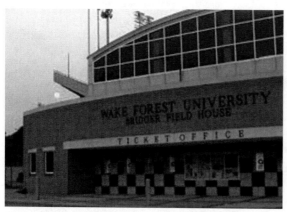

Bridger Field House

As chair of the University Traffic Commission, Mary Gerardy wrote to President Hearn on August 13 to ask him to approve the hiring of "a parking consultant to study the situation and develop a Parking Master Plan for the Reynolda Campus." She noted that "[d]uring the 1996–1997 academic year, the Traffic Commission blocked registration for students who owed parking fines in excess of $250.00. As a result, we collected over $100,000 more in parking fines than in previous years. Therefore, we have the funds to pay for a consultant," which she estimated would cost $40,000.

The December 1997 issue of *Wake Forest University Magazine* reported that membership in the major gift clubs had more than doubled in the last seven years. It now stood at 2,600 members.

The Calloway School of Business and Accountancy was awarded a $125,000 grant from the James S. Kemper Foundation. Funded over five years, it supported risk-management education and research.

A scholarship fund for international students was established in honor of former Dean Robert Dyer and his wife, Mary, in March 1998. In addition, the University created 175 merit-based scholarships of $2,000 each for international studies as part of the Plan for the Class of 2000. The Kutteh Family Scholarship was awarded for the first time to Jonathan Steven McKinna of Statesville.

Hickory native Sanford L. Steelman endowed the Margaret A. Steelman Lectureship at the School of Divinity in honor of his wife. It was the first endowed lectureship for the school and supported a focus on Judeo-Christian topics. The Henry R. Luce Foundation, Inc., awarded the school $150,000 to develop a series of multidisciplinary courses designed to provide students with the broad skills required to meet the needs of America's changing congregations.

WFDD raised more than $228,000 during its fundraising campaign in October. In January, it once again aired the weekly variety show *A Prairie Home Companion*, and on May 22 it hosted its fiftieth anniversary celebration, honoring the pioneers who founded it and those who helped it develop. Jack Thomas, station manager for 1951–1952, and Julian Burroughs, station manager for 1958–1981, were among the special guests.

As a community-building venue for families on both campuses, Graylyn Pool received scheduled improvements costing $350,000. Repairs included a completely new pool and pool deck, updated or replaced filter and drainage systems, addition of an up-to-code handrail system, and a renovated bathhouse.

The University Police bought three new vehicles: two GEO Trackers for parking management to replace two 1973 postal Jeeps, and a new twelve-passenger van to replace an older seven-passenger University Shuttle van. More students were taking advantage of the shuttle service, according to Police Chief Regina Lawson.

The University's endowment grew by $137 million from July 1, 1996, to June 30, 1997, for a total of $614.7 million, according to Lou Morrell, Vice President for Investment and Treasurer. The rate of return was 28 percent. Morrell stated that since June 30, 1990, when the endowment was $318 million, it had almost doubled. In a parallel event affirming Morrell's expertise as an investor,

Lou Morrell

the National Association of College and University Business Officers (NACUBO) presented him with the Rodney H. Adams Award "in recognition of outstanding contributions to professional development and research activities in the fields of endowment and investment management."

In February, the Trustees set tuition at $20,450 for the 1998–1999 academic year for all undergraduates except seniors, the first time tuition had exceeded $20,000. Seniors had their tuition set at $17,150 because they were not included in the Plan for the Class of 2000.

Summing Up the Year

The Year of Religion in American Life was filled with blockbuster events: Rabbi Harold Kushner, Bill Moyer, Tony Campolo, and a host of other religious and spiritual men and women graced large and small Wake Forest events as Frederick Buechner's classic *The Sacred Journey* was required reading for students, faculty, and administrators.

A shake-up in the senior administration saw Provost Dave Brown leave that office to begin a new tech adventure in partnership with IBM. He would become Vice President and Dean of a joint initiative to promote technology in academia, the International Center for Computer Enhanced Learning (ICCEL). Instead of searching for a new provost immediately, the President brought back Ed Wilson to oversee the academic part of the office and promoted Sam Gladding to administer the academic support areas of the Provost's Office, such as Admissions, Financial Aid, and the Registrar's Office.

Construction continued—a new information systems building near Worrell Professional Center and an 80,000-square-foot classroom building on the Magnolia Court between Carswell and Calloway Halls. To avoid the electrical problems of past years, an electrical substation was built just off campus. Bridger Field House was rebuilt, and many other structures on or near campus, such as Graylyn Pool, received facelifts or significant improvements. Amid all of the changes on the Reynolda Campus, the Bowman Gray School of Medicine was renamed the Wake Forest University School of Medicine to clarify its connection to the University. Its campus would now be called the Bowman Gray Campus. Its clinicians achieved new recognition in a number of specialties.

At the College, the judicial system was reformed yet again. A teaching and learning center was set up to serve faculty. A sorority and a fraternity shut down, but Greek life remained popular, and students, faculty, and administrators continued to excel. The baseball team won the ACC Tournament for the first time in twenty-one years. Even with tuition going over $20,000, students were excited about the new technology initiatives, first-year seminars, study and service at home and abroad. Harmony and anticipation dominated the landscape, as problematic areas were acknowledged and addressed.

CHAPTER SIXTEEN
1998–1999

Speaking with a Southern Accent:
Culture and Unity

We spent this year thinking about globalization and diversity. We may have had it wrong in this theme year. Instead of pondering globalization and diversity, perhaps we should have been reflecting on the opposite idea—globalization and unity. Human unity and solidarity may provide the basis upon which we can build a global foundation more secure than mere toleration or acceptance. Pro Humanitate is an ethical imperative. The culture toward which we labor in common is a world culture. This next world is a world made safe for human and creature habitation, a world where differences are resolved through negotiation based on mutual respect—a world where the needs of the least among us are met by the efforts of all.

Thomas K. Hearn Jr., May 17, 1999;
Charge to the Graduates, Wake Forest University Commencement

The third theme year, "The Year of Globalization and Diversity: Conflict or Harmony?" both questioned and celebrated the world's increasing intercommunication and diversity. On September 17, Oscar Arias Sanchez, former President of Costa Rica and Nobel Peace Prize recipient, spoke at the opening convocation. An Ethnic Heritage Faire on October 17 offered glimpses into African, Asian, Greek, Indian, Italian, Latin American, Native American, and Spanish cultures through exhibits and foods. The Middle Eastern dance troupe Magic Carpet, the steel band Shadz, and the mariachi band Los Viajeros performed. Student groups, such as Islam Awareness, set up booths and exhibits. Later in the year, the Chilean folk music group Inti-illimani performed, and a panel discussed the media's influence on cultural perceptions. Nigerian poet, playwright, and political activist Wole Soyinka, who received the 1986 Nobel Prize for Literature, spoke at Founders' Day Convocation on February 2. The year also featured a foreign film festival. Candyce Leonard (Humanities) compiled and edited a companion guide that detailed the events.

267

In late July, construction began on a two-story addition to Wingate Hall for the new Divinity School. Slated for completion in spring 1999, the 2,000-square-foot rotunda was part of a $4.25 million renovation that would include a new entrance to Wingate, complete with limestone columns, and improvements to the adjoining Wait Chapel. Eight new offices would house the school's dean, administrative staff, and faculty.

The two-story, 70,000-square-foot Information Systems building opened in August and was officially dedicated November 3. Just north of the Worrell Professional Center, it housed Information Systems staff; the ROTC department; a dining area and food court offering Chick-Fil-A, Boar's Head Deli, Pan Geo's, Starbuck's Coffee, and Krispy Kreme; a bookstore for law and business students; and the International Center for Computer-Enhanced Learning (ICCEL).

National recognition continued. In its annual survey of "America's 100 Most Wired Colleges," a detailed guide to Internet use in higher education published in May 1999, *Yahoo! Internet Life* ranked Wake Forest third among all schools, after Case Western Reserve and MIT, and first among liberal arts institutions. The Admissions Office sent a postcard announcing the rankings to student applicants.

U.S. News & World Report ranked the University twenty-ninth among national universities in its 1999 "America's Best Colleges" issue. Wake Forest received high marks for its small class sizes, low student/faculty ratio, high graduation and retention levels, financial resources, and percentage of alumni giving. Among "schools that offer the best value," Wake placed thirty-sixth. The May 5 issue of the *Princeton Review* ranked Z. Smith Reynolds Library among the top ten great libraries in the nation. During the year, the library moved from the Dynex catalog system to the Voyager online catalog system.

U.S. News & World Report also ranked the Babcock Graduate School of Management thirty-sixth in its annual survey of America's accredited business schools. The Babcock School was included among *Business Week*'s top fifty graduate business schools for 1998–1999, perhaps due to the implementation of its 3/38 plan, which was in its second year. The plan divided the entering class into three sections of thirty-eight students each. Students would take the same courses but be better able to work closely in groups. Career concentrations were increased to thirteen, and sixteen new professors were hired, knocking the student/faculty ratio down to 3-to-1. The student job placement rate was 99 percent, and scores on the Graduate Management Admission Test (GMAT) improved from 615 to 633. Overall, the school had 148 full-time MBA students: 55 in the executive program, 48 in the evening program, and 45 in the Charlotte-based program.

Although the University played down its rankings, President Hearn conveyed their importance in a March 2 memo to the Board of Trustees:

> "Were Wake Forest to fall from the top tier of private institutions in the region and the nation, our future would be compromised. . . . We must compete on value, not price, by offering quality educational programs that public universities do not and will not be able to provide. . . . Private universities are the standard of excellence for all higher education. . . . The only strategic outcome for

Wake Forest is to secure ourselves firmly within the most successful group of private universities. We must measure ourselves—financially, academically, and otherwise—against that standard. . . . Situating ourselves firmly in the upper tier of private institutions is necessary to preserving Wake Forest's fundamental values. . . . Let me reiterate that we can only serve our historic constituency to the extent that we are successful in achieving the status of a national institution which 'speaks with a Southern accent.'"

Hearn estimated the entering class size for fall 1999 at 950, which was just the size the University wanted.

The Wake Forest Information Network (WIN) went online in July, providing a secure portal to an array of new intranet services tailored to students, faculty, staff, and alumni. Services included a campus and alumni directory, class schedules, advisees' grades, class rosters, and class "look book." Online registration and admissions would be added as the year went by, according to Anne Yandell, Director of Business Application Development, who had shepherded the WIN project since its inception in 1997. The last registration involving long lines in the Green Room took place in early January 1999. Beginning April 5, students could register for courses online through WIN's Student Services web page. At the same time, Netscape replaced LotusNotes for email.

Jay Dominick, Assistant Vice President for Information Systems on the Reynolda Campus, and Paul LoRusso, Vice President and Associate Dean for Information Services on the Bowman Gray Campus, headed efforts to secure the University against the Y2K bug; many programmers used 9999 as a code for *end of function*, and some feared that on January 1, 2000, unless they were reprogrammed to recognize the new century, computers would crash.

Jay Dominick was in charge of making sure the Y2K bug did not affect Reynolda Campus computers. He is at left in this photo, showing parents and students a Wake Forest laptop.

Academics

Wake Forest hired fifty-four new faculty members for the 1998–1999 academic year: thirty-eight to teach in the College of Arts and Sciences, eight in the Babcock Graduate School of Management, four in the Calloway School of Business and Accountancy, three in the School of Law, and one in the School of Divinity, which would open in fall 1999. Most replaced retiring faculty or were adjuncts.

Led by the American Association of University Professors (AAUP), faculty continued to ask why their salaries were comparatively low, while the President's salary in particular was high at $424,000. An *Old Gold and Black* editorial on November 19 took up the controversy, stressing the need for better compensation, and questioning whether the plan to hire forty more permanent faculty, as outlined in the Plan for the Class of 2000, could be achieved.

The Academic and Community Engagement (ACE) Fellowship program was initiated with support from the Fund for Leadership and Ethics. It assisted select faculty in introducing service-learning techniques into their classes to concretely attack social problems in Winston-Salem. Paige Wilbanks, Director of Volunteer Services, and Katy Harriger, Associate Professor of Political Science, conceived the idea.

The curriculum review committee, chaired by Associate Dean Claudia Thomas, made eighteen recommendations, which were considered individually at faculty meetings beginning on November 9. The first noted that most Wake Forest courses were worth four credits, but only three at most other universities; the faculty voted to change four-credit classes to three credits, and five-credit classes to four. On November 30, they voted to reduce the number of credits needed to graduate to 112, beginning with the entering class in 2000. Departmental requirements for majors were limited to thirty-eight credits, and students were allowed to take no more than forty-two credits in a single department. Later meetings approved, in principle, recommendations for students to take courses in the areas of multiculturalism and quantitative reasoning, and at the March 1 meeting the faculty recommended the establishment of a math center to assist students.

The Divinity School hired a varied founding faculty. Frank Tupper (Theology) had been a Visiting Professor of Religion at Wake Forest since 1997; Sam Weber (Early Church History and Spiritual Formation) was the first Catholic monk of the Order of Saint Benedict to teach at Wake Forest; and Phyllis Trible (Old Testament and Associate Dean) had been a Professor at Union Theological Seminary in New York before joining Wake Forest University in July 1998. Meanwhile, Dean Bill Leonard explored religious practices ranging from snake handling to Catholicism in editing a new essay collection, *Christianity in Appalachia: Profiles in Regional Pluralism.*

The Department of Counseling was named the 1999 Robert Frank Outstanding Program by the Association for Counselor Education and Supervision (ACES). It was selected from among hundreds across the country, including much larger programs offering doctoral degrees.

Allen Mandelbaum, Kenan Professor of Humanities, was awarded the Gold Medal of the City of Florence on June 3 as part of a ceremony honoring the 735th anniversary of Dante's birth. It was the first time a translator of Dante had been so honored.

Dale Martin and Ralph Tower were each selected for a chaired professorship honoring Wayne Calloway, the late PepsiCo executive and namesake of the Calloway School of Business and Accountancy, while Gordon McCray was named the Bell-South Mobility Technology Faculty Fellow. Stanley W. Mandel was named director of the new Center for Entrepreneurship and Family Business in the Babcock Graduate School of Management.

John E.R. Friedenberg (Theatre) became the new director of the theater upon the retirement of Harold Tedford, who had held the position for thirty-two years.

Funded by a state grant, Chemistry Professor Robert Swofford trained Forsyth County middle and high school science and math teachers to use technology more effectively in their classrooms during the year. Steve Messier (Heath and Sports Science) received national attention for his research on arthritis and aging. In Psychology, Robert Beck became the University Ombudsman, and adjunct Professor C. Drew Edwards published *How to Handle a Hard-to-Handle Kid*, which explained why some children appear especially challenging and suggested specific strategies for parents to address and to correct problem behaviors.

Education Professor John Litcher was presented with the Donald O. Schoonmaker Faculty Award for Community Service. Charles M. Allen, Professor Emeritus of Biology, received the Jon Reinhardt Award for Distinguished Teaching.

On January 18, Maya Angelou read Martin Luther King's "Letter from Birmingham Jail" in Wait Chapel. Written in 1963 after King was arrested during a demonstration, the letter became a classic of the civil rights movement. Later in the year, to commemorate her seventieth birthday, Winston-Salem State University threw a birthday party for Angelou.

Administration and Staff

The administration also witnessed change, transitions, and achievements. Margaret Perry, who had served the University for fifty-one years, stepped down as Registrar and assumed a new position as Registrar Archivist in the middle of the summer. Lu Leake became interim registrar on August 1, 1998, while a national search started. Dorothy A. "Dot" Sugden (MA '85) was named Registrar in May 1999. She had a master's degree in mathematics and years of experience in data analysis at Wake Forest. Nancy Respess was named Assistant Registrar and Director of Registration. Policy also changed: from the first of January, transcripts were available to students for free.

ICCEL celebrated its first anniversary in January 1999. It was already serving K–12 schools and corporations as well as institutions of higher education. In fall 1998, it donated more than seven hundred used Wake Forest laptops to the Winston-Salem/Forsyth County school system. James "Jay" L. Dominick was promoted to its Associate Dean while maintaining his responsibilities as Assistant Vice President for Information Systems and Chief Information Officer.

Three information systems staff members were promoted. Tommy Jackson ('88), who had been Networking Director for a year, became Director of Networking and Telecommunications. Ron Rimmer was named Director of Business Computing, and

Anne Yandell Bishop (MBA '97) was promoted from Director of Business Application Development to Director of Intranet Development.

Paul W. Barnes ('90, MBA '98) was appointed Director of MBA Annual Programs for the Babcock School. In University Advancement, Kevin P. Cox (MA, '81) was named Assistant Vice President. Bryan Link joined the staff as Director of Development and Alumni Affairs for the School of Law. Mark Aust ('87) was named Director of Wake Forest Clubs, while Tim Snyder ('88) became Director of Advancement Technologies. David McConnell ('95) was named Assistant Director of the College Fund, and Cathy Chinlund was named Director of Advancement Records and Technology Operations, with Tammy Wiles as her Assistant Director; David Davis ('98) was hired as Manager of Technical Development. Cheryl V. Walker ('88) was promoted to Associate Director of Media Relations. Julie Leonard joined the University News Service as a media relations officer.

Effective February 15, the Reynolda and Bowman Gray Campuses consolidated their respective departments into a single Internal Audit Department, reporting to Gary L. Eckenroth, who became the new University Compliance Officer.

Among individual recognitions, Bill Starling ('57) was presented a resolution of appreciation from the Wake Forest Alumni Council during its summer meeting on the fortieth anniversary of his tenure in the Admissions Office. President Hearn was honored October 1, 1998, at a dinner celebrating his fifteenth year as president, while John G. Medlin Jr. of Winston-Salem was elected Chair of the Board of Trustees.

Paul Brown, Program Director at WFDD, won the National Federation of Community Broadcasters' 1998 Silver Reel Award for Special Entertainment Program for his music documentary, "Breaking Up Christmas: A Blue Ridge Mountain Holiday." The program was distributed by NPR and recorded on a compact disc.

Athletics

The baseball team won the ACC Championship for the second year in a row on May 22. Under Head Coach George Greer and Pitching Coach Bobby Moranda, the team had a win-loss record of 43–23, best in the team's history. One of the highlights of the season was junior Mike MacDougal pitching the Deacons' first no-hitter in sixty years against Duke on March 12.

The Sports Marketing Department set up a new group, the Deac Freaks, to cheer at football games. Its President, senior Sedrick Jackson, was also President of the Screamin' Demons, the cheering group for basketball games. Students could be members of both and received transport and tickets to one away game.

To pump up school spirit and to get students excited about an upcoming basketball game with Georgia Tech, the three co-hosts of the WAKE television show *Sportsline*—Drew Brown, Daniel Ogle, and Dave Whalen—staged a twenty-hour marathon show on February 15–16. Despite their effort and a Wake Forest win over Tech, the Deacons finished the season with a 16–12 overall record and a second-round defeat in the National Invitational Tournament, falling to Xavier University 87–76.

The women's soccer team, ranked seventeenth nationally, was invited to the NCAA tournament but was defeated by the University of Georgia in the first round, 5–2. The Deacons finished the season 13–7–1. At the end of the season, the men's soccer team, ranked twenty-first nationally, lost 1–0 to ACC champion Duke but finished the season with a winning record of 11–7–1. The volleyball team finished the season 21–12, a dramatic turnaround from their 1997 season record of 8–24.

C.J. Leak, who played for Independence High School in Charlotte and was considered to be the sixth best quarterback in the country, signed a national letter-of-intent to play under Coach Jim Caldwell. His high school coach was less than pleased. Leak played for two seasons and then transferred to the University of Tennessee.

Plans were announced for a new intercollegiate basketball facility, a four-story, 60,000-square-foot Student-Athlete Enhancement Center. Construction was scheduled to begin in late summer 1999 so the facility would be ready for the start of basketball practice in October 2000.

A men's basketball scholarship was named in memory of long-time Deacon Club member Leslie M. Morris ('41, MD '43) of Gastonia by his widow, Mary Alice King Morris, and his son, Leslie Morris Jr. ('67).

Desmond Clark became the ACC's all-time leading pass receiver. He was a bright spot in a disappointing 1998 football season, when the team went 3–8 on the season. The October 22 *Old Gold and Black* praised not only Clark but quarterbacks Rusty LaRue ('96) and Brian Kuklick, whose passes made Clark's achievement possible. Both Clark and Kuklick were chosen to play in the postseason Blue–Gray game. In another honor, Head Coach Jim Caldwell was chosen as an assistant coach in the East–West Shrine Bowl.

Janelle Kraus, a 1997 All-American, won her second consecutive women's cross country ACC championship. The team rose as high as sixth in the national poll while winning four of five regular season meets.

The Arts

The first public exhibition of the J. Donald Nichols ('66) collection, "American Abstract Art of the 1930s and 1940s," was held in the Fine Arts Gallery from August 28 through October 11. Considered the best and most comprehensive private collection of abstract art from that era, it featured more than two hundred paintings, drawings, and sculptures by such artists as Willem de Kooning, Joseph Albers, and Stuart Davis.

The University Theatre staged Thorton Wilder's *The Match Maker* and hosted a symposium in conjunction, *Thornton Wilder's Legacy*, on September 25–26. A. Tappan Wilder, nephew of the playwright; Robin Wilder, editor of Wilder's letters; and Wilder's biographer Penny Niven (MA '62)

Desmond Clark

Janelle Kraus

attended. Other performances through the year included Caryl Churchill's *Mad Forest*, Henrik Ibsen's *Hedda Gabler*, and *Closer than Ever* by Richard Maltby Jr. and David Shire. *The Fantasticks*, a parody of *Romeo and Juliet*, was the first musical performed in the Ring Theatre.

The Secrest Artists Series included performances by pianist Chitose Okashiro; Hesperion XX, an early music ensemble; clarinetist David Shifrin and the Muir String Quartet; the Doc Severinson Big Band; actress Claire Bloom presenting "Portraits of Shakespeare's Women"; and the Russian State Symphony Orchestra.

The Student Union sponsored a continuing musical series ranging from karaoke night to such professional musicians as the Dave Matthews Band and Jazz and Blues. Comedian Jim Breuer, best known for his Goat Boy character on *Saturday Night Live*, performed in Wait Chapel on October 16. He was followed weeks later by Roger McGuinn, best known as founder of the folk rock band The Byrds in the 1960s. Yaron Svaroy, an Italian journalist, and film director Spike Lee spoke in Wait Chapel. The latter event was co-sponsored by the Office of Multicultural Affairs.

Campus and Student Life

At a mandatory meeting during orientation, new students heard from psychologist Jane Elliott about the detrimental effects of racism on children and society. Waving off initial applause, she promised, "I'm going to offend everybody in the audience in the next five minutes," and she went on to discuss the various types of racism in American society. The former third-grade teacher conducted a famous experiment in her classroom the day after Martin Luther King was assassinated, treating blue-eyed students differently from brown-eyed students. The childrens' reactions were subsequently printed in the newspaper, and Elliott became an icon in the field of the psychology of racism.

For the second year in a row, applications for undergraduate admission were down. In 1997–1998, the drop was 3 percent, but it was 12–15 percent in 1998–1999, although the quality of applicants did not vary. In her "The Last Word" column in the March 1999 *Wake Forest Magazine*, Vice President for University Advancement Sandra C. Boyette stated that enrollment in the college and the Calloway School stood at about 3,800, and about 60 percent of the student body was from the South.

Jenny Blackford was Editor-in-Chief of the *Old Gold and Black*; Kayamma Lewis was Editor-in-Chief of *The Howler*; and Student Government President was Susan Eggers.

Of the Class of 2000, which was the first class to receive laptop computers, 940 students, now juniors, traded in their IBM 365 computers for updated 380XD models that were theirs to keep after graduation. Features of the updated computers included Netscape mail and updated hardware.

The University placed new restrictions on tailgating. Students were limited to one vehicle per parking place. They could not have gas-powered generators or external stereo systems, and they had to leave the tailgate area for the game twenty minutes before kickoff.

Short scenes from a movie, *The Girls' Room*, were filmed on campus and in Reynolda Gardens during September. The filming did not stir much excitement, but the appearance of three Wake Forest women in the October special issue of *Playboy* did. Opinions about the appropriateness of their appearance varied widely across campus. Nevertheless, a signing was held at Walden Books in Hanes Mall soon after publication. Emily Wade, Emily Woodall, and Brianna Lorenz (a false name) signed their photos in the "Girls of the ACC" edition.

At a less controversial media event, five hundred copies of *Poor Horatio*, an independent literary magazine, were distributed on campus at the start of the school year, the work of Heather Chappell and Ernie Nesbitt. The magazine was funded by advertisements from local businesses. In an October 10 editorial, the *Old Gold and Black* praised it as "providing a fresh and humorous perspective on student life and life in general." In November, *The Fine Print*, the school's first fully student-organized online magazine, was unveiled by seniors Charles Murphy and David Brooks. It had several interactive features; one allowed students to give feedback. Gordon McCray (Calloway) was the faculty advisor.

With twelve graduates serving as volunteers, Wake Forest ranked twenty-first nationally among smaller colleges and universities promoting the Peace Corps. Sophomore Martin Price initiated a Unite for Peace candlelight vigil in front of Wait Chapel on October 29. Students and faculty gathered to speak out against hatred and in support of human dignity. The aim was to oppose messages of the Westboro Baptist Church, which had planned to protest the inclusive language adopted by the Board of Trustees concerning nondiscrimination against people with sexual orientations other than heterosexuality. The church finally staged a demonstration outside the Reynolda Road entrance to the University on November 28, while students were on Thanksgiving break. It was small, brief, and peaceful.

The Black Student Alliance published a minority undergraduate student directory. The twenty-two-page directory included more than 350 black, Hispanic, and Asian students on and off campus in hopes of encouraging unity and ensuring that they could get in touch with one another. On February 25, the Alliance for Racial and Cultural Harmony (ARCH) sponsored a two-hour forum on interracial dating called *Jungle Fever*, named after the 1991 Spike Lee film about an interracial affair. The March 4 *Old Gold and Black* reported that the well-attended event at Shorty's was divided fairly equally among students of all races—whites, blacks, Hispanics, Asians, and Native Americans. The consensus among those present was that interracial dating should be not just socially accepted but encouraged, if it leads to true love.

The Benson University Center hosted the Ethnic Heritage Faire in October. Center Director Joanna Iwata and twelve students organized a wide range of multicultural experiences, including performances by a mariachi band and a Caribbean steel drum band, Indian dancers and an African dance ensemble. Booths representing Africa, the Dominican Republic, France, Japan, the Middle East, and Spain were set up. In a parallel event, the Wake International Students Association sponsored its

Students dancing at the Black and Gold Ball

first dinner to welcome new international students to campus.

Kim Gandy, Executive Vice President of the National Organization for Women (NOW), spoke on March 30 on "The New Face of Civil Rights: The Shift from Minorities to Gays and Lesbians," sponsored by the Women's Studies Program, Student Union, Gay/Straight Student Alliance, Women's Issues Network, and the Winston-Salem chapter of NOW. Pugh Auditorium was packed. Gandy's address was followed a week later, on April 6, by writer, feminist activist, and social critic bell hooks (nee Gloria Watkins) whose address "Love, Race and Domination" examined topics such as African American feminism, the civil rights movement, and capitalism.

The Black and Gold Ball, a formal dance for all students, was reinstated by Residence Life and Housing after an eight-year absence. It was the grand finale of Residence Hall Week (November 12–20), a celebration promoting community spirit.

More than one hundred Wake Forest students went hungry for thirty hours on March 26–27 as part of the annual World Vision Thirty-Hour Famine to help fight hunger and poverty around the world. More than one hundred students from various campus organizations participated in WILD (Winston-Salem into the Lives of Deacs) on April 8. The community effort was in honor of National Youth Service month. Students volunteered at twelve community service agencies, doing yard work at the Ronald McDonald House, tutoring middle school kids at the YMCA, sorting food at the Second Harvest Food Bank, and working on trails at SciWorks.

After nearly a decade of performances, the Agape women's ensemble decided to disband because of differences over whether group members should hold to a literal interpretation of the Bible or include Christians of varying beliefs. Out of the breakup, two new women's a cappella groups were formed: One Accord and SOUL (Sisters of Universal Love).

The Merit-based Scholarship program organized an evening of dessert and discussion in the Oak Room in Reynolda Hall on the theme "Racism around Us." Nat Irvin, a writer for the *Winston-Salem Journal*, was the featured speaker, and the November 17 event was attended by students, faculty, and staff.

In December, Jennifer Bumgarner, a senior from Hickory majoring in Political Science, was named one of thirty-one Rhodes Scholars nationally and was the seventh from Wake Forest since 1986. She served on the editorial board of the *Philomathesian* and as a representative on the Commission on the Status of Women. In February, she was again honored as one of twenty students selected for *USA Today*'s 1999 All-USA College Academic First Team, which came with a cash award of $2,500. When asked what she would do with the money, Bumgarner replied that she would save it for her studies at Oxford.

Sarah Graham, a junior, won the Army Physical Fitness Test (the varsity sport of ROTC) with 347 points, the highest score for both men and women, at the ROTC Ranger Challenge event at Fort Jackson, South Carolina. Twenty-six teams from fifteen schools in North and South Carolina competed. Graham's reaction: "My score was higher than any of the Citadel guys, which is kind of cool."

Freshman Melissa Poe, who, when she was nine years old, founded a nonprofit children's environmental organization that had grown to more than 300,000 members, received a *Seventeen*/Cover Girl Volunteerism Award for her commitment to protecting the environment. The award came on top of one she had received during the summer, when she was declared a Disney Eco Hero and featured in an exhibit at Disney's Animal Kingdom.

Melissa Poe

Amy Powell, a sophomore, was named the top variety debater at the U.S. Naval Academy Debate Tournament in February. She beat more than seventy other debaters for the title. Senior Daveed Gartenstein-Ross, also a member of the debate team, was chosen as one of two U.S. representatives to the 1999 International Debate Tours.

The Maia Witzl and Julie Hansen Chi Omega Scholarships, created by their sorority sisters to honor the two young women killed by a drunken driver in 1996, were awarded for the first time. Recipients were Lindsay Bricolo, a senior at Glenn High School, and Kerri McDermott, a senior at Mt. Tabor High School.

In Greek life, Phi Mu sorority started a new chapter, which was officially chartered at the University with twenty-eight members on October 25. Women's rush started January 8 and included 333 participants. Men's rush ended with 175 men pledging.

Finances, Facilities, and Alumni

In a memo to Reynolda Campus faculty and staff on January 8, President Hearn explained new budget guidelines for the upcoming academic year, 1999–2000:

> During the past five years, Reynolda Campus expenses have increased by 56 percent, a total of $75 million. There are now important reasons to restrain increases in tuition, the largest revenue item in our budget. . . . We must restrain the growth in tuition to make it possible to retain 'need-blind' admissions. . . . We must moderate salary increases and reduce those other expenditures.

He pointed out that inflation was running at less than 1.5 percent, which meant budgeting should be easier than if costs were rapidly escalating.

> I have asked the vice presidents to work with me in eliminating $1.2 million in costs from the administration's operating costs. That goal will be met. This work can prove beneficial to us in identifying savings and can be achieved without the kinds of stringent measures—layoffs and cutbacks—that have occurred at other universities.

Phi Mu sisters

Just before Christmas, R.J. Reynolds had cut one thousand jobs.

I emphasize the University remains financially sound. A recent credit evaluation by Standard and Poor's found us to be in excellent condition, affirming our AA credit standard in a very positive report. It is precisely because our University is in a healthy condition that each of us must work to maintain its fiscal integrity, while making every effort to keep Wake Forest affordable for students from all income groups, now and in the future.

Hearn had asked the Budget Advisory Committee to prepare a budget based on an undergraduate tuition increase of less than 5 percent. The actual tuition increase for 1999–2000 was 4.7 percent, raising tuition to $21,420.

Wake Forest staff were unhappy with a salary increase of just 2.5 percent for 1999–2000. At a Speak Out on March 17, Lou Morrell, Vice President for Investments and Treasurer; Jim Ferrell, Director of Human Resources; and Kathy Fansler, a computer support consultant answered questions about the University's financial health and current salary policies.

In October 1998, Wake Forest University Baptist Medical Center launched the public phase of its $100 million capital campaign, emphasizing endowment development for education, research, and patient care. "Sustaining the Miracle: The Campaign for the Medical Center" had already attracted $64 million in pledges in its quiet phase. It was scheduled to conclude in June 2001.

One of the biggest financial surprises of the year occurred when Winston-Salem businessman Thomas Jack Lynch, who died in December 1995 at seventy-nine years old, left the Philosophy department $2.6 million in his will. His estate could not be settled until July 1998 because it was so large: $13.5 million. He had established the Thomas Jack Lynch Philosophy Endowment Fund in 1985. He specified that the new fund was "to be used for visiting professorships, visiting philosophers in residence, faculty sabbaticals, and special seminars, and not for the department's regular expenses."

Another nice surprise came in November 1998 when the Davis family of Winston-Salem—Egbert L. Davis Jr. ('33), Thomas H. Davis (LLD '84), and Pauline

Davis Perry—donated their family's home, Sunnynoll, to the University along with six acres of land at the corner of Reynolda and Polo roads. The residence alone was valued at $1.7 million. More surprising still, Amos Swann from Kodak, Tennessee, who had no University ties, bequeathed $1.1 million to Wake Forest to be used for need-based scholarships for undergraduates from Tennessee.

Information Systems Building

The Divinity School received a $200,000 grant from the Jessie Ball DuPont Fund to establish a professorship in homiletics, or the art of preaching.

WFDD listeners pledged a record $257,211 during the fundraising campaign that began October 17 and ended November 4—despite an interruption on October 21, when the main antenna failed.

Polo Hall, a 72,000-square-foot residence, opened in August. The $10.6 million building offered 194 upper-class students apartment-style living without having to deal with a landlord or electric bills. Preference was given to non-Greek students. Simultaneously, nine houses on Student Drive were closed because of poor conditions. At the same time, the Information Systems Building opened. It was a 70,000-square-foot, $6 million facility that housed Information Systems, ICCEL, and for a brief time campus ministry.

Student Health Services moved into the old ROTC space on the lower level of Reynolds gymnasium on February 2 and took the name of the late George C. Mackie, long-time college physician on the old campus (1930–1956). The facility included the Taylor Wellness Center, named for Mary Ann Hampton Taylor, who directed Student Health Services from the late sixties until her retirement in 1991, and a conference room named for Paul S. Garrison, her predecessor. Campus Ministry moved into Kitchin Residence Hall, where Student Health Services had been located.

The Music Department opened a new lounge in the Scales Fine Arts Center that allowed students to meet and to practice informally. Previously, students gathered in the halls and sat on the floor of the Scales lobby for casual interactions.

A ceremony was held on October 23 to dedicate a campus street near the Worrell Professional Center in honor of the late Carroll Weathers, Dean of the School of Law from 1950 to 1970. Robert K. Walsh, the present Dean, and members of the Weathers family spoke. At the medical center, the clinical sciences building was renamed the Richard Janeway Clinical Sciences Tower in honor of the former Executive Vice President for Health Affairs.

The Wake Forest Ministerial Council established a scholarship to honor long-time University Chaplain Edgar D. Christman and his wife, Jean Sholar Christman. The scholarship would be awarded to an undergraduate chosen through the William Louis Poteat Scholarship program.

For the first time, the sixty-member Alumni Council of the undergraduate college had 100 percent participation in the College Fund.

Polo Hall

Summing Up the Year

The 1998–1999 academic year focused on globalization and diversity. Celebrations of cultural contributions alternated with programs and seminars considering racism. As the third most-wired campus in the United States, Wake Forest championed connection; for example, the new Wake Information Network (WIN) made intranet communication easier, especially student registration. Student achievement remained strong, highlighted by Jennifer Bumgarner, Wake Forest's seventh Rhodes Scholar since 1986 and one of twenty students selected for *USA Today*'s 1999 All-USA College Academic First Team. In athletics, the Diamond Deacons won the ACC baseball championship for the second straight year, and Desmond Clark set a new record for the most passes caught in the ACC.

The faculty began implementing findings from a curriculum review. Due to budget tightening, some faculty and staff members grumbled about inadequate compensation and meager raises, while they felt administrators were overcompensated. The Information Systems Building (later known as University Services Building, and renovated and renamed Alumni Hall in 2012) and Polo Residence Hall both opened, and construction started on the rotunda at the rear of Wingate Hall to create offices for the School of Divinity. The Davis family, who financed a good deal of the rotunda, also donated their estate, Sunnynoll, to the University.

At commencement, the baccalaureate service featured the new Dean of the Divinity School, Bill Leonard, and Nigerian Cardinal Francis Arinze addressed 828 undergraduates and 618 graduate and professional school students on "The Role of Religion in a World Seeking Harmony" as the 156th commencement speaker. The temperature was a cool fifty-two degrees, with a rainy mist; for the first time, tickets were required for commencement, and students were each issued two parking passes.

CHAPTER SEVENTEEN
1999–2000

A Divinity School, Vienna, Anticipation, and Controversy

In recent moral history, no event stands out like the Holocaust. The lessons of this tragedy-too-great-for-speaking repudiate moral relativism. The relativist says that good and right are culturally determined. But, it did not matter morally that the Nazi Government was legitimate or whether this terror was the result of generally accepted anti-Semitic social norms. Observations of social mores are irrelevant to the moral assessment of what happened. The Holocaust taught us, vividly, and I would have thought forever, that human beings possess rights not bestowed by governments or dependent upon social mores.

Thomas K. Hearn Jr., May 15, 2000;
Charge to the Graduates, Wake Forest University Commencement

A major event of the 1999–2000 academic year was the opening of the School of Divinity in August. The inaugural class comprised twenty-four students, nineteen women and five men. The idea had been discussed since the mid-1940s, but long-range planning began in earnest in April 1989, three years after Wake Forest ended its relationship with the Baptist State Convention of North Carolina. Although a $15 million endowment was needed for the school to be self-sustaining, by 1999 University officials realized that building an endowment was a slow process, and skepticism about the project was growing. Rather than lose the good will of those who had already contributed and pledged around $10 million, they pushed ahead. The dedication ceremony was held on October 12–13, and the theme for the opening convocation was "Theology at the Threshold of the Twenty-First Century."

Wake Forest defined the new school as "Christian by tradition, ecumenical in outlook, and Baptist in heritage" (Bill Leonard, personal interview, July 27, 2012). Feeling that the University's Baptist heritage would inform but not insulate the

Participants in the Divinity School inauguration gather on the quad after the ceremony

school's mission, it became the first university-based divinity school in the United States to start without a formal denominational affiliation. The curriculum developed around its mission. Traditional seminary subjects, such as biblical, theological, and historical studies, were combined with an art-of-ministry program that required a senior project/thesis or third-year internship. Another distinctive feature was a required off-campus experiential learning course that took students to Appalachia and New York City, as well as Egypt, Cuba, Israel, Nicaragua, and Romania.

Jill Crenshaw was hired as Director of Ministry Studies. James Dunn was Resident Professor of Christian Ethics and Public Policy. Crenshaw and Dunn, along with Bill Leonard and Phyllis Trible, established the curriculum and refined it before the first classes were offered. Adjunct professors taught all other courses. The school

Bill Leonard became the first dean of the Wake Forest Divinity School

granted a Master's of Divinity degree (M.Div), the standard degree for ministers in the United States.

Leonard's mission was to make the Divinity School a part of the University, which meant connecting with the Schools of Law and Medicine and formalizing a dual-degree agreement with the Counseling program. In addition to teaching, he and Wade Stokes (Development) were charged with fundraising and received grants from the Carpenter, Henry Luce, Jesse Ball DuPont, and Cannon foundations. Upon his arrival, Leonard had to raise $2 million.

The second major story of the year was the October 3 dedication of the 7,200-square-foot Flow Haus, a stately, three-level 1890s home in Vienna, Austria. The house was a gift from Trustee Vic Flow ('52) and his wife, Roddy. The first fourteen students to live in the Flow Haus began their studies on August 25 under German Professor Larry West. They focused on the German language, while taking courses in medieval literature, art, music, architecture, and theatre.

A third major story was a controversy that erupted in the fall, when the Wake Forest Baptist Church, an autonomous congregation that met in Wait Chapel, allowed the University Chaplain, who was a member, to perform a same-sex union ceremony. Prior to the event, Board of Trustees Chair John Medlin appointed an ad hoc committee, chaired by Michael G. Queen ('68), pastor of Wilmington's First Baptist Church, to study the question. The Trustees noted that the church should decide but asked that the ceremony not use University facilities. Queen met with church officials on several occasions, informing them of the request, and President Hearn delivered a formal message from the Trustees to the church on September 8. The church went ahead with the ceremony using University facilities.

Two news reporters, Paul Brown and Michelle Johnson, resigned from WFDD in protest to what they perceived as censorship and an infringement of their first amendment rights when they were asked to limit their coverage of the event to a University news release containing the full text of a Trustee report. Some faculty were also upset that the Trustees and administration acted without consulting them and that the Trustees' wording struck them as discriminatory. At their October meeting, the faculty passed a resolution calling on the President and Trustees to assure them of academic freedom and to reaffirm the University's nondiscrimination policy. Vice President Sandra Boyette, who was responsible for WFDD, told the University Senate that neither she nor her staff asked the station to limit its coverage of the Trustee response.

In response, the President appointed an interim advisory committee composed of Miles Foy (Law), Katy Harriger (Political Science), Michael Hazen (Communication), Wayne King (Journalism), and Harry Titus (Art) to address editorial concerns at the station, while an editorial policy was developed for the news staff. At Boyette's request, President Hearn later moved responsibility for the station from University Relations to the Provost's Office.

On a happier note, the University teamed with the Winston-Salem Convention and Visitors Bureau in fall 1999 to submit a bid to bring a 2000 presidential debate to campus. On January 6, 2000, the Commission on Presidential Debates (CPD) announced that it had selected Wake Forest to host the second of three debates on Wednesday, October 11, 2000, at 9 p.m. in Wait Chapel. The other two debates would be held at the John F. Kennedy Memorial Library in Boston and Washington

The Flow Haus

University in St. Louis. A vice presidential debate would be held at Centre College in Danville, Kentucky. Perhaps the strongest aspect of Wake Forest's application was its proposal, as the third most-wired campus in America, to incorporate the Internet's burgeoning capabilities and to appeal particularly to younger voters. A Presidential Debate page was mounted on the Wake Forest website, and Art Director Samantha Hand created the University's logo. Wake Forest was required to recruit sponsors to

Vic and Roddy Flow

provide a total of $550,000 to the commission for debate production, and to build anchor booths and camera platforms in Wait Chapel that would reduce the seating capacity to about 1,200. President Hearn held a news conference at Graylyn to announce the awarding of the debate.

Academics

Forty-five new faculty were hired at the start of the academic year, most of whom replaced faculty who had left or retired. *U.S. News & World Report*'s 2000 guide to America's Best Colleges ranked Wake Forest twenty-eighth on the basis of its small classes, low student/faculty ratio, high graduation and retention rates, financial resources, and alumni giving. The Calloway School of Business and Accountancy was also ranked twenty-eighth among the best undergraduate business programs. Calloway students achieved the highest passing rate in the country on the Certified Public Accountant (CPA) exam—nearly 83 percent compared with the average 24 percent elsewhere—catapulting Wake Forest into the number one spot in this category, more than seventeen points ahead of its nearest competitor, the University of Virginia. As a part of its growth, the Calloway School proposed an undergraduate degree program in management information systems for implementation in fall 2000. Senior Vice President Ed Wilson recommended its approval to the President in a September 23 memo.

The University was ranked nineteenth among America's top fifty most-wired universities and research institutions, according to *Yahoo! Internet Life* magazine. The American Productivity & Quality Center (APQC) and the American Assembly of Collegiate Schools of Business (AACSB), an international association for management education, designated Wake Forest one of six best-practice organizations for its innovative use of information technology in education.

Faculty recognition

In the Art department, Bernadine Barnes was named the first McCulloch Family Fellow. She joined the faculty in 1989, and her area of expertise was Renaissance art. Charlotte C. Weber, member of the Board of Trustees from 1993–1997, funded the Charlotte C. Weber Chair of Art, only the second endowed chair for a specific department. David M. Lubin, an expert on twentieth-century American art and culture, joined the Art department as the first Weber Chair. Weber also endowed the Charlotte C. Weber Faculty Award in Art with a gift of $2.5 million. With David Levy (Music), David Faber formulated a plan to exhibit student art throughout the year rather than only once. The Beethoven Gallery in the Scales Fine Arts Center, beside Brendle Recital Hall, was set aside exclusively for the display of student art.

Margaret Supplee Smith and Winston-Salem writer Emily Herring Wilson (MA '62) co-authored a book commissioned by the North Carolina Division of Archives and History, *North Carolina Women: Making History*. It described the many women who influenced North Carolina history. A copy was placed in every middle school and high school library in the state through a gift from Wachovia Bank. Both Smith and Candelas Gala (Romance Languages) were named Wake Forest Professors.

Wake Forest chemistry graduate student Thomas Poole and professor Bruce King talk about their research

S. Bruce King (Chemistry) was awarded one of six 1999 Henry Dreyfus Teacher-Scholar Awards. The $60,000 awards, given by the Camille and Henry Dreyfus Foundation, recognize early-career faculty for their teaching, mentorship, and research, primarily with undergraduates, in the chemical sciences. Funds provided salary support, research equipment, and supplies for undergraduate student researchers in King's lab. Biology Professor Gerald Esch won the 1999 Mentor Award from the American Society of Parasitologists, recognizing his extraordinary leadership in training young scientists and influencing the research and graduate education of a department, college, or institution.

Fred Howard (Mathematics and Computer Science) was elected President of the Fibonacci Association, an international, 700-member group focused on the study of elementary number theory and combinatorial analysis.

At the Calloway School, Annette Lytle Ranft (Business) was named the Exxon-Wayne Calloway Faculty Fellow. Clay Hipp (Calloway) stepped down as the University's judicial officer to work full-time as a senior lecturer.

Allan Louden (Communication) received the George Ziegelmueller Award from the National Debate Tournament Board of Trustees in May 2000. The award was presented to a faculty member who had earned distinction in the communication profession while coaching debate teams to competitive success at the National Debate Tournament. Wake Forest's performance at the tournament in the last ten years included a national championship in 1997, three final-four teams, four final-eight teams, six top sixteen teams, and eleven other teams who qualified for the elimination rounds. The debate squad had been ranked among the nation's top ten programs in every year of the preceding decade.

Mary Wayne-Thomas's theatre costume designs were the subject of an exhibit in the Scales Fine Arts Gallery in September 1999

David Coates (Political Science), who taught and wrote comparative studies about United States and European systems of economics, politics, and social order, was named the Worrell Professor of Anglo-American Studies beginning July 1, 1999.

In the Music department, Dan Locklair, composer-in-residence, was awarded a North Carolina Arts Council Artist Fellowship. On February 1, Teresa Radomski and Louis Goldstein directed a program by contemporary composers John Cage and George Crumb entitled "Rainsticks and Ancient Voices."

Donald H. Wolfe, Professor and Chair of Theatre, was presented the Marian A. Smith Distinguished Career Award by the North Carolina Theatre Conference at its annual meeting. Mary Wayne-Thomas's twenty-year career with the department as a designer and creator of costumes was the subject of a September exhibit at the Scales Fine Arts Gallery. It traced the design process from artist renderings and fabric swatches to the final costume.

The Divinity School named Brad R. Braxton, a Baltimore Baptist minister, as the Jessie Ball duPont Assistant Professor of Homiletics and Biblical Studies.

Jeanne Simonelli, an applied cultural anthropologist, was appointed the new chair of the Department of Anthropology. The department had thirty-five majors, three full-time professors, one half-time professor and museum director, one full-time temporary faculty member, and adjuncts.

Calloway School of Business and Accountancy

Sarah Watts (History), Chair of the Student Life Committee, and Vice President Ken Zick undertook a study of the campus climate for gay students in March.

The Physics Department received an IBM SP-2 supercomputer that could "simulate different types of cosmic collisions to see what kind of gravity waves each lets loose," allowing the pursuit of various questions related to condensed matter physics.

The Women's Studies program and the Women's Health Center of Excellence at the School of Medicine sponsored a series of events September 13–18 as part of the second annual fall initiative on violence against women. The cardiac rehabilitation program, the first in North Carolina and one of the first in the nation, celebrated its twenty-fifth anniversary on May 2. It had helped over 3,000 individuals. Its medical director, Henry S. Miller Jr., was recognized for his many contributions.

As the Calloway School of Business and Accountancy observed its fiftieth anniversary, it was ranked in the top 10 percent of American undergraduate business schools by *U.S. News & World Report*'s college guide. Founded in 1949 as the Wake Forest School of Business Administration, it offered bachelor of science (BS) and bachelor of business administration (BBA) degrees, and students were enrolled for all four years. In 1952, it offered only the BBA, and students entered in their junior year after two years of liberal arts education. It now offered four degrees: a BS in analytical finance, a BS in business, a BS in mathematical business, and a BS/MS in accounting. The liberal arts requirement held. The school had thirty-five full- and part-time faculty members and some 405 students.

The Graduate School held its first hooding and awards ceremony in May on the Saturday preceding Monday's commencement exercises in Wait Chapel.

The Wake Forest University Press sponsored a week-long Irish Festival in March. The celebration of Irish culture included a four-night Irish film series, Irish bands, Irish poetry, the Triad Irish Dancers, and Irish storytelling. The Museum of Anthropology hosted a special exhibit, "Queen Anne's Revenge: The Search for Blackbeard's Flagship," from August 20 to September 14.

Administration and Staff

On November 9, the President sent a memo to faculty about communication between faculty and administration.

> . . . as we together pursue our educational mission, the University administration and the faculty must maintain effective dialogue. To the extent that members of the faculty do not believe that their opinions are adequately heard and valued,

misunderstanding and mistrust result. In the end, this is a matter for which I am responsible. I believe that our processes are imperfect and we depend too much on the use of intermediaries between the faculty and this office.

I am prepared to work for better communication and those improved relationships which enhance trust. The deans will be arranging opportunities for me to meet with members of our faculty. I am eager to provide an opportunity for every faculty member who wants to participate.

I hope these gatherings can be primarily listening sessions for me. I want to hear from you directly about communication and other issues and to discover what method or venues you regard as most useful in securing a direct faculty voice in the administration. When these discussions are concluded, I will report back to you with a plan to implement the necessary changes we have identified.

On December 1, Hearn wrote Carole L. Browne, President of the University Senate, to announce his intention to attend its meetings whenever possible. "This should allow us to have one regular forum in which faculty leadership and the administration can confer on a regular basis."

On January 14, he addressed a large audience of faculty and staff in Pugh Auditorium. He was responding to meetings with faculty in the previous semester that resulted from the widespread complaints voiced during the Wake Forest Baptist Church/WFDD controversy. Faculty felt they had little input into administrative decisions and policy formation. Hearn said that the meetings made clear that beneath last fall's controversy lay strong feelings about the faculty salary plan and last year's pay raises. Some faculty accused the administration of reneging on the goal set forth in the Plan for the Class of 2000 (now called the Wake Forest Undergraduate Plan) to boost average faculty salaries at all ranks to a level above the average at comparable institutions. Although the President noted that salaries for continuing faculty had risen an average of 5 percent this year, which had been the goal, he acknowledged that joint-admission institutions had matched or outpaced Wake Forest's salary increases.

Further, the Trustee decision regarding the use of Wait Chapel for a same-gender union ceremony had made it clear that the University needed a general policy on the use of all campus facilities, not just use of facilities by extramural groups for religious meetings. The discussion continued through the spring, and appropriate campus groups were consulted.

In another reaction to the controversy, at the request of Sandra Boyette, President Hearn moved oversight of WFDD from University Relations to the Provost's Office. On October 25, he wrote a memo to Vice Presidents and Deans: "Effective immediately, the supervision of WFDD is being moved to Associate Provost Samuel Gladding." On February 4, Gladding sent a letter to the campus community outlining what was being done in regard to the station, but on February 9, an ad hoc University Senate committee issued an eighteen-page report on the fall controversy. At a subsequent subcommittee meeting, Gladding attested that most of the recommendations of the report were being implemented, including new staff appointments, a formal statement supporting WFDD's editorial integrity, and a newly established advisory board. Paulette Cott was promoted to News Director, and Bob Workmon to Program

Leon Corbett; Reid Morgan

Director. Kimberlea Daggy was promoted to Music Director.

Y2K turned out to be YAWN2K. The rollover to 2000 was a nonevent at Wake Forest, as Assistant Vice President and Chief Information Officer Jay Dominick reported. Planning to work from 10 p.m. New Year's Eve until 10 a.m. New Year's Day, he went home at 3 a.m. having tested "everything I knew how to test." He also called off plans to have the staff report at 10 a.m. on New Year's Day to fix faulty programs. Before January 1, the University had set up two phone lines to address the Y2K problem, but neither was needed. The medical center also took precautions and had hundreds of extra nurses on duty for the rollover. "A nurse was stationed at the bed of every patient requiring electrical or mechanical equipment. In addition, 132 extra doctors were on hand as a precaution, not so much for the patients already at the medical center, but for those who might show up," explained Paul LoRusso, Vice President and Associate Dean of Information Services at the medical center.

The year brought changes among administrative staff. Leon Corbett announced his retirement effective July 1, 2000, although he continued to serve as Senior Counsel, Secretary to the Board of Trustees, and Corporate Secretary. Reid Morgan became General Counsel and manager of the Legal Department and continued as Assistant Secretary to the Board of Trustees.

President Hearn outlined his retirement plan to Hubert B. Humphrey, a Trustee from Greensboro, in an April 3 letter. He said he would retire at age seventy and give the Board of Trustees a full year's notice to ensure an orderly search for his replacement. He had taken on another responsibility as Chair of the Center for Creative Leadership's Board of Governors.

The Office of Career Services promoted Carolyn Couch to associate director. In the same office, Patrick Sullivan became Assistant Director for Technology and Experiential Education, and Allison Corkey was named Assistant Director for Career Development.

Rebecca (Becky) Glen Hartzog was named the new Associate Chaplain and Baptist campus minister. Donald "Buz" Moser, former commander of the Military Science department, became the new Director of University Stores, including the bookstore and its textbook section, the Deacon Shop, the Information Systems bookstore, the Bridger Field House shop, merchandise sales at basketball and football games, and vending and catalog sales.

Pia Wood, Director of the Undergraduate International Studies Program at Old Dominion University, replaced Richard Sears (Political Science) as Director of

International Studies. Sears returned to full-time teaching, and Wood was also given an academic appointment in the Department of Political Science. International studies was to become one of Wake Forest's highest priorities for the next decade. Approximately 50 percent of students studied abroad before graduating, and to ensure they received adequate information on programs

Donald "Buz" Moser

other than those run by Wake Forest, they were required to attend an information session and to make an advising appointment with a staff member in International Studies.

In University Advancement, Betsy J. Chapman ('92, MA '94) was named Director of Alumni Programs, and Lori Dishman (MA '98) became Director of Gift Stewardship. The Office of Research and Sponsored Programs changed its name to the Division of Research Programs and Partnerships.

The Calloway School announced four new administrative positions. Helen Akinc was promoted to Assistant Dean for Student Professional Affairs; J. Kline Harrison was named Associate Dean for Curriculum and Administration; Betsy Hoppe was named Assistant Dean for Student Academic Affairs; and Dale Martin was promoted to Associate Dean for Academic Programs and Resources. Yvonne Stewart became the Director of the Arthur Andersen Accounting Research and Information Center.

Human Resources, which had been managed by Lou Morrell, was transferred to John Anderson. Ralph D. Pedersen was named its new director in mid-January 2000, succeeding James (Jim) L. Ferrell, who retired January 7 after twenty-five years of service. Pedersen had been Director of Human Resources at the University of Utah since April 1996, and before that he had held a similar position for a decade at UNC-Charlotte. He was a retired Army lieutenant colonel.

The University Editor's Office received the Grand Gold Medal for Overall Publication Programs, the top award in the national Council for Advancement and Support of Education (CASE) Circle of Excellence competition.

Richard Janeway (Medicine) received the Medallion of Merit, the University's highest award. David G. Brown published *Always in Touch: A Practical Guide to Ubiquitous Computing*, which discussed the power of computers to connect, especially on a college campus.

In an unrelated but fun event, Kevin Jasper, a programmer/analyst in the Information Systems department, won the 2000 National Hollerin' Contest held in Spivey's Corner, North Carolina.

Athletics

Wake Forest beat Notre Dame for the NIT men's basketball championship at Madison Square Garden on March 30, and a celebration rally was held in Reynolds gym on April 4. The team's final record was 22–14.

Club Rugby

The football team also did well, compiling a 7–5 record and winning the Jeep Eagle Aloha Bowl in Honolulu on Christmas day, beating Arizona State 23–3. The season and the bowl victory would be among the high-water marks of Head Coach Jim Caldwell's tenure at Wake Forest, the first winning season since 1992.

In women's sports, the volleyball team went 25–9 (10–6 in the ACC) for its most successful season in history and its second consecutive twenty-win season. The team was led by Trina Maso de Moya, ACC Volleyball Player of the Year. Head Coach Mary Buczek was honored as the ACC's Coach of the Year. The field hockey team went 18–4 (2–2 in the ACC) and and was third in the nation, its highest national ranking ever. Head Coach Jennifer Averill was named Coach of the Year by both the ACC and the

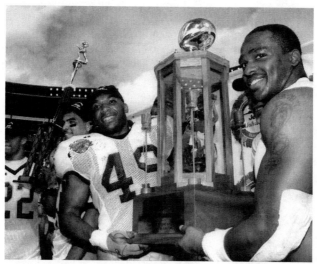

The football team celebrates after winning the Jeep Eagle Aloha Bowl

National Field Hockey Coaches Association (NFHCA).

The women's tennis team finished the season with an overall record of 18–1 and was ranked second in the nation. It was defeated in the ACC tournament by Duke. In women's cross country, Head Coach Francie Goodridge's contract was not renewed, and she left before the start of the season. Annie Schweitzer Bennett was hired as her replacement. At one point, the team was ranked nineteenth nationally. It was anchored by Janelle Kraus, who finished her career with a school-record twelve individual titles.

Trina Maso de Moya

The women's soccer team went 16–6–1 (4–3 in the ACC) and enjoyed its most successful season in the six-year history of the program. It advanced to the championship match of the ACC Tournament for the first time and earned a national ranking of seventh. It received a bid to the NCAA Tournament for the fourth consecutive season and advanced to the round of sixteen teams.

The men's soccer team went 13–3–5 (2–1–3 in the ACC) for third place in the ACC. It had been ranked as high as third in the nation by the National Soccer Coaches Association of America (NSCAA), its highest ranking to that time.

The men's soccer team had their best season ever

While the baseball team did not win the ACC title again, they had a winning record (41–20–1), went to the NCAA Regionals, and were ranked twentieth in the country at the end of the season. Men's Cross Country Coach John Goodridge resigned in August to protest the termination of his wife's contract and was replaced by Bill Dellinger, the legendary coach at Oregon for twenty-three years, who had just retired. The squad finished third at the ACC Championships and fifth at the NCAA Regional Championships.

Overall, Wake Forest was one of only ten schools in the country and the only ACC school to participate in postseason play in football, men's basketball, and baseball during the 1999–2000 academic year. A third of Wake Forest's varsity athletes—110—made the ACC Academic Honor Roll, earning a 3.0 grade point average or better.

In individual accomplishments, Barbara Walker was named Associate Athletic Director and Senior Women's Administrator. She was in charge of thirteen sports, including men's golf, men's and women's tennis, men's and women's soccer, men's and women's track and field/cross country, women's basketball, volleyball, baseball, and field hockey.

In another change in the athletic department, Jim Davis became Assistant Athletic Director of Media Relations when John Justice left after sixteen years to join International Sports Processes, a sports marketing firm in Winston-Salem. Davis left after only a month, and Jen Hoover was named interim director.

Ground was broken for the new student-athletic enhancement center on April 25. It was projected to cost $9.5 million and to open in fall 2001. Wake Forest students were athletically active on a number of levels. Probably the largest increase in participation was on the club and intramural levels. Max Floyd reported that participation had grown 78 percent since 1994–1995, when about 3,500 students participated in intramural sports. By 1999–2000, participation had increased to 6,233, and the variety of sports had grown; for example, there was a club rugby team and a club ice hockey team.

The Arts

The University Theatre staged four productions during the year: Fay Kanin's *Good-bye, My Fancy*; Tom Stoppard's *Arcadia*; Anna Deavere Smith's *Twilight, Los Angeles, 1992*; and Gilbert and Sullivan's *H.M.S. Pinafore*.

Jane Mead, poet-in-residence, gave a reading on November 16 in the Scales Fine Arts Center's Ring Theatre. African American poet Nikki Giovanni spoke about her life and work on November 18.

The Secrest Artists Series featured five concerts. They began in October with the Vienna Chamber Orchestra, followed in November when Rick Benjamin's Paragon Ragtime Orchestra accompanied a Charlie Chaplin film festival. Guitarist Christopher Parkening and special guest artist Jubilant Sykes, baritone, presented "Braziliana!," an evening of music from South America in January. "The

Barbara Walker

The production of H.M.S. Pinafore was very popular

Mandinka Epic," a spectacle of music, song, and dance from the heart of West Africa, came to the University in February. The last performance in the series was the female a cappella ensemble Anonymous 4, who focused on music from the 11th century.

Music researcher Elizabeth Jordan presented "The Holocaust: Musicians and Choices" on September 9. Her lecture focused on the Third Reich's effect on music and musicians. It specifically examined songs that were composed in concentration camps and ghettos, and other songs that had psychological importance among prisoners and survivors. In April, playwright Claudia Stevens performed a one-woman musical drama, "An Evening with Madame F," a mixture of music, song, and drama, to depict the experience of Fania Fenelon, an Auschwitz inmate forced to provide musical entertainment to the Nazis.

In October, mezzo-soprano Grace Johnson and classical guitarist Michael Nicolella gave separate performances in Brendle Recital Hall, and the Wake Forest Concert Choir premiered "Shepherds Rejoice," two Christmas anthems by composer-in-residence Dan Locklair.

The Scales Fine Arts Gallery displayed "New Acquisitions to the Wake Forest University Print Collection" on March 13–29. A slide lecture by one of the artists, Warrington Colescott, was held on March 17. (Every four years, starting in the mid-1960s, the University sponsored an art-buying trip to New York City, where selected students used University money to buy original art works that were then brought back to campus and usually displayed in campus buildings. The new acquisitions were usually first displayed as a group such as the one mentioned at the opening of this paragraph.)

The Student Union sponsored performances by singer Rodie Ray, singer and songwriter Del Suggs, The Mike Plume Band, Neintown Steel and Mark Firehammer, acoustic pop trio Guster, Grammy-nominated banjo virtuoso Bela Fleck and the Flecktones, and *Saturday Night Live* comedian Kevin Nealon.

Campus and Student Life

At the end of August, 982 freshmen moved into their residence halls and began orientation activities. The first-year class comprised 505 women and 477 men from forty-four states and seven foreign countries. With their arrival, the University reached a milestone in its technology initiative. All undergraduates now had their own IBM ThinkPad computer for use inside and outside of the classroom. The complete estimated cost to a student for the 1999–2000 academic year, according to the Wake Forest webpage, was $27,620.

The year's theme was "Science and Technology: The Next Millennium," chaired by William E. Conner (Biology). The opening convocation on September 16 was to feature James D. Watson, author of *The Double Helix* and Nobel Prize winner for the discovery, with Francis Crick, of the molecular structure of DNA, but it was canceled due to the threat of Hurricane Floyd. The rest of the year featured a plethora of programs on topics like genetics, technology, cloning, encryption, and sustainability, as well as a film series and a number of related first-year seminars. On Founders' Day, February 10, David Suzuki, award-winning geneticist, environmentalist, and host of the television series *The Nature of Things*, spoke.

The Templeton Guide: Colleges that Encourage Character Development, published in October by the John Templeton Foundation, named Wake Forest University to its annual Honor Roll of one hundred colleges committed to the development of conscience, character, citizenship, and social responsibility among students. Wake Forest was one of only three North Carolina schools included, recognized for outstanding academic honesty, substance-abuse prevention programs, and student leadership programs. The guide named President Thomas K. Hearn Jr. as one of the top fifty college presidents for demonstrating leadership and character.

Wake Forest and Winston-Salem State celebrated the fortieth anniversary of the student sit-in at the Woolworth's lunch counter at Fourth and Liberty

The Year of Science and Technology logo

Chinese New Year Festival

Streets to protest segregation. The celebration, "Leadership and Civil Rights: Retrospective and Prospective Visions," featured free and public events at both universities and in downtown Winston-Salem on February 23–24, 2000. Event highlights included the dedication of a commemorative historical marker by Winston-Salem Mayor Jack Cavanagh, panel discussions with the former student participants and local civil rights leaders, and a Unity Sing with music groups from both universities. The celebration grew out of a Civil Rights Symposium called "Leadership and Civil Rights" held on the Wake Forest campus and organized by Susan Faust (Communication) and Mary Dalton (Communication). As a companion project, Dalton and Faust produced a forty-five minute video documentary on the sit-in and its ramifications, *I'm Not My Brother's Keeper: Leadership and Civil Rights in Winston-Salem, North Carolina*. It aired on North Carolina public television on September 29. With a grant from the Fund for Leadership and Ethics, Dalton and Faust sent copies to every public library in North Carolina, including public university and community college libraries, and all Winston-Salem/Forsyth County middle schools for inclusion in their North Carolina curriculum.

On March 1, University of California, Santa Cruz Professor Angela Davis, who gained national attention as a political activist in the 1960s, spoke. The turnout for her presentation was modest.

Students, faculty, staff, and alumni made a three-day trek to the former campus for a celebration of University history. Provost Emeritus Ed Wilson ('43) delivered an address, "Unrivaled by Any," on Saturday, April 1, in Binkley Chapel.

The first campus-wide program to celebrate the Chinese New Year was held on February 13 in the theater lobby of the Scales Fine Arts Center. It was organized and executed by Cristina Yu of Z. Smith Reynolds Library with a grant from the Fund for Leadership and Ethics. It featured demonstrations and hands-on activities highlighting various aspects of Chinese culture, including calligraphy, face painting, paper folding, tea tasting, and acupuncture. It attracted over two hundred participants, including many students, and became an annual event.

A campus memorial service was held on September 18 in Wait Chapel for Kathryn Ann "KC" Clendenin, a rising junior, who died suddenly on Wednesday, June 16,

First Sit-In Victory in North Carolina marker

in Virginia, where she was spending a second summer as a counselor at the United Methodist Church's Camp Highroad. Family, friends, and classmates of KC recalled her joy in being a Wake Forest student and her participation in the University orchestra in stories and songs.

Khalid Jones was Student Government President. Robert Numbers II was Editor-in-Chief of *The Howler*; Jenny Blackford and Theresa Felders were Editors-in-Chief of the *Old Gold and Black*. Sheereen Miller was the Student Trustee.

The *Old Gold and Black* published an anti-Semitic brochure, "The Revisionist," as an advertising insert on March 14. It aroused "anger and deep concern" on and off campus. In a March 21 memo to the University community, President Hearn stated that "the content of the brochure is offensive and deplorable . . . the decision to include the insert was made without consultation within the student newspaper's editorial staff and no conferral with the larger community." It "caused harm to others" as well as the University community. "We apologize for the harm done to individuals and to our community. We must be about the work of reconciliation." The Anti-Defamation League (ADL) expressed its gratitude to Hearn for this response.

The Student Environmental Action Coalition and the campus chapter of Amnesty International hosted an Earth Day celebration on April 7. Before the event, students participated in a Campus Sweep, picking up litter.

The Deacon Angels, a group of young women who helped recruit football players by showing them around campus, were chartered as an official student group and then roundly criticized for perpetuating sexism.

In an effort to bring together different elements of the campus, Student Union, the Interfraternity Council, and the Panhellenic Council combined their annual Springfest and Greek Week into a joint Deacon Days celebration in mid-April. The event featured the Quad 500, a relay race; a Greek sing; and an initiative to take a faculty member to lunch.

Kathy Smith (Political Science) sponsored The Tie that Binds, a program that sought to cross bridges of race, ethnicity, and socioeconomic status to promote cultural awareness and respect. She and nine students volunteered at the Tbilisi Youth House for Internally Displaced Persons in the Republic of Georgia for two weeks after the semester ended.

The Quad 500

The number of STARS (Student Technology AdvisoRS) increased to forty. Under the direction of Andrea Ellis and funded by an anonymous grant, they were enlisted to educate faculty in the use of technology. Since their modest beginning when the Plan for the Class of 2000 was put in place, STARS had helped sixty-six faculty in twenty-seven departments, including some in Medical and Law Schools.

The student-initiated Brian Piccolo cancer drive turned twenty and by fall 1999 had raised over $435,000 to support cancer research and treatment through Wake Forest's Comprehensive Cancer Center. In another act of giving, seniors Karen Stephan Borchert and Jessica Jackson Shortall created Homerun to provide home-cooked meals for the sick and needy. In 2006, they would partner with DC Central Kitchen to form Campus Kitchens at thirty-three universities nationwide.

Junior Dan Durand and seniors Kevin Woods and Jacob Kline won the International Mathematical Contest in Modeling. They competed against approximately four hundred teams representing several countries. Over four days in February, they were closeted together to draft a forty-page solution to an open-ended, real-world math problem. To celebrate the victory, the Math Club rolled the Quad.

Jessica Esther Posner, a junior history major with a minor in Latin American studies, was one of sixty-one students awarded a 2000 Truman Scholarship. She planned to seek a master's degree in public health with a focus on women's reproductive health.

A junior, Ann Marie Collins, was diagnosed with bacterial meningitis in early October and treated at the medical center. Those who had close contact with her were urged to visit health services to receive a single tablet of Ciprofloxacin, also known as Cipro. Approximately 150 students responded. Collins recovered.

Theta Chi, Sigma Chi, and Kappa Kappa Gamma received special recognition plaques for fundraising in support of the Rape Aggression Defense (RAD) program in a ceremony organized by University Police. Drew Fletcher, former President of Theta Chi, received an individual award for his role in planning the event, conceived by Patrol Officer Thomas Slater. The money was used to sponsor the free participation of forty-four women in, and to achieve full accreditation of, the program.

Kappa Sigma returned to campus after a two-year suspension.

Facilities, Finances, and Alumni

The opening of East Hall (later Greene Hall), slated for July 23, was delayed by a faulty first-floor concrete pour that had to be redone. Claudia Thomas Kairoff coordinated the effort to find space for 180 classes until the first week of October. Her biggest challenge was Romance Languages: eighty-three of its classes met five days a week. At the same time, several classrooms in Tribble Hall were upgraded to include multimedia presentations. Emergency power capability was upgraded in Reynolda and Winston halls, too.

The two-story addition to Wingate Hall was completed in late July and became the main entrance to the Divinity School, while Kitchin Residence Hall's lower level was renovated from the Student Health Center to the Office of Campus Ministry. With the installation of new fire alarms and smoke detectors in Collins, Kitchin, Palmer, and Piccolo residence halls, the three-year plan to upgrade fire alarm protection

Pan Geos

equipment in all of the residence halls was completed. Sprinklers were also installed. The final stage of work was scheduled for the summer of 2000.

On May 16, the University donated more than 580 sets of furniture from Kitchin, Efird, Huffman, Palmer, and Piccolo residence halls to the Hurricane Floyd relief effort in eastern North Carolina, and about 250 more that the University had in storage were donated a few days later. Wake Forest employees, volunteers from area churches, businesses, and the Baptist Men of North Carolina moved the donated furniture.

The Wachovia Bank branch on campus shortened its hours from 9 a.m. to 5 p.m. to 10 a.m. to 2 p.m., causing displeasure among students, staff, and faculty. The bank justified its new hours, stating that 70 percent of its business occurred between 10 a.m. and 2 p.m.

Pan Geos Granary, a ubiquitous Mexican eatery that served healthy food, took the place of Taco Bell in the Benson Food Court when Taco Bell sales declined. Because of the emphasis on fresh food, it was open only from 10:30 a.m. to 1:30 p.m. and 5 p.m. to 7:30 p.m.

The chains that had surrounded the Quad for over a decade were removed on the recommendation of the Capital Planning Committee. Former head groundskeeper Melvin Layton had them put up in an effort to preserve the grass.

From fall 1998 to spring 1999, Parking Management issued 18,321 parking tickets. During summer 1999, a parking lot near Polo Residence Hall was paved, and utilities were moved to prepare for construction of a new building for basketball practice and athletics education behind the Athletic Center. At a speak-out in Pugh Auditorium on April 5, John Anderson, Vice President for Finance and Administration, said that plans were being prepared for a day-care center in the meadow area north of Reynolda Village and for a parking deck on the lot behind the Scales Fine Arts Center. The day-care center would have space for about 150 children; the parking lot 250 spaces. Each was projected to cost $4.5 million. One, but not both, of these projects would be submitted to the Trustees at their October 2000 meeting. Anderson said that contrary to popular belief, faculty and staff parking was in shorter supply than student parking.

Wake Forest became one of the first institutions in North Carolina to implement the American Heart Association's Public Access to Defibrillation program. Staff members and students were trained to use automated external defibrillator machines specifically designed for nonmedical personnel with only a few hours of training.

A $150,000 grant from the Starr Foundation benefited the Wake Forest Research Fellowship program, which enables students to join faculty mentors as junior partners in scholarly research projects. Juniors and seniors selected for the program received $2,000. A $228,305 grant from the Charles E. Culpepper Foundation supported a three-year summer program allowing faculty to create and to use new ways of teaching with technology. WFDD received a grant from the Winston-Salem Foundation that allowed the station to fund a new cultural program, "Live from Studio A." Hosted by Kimberly Daggey, the show featured local musicians, and the station acquired a restored 1923 Steinway piano for live performances.

The Henry Luce Foundation awarded $255,356 to fund four Clare Booth Luce Scholarships for outstanding undergraduate women in science, mathematics, or computer science. In both fall 2000 and 2001, two scholarships were awarded to cover tuition, room and board, and other fees and expenses for their junior and senior years. Edwin Andrews and his wife, Nancy, of Asheville established a scholarship in the Divinity School in honor of his father.

The Duke Energy Corporation awarded the Calloway School of Business and Accountancy $500,000 in honor of the late Thomas H. Davis, a member of Duke Energy's board of directors from 1978–1990. Davis designated the University as the recipient of his memorial gift, which was added to the endowment for the Calloway School's Thomas H. Davis Chair of Business, held by Umit Akinc. The Kirby Foundation gave $5 million for construction of a new wing on Calloway Hall. The gift was the largest from a foundation outside of Forsyth County and the largest gift ever to the Calloway School. The 50,000-square-foot addition was projected to cost about $14 million and would be located at the back of Calloway Hall. Nearly four hundred students enrolled in the Calloway School annually, and one in five Wake Forest students earned a degree from it.

The Trustees approved a 4.6 percent full-time tuition hike for undergraduates, to $22,410 for the 2000–2001 academic year. Full-time tuition for 1999–2000 was $21,420. On February 5, they also approved a salary opportunity fund, devised by Lou Morrell. It separated $35 million in unrestricted money from the University's endowment pool and invested it aggressively. The idea was to raise faculty salaries to the mean of a group of peer institutions over the next two years. Davidson, Duke, Emory, Richmond, UNC-Chapel Hill, UVA, Vanderbilt, Washington & Lee, and William and Mary were considered peer-comparable, or joint admission, institutions at the time. The plan called for spending $2.2 million during the next two years to lift faculty salaries through merit raises to the average of the joint admissions group. An additional $1 million was to be spent to boost staff salaries. This money was in addition to increases already scheduled as part of the University's long-range financial plan, which called for 3.5 percent faculty raises and 2.5 percent staff raises for 2000–2001.

On April 28, the Board of Trustees approved a total operating budget of $584 million for the 2000–2001 fiscal year beginning July 1. The new budget included $384 million for the Bowman Gray Campus and $200 million for the Reynolda Campus, increases of 11 percent and 4 percent, respectively.

In an April 10 memo to the University community, President Hearn wrote:

"The Heritage and Promise Campaign which ended in 1995 was our first attempt at a national funding effort, and it successfully brought in $172 million against a goal of $150 million, which put it $22 million over its target. That campaign . . . was heavily devoted to bricks-and-mortar, because our early planning processes had identified space as the primary obstacle to academic growth."

Hearn stated that even with a healthy growth in endowment, Wake Forest was still "70 percent tuition-dependent." The University endowment had a market value of $974.2 million at the end of February 2000, which included stocks and bonds as well as real estate. The Reynolda Campus represented 53 percent and the Medical School 47 percent. The University spent 5.3 percent of its endowment each year, but the Reynolda Campus endowment was 48 percent restricted.

The Campaign for Wake Forest University: Honoring the Promise was announced privately. It concentrated on raising endowments for scholarships and faculty support.

It would be announced publicly in the spring of 2001 and run for five years. Joining Hearn as campaign co-chairs were Victor I. Flow Jr. ('52), William B. Greene ('59), J. Donald Nichols ('66), A. Alex Sink ('70), C. Jeffrey Young ('72), and Alice K. Horton. In the previous campaign, more than one hundred scholarships were funded, and the number of endowed chairs and professorships grew from nineteen to forty-three.

Wake Forest University Baptist Medical Center surpassed its $100 million goal ($103 million) in its capital campaign, Sustaining the Miracle, the largest in its history. It began in July 1996 and concluded in June 2001. Funding priorities were creating centers of excellence in such areas as aging and cancer; endowment support for faculty, students, and academic programs; and general funding and annual support for special programs.

Among alumni, Eddie Timanus ('90) of Reston, Virginia, became the first blind contestant to compete on *Jeopardy*. He became an undefeated champion after five wins and took home two cars and nearly $70,000. Law school alumnus Ed Wilson Jr. ran for the Democratic nomination for Lieutenant Governor.

Summing Up the Year

The opening of the School of Divinity in August was a highlight of the year. The dream that had been nurtured since disaffiliation with the Baptist State Convention of North Carolina in 1986 was now a reality. It became the University's sixth major academic unit.

Another celebration came with the announcement on January 6, 2000, that the Commission on Presidential Debates (CPD) had selected Wake Forest to host the second of three debates on October 11, 2000, in Wait Chapel. It would be the second time in twelve years the University had been so honored.

The third major story of the year was the dedication of the Flow Haus in Vienna, Austria, the third major overseas residential property, and a gift from trustee Vic Flow ('52) and his wife, Roddy. The first fourteen students arrived in late summer, and President Hearn joined Peter Csendes, Deputy Chief of the Viennese Archives, to speak at the October ceremony that officially marked its dedication.

The last significant story of the year involved controversy. The autonomous Wake Forest Baptist Church conducted a same-sex union ceremony in Wait Chapel, a University facility. Two WFDD news reporters resigned their positions because they felt they had been prevented from fully covering the story. As a result, oversight of WFDD was transferred from University Advancement to the Office of the Provost, and the station drafted a statement on integrity and responsibility.

The baccalaureate service featured author and novelist Reverend Frederick Buechner, whose book was required reading during the Year of Religion and American Life. The 157th commencement speaker was John Chambers, President and Chief Executive Officer of Cisco Systems, Inc., a worldwide leader in networking for the Internet. The combination of theology and technology appeared to be an appropriate way to end the year.

CHAPTER EIGHTEEN
2000-2001

A Presidential Debate, the Beginning of a Campaign, and the Z. Smith Reynolds Gift

As blessings—uncertain and undeserved—the rewards of our lives are rendered sacred. Suffering can teach us, if we are wise, that we live by grace.
    Your neighbor is anyone who, on your life's way, needs your compassion and care. Each person is your neighbor in the neighborhood that is the world.

Thomas K. Hearn Jr., May 21, 2001;
Charge to the Graduates, Wake Forest University Commencement

At the beginning of the 2000–2001 academic year, Wake Forest had an enrollment of 3,938 undergraduates. Of the 536 women and 499 men in the first-year class, 7 percent were African American and 12 percent overall were minorities. The University's graduate programs upped the total enrollment of the University to 6,235 students: the Graduate School of Arts and Sciences had 577 students; the Babcock Graduate School of Management, 615; the School of Medicine, 442; the School of Law, 477; the Divinity School, 50; and the Allied Health Program, 136. The student/faculty ratio was an enviable 10.5 to 1, with 348 full-time undergraduate faculty offering thirty-four majors. Average SAT scores of the entering students reached a new high, between 1210 and 1390, and in an unusual move, the University accepted fifty of them for enrollment in January rather than August because more had enrolled than expected, and there were not enough rooms in the fall. At $22,410, tuition was also at an all-time high.

For the second consecutive year, Wake Forest ranked twenty-eighth among national universities and colleges in *U.S. News & World Report's* 2001 guide *America's Best Colleges*. The guide also ranked Calloway School of Business and Accountancy twenty-eighth among the nation's best undergraduate business programs. For the second year in a row, Calloway students achieved the highest passage rate in the country on the Certified Public Accountant (CPA) exam; twenty-two out of twenty-five students who took the exam passed. Second-place University of Virginia was seventeen points behind!

The *Financial Times of London* ranked the Babcock Graduate School of Management fifty-fifth among the world's hundred best graduate business schools, thirty-sixth among U.S. business schools, twenty-second among private U.S. business schools, and tenth among nondoctoral degree-granting graduate business schools. It was also ranked first in North Carolina and the southeast and eleventh among the world's top fifty business schools in a survey of corporate recruiters conducted by *The Wall Street Journal*.

Against this setting, there were three major stories for the year: a presidential debate, the start of another national capital campaign, and a new pledge of financial support from the Z. Smith Reynolds Foundation.

The Presidential Debate

Wake Forest was in the spotlight for the second time in twelve years, as a nationally televised debate between George W. Bush and Al Gore was held in Wait Chapel on October 11.

Wait Chapel was originally designed to seat 2,400, but over the years renovations had reduced main-level seating to 1,588 and balcony seating to 662. For the 2000 presidential debate, all balcony seats and some main-level seats were removed, leaving about 1,200 seats. A ticket was a prized commodity, and more than 1,500 students volunteered to help in preparations and follow-through.

Before the debate was secured, Wake Forest had to convince the Commission on Presidential Debates that it could support the event financially. Enterasys Networks was the leading sponsor, and as they had in 1988, Wachovia Corporation and US Airways joined. Other sponsors included BellSouth, Duke Energy (an in-kind gift), Idealliance, the *Winston-Salem Journal*, TITAN Technology Partners, Panasonic, Opinioneering Corporation, Flow Automotive Company, and Mr. and Mrs. Charles D. Peebler Jr. of New York City, who were members of the Parents' Council.

In other preparations for the debate, the University created a dedicated website, http://debate.wfu.edu, to regularly update information. "Our preparations for the debate have sparked creativity throughout the University community," said President Hearn "Since learning of our selection as a debate site last January, students, faculty and staff have been exploring how to make the most of this extraordinary educational opportunity."

2000 Presidential Debate logo

Professors designed and taught related courses. Allan Louden (Communication) offered Great Teachers: Presidential Debates; Kathy Smith (Political Science), Topics in Public Policy: Debates and Campaigns; and David G. Brown (Economics/ICCEL), a first-year seminar titled Ways of Thinking about Presidential Campaigns. In the days leading up to the debate, the Political Science department organized a conference on Debatable Issues in the Presidential Campaign, featuring twelve panel discussions (October 3–6), and the School of Law hosted a Presidential Election Symposium from October 6–8. Both programs featured outstanding outside speakers and University faculty.

In addition, the University hosted an interactive online educational project. More than 2,200 high school students in Advanced Placement U.S. History and Government classes at more than seventy high schools nationwide participated for nine weeks in Linking Debatable Issues: The Wake Forest Advanced Placement Electoral Project. In other electronic initiatives, Wake Forest students encouraged debate and voting through partnerships with Opinioneering Corporation and SpeakOut.com. A panel of students developed and led real-time online discussions on important topics related to the presidential election.

On the day of the debate, at a party in a tent outside of Davis Chapel, the candidates met. Using an online registration system, the University selected seventy-five undergraduates, fifteen graduate students, and ten faculty/staff as potential ticket winners. In actually, the University had 220 tickets, and more than 150 undergraduates attended.

On the night of the debate, moderated by Jim Lehrer of the *MacNeil-Lehrer News Hour* on PBS, more than four hundred students, alumni, faculty, and staff gathered

President Hearn greets Al Gore on his arrival for the 2000 Presidential Debate

on the Magnolia Quad to watch a live broadcast on a giant screen, while select guests, including retired four-star general and statesman Colin Powell and North Carolina Senator John Edwards and his wife Elizabeth, gathered in Pugh Auditorium in the Benson University Center to do the same. Security was tight. A suspicious package found on Poteat Field was blown up by the bomb squad. After the debate ended, students rolled the Quad with red, white, and blue streamers.

The rock band Hootie and the Blowfish, rap artist Rah Digga, and alternative singer Daniel Cage gave a free concert in the Lawrence Joel Coliseum, sponsored by Rock the Vote, a nonpartisan group working to increase youth participation in the political process. The music began at 7 p.m., but there was an intermission from 9 p.m. to 10:30 p.m. so the crowd could watch the live telecast of the debate. Benson served as the media center. It housed approximately 750 of 2,500 media representatives starting on October 9, twice as many as in 1988, according to University reporter Kevin Cox. During the debate, the phones went out but came back on in time for reporters to file their stories. As many as a thousand volunteers provided clerical, computer, and technical support, hospitality, and directions. Volunteers signed up on a website until September 17, and training was held on September 18–20. Preference was given to undergraduates.

The University granted public gathering permits to several groups, including American Atheists, Falun Gong (Falun Dafa), West Triangle Chapter Million Mom March, and the Libertarian Party of Forsyth County. One permit was granted to a private citizen. Demonstrators could gather in a designated area near the University Parkway entrance from 6 p.m. until 1 a.m. on debate night. The number of applicants for undergraduate admission to the University rose after the presidential debate, just as it had after the first presidential debate on campus twelve years before.

Honoring the Promise Campaign

A second major story of the year was the launch of the Honoring the Promise Campaign on April 26, 2001. Wake Forest began this $450 million capital campaign with $300 million designated for the Reynolda Campus. It was the second major campaign in a decade and included both campuses of the University. Called Honoring the Promise, its primary goals were to raise funds for student scholarships and faculty support. It was ambitious, striving for triple the amount of the Heritage and Promise campaign of the early 1990s, which had a goal of $150 million. During the quiet phase of the campaign before April, over

Students rolled the quad with red, white and blue streamers after the debate

$264 million was raised, $140 million by the Reynolda Campus and $124 million by the School of Medicine.

The campaign was kicked off with a speech by President Hearn and then a Deacons on Parade event, modeled on Chicago's public art exhibit, Cows on Parade, held in 1999. Five hundred buttons with the words *Deacons on Parade* were distributed before the fiberglass figures were walked around the quad so everyone could see them. Nineteen seven-foot-tall Deacons, made of fiberglass and decorated by students and faculty, were a part of the procession around the Quad. They included the Wake Forest Signature Deacon; Dr. Deacon; Four Muses Deacon; Calloway Deacon; Baptist Student Union Deacon; Devoted Deacon; Athletics Deacon; Presidential Deacon; Tim Duncan Deacon; Greek Deacon; Babcock's Manager of the Global Future; Deacon and the Technicolor Dream Coat; Solid Gold Deacon; Golf Deacon; Joe Judge; Liberated Form; 2000 Presidential Debate Deacon; Cadet Deacon; and Sequin Deacon.

Most of the Deacons were sold at auction during Homecoming Weekend of 2002 (October 26–27) and raised $35,000, most of which went toward the student-supported goals of the campaign, but each group who decorated a Deacon also received some funds. Jennifer Richwine was the Director of Campaign Programs, which ran through June 30, 2006, and eventually raised $689 million. The campaign's rationale, according to President Hearn, could be summed up in a sentence: "It is time to move Wake Forest again, not in place but in purpose."

The Z. Smith Reynolds Foundation Gift

A third major story of the year was the Z. Smith Reynolds Foundation of Winston-Salem making a pledge in perpetuity of 3 percent of its annual income to Wake Forest.

Deacons on Parade

The pledge, announced at a November 3 press conference, was the largest long-term commitment ever made to Wake Forest by a foundation, equivalent to adding $15 million to the endowment. The first gift was predicted to be approximately $750,000; 25 percent would fund scholarships for North Carolina students from middle income families; 20 percent, Gordon scholars; and 15 percent, Reynolds scholars. Another 20 percent would be used as salary supplements for promising young faculty and to establish new Reynolds Professorships. The last 20 percent would be used for special undergraduate programs and needs. The Reynolds Foundation was giving the University $1.2 million annually at the time the gift was announced.

Academics

Amanda Carlson and Matt Silversten ('98) suggested a theme for 2000–2001: The Year of Ethics and Honor. Co-chaired by Mary Foskett (Religion) and Sam Gladding (Associate Provost), activities included an address by Stephen L. Carter, author of the 1994 best-seller *The Culture of Disbelief: How American Law and Politics Trivialize Religious Devotion* and the 1999 book *Civility*, at the fall convocation. At Founders' Day, lawyer and Harvard Professor Mary Ann Glendon spoke on "One Nation: Two Cultures," addressing human rights in the United States and abroad.

The year also featured a panel discussion on business ethics; a lecture on athletics and ethics by *Sports Illustrated* writer John Feinstein; a symposium on law and morality led by Columbia University Law Professor Patricia J. Williams; a lecture by Arthur Schwartz of the John Templeton Foundation on character education; a program on "Moral Outlook in the Poetry of Robert Frost," led by President Hearn; a conversation on human sexuality from a Christian perspective hosted by pastor and sociologist Tony Campolo and his wife Peggy, who held opposing views on homosexuality; a film series; and a University Orchestra concert, "Ethics Exemplified," led by David Hagy, in which pieces by Mozart, Hindemith, Mahler, and others were selected to reflect aspects of ethics. J. Philip Wogaman, President Bill Clinton's pastor, delivered a series of lectures, and Robert Audi, Charles J. Mach Distinguished Professor of Philosophy at the University of Nebraska, presented the A.C. Reid Lectures during March and April on "Moral Value and Human Diversity" as part of the Year of Ethics and Honor.

Academic programs and individual faculty efforts were strongly rewarded. The Andrew Mellon Foundation contributed $45,000 to the International Studies Program to extend its activities beyond the classroom and into campus life. The U.S. Department of Education also awarded it $216,557 to expand the Latin American Studies Program. Steven Folmar, Visiting Professor of Anthropology, used funding from the Forsyth Early Childhood Partnership to provide the first cultural competency training offered to North Carolina teachers and other professionals working with Smart Start, a program for children five years and younger. In another first, Folmar took undergraduate students enrolled in SPIN

Z. Smith Reynolds

F O U N D A T I O N
Z. Smith Reynolds Foundation

(Summer Program in Nepal) to that country to learn about its religious and cultural diversity.

Linda Nielsen (Education) received the Outstanding Volunteer Award for 2000 from Today's Woman Health and Wellness Center. Steve Nickles (Babcock, Law) was confirmed by the U.S. Senate to a position on the newly created Internal Revenue Service Oversight Board, while Carol Anderson (Law) was named President of the Forsyth County Bar Association for 2000–2001.

In the Music department, David B. Levy and Stewart Carter contributed to the second edition of the *New Grove Dictionary of Music and Musicians,* long regarded as the standard music encyclopedia in the English language. Angela Hattery's book *Women, Work, and Family: Balancing and Weaving,* examining the ways mothers with young children resolve the conflict between job and family, was published by Sage. In Sociology, Charles F. Longino Jr. was elected President of the Association for Gerontology in Higher Education (AGHE); Earl Smith, Rubin Professor of American Ethnic Studies, was elected the twenty-first President of the North American Society for the Sociology of Sport; and Catherine T. Harris was elected President of Alpha Kappa Delta, the International Sociology Honor Society.

The Calloway School of Business and Accountancy named Jonathan Duchac the first Merrill Lynch Professor in Accounting and Paul Juras the Pricewaterhouse-Coopers Professor for Teaching Excellence. Don Robin became the first J. Tylee Wilson Chair of Business Ethics, a position made possible by a $1 million gift from

Year of Ethics and Honor logo

BellSouth Corporation. In the spring, Robin became Editor of the *Journal of the Academy of Business Education*.

In Health and Exercise Science, Paul Ribisl gave a keynote address, "The New Y2K Problem: Obesity: Genes, Gluttony, or Sloth," at the fifteenth annual meeting of the American Association of Cardiovascular and Pulmonary Rehabilitation. Shannon Mihalko found a link between exercise and breast cancer survivors' quality of life.

Robert M. Helm, Worrell Professor of Philosophy, was honored at the International Symposium of Philosophy in Zacharo, Greece, for his contribution to the science of philosophy and the cultural development of Greece.

Leadership and Civil Rights in Winston-Salem, a documentary written by Mary Dalton (Communication), debuted on February 23 in Carswell Hall's Annenberg Forum. It told the story of the Winston-Salem Woolworth's sit-in, where black students from Winston-Salem State University and white students from Wake Forest University joined together to protest segregated lunch counters on February 23, 1960.

Maya Angelou (Humanities) was one of twelve recipients of the National Medal of Arts. Her long-time friend, Dolly McPherson (English), the first African American woman to join the Wake Forest faculty in 1974, retired. She taught classes in British literature, African American fiction, and autobiography. Doyle Fosso, Professor Emeritus of English, received the Jon Reinhardt Award for Excellence in Teaching, while Willie Pearson Jr. received the Donald O. Schoonmaker Faculty Award for Community Service.

At Founders' Day, Vic Flow was awarded the University's highest honor, the Medallion of Merit. Angela Hattery (Sociology) was awarded the Kulynych Family Omicron Delta Kappa Award for Contribution to Student Life. Nina Lucas (Theatre and Dance) was awarded the Reid-Doyle Prize for Excellence in Teaching. Kathleen Kron (Biology) and James Schirillo (Psychology) received the Award for Excellence in Research. Patricia J. Roberts (Law) was presented the Joseph Branch Excellence in Teaching Award. Ajay Patel (Babcock School) received the Kienzle Teaching Award.

Sally Shumaker (Medical School) became director of the newly created Office of Intercampus and Community Program Development. Her goal was "to discover innovative ways to enhance graduate and undergraduate education and research on both campuses and to integrate programs cross-campus and within the community."

In departmental changes, Computer Science split from Mathematics and became its own department with eight full-time faculty members. The Department of Mathematics had been renamed the Department of Mathematics and Computer Science in 1984. Both departments were housed in Calloway Hall. Jennifer Berg became Chair of Computer Science, while Richard Carmichael chaired Mathematics.

Margaret Thatcher, former Prime Minister of Great Britain, delivered the Babcock School's Broyhill lecture in Wait Chapel on February 16.

Walter Brueggemann, McPheeters Professor of the Old Testament at Columbia Theological Seminary in Decatur, Georgia, presented three lectures as part of the Divinity School's J.T. Albritton series on March 4–5. Nobel Prize-winning author Derek Walcott offered a writing workshop, book signing, and talk on April 10, co-sponsored by the English and History Departments.

The History of Economics Society held its twenty-eighth annual meeting in Worrell Professional Center from June 29 to July 2. Dan Hammond (Economics),

President-Elect of the society, hosted the event. The Department of Music, represented by Stewart Carter, in conjunction with the Historic Brass Society, hosted the seventeenth annual Early Brass Festival from June 29 to July 1 in Brendle Recital Hall.

College faculty voted to switch from the academic credit system to an hours system. Students who entered the University in fall 2001 would earn hours instead of credits for their coursework. In general, a class that met three hours per week would be worth three hours toward the 112 hours required for graduation. In the 1970s, the University briefly experimented with a schedule that included a January term, necessitating the use of credits, and after abandon-

Margaret Thatcher

ing it never switched back to its previous hours' system. To ease the transition, both systems would run concurrently for up to six years.

Wayne Silver (Biology) directed the new neuroscience minor, first offered in the fall semester. A twenty-hour minor in health policy and administration was also added.

Wake Forest University Press celebrated its twenty-fifth anniversary in March during the annual Irish Festival. The major publisher of contemporary Irish poetry in North America was still one of the smallest university presses in the country. President Hearn commemorated the tenth anniversary of the Tokai–Wake Forest undergraduate exchange program in a November 25 letter to Tatsuro Matsumae, President of the Tokai University Educational System.

The Department of English named its faculty lounge after esteemed poet A.R. Ammons ('49), who died February 25 in Ithaca, New York. He won the National Book Award for Poetry in 1973 and 1993. He visited Wake Forest on several occasions to read and to teach classes.

The Women's Studies Library opened on September 5. Four years in the making, it was located in C113 Tribble Hall and housed 450 books, seventy compact discs, and twenty-five videos.

Administration and Staff

In an August 23 letter, President Hearn responded to Claudia Thomas, Chair of the Committee to Implement the Report on the Status of Women. He enlisted Ralph

Pedersen, Director of Human Resources, to help her monitor and evaluate progress toward the goals and keep the administration informed. In one response, the University Police Department secured a $200,000 grant from the U.S. Department of Justice to develop strategies to combat violence against women on campus. In disappointing news, the Trustees deferred construction of a day-care center ($5 million), estimating it would cost $250,000 a year for the University to subsidize it. However, they did approve faculty representation on Trustee Committees. Faculty chosen by the Senate would begin to serve in April 2001. In a November 8 letter, Senate President David Levy (Music) thanked President Hearn for this decision and the other "good work you do on our behalf [that] often goes unseen and unacknowledged."

On the Reynolda Campus, beginning September 1, certain benefits already provided to spouses of full-time University employees were extended to same-gender domestic partners, including health and dental insurance and tuition concessions. On November 3, President Hearn wrote that three recommendations from Ralph Pedersen and the Senate were being implemented: increasing the allowable contribution of pre-tax dollars to the medical flexible spending account from $2,000 to $4,000; a six-week paid maternity leave policy for staff; and changing the qualification for long-term disability so that employees received help when unable to do their job, rather than when totally disabled.

On September 13, Edwin Wilson was appointed Chair of the Provost Search Committee, with Reid Morgan providing staff support. Members of the committee were Deborah Best (Psychology), Stewart Carter (Music), Timothy Davis (Law), Mary DeShazer (English), Frederick Harris, Betsy Hoppe (Calloway School), Bradley Jones (Chemistry), Bill Leonard (Divinity), Minta McNally (Alumni Relations), John Moorhouse (Economics), and Sally Shumaker (Medical School).

In new appointments announced July 1, 2000, Doug Edgeton (Medical School) was appointed Senior Vice President for Health Affairs. Reid Morgan was named General Counsel, replacing Leon Corbett, who became Senior Counsel. At WFDD, Linda Ward became Executive Director of Station Development, while Jay Banks ('74, MBA'76) became interim station manager for six months until taking on the position permanently in April. Larry Schooler and Renee Boyd joined as general assignment reporters for the news staff.

Mary Gerardy, Assistant Vice President for Student Life, was appointed Coordinator of Gay and Lesbian Students as the result of a study conducted by the Student Life Committee at President Hearn's request. Its most disturbing finding was that both subtle and direct harassment and hostility were frequently directed toward gay students. In her new role, Gerardy provided information, support, and programming for gay and lesbian students and acted as a staff liaison and resource for other campus constituencies addressing concerns. A lounge in the Benson University Center was authorized for the Gay-Straight Student Alliance.

Nancy Crouch was promoted to Assistant Chief Information Officer and Anne Bishop to Director of Research and Development in the Information Systems Department. Robin M. Sorensen was named Assistant Director of Institutional Research.

District III of the Council for the Advancement and Support of Education (CASE) gave the University Advancement office its highest recognition in the institutional projects category for its involvement in the presidential debate. The University

Editor's office won a couple of awards, and the Babcock Graduate School of Management won Merit Awards in the media relations and publication categories.

Wake Forest also received the Pioneer Award at the Fourth Annual Conference on Ubiquitous Computing at Seton Hall University, recognizing the comprehensive technology initiative in 1996, which provided students, faculty, and staff with laptop computers.

Tim Auman

Dean Gordon Melson became President-Elect of the Conference of Southern Graduate Schools, and Tim Auman, United Methodist campus minister, was named Campus Minister of the Year by the United Methodist Foundation for Higher Education. More than 350 campus ministers from across the nation were considered for this honor.

Randal L. Hall, an Assistant Director of Scholarships, published *William Louis Poteat: A Leader of the Progressive-Era South*, and signed copies at a public reception on September 14 in the University Bookstore. Poteat was President of Wake Forest College from 1905–1927 and one of the most outspoken liberals of his time, openly teaching evolution. Two of Poteat's granddaughters, Diana Hobby and Sylvia Lowe, attended the reception. In another book event, Russell Brantley, the University's Director of Communication from 1953 to 1987, read from his book of poetry, *Fetch-Life,* on November 15 in Z. Smith Reynolds Library. A book signing followed, with sales benefiting the library.

Bill Starling announced plans to retire at the end of the 2002 academic year. In a November 16 memo to the President, Associate Provost Gladding recommended that Starling's duties be divided between Martha Allman, who would become Director of Admissions and Bill Wells, Director of Financial Aid. In addition, the Admissions Oversight Committee recommended to the President that Bill Starling be named Dean of Admissions and Financial Aid in spring 2001 and the title discontinued after his retirement. Unfortunately, his service as dean was short-lived. He died unexpectedly on June 18 at age sixty-five, having served in the Wake Forest Admissions Office for forty-three years.

Athletics

Wake Forest lost its head coaches for both men's basketball and football during the year. One was a surprise; one was inevitable. On April 12, 2001, men's basketball Head Coach David Odom resigned after twelve years and moved to the University of South Carolina, leaving some in shock and many disappointed. During his tenure, Odom established himself as a premier coach with a 240–132 record and a .645 winning percentage. He led Wake Forest to seven straight NCAA tournament appearances and one National Invitational Tournament championship. He was ACC Coach of the Year in 1991, 1994, and 1995, and he coached three All-Americans: Rodney Rogers ('93); Randolph

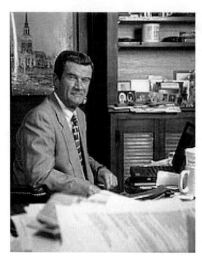

Bill Starling

Childress ('95); and Tim Duncan ('97). The Deacons record for the 2000–2001 season was 19–11, with a first-round loss in the NCAA tournament to Butler, 79–63. Skip Prosser, 50, head coach at Xavier for the past eight years, became the new head coach for men's basketball. He had won more than two-thirds of his games (165 wins, 78 losses) at Xavier and Loyola (Maryland) and coached Xavier to six 20-win seasons in seven tries, reaching postseason play six times (four NCAA tournaments and two NIT invitations). He also took Loyola (Maryland) to the NCAA tournament and won the Metro Atlantic Conference with a 17–13 record.

The football team reverted to a losing record of two wins and nine losses as the Jim Caldwell era came to a close. Overall, Caldwell compiled a 26–63 record in eight years, with an overall winning percentage of .292 and an ACC record of 12–52 (.188). The all-time winning percentage for Wake Forest through the 2000 season was .395. In mid-December 2000, Jim Grobe, age forty-eight, was appointed head coach, and he took over the Wake Forest football program with eight of his assistant coaches from Ohio University.

On a brighter note, the field hockey team finished the season with an 18–4 record and competed in the NCAA Final Four. Overall, Wake Forest finished thirty-third nationally in the Sears Directors' Cup standings, the fourth consecutive year the Athletics Department had improved its national ranking. It finished 120th in 1997–1998, 110th in 1998–1999, and fiftieth in 1999–2000. Among private schools, Wake Forest ranked eighth.

In September 2000, Darius Songaila ('01) helped the Lithuanian basketball team capture a bronze medal at the Olympics in Sydney, Australia. Other Wake Forest representatives on the USA Olympic Team were Hunter Kemper ('98) in the triathlon; Andy Bloom ('96) in the shotput; Steve Brown ('91) in the 110-meter high hurdles for Trinidad and Tobago; and Tim Duncan ('97) as a member of the USA men's basketball Dream Team.

Barry Lawing (MA '84) published a history of Deacon basketball, *Demon Deacon Hoops*, covering the program from its inception in 1906 through the 2000 season.

Carol Merritt, a first-year student, shattered two University track records in the Wake Forest Relays at Kentner Stadium. She ran the 100-meter dash in 11.97 seconds and the 200-meter dash in 24.98 seconds. She went on to break the Wake Forest record in the 400-meter dash at another meet. Sophomore Liz Washam took second place in the pole vault, tying a school record of 10 feet 4 inches. The men's track team also did well in the relays, capturing six first-place finishes. In the Raleigh Relays, Sara Day broke a Deacon record in the 10,000 meters with a time of 33:30.23 and qualified for the NCAA meet. In the Florida Relays, junior J.K. Kuretich shattered the school record in the decathlon, amassing 7,062 points for a second-place finish.

Dianne Dailey was inducted into the National Golf Coaches Association Hall of Fame. Head baseball coach George Greer picked up his 600th career win against Virginia on April 8. Equally impressive, the Deacons captured their third ACC championship in four years, beating North Carolina State 17–4 on May 20. Senior Dave Bush was named the tournament's most valuable player. In the NCAA regional finals, the Deacons lost to Tennessee, 6–2.

Skip Prosser

The Arts

The University Theatre produced four plays on its Mainstage: a modern version of Aristophanes's *Lysistrata*, Max Frisch's *Biedermann and the Firebugs,* Joan Ackermann's *Off the Map,* and Richard Brinsley Sheridan's *School for Scandal.* In addition, the Ring Theatre was renovated and rededicated on August 17, 2000, with Dean Paul Escott and Jonathan Christman (Theatre) cutting the ceremonial ribbon. The Ring was converted from a circle to a semi-proscenium that afforded better production flexibility and better sight lines. Playwright Arlene Hutton's provocative one-act show, *I Dream Before I Take the Stand,* was performed there with Cynthia Gendrich, Assistant Professor of Theatre, and actor D.A. Oldis in the leading roles.

The Secrest Artists Series included flutist Eugenia Zukerman and harpist Yolanda Kondonassis in September; the Takacs String Quartet in October; and Bang on a Can, playing contemporary classics in November. The spring semester line-up featured mezzo-soprano Denyce Grave and the Winston-Salem Symphony in February and violinist Eileen Ivers in March.

The Department of Music presented Teresa Radomski, soprano, and Jacqui Carrasco, violinist, in a September 10 concert, and a celebration of American composer Aaron Copland's one-hundredth birthday on September 14 featured Louis Goldstein performing Copland's "Piano Fantasy." Pianist Peter Kairoff, violinist Jacqui Carrasco, and horn player Robert Campbell performed music of Johannes Brahms in concert on November 12.

The Wind Ensemble premiered two new works on December 5. The first, "Pilgrim's Lot" by Dan

Jim Grobe

Locklair, was composed for the fifty-member campus group and dedicated to Kevin Bowen, director of instrumental ensembles at Wake Forest, and to the University's band program. The other, "Empire of Light" by Johan de Meij, was commissioned by a consortium of eight university bands in the ACC Band Directors Association, with each institution participating in the premiere by performing it on their own campuses.

Phil Hanes gave two extraordinary paintings to the University: a Copley appraised at between $900,000 and $1,000,000, and "Woman in a Spanish Shawl" by William Merritt Chase, valued at $1,000,000 by Christie's.

Ben Harper and the Innocent Criminals played in Wait Chapel on February 26. Emmy-winner Mike Reiss, producer of *The Simpsons*, spoke on April 9, and *Saturday Night Live* star Darrell Hammond, best known for his impression of former President Bill Clinton, performed on April 24, both sponsored by the Student Union. T.J. Cross, a nationally recognized comedian who starred in the film *Gone in 60 Seconds*, headlined the University's third annual Comedy All-Stars Show.

Darius Songaila

Campus and Student Life

For the first time in school history, Wake Forest's 1,035 freshmen climbed onto twenty-six city buses during orientation to tour Winston-Salem on Saturday, August 26. The incoming freshmen visited downtown, Bethabara Park, the North Carolina School of the Arts, and Old Salem. The last stop, at 6 p.m., was the Summer on Trade Street celebration in the Arts District.

Three accounting students in the Calloway School of Business and Accountancy earned the highest scores in North Carolina on the May 2001 Certified Public Accountant (CPA) exam. Wendel Kralovich, Kirk Sonnenfeld, and Brian Branson were awarded medals for their performance. Since 1997, when the Calloway School first offered a master's degree in accountancy, students' passage rate had ranked either first or second in the nation. Despite this excellent performance record, on November 21, President Hearn wrote Jack Wilkerson that "contrary to the original idea that it would be self-supporting," the master's of accounting program had become "a scholarship obligation." In any case, a group of accounting and analytical finance students, led by Professor Yvonne Hinson, turned the main downtown bus station into a temporary income tax preparation office, offering four three-hour sessions from February 20 to March 3 to help people who could not afford assistance.

Over 120 students participated in a Thirty-Hour Famine sponsored by World Wide on March 23. The event was headed by junior Brian Gross and raised funds to stop child deaths due to starvation. Thirty students participated in Habitat for Humanity's shantytown project, spending the night on the Mag Quad to increase awareness of homelessness and to raise money for the organization.

Wake Forest students started D.E.S.K. (Discovering Education through Student Knowledge) in the spring, painting desks and giving them to at-risk Old Town Elementary School students who needed a place to study in their homes.

The Lilting Banshees' spring semester show was *Six Degrees of Kevin Cox*, featuring funny sketches about media relations specialist Cox and other Wake Forest personalities and events. After five years

Lysistrata

(1996–2001), the Discovery Series started by Benson University Center Director Joanna Iwata had offered twenty-nine talk shows, which had enlisted seventy guests representing twenty academic departments and community agencies, and were attended by more than six hundred students, faculty, and staff. Step teams from nearly ten organizations and three states went toe-to-toe on January 19 for the first Dr. Martin Luther King Jr. Step Show Invitational, One Step Closer to the Dream.

Amanda Carlson was elected President of Student Government. Jessica Von Herbulis was President of the Student Union. Brian Schiller was Editor-in-Chief of the *Old Gold and Black*, and *Howler* co-Editors-in-Chief were Heather Seely and Robert Numbers II.

Adam Dickey, Corey Houmand, and Andy Pruett teamed up to win the Mathematical Contest in Modeling, competing against nearly five hundred teams representing 230 institutions from eleven countries. The annual contest challenges undergraduate teams to use applied mathematics to solve open-ended, real-world problems. Steve Robinson and Miaohua Jiang (Mathematics) prepared the Deacon team. Working long into the night over the four-day contest, the three created a twenty-six-page mathematical model to evacuate the South Carolina coast in the event of a hurricane. The previous year, a Wake Forest team took second place, and another won in 1996 with a mathematical model for the best placement of sensors to detect submerged submarines. The winning students and their friends rolled the Quad in celebration of their victory. Wake Forest first participated in the contest in 1995, when interested students pressed Robinson and Associate Professor Ed Allen to organize a team. The department then created Problem-Solving Seminar/Math 165, a one-credit course for potential contest entrants.

Individual students demonstrated their initiative as well. Derrick Thompson, a sophomore, helped found a technology group through the University's new Knowledge 2 Work program, which helped students with strong computer skills from middle and lower income families earn an hourly wage by performing technical work for local non-profit groups, corporations, and individuals. Maria Toler, a junior, started and managed her own company, Collegeboxes, a door-to-door, student-run storage service. Students registered online, were supplied with packing materials, and had their boxes picked up

D.E.S.K.

from their door, stored over the summer, and delivered back to them in the fall. Jonathan Kelly, a junior chemistry major and the student representative on the Board of Trustees, used a grant from the University's Fund for Ethics and Leadership to create a leadership program for black male high school students. He designed a weekend retreat, Men of Distinction: Wake Forest University Academy for Future Leaders, on campus on November 10–12. High school sophomores and juniors from across North Carolina were paired with student volunteers and stayed in residence halls during the program. Kelly was later re-elected as the Student Trustee to the Board of Trustees.

Amanda Carlson

Senior Alan Trammell was one of forty American students of demonstrated academic excellence and leadership potential who received a British Marshall Scholarship, financed by the British government, to continue their studies for two years at any British university. Trammell chose the London School of Economics. He was also named to the second team of *USA Today*'s All-USA College Academic Teams; classmate Jessica Posner was named to the third team.

Jonathan Kelly

Two Calloway students, Ricky Van Veen and Rob Holland, took top awards at the 2001 Central Atlantic States Regional Entrepreneur Awards. Van Veen earned first place for his website, CollegeHumor.com. Holland took second place for Exidos Films, his multimedia production company, which taped school productions. The students were nominated for the awards by Page West, Associate Professor of Business.

Sophomore Brooke Bavinger and senior Winston Irwin received the Outstanding Volunteer of the Year 2000 Award from Independence High School, an alternative school for teenagers with special circumstances or academic problems that made it difficult for them to attend regular schools.

In Greek life, the Interfraternity Council started an Alcohol SpeakOut program. It had two objectives: first, to honor two Chi Omega students, Maia Witzl and Julie Hansen, who were killed by a drunken driver in 1996; and second, to raise student awareness about the consequences of irresponsible drinking.

Kappa Alpha was found guilty of having a secret pledge class, hazing, deception, and contempt for the judicial system in an April ruling by Dean of Student Services Harold Holmes, and its charter was revoked by the University. Another fraternity, Delta Sigma Phi, disbanded, citing problems with regulations imposed by the University and its national organization.

Facilities, Finances, and Alumni

Yahoo! Internet Life magazine ranked Wake Forest the nineteenth most-wired institution in a survey of U.S. universities and research schools. At the same time, the University began moving toward a wireless environment, installing the hardware to enable wireless access in 140 spots on campus, including residence halls, lounges, the library, and certain popular outdoor areas.

In October, Wake Forest was honored with the 2000 Educause Award for Excellence in Campus Networking. The annual award recognized the University's use of strategic, integrated, and innovative network technology.

On July 13, President Hearn asked Vice President Wilson to chair a task force to draw up "explicit guidelines on the reservation of space on the Reynolda Campus." He informed Wilson that Vice President Anderson was to head another task force to make recommendations "on appropriate rationale and charges in renting these spaces." One area that was not on any administrator's list was a parking deck that the Trustees had not approved because of the $5.5 million cost.

The master plan for Reynolda Campus development received its first update in a decade. It focused on minimizing the impact of automobiles and incorporated many of the landscape recommendations prepared by a consultant in 1998, including narrowing the perimeter road into a "village lane," eliminating on-street parking, widening pedestrian walkways, and converting Gulley Drive between Tribble Hall and the South Campus residence halls to a two-way thoroughfare with specialty paving and no on-street parking. In February, an extensive physical survey of the campus was part of a long-term project to provide individuals with disabilities equal access to academic, social, and recreational activities.

The Wait Chapel bell tower was named in memory of Annie Pearl Shore Davis, mother of the late Thomas H. Davis, Egbert L. Davis Jr., and Pauline Davis Perry, who gave major gifts to support the Divinity School. In October, two students, Stephen Herman and Ty Webb, were walking back from a Chi Rho practice when they spotted a deer in Wait Chapel. Although exhausted and bleeding from the mouth, the deer eventually found its way out.

Beginning on May 14, the University moved furniture out of residence halls and into tractor-trailer trucks to support the Baptist State Convention of North Carolina's ongoing relief effort in response to Hurricane Floyd in 1999. The University donated four hundred bunk beds and desks and 230 dressers to the effort. Local companies loaned the trucks and drivers. It was the second year Wake Forest had made such a large donation, according to Michael Logan, who facilitated the project. In the previous spring, the University had given more than seven hundred sets of furniture that included beds, dressers, mirrors, hutches, desks, and chairs. Twenty tractor-trailer trucks were needed to move them to eastern North Carolina.

Work on the Student Athlete Enhancement Center was on schedule with occupancy anticipated for the fall. Groundbreaking for an addition to the back of Calloway Hall was scheduled for February 2002. BB&T Corporation made a $500,000 commitment to support the construction, which would bring all of the Calloway School's offices and classrooms under one roof.

Shuttle service between the Bowman Gray and Reynolda Campuses was offered on a trial basis in the 2000–2001 academic year.

On April 27, the Board of Trustees approved a total budget of $678 million for the 2001–2002 fiscal year. The new budget included $461 million for the Bowman Gray Campus and $217 million for the Reynolda Campus. Full-time undergraduate tuition increased 5 percent from $22,410 to $23,530. The *Old Gold and Black* pointed out in an above-the-fold front-page story on March 29 that the proposed $1,120 tuition hike would mean that, over the past ten years, tuition had risen 142.6 percent from the 1991 price of $9,700.

An anonymous donor gave $4 million to endow a scholarship fund for lower- and middle-income students and other students from the University's traditional constituency. The Heritage Scholarship was given to thirty-two new and returning students in fall 2001. K. Wayne Smith ('60), a former member of the Board of Trustees, established a scholarship for high school seniors from his hometown of Newton.

Eleanor Reid Forrow and her husband, Brian D. Forrow, of Greenwich, Connecticut, gave $100,000 to the Divinity School in honor of her late parents, Albert Clayton Reid and Eleanor Jones Reid. The gift was designated to encourage and to promote the practice of pastoral care. Lynn Durham of Midland, Texas, also gave the school $100,000 for scholarships. The school used a $50,000 grant from the Tannenbaum-Sternberger Foundation of Greensboro to establish and support a partnership with the Greensboro Urban Ministry, and in spring 2001 created a denominational studies emphasis, with specific programs for Baptist and Presbyterian students.

The Charles M. Allen Professorship was established in January 2001. Allen taught in the Biology department from 1941 until 1989. He started the Artists Series in 1958 and ran it for twenty years, and he made valuable contributions to the design of the Scales Fine Arts building and other campus projects during the Scales administration.

The new Pro Humanitate Fund for Service-Learning in Action received a grant for $384,000 from an anonymous donor to help faculty integrate community service into their courses. The new program built on the success of the Academic and Community Engagement (ACE) Fellowship program, which introduced selected faculty to service-learning techniques, so they could include community service as a course requirement. The new fund allowed more professors to complete the training and provided grants to faculty engaged in community-based research.

The Law School received a $150,000 grant from the Jessie Ball duPont Charitable and Educational Fund to benefit

Will Campbell

students who pursued work in the public interest. Graduates meeting certain guidelines, including State Bar membership and employment as a public interest lawyer, were eligible to receive an award equal to 10 percent of student debt.

On March 26, President Hearn wrote a memo to faculty and staff, announcing, "As of December 31, 2000, the market value of our endowment was $894,369,000, down about 7.7 percent from the close of the last fiscal year. Total 2000 calendar-year return, however, was 15.8 percent." By December 31, 2000, the Reynolda Campus had also received $21.8 million in gifts, the best half-year fundraising performance in school history. Trustee William B. Greene Jr. ('59), co-chair of the upcoming capital campaign, made a $5 million unrestricted commitment to support the endowment. East Hall was renamed in his honor, and the dedication took place on October 5. Greene's gift came just four months after the Kirby Foundation gave $5 million to expand Calloway Hall; Greene and Calloway were both members of the Class of 1959.

Wake Forest University Baptist Medical Center's capital campaign surpassed its $100 million goal a year ahead of schedule, with $109 million raised.

The E. Rhodes and Leona B. Carpenter Foundation of Philadelphia gave the Divinity School $100,000 to support a visiting professor of Jewish studies and pledged another $212,000 if the school raised $448,000 for a $700,000 endowment to fund the position permanently.

Will Campbell ('48), renowned civil rights activist and author of sixteen books on the South, received the National Humanities Medal in December.

Summing Up the Year

The most publicized story of 2000–2001 was the presidential debate between Al Gore and George W. Bush. It was the second presidential debate hosted by the University and, like the first, created a great deal of excitement and national exposure. Applications for admission increased following the debate. A second major story was the launching of a second capital campaign within a decade. Known as "Honoring the Promise," its goal was $600 million, with the majority of the money going to the Reynolda Campus. It was kicked off publicly in late April with a speech by the President and a parade of nineteen seven-foot-tall fiberglass Deacons that were each decorated

Barbara Bush

by a campus group. A third important event of the year was a gift from the Z. Smith Reynolds Foundation that guaranteed Wake Forest 3 percent of its annual income in perpetuity in addition to the $1.2 million dollars the Foundation was already giving the University each year.

The theme for the year was Ethics and Honor. Among many programs, the University celebrated the fortieth anniversary of students' participation in the 1960 sit-in for integration in downtown Winston-Salem, as well as the publication of a book by Randal Hall on William Poteat, who embodied human virtue.

The college switched from credits to hours, and computer science became its own department apart from mathematics. A neuroscience minor was offered for the first time. Domestic benefits were granted to gay and lesbian couples, and more benefits were given to all employees. On a sad note, Bill Starling, the long-serving director of admissions and an institution at the University, unexpectedly died.

Athletically, the baseball team won its third ACC title in four years and went to the NCAA Tournament. The field hockey team also distinguished itself. However, two coaches, Dave Odom in basketball and Jim Caldwell in football, ended their tenure at Wake Forest. Their replacements were Skip Prosser and Jim Grobe, and both would go on to have very successful careers at Wake Forest.

Alumni and friends continued their generous support, such as an anonymous gift of $4 million and the Z. Smith Reynolds Foundation's gift in perpetuity. The University was also altruistic, sending furniture to eastern North Carolina to help families devastated by Hurricane Floyd and supporting mechanisms to teach community service in the classroom. Will Campbell ('48), an author and civil rights activist, was the recipient of the National Humanities Medal.

The 158th commencement brought former First Lady Barbara Bush to speak.

President Hearn's "Charge to the Graduates, Commencement 2001" stood out most. He emphasized actions over affect and concluded: "Love is not a feeling, not an emotion, but a way of living. Feelings come and go but those who practice love know that its requirement is that we live in compassionate regard for every life we contact."

CHAPTER NINETEEN
2001–2002

September 11, Reynolda House, and Health Sciences

The only measure of our capacity to love people and ideals beyond our immediate circle of affection is the willingness, readiness and capacity to sacrifice—and to suffer if need be—that the objects of our devotion and the moral and spiritual aims of our lives be advanced. To love is to serve, if need be to sacrifice, for the purposes to which we devote our lives.

Thomas K. Hearn Jr., May 20, 2002;
Charge to the Graduates, Wake Forest University Commencement

Students had hardly settled into a routine at the start of the academic year when the terrorist attacks on New York City and Washington, DC, occurred on September 11, 2001. An alumnus, Mark Schurmeier ('79), was killed in the north tower of the World Trade Center when it collapsed. He was forty-four years old. The attacks affected life on the Reynolda Campus as well, often in unexpected ways. Behaviors ranged from anxiety, caution, prevention, and reassurance to positive action and resolve. In an immediate response, Sam Gladding (Associate Provost/ Counseling) spent a week after the attacks working with the Red Cross at Pier 94 in New York City, providing psychological first aid to families in grief who lost love ones from the attacks on the World Trade Center. On September 17, President Hearn wrote to parents, assuring them that Wake Forest was committed to care for students' needs, both their physical safety and emotional well-being. He ended: "We remain committed to each other, to our country, and to principles of good." The University also reached out to alumni and parents in the Washington and New York areas by phone.

A group of students led by Jonathan Willingham and Jay Cridlin organized a series of events that explored questions raised by the attack. A theme had not been set for the year, so they called it The Year of Unity and Hope: *Pro Humanitate* at

Sam Gladding

Work. The first event was a September 26 forum in Brendle Recital Hall called *Understanding September 11*. The forum was led by Charles "Hank" Kennedy (Political Science) and Charles Kimball (Religion), experts on the Middle East, who explained the history of American relations with countries in that region. In late October, poet Jane Mead (English) hosted An Evening of Poetry and Silence, where participants were invited to read original poems or favorites by others in remembrance of the victims, and donations were collected for the Red Cross September 11 Fund and the Help Afghan Women Campaign. In a second forum on November 1, *Responding to Conflict: Military, Diplomatic, and Humanitarian Approaches*, Michael Hughes (History), Nagesh Rao (English), and George K. Walker (Law) discussed how the United States and its allies were responding to the terrorist attacks. On November 7, Political Science faculty Michaelle Browers, David Coates, Hank Kennedy, and Richard Sears hosted a teach-in called "Why Do They Hate Us? The War on Terrorism."

Students, faculty, and staff raised more than $10,000 to benefit charities supporting victims of the 9/11 attacks during a campus-wide fund drive held between mid-September and mid-October. Organized by the Volunteer Service Corps, the project drew more than a thousand student participants. In addition, the College Book Store sold greeting cards featuring the logo that student Melissa McGhie designed for the Year of Unity and Hope: a stained glass window of reds, blues, and golds, with a candle flickering in the center. The Year of Unity and Hope also sponsored a Book of Days similar to the one published during the Year of Religion in 1996–1997. Students, faculty, and staff contributed their thoughts and stories on the year's theme for publication online.

Melissa Poe and Jill Bader began a project called Helping Hands in late October. They asked a supplier to sell them gloves at a discount, and students at Sherwood and Jefferson Elementary Schools decorated more than five hundred pairs bearing messages of thanks and encouragement that were then sent to the clean-up crews still working around the clock in the rubble of the World Trade Center.

In the spring, Doug Waller ('71), congressional correspondent for *Time* magazine, spoke about his experiences as a journalist during times of crisis, including his contributions to *Time*'s coverage of the September attacks. At another spring event, Joe Stork of Human Rights Watch spoke on "Terrorism, War, and the Middle East: The Human Rights Dimension."

Melissa Poe and Jill Bader with Helping Hands school children

In a major internal event, Wake Forest entered into an affiliation with the Reynolda House Museum of American Art on January 15. While the University would now elect its Board of Trustees, the museum would remain independent and self-governing. Executive Director Barbara Millhouse would continue in her position, and Wake Forest would provide a temporary director until a replacement was found for John Neff, who had recently departed. John Anderson initially assumed the responsibility, assisted for a few months by Associate Provost Sam Gladding.

At the time, Reynolda House was in a capital campaign to raise $12 million to construct a 29,000 square foot, three-story educational wing that would include a visitors' center, gallery, multipurpose room, library and archives, classrooms, and studio space. It had raised $9.4 million, and the University agreed to make up any shortfall as well as any annual budget shortfall during the transition.

Reynolda House opened to the public in 1967 and provided a wide range of interdisciplinary educational programs for adults and children. The house was completed in 1917, and it served as the primary residence of tobacco magnate R.J. Reynolds and his wife, Katherine. In the late 1940s, Charles and Mary Reynolds Babcock donated three hundred acres of the estate to Wake Forest for the construction of the Reynolda Campus and, later, Reynolda Gardens and Reynolda Village. In 1964, the Babcock family placed Reynolda House and the surrounding nineteen acres into a nonprofit institution to create a center of American art. Now, Reynolda House entered into a semi-autonomous partnership with Wake Forest, similar to the health sciences agreement forged between the University and the Medical School.

Signing the Reynolda House agreement, left to right: President Hearn, Barbara Millhouse, and Wake Forest Trustee Chair William B. Greene, Jr.

In another major development, the Board of Trustees created a new corporation, Wake Forest Health Sciences (WFHS), as a wholly owned, nonprofit subsidiary. Richard Dean, Senior Vice President for Health Affairs, was appointed its President. It included Wake Forest University School of Medicine, One Technology Place downtown, ten dialysis centers throughout the region, Amos Cottage Rehabilitation Hospital, and co-ownership of Wake Forest University Baptist Behavioral Health (formerly Charter Hospital). The new corporation "simply formalizes the way we do business," said President Hearn. "The medical school administration has for a long time managed the medical enterprise for the University."

WFHS had its own board of directors. The Board of Trustees' eight-member health affairs committee oversaw the medical school and constituted the core of the WFHS board, which was allowed to have up to thirteen additional members. Hearn became one of its officers and was responsible for appointing its President. Under the new structure, the Dean of the medical school reported to the WFHS President, although his appointment involved both the University and WFHS Presidents. Medical school faculty remained part of the University faculty, and degrees from all School of Medicine graduate and professional programs continued to be awarded by the University.

Academics

Wake Forest was ranked twenty-sixth among 249 national universities—tied with UCLA and two spots up from the previous year—in the new edition of *U.S. News & World Report*'s annual guide. The University earned high marks for its small classes, low student/faculty ratio, high freshman retention rate, alumni giving, and financial resources. *Yahoo! Internet Life* magazine ranked it twentieth among America's top 100 "most wired colleges," the only North Carolina school ranked in the top twenty, and the homepage, http://www.wfu.edu, won the award for best web portal. The School of Law's LLM program for international students was ranked eighth in the nation by American Universities Admissions Program, a private student-recruiting firm.

Michael Hyde

Many faculty achieved international and national recognition. Poet-in-residence Jane Mead won a 2002 Guggenheim Fellowship from the John Simon Guggenheim Memorial Foundation for "exceptional creative ability in the arts." George Aldhizer (Calloway) received the Institute of Internal Auditors' 2001 Leon R. Radde International Educator of the Year award at its international conference in Buenos Aires, Argentina. The National Communication Association honored Michael Hyde, University Distinguished Professor of Communication Ethics, with two awards for his book, *The Call of Conscience: Heidegger and Levinas, Rhetoric and the Euthanasia Debate*: the Diamond Anniversary Book Award, given yearly to the most outstanding scholarly book, and the Marie Hockmuth Nichols Award for Outstanding Scholarship in Public Address.

John Llewellyn (Communication) analyzed the professional language of Division I men's college basketball coaches for nearly two decades. His research revealed four recurring themes among both winning and losing coaches, and he contributed a chapter on this language, "Coachtalk," to *Case Studies in Sport Communication* (Praeger, 2003), edited by Robert S. Brown and Daniel J. O'Rourke III.

Michael Kent Curtis (Law) received the Mayflower Cup for his book *Free Speech, the People's Darling Privilege: Struggles for Freedom of Expression in American History* (Duke University Press, 2000). The annual award from the North Carolina Literary and Historical Association recognizes the best nonfiction work by a North Carolinian. The book also received the national Hugh M. Hefner First Amendment Award.

Mark Welker (Chemistry) spent the 2001–2002 academic year as a program officer with the National Science Foundation in Arlington, Virginia. Ron Dimock (Biology), Dilip Kondepudi (Chemistry), and Paul Ribisl (Health and Exercise Science) were named Wake Forest Professors. Herman Eure (PhD '74, Biology) received the Jon Reinhardt Award for Excellence in Teaching.

The Divinity School named Jill Crainshaw ('84) Associate Dean for Vocational Formation. Previously, her title was Director of Vocational Development. Through an anonymous gift made available in 2001, Doug Bailey, for twenty-three years the rector of Trinity Episcopal Church in Memphis, became Professor of Urban Ministry and brought his own nonprofit Center for Urban Ministry to the Divinity School.

The Babcock Graduate School of Management launched the Babcock Demon Incubator on November 13 in the 1,200-square-foot basement of a University-owned house on University Drive. It could host between three and five tenants at one

Doug Bailey

time until they could find permanent homes. Directed by Paul Briggs, a former Duke Energy executive, the goal was to assist local entrepreneurs in starting and succeeding in their own businesses. The Babcock School also sponsored a conversation with Michael Dell, CEO of Dell Computers, in Wait Chapel as part of the 2002 Broyhill Executive Lecture Series. Instead of a formal lecture, Babcock Dean Charles Moyer led Dell through questions and answers.

The first lecture in the Joseph A. Jones Finance Lecture Series was presented by Sarah Ketterer, CEO and portfolio manager of Causeway Capital Management LLC, a leading Los Angeles-based asset management firm. The Jones Lecture Series was established through a gift from Joseph A. Jones, a 1961 graduate of the Calloway School.

To commemorate the 250th anniversary of the Wachovia settlement, the History Department sponsored a symposium on April 4–6 exploring the influence of German Moravians. Also in April, married theologians Jurgen Moltmann and Elisabeth Moltmann-Wendel delivered talks as part of the Margaret A. Steelman Lecture Series at the Divinity School.

Wake Forest received a five-year, $1.9 million grant from the Lilly Endowment of Indianapolis to establish a center for undergraduate vocational exploration. Administered by Bill Leonard and Paul Escott, it was named after the University's motto, *Pro Humanitate*, for the good of humanity, and opened in 2002. The center coordinated service-learning courses, international service trips, and nonprofit internships for students. The Lilly Endowment awarded $55.3 million to twenty-eight American colleges and universities to support research to develop new academic courses, such as first-year seminars, service-learning initiatives that would prompt reflection on vocation, scholarships for students interested in vocations within the ministry, and a theme house where they would reside together. The Divinity School hosted summer programs for high school seniors and college undergraduates considering questions of calling and vocation related to their faith, and Bill Leonard discussed these initiatives on UNC-TV's *North Carolina People with William Friday* on October 19 and 21.

To encourage a commitment to community service and later legal pro bono work, the Law School dedicated a day of its five-day orientation program to a community service project. On August 15, the entire entering class, in addition to faculty and staff, helped build the foundations for six Habitat for Humanity houses in the Neals Place development in Winston-Salem.

Wake Forest and Virginia Tech announced a plan to establish a joint School of Biomedical Engineering and Sciences (SBES) in October. The aim was to maximize collaboration among researchers and educators in biology, engineering, and medicine, and to advance fundamental discoveries leading to improved healthcare technologies. In support, the School of Medicine established a Center for Biomedical Engineering with participation by thirteen departments, which put up $1.5 million to launch the SBES. This center administered

Logo for School of Biomedical Engineering

the program at Wake Forest, while Virginia Tech already had a parallel center.

The School of Medicine also established the Maya Angelou Research Center on Minority Health to develop methods to close the health gap between minorities and other Americans. The University sought a $20 million endowment for its operations.

In the Political Science Department, Jack Fleer and Dick Sears retired. Both came to the University in 1964. Fleer was department chair from 1969 to 1977 and from 1985 to 1997, and he directed the Boys' State summer program, sponsored by the American Legion, on the Wake Forest campus from 1965 to 1977. Sears was instrumental in gaining a $500,000 grant from the Pew Memorial Trust to start the international studies program, which he directed until 1999. He was awarded the Donald O. Schoonmaker Faculty Award for Community Service during the 2001 Opening Convocation.

In a reflective speech covering politics and the life of the mind, world-renowned presidential historian and journalist Doris Kearns Goodwin delivered the Founders' Day Convocation address on February 21.

The Tie That Binds switched its emphasis from the Republic of Georgia and instead traveled to Eagle Butte, South Dakota, to work with the Cheyenne River Reservation's Youth Project from May 12 to May 25. Faculty advisor Ulrike Wiethaus (Humanities) accompanied the eleven students on the trip.

Minors in Japanese and Chinese were offered by the Asian Studies Department. The Department of Music established two different majors: Music Performance, and Music in the Liberal Arts. The latter encompasses music history, music theory, composition, and conducting.

Jack Fleer and Dick Sears

Throughout the year, some faculty complained that they were not being adequately compensated in comparison with their counterparts at other institutions. The President responded in an April letter that salaries had improved over the past three years, 17.6 percent for full professors, 15.9 percent for associate professors, and 14.4 percent for assistant professors. He also promised that the salaries and operating budget would increase during the 2002–2003 academic year. Nevertheless, the argument continued, with each side claiming the other's figures were inaccurate or misleading.

Thirty-eight new faculty joined the Reynolda Campus: thirty-two became part of the College of Arts and Sciences; three, the Calloway School of Business and Accountancy; two, the School of Law; and one, the Babcock Graduate School of Management.

In a faculty-related event, the Wake Forest Club, composed of the wives of male faculty members for the most part, ceased operations. Numbers and interest in the club had dwindled over time since its inception in 1948. In addition, many spouses of faculty members were working full-time.

Administration and Staff

On March 14, President Hearn named William (Bill) C. Gordon ('68, MA '70), President of the University of New Mexico since 1999, the next Provost, to begin on September 1. Gordon had been an active leader during his student days, and he was named "Man of the Year" by the *Old Gold and Black* in 1968. He was attracted back to the University because he thought Wake Forest combined the best features of both a liberal arts college and a research university.

In another senior appointment, William B. Applegate was named Dean of the School of Medicine and Senior Vice President of Wake Forest Health Sciences effective April 1, 2002. Richard H. Dean, President and CEO of WFHS, made the announcement on February 6. Applegate was Chair of the Department of Internal Medicine, a position he assumed in January 1999, and Co-chair of Wake Forest University Physicians. C. Douglas Maynard, recently retired Chair of Radiology, served as Acting Dean and chaired the search committee when James N. Thompson resigned effective July 1, 2001. A member of the faculty since 1979, Thompson became Dean in 1994 and was named a Vice President in 1997. He remained on the faculty as a professor of otolaryngology.

Phil Hendrix was appointed the Reynolda Campus Director of Purchasing. David Fyten, former University editor and Assistant Vice President for Public Affairs, stepped down to become a part-time staff writer and to pursue other opportunities. Cherin Poovey, former Director of Publications and Associate University Editor, was named Director of Creative Services.

Bill Gordon

Kerry M. King ('85), formerly Director of University Rela-
tions Communications, became Associate Director in
January 2002, and *Window on Wake Forest* went online on
January 1, 2002.

John R. Woodard ('61) retired as head of the University archives and director of the library's North Carolina
Baptist Historical Collection after thirty-six years. He was
an institution unto himself.

Jay Banks ('74, MBA '76) was appointed the new station manager of WFDD in September 2001, and six people joined the staff: Evan Richey, operations coordinator;
Denise Franklin, senior news host and editor; Anna Cox,
membership coordinator; Shelia Thrower, underwriting

William Applegate

associate; Marian Wilson, musical host; and Marie Sher-
man, administrative assistant. Banks would later become the director of major giving
at the station.

Linda McKinnish Bridges (Religion) was named an Associate Dean of the College. She also taught in the Divinity School during the 2001–2002 academic year.

John P. Anderson, Vice President for Finance and Administration, was elected to
the Board of Directors of MCNC, a nonprofit corporation known for maintaining
advanced equipment and expertise in emerging technologies.

QualChoice was no longer available as a health insurance vendor, and the University went back to Blue Cross/Blue Shield.

The University Police secured a $200,000 grant from the United States Justice
Department to establish the Center for Awareness, Response, and Education (CARE)
in an effort to combat the problem of sexual assaults on campus. CARE had two
teams: 1) education and awareness; and 2) crisis response. Its office was located in the
University Police Communication Office.

Athletics

In his inaugural term, Head Football Coach Jim Grobe led the team to six wins and
five losses overall and compiled a 3–5 record in the ACC, including wins over Virginia and North Carolina. Even though the team did not go to a bowl, senior Michael
Collins earned All-ACC first-team honors.

For the first time since 1996, Midnight Madness returned to Reynolds gym on
October 12–13, as the men's basketball team held an intrasquad game before a student audience. It was not the only time fans had something to cheer about, as the
team compiled a 21–13 record and advanced to the second round of the NCAA tournament before losing to Oregon, 92–87. In other basketball news, President Hearn
wrote John Swofford, Commissioner of the ACC, to regulate "coach to referee" conduct in conference basketball games. He thought some coaches were manipulating
the referees through various tactics.

The field hockey team was ranked number one for three weeks during the 2001
season and advanced to the NCAA semi-finals. The baseball team was ranked as high
as third nationally during the spring season and finished with a 47–13–1 record before

Jay Banks ('74, MBA '76)

losing in the NCAA regional playoffs to Richmond. The men's tennis team broke into the top twenty-five nationally for the first time in its history, reaching number 22 in late March after a 10–1 start.

Men and women's club crew teams were formed, and both had success. The men's team won a set of medals at a regatta in Washington, D.C., and the women's team won the novice division at the West Virginia Governor's Cup. The teams were coached by Sam Williamson, captain of the men's team, and Ben Cook, who had rowed for Clemson for four years. The women's team captain was Jill Coleman. Combined, they had about twenty-five members and practiced on Salem Lake.

The volleyball team finished with a 20–11 record (10–7 in the ACC). Seniors Maso de Moya and Margaret Davidson earned all-ACC honors and were selected for the first and second teams, respectively.

In women's tennis, junior Bea Bielik won the NCAA singles title in spring 2002 to become the first Wake Forest female athlete to win a national title. She was also named the ACC Female Athlete of the Year in July 2002, the first time a Wake Forest woman had won. Bielik was given the Marge Crisp Award as the top female athlete at Wake Forest. She teamed with Janet Bergman to win doubles titles in many tournaments over the year as well, and they came in second in the NCAA doubles competition.

Dianne Dailey was selected LPGA Coach of the Year, while head men's track and field coach Noel Ruebel resigned and was replaced by Gary Sievers. Seniors Rachel Burns (women's track) and Maren Haus (tennis) received the ACC's Jim Weaver Award, recognizing exceptional achievement on the field and in the classroom. Nathan Sisco, a junior, won the 2001 individual ACC cross country championship. He was only the second Deacon to do so. Later in year, Sisco and teammate Chris Estwanik qualified for the NCAA championships.

In addition to student-athlete achievements, Doug and Elizabeth Manchester made a substantial monetary contribution to Wake Forest, and the Athletic Center, built in 1979, was renamed in their honor to become known as the Manchester Athletic Center.

The Arts

The University's Writers Reading series began on October 11 with a poetry reading by Carl Phillips. Other participants included novelist Julie Edelson (English, MALS); poet, scholar, and journalist Ted Genoways; and novelist and Duke University English Professor Joe Ashby Porter. The University Theatre produced John Guare's *The House of Blue Leaves*; William Shakespeare's *A Midsummer Night's Dream*; Sam Shepard's *A Lie of the Mind*; and Frances Hodgson Burnett's *The Secret Garden*. The Anthony Aston Players performed *All in the Timing*, a one-act play by David Ives, and *The Boys Next Door* by Tom Griffin in the Ring Theatre.

After two years of trying, the Women's Initiative for Support and Empowerment (WISE) brought the feminist play *The Vagina Monologues* by Eve Ensler to campus. It features a group of women speaking candidly and passionately about their bodies. Besides focusing on issues unique and important to women, the event raised money for organizations that benefited women. The *Old Gold and Black* praised the staging, and both performances in the Ring Theatre sold out.

The Secrest Artists Series held six events during the year, starting with a concert by the Venetian baroque ensemble Accademia di San Rocco in celebration of the thirtieth year of the Wake Forest residential study program in Venice. Russian piano virtuoso Arcadi Volodos was followed by the Salzburg Marionette Theatre, which performed Mozart's *The Magic Flute* in November. During the second half of the year, the Prague Radio Symphony Orchestra performed along with the Philadelphia Dance Company (Philadanco). The series concluded with the all-female Cuban string orchestra Camerata Romeu in March.

Jewels in Our Crown: Treasures from the Wake Forest Art Collections showcased about fifty of the more than 1,300 works of art owned by the University. Mounted in the Fine Arts Gallery of the Scales Fine Arts Center from August 24 through October 14, the show was curated by Kathryn McHenry to celebrate the sixtieth anniversary of Wake Forest's collection of major works of art. Paintings from seven of the nine collections were included. From February 8 through March 24, *Portraits and Personnages* featured fifty human characterizations on paper from the personal art collection of the late French modern artist Jean Dubuffet.

On November 3, the Music Department sponsored a Bellini 200th Birthday Bash to celebrate the Italian composer Vincenzo Bellini. The concert featured Teresa Radomski, soprano; Laura Ingram-Moore, soprano; Richard Heard, tenor; and Peter Kairoff, piano. Twenty-two voice students also performed.

Student Government sponsored a performance of Second City, the improvisational comedy troupe, in Brendle Recital Hall on September 17; another by the rock band Blues Traveler on September 28; and comedian and actor Bill Bellamy on October 11. In the second semester, it brought in contemporary Christian musicians Andrew Peterson and Derek Webb. Acoustic Syndicate, a North Carolina band, headlined the Springfest concert on April 18 in Wait Chapel, along with The Iguanas, from New Orleans, and Georgia Avenue, a student band from Virginia.

Bea Bielik

Campus and Student Life

The entering class totaled 991, 491 men and 500 women, with only four states not represented: Alaska, Montana, Utah, and New Mexico. Students arrived at a historic time as both a public and private celebration of the fiftieth anniversary of the Reynolda Campus groundbreaking took place on October 29 with a luncheon and special program. Descendants of many of the key participants in the October 15, 1951, ceremony, at which President Truman spoke, were on hand. Ed Wilson noted the groundbreaking was second in importance only to the founding in the history of the University.

Over the summer of 2001, Assistant Professor of Economics Sylvain Boko led a study abroad trip to Benin, West Africa, and in spring 2002, student-participants Brett Bechtel, Rosita Najmi, and Lisa Biedrzycki coordinated Project Bokonon, which means *medicine man* in Benin's native Fon language. They raised money to buy basic medical supplies like needles, gloves, and bandages for several open-air hospitals in Benin, including the hospital where Boko was born.

In a bizarre incident related to 9/11, Jordan Munn, a sophomore, received a suspicious package on February 12. After partially unwrapping it, he called University police because it looked like a bomb, and the only return address was "I Will Winn, Tulsa, Oklahoma." University police called the Winston-Salem bomb squad, who evacuated Poteat Hall using the fire alarm. Examined by x-ray and explosives-detecting dogs, the package was a hoax, but students could not return to the area for over four hours.

The City of Joy Scholars trip was affected by 9/11. The group traveled to Mexico to volunteer in one of the homes established by Mother Teresa because going to Calcutta, India, was deemed too dangerous. Other service trips went off as planned. A group of Catholic students traveled to Costa Rica to work with Nicaraguan refugees, and the Honduras Outreach Project and Exchange (HOPE) Scholars Program took ten students to dig latrines, restore houses, and repair roads in the Agalta Valley, a remote mountainous region of Honduras devastated by 1998's Hurricane Mitch.

On February 19, Peace Corps Chief of Staff Lloyd O. Pierson informed President Hearn that Wake Forest ranked ninth nationally among colleges and universities with alumni currently serving as Peace Corps Volunteers. At the time, fourteen alumni were serving. In response to a speech by Jessica Jackson ('00) about her experiences in the Peace Corps in Uzbekistan, the entire student body collected and sent 2,640 pounds of literature to village libraries. Jackson said that Uzbekistan citizens saw their ability to read English as one of the main ways to achieve a better life. Student Government and the executive committee of the Year of Unity and Hope paid to ship the books.

David L. Horne, a Pan-African studies professor at California State University-Northridge and leading reparations advocate, was the keynote speaker for Martin Luther King Jr. Day. On February 22, Wake Forest, Winston-Salem State University, and the city of Winston-Salem commemorated the forty-second anniversary of one of North Carolina's first successful lunch-counter sit-ins with a rededication of a historical marker at the corner of Liberty and Fourth Streets. President Hearn, the chancellor of Winston-Salem State, and the mayor of Winston-Salem spoke, and William Stevens, one of the Wake Forest students who participated in the 1960 sit-in, attended. Susan Faust coordinated the event.

The Office of Multicultural Affairs held a Multicultural Male Summit on April 12–13 for 150 minority male students at North Carolina universities. Author Cornel West, Professor of Afro-American Studies at Harvard, was the keynote speaker.

Jordan Brehove was Student Government President, and Sean Prince was selected as the Student Trustee for 2002–2003. *Howler* Editor-in-Chief was Jennifer George, and Will Wingfield was Editor-in-Chief of the *Old Gold and Black*, which won a Pacemaker Award for general excellence from the Associated Collegiate Press. The award annually recognizes the best college newspapers in the nation.

On-campus parking improved because all 246 first-year students who had cars were required for the first time to park in a satellite lot across Polo Road between 7 a.m. and 5 p.m. Monday through Friday. Lot P east of Wait Chapel, formerly reserved for faculty and staff during weekday business hours, was now reserved for them around the clock. It reduced the number of student cars left illegally in the lot during the day after parking legally at night.

On the night of April 14, just before Campus Day, several Christian organizations chalked sidewalks on the Quad with biblical verses and religious quotes to show prospective students that Jesus was active on campus. Their actions drew mixed responses. Chalking was not permitted except on the sidewalks between the Magnolia Court and Benson University Center.

Maura Proulx, Jackie Shock, and Kristin Zipple chose to delay their professional careers to spend one year volunteering with Catholic service organizations after graduation. The three women, members of the Wake Forest Catholic Community, organized a campus visit in the spring by Jonathan Kozol, author of *Death at an Early Age* (published in 1967), and long-time proponent of social justice and education equality.

Senior Mary Claire Butts appeared on a college cheerleading edition of the NBC game show *The Weakest Link* in the spring of 2002. She was not only a cheerleader but a history major with minors in Spanish and international studies. She won and brought home $74,000. Two first-year students, Anna Hight and Emily Word, were guests on *The Sally Jessy Raphael Show* because they were born on the same day in the same hospital and years later attended the same University and pledged the same sorority.

Jamie Dean, a visually impaired first-year student, and his seeing-eye dog, Paul, quickly learned to navigate the campus. Dean became a leader on campus.

The Washington-based Harry S. Truman Scholarship Foundation awarded Lindsay J. Littlefield, a junior, one of its sixty-four merit-based, $30,000 scholarships ($3,000 for her senior year and $27,000 for graduate school). The award supports college students who wish to attend graduate or professional school to prepare for careers in government or other public service.

Cynthia Gillikin, a sophomore biology major, was named a 2002–2003 Goldwater Scholar, one of 309 out of more than 1,100 applicants to receive $15,000 toward the cost of tuition for her junior and senior years. The program aims to encourage

Mary Claire Butts

outstanding students to pursue careers in mathematics, the natural sciences, and engineering.

Student teams won two of the six Outstanding Awards presented at the annual Mathematical Contest in Modeling for solving a problem involving airline overbooking. They were among 522 teams representing 282 institutions from eleven countries. The first team, composed of seniors Corey Houmand, John Bowman, and junior Adam Dickey, won the Outstanding Award in the 2001 competition. The second team, juniors Elizabeth Perez, Crystal Taylor, and Anthony Pecorella, competed for the first time.

Junior Tyler Overstreet and senior Kyle Voorhees, "Bigs" with the Forsyth County Big Brothers/Big Sisters program, organized a kickball tournament on Davis Field on April 6 that brought together local children in need of a mentor and volunteers who might be willing to make the commitment to become a big brother or sister.

David Willhoit and Matt Hinson started Wake Works to train students in the art of banquet food service. The group began in October after Hinson, who was working as a waiter at the Adam's Mark Hotel, noticed the poor quality of the temporary staff. The company worked with students' schedules, and the training was administered online.

Senior Levar Hairston died from sickle cell disease on July 26, one semester short of graduation. At his funeral, Associate Dean William Hamilton called him "a good man, a good friend, and a good student." In honor of his dedication and perseverance, the Calloway School created the Levar Antwain Hairston Award, annually given to a Calloway student who overcame hardships in pursuit of the degree.

The 2001 Student Trustee Jonathan Kelly, who organized a leadership program called Men of Distinction for male high school students, organized a similar program, Women of Courage and Valor: Changing the Face of Tomorrow, for their female counterparts. The program took place on April 19.

In Greek life, Sigma Pi pledges dressed in Nordic gear clashed on the upper Quad March 1 in Vikingfest. The action was anything but festive, as the young men fought each other in front of Reynolda Hall. The Big Kahuna Festival was just the opposite: Delta Kappa Epsilon (Deke) pledges, dressed as Pacific Islanders, lugged one of the senior members of the fraternity from his house on Polo Road to the upper Quad to comment on social life and a few individuals.

A misdemeanor citation for abandonment of an animal and allowing livestock to run at large was issued to members of the Sigma Phi Epsilon fraternity, who brought a pig to an off-campus party on April 20 and left it there after the party ended. After an investigation, the University suspended the Zeta chapter for three years.

The Zeta Omicron chapter of Kappa Alpha Theta sorority voted to disband in the spring, the third Greek organization to exit campus in six months. The reason was low membership. Ironically, more than three hundred men and three hundred women took part in spring rush.

On Valentine's Day, members of the Alpha Phi Alpha fraternity laid roses at the doors of every minority woman on campus. The Panhellenic Council sponsored the Sixth Annual Breast Cancer Fashion Show on November 13, raising more than $2,000 for breast cancer research.

Facilities, Finances, and Alumni

The 3,600-square-foot art gallery in the Scales Fine Arts Center was named for Phillip and Charlotte Hanes. The formal announcement and dedication came at a reception in the gallery on September 7, during President's Weekend. Hanes, who received an honorary Doctor of Laws degree from Wake Forest in 1990, was known locally for his leadership and support of the arts, having helped shape the North Carolina School of the Arts, the Southeastern Center for Contemporary Arts (SECCA), and the Roger L. Stevens Center for the Performing Arts, all in Winston-Salem.

The Benson Center food court was renovated over the summer to increase the number of food options while decreasing the time spent waiting in line. The area had not been changed since it opened in 1990. Construction of the 50,000-square-foot Student Athlete Enhancement Center (SAEC), which took fourteen months and cost $10.8 million, continued through the summer and was completed in October. It was named in honor of Kenneth D. Miller ('76) of Greensboro and became known as the Miller Center. Originally conceived for the benefit of student-athletes, with study and computer rooms, practice gyms for men's and women's basketball, and team locker and meeting rooms, the Miller Center also included a state-of-the-art fitness center and aerobics room that were open to all students, faculty, and staff. The previous fitness center in Benson was gutted and converted into offices for Residence Life and Housing staff.

Graylyn International Conference Center launched an extensive renovation as the University took over its management on July 1, spending approximately $2.5 million for improvements, including new air conditioning equipment and renovation of sixteen guestrooms in the Manor House and forty-five guestrooms in the mews. In the fall, Graylyn was inducted into the prestigious International Association of Conference Centers of North America and recognized with three of the industry's top awards for 2001: its second consecutive Stars of the South Award from *Meetings South* magazine, its fourth consecutive Gold Key Award from *Meetings & Conventions*, and its twelfth consecutive Award of Excellence from *Corporate & Incentive Travel*.

The 1956 M.P. Miller pipe organ in Wait Chapel was repaired. Renovations occurred over a three-year period and included a new four-manual console and tonal additions by the Schantz Organ Company of Orrville, Ohio. Nearly 750 pipes were added, bringing the total to more than four thousand.

For the third year in a row, the University donated more than five hundred pieces of used furniture to flood relief efforts of the Baptist State Convention of North Carolina and other nonprofit groups in North Carolina and Virginia. Ironically, the Convention, in an almost inconsequential move, voted in November to break all formal ties with the University and designate it a "historical educational institution" rather than an affiliated institution.

Miller Center

In financial matters, three PepsiCo executives, Donald M. Kendall, Roger A. Enrico, and Steven S. Reinemund, contributed a total of $500,000 to support the Calloway School of Business and Accountancy. The gift was used to create the Four Chairmen's Bridge, an arched bridge with wrought iron railing that would define the main entrance to the Calloway School. The bridge was named for each of the three donors and the late Wayne Calloway ('59), chair and CEO of PepsiCo, Inc.

The Annenberg Foundation awarded $250,000 to the Presidential Scholarship program, which rewards students with extraordinary talent in the areas of dance, writing, music, theatre, studio art, community service, debate, entrepreneurship, and leadership. In recognition of the gift, one of the scholarships was renamed the Annenberg Presidential Scholarship.

With a gift of nearly $7 million from the estate of the late barbecue restaurateur William Keith Stamey of Greensboro, who died in June 2000, the University established scholarships ranging from $1,000 to $15,000, depending on need, to assist sixty-two freshmen and returning students. It was the largest single gift made to Wake Forest by an individual, according to James Bullock, Director of the University's Honoring the Promise capital campaign, and it established the University's fourth-largest endowed scholarship fund, after the Reynolds, Carswell, and Hankins scholarships.

Wachovia Bank gave a $2 million gift to the Babcock Graduate School of Management to endow the Wachovia Scholars program, which aimed to increase student diversity. It provided up to 100 percent of tuition, books, and room and board costs for six full-time MBA students from underrepresented groups.

The F.M. Kirby Foundation donated $5 million for the four-story Kirby wing of Calloway Hall; groundbreaking took place on October 4. The Kresge Foundation also made a $750,000 commitment. The expansion would allow the Computer Science and Mathematics Departments to house all of their classrooms and faculty offices in Calloway Hall, and the Calloway School of Business and Accountancy would have its own space for the first time. In the last eight years, Calloway enrollment had increased 33 percent, and its faculty had increased by 50 percent, making space increasingly tight. The total cost for the expansion would be $14 million.

The front of the Calloway building, facing the Magnolia Court, was renamed in honor of Doug and Elizabeth Manchester, who made a substantial contribution

Four Chairmen's Bridge to Calloway Hall

to the University. The entrance now was known as Manchester Hall. The Magnolia Court was renamed Manchester Plaza as well, although most students, faculty, and staff continued to call it the Magnolia Court.

On January 10, President Hearn wrote Dick Dickson, President of Paradies Shops in Atlanta, that it was "a continuing source of consternation here that your operations at Piedmont Triad International Airport sell Duke and Carolina merchandise, but Wake Forest materials, in our home airport, are not offered." He asked that a company representative contact Donald J. "Buz" Moser "to make arrangements to have our products in our airport." Dickson replied on January 16 that Wake Forest merchandize would be sold at the airport forthwith.

President Hearn spoke and Chaplain Christman prayed at a dedication ceremony on September 20 as most Christian campus ministries moved into centralized office space in Kitchin House. A few Christian groups, such as Campus Crusade and Forest Fire, as well as the Jewish Student Organization and Islam Awareness, were not housed in Kitchin. Harold "Hal" and Rita Roser gave $350,000 to endow a new fund to support students in performing Christian service.

The Admissions and Welcome Center was named in memory of long-time Dean of Admissions William G. Starling ('57), who died on June 18, 2001. Starling's fraternity brother Bill Cobb ('58), his wife, Rhoda, and the Cobb Foundation made a gift to rename the building to mark Starling's retirement, planned for 2002. The dedication was held during Homecoming weekend on October 26, and a portrait of Starling that would be hung in the center was unveiled.

The endowment fell by $175 million (down 13.95 percent) during 2000–2001 for an end-of-the-year total of $812,389,000. In a November 15 memo, President Hearn reminded faculty and staff that the nation was in a recession and that Wake Forest's financial aid to undergraduates had "*more than doubled* in the last five years as we strive to retain our need-blind admissions policy and maintain economic diversity in the student population. . . ." He stated that the campaign for Wake Forest was moving ahead with no changes anticipated and that the University had already generated more than half of the Reynolda Campus pledges, $156.3 million, toward the $300 million goal. He added, "Unlike some other universities, we will have budgeted increases in salaries and operating items for 2002–2003." Nonsalary operating budgets were expected to grow by a modest 1 percent. "In summary, as we begin our annual budget process, we face a 10 percent decline in available unrestricted endowment income; continued pressure on tuition rates; increased financial aid expenditures; insurance cost increasing at double-digit rates; and a sluggish economy."

On March 22, the Board of Trustees approved a total budget of $734 million for the 2002–2003 fiscal year: $507 million for the Bowman Gray Campus and $227 million for the Reynolda Campus, increases of 8 percent and 4 percent, respectively. Full-time undergraduate tuition for the fall of 2002 increased by 5 percent to $24,750 from $23,530. In 2001–2002, 67 percent of undergraduates received financial aid; 32 percent received need-based financial aid; and 42 percent of undergraduates from North Carolina received need-based aid.

Bill Starling's portrait is unveiled

In April 2002, the goal for the Honoring the Promise campaign was raised from $450 million to $600 million to reflect a greater need for funding of University priorities and the fact that fundraising efforts were going so well.

Mary Easley ('72, Law '75), a Double Deacon and wife of Governor Michael Easley, gave the Opening Convocation address on September 13, "Competence, Confidence, and the Comfort Zone: How to Color Your Life outside the Lines."

Summing Up the Year

The $450 million capital campaign became the $600 million campaign as fundraising went well and University needs continued to grow. The University struck a partnership affiliation with Reynolda House Museum of American Art and created Wake Forest Health Sciences to simplify administration of the medical school. All three major changes took place as people struggled to cope, both nationally and locally, with the horror of the terrorist attacks in New York City and Washington, D.C. Wake Forest students, faculty, and administrators responded quickly, decisively, and humanely, contacting parents and alumni in the affected areas, holding teach-ins, and sending gloves and messages to first responders.

Students and faculty volunteered for service trips to help the less fortunate and started new initiatives like Project Bokonon in Benin. Student-athletes studied and played hard, and one, Bea Bielik, became the first woman in Wake Forest history to win an individual national title. Other students won Truman and Goldwater awards and continued a tradition of academic excellence.

The academic year wrapped up for most students and faculty on the third Sunday and Monday in May with a baccalaureate service featuring Children's Defense Fund Founder Marian Wright Edelman and an address by 160th commencement speaker Senator John McCain. Approximately 1,521 undergraduate and graduate students received diplomas and made their way out into a less secure world than they had known when they matriculated into the University.

CHAPTER TWENTY
2002–2003

Transitions, Field Hockey, a Centennial, and Remembrance

My father loved to quote these familiar lines [from Phillips Brooks]:
   Do not pray for easy lives. Pray to be stronger men [and women]! Do not pray for tasks equal to your powers. Pray for powers equal to your tasks.
   I offer that benediction to you as you leave these halls to enter your varied fields of service.

Thomas K. Hearn Jr., May 19, 2003;
Charge to the Graduates, Wake Forest University Commencement

On July 1, 2002, Bill Gordon ('68, MA '70) returned to Wake Forest to become its Provost. A native of Rome, Georgia, he entered Wake Forest as an undergraduate in 1964 on a baseball scholarship but an injury forced him to pursue other interests. He did so with passion, becoming business manager of the *Old Gold and Black* and Student Government treasurer. He stayed on an extra two years to earn a master's degree in psychology and then earned his PhD in experimental psychology at Rutgers University. He taught for five years at the State University of New York at Binghamton and joined the University of New Mexico faculty in 1978. He served as Chair of the Psychology Department, Dean, and Provost before being named President in 1999. He returned to Wake Forest highly regarded for his commitment to the teacher-scholar ideal and the liberal arts tradition. He was an excellent fit, and his organizational abilities and skills at writing and public speaking won praise and admiration on campus and off.

The campus was also excited when the field hockey team won a national championship under Head Coach Jennifer Averill. The Deacons defeated Penn State 2–0 in the first national championship for a Deacon athletic team since men's golf in 1986 and the first national championship for a women's team. Averill, who began

347

her tenure in 1992, was named ACC, South Region, and National Coach of the Year, while Kelly Doton was named ACC Player of the Year.

The medical school celebrated its centennial with the theme The Legacy of Yesterday, the Promise of Tomorrow. A book on the school's history, *One Hundred Years of Medicine: Legacy and Promise*, was published. Scientist and entrepreneur Craig Venter, a pioneer in sequencing the human genome and cloning, was the fall convocation speaker for both campuses on October 10 in Wait Chapel. The medical school hosted tours of its facilities in October, and a Mini-Medical School for the general public offered programs on genetics, radiology, cancer, cardiology, physiology, and pharmacology.

Jennifer Averill

To commemorate the one-year anniversary of 9/11, the University planned a Day of Remembrance with meditations, music, and continuous screening of the HBO documentary film *In Memoriam/New York City/September 11, 2001* in Benson University Center. The upper quad was decorated with flags of all the nations that lost citizens in the terrorist attacks. From the steps of Wait Chapel, students, faculty, and staff took turns reading aloud the names of the more than three thousand victims. President Hearn began at 10:30 a.m. Over six hundred students took the Celebrating the American Spirit Service Pledge, sponsored by the Office of Volunteer Services and many student organizations, to serve the local community in

2002 Field Hockey Team

some way during the 2002–2003 academic year in honor of the victims. After an interfaith worship service in Wait Chapel, a candlelight vigil circled the quad.

Academics

U.S. News & World Report ranked Wake Forest twenty-fifth in the national research university category, up one place from the year before, and thirty-first among "Great Schools at Great Prices." It noted that 63 percent of Wake Forest classes had fewer than twenty students, and 93 percent of first-year students return for their sophomore year. It also ranked the Calloway School of Business and Accountancy twenty-fifth among the country's top undergraduate business programs.

At the beginning of the academic year, the University officially offered thirty-four majors to approximately 3,900 undergraduates. Thirty-nine new faculty members joined the Reynolda Campus: thirty-two in the College of Arts and Sciences, one in the Calloway School, four in the Divinity School, and two in the School of Law. George Graham, the incoming A.C. Reid Professor of Philosophy, arrived in the spring semester. The Board of Trustees approved a plan to split the counseling program off from the Education Department as a new Counseling Department.

According to a new agreement, Wake Forest students wishing to study in Japan could do so on the Kansai Gandai campus. The program was directed by Jay Ford (Religion). Previously, Wake Forest students had studied as a cohort with a faculty advisor at Tokai University (1991–2001). At Kansai Gandai, they could choose among many more classes and participate in campus life much more fully.

The Harry S. Truman Scholarship Foundation recognized Wake Forest as one of four 2002 Truman Scholarship Honor Institutions. The award recognized Wake Forest for sustained success in helping outstanding students win Truman Scholarships and pursue careers in public service. Eleven students had received Truman Scholarships since 1977.

Daniel B. Kim-Shapiro (Physics) was awarded a five-year, $1.5 million grant from the National Institutes of Health to study the effects of nitric oxide in sickle cell blood. Governor Easley appointed Mark Welker (Chemistry) to a four-year term on the North Carolina State Board of Science and Technology.

In Psychology, Mark Leary published research showing that social approval and disapproval affect virtually all people's feelings about themselves, even those who adamantly claim they are not affected. William Fleeson was awarded the 2002 Theoretical Innovation Prize by the Society for Personality and Social Psychology. He presented his findings—that acting extroverted can make people happier—to the University community on March 19 in a lecture titled, "Moving Personality Forward: Integrating the Process and the Structure Approaches."

Charles Kimball (Religion) published *When Religion Becomes Evil: Five Warning Signs* (HarperOne), that sought to make sense of the evil perpetrated in the name of religion, such as the 9/11 attacks. *Publishers Weekly* named it one of the best fifteen books on religion in 2003. Brad R. Braxton (Divinity) published *No Longer Slaves: Galatians and African American Experience* (Liturgical Press), which interpreted the

New Testament message of Paul to the Galatians from the perspective of modern African Americans. Margaret Bender (Anthropology) wrote *Signs of Cherokee Culture: Sequoyah's Syllabary in Eastern Cherokee Life* (University of North Carolina Press), based on her extensive fieldwork among the Eastern Band of Cherokee in western North Carolina. The book explained how their writing system was used in special and subtle ways to shape a shared cultural identity.

David L. Faber (Art), co-authored a top-selling drawing textbook, *A Guide to Drawing* (6e), by revising more than 40 percent of the content for a new edition. David Lubin, Charlotte Weber Professor of Art, presented a slide show and lecture on April 23 in the Scales Fine Arts Center. Following on the publication of his *Shooting Kennedy: JFK and the Culture of Images* (University of California Press), he showed and discussed photographs and film stills of Jack and Jackie from the time of their courtship in 1953 to John's death and funeral ten years later. Lubin pointed out the influence of these images on American art, popular culture, and history. The event was sponsored by the Euzelian Society.

Mary Dalton (Communication) made a local artist the focus of a fifteen-minute documentary that aired on UNC-TV September 21. *Sam McMillan: The Dot Man* revealed the passion behind the artwork he produced and the life he led.

The Ewing Marion Kauffman Foundation awarded the Calloway School of Business and Accountancy a $47,300 grant to foster undergraduate entrepreneurship. It was used to support the Center for Undergraduate Entrepreneurship, an interdisciplinary hub that provided physical facilities and business mentoring to undergraduate liberal arts students. Also in the Calloway School, Gordon E. McCray ('85) was named Associate Dean. Paul Juras was again named PricewaterhouseCoopers Professor for Teaching Excellence, while Page West was named Benson-Pruitt Professor and Director of the Business Degree Program. Lee Knight was appointed Director of the Accounting Program; James Cotter, Director of the Analytical Finance Program; and Bruce Lewis, Director of the Information Systems Program. Yvonne Hinson joined others in Forsyth County to form the Forsyth Working Families Partnership, a coalition of local nonprofit organizations formed to educate the community about the Earned Income Tax Credit, a tax refund available to working families with incomes around $32,000 or less.

Composer-in-Residence and Professor of Music Dan Locklair wrote an original piece in honor of retired University Chaplain Ed Christman ('50, JD '53). The piece was commissioned by Mary Ann Hampton Taylor ('56, MD '60), former Director of the Student Health Service, and her husband, Gerald Taylor ('58), a retired dentist. "O Sing to the Lord a New Song" set Psalm 96, Christman's favorite, as a five-minute composition for chorus and piano. It premiered on December 4, 2002, at the Holiday Choral Concert under the direction of Brian Gorelick. A second performance was held three days later at the annual Love Feast in Wait Chapel. The Louisville Orchestra in Kentucky premiered Locklair's Symphony No. 1, *Symphony of Seasons*, inspired by "The Seasons," a collection of poems by eighteenth-century British poet James Thomson, in October.

Under the direction of rare-books librarian Sharon Snow of Z. Smith Reynolds Library and with a $23,500 grant from the federal Institute for Museum and Library

Services to the NC-ECHO (Exploring Cultural Heritage Online) project, the papers of Samuel and Sarah "Sally" Wait were digitized.

In the Counseling Department, Sam Gladding was elected President of the American Counseling Association, the world's largest counseling organization, with a membership of more than 56,000 in the United States and fifty other countries. Donna Henderson was elected President of the Association for Counselor Education and Supervision (ACES), a division of the American Counseling Association.

At the Divinity School, Katherine "Kitty" E. Amos became the first Associate Dean for Academic Affairs and an Associate Professor of Christian education and spiritual formation. Douglass Bailey ('60) became the Executive Director of the Center for Urban Ministry, and Neal Walls became an Associate Professor of Old Testament interpretation.

Winston-Salem State University held a Maya Angelou Day in appreciation of all her accomplishments. Angelou (Humanities) spoke to over two thousand students, faculty, and staff about tolerance and equality. Ed Wilson ('43), who retired from active teaching in 2002, was one of seven individuals to receive the North Carolina Award, North Carolina's highest civilian honor, during the fall. An endowed chair at Wake Forest was also established in his honor, the Edwin G. Wilson Chair in English Literature.

In Education, Linda Nielsen offered a course, Women's Studies Internships, which gave student volunteers a chance to serve Winston-Salem's poor, neglected, and abused women and girls. Patricia Cunningham and Dorothy Hall developed a phonics curriculum, Month by Month Phonics, which was adopted by the New York City public school system and featured in a *New York Times* story in January 2003.

The West African country of Benin awarded Sylvain Boko (Economics) its highest honor, Knight of the National Order of Benin, at a July 26 ceremony in Cotonou.

The campus held a candlelight vigil around the Quad in remembrance of those who died in the 9/11 attacks in 2001

President Mathieu Kerekou presented Boko with a presidential medal during the ceremony.

James Wilson (History) was one of twelve recipients of the Peace Corps' Franklin H. Williams Award at a June 4 ceremony in Washington, D.C. It honors Peace Corps volunteers of color who have put their overseas experiences to work in their communities and professions to promote better understanding.

Debate Team Coach Ross Smith was named Coach of the Year in the Southeast Region in March, and Assistant Coach Jarrod Atchison ('02) was named Graduate Assistant of the Year by the National Debate Tournament. Smith, who became the coach in 1984, was National Coach of the Year in 1997 and District VI Coach of the Year in 2000. He had led more teams to the elimination rounds of the National Debate Tournament than any other coach in the last decade, and his teams had won every major intercollegiate invitational and round robin tournament at least once. Atchison earned the best regular season record in the history of Wake Forest debate during his senior year. He was named the second best speaker in the country in 2002.

Andrew V. Ettin (English) was presented with the Donald O. Schoonmaker Faculty Award for Community Service at the Opening Convocation, and Katy Harriger (Political Science) received the Jon Reinhardt Award for Excellence in Teaching. Former U.S. Senator Bill Bradley, also a member of the Basketball Hall of Fame, delivered the Founders' Day Convocation address, "America: The Path Ahead," on February 27.

Charlie Moyer resigned as Dean of Babcock School to return to the classroom effective June 2003. He became Dean in 1997. Soon after his announcement, Provost Gordon appointed a search committee for his replacement, chaired by Ken Middaugh, Associate Dean for Management Education.

A year-long seminar series, Curing and Caring: The Present State and Future of Bioethics in America, brought nationally and internationally known researchers and specialists to both the Reynolda and Bowman Gray Campuses to speak on ethical questions in biology and medicine. The events were sponsored by the University's Bioethics Task Force with grant support from the Fund for Ethics and Leadership.

With the country at war in Iraq, a group of concerned faculty led by Will Fleeson (Psychology) organized the group Faculty Raising Dialogue. It offered public panel discussions on February 4 and March 25. On March 3, students and faculty read Aristophanes's antiwar comedy, *Lysistrata,* in Shorty's. More than 650 readings of the play took place on that day in thirty-eight countries.

Carol Meyers (Duke), Margaret A. Farley (Yale), and Katie Cannon (Union Theological Seminary, Richmond) spoke on feminist and womanist theology during the inaugural Phyllis Trible Lecture Series in the Divinity School on March 18 and 19. Michael E. Dyson, Avalon Professor in the Humanities at the University of Pennsylvania, gave the keynote address at the University's

Sylvain Boko

Multicultural Male Summit on March 29. More than two hundred people, including students, attended workshops, forums, and lectures in Greene and Carswell Halls. The theme of the summit was "Identity: Who am I? . . . Why am I?"

A symposium on the life and legacy of Thomas Dixon Jr. (1883) was held April 10–13. Organized by Randal Hall ('94), Associate Director of Merit-Based Scholarships, and Michele Gillespie, Associate Professor of History, with assistance from Divinity School Dean Bill Leonard, it examined race, religion, gender, and the power of popular fiction and film. Dixon was a nationally prominent minister, lecturer, and writer at the turn of the twentieth century. A proponent of urban social reform through Christianity, he was also an advocate of subservient roles

Ross Smith

for women and a virulent racist, whose books were the basis of D.W. Griffith's monumental silent film *The Birth of a Nation*, which harshly stereotyped blacks and justified the rise of the Ku Klux Klan.

On April 1, the University hosted a technology consortium for faculty and staff of southeastern colleges and universities. It brought together leaders in higher education technology to share ideas and discuss effective uses of classroom and campus technology. David G. Brown, Dean of the International Center for Computer Enhanced Learning (ICCEL), delivered the keynote address.

Randy S. Casstevens ('87, MBA, '95), Chief Financial Officer of Krispy Kreme, spoke on corporate responsibility as a part of the Calloway School's Joseph A. Jones Finance Lectureship. An even larger luminary, Ron Clark, *Oprah Magazine*'s first "Phenomenal Man," spoke on February 11 in Brendle Recital Hall. A fifth-grade teacher at Public School 83 in Harlem and the 2000 Disney American Teacher of the Year, Clark's innovative pedagogy gained national recognition. ABC turned his life story into a *Sunday Night Movie of the Week*. He spoke on "Teaching through Adversity— Facing Challenges and Making a Difference" and returned to campus in mid-April to

sign copies of his new book, *The Essential 55: An Award-Winning Educator's Rules for Discovering the Successful Student in Every Child* (Hachette).

On March 19, W. Deen Mohammed, the leader and international spokesman for the American Society of Muslims, presented a lecture, "Respecting Human Dignity: A Prerequisite for 21st-Century Leaders." A few days later, on March 24, the

Michele Gillespie

Randal Hall

Retired Reverend William E. Swing, Episcopal bishop of California and founder and President of the United Religions Initiative (URI), spoke on how people of different global faith traditions can talk to and embrace one another.

Administration and Staff

Murray C. Greason Jr., an attorney with Womble Carlyle Sandridge & Rice in Winston-Salem, was elected Chair of the Board of Trustees. L. Glenn Orr of Winston-Salem, President of the Orr Group, was elected Vice Chair. Leon Corbett ('59, JD '61), Senior University Counsel and Secretary of the Board of Trustees since 1983, retired. Reid Morgan ('75, JD '79) was promoted to Vice President effective July 1, 2002. He continued as Secretary of the Board of Trustees and University Health Services and oversaw the legal offices on both the Reynolda and Bowman Gray Campuses.

Betsy Taylor (Counseling Center) was named Director of the new Pro Humanitate Center. She coordinated activities funded by a $1.9 million grant from the Lilly Endowment to encourage students to plan their careers with service to humanity in mind. Charles Kimball (Religion) headed a committee looking at another part of the Lily grant that dealt with institutional identification. In mid-June, the Summer Institute for Vocational Formation, sponsored by the Pro Humanitate Center, brought fourteen high school juniors and seniors to the campus for two weeks of activities focused on faith and vocation.

In the fall, Associate Dean of the College Linda McKinnish Bridges (Religion) was named Interim Director of the Women's Studies Program until Anne Boyle (English) became Director in January. Stephen L. Whittington was named as the new Director of the Museum of Anthropology; Lori Messer became the new Director of the Office of Research and Sponsored Programs.

Cherin Poovey was promoted to Assistant Vice President for University Advancement. She retained her title as Director of Creative Services. David Barksdale ('86) joined the University as Director of the College Fund and Annual Support.

In Information Systems, Jamie Barras became Director of Project Management; Kriss Dinkins, Director of Support and Outreach Services; Todd Edwards, Director of Media Solutions; Tommy Jackson, Director of Information Technology Security; Lynda Mitchell, Director of Technology Initiatives; and Lee Norris, Director of Information Technology Infrastructure.

Murray Greason

University Chaplain Ed Christman ('50, JD '53), retired on June 30 at age seventy-three. He had served as Baptist campus minister and Assistant University Chaplain since 1961 and became University Chaplain in 1969. He was instrumental in starting the Preschool Conference, the Volunteer Service Corps, and the annual Christmas Love Feast. He was famous in the 1990s for his orientation speeches, in which he included hundreds of students' names.

Cecil Price, Director of Student Health Services, and Janet Williamson, an administrator in the Office of Creative Services, were named Employees of the Year in 2002 at the Staff/Employee Awards Recognition Banquet on October 29, sponsored by the Department of Human Resources. The University awarded each $1,000.

Athletics

The football team enjoyed the first back-to-back winning seasons since 1987–1988 with a 7–6 win-loss record. They finished with a convincing 38–17 win over Oregon in the Seattle Bowl on December 30. After a successful first two years, the University and Head Coach Jim Grobe agreed to a ten-year contract extension in January 2003.

One of the highlights of the successful basketball season of 2002–2003 was a 90–84 win over Duke on February 13 at the Joel Coliseum. The Deacons won the regular season ACC title, and Head Coach Skip Prosser was named ACC Coach of the Year after compiling a record of 25–6. Josh Howard was honored as the ACC Player of the Year, named an Associated Press First-team All-American, and his number was retired. Mayor Allen Joines even proclaimed a day in honor of the Winston-Salem native. Unfortunately, although the Deacons were seeded number two in the NCAA Tournament, they lost in the second round to Auburn, 68–63.

Brian Fleishman, head coach of the women's tennis team, was named National Coach of the Year, Southeast Regional Coach of the Year, and received the 2002 Coach Verdieck Award for College Coaching.

The women's track and field team was ranked as high as fourth in the nation by the FinishLynx NCAA poll after their second place finish in the NCAA Pre-National Invitational meet on October 19. Annie Schweitzer-Bennett was named ACC Coach of the Year and NCAA Southeast Region Coach of the Year. Runner Anne Bergasel was recognized as All-ACC, All-American, Academic All-American, and All-Southeast Region. She had some amazing performances during the year. At the Stanford Invitational, which was the first time Bergasel ever ran the 10,000-meter event, she knocked six seconds off the Wake Forest record set by Sara Day in 2001. Day, who happened to be working at the meet as a volunteer, was the first to congratulate Bergasel.

The student-athlete graduation rate for 2001–2002 (the most recent

Ed Christman

Josh Howard

data available) was announced in September. It was at 74 percent, the highest it had been in three years, and right behind Duke and Virginia in the ACC.

Controversy over installing lights for night games at Gene Hooks baseball stadium erupted when the Faculty Drive Neighborhood Association complained that the lights would be disruptive and lower property values. After much discussion, Athletic Director Ron Wellman worked with the baseball team to use Ernie Shore field for night games in 2003, and the idea of new lights was dropped.

President Hearn wrote Wellman on May 2, stating, "I am revising our proposed new annual financial commitment to the department. Formerly at $375,000 per year for three years beginning in '03–'04, it is being revised as follows [$500,000 for '04–'05], showing the existing $250,000 per year/four-year program with cumulative totals." The new annual commitment was to be funded in part by a new student activity fee of $200 per year beginning in 2004–2005. This fund would be shared between athletics and student affairs. Hearn went on to say, "The academy was not formed for athletics, but at Wake Forest we are glad to identify the athletics program as part of that mission. To exist in tension means that athletics must be a part of the academy in fundamental respects, including the sharing of resources in a reasonable manner to preserve our overall excellence." After receiving the letter, Wellman turned down a job as University of Tennessee Athletic Director on May 6 and signed a new long-term contract with Wake Forest.

Anne Bergasel

Club Ultimate Frisbee became the latest rage on campus. Men's, women's, and mixed gender teams traveled and did well against other university clubs.

Individual student performances shone. James D'Antona was ACC Player of the Year in baseball, and Calvin Pace was ACC Defensive Football Player of the Year. Bill Haas and Nuria Clau were the ACC

Golfers of the Year. Christy Williams was ACC Rookie of the Year in volleyball. Lauren Gregg, a member of the Equestrian Club, placed fourth at the National Finals of the International Horse Show Association. It was the second year she had qualified for the National Finals. Katie Bason, a sophomore, was chosen for the Under-21 Women's Baseball League's Team America. She played in two World Series for women, facing other women's teams from around the world in the fall. Tennis player Bea Bielik gave up her senior year to turn professional.

Barry Faircloth ('93) was named Associate Athletic Director for Development, succeeding Mike Pratapus ('85, MAEd '88). Faircloth's responsibilities included all athletic fundraising, including the Deacon Club's.

The Women's Athletic Program, which started under the tutelage of Marge Crisp and Dot Casey, celebrated its thirtieth year.

Barry Lawing ('84), author of *Demon Deacon Hoops: History of Wake Forest Basketball in the Twentieth Century*, and Jim Early ('62), author of *The Best Tarheel Barbecue, Manteo to Murphy*, signed copies of their books at the University bookstore on October 12.

The Arts

The University Theatre produced Christopher Durang's *The Marriage of Bette and Boo*; Anton Chekhov's *The Cherry Orchard*; Tennessee Williams's *Vieux Carre*; and a 1746 comedy by Goldoni, *Servant of Two Masters*. The student theatre group, the Anthony Aston Players, presented *Lear's Daughters* by Elaine Feinstein and *Wisdom Teeth* by Wake Forest sophomore J.M. Picard in the Ring Theatre.

The Department of Theatre joined with the Southeastern Center for Contemporary Art (SECCA) to present internationally acclaimed performance artist Tim Miller on March 20. He performed a recent work, "Glory Box," a politically charged exploration of his struggles for immigration rights for gay people and their partners.

The Secrest Artists Series included performances by Canadian tenor Ben Heppner; the Ahn Trio, sisters from Seoul on piano, violin, and cello; the Eos Orchestra, a New York City chamber orchestra; and Red Priest, the British early music ensemble.

The Student Union brought the Pat McGee Band to perform at orientation in August on Davis Field; hypnotist Tom Deluca, who performed in Wait Chapel in October; Nine Days, another popular band; and bluegrass revival band Nickel Creek. Barry Drake gave a multimedia presentation and lecture, "60's Rock—When the Music Mattered," in March in Carswell Hall, while Jars of Clay and Caedmon's Call, two popular Christian rock groups, played in Wait Chapel in April.

On February 8, the International Championship of Collegiate A Cappella (ICCA) South Quarterfinals were held in Wait Chapel. David Bellugi, a recorder virtuoso from Florence, Italy, performed March 18 in Brendle Recital Hall, accompanied on the harpsichord by Peter Kairoff (Music). On March 22, Dale Backus ('90), a former Wake Forest football player and now a freelance classical pianist, performed in Brendle. The University Concert Choir presented Daniel Bollius's oratorio *Harmonic Representation of the Conception and Birth of St. John the Baptist* on April 4 in Brendle Recital Hall. The performance was a signature event of the Conference of the

Ultimate Frisbee became a popular club sport

Society for Seventeenth-Century Music, which brought sixty scholars from around the world to campus. Giovanni Umberto Battel, Director of the Venice Conservatory of Music and internationally known pianist, played on April 11 as part of an exchange program.

"Breaking Boundaries," a collection of fifty works by former artists-in-residence at the Atlantic Center for the Arts in New Smyrna Beach, Florida, was displayed on the lower level of the Charlotte and Philip Hanes Art Gallery from late August to early October. The upstairs gallery featured paintings by Art alumnus William Crow ('95). In October, *Corapeake*, a multimedia documentary about the small North Carolina town by photographer Kendall Messick ('87), was shown in the upstairs gallery, and "Pattern and Possibility," a show of watercolor paintings by poet A.R. Ammons, was exhibited downstairs. From November through January, "Treasures II: Selected Works from the Wake Forest Art Collections" featured thirty works in the downstairs gallery, while the upstairs gallery showed "Fair Witness," a multimedia installation by artist and musician John Richard Blackburn. In February and March, "Seeing Italy through Prints," a collection of works from the sixteenth to the eighteenth century by such artists as Raphael, Titian, and Michelangelo, graced the gallery.

Provost Emeritus Ed Wilson and Mary Dalton (Communication) read from Martha Mason's ('60) new book, *Breath: Life in the Rhythm of an Iron Lung*, on April 8. Mason, a resident of Lattimore in Cleveland County, transferred to Wake Forest in 1958. She arrived on campus encased in an 800-pound iron lung, where she had spent most of her life from age eleven. After her 1960 graduation at the top of the first class to graduate from the Winston-Salem campus, she returned home. In *Breath*, she wrote the compelling story of her idyllic childhood, the year she spent on hospital polio wards, her days at Wake Forest, and her life as an adult.

Campus and Student Life

The 1,012 students in the first-year Class of 2002 represented forty-one states and fifteen foreign countries. Of the 496 men and 516 women, 31 percent were from North Carolina; 45 percent were ranked in the top five percent of their high school graduating classes; 14 percent were minorities. The Graduate School welcomed 160 students; there were 119 new, full-time MBA students; 169 first-year students in the School of Law; thirty-two first-year Divinity School students; and 108 first-year medical students.

The *Old Gold and Black* reported at the end of the academic year that Wake Forest students participated in 130 clubs and organizations. While some groups were specialized, with as few as ten members, others, like Student Union, were large and covered a wide range of interests. Max Floyd, Director of Campus Recreation, stated that 88 percent of women and 90 percent of men were involved in intramurals and club sports. Over half of the student body volunteered in some way and gave generously, often through their Deacon Dollars, to good causes like the Brian Piccolo Cancer Drive, which collected over $48,000 that year.

An estimated 57.8 percent of undergraduates received credit for study abroad in the 2002–2003 academic year. According to *Open Doors 2004*, a report published by the Institute of International Education, Wake Forest was at the top of the list of "Selected Institutions by Estimated Undergraduate Participation in Study Abroad: Top 20 Doctoral/Research Institutions, 2002–2003."

A new Wake Forest tradition began just before winter break, the Lighting of the Quad. Initiated by a number of student groups, the quad was strung with lights, and hot chocolate and cookies were offered. A large Christmas tree was placed in front of Reynolda Hall and lit after representatives of a variety of interfaith campus groups—Jewish, Christian, Islam, and Baha'i— spoke, and various campus a cappella groups sang.

Thomas Richard Jones, convicted of first-degree murder in connection with the 1996 wreck that killed sophomores Julie Hansen and Maia Witzl, pleaded guilty to two counts of second-degree murder during a retrial in January 2003. He was sentenced to between fifteen and eighteen years in prison minus the 6.5 years he had

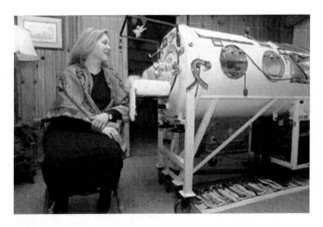

Martha Mason talks about her life in an iron lung to Mary Dalton

already served. The North Carolina Supreme Court overturned the first-degree murder conviction in 1997, ruling that there was no legal basis for charging an impaired driver with first-degree murder.

The war with Iraq, which started March 19, elicited an array of responses from students. Some demonstrated at a University entrance to show support for the U.S. administration and military troops. Candlelight vigils on campus and in downtown Winston-Salem protested military action. An ongoing campus drive gathered items needed by U.S. soldiers, and several forums and panel discussions examined the topics of war and U.S. foreign policy.

In the Wake Alternative Break, two groups of ten to twelve students volunteered with local agencies in Atlanta and New Orleans March 8–16, working from 10 a.m. until 3 p.m. each day. After exams, ten Wake Forest students spent two weeks volunteering on a Navajo reservation in Ganado, Arizona, beginning May 14. They worked with the elderly living in both independent and assisted settings, doing lawn care, minor home repairs, painting, and roofing.

In a study conducted by consultant Alan Cox, undergraduates in focus groups suggested ways to improve the University's intellectual climate:

- develop intellectual discussion groups among students and faculty that meet several times during a semester;
- offer more small seminars;
- promote interdisciplinary events and connect class work with extracurricular activities;
- provide more flexibility in the classes students can take;
- offer more pass/fail courses in the humanities for juniors and seniors;
- encourage more interaction between students and faculty outside of class, including open-door office hours;
- encourage students to align with others of similar interests to promote the intellectual climate outside of the classroom and have requirements for participation;
- offer team-taught, interdisciplinary classes that combine and relate liberal arts material; and
- minimize the number of lecture classes in favor of discussion.

The Wake Forest Army ROTC unit was included in the top 15 percent of Cadet Command's 271 units for 2002–2003. The high ranking owed much to the first- and third-place performances of the two teams entered in the national Ranger Challenge competition at Fort Jackson, South Carolina.

For the fifth time in as many years, the Wake Forest math team took top honors in Mathematics in Modeling, an international math competition. Coached by Assistant Professor of Mathematics Hugh Howards, the 2003 team was composed of Dana Lindemann, a senior physics major; Robert Haining, a junior computer science major; and Neal Richardson, a junior political science major. They used applied mathematics to devise the best way to handle baggage security claims at airports. Approximately seven hundred teams from colleges and universities around the world competed.

Lighting of the Quad

For the third time in five years, Calloway School accounting students ranked first in the nation for their performance on the 2001 Certified Public Accountant (CPA) exam. Senior Eric Almond received a bronze medal for the third highest score in North Carolina in 2002.

In cooperation with the administration, Student Government made plans to turn the former Delta Sigma Phi lounge in Taylor House into a coffee shop. At the same time, Rhoda Channing, head of Z. Smith Reynolds Library, told Student Government that the library was exploring the installation of a cybercafé. The only thing the two proposals had in common was coffee. In the spring, Campus Grounds opened in Taylor House, but the funding that would enable it to serve coffee came later.

The centennial edition of *The Howler* won two national awards: the Columbia Scholastic Press Association's Silver Medal for college yearbooks, and a first-class award with one mark of distinction from the Associated Collegiate Press. The yearbook's cover stood out, and these awards were just below the top category of All-American.

The Democracy Fellows, a group of twenty-eight sophomores participating in a four-year project in which they deliberated over community concerns, sponsored a two-hour campus-wide forum on building community. It took place on October 8 and involved over a hundred students, staff, faculty, community members, and alumni. Program co-founders Katy Harriger (Political Science) and Jill McMillan (Communication) facilitated the forum and wrote up its recommendations.

Rising senior Sarah Hubbard, a chemistry major, was one of three hundred in the nation awarded a Barry M. Goldwater Scholarship, the premier undergraduate award for students in mathematics, the natural sciences, and engineering. She received $7,500 toward the cost of tuition during the 2003–2004 academic year.

Rising senior Jennifer Harris, an economics and political science major, was named a Truman Scholar, one of seventy-six students selected by the Harry S. Truman Scholarship Foundation. Harris was also one of twenty students named to the second team on *USA Today*'s fourteenth All-USA College Academic Team, which honored students for outstanding intellectual achievement and leadership. Rosita Najmi, also a rising senior, earned an honorable mention.

Matt Hinson, a senior history major, won first place in the central Atlantic region in the 2003 Global Student Entrepreneur Awards. He was the second Wake Forest student to win this award in the past three years. Ricky Van Veen, a business major, won in 2001 for a profitable website he had created, http://www.collegehumor.com.

Michael White published the last of his popular "Abercrombie and Wake" cartoons in the *Old Gold and Black* in April. The cartoon, featuring the sparring of two "typical" Wake Forest students, ran regularly for three years. Even when he was studying abroad, White sent "Abercrombie and Venice" to the paper.

In his last Heath and Exercise Science class on bowling, senior Mike Vredenburg scored a perfect 300.

Ryan Ramsey was Student Government President; Will Wingfield was Editor-in-Chief of the *Old Gold and Black*; Alan English was Editor-in-Chief of *The Howler*; and the Student Trustee was Jonathan Kelly.

Riley Hollingsworth, Special Counsel to the Federal Communications Commission, was honored by the Amateur Radio Club on March 6. The club, founded in 2001, created a chapter for alumni. Hollingsworth was its inaugural member.

At a recognition banquet, the Order of the Omega, the Greek honor society, presented awards to the fraternity and sorority member who contributed most to both campus life and the Winston-Salem community during the year. The first recipients were Brett Bechtel of Theta Chi and Tyler Overstreet of Kappa Kappa Gamma.

In anticipation of pledge night and in support of love, the Student Union sponsored a lecture by Boston College Professor Michael Christian, author of *The Art of Kissing* under the pseudonym William Cane. He did not lecture so much as engage students in demonstrations. Eight volunteers, four men and four women, followed his instructions to show how to "liplock," "neck kiss," "bite kiss," "French kiss," "vacuum kiss," and, most important, avoid "hickies." The demonstrations and what followed on pledge night were not the same.

Facilities, Finances, and Alumni

Seniors Nazlia Alimohammadi of Winston-Salem and Anna Clark of Durham, North Carolina, created a sculpture in front of Salem Hall as a part of a public art course taught in fall 2002 by Associate Professor of Art David Finn. It is a picnic table, called "Periodic Table" in reference to Mendeleyev's periodic table of the elements; the benches even reproduce the auxiliary groupings of the rare earth elements. Alimohammadi built the steel structure, and Clark hand-painted the tiles mounted on the surface. The student affiliate chapter of the American Chemical Society provided funds, and Assistant Professor of Chemistry Paul Jones served as project liaison.

Work began on a new 33,000-square-foot wing to Reynolda House in May, scheduled for completion in fall 2004. The new wing was designed to provide room for historical displays, changing exhibitions, two art studios, a library, and new bathrooms. The plan included efforts to restore the house to its original 1917 appearance.

An ice storm in early March left more than 350,000 Triad residents without power, closed local schools, and sent trees and limbs crashing onto homes and cars. The Reynolda Campus lost one ash tree on the Quad, which had to be replaced, and a few magnolias and crepe myrtles. A number of trees fell in wooded areas around campus. Bill Sides, Director of Facilities Management, said that cleaning up these wooded areas and pruning large oak trees and replacing ornamental trees on campus could take several years. The University's electric substation and buried high-voltage distribution lines prevented outages.

WFDD stopped broadcasting the 11 a.m. worship service of the Wake Forest Baptist Church, ending a long tradition. Thus the church started broadcasting on WSJS. On October 30, WFDD sponsored a day-long forum on Ethics and News Leadership in the Media for journalism students at Wake Forest and surrounding colleges. News director Denise Franklin welcomed attendees, and Reid Ashe, President and Chief Operating Officer at Media General, gave the keynote address.

Graylyn International Conference Center was awarded the Gold Key award by the 70,000 subscribers to *Meetings & Conventions* magazine for the third year in a row. Graylyn also received a Pinnacle Award from *Successful Meetings* magazine. More than 75,000 meeting, incentive travel, and convention planners were asked to select sites and destinations on the basis of the quality of their facilities and services.

On August 13, the School of Medicine announced plans for a 180-acre expansion of the Piedmont Research Park in downtown Winston-Salem. The park covered eleven acres and had four buildings housing six hundred employees. As Chair of Idealliance, the nonprofit organization supervising the plans, President Hearn said the expansion would eventually rank with the moves of the medical school and college to Winston-Salem as one of the major events in University history.

A Chick-Fil-A restaurant opened in Benson University Center in February. It was extremely popular. ARA had made other changes to its food services at the start of the academic year. The most popular food station, the Roasting Pit, which offered home-cooked vegetables and hand-carved meats, was renamed the Home Zone. Parmigianos, an Italian favorite that served mostly pasta dishes, was updated to Bene Pasta. Café Features, which offered a variety of traditional American foods, became World's Fare. Homemade soup stations, called Kettle Classics, were added to the Reynolda Hall cafeteria, the Benson Center food court, and the food court in the Information Systems building. Finally, the dessert stations across campus were renamed Tummy Yummy. They served traditional desserts, such as pies and cakes, as well as healthier, low-fat options. In addition, Aramark hosted a dining etiquette program for students. Dining with the Director offered an eight-course meal where students learned how to use their utensils and set a table properly.

In financial matters, the University became self-insured, with third-party administrator ACS Benefits processing all claims. Gloria Muday (Biology), chair of the Senate ad hoc committee on healthcare, wrote President Hearn on May 16 about

Nazlia Alimohammadi and Anna Clark

disappointments with the University's contribution to health insurance for the coming year.

> The budgeted contribution by the University of $5.7 million with its matched employee premium contribution of $3.8 million is $800,000 short of the cost of maintaining our current health insurance plan for next year. . . . To maintain the current health insurance plan, we request that the University contribute 60 percent of the total costs, rather than just 60 percent of the premium costs. That would require a contribution of $6.2 million, which represents an increase in $500,000 over the current budget.

Before this letter, however, President Hearn had sent a memo to Reynolda Campus faculty and staff on April 2 notifying them that, for each of the past two years, the loss on the endowment had averaged 9.6 percent, and the University was entering a period of austerity. He said that despite cost cuts and freezes worth $2.1 million in savings, intended to prioritize "salary increases and essential programs and services," he was asking "budget unit directors to make further reductions, totaling $1 million in the fiscal year 2004 budget." In a July 26 memo to vice presidents, he wrote: "Given the uncertain economic environment, I am asking John Anderson to initiate contingency planning in the event that we face a worsening revenue situation."

On April 4, the Board of Trustees approved a total budget of $749 million for the 2003–2004 fiscal year. It included $511 million for Wake Forest Health Sciences and $238 million for the Reynolda Campus. Full-time undergraduate tuition was increased 7 percent to $26,490 from the 2002–2003 tuition of $24,750.

G. Eugene Boyce (Law '54) and the law firm of Womble Carlyle Sandridge & Rice established the Judge Donald L. Smith Professorship for Studies in Constitutional and Public Law. The Class of 1997 established the Matthew James Alexander Memorial Fund, which provided need-based funds to a student who wished to follow Matt's dream and study in the Dijon program in France. Matt was killed on July 17, 1996, when TWA flight 800 crashed off the coast of Long Island, New York.

The twenty members of the first graduating class of the Divinity School established an endowed fund to provide scholarships for future students. Each member of the Class of 2002 agreed to contribute to the Inaugural Class Scholarship Fund for five years. Sylva Billue pledged $20,000 to establish the Phyllis Trible lecture series, named in honor of the University Professor of Biblical Studies, who was one of the Divinity School's first faculty members.

Glenn Orr

Glenn Orr received the *Pro Humanitate* Award in recognition of his exemplary leadership and service to the University. The L. Glenn Orr Professorship in Banking and Financial Services at the Babcock Graduate School of Management was also established. Frank Holding ('52, LLD '09) and Howard Twiggs received the Distinguished Alumni Awards during President's Weekend.

Best-selling author Davis Bunn ('74) returned to campus to speak in Wait Chapel on February 20, sponsored by the *Pro Humanitate* Center, Campus Ministry, and the Divinity School. Attracting both religious and secular readers, his novels address Christian moral values.

Bob Ehrlich (JD '82) became the first Republican governor of Maryland since Spiro Agnew.

Summing Up the Year

The big news for 2002–2003 was the new Provost, William Gordon ('68, MA '70). The search had taken two years. Thus, the chief academic duties of the University had been split for four years between Ed Wilson and Sam Gladding. Gordon had been President of the University of New Mexico, and he had a stellar background of administrative experience, having served at all levels within the academy.

In other good news, the field hockey team under Head Coach Jennifer Averill won the ACC Championship, defeating Maryland 4–0, and then won the NCAA Championship, defeating Penn State 2–0. It was the first national championship for a Wake Forest team since 1986, when the men's golf team captured the title, and it was the first national championship for a Wake Forest women's team.

The Medical School celebrated its centennial year with the theme, "The Legacy of Yesterday, the Promise of Tomorrow." Craig Venter, pioneer and pacesetter in the race to decode the human genome, was the opening convocation speaker for the occasion. Although the whole University adopted the theme, the Year of Health and Medicine, most events associated with it were held at the Medical School.

On a somber note, a Day of Remembrance was held on the Reynolda Campus to commemorate the one-year anniversary of September 11. The upper quad was decorated with flags of all the nations that lost citizens during the terrorist attacks. Students, faculty, and staff took turns reading aloud the names of the more than three thousand victims on the steps of Wait Chapel. The day ended with an interfaith worship service to commemorate the events of the day as a candlelight vigil encircled the Quad. The 159th graduation speaker was Michael R. Bloomberg, mayor of New York City.

CHAPTER TWENTY-ONE
2003–2004

Brain Cancer, a Sixth Theme Year, and Another Field Hockey Title

We must never reach the point of abandoning the better and more hopeful possibilities of life, even in great difficulty. The profound balance between our frail human condition and the dauntless human spirit to be and to achieve is ever-refined by our experience, bringing us closer to a true understanding of life and ourselves. To see each other, our families, our endeavors, and ourselves with this perspective allows us to live our lives fully and without regret.

Thomas K. Hearn Jr., May 17, 2004;
Charge to the Graduates, Wake Forest University Commencement

In early October, President Hearn announced that he had been diagnosed with brain cancer at age sixty-six. Since he would have to undergo two surgeries, chemotherapy, and radiation, Provost Bill Gordon ('68, MA '70) became Acting President in November. A former university president, he was well equipped to step in.

In April, the President returned to campus and announced that he would reassume his duties as President but retire at the end of the academic year 2004–2005. During his remaining time, he had three priorities: completing the Honoring the Promise capital campaign, which had raised $505 million to that point; developing the Piedmont Triad Research Park; and advancing the new collaboration with Reynolda House. Hearn told friends that, since his surgery, he tired more easily and had a hard time reading long *New York Times* articles. In response, he shortened his schedule, kept up with his regular duties, but left some of the more contentious duties, such as faculty relations, to Provost Gordon.

"I have no regrets," he said. He did not feel fate had treated him unfairly, and in his charge to the Class of 2004 at commencement, which he titled "Lessons in Happiness," he dealt with the theme of adversity.

Fostering Dialogue logo

The theme for the year was Fostering Dialogue: Civil Discourse in an Academic Community. The sixth theme year was co-chaired by Claire Hammond (Economics) and Ed Allen (Mathematics), and the logo was designed by Craig Fansler (Z. Smith Reynolds Library). It featured two faces in profile with olive branches extending from their mouths and growing together.

Activities included presentations by Pulitzer Prize-winning playwright Tony Kushner (*Angels in America*); Steven Brams, game theorist and political analyst; and Tim Wise, senior advisor at Fisk University's Race Relations Institute. Michaelle Browers (Political Science) organized a series of six films on gender, identity, and social change. The official kick-off event was an agora, or outdoor discussion, on the Magnolia Court in mid-November. Senior administrators, students, and other members of the University community discussed the ways that dialogue occurs on campus. Before the discussion, four senior administrators spent a day shadowing students, going to classes, eating with them, and attending student events.

Paul D. Escott, who had served as Dean of the College since 1995, announced in September 2003 that he would resign as Dean effective June 30, 2004, but remain as Reynolds Professor of History. Provost Gordon appointed a committee to conduct a national search for his successor. Chaired by Richard Carmichael (Mathematics), it included Anne Boyle (Women's Studies/English), Herman Eure (Biology), George Graham (Philosophy), Claire Hammond (Economics), Jennifer M. Harris (senior), Nina Lucas (Dance), Minta McNally (University Advancement/Alumni Activities), Gordon Melson (Graduate School of Arts and Sciences), James Powell (Classical Languages), and Jack Rejeski (Health and Exercise Science). After a seven-month search, the committee made its recommendations, and the Provost announced on May 4 that Deborah L. Best ('70, MA '72) would be the new Dean. A Wake Forest Professor known internationally for her scholarship on development, she joined the faculty in 1972 and chaired the Psychology Department from 1994 to 2002.

In November, the field hockey team won a second national championship, defeating Duke 3–1 in Amherst, Massachusetts, and making Wake Forest only the third school ever to win back-to-back field hockey championships. The Deacons finished the year 22–1 and won the ACC Tournament for the second straight year. Head Coach Jennifer Averill (156–84–3) was again named ACC and National Coach of the Year, and senior Kelly Doton was again National Player of the Year. Six players

were named to the NCAA
All-Tournament Team; four
received All-American Hon-
ors; three were named First
Team All-Americans; and
three were named to Junior
National Field Hockey
Teams.

Academics

U.S. News & World Report's
2004 guide, "America's Best
Colleges," ranked Wake For-

Deborah Best and Bill Gordon

est twenty-eighth among national universities, down from twenty-fifth in 2003. The
Calloway School of Business and Accountancy ranked twenty-first, up from twenty-
fifth the previous year. *Forbes Magazine* and *The Princeton Review*'s list of the Top 25
Most Connected Campuses ranked Wake Forest second, and it was the only North
Carolina school in the Top 15. The *National Jurist* ranked the School of Law as a
best value among private law schools based on its comparatively moderate tuition,
above-average bar exam pass rates, and excellent student/faculty ratio. For the second
consecutive year, the Babcock School of Management was ranked in the top 10 percent of the nation's MBA schools in a survey released by *U.S. News & World Report.*
The part-time MBA program was ranked twenty-fourth, and the entrepreneurship
program twenty-sixth.

Wake Forest's 2003 Field Hockey Team: National Champions

Fifty new faculty members, most visitors, joined the Reynolda Campus: thirty-nine in the College of Arts and Sciences; six in the School of Law; three in the Babcock Graduate School of Management; and two in the Calloway School of Business and Accountancy. Because of financial concerns, the Trustees announced a freeze on faculty salaries and operating budgets for 2004–2005, and College faculty responded by passing two resolutions that were sent to the Board. One asked that faculty salaries be adjusted to accommodate increases in inflation, and the other for a plan to fulfill the promise to raise faculty salaries in the Plan for the Class of 2000.

The University worked with IBM technicians to replace a faulty component in the IBM R40 ThinkPad, distributed to freshmen and juniors in August, that caused freezing and problems with restarting and connecting to the network. Beginning April 8, IBM installed a wireless card in all R40 student computers that were dropped off for repair.

On December 15, Wake Forest was selected as one of eight Kauffman Campuses by the Ewing Marion Kauffman Foundation, receiving a $2.16 million grant to create a sustainable culture of entrepreneurship on campus. The grant was matched by University fundraising, and the University became a national model for incorporating entrepreneurship into a liberal arts curriculum. The five-year plan included establishing a university-wide Office of Entrepreneurship and Liberal Arts with Elizabeth J. Gatewood as director; adding new entrepreneurship courses and faculty; creating a Center for Entrepreneurship; and developing a fifth-year entrepreneurship institute for recent graduates pursuing new ventures.

As part of theme-year activities, Chaplain Timothy Auman gave the keynote address at fall convocation on "The Conversion of Language," exploring how free people with passionate interests and beliefs can communicate openly without turning dialogue into discord. Thomas C. Taylor, Professor Emeritus of Accountancy, received the Donald O. Schoonmaker Faculty Award for Community Service, while Biology Professor Peter D. Weigl received the Jon Reinhardt Award for Excellence in Teaching.

Award-winning professor, poet, activist, and humanitarian Sonia Sanchez was the keynote speaker at the Sisters Inspirational Summit, *More than a Woman of Color: A Woman's Worth in 2003*. Her speech on October 4 concluded a daylong series of workshops and lectures attended by more than two hundred students from colleges and universities across the state. The event was organized by seniors Hattie Mukombe and Monica Somerville.

John Haldane, Professor of Philosophy and Director of the Centre for Ethics, Philosophy and Public Affairs at the University of St. Andrews, Scotland, spoke on October 14 at the Benson University Center, sponsored by the Philosophy Department. His lecture, "Going Public: The Morality and Politics of Disclosure," discussed the morality of the increasingly common practice among the media of exposing the private lives of politicians and other public figures.

Marsha Sinetar, an organizational psychologist, pioneering educator, and best-selling author on the topic of fulfilling careers, discussed "The Heart of Vocation" on November 3 in the Benson University Center. Her lecture was sponsored by the *Pro Humanitate* Center, the Office of Career Services, and the Calloway School of Business and Accountancy.

The University hosted *Native American Indian Sovereignty: An Interdisciplinary and Cross-Cultural Symposium* on November 6 as part of Fostering Dialogue. David Wilkins, a Lumbee representative and Professor of American Indian Studies at the University of Minnesota, Twin Cities, gave the keynote address. Ulrike Wiethaus (Humanities) organized the event.

Hoda Hosseini, co-founder of the Broward County Institute for the Healing of Racism in Florida, took part in a conference on diversity, The Destiny of America: RACE-ing into the Twenty-first Century, on February 12. On February 19, the Student Union sponsored a lecture by race-relations expert and author Daryl Davis, "A Black Man's Odyssey into the Ku Klux Klan." It focused on confronting prejudices, overcoming fears, and forging peace with adversaries. The third annual Multicultural Male Summit featured playwright James H. Chapmyn, performing his multimedia "One Race, One People, One Peace" program on April 3.

Public and academic lecturers for the year were varied. Alex Vesely, who taught Wake Forest graduate counseling students at Flow House, visited September 18–19 to speak on his grandfather "Viktor Frankl's Legacy: Man's (and Woman's) Continued Search for Meaning" and lead a workshop on "Logotherapy: Helping Clients Find Meaning in Their Lives." On October 9, Emilie Townes, of the Union Theological Seminary in New York, delivered "Legends are Memories Greater than Memories" as the Divinity School's 2003 Margaret A. Steelman Lecture. Candace Bushnell, author of the best-seller *Sex and the City*, spoke on "Sex and the City: An Honest Look at Love and Relationships" on October 22 in the Benson Center. She discussed her books, her life, and the rise of what she described as her "semi-famous" career. The event was sponsored by the Student Union.

Donald C. Johanson, America's best known paleoanthropologist, spoke on "The Origin of Humankind: The View from Africa" in Wait Chapel on February 26. In 1974, he discovered the 3.18 million-year-old hominid skeleton popularly known as Lucy, which had an extraordinary influence on contemporary understanding of early hominid evolution. Physician, social activist, and clown Patch Adams presented "The Joy of Caring," a lecture on love and service, in Wait Chapel a few days later to raise money for Mother Teresa's Sisters of Charity and his own free hospital, The Gesundheit! Institute. The next month, on March 23, Orson Scott Card, best-selling author of *Ender's Game* and its sequel, *Speaker for the Dead*, gave a free public lecture entitled "On Science and Science Fiction."

Thomas Keating, a Cistercian Trappist priest, monk, and former abbot, led a program on "Prayer, Peace, and Dialogue," sponsored by the Divinity School, on April 5–6 in Wait Chapel. On April 5, the Department of Music hosted a lecture on George Gershwin's *Porgy and Bess* by Howard Pollack, author and Professor of Music History at the University of Houston. It also co-sponsored the thirty-third annual conference of the American Musical Instrument Society (AMIS) on May 19–22 in historic Old Salem.

Dennis W. Archer, President of the American Bar Association, spoke at the Law School on "Challenges in the Future for the Legal Profession" on April 13. The next day, the Student Union presented "Heads vs. Feds: The Great Debate." Steven Hager, former Editor-in-Chief of *High Times* magazine, and Robert Stutman, a twenty-five-year veteran of the U.S. Drug Enforcement Administration

(DEA), discussed the controversies involved in legalizing marijuana. On April 15, Raúl Muñoz Leos, Director General of Petróleos Mexicanos (Pemex), delivered the 2004 Broyhill Executive Lecture, "Democratic Values and the Development of Energy."

Pulitzer Prize-winning journalist Anna Quindlen, well known for her prestigious "Last Word" column in *Newsweek* and her best-selling novel *Blessings*, gave the Founders' Day Convocation address on February 19 in Wait Chapel. Provost Emeritus Edwin G. Wilson received the Medallion of Merit, the University's highest honor. James Cotter (Calloway School) received the Kulynych Family Omicron Delta Kappa Award for Contribution to Student Life. The Award for Excellence in Research was presented to Clifford Zeyl (Biology), and the Reid-Doyle Prize for Excellence in Teaching was awarded to Hugh Howards (Mathematics). Michael Green, Bess and Walter Williams Distinguished Chair in Law, was awarded the Joseph Branch Excellence in Teaching Award. Michelle Roehm, Associate Professor of Marketing, and Michael Lord, Associate Professor of Management, were presented the Cowan Faculty Research Prize, and the Kienzle Teaching Award was presented to Ram Baliga, John B. McKinnon Professor of Management.

Three faculty were appointed as Z. Smith Reynolds Foundation Fellows: Margaret Bender (Anthropology), Miles Silman (Biology), and Angela Hattery (Sociology). Cindy Gendrich (Theatre and Dance) was appointed a Junior Faculty Fellow.

Filmmaker Magazine named Brett Ingram (Communication) one of the top "25 New Faces of Indie Film 2003." He directed *Monster Road*, about clay animator Bruce Bickford, which premiered and was named best documentary at the Slamdance Film Festival in Park City, Utah, on January 21. In late September, David Finn (Art) showed nine marble shoes, or "Ghosts," in the windows of Huggins Shoe Repair (formerly Hines Shoes) on West 4th Street in downtown Winston-Salem. After five months' work, he and several of his students finished a twenty-two-foot tower at Diggs Elementary School. It was covered with a thousand ceramic tiles decorated by the children, each representing an academic area of concentration, such as ecology, math, or the arts.

Dan Locklair (Music) received a 2003–2004 award from the American Society of Composers, Authors, and Publishers (ASCAP). His composition "The Peace May Be Exchanged" from *Rubrics*, a five-movement suite for organ, was performed as part of the organ prelude at the June funeral service of former President Ronald Reagan at the National Cathedral in Washington, D.C.

In the History Department, Sarah Watts published *Rough Rider in the White House: Theodore Roosevelt and the Politics of Desire* (University of Chicago Press) and was promoted to Professor, the first woman to achieve that rank in the department. Ed Hendricks completed a two-year effort to produce an electronic version of the *History of Wake Forest College* book series. All four books, which spanned the founding in 1834 through the end of the Tribble administration in 1967, were collected on one CD and available for purchase at the College Bookstore and the Wake Forest College Birthplace Society on the old campus.

David Coates (Political Science), Worrell Professor of Anglo-American Studies and co-author of the recently released *Blair's War* (Polity), discussed the book on April 22. Bill Leonard (Divinity) saw his fifteenth book, *Baptist Ways: A History*,

published by Judson Press.
It traced significant aspects
of the Baptist movement
from the seventeenth to the
twentieth century.

Jack Rejeski (Health
and Exercise Science)
edited a special supplement
on preventing disability in
older adults in the October
2003 issue of the *American
Journal of Preventive Medi-*

David Finn

cine. In an article published in the *Journal of Computer-Mediated Communication,*
Ananda Mitra (Communication) proposed that blogs had changed the way we consider space, time, and voice and that blogging gave a voice to a previously excluded
element of society.

Miles Silman (Biology) and collaborators at Florida Institute of Technology
documented climate change and changes in forest composition over the past 48,000
years in one of the world's biodiversity hot spots, the eastern slope of the Peruvian
Andes. It was the first continuous record of Andean climate change.

Barry Maine (English) was named Director of Interdisciplinary Honors, succeeding James Barefield (History), who retired in the spring of 2004. Maine joined
the faculty in 1981 and chaired English from 1987 to 1996. George Graham became
the University's first A.C. Reid Professor of Philosophy. His special interest was in
mental health. Noted scholar Sidney A. Shapiro, an expert in administrative law and
regulatory policy, was hired as University Distinguished Chair in Law.

The Calloway School of Business and Accountancy named six faculty mem-
bers Calloway School Entrepreneurship Fellows for the academic year: Sheri
Bridges (Business); Jonathan Duchac (Accountancy); Paul Juras (Accountancy);
William Marcum (Finance); Annette Ranft (Strategic Management); and Julie
Wayne (Business). The fellowships allowed them to develop curricula tailored
to the needs of liberal arts students who aspired to careers as entrepreneurs.
Two T.B. Rose Fellowships were awarded to James Cotter and Page West. Bruce
Lewis was awarded the Cooper Family Fellowship in Information Systems. At
an annual awards ceremony in the spring,
Cotter received the Undergraduate Student
Teaching Award, and Lee Knight, named
Hylton Professor of Accountancy earlier,
received the Graduate Student Teaching
Award. According to a study in the journal
Advances in Accounting, she was one of the
most prolific researchers in her field, cred-
ited with forty-three articles since earn-
ing her doctorate in 1981. Dale Martin
(Accountancy) received the Horace Kelly
Alumni Teaching Award; Duchac received

Cindy Gendrich

Ajay Patel

the T.B. Rose Instructional Innovation Fellowship, and Denise McManus (Business) received the Faculty Scholarship Award.

In February, the Calloway School received a $63,000 grant from the Jessie Ball duPont Religious, Charitable, and Educational Fund to support the transition of many duties of the Forsyth County Working Families Partnership to the Forsyth County United Way.

The North Carolina Bar Association awarded the 2004 Law Student Pro Bono Award to the School of Law's Domestic Violence Advocacy Center (DVAC). About one hundred students volunteered to work with local attorneys representing domestic abuse victims or with Family Services to assist victims and their families.

Faculty approved a new interdisciplinary film studies minor; Romance Languages, Theatre, and Humanities were the participating departments. They also voted to eliminate starting their regular business meetings with a prayer.

A Theatre Department seminar co-taught by Cindy Gendrich and Leah Roy in fall 2003 sent young student actors to perform short scenes in Sociology, Political Science, History, and other courses. ClassAct allowed professors to use these live performances to facilitate discussion and to engage their students, while the theatre students honed their acting and directing skills.

The graduate counseling program, long a part of the Education Department, became a separate department in 2003, with Associate Provost Sam Gladding ('67, MAEd '71) serving as Chair. The East Asian Languages and Literature program also became a department, with David Phillips, Associate Professor of Japanese and former program coordinator, as Chair. A new Charlotte Saturday MBA program began in January 2004.

Administration and Staff

The continuing tension in faculty and administrator relationships increased after the April 2004 announcement that salaries and operating budget allocations to academic departments were frozen for the 2004–2005 academic year.

Provost Gordon appointed Chemistry Professor Mark Welker to a new half-time position as Associate Provost of Research. Timothy L. Auman, United Methodist campus minister since 1998, was appointed University Chaplain in July 2003, succeeding Ed Christman, who had retired after thirty-four years in that position. Associate Dean and Professor Ajay Patel was named interim Dean of the Babcock Graduate School of Management in August 2003 and then Dean in April 2004. He replaced R. Charles Moyer, who resigned in July 2003.

Tom Phillips ('74, MA '78) was named Director of Wake Forest Scholars, a new position in which he assisted undergraduates in applying for postgraduate scholarships and fellowships. Previously, he was Director of Merit-Based Scholarships, informing the selection of Reynolds, Carswell, and Gordon scholars.

Lynn Sutton, Associate Dean of the Library System at Wayne State University, became Director of Z. Smith Reynolds Library. She succeeded Rhoda Channing, who died in 2003. Danny Kemp was hired as Director of Software Solutions for the University's Information Systems Department.

Kenneth Overholt, Deputy Chief of Police, was awarded the Law Enforcement Medal from the Sons of the American Revolution.

Tom Phillips

Athletics

Virginia Tech, Boston College, and the University of Miami joined the Atlantic Coast Conference on July 1, 2004, expanding the Conference's membership to twelve. The change signaled that the ACC was increasing its emphasis on football. Richard Carmichael ('64, Mathematics) was appointed faculty athletics representative beginning July 1, replacing Ed Wilson, who had served as President of the ACC during the 2002–2003 academic year.

The football team suffered its first losing season under Head Coach Jim Grobe with five wins and seven losses. Nonetheless, three players were selected to the All-ACC Team: Tyson Clabo, Eric King, and Ryan Plackemeier. These three first-team selections were the most since 1992.

The men's basketball team had another stellar year, including a 90–84 come-from-behind victory over Duke in which Chris Paul scored 19 points in the final twenty minutes. On March 18, all television monitors in Benson University Center and in Pugh Auditorium were tuned to the Demon Deacons' first NCAA Tournament game against Virginia Commonwealth University. A week later, on March 25, fans gathered in the Magnolia Courtyard to watch the team take on St. Joseph's in the semi-final of the East Regional. The Student Union sponsored the outdoors big-screen display.

Josh Howard ('03) was selected by the Dallas Mavericks in the first round of the National Basketball Association draft in June. Calvin Pace ('03) was a first-round pick in the National Football League draft, and Kyle Sleeth ('03) was a first-round pick in the Major League Baseball draft—a trifecta for Wake Forest athletics.

All-American Jeremiah White was named ACC Player of the Year, a first for Wake Forest men's soccer. He and teammates William Hesmer and Michael Parkhurst were also named first-team All-ACC. *Lynn Sutton*

Richard Carmicheal

Chris Paul

Jeremiah White

Unfortunately, while they had a winning season, the team was eliminated in the second round of the NCAA Tournament by Virginia. The women's soccer team also had a successful season but was eliminated by UNC-Greensboro in the first round of the NCAA Tournament.

Nikeya Green earned All-American honors at the NCAA Indoor Track Championships. Annie Bersagel was selected for the second time as an All-American in cross-country. Sean Moore, a freshman golfer, captured an ACC medal with a score of 205, 11 under par. He was the first Deacon to win the honor since Tim Straub in 1989, becoming the University's nineteenth individual winner. Bill Haas ('04) received the prestigious Ben Hogan Award, presented annually to the top men's golfer in the amateur ranks, on May 17. Haas was ACC Player of the Year for the second straight year and only the fifth player ever to earn All-ACC honors four times. He was also the fourth student-athlete in the last ten years to be named a National Player of the Year. Others were Kelly Doton ('04), field hockey; Bea Bielik ('03) tennis; and Tim Duncan ('97), men's basketball. The golf team finished the ACC tournament in second place.

The dance team finished twenty-first and the cheer team in the top twenty at the 2004 UCA/UDA College Nationals competition in Orlando in mid-January. Wake Forest had not sent a team to the nationals in over ten years. The equestrian team, a club sport, had one of its most successful seasons.

Mark Petersen, former Associate Head Coach for the men's basketball team at the University of Minnesota, was named Head Women's Basketball Coach, succeeding Charlene Curtis. Assistant athletic trainer Adam Pecina was selected by the United States Olympic Committee to provide sports medicine to the men and women's teams at the 2004 Olympics in Athens, Greece.

Wake Forest placed fifth among private schools and fourth in the ACC in recording its highest finish ever in the 2002–2003 National Association of

Collegiate Direc-
tors of Athletics
(NACDA) Director's
Cup Standing. The
overall ranking of
thirty-two was ten
places higher than
in 2001–2002 and
one spot higher than
its previous highest
ranking of thirty-
three in 2000–2001.

Bill Haas

Jim Grobe named the foyer of the Pruitt Football Center in honor of Bill Faircloth ('64), Assistant Athletic Director for Football. A new Deacon Shop opened in
Hanes Mall in Winston-Salem as a partnership between University Stores and the
Athletics Department. Buz Moser, Director of University Stores, played a major role
in setting it up. Sports commentator Dick Vitale signed copies of his book, *Dick
Vitale's Living a Dream*, at the College Book Store on February 18. The bookstore
sponsored a Wake Forest spirit contest in connection with the signing, awarding
three prizes to the most spirited students.

The Arts

The University Theatre staged productions of Tony Kushner's *Angels in
America*, Ann-Marie MacDonald's
*Goodnight Desdemona (Good Morn-
ing, Juliet)*, Murray Ross's *Monkey
Business*, and James Lapine and Stephen Sondheim's *Into the Woods*. A fire
destroyed the set for *Into the Woods* on
April 3, and the play was moved from
the MainStage Theatre to Brendle
Recital Hall. Student-directed plays
were part of the Fall Studio Series in
the Ring Theatre: *Fifty Years Ago* by
Murray Schisgal, *Betrayed by Everyone* by Kenneth Lonergan, and *Tinkle
Time* by Dana Coen. On November
19, the Student Union sponsored
a lecture by Beth McCarthy Miller,
award-winning director of *Saturday
Night Live*, in the Benson University
Center.

The Student Union also sponsored a performance by the Roots,

Angels in America

a hip-hop band, in Wait Chapel on September 25. Their eclectic style conveyed a poetic urban message. Homecoming Weekend was kicked off with a performance by the ColorBlind Comedy Tour, featuring comedians Cocoa Brown and JJ, October 9 in Wait Chapel. The event was co-sponsored by the Student Union and Unified Rhythms Hip Hop Dance Squad. Founded in 2001, Unified Rhythms was a multicultural group of women who aimed to balance cultural diversity on campus through service, leadership, music, and dance.

With an all-student cast, chorus, and orchestra, the Department of Music staged Henry Purcell's opera *Dido and Aeneas*, the story of two tormented lovers. The sold-out performances took place on October 24–25 in Brendle Recital Hall. The department presented Giovanni Umberto Battel, internationally renowned pianist and director of the Venice Conservatory of Music, on November 16.

The Secrest Artists Series included performances by the National Symphony Orchestra with conductor Leonard Slatkin; pianist Orion Weiss; the American Brass Quintet; the St. Lawrence String Quartet featuring clarinetist Todd Palmer; the Brad Mehldau Jazz Trio; and the Masters of Mexican Music.

In the fall semester, the Dillon Johnston Writers Reading Series featured novelists Julianna Baggott, Rita Ciresi, and Paul Eggers.

"Pixerina Witcherina," an exhibition of works by contemporary female artists who addressed the complex history of women and storytelling, opened in August at the Charlotte and Philip Hanes Gallery. The title was taken from a language British author Virginia Woolf invented to share secrets with her niece and referred to the polarization of women's roles in fairy tales as either innocent, flirtatious pixies or evil, plotting witches. The exhibit was followed by "INSIDE/OUTSIDE Contemporary Cuban Art," a mixed-media exhibit of recent work from artists born and educated in Cuba. The end of the year saw a retrospective of seventy-nine photographs displaying a broad range of creative approaches by Sam Abell, a contributing photographer-in-residence at the National Geographic Society. Abell discussed his work at the opening on February 6.

Campus and Student Life

Wake Forest welcomed 1,009 new first-year students at orientation on August 20. The class represented forty states and ten foreign countries; 27 percent were North Carolina residents; 41 percent graduated within the top 5 percent of their high school classes. The incoming class included 520 women and 489 men; 13 percent were minorities. Classes began on August 27 for everyone except the School of Law's 194 students, who started on August 25.

Elizabeth Bland was Editor-in-Chief of the *Old Gold and Black*. Jennifer George was Editor of *The Howler*. Maeve Goff was Student Government President, and Dana Givens, Student Union President. Rising senior Ashlee Miller was chosen as the Student Trustee.

Controversy started early over an article in *The Howler* that questioned whether the homecoming king and queen selection was representative. For the past twelve years, the king and queen had been black, although minorities represented only a fraction of the student body. Many students called the editorial racist, and editor Alan

English apologized and explained that it was meant to raise questions rather than single out a particular group. While the editorial lacked sensitivity, the 2003 *Howler* had style and earned awards from the American Scholastic Press and the Associated College Press, including Best University Yearbook among universities with more than 2,500 students based on its superior content presentation, page design, photography, structure, and creativity.

Another controversy arose over the appropriateness of a replica of a plaque from the old campus, placed outside Tribble Hall in 1999, referring to janitor Tom Jeffries, who died in 1923, as "Dr. Tom." In spring 2004, a new plaque placed beside the old one explained who Tom Jeffries was. Research conducted by Biology Professor Herman Eure (PhD '74) and Vice President Sandra Boyette explained that Jeffries was the only University employee at the old campus to have a formal funeral procession. Faculty and staff served as his pall bearers.

An advisory committee chaired by Mary Gerardy, Associate Vice President, was appointed to recommend allocations of a portion of the new $100 annual student activities fee approved in fall 2002 by the Board of Trustees. On the recommendation of Student Government, half was earmarked for a future student recreation center; the other half for campus-wide enhancements to social, recreational, and community-building activities.

Although over 50 percent of Wake Forest students reported studying abroad in 2003, Joel Cohen, an economics and political science major, set a record as he headed to France for the fall semester. That trip marked his fourth study abroad experience. He had already studied in England, Argentina, and Brazil. With the increase in study abroad, the Center for International Studies issued new requirements for insurance. Director Pia Wood announced them in an email on November 17. On campus, Student Health Service treated more than 160 students for gastrointestinal illness soon after spring break, according to Director Cecil Price.

Technology Quarters, on the third floor of Luter Residence Hall, were open to twelve first-year students who were interested in learning about computers and willing to test new technology the University was considering for campus use. The new theme housing was the brainchild of Information Systems staff.

In the latest effort to incorporate technology into the learning process, students used hand-held computers in the classroom and for research over the summer. Information Systems research and development staff worked with faculty to develop software that matched the particular needs of their subject; for example, Bill Conner (Biology) used them in a course on animal behavior. However, the hand-held computers were not adopted for the University as a whole.

The University developed and implemented the Deacon Electronic Account Center (DEAC) in December 2003. It offered an online system for paying tuition and other costs, checking monthly statements listing long-distance telephone and other routine charges, and viewing regularly updated student account activity.

President Hearn worked with Governor Easley and a number of state agencies to organize the North Carolina Presidents' Summit on Alcohol Use & Abuse at the executive mansion in Raleigh on September 24. Forty college and university presidents and chancellors attended and were asked to sign a statement of commitment to address excessive drinking and its consequences.

The University ruled that, starting with the entering class of 2004, all students had to live on campus through their sophomore year. The idea—that Wake Forest was best experienced on campus—was generated by Connie Carson, Director of Residence Life and Housing, and Martha Allman, director of Admissions.

Wake Forest students demonstrated their quality both in teams and as individuals. President Hearn was informed on March 23 by Major General Alan W. Thrasher that the University's Army ROTC unit was in the top 15 percent of Cadet Command's 271 units for the 2002–2003 school year.

A team of five students from the Calloway School was one of five national winners in PricewaterhouseCoopers' inaugural xTREME Accounting (xACT) Competition held in New York City on January 22–23. Graduate students Karen Ludwick and Jonathan Fenton, junior Elizabeth Ellis, and sophomores Joshua Hemphill and Roxanna Drake, coached by George Aldhizer (Accountancy), competed against 220 teams from twenty-eight schools.

Yvonne Hinson and her accounting students again offered free tax-filing assistance to local residents. Their services began February 3 at the Goodwill Industries building. In 2003, the group assisted around 1,700 local taxpayers, returning between $30,000 and $40,000 in tax credits to them.

The fifth annual Babcock Elevator Competition took place on March 26–27. The first round consisted of two, twenty-eight-floor elevator rides at the Wachovia

Center during which teams pitched their business plans to a venture capitalist. The only thing the students could leave behind when the rides ended was a business card. Organized by the Babcock School's Angell Center for Entrepreneurship, the competition was believed to be the only one of its kind in the country. Babcock students also used their business knowledge to help the rector of the Haiti Nazarene Theological Seminary, who was struggling with the costs associated with running the school. The students worked with Stan Davis (Accounting) to develop tactical plans that included accounting systems and management strategies.

The annual Stop, Drop & Go program, in which students collected residence hall items discarded in the spring and sold them to the public in the fall, entered its third year. Four students started it to provide affordable goods to the community and to raise money for charities. At its yard sale on September 13, the program raised $1,750 for Crisis Control.

Hit the Bricks, a unified, yet competitive, fundraiser for the Brian Picollo Cancer Fund, ran from 11 a.m. to 7 p.m. on September 25. Teams of ten from fraternities, sororities, and open groups

Martha Allman; Connie Carson   raced each other around the brick Quad. Prizes

were awarded in different categories. Lambda Chi Alpha won the fraternity division; Pi Beta Phi won the sorority division; and the open division was split between the Volunteer Service Corps, which completed the most laps, and the "Bostwick Babies," who raised the most money. Over $5,000 was raised. University bookstore manager Buz Moser provided all the prizes for the winners, worth $8,000.

Senior business major Nick Gray and computer science graduate student Ryan Farley created BuddyGopher, which enabled instant-messenger users to read the away-messages of everyone on their buddy list simultaneously. Before BuddyGopher, instant-message systems required users to click on each person in their address book, or buddy list, to read their away-message.

Jennifer Harris, a political science and economics major, was named a Rhodes Scholar, the eighth Wake Forest student to receive the prestigious scholarship since 1985. She announced plans to study international relations at Oxford University. She was also one of seventy-six students to receive a Truman Scholarship and was named to the second of *USA Today*'s All-USA College Academic Teams.

Anjali Garg, a rising senior and a Presidential Scholar in debate, was also named a 2004 Truman Scholar, the thirteenth Wake Forest student in seventeen years to receive this award to support careers in public service.

Rosita Najmi was one of twenty students selected to the first of *USA Today*'s 2004 All-USA College Academic Teams, honoring outstanding intellectual achievement and leadership. The announcement was made February 12. Najmi was an economics major and co-founded Project Bokonon, which provided medical supplies to hospitals in Benin, West Africa. In fall 2003, she was named one of *Glamour* magazine's top ten college women of the year and received $1,500, a trip to New York City, and opportunities to meet with important female professionals.

Senior Lee Norris starred as Mouth McFadden in the television series *One Tree Hill*, which premiered on the WB network on September 23. A special viewing was held in Annenberg Auditorium on that night. Norris had previously starred in the television series *Boy Meets World*. Senior Jim Fitzpatrick, an analytical finance major, battled wits with two other college students on *Jeopardy*'s College Championship on November 13.

Margaret Elizabeth "Meg" Hudson died on November 21 after a long battle with pulmonary hypertension. She was twenty-one years old.

In Greek life, two Delta Kappa Epsilon (DKE) houses were razed to make way for a new, 6,500-square-foot house that cost $260,000. DKE alumni raised most of the money and took care of building permits.

The student life committee voted on October 9 to allow Kappa Alpha to colonize at the University according to a plan and schedule submitted by the fraternity's national representatives. The committee's resolution stipulated that Kappa Alpha would not be chartered on campus until August 2004. The Tau chapter of Kappa Alpha had lost its charter at Wake Forest in 2001.

The Zeta Lamba chapter of Chi Omega returned their charter to the sorority's national organization in early September rather than live with social probation restrictions. After several weeks, the sorority voted to return to campus, and the chapter was reorganized and reinstated. The national Lambda Chi Alpha fraternity presented its Grand High Alpha award, its highest honor, to Wake Forest's Theta Tau chapter to commemorate its community service, campus involvement, and academic

Students raced each other in Hit the Bricks; faculty and staff were a bit less competitive

record. Delta Zeta established a Pi Delta colony, with its first round of recruitment in January 2004.

Facilities, Finances, and Alumni

Calloway School faculty returning from summer vacation in early August 2003 found a much-anticipated present: a new building! "It was kind of like Christmas. We were so excited to move in," said Dean Jack Wilkerson. The 57,000-square-foot Kirby Hall brought all the Calloway School's classrooms and offices under one roof for the first time. The $14 million facility, dedicated April 1, included eleven classrooms, forty-two faculty offices, two student labs, and space for the Center for Entrepreneurship.

Trustee and Wake Forest parent Alice Kirby Horton, director of the F.M. Kirby Foundation, was responsible for its $5 million contribution to the building in recognition of her parents, Fred and Walker Kirby. The 49,000-square-foot addition to Calloway Hall was completed in the summer.

President Hearn spoke at the dedication of the Kirby Wing

Martin Hall was dedicated on October 9. It was named after Zeno Martin Sr. ('26), who served as mayor of Marion, North Carolina, and business manager of Meredith College, near Raleigh. Completed in 1994, Martin Hall was formerly known as North Hall. It was a three-story residence for ninety-five upperclassmen on the northwestern edge of campus. A faculty office at the School of Law was named in honor of Julius H. Corpening ('49), Assistant Vice President for University Relations. Corpening retired at the end of 2004, having spent thirty of his thirty-seven years at the University promoting the Law School to alumni and donors.

On July 31, an ice cream and lemonade social was held for invited members of the Wake Forest community and the craftsmen who had spent the past two summers laying bricks for the Young Student Walk on University Plaza. The celebration was held in the main lounge of Reynolda Hall. The event signaled the official opening of the Young Student Walk, which was named in memory of the late J. Smith Young, a

Julius Corpening, third from left, surrounded by family — Katie Corpening '09, second from left, with her mother, Cindy, Julius '49, and Jay '76

Minta Aycock McNally, assistant vice president for alumni activities at Wake Forest University (second from left), talks with Larry Young Hines (from left), Lynn Young and Mary Craven Hines, members of J. Smith Young's family, as they get their first look at the Young Student Walk plaque embedded into the sidewalk outside Reynolda Hall.

1939 graduate of Wake Forest and a Life Trustee who died in May 2001. He received the Distinguished Alumni Award in 1966. One of his sons, Jeff Young ('72), a Trustee, attended the ceremony. Crews installed approximately 200,000 bricks, new planters, railings, expanded seating areas, and improved drainage as part of the project. An approximately 600-pound bronze rendering of the University's seal was set in the brick in front of Reynolda Hall.

Other summer construction projects included renovations to the Pruitt Football Wing at the Athletic Center and the main lounge in Taylor residence hall.

Graylyn International Conference Center was awarded three meeting and conference industry awards for 2003: the Gold Key Award from *Meetings & Conventions* magazine for the fourth consecutive year, a Pinnacle Award from *Successful Meetings* magazine for the seventh time, and *Corporate & Incentive Travel* magazine's Award of Excellence.

Aramark, the University's food service provider, added several menu options to its campus dining areas, a new convenience store, a coffee shop, and special dinners in the Magnolia Room. Bodega, a new convenience store featuring candy, beverages, health and beauty aids, and other items, opened in the Benson University Center food court. A new coffee shop, Campus Grounds, opened in Taylor residence hall on September 3 with a ribbon-cutting ceremony on September 15. It offered espresso, cappuccino, iced coffee beverages, and baked goods and was open until 1:30 a.m. Aramark now offered dinner in the Magnolia Room two nights a month in addition to its daily lunch features, including a soup and salad bar, vegetables, and three entrée options.

Wake Forest donated twelve computers and printers, paper, and ink cartridges to Cisco Systems' Networking Academy at Kabul University. It donated to similar technology support programs in Ghana and Central America and gave away or sold

Colin Powell

at reduced rates computers and equipment to various other groups, including the Winston-Salem/Forsyth County school system.

Continuous daily shuttle service for all students, faculty, and staff began on the Reynolda Campus during spring semester 2004. The University Police shuttle expanded its operations to run every forty minutes, with the exception of seventy-minute breaks from 12:30 p.m. to 1:40 p.m., and from 7 a.m. to 6:10 p.m., Monday through Friday. Night shuttle service continued to operate from 6 p.m. to 3 a.m., seven days a week. Chief Regina Lawson said the new daily service was a joint effort between University Police and Student Government.

The endowment was valued at $725 million at the end of the 2002–2003 academic year. After two years of losses, it posted a 3.2 percent gain. In April, the Board of Trustees approved a total budget of $812 million for the 2004–2005 fiscal year beginning July 1. It included $563 million for Wake Forest Health Sciences and $249 million for the Reynolda Campus. Full-time undergraduate tuition increased 6.5 percent from $26,490 to $28,210 for 2004–2005.

The Presidential Scholarships program celebrated its fifteenth year. Former Board of Trustees Chair Hubert B. Humphrey Jr. ('48), who died March 18, 2003, left $750,000 to the study-abroad fund he had established in his name in 1996.

Martha Mason ('60), author of *Breath*, was awarded the University's *Pro Humanitate* Award on September 5.

Summing Up the Year

The year began with a shock: President Hearn was stricken with brain cancer and had to delegate his duties to Provost Bill Gordon for almost six months. When he returned to work on April 19, he soon realized he could not stay on. He announced his retirement for July 1, 2005, and committees formed to begin the search for the thirteenth president.

The sixth theme year reflected one of President Hearn's long-term priorities: Fostering Dialogue: Civil Discourse in an Academic Community. Speakers and events were hosted to prompt discourse on immediate concerns, such as administrator/student relationships, and controversial subjects, such as sexuality and race.

Deborah Best (Psychology) was selected as the new Dean of the College. The Quad's concrete sidewalks were replaced with brick as the Young Student Walkway was finished. Martin Hall, a new residence for upperclass students, and Kirby Hall, a new home for the Calloway School of Business, were completed and occupied.

The campus celebrated another field hockey championship. Coach Jennifer Averill guided the team to a 22–1 season and beat Duke 3–2 in overtime for both the ACC and NCAA championships. Six Deacon women were named to the All-ACC team: Kelly Dostal, who scored the winning goal, Maeke Boreel, Claire Laubach, Kelly Doton, Katie Ridd, and Lucy Shaw.

Although the academic year did not officially end for another five weeks, it wrapped up for most students and faculty at commencement, with the baccalaureate service featuring noted author and Episcopal priest John R. Claypool of the McAfee School of Theology at Mercer University, and Secretary of State Colin Powell delivering the 160th commencement address. Powell was the fourth Republican in a row to speak, following Barbara Bush, John McCain, and Michael Bloomberg, but he was the first African American to speak since Governor Wilder of Virginia in 1991. A crowd of 15,000 assembled on the University Plaza to hear him address approximately 1,600 graduates.

CHAPTER TWENTY-TWO
2004–2005

The End and Start of an Era

My two decades plus at Wake Forest have passed like a mere season or so. There was always something important to do, some issue crying for our time and attention. I have given myself across the years mostly to those objects of concern. Our basic need has been to establish ourselves as a national rather than a regional institution. I believe that ambition has been largely realized . . . . I urge you to practice this art of community if your groups are to succeed. That too is a part of this message of Pro Humanitate. We must grasp to the very ends of our collective reaches. We can—as we already have— accomplish what seems beyond our reach. Achieving more than we thought possible or probable has become a Wake Forest metaphor.

Thomas K. Hearn Jr., May 16, 2005;
Charge to the Graduates, Wake Forest University Commencement

The major story of 2004–2005 was the change of the top leader at the University. Thomas Hearn retired June 30, 2005. His twenty-two year service as President was the longest of any Wake Forest President except Washington Manly Wingate, who served from 1854 to 1879. At a formal retirement dinner for the president and his wife, Laura, on April 15, Murray Greason, Chair of the Board of Trustees, announced that the broad green lawn stretching from Wait Chapel to Reynolda Hall would now be called Thomas K. Hearn Jr. Plaza.

On April 25, the Department of Music presented a Gilbert and Sullivan Gala in honor of the President. It surprised and pleased him, and featured the Wake Forest orchestra directed by David Hagy and student performers taught and coached by Teresa Radomski and Jim Dodding. In another marker event, the University celebrated commencement on May 16, announcing that it had met its $600 million capital campaign goal thirteen months ahead of schedule, thanks in part to a major gift from the Hearns. The total raised was $617 million at the time of the announcement,

The Quad was named Hearn Plaza in honor of Thomas K. Hearn Jr.

with $361 million for the Reynolda Campus and $256 million the Bowman Gray Campus.

Hearn retired to an office on the fourth floor of the Z. Smith Reynolds Library soon after commencement and would work there until his death in 2008. He used that time to reflect on his presidency and to receive both visitors and accolades. For example, he received the 2005 Chief Executive Leadership Award by the Council for the Advancement and Support of Education (CASE) District III.

A presidential search committee and two advisory committees were formed in the summer of 2004, and the A.T. Kearney Executive Search firm was retained to assist them. Murray Greason ('59, JD '62), Winston-Salem attorney and chair of the trustees, chaired the search committee, which included six other Trustees—L. Glenn Orr Jr., K. Wayne Smith ('60), William B. Greene Jr. ('59), Simpson O. Brown Jr. ('77, MBA '86), Deborah Dixon Lambert ('78), and James A. Dean; two current faculty members, Judy Karen Brunso-Bechtold (Neurobiology and Anatomy) and Michele K. Gillespie (History); two retired faculty members, C. Douglas Maynard ('55, MD '59) and Edwin G. Wilson ('43); and Bobbi Acord ('86, JD '89), President of the Law Alumni Council. Nine of the twelve members were alumni.

The search committee met for the first time from July 29 to August 1 at the Summer Leadership Conference, a gathering of alumni leaders and volunteer board members from the College, Calloway School, graduate and professional schools. The committee also scheduled four campus forums in September for alumni and others to share their opinions. Individuals were encouraged to visit a website devoted to the presidential search; to read the first draft of a candidate profile describing the attributes desired in the next president; and to email comments to the committee.

The faculty advisory committee was composed of Chester "Chet" Miller (Babcock), Gordon E. McCray ('85, Calloway), Douglass M. Bailey ('60, Divinity), Charles P. Rose Jr. (Law), Judy Brunso-Bechtold (Neurobiology and Anatomy), Michele K. Gillespie (History), Katy J. Harriger (Political Science), Richard E. Heard (Music), Win-Chiat Lee (Philosophy), Barry G. Maine (English), Eric "Rick" Matthews (Physics), and Gloria K. Muday (Biology).

The volunteer boards and councils advisory committee was made up of Bobbi Jo Acord ('86, JD '89, Atlanta), Thomas Rannels Blank ('74, Arlington, VA), Shelmer Doyle Blackburn ('82, Raleigh), Fred Guthrie Crumpler (JD '57, Winston-Salem), David Wright Dupree (MBA '78, Washington, DC), Mr. and Mrs. James M. Hoak Jr. (Dallas, Parents Council), Ann A. Johnston (MBA '81, Winston-Salem), Bradley David Kendall ('89, Atlanta), Mitesh Bharat Shah ('91, Atlanta), James Thomas Stone ('70, Raleigh), Mary Ann Hampton Taylor ('56, MD '60, Winston-Salem), George Todd Turner ('95, Raleigh), and John W. Wagster ('57, Nashville).

On January 21, after a ten-month national search, the Board of Trustees elected Nathan O. Hatch, Provost of the University of Notre Dame, thirteenth President of Wake Forest beginning July 1, 2005. Hatch, a fifty-eight-year-old Presbyterian and native of Columbia, South Carolina, was Andrew V. Tackes Professor of History at Notre Dame and one of the most influential scholars in the history of religion in the United States. Besides his academic and administrative experience, he had extensive experience in strategic planning and strengthening undergraduate, graduate, and professional education.

A presidential transition committee composed of faculty, staff, students, trustees, alumni, and parents met for the first time on January 27. It was to advise on various aspects of the transition, including Hatch's early activities with the campus community and such events as the inauguration in the fall. It was chaired by K. Wayne Smith, a Trustee

President Hearn held up a stuffed dog symbolizing the Honoring the Promise achievement of its goal of $600 million

who served on the presidential search committee. The Vice Chairs were Trustee Jeanette Hyde of Raleigh and Ed Wilson. Twelve faculty members, representing the undergraduate, graduate, and professional schools, included Chet Miller (Babcock), Gordon McCray (Calloway), Douglass Bailey (Divinity), Charles P. Rose Jr. (Law), Judy Brunso-Bechtold (Neurobiology and Anatomy), Michele Gillespie (History), Katy Harriger (Political Science), Harry Titus (Art), Win-Chiat Lee (Philosophy), Barry Maine (English), Rick Matthews (Physics), and Gloria Muday (Biology). Muday was President of the University Senate, and Titus President-Elect. The two students were senior Jamie Dean, student member of the Board of Trustees, who also served on the presidential search committee, and Kamieka Hairston, an MBA student. Also on the committee were Nancy Kuhn of Washington, D.C., representing the College Alumni Council; Matt and Llew Ann King of Brentwood, Tennessee, representing the Parents Council; and Barbara Walker, Senior Associate Athletic Director, representing the administrative staff.

Academics

The Reynolda Campus welcomed fifty-four new faculty members during 2004–2005. Forty-six joined the College of Arts and Sciences; six, the School of Law; and two, the Calloway School of Business and Accountancy.

Nathan and Julie Hatch received Wake Forest tie-dye shirts on their arrival to Wake Forest

Pulitzer Prize-winning playwright Tony Kushner gave a free, public lecture on September 9 in Wait Chapel. Lee Hamilton, former congressional representative from Indiana, Director of the Woodrow Wilson International Center for Scholars in Washington, D.C., and Vice Chair of the 9/11 Commission, delivered the fall convocation address on October 28. Charles Richman (Psychology) was presented with the Donald O. Schoonmaker Faculty Award for Community Service, and Sarah Watts (History) the Jon Reinhardt Award for Distinguished Teaching.

James Carville, Democratic Party strategist, author, and co-host of CNN's *Crossfire*, was the Founders' Day speaker in February 2005. His remarks emphasized the importance of overcoming failure. After he spoke, James Powell (Classical Languages) was awarded the Kulynych Family Omicron Delta Kappa Award for contribution to student life. The Reid-Doyle Prize for Excellence in Teaching was presented to Martin Guthold (Physics). The Award for Excellence in Research was presented to Ulrich Bierbach (Chemistry). The Kienzle Teaching Award went to Jonathan Pinder and the Cowan Faculty Research Prize to Timothy Smunt, both Babcock faculty. Simone Rose (Law) was awarded the Joseph Branch Excellence in Teaching Award, and Wake Forest's highest honor, the Medallion of Merit was given to Timothy Pennell of Winston-Salem and Willis "Doc" Murphrey III of Roanoke Rapids.

David Lubin, Charlotte C. Weber Professor of Art, was honored by the Smithsonian American Art Museum in the fall for his book *Shooting Kennedy: JFK and the Culture of Images*. The book was published in November 2003 on the fortieth anniversary of the Kennedy assassination.

James Carville

Mark Leary (Psychology) published a new book in August 2004, *The Curse of the Self* (Oxford University Press), discussing how self-reflection was a mixed blessing, helpful in planning ahead and solving problems but creating anxiety about future performance. Leary suggested quieting and reducing unnecessary self-consciousness through meditation.

David Evans (Anthropology) published a novel, *The Judas Bird: A*

Modern Treasure Tale (Alliance Books). Dan Locklair (Music) released a new CD, *Chamber Music.*

In the Sociology Department, Charles Longino Jr., Director of the Reynolda Campus Gerontology Program, was elected President of the Gerontological Society of America, the oldest and largest national multidisciplinary organization devoted to the advancement of gerontological research. He was past President of the Asso-

Chuck Longino

ciation for Gerontology in Higher Education and the Southern Gerontological Society as well as Editor of the *Journal of Gerontology: Social Sciences* at the time of his election. Ian Taplin and Saylor Breckenridge documented the rapid growth of retail wineries and commercial wine production in North Carolina, and their study was published in the book series *Research in the Sociology of Work.*

Daniel B. Kim-Shapiro (Physics) was awarded a five-year, $518,400 Independent Scientist Career Development Award (K02) by the National Heart, Lung, and Blood Institute (NHLBI) of the National Institutes of Health (NIH) for his project, "Nitrite and Nitric Oxide in Sickle Cell Blood."

Mary Lynn Redmond (Education), Director of Foreign Language Education, helped high school students at a foreign language camp June 13–16 to develop French and Spanish language skills.

Sam Gladding (Counseling) was named to the Hall of Fame of the University of Alabama at Birmingham's counselor education program. Gladding, the first person to receive this honor, taught at UAB from 1984 to 1990.

Ananda Mitra (Communication) became the first Director of the Survey Research Center after serving as interim director since its establishment in September 2003. The center was founded on the recommendation of an intercampus task force led by Sally Shumaker, Professor of Social Sciences and Health Policy at the medical school and Director of the Office of Intercampus and Community Program Development. It assisted faculty research by moderating focus groups, designing questionnaires, sampling, computer-aided telephone interviewing, mail data collection, web-based data collection, and data analysis.

The Arthritis Foundation named Wake Forest University's

Daniel B. Kim-Shapiro

Arthritis, Diet, and Activity Promotion Trial (ADAPT) one of the ten greatest advances of 2004. Stephen Messier, Professor of Health and Exercise Science, was the principal investigator. The study was a joint effort with Wake Forest Baptist Medical Center.

As film studies became a minor, the University premiered two documentary films produced by Communication Department faculty in October. The first, *The Life-Giving Gift of Acknowledgment*, was produced by Michael Hyde, Mary Dalton, and Steve Jarrett and directed by former faculty member and award-winning film-maker Brett Ingram. It incorporated the theme from the 2003–2004 academic year, Fostering Dialogue. The second documentary, *Building Pro Humanitate: A Video Diary of Service in Vietnam*, was again produced by Dalton and directed by Ingram. It centered on twelve students who took a service trip to Vietnam, teaming up with Vietnamese students to build a school in a remote village, and touring cultural sites around the country during their second week.

The University also hosted a film forum on actor Pat Hingle January 15–16 in Pugh Auditorium. Hingle, who lived in Wilmington, North Carolina, had been in more than 110 motion pictures and numerous television shows since the early 1950s. Curtis Gaston, visiting lecturer in Communication, organized the forum, co-sponsored by the Communication Department and the Film Studies Program. On January 19, following the opening weekend of Paramount's *Coach Carter*, starring Samuel L. Jackson, Ken Carter himself spoke on "Average Is Just Not Good Enough. PERIOD!" He was famous for locking his undefeated, state-play-off-bound high school basketball team out of the gym and forcing them to hit the books and "rise as a team."

The Center for International Studies hosted a six-week series of lectures and discussions on current foreign policy. Great Decisions Forum 2005 was coordinated by Yomi Durotoye (Political Science). In the Babcock Leadership Series, Jeffrey Hollender, President and Chief Executive Officer of Seventh Generation, delivered a lecture on "What Matters Most" on January 31 in the Worrell Professional Center. He was followed the next day by William Johnson, Chair, President and Chief Executive Officer of H.J. Heinz Company.

William Glasser, an internationally known psychiatrist and author of *Reality Therapy*, led a workshop on February 21. He created reality therapy in 1965.

Tim Tyson, an expert on twentieth-century black freedom movements in the U.S. South and author of *Blood Done Sign My Name*, spoke on March 15 in Wait Chapel. Clifford Will, one of the world's leading authorities on Albert Einstein's theory of general relativity, spoke on March 17 in Pugh Auditorium, sponsored by the Physics Department, as part of the 2005 World Year of Physics, a celebration commemorating the one hundredth anniversary of five papers by Einstein that influenced all areas of modern physics.

Steven Feierman, an expert on the history of health and healing in Africa, presented the Clonts Lecture in History on March 21. The next

Ananda Mitra

day, ethicist William F. May delivered a keynote address, "The Public Obligation of the Professional," in Wait Chapel. He explored how the professions of medicine, law, politics, engineering, media, ministry, business, and academia struggle with their dual identity as a means to a livelihood and a calling to public service.

In spring 2005, the English Department launched its first annual Kenan Lecture Series, Chaos in American Literature and Science. Its three lectures were free, open to the public, and funded by the W.R. Kenan Jr. Professorship of Humanities. On March 23 at the Scales Fine Arts Center, Roger Gilbert, English Professor at Cornell University, discussed poet A.R. Ammons ('49): "From Whiteville to Ithaca: A.R. Ammons' Scenic Route." Gilbert was working on a critical biography of the North Carolina native at the time.

On March 24, Robert E. Rubin, former U.S. Treasury Secretary and Director and Chair of the Citigroup, Inc., executive committee, delivered the 2005 Broyhill Executive Lecture. Judge John G. Roberts Jr. of the United States Court of Appeals for the District of Columbia Circuit spoke at the second annual Jeff Rupe Memorial Lecture in the Law School's courtroom-auditorium.

Wake Forest University Press, the premier publisher of Irish poetry in North America, hosted the eighth annual Irish Festival. It started on March 12 with Irish Festival Community Day on Davis Field, which drew more than 3,500 people and featured Irish cultural activities, including music, dancing, storytelling, and arts and crafts. Other events had a small cover charge but included a concert, dancing, storytelling, a poetry contest, and poetry readings.

The Calloway School of Business and Accountancy named three Accounting faculty members to PricewaterhouseCoopers-endowed appointments in fall 2004: Terry Baker, George Aldhizer, and Yvonne Hinson. Hinson already had an appointment, but her PricewaterhouseCoopers endowment was extended through 2006.

Deborah A. Nolan, Associate Director of Z. Smith Reynolds Library, was selected as one of the fifteen best academic library leaders in the nation to participate in the 2005 UCLA Senior Fellows Program.

The Health and Exercise Science Department's twenty-nine-year-old cardiac rehabilitation program was reorganized. Patients in the early stage of cardiac rehabilitation now went to the J. Paul Sticht Center on Aging and Rehabilitation at the medical center. The Reynolda Campus program continued

Cardiac rehabilitation program: Pete Brubaker talks with a participant

its focus on long-term exercise maintenance for cardiac patients but expanded to provide exercise and lifestyle programs for those living with other chronic diseases and conditions, such as pulmonary disease, diabetes, and obesity. To reflect the program's new mission, its name changed to the Healthy Exercise and Lifestyle ProgramS (HELPS).

Katy Harriger (Political Science) and Jill McMillan (Communication) continued their research project, Democracy Fellows, which looked at the effects of public deliberation on college students. Before orientation, first-year students were asked to closely follow the 2004 presidential race; during their first week at Wake Forest, they attended a panel discussion and a small group meeting with academic advisors to consider the major questions. The program was designed to teach them that college is a place to think and to demonstrate that politics can be discussed without conflict or argument.

The Museum of Anthropology was one of two museums in North Carolina to receive a 2004 Museums for America grant from the Institute of Museum and Library Services. The $54,869 grant funded a new computerized data management program to replace the outmoded catalog system. The museum also established a fifteen-member advisory board in July: from Winston-Salem, Stanley Bohrer, Tyler Cox, Yomi Durotoye (Political Science), Kikuko Imamura (International Studies), Marjorie Northrup, Barbee Oakes (Multicultural Affairs), Daisy Rodriguez, Joti Sekhon, and Paul Thacker (Anthropology); from Rural Hall, Ulrike Wiethaus (Humanities); from Lewisville, Hobie Cawood, Marisa Estelrich, and Willie Everett; Ruth Revels of Greensboro; and Cristopher Avila of Stoneville. The Wachovia Historical Society and the Mission Society of the Moravian Church South, Inc., gave the museum over twenty thousand archaeological artifacts and 239 objects collected by Moravian missionaries. They had been on loan to the museum since 1983. The artifacts, including pottery, stone axes, spear points, and shell jewelry, provide glimpses of Native American life along the Yadkin and Pee Dee Rivers from about 8000 B.C. to 1700 A.D. They were part of the Douglas Rights Collection, gathered in the 1930s and 1940s by the Reverend Rights, a founder of the North Carolina Archaeological Society and well-known Winston-Salem Moravian minister.

Laura Hearn

Administration and Staff

Laura Hearn received the *Pro Humanitate* Award from Murray Greason, Chair of the Board of Trustees, at a Wake Forest Society dinner on February 25. It recognized her generosity in welcoming thousands into the President's home and contributing to the landscaping and beautification of the Reynolda Campus and her careful restoration of the Shipman garden at the President's house.

Ed Christman, who retired as chaplain in 2003, received the first Divinity School Distinguished Service Award on March 22.

Kerry M. King ('85) and Judy Swicegood were named Employees of the Year for 2004. King had worked at the University for fifteen years and was Associate Director of Creative Services in University Advancement. Swicegood had worked at the University for twenty years and was the administrative coordinator of the Physics Department.

Hu Womack

Mark E. Welker (Chemistry) was named Associate Provost for Research effective July 1. In February 2005, Brenda Balzer became interim Director of Human Resources. Ginny Bridges Ireland was named acting Director of Admissions and Student Services at the Divinity School, and Michelle Adkins was named Director of the new Reynolda Campus Environmental Health and Safety Department. Mary Dawne Clark ('83) became the new Director of Annual Support and the College Fund in University Advancement, and Melissa Combes (MBA '97) was named Director of Development for the Babcock Graduate School of Management and the Calloway School of Business and Accountancy.

Hu "Giz" Womack, information technology specialist at Z. Smith Reynolds Library, appeared on one of seven Triad Equality Alliance billboards in October celebrating National Coming Out Day on October 11. The billboard aimed to move the community toward greater acceptance of lesbian, gay, bisexual, and transgender family members, friends, and neighbors. Security officer George McBride, "the friendly, white-haired man with the bowl of mints" who kept watch from 6 p.m. to 1 a.m. in the foyer of Z. Smith Reynolds Library, retired June 3 after ten years with the University.

L. Glenn Orr of Winston-Salem was elected the new Chair of the Board of Trustees, and Murray Greason was elected Vice Chair. Alexandria J. Reyes, a junior, was elected as the student member of the Board.

Athletics

In 2004, the football team went 4–7 for the second losing season in a row for Coach Jim Grobe. In much better news, Wake Forest not only hosted the 2004 Division I Field Hockey Championship at Kentner Stadium, but the team won its third consecutive NCAA National Championship, beating Duke 3–0 on November 21. The men's soccer team won the ACC regular season title.

With a 15–14 record, the women's basketball team was invited to the Women's National Invitational Tournament. It was their first postseason appearance since 1987–1988. They advanced to the third round, where they lost to West Virginia 65–52 after defeating Charlotte and South Florida.

At men's basketball games, the number of Screamin' Demons was capped at 2,210 and reached capacity by late October; 200 tickets were allocated to the medical school, and ninety for the band, for a total of 2,500 student tickets. Adding to the excitement, Noel Shepherd ('90), an account executive with WXII-12, danced in the aisles to the song "Jump Around" by House of Pain. Wearing a Deacon tie-dye shirt and floppy tie-dye hat, he was known to the crowd as NazT Deac.

The basketball floor in Lawrence Joel Memorial Coliseum was replaced after fourteen years, as was the grass at Groves Stadium. New track and turf were added to Kentner Stadium, and FieldTurf, a product as soft as grass but much easier to maintain, was laid down on the football practice field.

President Hearn was appointed Chair of the Knight Commission, assuming duties on March 1, 2005, from William Friday. Hearn had been a member since 1989. The Club Crew team honored the President by naming a newly acquired racing shell the Thomas K. Hearn. On March 31, President and Mrs. Hearn formally christened the shell on the Magnolia Quad with water from Belews Lake, where the team practiced, and champagne over its bow.

In another club sport, the ice hockey team finished second in the Piedmont Hockey Association for the second straight year. A twenty-eight-team intramural dodgeball league was formed in the fall. Regular season games were played on the basketball courts outside Collins Residence Hall.

George Greer resigned as baseball coach after seventeen years and 608 wins, the winningest baseball coach in Wake Forest history. He was replaced by Rick Rembielek, age forty-three, the winningest coach in any sport in Kent State University history.

"Our Reality," a theater piece based on the experience of student-athletes, was presented August 29 in the MainStage Theatre. Many student-athletes had taken a summer-session class taught by Sharon Andrews and Brook Davis. The play dramatized their insights into the life of an athlete on campus.

A campus-wide effort to study the athletics program was part of the NCAA Division I certification program to assure integrity in college and university sports. Standards were established in 1993, and Wake Forest was first certified in 1995. Vice Presidents Sandra Boyette and Ken Zick co-chaired the steering committee that oversaw the study; Robert Walsh, Dean of the School of Law, chaired

Women's 2004 field hockey team

the subcommittee on governance and rules compliance. Toby Hale, Associate Dean of the College, chaired the subcommittee on academic integrity, and Harold Holmes, Associate Vice President and Dean of Student Services, chaired the subcommittee on equity, welfare, and sportsmanship. The steering committee and the subcommittees included students, faculty, staff, alumni, and trustees. Mike Piscetille, a junior and track-and-field letterman, represented the University and ACC student-athletes on the NCAA rules and policies committee.

The Arts

Plays produced on the Mainstage Theatre during the year were David Hare's *The Secret Rapture*, Joseph Heller's *Catch-22*, Sophocles's *Antigone*, and William Shakespeare's *Twelfth Night*.

Noel Shepherd as NazT Deacon

President and Mrs. Hearn christen the Thomas K. Hearn Jr. shell

The fall Studio Series in the Ring Theatre featured performances of *The Actor's Nightmare*, *Hidden in This Picture*, and *Blind Date*, one-act plays directed by theatre majors. The Anthony Aston Players performed three original one-act plays written by senior Amy Currie.

In observance of Domestic Violence Awareness Month and as part of Amnesty International's Year of the Arts and Human Rights, "Domestic Disturbance: An Evening of Performance and Discussion about Abuse" was presented on October 23 in the Ring Theatre. Initiated by senior Lakshmi Krishnan, President of the University's Amnesty International chapter, the event was designed to raise awareness about different forms of domestic violence.

The Secrest Artists Series featured performances by award-winning vibraphonist-composer Stefon Harris and his jazz quintet, Blackout; The English Concert with Andrew Manze; A Scottish Christmas with Bonnie Rideout; violinist Joshua Bell; and the Tuscan Sun Festival Tour with the New European Strings Chamber Orchestra.

Classical guitar duo Murray Holland and Duane Corn performed a free concert in Brendle Recital Hall on February 4. On February 13, the Music Department co-sponsored a benefit concert for Cancer Services, Inc., of Winston-Salem. It featured cancer survivor and renowned opera singer Diane Thornton and pianist Ruskin Cooper. Admission was free, but donations to Cancer Services were accepted at the door, and all proceeds went to help local cancer survivors and their families.

The Music Department presented Italian recorder virtuoso David Bellugi, performing with Peter Kairoff, harpsichordist and Professor of Music, on March 29 in Brendle Auditorium Recital Hall. On April 7–8, *L'isola disabitata*, a salon opera by Manuel del Pópulo Vicente García (1775–1832), also premiered in Brendle. Composed in 1831, the opera was never published or performed. Teresa Radomski, Professor of Music and vocal director for the production, transcribed the original manuscript. Jim Dodding, Professor of Theatre, directed.

Student Union sponsored comedy hypnotist Tom DeLuca during Family Weekend in October and the band O.A.R. (Of a Revolution), which performed in Wait Chapel November 12. Bill Rancic, winner of the first season of Donald Trump's reality show, *The Apprentice*, spoke and signed books in January. Live music with Rob Gonzalez and a five-course dinner were featured in February. Musician and historian Barry Drake gave a multimedia presentation and lecture, "80's Rock—Music in the Video Age," on March 30 in Pugh Auditorium. Finally, actor, playwright, and stand-up comedian Lewis Black performed on March 31 in Wait Chapel.

The Alban Elved Dance Company, in collaboration with faculty from the Computer Science Department, presented *Free Space 2004—The Bridge*, the third in a series of performances combining dance and technology. Staged in the Scales Fine Arts Center in early December, the production incorporated digital poetry, multimedia interpretations, mathematical interplay, technology, and people, and was designed to encourage audiences to explore their creative relationship with technology.

The Charlotte and Philip Hanes Art Gallery celebrated the opening of the academic year with two exhibits, "Inside the Ropes" by Ted Potter, and "Monumental Micros." In the lower gallery, "Inside the Ropes" featured large-scale expressive paintings by Potter, a former director of the Southeastern Center for Contemporary Art

(SECCA). "Monumental Micros," displayed in the upstairs gallery, was a joint exhibition of small works by members of the Philadelphia Sculptors and Sculptors, Inc., of Baltimore. Works no larger than a box of safety matches represented over forty artists. These exhibits were followed by more than forty multimedia works by fourteen Art Department faculty and staff members. In February, the downstairs gallery featured "Young Americans—Modern Romanticism," in which various artists used traditional genres to address current topics and popular culture. The upstairs gallery showed "Memoirs of a Beast," a mixed-media installation by Judith Page.

Campus and Student Life

The first-year class was selected from the largest number of applicants ever and was the largest ever. Of the 1,125 new students, 17 percent were minorities; 26 percent were from North Carolina; and the numbers of men and women were equal. Applications had increased 20 percent over the previous year to 7,481, nearly 1,200 more than in 2004 and 950 more than the previous record year, 1997. Twenty-three North Carolina Baptist students were awarded the William Louis Poteat Scholarship, each valued at $11,200 and renewable for four years, for a total value of $44,800.

As students unpacked, they had access to a container specifically designated for recycling cardboard. Jim Coffey, in charge of the University's recycling program, stated that in addition to capturing a large amount of recyclables that would have been thrown away, the cardboard was hauled away for free through a partnership with Paperstock and Triad Waste Solutions.

The primary parking option for first-year students was the Student Drive lot off of Polo Road. Additional parking was available in Lot A at the First Assembly of God on the west side of Long Drive and the Reynolda Village satellite parking lot. A new policy let students replace their Deacon Cards once a year at no cost, and in another change, the election of homecoming kings and queens was shifted from a paper ballot to online using WIN. By the end of 2004–2005, 49 percent of graduating seniors reported studying abroad.

In its October issue, *Black Enterprise* magazine named Wake Forest thirty-first in its list of the fifty best public and private colleges for African Americans. *U.S. News & World Report's* edition of *America's Best Colleges* rated the University as a whole at twenty-seven, one spot up from the previous year. The Babcock Graduate School of Management was ranked thirty-sixth; the School of Law, thirty-fourth; and Baptist Medical Center fortieth for research.

Student leaders included Tom Clark and Angel Hsu, Editors-in-Chief of the *Old Gold and Black*; Richard E. "Trip" Chalk III, Student Government President; and Stephen Evans, Editor-in-Chief of *The Howler*. The *Old Gold and Black* received the Online Pacemaker Award from the Associated Collegiate Press for its website, the highest honor for college student publications on the web.

Big Ron and the Have Mercy Blues Band kicked off the new Bookstore Lunchtime Music Series from 11 a.m. to noon on September 16. The weekly series of Thursday concerts, held in front of the college bookstore, were free and open to the public. University Stores initiated them as a way to thank the campus and local community for their business and to give local talent a venue to promote their music. Groups in the Bookstore Lunchtime Music Series ranged from the Wake Forest Gospel Choir to the Winston-Salem Symphony Ensemble.

The second annual Sister's Inspirational Summit, *The Spirit of a Woman*, was held on October 2. The all-day summit included several workshops led by local women focusing on various aspects of women's health and lives, a banquet, a keynote address by award-winning poet Nikki Giovanni, and a book signing. The Asian Student Interest Association (A.S.I.A.) and the Indo-U.S. Association of Winston-Salem co-hosted a Diwali celebration on November 14. The Indian Festival of Lights marked the first time the University had collaborated with the community for this festival, attended by more than five hundred people. It became a new annual event.

Diversity Days (March 17–20) included a variety of programs reflecting different cultural heritages: students dressed in ethnic costumes, and international music, ethnic foods, and an international fair featuring various student organizations were sponsored by the Race Relations Committee of the Student Government, the Office of Multicultural Affairs, and the Resident Student Association.

Student volunteers from various campus organizations hosted the third annual Kickball for Kids, an on-campus field day for as many as one hundred children in Big Brothers/Big Sisters (BBBS) of Forsyth County on April 2. It provided the opportunity for current big brothers and big sisters and their "littles" to enjoy a day of fun and paired children on the waiting list with a college student for the day.

The Disabilities Awareness Coalition (DAC) hosted the second-annual Meg Hudson Memorial Arts Festival on April 22. It included an art show, silent auction, and concert. It was created in honor of junior Margaret "Meg" Hudson, a DAC member who died from a rare heart and lung condition in fall 2003. All proceeds from the festival went to the National Down Syndrome Society.

Student Union started a new tradition in the spring, an outdoor semi-formal dance under a tent on the Magnolia Court called Shag on the Mag. It was the idea of Joseph Bumgarner, and with help from Kathy Arnett, Patrick Brennan, and a gift of $50,000 from the new Student Activities Fund, Shag on the Mag was the highlight of Springfest. Lasting from 10 p.m. to 2 a.m., it attracted almost a thousand students, who danced to the music of The Embers.

Also during the spring of 2005, Mike Ford, Director of Student Development, came up with another idea that students really liked. It was another fundraiser for the Brian Piccolo Cancer Fund. Instead of running, as in Hit the Bricks, this twelve-hour event was a dance marathon. Students could dance by themselves, with a partner, or with a group. It didn't matter—what counted was that students stay on their feet dancing, except for official breaks, and that they pledge or get pledges for each hour that they danced. The event was called "Wake 'N Shake."

To connect Wake Forest students who spoke Spanish with organizations in Winston-Salem that needed them, senior Jessie Lee Smith started Aprender y Enseñar (To Learn and To Teach). Using a website, the students were matched with local agencies based on their interests, Spanish-speaking ability, and schedule. In addition to providing much-needed volunteers, the program helped undergraduates practice Spanish and better understand Hispanic culture.

Shag on the Mag

Project for Freedom and Justice, a local nonprofit organization assisting the wrongfully imprisoned, received help from students enrolled in a first-year Sociology seminar, Gender, Power, and Violence, taught by Angela Hattery and Earl Smith. The students processed letters from inmates to help identify prisoners who were good candidates for assistance.

Three student groups spent a part of their winter recess serving the poor and disadvantaged in other countries. In December and January, thirty-seven student volunteers and seven faculty or staff advisors traveled to India, Costa Rica, and Vietnam. The City of Joy Scholars Program took eleven student volunteers to Calcutta, India, to work with the Missionaries of Charity. Students changed beds, bathed patients, cleaned wards, and fed and comforted the sick and dying. Twelve other students traveled to Lam Dong Province in Vietnam with the University's Peacework Ambassadors

Wake 'N Shake

Program. They helped build a school in a poor, rural village near Dalat. The Wake Forest Catholic Campus Ministry sent twelve Wake Forest students and one Salem College student to work with Nicaraguan refugees in Alajuelita, Costa Rica. The students painted a school and volunteered in children's programs.

On February 5, undergraduate students hosted a benefit concert in Wait Chapel, sponsored by the University Tsunami Relief Committee, an organization made up of several campus organizations. The dance team and the a cappella groups Innuendo, Demon Divas, and Chi Rho performed. A "rappers' showdown" was also featured. First-year student Ritu Bhattacharya came up with the idea for the benefit to raise money for the American Red Cross Tsunami Relief Fund. The Divinity School's Student Leadership Council held a benefit pancake breakfast almost a month later to raise money for the same organization.

Technology Quarters, the off-campus house, took off with the cooperation of the Information Systems Department. Nine students, sophomores and higher, learned about new technology, shared technical expertise, and helped the University test new software and hardware considered for campus use. The program built on the previous year's experiment in which first-year students interested in technology lodged on a floor in Luter Residence Hall. Jay Dominick (MBA '95), Assistant Vice President for Information Systems, said, "Students are the experts on what technologies they want and how they want to use them."

A sculptural chess table, "Lateral Thinking," was designed and built by Art Professor David Finn and two students, Steve Gurysh and Heather Hans, in cooperation with the Winston-Salem Scholastic Chess Association. It was presented to the city at Rock the Block festivities on October 15. The project was the first completed by Art Pro Humanitate, an informal group of art students formed by Finn to work on Winston-Salem community projects.

Groups and individual students achieved recognition. The Lilting Banshees Comedy Troupe was one of nine selected to perform at the Chicago Improv Festival. Junior Kelly Williamson started the first campus-wide prom-dress drive, sponsored by the Volunteer Service Corps, the Wake Forest chapter of Delta Sigma Theta sorority, and the Salvation Army Thrift Store. Once the dresses were collected, they were given to the thrift store, where high school students could buy them at a discount.

First-year student Allie Walker appeared on the *Oprah Winfrey Show* September 17 with her twin sister, Elli. They were both given makeovers by Oprah's stylist Mischa Barton and, prior to the show, were flown to Los Angles and Chicago. Senior Aaron Mass appeared on *Who Wants to Be a Millionaire?* on February 21–22. Mass, an economics major, was one of eight students from universities across the country selected for the show's College Week.

For more than two months in the summer, ten students—Aja Brooks, Rebecca Cook, Cameron Latimer, Terrell Nicholson, Kyle Layman, Polly Elbertse, Jennifer Holland, Jeanetta Craigwell-Graham, Ashleigh Lawrence, and William Murphy—from diverse cultural and racial backgrounds participated in an internship program designed to celebrate the fortieth anniversary of Freedom Summer in 1964. The students worked with local groups in Winston-Salem, Raleigh, Charlotte, and Oxford, Mississippi on projects addressing education reform, economic justice, neighborhood development, healthcare access, organizational development, immigrant rights, and voter rights and education. Steve Boyd (Religion) was active in the project.

Senior Rebecca E. Cook, a Carswell Scholar and biology major, who had worked to improve healthcare for premature babies in Kenya, was named a Rhodes Scholar. The daughter of missionaries serving in Kenya, Cook was the ninth Wake Forest student to be named a Rhodes Scholar since 1986. She was also Co-Founder and Co-President of the Wake Forest Student Global AIDS Campaign. In Winston-Salem, she was involved with CHANGE (Communities Helping All Neighbors Gain Empowerment) and named to the second team in *USA Today's* annual All-USA College Academic Team program for 2005.

Martha Napier, a sophomore presidential scholar, organized a project called "Illitics: Illustrate Your Politics." It gave students a chance to express their political beliefs and reactions to the upcoming 2004 presidential election. She set up an outdoor collage on the Magnolia Court on November 1, the day before Election Day, on which students could write their thoughts about the election, hang articles or other print-matter from the Internet, or express their political views in any other way that could be attached to the wall. Students were encouraged to bring their own materials, but Napier provided red, white, blue, and black paint, newspapers, and magazines.

Three Wake Forest women appeared in the October Girls of the ACC issue of *Playboy*, which the magazine presented for the first time since 1998. Erika Harris, a sophomore, returned home in November to compete in the Miss Illinois competition and represent her home state in the Miss USA Pageant.

Lilting Banshees

Rebecca E. Cook

Facilities, Finances, and Alumni

The Professional Grounds Management Society (PGMS) gave Wake Forest a Grand Award for Landscaping in its 2004 Green Star Awards competition. The award was formally presented to University representatives on November 6 at an awards program in Charlotte.

WFDD changed its format from classical music and news to a news/talk-show format. The move put it more in line with its chief competitor, WUNC, which broadcast to Greensboro, but the transition sparked an outcry from some listeners who would now hear classical music only from 8 p.m. to 5 a.m.

In the summer of 2004, Wake Forest completed installation of its most efficient wireless network to date. The Next-Generation Network ran at 54 megabits per second and placed the University among a small group of higher education institutions offering high-speed wireless Internet access in every campus building.

Graylyn International Conference Center was awarded a 2004 Pinnacle Award for the eighth year and a 2004 Gold Key Award for the fifth consecutive year, two of the meeting and conference industry's top awards. Graylyn was also named 2004 Employer of the Year by the Mayor's Council for Persons with Disabilities (MCPD) in Winston-Salem. Mayor Allen Joines presented a plaque to Graylyn at an awards banquet on October 19.

Reynolda Park was created in the parking lot behind Reynolda Hall between the renamed Calloway Center and Kitchin Residence Hall. It featured extensive sidewalks using more than 100,000 bricks, about half the number used in University Plaza. Lighting, trees, grass, an irrigation system, and a new emergency phone were added. The drive around Reynolda Park was one way, eliminating the need for large delivery trucks to back up to the loading dock from the street. Walls were built to screen the loading dock and dumpsters from public view. A walkway was installed in parking lot Q with ramps on both sides. Before the walkway, handicapped students in Polo Hall had no way to get to the rest of the campus.

The Sundry Shop was moved from Davis House to the former Oak Room in Reynolda Hall next to the Pit. The new convenience store was called the C3. In place of the Sundry Shop in Davis, a full-menu Subway opened.

Reynolda House opened its new $12 million, 30,000-square-foot wing on April 23 and invited the public to see it on Community Day. The rest of the house had been restored to its 1917 condition.

The endowment achieved a 17 percent investment return for the twelve-month period ending June 30, 2004. Its total market value was $812.2 million at the end of the 2003–2004 fiscal year. On April 1, the Board of Trustees approved a total budget of $1.011 billion for the 2005–2006 fiscal year, beginning July 1. It included $742.7 million for Wake Forest Health Sciences and $269 million for the Reynolda Campus, with a 3.5 percent increase for Reynolda Campus faculty and staff pay raises. They also approved a 6.7 percent increase in full-time undergraduate tuition for 2005–2006 to $30,110, up from $28,210.

David N. Gill ('77) and Diane P. Gill ('77) of Knoxville, Tennessee, established the Reverend Sumner H. Gill and Mrs. Lois C. Gill Scholarship in the Divinity School. The full-tuition scholarship was created to honor the life ministry of Sumner and Lois Gill. James M. and Marilyn Dunn of Winston-Salem gave $100,000 to the Divinity School to establish the Bill and Judith Moyers Scholar Program, which provided funding for one Divinity School student a year to serve as an intern at the Baptist Joint Committee on Religious Liberty in Washington, D.C. The gift, starting in 2006, was intended to recognize the contributions of award-winning journalist Bill Moyers and his wife, Judith, to American public life.

Rocky Mount businessman John E. "Jack" Bishop committed $100,000 through an estate gift to endow the Jack and Jean Bishop Scholarship, which assists Calloway students from the Rocky Mount area with a scouting background. The Reznick Group, one of the top twenty accounting firms in the nation, pledged $250,000 to the Calloway accounting program. Scottish Holdings, Inc., pledged $500,000 to the enterprise risk management program at Calloway School.

Richard Burr ('78), who was running for the U.S. Senate seat being vacated by John Edwards, came back to campus to campaign at a rally in Shorty's. Alan Williams ('04), a basketball walk-on for both Skip Prosser and Dave Odom, published a tell-all book, *Walk-on: Life from the End of the Bench* (New Heights Press). Colin Creel ('96) signed copies of his book *Perspectives: A Spiritual Life Guide for Twentysomethings* (Relevant Books) at the College Bookstore. Liz Richardson ('03), a Peace Corps volunteer in Togo, Africa, won the *Vanity Fair* essay contest for "My American Home," in which she explained U.S. society and culture to the rest of the world.

Summing Up the Year

After twenty-two years, a heart condition, and brain cancer, President Thomas K. Hearn left his position at Wake Forest on a high note. Thirteen months earlier than expected, the Honoring the Promise capital campaign had exceeded its $600 million goal by $17 million. In addition, during his twenty-two years Hearn had led the University through its first two national capital campaigns, which brought in over $1 billion overall, and had substantially built Wake Forest's infrastructure and national reputation. In gratitude for Hearn's long and productive service, the Board of Trustees voted to name the Quad Hearn Plaza.

As significant as the Hearn administration had been, friends and alumni looked forward to greeting the thirteenth President, Nathan O. Hatch. He had a sterling academic and administrative reputation. His work in many capacities at Notre Dame, especially his ten years as Provost, gave him a wide perspective on higher education and prepared him to take the helm at Wake Forest. The University had many reasons to be proud at the end of the 2004–2005 academic year—another Rhodes scholarship, a third straight field hockey national championship, an ACC championship for men's soccer, international and local service from Calcutta, India, to nearby Old Town Elementary School by students, the growth of study abroad, significant development of the endowment, and recognition for faculty and staff accomplishments. In addition, a new altruistic tradition was started by students; Wake 'N Shake and a new spring dance event, Shag on the Mag, were founded.

Arnold Palmer and President Hearn

Professional golfer Arnold Palmer ('51) ended the traditional academic year as the 161st commencement speaker. His involvement with the University from the Tribble era through the Scales presidency to the conclusion of the Hearn years reflected its place in his world and the wider world, as he wished new graduates and the President well in their new lives.

EPILOGUE

Life is infinitely precious, and our grasp on it is but frail.

Thomas K. Hearn Jr.

Thousands of words have been written about Thomas K. Hearn Jr. and his tenure as President of Wake Forest from 1983 to 2005. The man, the University, and the times were dynamic. When reflecting on these twenty-two years, they can be viewed as both exciting and transformational, with many people within the institution—faculty, staff, and students—as well as those outside of it, such as alumni, businesses, and foundations, shaping the present and the future. Accomplishments of the era included:

- a change from restrictive denominational governance controlled by the Baptist State Convention of North Carolina to independent governance by a self-perpetuating Board of Trustees open to all individuals who shared the University's values;
- growth from a strong regional university to a top-thirty national institution of higher education;
- bold technology moves, such as the Plan for the Class of 2000, providing laptop computers to all faculty and students beginning in the fall of 1996;
- a strengthening of the liberal arts tradition on the undergraduate level with the approval of double majors, double minors, and interdisciplinary minors, such as film studies;
- the growth of new departments—for example, East Asian Languages and Literature, Communication, Computer Science, and Theatre;
- a renewed focus on the first-year experience, including first-year seminars and substance-free housing;

407

- a reinforcement and extension of graduate and professional education, including the establishment of a joint School of Biomedical Engineering and Sciences (SBES) with Virginia Tech;
- an expansion into international experiences and education abroad, such as the Flow Haus in Vienna, Austria, and international arrangements with Kansai Gandai University in Japan;
- curriculum reform and a change from credit units to semester hours;
- a building program supporting academic space and student housing—unparalleled in the history of the University except during the Tribble years—by adding structures such as Olin, Benson, Greene, Kirby, Worrell, Polo, Collins, Martin Information Systems, the Wilson Wing of the ZSR Library, and an addition to Winston Hall;
- the construction of Kentner, Hooks, and Spry Stadiums;
- significant financial support for the building of the Lawrence Joel Coliseum;
- rebuilding of Bridger Field House and extensive renovations to Groves Stadium, including the President's Box;
- recycling of glass and paper in academic and residential buildings;
- a tightening of security to protect students, faculty, and staff, including the construction of gates and key card entry systems;
- the construction of a power substation;
- a beautification plan and program that was continuously implemented and renewed, especially after the removal of the elms from the Quad;
- the establishment of a new professional school, the School of Divinity;
- the establishment of interdisciplinary professional degrees, such as MD/PhD, MD/MBA, MDiv/MA, and JD/MBA;
- the greater integration of the medical school into the rest of the University, including changing the name of the school from the Bowman Gray School of Medicine to the Wake Forest University School of Medicine;
- the creation of a cappella singing groups, such as Chi Rho, Plead the Fifth, One Accord, SOUL, and Demon Divas;
- the expansion of the Babcock Graduate School of Management to Charlotte and the founding of the school's evening program;
- an equalization in admissions between men and women to 50/50;
- an increase in the number of women faculty and greater attention to women's issues;
- a conscious and direct effort to address discrimination and hostility issues related to gay and lesbian individuals and groups;
- an increase in black student enrollment from about 3 percent to 9 percent and an overall increase in minority enrollment to about 15 percent;
- a major increase in need-blind financial aid from around $2.5 million to $60 million;
- a greater emphasis on student development through organizations such as the Volunteer Service Corps and preschool programs such as SPARC;
- a loosening of *en loco parentis* rules and a growth in freedom for students;
- an emphasis on preventive maintenance of buildings and upgrading residential space with air conditioning and smoke detectors;

- an emphasis on leadership, ethics, and civic responsibility through such programs as LEAD and LEAD II;
- a respect for the past in making treks back to the old campus in 1984 and 1992, as well as providing financial support for the Calvin Jones House, the birthplace of Wake Forest;
- new opportunities for undergraduates to participate in research and more support for faculty to engage in research;
- a unifying annual focus on themes such as art, religious life, dialogue, medicine and honor;
- increased focus on service, including the building of two Habitat for Humanity houses on campus in 1992 and 1995 and the start of service trips abroad during break periods, e.g., City of Joy, the Tie that Binds, and HOPE;
- the continued vigilance to field athletic teams that had academic integrity;
- the supporting of traditions such as "rolling the Quad" and the Moravian "love feast," while creating new traditions, such as "Hit the Bricks," "Lighting of the Quad," "Wake and Shake," "Project Pumpkin" and "Shag on the Mag";
- two nationally televised presidential debates in 1988 and 2000;
- the winning of four national NCAA titles—three in field hockey, one in men's golf—plus an individual NCAA women's tennis title by Bea Bielik and numerous individual and team ACC championships in baseball, men's and women's soccer, men's and women's cross-country, men's basketball, and women's tennis;
- an expansion of intramural and club sports, e.g., ice hockey, rugby, ultimate Frisbee, as well as improvements to athletic fields and facilities;
- the awarding of nine Rhodes scholarships to Richard Chapman (1986), Maria Merritt (1987), E. Scott Pretorius (1988), Robert Esther (1991), Carolyn Frantz (1994), Charlotte Opal (1997), Jennifer Bumgarner (1998), Jennifer Harris (2004), and Rebecca Cook (2005) — and numerous Goldwater, Truman, Beinecke, Luce, and Fulbright scholarships;
- the establishment of centers such as math and teaching, and the expansion of the learning assistance center;
- the colonization of women's societies into chapters of national sororities;
- an increase in lounge space for women's sororities;
- the first official celebration of Martin Luther King Jr. Day by the University;
- significant growth in faculty and staff salaries and Human Resources benefits;
- a dramatic increase in the endowment to more than $800 million by the end of 2005;
- the growth and strengthening of student applications for admission;
- the expansion of the Z. Smith Reynolds Library and a dedication to library services throughout the University, including digitalization of the library catalogue and important papers;
- the opening of Graylyn as a profit-making, high-end conference center;
- the establishment of the faculty teacher-scholar model;
- the creation of dozens of new endowed faculty chairs and of hundreds of new student scholarships, such as the Poteat and Stamey;
- the national and international success of academic teams in mathematics, physics, and debate;

- the expansion of business degree specialties from the Calloway School: BS in analytical finance, BS in business, BS in mathematical business, and a BS/MS in accounting;
- the initiation of the Summer Management Program;
- the creation of new spaces, such as Shorty's and Campus Grounds, where students could hang out;
- a formal affiliation with and expansion of the facilities at Reynolda House;
- the successful conclusion of two major capital campaigns: Heritage and Promise (over $172 million) and Honoring the Promise (over $600 million);
- excellent stewardship of the RJR Headquarters Building and Reynolda Village; and
- exploration of, initiation into, and innovation in what would become the Wake Forest Research Park downtown and later Innovation Quarter.

Overall, the Hearn years witnessed a convergence of mostly uplifting and affirmative people, policies, and events that brought the University forward in both expected and surprising ways to the benefit of its constituents both on and off campus, as well as the state, the region, the nation, and the world. There were some rough patches, some personal and institutional setbacks and disappointments, but the trajectory was upward. The institution did not lose its values, but embraced them even more firmly. Congenial student-to-student and student-to-faculty interactions continued as a hallmark and defining value. Friendliness, honor, responsibility, and purpose were seen and felt throughout the institution, as they were in past decades. The University lived up to its motto, *Pro Humanitate.*

President Hearn brought Wake Forest into national prominence

President Hearn's name being added to the list of Wake Forest Presidents

The end of the era came with Tom Hearn's retirement in 2005 and his death three years later. He was direct about his funeral plans. Doug Bailey (Divinity), Bill Leonard (Divinity), and Weston Hatfield (Trustee and friend) were all with Laura Hearn a few days before the President died on August 18 and would all speak at his funeral. On the day of his death, he was surrounded by Laura; his three children, Thomas, Lindsay, and Will; and his step-daughter, Forrest. Ironically, serendipitously, and some would say appropriately, the former President's memorial service was held August 22, 2008, in Wait Chapel on Hearn Plaza only hours after the incoming freshman class had been welcomed in the same venue. The President Emeritus was seventy-one years old, but his legacy is timeless. As University of North Carolina President Emeritus William Friday said, "I believe Tom Hearn was one of a very few university presidents who really made a difference in the last decade of the twentieth century."

APPENDIX A

Departments and Faculty in the College, 1983–2005

American Ethnic Studies (AES)

Interdisciplinary Minor

1996–2004
Earl Smith (Sociology), Director

2004–2006
Earl Smith (Sociology), Director
Adjunct Instructor M. Beth Hopkins

Anthropology (ANT)

1983–1984
J. Ned Woodall, Chair
Professors E. Pendleton Banks, Stanton K. Tefft, J. Ned Woodall
Associate Professors David K. Evans, David S. Weaver
Adjunct Assistant Professor Jay R. Kaplan
Instructor/Curator, Museum of Man, Linda B. Robertson
Research Associate Ben P. Robertson

1984–1987
J. Ned Woodall, Chair
Professors E. Pendleton Banks, Stanton K. Tefft, J. Ned Woodall
Associate Professors David K. Evans, David S. Weaver
Assistant Professor/Curator, Museum of Man, Linda B. Robertson

Adjunct Assistant Professor Jay R. Kaplan
Instructor/Research Associate Ben P. Robertson

1987–1988
David S. Weaver, Chair
Professors E. Pendleton Banks, David K. Evans, Stanton K. Tefft, J. Ned Woodall
Associate Professor David S. Weaver
Adjunct Associate Professor Jay B. Kaplan
Instructor/Research Associate Ben P. Robertson
Director/Curator, Museum of Man, Mary Jane Berman

1988–1989
David S. Weaver, Chair
Professor E. Pendleton Banks, David K. Evans, Stanton K. Tefft, J. Ned Woodall
Associate Professor David S. Weaver
Adjunct Associate Professor Jay R. Kaplan
Instructor, Director/Curator, Museum of Anthropology, Mary Jane Berman
Instructor/Research Associate Ben P. Robertson
Research Associates Lawrence E. Abbott, Perry L. Gnivecki

1989–1990
David S. Weaver, Chair
Professors E. Pendleton Banks, David K. Evans, Stanton K. Tefft, David S. Weaver, J. Ned Woodall
Adjunct Associate Professor Jay R. Kaplan
Instructor, Director/Curator, Museum of Anthropology, Mary Jane Berman
Visiting Instructors Perry L. Gnivecki (Research Associate), Douglas E. Reinhardt

1990–1994
David S. Weaver, Chair
Professors E. Pendleton Banks, David K. Evans, Stanton K. Tefft, David S. Weaver, J. Ned Woodall
Assistant Professor, Director/Curator, Museum of Anthropology, Mary Jane Berman
Visiting Assistant Professor Dorothy J. Cattle
Adjunct Professor Jay R. Kaplan

1994–1995
David S. Weaver, Chair
Professors E. Pendleton Banks, David K. Evans, Stanton K. Tefft, David S. Weaver, J. Ned Woodall
Assistant Professor, Director/Curator, Museum of Anthropology, Mary Jane Berman
Visiting Assistant Professor Dorothy J. Cattle

Adjunct Professor Jay R. Kaplan
Adjunct Assistant Professor Steven Folmar

1995–1996
David S. Weaver, Chair
Professors David K. Evans, Stanton K. Tefft, David S. Weaver, J. Ned Woodall
Assistant Professor, Director/Curator, Museum of Anthropology, Mary Jane
 Berman
Visiting Assistant Professors Dorothy J. Cattle, Nancy L. Nelson
Adjunct Professor Jay R. Kaplan
Adjunct Associate Professor Sara A. Quandt
Adjunct Assistant Professor Steven Folmar

1996–1997
David S. Weaver, Chair
Professors David K. Evans, Jay R. Kaplan, Stanton K. Tefft, David S. Weaver, J. Ned
 Woodall
Associate Professor, Director/Curator, Museum of Anthropology, Mary Jane
 Berman
Visiting Assistant Professor Nancy L. Nelson
Adjunct Associate Professor Sara A. Quandt
Adjunct Assistant Professors Dorothy J. Cattle, Steven Folmar

1997–1998
Toby A. Hale, Acting Chair
Professors David K. Evans, Jay R. Kaplan, Stanton K. Tefft, David S. Weaver, J. Ned
 Woodall
Associate Professor, Director/Curator, Museum of Anthropology, Mary Jane
 Berman
Visiting Assistant Professor Nancy L. Nelson
Adjunct Associate Professor Sara A. Quandt
Adjunct Assistant Professors Steven Folmar, Ronda C. Stavisky
Adjunct Instructor Beverlye H. Hancock

1998–1999
Carole L. Browne, Acting Chair
Professors David K. Evans, Jay R. Kaplan, Stanton K. Tefft, David S. Weaver, J. Ned
 Woodall
Associate Professor, Director/Curator, Museum of Anthropology, Mary Jane
 Berman
Visiting Assistant Professor Nancy L. Nelson
Adjunct Associate Professor Sara A. Quandt
Adjunct Assistant Professors Steven Folmar, Ronda C. Stavisky
Adjunct Instructor Beverlye H. Hancock

1999–2000
Carole L. Browne, Acting Chair
Professors Jay R. Kaplan, Stanton K. Tefft, David S. Weaver, J. Ned Woodall
Associate Professor, Director/Curator, Museum of Anthropology,
    Mary Jane Berman
Adjunct Associate Professor Sara A. Quandt
Adjunct Assistant Professor Steven Folmar
Adjunct Instructor Beverlye H. Hancock

2000–2001
Jeanne M. Simonelli, Chair
Professors Jay R. Kaplan, Jeanne M. Simonelli, Stanton K. Tefft, David S. Weaver,
    J. Ned Woodall
Associate Professor, Director/Curator, Museum of Anthropology,
    Mary Jane Berman
Adjunct Associate Professor Sara A. Quandt
Adjunct Assistant Professor Steven Folmar
Adjunct Instructor Beverlye H. Hancock

2001–2003
Jeanne M. Simonelli, Chair
Professors Jay R. Kaplan, David S. Weaver, J. Ned Woodall
Associate Professor, Director/Curator, Museum of Anthropology,
    Mary Jane Berman
Assistant Professor Margaret C. Bender
Visiting Assistant Professor Steven Folmar
Adjunct Associate Professors Thomas A. Arcury, Sara A. Quandt
Adjunct Instructor Beverlye H. Hancock

2003–2004
Jeanne M. Simonelli, Chair
Professors Jay R. Kaplan, Jeanne M. Simonelli, J. Ned Woodall
Assistant Professors Margaret C. Bender, Ellen Miller
Adjunct Professor Thomas Arcury
Adjunct Associate Professor and Director, Museum of Anthropology,
    Stephen Whittington
Adjunct Assistant Professor Betty Duggan
Adjunct Instructors Beverlye H. Hancock, Kenneth Robinson
Lecturer Steven Folmar

2004–2005
Jeanne M. Simonelli, Chair
Professors Jay R. Kaplan, Jeanne M. Simonelli
Assistant Professors Margaret C. Bender, Ellen Miller, Paul Thacker
Adjunct Professors Thomas Arcury, Sara A. Quandt

Adjunct Associate Professor and Director, Museum of Anthropology,
    Stephen Whittington
Adjunct Assistant Professor Garth Green
Adjunct Instructors Beverlye H. Hancock, Kenneth Robinson
Lecturer Steven Folmar

2005–2006
Jeanne M. Simonelli, Chair
Professors Jay R. Kaplan, Jeanne M. Simonelli
Associate Professor Margaret C. Bender (Z. Smith Reynolds Foundation Fellow)
Assistant Professors Ellen Miller, Paul Thacker
Adjunct Professors Thomas Arcury, Sara A. Quandt
Adjunct Associate Professor and Director, Museum of Anthropology,
    Stephen Whittington
Adjunct Assistant Professor Garth Green
Adjunct Instructors Beverlye H. Hancock, Kenneth Robinson
Lecturer Steven Folmar

ART (ART)

1983–1984
Margaret S. Smith, Chair
Associate Professors Marvin S. Coats, Robert Knott, Margaret S. Smith
Assistant Professors Gary A. Cook, Paul H. D. Kaplan, Andrew W. Polk III
Visiting Professor Terisio Pignatti (Venice)
Instructors Elizabeth A. Sutherland, Harry B. Titus Jr., Norman Tuck
Lecturer David Bindman (London)
Gallery Director Victor Faccinto

1984–1985
Margaret S. Smith, Chair
Associate Professors Robert Knott, Margaret S. Smith
Assistant Professors Gary A. Cook, Paul H. D. Kaplan, Andrew W. Polk III,
    Harry B. Titus Jr.
Visiting Professor Terisio Pignatti (Venice)
Instructors Deborah Fanelli, Elizabeth A. Sutherland
Lecturers Brian Allen (London), David Bindman (London),
    Richard T. Godfrey (London)
Gallery Director Victor Faccinto

1985–1986
Margaret S. Smith, Chair
Associate Professors Robert Knott, Margaret S. Smith
Assistant Professors Gary A. Cook, Paul H. D. Kaplan, Andrew W. Polk III,
    Harry B. Titus Jr.

Visiting Professor Terisio Pignatti (Venice)
Visiting Assistant Professor David Faber
Instructors Deborah Fanelli, Elizabeth A. Sutherland
Lecturers Brian Allen (London), David Bindman (London),
    Richard T. Godfrey (London)
Gallery Director Victor Faccinto

1986–1987
Margaret S. Smith, Chair
Professor Terisio Pignatti (Venice)
Associate Professors Robert Knott, Margaret S. Smith
Assistant Professors Gary A. Cook, Paul H. D. Kaplan, Harry B. Titus Jr.
Visiting Assistant Professor David Faber
Instructors Deborah Fanelli, Catherine L. Turrill
Lecturers Brian Allen (London), David Bindman (London)
Gallery Director Victor Faccinto

1987–1988
Margaret S. Smith, Chair
Professors Terisio Pignatti (Venice), Margaret S. Smith
Associate Professors Paul H. D. Kaplan, Robert Knott
Assistant Professors David Faber, Harry B. Titus Jr.
Visiting Assistant Professor Sarah Ferguson
Instructor Deborah Fanelli
Lecturers Brian Allen (London), David Bindman (London)
Gallery Director Victor Faccinto

1988–1989
Paul H. D. Kaplan, Acting Chair
Professors Terisio Pignatti (Venice), Margaret S. Smith
Associate Professors Paul H. D. Kaplan, Robert Knott
Assistant Professors David Faber, Harry B. Titus Jr.
Visiting Assistant Professors Sarah Ferguson, Page H. Laughlin, Norman Tuck
Adjunct Assistant Professor Mary Ellen Carr Soles
Lecturers Brian Allen (London), David Bindman (London), Martine L. Sherill
Gallery Director and Lecturer Victor Faccinto

1989–1990
Harry B. Titus Jr., Acting Chair
Professors Robert Knott, Terisio Pignatti (Venice), Margaret S. Smith
Associate Professor Paul H. D. Kaplan
Assistant Professors David Faber, Harry B. Titus Jr.
Visiting Assistant Professors Anthony Colantuono, David Finn, Page H. Laughlin
Visiting Instructors L. Susan Forster, Alix Hitchcock
Lecturers Brian Allen (London), David Bindman (London)
Gallery Director and Lecturer Victor Faccinto

1990–1991
Harry B. Titus Jr., Chair
Professors Robert Knott, Terisio Pignatti (Venice), Margaret S. Smith
Associate Professor Harry B. Titus Jr.
Assistant Professors Bernadine Barnes, David Faber, Page H. Laughlin
Visiting Assistant Professor David Finn
Visiting Instructor Alix Hitchcock
Lecturers Brian Allen (London), David Bindman (London)
Gallery Director and Lecturer Victor Faccinto

1991–1992
Harry B. Titus Jr., Chair
Reynolds Professor Terisio Pignatti (Venice)
Professors Robert Knott, Margaret S. Smith
Associate Professors David L. Faber, Harry B. Titus Jr.
Assistant Professors Bernadine Barnes, Page H. Laughlin
Visiting Assistant Professor David Finn
Visiting Instructors Richard P. Faude, Margaret C. Gregory, Alix Hitchcock
Lecturers Brian Allen (London), David Bindman (London)
Assistant Lecturer Katie Scott (London)
Gallery Director Victor Faccinto

1992–1993
Harry B. Titus Jr., Chair
Reynolds Professor Terisio Pignatti (Venice)
Professors Robert Knott, Margaret S. Smith
Associate Professors David L. Faber, Harry B. Titus Jr.
Assistant Professors Bernadine Barnes, Page H. Laughlin
Visiting Assistant Professor David Helm
Visiting Instructors David Finn, Margaret C. Gregory, Louise Lackey-Zachmann
Lecturer Brian Allen (London)
Assistant Lecturer Katie Scott (London)
Gallery Director Victor Faccinto

1993–1994
Harry B. Titus Jr., Chair
Reynolds Professor Terisio Pignatti (Venice)
Professors Robert Knott, Margaret S. Smith
Associate Professors David L. Faber, Harry B. Titus Jr.
Assistant Professors Bernadine Barnes, Page H. Laughlin
Visiting Assistant Professor David Helm
Visiting Instructors Margaret C. Gregory, Alix Hitchcock
Lecturer Brian Allen (London)
Assistant Lecturer Katie Scott (London)
Gallery Director Victor Faccinto

1994–1995
Harry B. Titus Jr., Chair
Reynolds Professor Terisio Pignatti (Venice)
Professors Robert Knott, Margaret S. Smith
Associate Professors David L. Faber, Page H. Laughlin, Harry B. Titus Jr.
Assistant Professor Bernadine Barnes
Visiting Assistant Professors David Helm, Nancy Kelker
Visiting Instructors Margaret C. Gregory, Alix Hitchcock
Lecturer Brian Allen (London)
Assistant Lecturer Katie Scott (London)
Gallery Director Victor Faccinto

1995–1996
Harry B. Titus Jr., Chair
Reynolds Professor Terisio Pignatti (Venice)
Professors Robert Knott, Margaret S. Smith
Associate Professors David L. Faber, Page H. Laughlin, Harry B. Titus Jr.
Assistant Professor Bernadine Barnes
Visiting Assistant Professor David Helm
Visiting Instructor Alix Hitchcock
Lecturer Brian Allen (London)
Assistant Lecturer Katie Scott (London)
Gallery Director Victor Faccinto

1996–1998
Robert Knott, Chair
Reynolds Professor Terisio Pignatti (Venice)
Professors Robert Knott, Margaret S. Smith
Associate Professors David L. Faber, Page H. Laughlin, Harry B. Titus Jr.
Assistant Professor Bernadine Barnes
Visiting Assistant Professor David Finn
Visiting Instructor Alix Hitchcock
Lecturer Brian Allen (London)
Assistant Lecturers Maria A. Chiari (Venice), Katie Scott (London)
Gallery Director Victor Faccinto

1998–1999
Margaret S. Smith, Chair
Reynolds Professor Terisio Pignatti (Venice)
Professors Robert Knott, Margaret S. Smith
Associate Professors Bernadine Barnes, David L. Faber, Page H. Laughlin,
    Harry B. Titus Jr.
Assistant Professors David Finn, John R. Pickel
Visiting Instructor Alix Hitchcock
Lecturer Brian Allen (London)

Assistant Lecturers Maria A. Chiari (Venice), Katie Scott (London)
Gallery Director Victor Faccinto

1999–2000
Margaret S. Smith, Chair
Reynolds Professor Terisio Pignatti (Venice)
Professors Robert Knott, Margaret S. Smith
Associate Professors Bernadine Barnes, David L. Faber, Page H. Laughlin,
    Harry B. Titus Jr.
Assistant Professors David Finn, John R. Pickel
Visiting Instructor Alix Hitchcock
Lecturers Brian Allen (London), Maria A. Chiari (Venice),
    Beatrice Ottersböck (Vienna), Katie Scott (London)
Gallery Director Victor Faccinto

2000–2002
Margaret S. Smith, Chair
Reynolds Professor Terisio Pignatti (Venice)
Wake Forest Professor Margaret S. Smith
Charlotte C. Weber Professor of Art David M. Lubin
Professor Robert Knott
Associate Professors Bernadine Barnes, David L. Faber,
    Page H. Laughlin, Harry B. Titus Jr.
Assistant Professors David Finn, John R. Pickel
Visiting Instructor Alix Hitchcock
Lecturers Brian Allen (London), Maria A. Chiari (Venice),
    Beatrice Ottersböck (Vienna), Katie Scott (London)
Gallery Director Victor Faccinto

2002–2003
Margaret S. Smith, Chair
Reynolds Professor Terisio Pignatti (Venice)
Wake Forest Professor Margaret S. Smith
Charlotte C. Weber Professor of Art David M. Lubin
Professors Robert Knott, Harry B. Titus Jr.
Associate Professors Bernadine Barnes (McCulloch Family Fellow),
    David L. Faber, David Finn (Z. Smith Reynolds Foundation Fellow),
    Page H. Laughlin
Assistant Professor John R. Pickel
Instructor Alix Hitchcock
Adjunct Instructor David C. Hart Jr.
Lecturers Brian Allen (London), Maria A. Chiari (Venice),
    Beatrice Ottersböck (Vienna), Katie Scott (London)
Gallery Director Victor Faccinto

2003–2004
Margaret S. Smith, Chair
Reynolds Professor Terisio Pignatti (Venice)
Wake Forest Professor Margaret S. Smith
Charlotte C. Weber Professor of Art David M. Lubin
Professors Robert Knott, Harry B. Titus Jr.
Associate Professors Bernadine Barnes, David L. Faber,
    David Finn (Z. Smith Reynolds Foundation Fellow), Page H. Laughlin
Assistant Professor John R. Pickel
Adjunct Assistant Professor Leigh Ann Hallberg
Instructors David C. Hart Jr., Alix Hitchcock
Lecturers Brian Allen (London), Maria A. Chiari (Venice),
    Beatrice Ottersböck (Vienna), Katie Scott (London)
Galley Director Victor Faccinto

2004–2005
Margaret S. Smith, Chair
Wake Forest Professor Margaret S. Smith
Charlotte C. Weber Professor of Art David M. Lubin
Professors Robert Knott, Harry B. Titus Jr.
Associate Professors Bernadine Barnes, David L. Faber, David Finn
    (Z. Smith Reynolds Foundation Fellow), Page H. Laughlin, John R. Pickel
Adjunct Assistant Professor Leigh Ann Hallberg
Instructors Alix Hitchcock, Jeffrey P. Thompson
Adjunct Instructors Kimberly Dennis, Jennifer Gentry
Lecturers Brian Allen (London), Maria A. Chiari (Venice), Beatrice
    Ottersböck (Vienna), Katie Scott (London), Yue-Ling Wong
Galley Director Victor Faccinto

2005–2006
Page H. Laughlin, Chair
Reynolds Professor of Film Studies and Professor of Art Peter Brunette
Wake Forest Professor Margaret S. Smith
Charlotte C. Weber Professor of Art David M. Lubin
Professors Robert Knott, Page H. Laughlin, Harry B. Titus Jr.
Associate Professors Bernadine Barnes, David L. Faber, David Finn
    (Z. Smith Reynolds Foundation Fellow), John R. Pickel
Assistant Professor Lynne Johnson
Adjunct Assistant Professor Leigh Ann Hallberg
Instructors Alix Hitchcock, Jeffrey P. Thompson
Adjunct Instructors Kimberly Dennis, Jennifer Gentry
Lecturers Brian Allen (London), Maria A. Chiari (Venice),
    Beatrice Ottersböck (Vienna), Katie Scott (London), Yue-Ling Wong
Galley Director Victor Faccinto

ASIAN STUDIES (ASI)

(The Asian Studies program became an interdisciplinary minor in 1992–1993. The change was first listed in the 1993–1994 *Bulletin*. In 2003–2004 the program's resources merged into two related programs: the interdisciplinary minor in East Asian Studies and the minor in Middle East and South Asia Studies. The change was first listed in the 2004–2005 *Bulletin*.)

1983–1991
Balkrishna Govind Gokhale, Director

1991–1992
Janice B. Bardsley, Coordinator

1992–1993
Win-chiat Lee, Coordinator

1993–1997
Win-chiat Lee (Philosophy), Coordinator

1997–2000
Wei-chin Lee (Politics), Coordinator

2000–2004
Charles H. Kennedy (Political Science), Coordinator

BIOLOGY (BIO)

1983–1984
Gerald W. Esch, Chair
Professors Charles M. Allen, Ralph D. Amen, Gerald W. Esch, Mordecai J. Jaffe, Raymond E. Kuhn, James C. McDonald, Robert L. Sullivan, Peter D. Weigl, Raymond L. Wyatt
Associate Professors John F. Dimmick, Ronald V. Dimock Jr., Herman E. Eure, A. Thomas Olive
Assistant Professors Ramunas Bigelis, Carole L. Browne, Robert A. Browne, Hugo C. Lane
Adjunct Professors Harold O. Goodman, Stephen H. Richardson
Adjunct Associate Professor J. Whitfield Gibbons

1984–1985
Gerald W. Esch, Chair
Professors Charles M. Allen, Ralph D. Amen, Ronald V. Dimock Jr., Gerald W. Esch, Mordecai J. Jaffe, Raymond E. Kuhn, James C. McDonald, Robert L. Sullivan, Peter D. Weigl, Raymond L. Wyatt

Associate Professors John F. Dimmick, Herman E. Eure, A. Thomas Olive
Assistant Professors Carole L. Browne, Robert A. Browne, Hugo C. Lane,
    William A. Thomas
Adjunct Professors J. Whitfield Gibbons, Harold O. Goodman,
    Stephen H. Richardson

1985–1986
Ronald V. Dimock Jr., Chair
Professors Charles M. Allen, Ralph D. Amen, Ronald V. Dimock Jr.,
    Gerald W. Esch, Mordecai J. Jaffe, Raymond E. Kuhn, James C. McDonald,
    Robert L. Sullivan, Peter D. Weigl, Raymond L. Wyatt
Associate Professors Nina Strömgren Allen, John F. Dimmick, Herman E. Eure,
    A. Thomas Olive
Assistant Professors Carole L. Browne, Robert A. Browne, Hugo C. Lane,
    William A. Thomas
Adjunct Professors J. Whitfield Gibbons, Harold O. Goodman,
    Stephen H. Richardson

1986–1987
Ronald V. Dimock Jr., Chair
Professors Charles M. Allen, Ralph D. Amen, Ronald V. Dimock Jr.,
    Gerald W. Esch, Mordecai J. Jaffe, Raymond E. Kuhn, James C. McDonald,
    Robert L. Sullivan, Peter D. Weigl, Raymond L. Wyatt
Associate Professors Nina Strömgren Allen, Herman E. Eure, Hugo C. Lane, A.
    Thomas Olive
Assistant Professors Carole L. Browne, Robert A. Browne, Wayne L. Silver,
    William A. Thomas
Adjunct Professors J. Whitfield Gibbons, Harold O. Goodman,
    Stephen H. Richardson

1987–1988
Ronald V. Dimock Jr., Chair
Professors Charles M. Allen, Ralph D. Amen, Ronald V. Dimock Jr., Gerald W.
    Esch, Mordecai J. Jaffe, Raymond E. Kuhn, James C. McDonald, Peter D. Weigl,
    Raymond L. Wyatt
Associate Professors Nina Strömgren Allen, Carole L. Browne, Robert A. Browne,
    Herman E. Eure, Hugo C. Lane, A. Thomas Olive
Assistant Professors Wayne L. Silver, William A. Thomas
Adjunct Professors J. Whitfield Gibbons, Harold O. Goodman, Stephen H.
    Richardson
Adjunct Assistant Professor Margaret Mulvey

1988–1989
Ronald V. Dimock Jr., Chair
Professors Charles M. Allen, Ralph D. Amen, Ronald V. Dimock Jr., Gerald W.
    Esch, Mordecai J. Jaffe, Raymond E. Kuhn, Peter D. Weigl, Raymond L. Wyatt

Associate Professors Nina Strömgren Allen, Carole L. Browne, Robert A. Browne, William E. Conner, Herman E. Eure, Hugo C. Lane, A. Thomas Olive
Assistant Professors Wayne L. Silver, William A. Thomas
Adjunct Professors J. Whitfield Gibbons, Harold O. Goodman, Stephen H. Richardson
Adjunct Assistant Professor Margaret Mulvey

1989–1990
Ronald V. Dimock Jr., Chair
Professors Charles M. Allen, Ralph D. Amen, Ronald V. Dimock Jr., Gerald W. Esch, Mordecai J. Jaffe, Raymond E. Kuhn, Peter D. Weigl, Raymond L. Wyatt
Associate Professors Nina Strömgren Allen, Carole L. Browne, Robert A. Browne, William E. Conner, Herman E. Eure, Hugo C. Lane
Assistant Professors James F. Curran, Wayne L. Silver, Ellen L. Simms, William A. Thomas
Adjunct Professors J. Whitfield Gibbons, Harold O. Goodman, Stephen H. Richardson
Adjunct Assistant Professors John M. Aho, Margaret Mulvey

1990–1991
Ronald V. Dimock Jr., Chair
Professors Ralph D. Amen, Ronald V. Dimock Jr., Gerald W. Esch, Mordecai J. Jaffe, Raymond E. Kuhn, Peter D. Weigl, Raymond L. Wyatt
Associate Professors Nina Strömgren Allen, Carole L. Browne, Robert A. Browne, William E. Conner, Herman E. Eure, Hugo C. Lane, Wayne L. Silver
Assistant Professors James F. Curran, Michael J. Foote, Ellen L. Simms, William A. Thomas
Adjunct Professors J. Whitfield Gibbons, Harold O. Goodman, Terry C. Hazen, Stephen H. Richardson
Adjunct Assistant Professors John M. Aho, Margaret Mulvey

1991–1992
Gerald W. Esch, Chair
Professors Ralph D. Amen, Ronald V. Dimock Jr., Gerald W. Esch, Mordecai J. Jaffe, Raymond E. Kuhn, Peter D. Weigl, Raymond L. Wyatt
Associate Professors Nina Strömgren Allen, Carole L. Browne, Robert A. Browne, William E. Conner, Herman E. Eure, Hugo C. Lane, Wayne L. Silver
Assistant Professors James F. Curran, Ellen L. Simms
Visiting Assistant Professor Jack K. Harris
Adjunct Professors J. Whitfield Gibbons, Harold O. Goodman, Terry C. Hazen, Stephen H. Richardson
Adjunct Assistant Professors John M. Aho, Margaret Mulvey

1992–1993
Gerald W. Esch, Chair
Professors Ralph D. Amen, Ronald V. Dimock Jr., Gerald W. Esch,
    Herman E. Eure, Mordecai J. Jaffe, Raymond E. Kuhn, Peter D.
    Weigl, Raymond L. Wyatt
Associate Professors Nina Strömgren Allen, Carole L. Browne,
    Robert A. Browne, William E. Conner, Hugo C. Lane, Wayne L. Silver
Assistant Professors James F. Curran, Gloria K. Muday
Visiting Assistant Professors Kathleen A. Kron, Anne M. Moore
Adjunct Professors J. Whitfield Gibbons, Harold O. Goodman,
    Terry C. Hazen, Stephen H. Richardson
Adjunct Assistant Professors John M. Aho, Margaret Mulvey

1993–1994
William E. Conner, Chair
Charles H. Babcock Professor of Botany Mordecai J. Jaffe
Wake Forest Professors Gerald W. Esch, Raymond E. Kuhn
Professors Ralph D. Amen, Ronald V Dimock Jr., Herman E. Eure, Peter D. Weigl
Associate Professors Nina Strömgren Allen, Carole L. Browne, Robert A. Browne,
    William E. Conner, Hugo C. Lane, Wayne L. Silver
Assistant Professors David J. Anderson, James F. Curran,
    Kathleen A. Kron, Gloria K. Muday
Adjunct Professors J. Whitfield Gibbons, Harold O. Goodman, Terry C. Hazen,
    Stephen H. Richardson
Adjunct Associate Professor Margaret Mulvey
Adjunct Assistant Professor John M. Aho

1994–1995
William E. Conner, Chair
Charles H. Babcock Professor of Botany Mordecai J. Jaffe
Wake Forest Professors Gerald W. Esch, Raymond E. Kuhn
Professors Nina Strömgren Allen, Robert A. Browne,
    Ronald V. Dimock Jr., Herman E. Eure, Peter D. Weigl
Associate Professors Carole L. Browne, William E. Conner,
    James F. Curran, Hugo C. Lane, Wayne L. Silver
Assistant Professors David J. Anderson, Stephen M. Gatesy,
    Kathleen A. Kron, Gloria Muday, Rosanne J. Spolski
Adjunct Professors J. Whitfield Gibbons, Terry C. Hazen, Stephen H. Richardson
Adjunct Associate Professor Margaret Mulvey
Instructor David W. Hall

1995–1996
William E. Conner, Chair
Charles H. Babcock Professor of Botany Mordecai J. Jaffe
Wake Forest Professors Gerald W. Esch, Raymond E. Kuhn

Professors Robert A. Browne, William E. Conner,
    Ronald V. Dimock Jr., Herman E. Eure, Peter D. Weigl
Associate Professors Carole L. Browne, James F. Curran,
    Hugo C. Lane, Wayne L. Silver
Assistant Professors David J. Anderson, Stephen M. Gatesy,
    Kathleen A. Kron, Gloria K. Muday, Rosanne J. Spolski
Visiting Assistant Professor Kathrin F. Stanger
Adjunct Professors J. Whitfield Gibbons, Terry C. Hazen, Stephen H. Richardson
Adjunct Associate Professor Margaret Mulvey
Instructor David W. Hall

1996–1997
William E. Conner, Chair
Charles H. Babcock Professor of Botany Mordecai J. Jaffe
Wake Forest Professors Gerald W. Esch, Raymond E. Kuhn
Professors Carole L. Browne, Robert A. Browne, William E. Conner,
    Ronald V. Dimock Jr., Herman E. Eure, Hugo C. Lane, Peter D. Weigl
Associate Professors James F. Curran, Wayne L. Silver
Assistant Professors David J. Anderson, Kathleen A. Kron, Gloria K. Muday,
    Rosanne J. Spolski, Brian W. Tague
Visiting Assistant Professors Eric K. Findeis, David W. Hall, Steven K. Rice,
    Kathrin F. Stanger, Eric J. Wetzel
Adjunct Professors J. Whitfield Gibbons, Terry C. Hazen, Stephen H. Richardson
Adjunct Associate Professor Margaret Mulvey

1997–1998
William E. Conner, Chair
Charles H. Babcock Professor of Botany Mordecai J. Jaffe
Wake Forest Professors Gerald W. Esch, Raymond E. Kuhn
Professors Carole L. Browne, Robert A. Browne, William E. Conner,
    Ronald V. Dimock Jr., Herman E. Eure, Hugo C. Lane, Peter D. Weigl
Associate Professors James F. Curran, Gloria K. Muday, Wayne L. Silver
Assistant Professors David J. Anderson, Kathleen A. Kron,
    Rosanne J. Spolski, Brian W. Tague
Visiting Assistant Professors Hanya E. Chrispeels, Eric K. Findeis,
    David W. Hall, Steven K. Rice, Kathrin F. Stanger-Hall
Adjunct Professors J. Whitfield Gibbons, Terry C. Hazen
Adjunct Associate Professor Margaret Mulvey

1998–1999
William E. Conner, Chair
Charles H. Babcock Professor of Botany Mordecai J. Jaffe
Wake Forest Professors Gerald W. Esch, Raymond E. Kuhn
Professors Carole L. Browne, Robert A Browne, William E. Conner,
    Ronald V. Dimock Jr., Herman E. Eure, Hugo C. Lane, Peter D. Weigl

Associate Professors James F. Curran, Kathleen A. Kron,
　　Gloria K. Muday, Wayne L. Silver
Assistant Professors David J. Anderson, Miriam A. Ashley-Ross,
　　Rosanne J. Spolski, Brian W. Tague, Clifford W. Zeyl
Visiting Assistant Professors Hanya E. Chrispeels, Steven K. Rice
Adjunct Professors J. Whitfield Gibbons, Terry C. Hazen
Adjunct Associate Professor Margaret Mulvey

1999–2000
Herman E. Eure, Chair
Charles H. Babcock Chair of Botany William K. Smith
Wake Forest Professors Gerald W. Esch, Raymond E. Kuhn
Professors Carole L. Browne, Robert A. Browne, William E. Conner,
　　Ronald V. Dimock Jr., Herman E. Eure, Hugo C. Lane, Peter D. Weigl
Associate Professors David J. Anderson, James F. Curran, Kathleen A. Kron,
　　Gloria K. Muday, Wayne L. Silver
Assistant Professors Miriam A. Ashley-Ross, Miles R. Silman, Rosanne J. Spolski,
　　Brian W. Tague, Clifford W. Zeyl
Visiting Assistant Professors Hanya E. Chrispeels, A. Daniel Johnson, Derek A.
　　Zelmer
Adjunct Professors J. Whitfield Gibbons, Terry C. Hazen
Adjunct Assistant Professor Jennifer C. Waters (Director of Imaging Facility)

2000–2001
Herman E. Eure, Chair
Charles H. Babcock Chair of Botany William K. Smith
Wake Forest Professors Gerald W. Esch, Raymond E. Kuhn
Professors Carole L. Browne, Robert A. Browne, William E. Conner, Ronald V.
　　Dimock Jr., Herman E. Eure, Hugo C. Lane, Peter D. Weigl
Associate Professors David J. Anderson, James F. Curran, Kathleen A. Kron,
　　Gloria K. Muday, Wayne L. Silver
Assistant Professors Miriam A. Ashley-Ross, Miles R. Silman, Brian W. Tague,
　　Clifford W. Zeyl
Visiting Assistant Professors A. Daniel Johnson, Pat C.W. Lord
Adjunct Professors J. Whitfield Gibbons, Terry C. Hazen
Adjunct Assistant Professor Jennifer C. Waters (Director of Imaging Facility)

2001–2002
Herman E. Eure, Chair
Charles M. Allen Professor of Biology Gerald W. Esch
Charles H. Babcock Chair of Botany William K. Smith
Wake Forest Professor Raymond E. Kuhn
Professors Carole L. Browne, Robert A. Browne, William E. Conner, James F.
　　Curran, Ronald V. Dimock Jr., Herman E. Eure, Hugo C. Lane,
　　Wayne L. Silver, Peter D. Weigl

Associate Professors David J. Anderson, Kathleen A. Kron, Gloria K. Muday
Assistant Professors Miriam A. Ashley-Ross, Miles R. Silman,
    Brian W. Tague, Clifford W. Zeyl
Visiting Assistant Professors Stephan G. Bullard, Hanya E. Chrispeels,
    A. Daniel Johnson, Pat C.W. Lord
Adjunct Professors J. Whitfield Gibbons, Terry C. Hazen
Adjunct Assistant Professor Jennifer C. Waters (Director of Microscopy)

2002–2003
Herman E. Eure, Chair
Charles M. Allen Professor of Biology Gerald W. Esch
Charles H. Babcock Chair of Botany William K. Smith
Wake Forest Professor Raymond E. Kuhn
Professors Carole L. Browne, Robert A. Browne, William E. Conner,
    James F. Curran, Ronald V. Dimock Jr., Herman E. Eure, Hugo C. Lane,
    Wayne L. Silver, Peter D. Weigl
Associate Professors David J. Anderson, Kathleen A. Kron (Z. Smith Reynolds
    Foundation Fellow), Gloria K. Muday, Brain W. Tague
Assistant Professors Miriam A. Ashley-Ross, Miles R. Silman,
    Clifford W. Zeyl (Z. Smith Reynolds Foundation Fellow)
Visiting Assistant Professors Stephan G. Bullard, Leslie D. Clifford, Pat C.W. Lord
Adjunct Professors J. Whitfield Gibbons, Terry C. Hazen
Lecturer A. Daniel Johnson

2003–2004
Herman E. Eure, Chair
Charles M. Allen Professor of Biology Gerald W. Esch
Charles H. Babcock Chair of Botany William K. Smith
Wake Forest Professors Ronald V. Dimock Jr., Raymond E. Kuhn
Professors Carole L. Browne, Robert A. Browne, William E. Conner,
    James F. Curran, Herman E. Eure, Hugo C. Lane, Wayne L. Silver,
    Peter D. Weigl
Associate Professors David J. Anderson, Kathleen A. Kron (Z. Smith Reynolds
    Foundation Fellow), Gloria K. Muday, Brian W. Tague
Assistant Professors Miriam A. Ashley-Ross, Douglas A. Fantz, Miles R. Silman,
    Clifford W. Zeyl (Z. Smith Reynolds Foundation Fellow)
Visiting Assistant Professor Pat C.W. Lord
Adjunct Professors J. Whitfield Gibbons, Terry C. Hazen
Adjunct Assistant Professor and Director of Microscopy Anita K. McCauley
Lecturer A. Daniel Johnson

2004–2005
Herman E. Eure, Chair
Charles M. Allen Professor of Biology Gerald W. Esch
Charles H. Babcock Chair of Botany William K. Smith

Reynolds Professor Susan Fahrbach
Wake Forest Professors Ronald V. Dimock Jr., Raymond E. Kuhn
Professors Carole L. Browne, Robert A. Browne, William E. Conner,
    James F. Curran, Herman E. Eure, Kathleen A. Kron (Z. Smith Reynolds
    Foundation Fellow), Hugo C. Lane, Gloria K. Muday,
    Wayne L. Silver, Peter D. Weigl
Associate Professors David J. Anderson, Brian W. Tague,
    Clifford W. Zeyl (Z. Smith Reynolds Foundation Fellow)
Assistant Professors Miriam A. Ashley-Ross, Douglas A. Fantz,
    Miles R. Silman
Visiting Assistant Professor Pat C.W. Lord
Adjunct Professors J. Whitfield Gibbons, Terry C. Hazen
Adjunct Assistant Professor and Director of Microscopy Anita K. McCauley
Lecturer A. Daniel Johnson

2005–2006
Herman E. Eure, Chair
Charles H. Babcock Chair of Botany William K. Smith
Charles M. Allen Professor of Biology Gerald W. Esch
Reynolds Professor Susan Fahrbach
Wake Forest Professors Ronald V. Dimock Jr., Raymond E. Kuhn
Professors David J. Anderson, Carole L. Browne, Robert A. Browne,
    William E. Conner, James F. Curran, Herman E. Eure,
    Kathleen A. Kron, Hugo C. Lane, Gloria K. Muday, Wayne L. Silver,
    Peter D. Weigl
Associate Professors Miriam A. Ashley-Ross, Miles R. Silman
    (Z. Smith Reynolds Foundation Fellow), Brian W. Tague,
    Clifford W. Zeyl (Z. Smith Reynolds Foundation Fellow)
Assistant Professor Erik C. Johnson
Visiting Assistant Professor Pat C.W. Lord
Adjunct Professors J. Whitfield Gibbons, Terry C. Hazen
Adjunct Assistant Professor and Director of Microscopy Anita K. McCauley
Adjunct Assistant Professor Hanya E. Chrispeels
Lecturer A. Daniel Johnson

BUSINESS AND ACCOUNTANCY (BUS & ACC)

The School of Business and Accountancy was established in 1980 as a separate "School," no longer a "Department" in Wake Forest College. Thus, bulletins from that time on had a separate section towards the back under the heading "School of Business and Accountancy" to differentiate the School from the College. Here the various policies and courses of the School were disclosed. Previously the business and accountany courses had been listed under the Department of Business and Accountancy as part of Wake Forest College along with the other departments and various courses in the arts, humanities, mathematic, sciences, etc.

From 1983–1984 through 1994–1995, the School of Business and Accountancy prefixed its courses with the codes BUS (for business courses) and ACC (for accountancy courses). The school changed its name to Wayne Calloway School of Business and Accountancy in 1995–1996.

This same information as described above is also listed under "School of Business and Accountancy" since this academic subject matter was a different school from Wake Forest College in the years 1983–2005.

1983–1984
Thomas C. Taylor, Dean
Professors Delmer P. Hylton, F. Jeanne Owen, Thomas C. Taylor
Associate Professors Umit Akinc, Leon P. Cook Jr., A. Sayeste Daser,
Arun P. Dewasthali, Carol Elbing, Stephen Ewing, Thomas S. Goho,
Dale R. Martin, Ralph B. Tower
Assistant Professor Michael Roberts
Instructors Olive S. Thomas, Robin Tower, Julie Yu
Lecturer Lee Stokes

1984–1985
Thomas C. Taylor, Dean
Professors Delmer P. Hylton, F. Jeanne Owen, Thomas C. Taylor
Associate Professors Umit Akinc, Leon P. Cook Jr., A. Sayeste Daser,
Arun P. Dewasthali, Carol Elbing, Stephen Ewing, Thomas S. Goho,
Dale R. Martin, Ralph B. Tower
Assistant Professors John S. Dunkelberg, Michael Roberts, Julie Yu
Instructor Olive S. Thomas
Lecturer Lee Stokes

1985–1986
Thomas C. Taylor, Dean
Professors Delmer P. Hylton, F. Jeanne Owen, Thomas C. Taylor
Associate Professors Umit Akinc, Leon P. Cook Jr., A. Sayeste Daser,
Arun P. Dewasthali, Carol Elbing, Stephen Ewing, Thomas S. Goho,
Dale R. Martin, Ralph B. Tower
Assistant Professor John S. Dunkelberg
Visiting Professor Eddie V. Easley
Instructor Olive S. Thomas
Lecturer Lee Stokes

1986–1987
Thomas C. Taylor, Dean
Professors Eddie V. Easley, Delmer P. Hylton, F. Jeanne Owen, Thomas C. Taylor
Associate Professors Umit Akinc, Leon P. Cook Jr., A. Sayeste Daser, Arun P.
Dewasthali, Stephen Ewing, Thomas S. Goho, Dale R. Martin, Ralph B. Tower

Assistant Professor John S. Dunkelberg
Adjunct Associate Professor Carol Elbing
Instructors Kim W. Driesbach, Timothy P. Summers
Lecturers Lee Stokes, Olive S. Thomas

1987–1988
Thomas C. Taylor, Dean
Professors Eddie V. Easley, Delmer P. Hylton, F. Jeanne Owen,
    Thomas C. Taylor
Associate Professors Umit Akinc, Leon P. Cook Jr., A. Sayeste Daser,
    Arun P. Dewasthali, Stephen Ewing, Thomas S. Goho, Dale R. Martin,
    Ralph B. Tower
Assistant Professors John S. Dunkelberg, Timothy P. Summers
Adjunct Associate Professor Carol Elbing
Instructors S. Douglas Beets, Kim W. Driesbach
Lecturers Lee Stokes, Olive S. Thomas

1988–1989
Thomas C. Taylor, Dean
University Professor K. Wayne Smith
Professors Eddie V. Easley, Delmer P. Hylton, F. Jeanne Owen,
    Thomas C. Taylor
Associate Professors Umit Akinc, Leon P. Cook Jr., A. Sayeste Daser,
    Arun P. Dewasthali, John S. Dunkelberg, Stephen Ewing,
    Thomas S. Goho, Dale R. Martin, Ralph B. Tower
Assistant Professor S. Douglas Beets
Adjunct Instructor Helen Akinc
Lecturers DeLeon E. Stokes, Olive S. Thomas
Adjunct Lecturer Horace O. Kelly Jr.

1989–1990
Thomas C. Taylor, Dean
University Professor K. Wayne Smith
Professors Eddie V. Easley, Delmer P. Hylton, F. Jeanne Owen,
    Thomas C. Taylor
Associate Professors Umit Akinc, Leon P. Cook Jr., A. Sayeste Daser,
    Arun P. Dewasthali, John S. Dunkelberg, Stephen Ewing,
    Thomas S. Goho, Dale R. Martin, Ralph B. Tower
Assistant Professor S. Douglas Beets
Adjunct Instructors Helen Akinc, Jules Laskey, Kaye Nifong,
    Robin Tower
Lecturers DeLeon E. Stokes, Olive S. Thomas
Adjunct Lecturer Horace O. Kelly Jr.

1990–1991
Thomas C. Taylor, Dean
Professors Eddie V. Easley, Delmer P. Hylton, F. Jeanne Owen, Thomas C. Taylor
Associate Professors Umit Akinc, Leon P. Cook Jr., A. Sayeste Daser,
　　Arun P. Dewasthali, John S. Dunkelberg, Stephen Ewing,
　　Thomas S. Goho, Dale R. Martin, Ralph B. Tower, Jack E. Wilkerson Jr.
Assistant Professors S. Douglas Beets, P. Candace Deans
Adjunct Instructor Helen Akinc
Lecturers Horace O. Kelly Jr., DeLeon E. Stokes, Olive S. Thomas

1991–1992
Thomas C. Taylor, Dean
Professors Eddie V. Easley, Delmer P. Hylton, F. Jeanne Owen, Thomas C. Taylor
Associate Professors Umit Akinc, Leon P. Cook Jr., A. Sayeste Daser,
　　Arun P. Dewasthali, John S. Dunkelberg, Stephen Ewing,
　　Thomas S. Goho, Dale R. Martin, Ralph B. Tower, Jack E. Wilkerson Jr.
Assistant Professors S. Douglas Beets, P. Candace Deans, J. Kline Harrison
Adjunct Instructor Helen Akinc
Lecturers Horace O. Kelly Jr., DeLeon E. Stokes, Olive S. Thomas, C. Michael
　　Thompson

1992–1993
Thomas C. Taylor, Dean
Professors Eddie V. Easley, Thomas C. Taylor
Associate Professors Umit Akinc, Leon P. Cook Jr., A. Sayeste Daser,
　　Arun P. Dewasthali, John S. Dunkelberg, Stephen Ewing, Thomas S. Goho,
　　E. Clayton Hipp Jr., Dale R. Martin, Ralph B. Tower, Jack E. Wilkerson Jr.
Assistant Professors S. Douglas Beets, P. Candace Deans, J. Kline Harrison
Instructor Paul E. Juras
Adjunct Instructors Helen Akinc, Emily G. Neese
Lecturers Horace O. Kelly Jr., DeLeon E. Stokes, Olive S. Thomas,
　　C. Michael Thompson

1993–1994
Dana J. Johnson, Dean
C. Michael Thompson, Assistant Dean
Professors Umit Akinc, Eddie V. Easley, Stephen Ewing, Dale R. Martin,
　　Thomas C. Taylor (Hylton Professor of Accountancy), Ralph B. Tower
Associate Professors S. Douglas Beets, Leon P. Cook Jr., A. Sayeste Daser,
　　Arun P. Dewasthali, John S. Dunkelberg, Thomas S. Goho,
　　E. Clayton Hipp Jr., Jack E. Wilkerson Jr.
Assistant Professors P. Candace Deans, J. Kline Harrison, Paul E. Juras
Adjunct Instructors Helen Akinc, Emily G. Neese
Lecturers Horace O. Kelly Jr., DeLeon E. Stokes, Olive S. Thomas,
　　C. Michael Thompson

1994–1995
Dana J. Johnson, Dean
C. Michael Thompson, Assistant Dean
Professors Umit Akinc (Thomas H. Davis Professor of Business),
    A. Sayeste Daser, Eddie V. Easley, Stephen Ewing, Dale R. Martin,
    Thomas C. Taylor (Hylton Professor of Accountancy), Ralph B. Tower
Associate Professors S. Douglas Beets, Arun P. Dewasthali,
    John S. Dunkelberg (Benson-Pruitt Professor of Business),
    Thomas S. Goho, E. Clayton Hipp Jr., Jack E. Wilkerson Jr.
Assistant Professors P. Candace Deans, Jonathan E. Duchac,
    J. Kline Harrison, Paul E. Juras
Instructors Helen Akinc, Katherine S. Hoppe
Adjunct Instructors Suzanne S. Buchanan, Cynthia R. Sutton
Lecturers Horace O. Kelly Jr., DeLeon E. Stokes, Olive S. Thomas,
    C. Michael Thompson
Visiting Lecturer Locke M. Newlin

1995–1996
Dana J. Johnson, Dean
Assistant Deans Horace O. Kelly Jr., C. Michael Thompson
Professors Umit Akinc (Thomas H. Davis Professor of Business),
    John S. Dunkelberg (Benson-Pruitt Professor of Business),
    Eddie V. Easley, Stephen Ewing, Dale R. Martin, Thomas C. Taylor
    (Hylton Professor of Accountancy), Ralph B. Tower
Associate Professors S. Douglas Beets, Helen M. Bowers (Kemper Faculty Fellow),
    Arun P. Dewasthali, Thomas S. Goho, J. Kline Harrison,
    E. Clayton Hipp Jr., Jack E. Wilkerson Jr.
Assistant Professors Jonathan E. Duchac, Paul E. Juras, Gordon E. McCray
Visiting Assistant Professors Dennis Cole, Steven J. Crowell
Instructors Helen Akinc, Katherine S. Hoppe
Lecturers Horace O. Kelly Jr., C. Michael Thompson
Visiting Lecturers David K. Isbister, Locke M. Newlin

1996–1997
Dana J. Johnson, Dean
Assistant Dean Katherine S. Hoppe
Professors Umit Akinc (Thomas H. Davis Professor of Business),
    John S. Dunkelberg (Benson-Pruitt Professor of Business),
    Eddie V. Easley, Stephen Ewing, Dale R. Martin, Thomas C. Taylor
    (Hylton Professor of Accountancy), Ralph B. Tower
Associate Professors S. Douglas Beets, Helen M. Bowers (Kemper Faculty Fellow),
    Arun P. Dewasthali, Thomas S. Goho, J. Kline Harrison, Jack E. Wilkerson Jr.
Assistant Professors Jonathan E. Duchac, Patricia A. Graybeal, Paul E. Juras,
    Gordon E. McCray, C. Michael Thompson, G. Page West III

Instructors Helen Akinc (Director of Student Services), Katherine S. Hoppe
Visiting Assistant Professors Dennis Cole, Kathryn R. Nickles
Visiting Lecturers E. Clayton Hipp Jr., David K. Isbister, Emily Neese,
Thomas Ogburn

1997–1998

Jack E. Wilkerson Jr., Acting Dean
Assistant Dean Katherine S. Hoppe
Professors Umit Akinc (Thomas H. Davis Professor of Business),
John S. Dunkelberg, Eddie V. Easley, Stephen Ewing, Dale R. Martin
(Price Waterhouse Professor of Accountancy), Thomas C. Taylor
(Hylton Professor of Accountancy), Ralph B. Tower, Jack E. Wilkerson Jr.
Associate Professors S. Douglas Beets, Helen M. Bowers
(Kemper Faculty Fellow), Arun P. Dewasthali, Thomas S. Goho,
J. Kline Harrison (Benson-Pruitt Associate Professor), Paul E. Juras
Assistant Professors Sheri A. Bridges, Jonathan E. Duchac,
Patricia A. Lobingier, Gordon E. McCray, G. Page West III
Visiting Assistant Professors Mark W. Huber, William M. Marcum,
Margaret C. Smith
Instructors Helen Akinc, Tamara M. Greenwood, Katherine S. Hoppe
Lecturers E. Clayton Hipp Jr., David K. Isbister, Debra R. Jessup, Thomas Ogburn
Adjunct Lecturers Robyn Earthman, Emily Neese
Executives-in-Residence Hunter Cook, John F. Ward

1998–1999

Jack E. Wilkerson Jr., Dean
Assistant Dean Katherine S. Hoppe
Professors Umit Akinc (Thomas H. Davis Professor of Business),
John S. Dunkelberg, Eddie V. Easley, Stephen Ewing, Dale R. Martin
(Price Waterhouse Professor of Accountancy), Donald P. Robin
(J. Tylee Wilson Professor of Business Ethics), Thomas C. Taylor
(Hylton Professor of Accountancy), Ralph B. Tower, Jack E. Wilkerson Jr.
Associate Professors S. Douglas Beets, Arun P. Dewasthali, Thomas S. Goho, J.
Kline Harrison (Benson-Pruitt Associate Professor), Paul E. Juras
Assistant Professors Sheri A. Bridges, Jonathan E. Duchac, Debra R. Jessup,
William M. Marcum, Patricia A. Lobingier, Gordon E. McCray, Yvonne H.
Stewart (Coopers & Lybrand Faculty Fellow), G. Page West III
Visiting Professor Donald H. Taylor
Visiting Assistant Professor Mark W. Huber
Instructors Helen Akinc, Anna M. Cianci, Tamara M. Greenwood,
Katherine S. Hoppe
Lecturers James L. Dominick, E. Clayton Hipp Jr., David K. Isbister,
Thomas Ogburn
Executives-in-Residence James H. Clippard Jr., Peter C. Valenti

1999–2000
Jack E. Wilkerson Jr., Dean
Assistant Dean Katherine S. Hoppe
F.M. Kirby Chair of Business Excellence Roger L. Jenkins
Professors Umit Akinc (Thomas H. Davis Professor of Business),
  John S. Dunkelberg (Kemper Professor), Eddie V. Easley, Stephen Ewing,
  Dale R. Martin (PricewaterhouseCoopers Professor of Accountancy),
  Donald P. Robin (J. Tylee Wilson Professor of Business Ethics),
  Thomas C. Taylor (Hylton Professor of Accountancy), Ralph B. Tower,
  Jack E. Wilkerson Jr.
Associate Professors S. Douglas Beets, Arun P. Dewasthali,
  Jonathan E. Duchac, Thomas S. Goho, J. Kline Harrison
  (Benson-Pruitt Associate Professor), Paul E. Juras
Assistant Professors Terry A. Baker, Sheri A. Bridges, Audrey A. Gramling
  (PricewaterhouseCoopers Faculty Fellow), Debra R. Jessup,
  Patricia A. Lobingier, William M. Marcum, Gordon E. McCray
  (BellSouth Mobility Technology Faculty Fellow), Yvonne H. Stewart
  (PricewaterhouseCoopers Faculty Fellow), G. Page West III
Instructors Helen Akinc, Anna M. Cianci, Tamara M. Greenwood,
  Katherine S. Hoppe
Visiting Instructor of Information Systems James W. Enyon
Lecturer in Accounting Maureen L. Carpenter
Lecturers in Business Andrew C. Ellis, E. Clayton Hipp Jr., David K. Isbister,
  Karen E. Mishra, Daniel Paul, Tracy D. Rishel
Executive-in-Residence Peter C. Valenti

2000–2001
Jack E. Wilkerson Jr., Dean
Associate Dean for Curriculum and Administration J. Kline Harrison
Associate Dean for Academic Programs and Resources Dale R. Martin
Assistant Dean for Student Professional Affairs Helen W. Akinc
Assistant Dean for Student Academic Affairs Katherine S. Hoppe
F.M. Kirby Chair of Business Excellence Roger L. Jenkins
Professors Umit Akinc (Thomas H. Davis Professor of Business),
  John S. Dunkelberg (Kemper Professor), Stephen Ewing, Dale R. Martin
  (Wayne Calloway Professor of Accountancy), Donald P. Robin
  (J. Tylee Wilson Professor of Business Ethics), Thomas C. Taylor
  (Hylton Professor of Accountancy), Ralph B. Tower (Wayne Calloway
  Professor of Taxation), Jack E. Wilkerson Jr.
Associate Professors S. Douglas Beets, Arun P. Dewasthali,
  Jonathan E. Duchac, Thomas S. Goho (Benson-Pruitt Associate Professor),
  J. Kline Harrison, Paul E. Juras
Assistant Professors Terry A. Baker, Sheri A. Bridges, Audrey A. Gramling
  (PricewaterhouseCoopers Faculty Fellow), Debra R. Jessup,
  Patricia A. Lobingier, William M. Marcum (Director of the
  Risk Management Faculty Fellow Program), Gordon E. McCray (BellSouth

Mobility Technology Faculty Fellow), Amy E. Randel, Annette L. Ranft (Exxon-Wayne Calloway Faculty Fellow), Yvonne H. Stewart (PricewaterhouseCoopers Faculty Fellow and Director of the Arthur Andersen Center), G. Page West III
Instructors Helen Akinc, Katherine A. Baker, John Bennett, Tamara M. Greenwood, Katherine S. Hoppe, Mary Martha McKinley
Visiting Instructors James W. Enyon, Karen E. Mishra
Senior Lecturer in Business E. Clayton Hipp Jr.
Lecturer in Business David K. Isbister

2001–2002
Jack E. Wilkerson Jr., Dean
Associate Dean for Curriculum and Administration J. Kline Harrison
Associate Dean for Academic Programs and Resources Dale R. Martin
Assistant Dean for Student Professional Affairs Helen W. Akinc
Assistant Dean for Student Academic Affairs Katherine S. Hoppe
F.M. Kirby Chair of Business Excellence Roger L. Jenkins
Professors Umit Akinc (Thomas H. Davis Professor of Business),
    John S. Dunkelberg (Kemper Professor), Stephen Ewing, J. Kline Harrison,
    Dale R. Martin (Wayne Calloway Professor of Accountancy), Donald P. Robin
    (J. Tylee Wilson Professor of Business Ethics), Thomas C. Taylor
    (Hylton Professor of Accountancy), Ralph B. Tower (Wayne Calloway
    Professor of Taxation), Jack E. Wilkerson Jr.
Associate Professors S. Douglas Beets, Arun P. Dewasthali,
    Jonathan E. Duchac, Thomas S. Goho (Benson-Pruitt Associate Professor),
    Gordon E. McCray (BellSouth Mobility Technology Faculty Fellow),
    G. Page West III
Assistant Professors Terry A. Baker (PricewaterhouseCoopers Faculty Fellow),
    Robert M. Ballenger (Cooper Family Fellow in Information Systems),
    Sheri A. Bridges, Yvonne L. Hinson (PricewaterhouseCoopers Faculty
    Fellow and Director of the Arthur Andersen Center), Debra R. Jessup,
    Paul E. Juras (PricewaterhouseCoopers Faculty Fellow), Patricia A. Lobingier,
    William M. Marcum (Citibank Faculty Fellow, Director of the Risk Management
    Faculty Fellow Program), Amy E. Randel, Annette L. Ranft (Exxon-Wayne
    Calloway Faculty Fellow)
Visiting Professors Lee G. Knight, K. Wayne Smith
Instructors Helen W. Akinc, Katherine A. Baker, Katherine S. Hoppe,
    Mary L. Kesel, Mary Martha McKinley, Karen E. Mishra, Karen D. Nard,
    Karen K. Rogalski
Senior Lecturer in Business E. Clayton Hipp Jr.
Lecturers in Business Tamara M. Greenwood, David K. Isbister,
    Wayne Forrest Morgan

2002–2003
Jack E. Wilkerson Jr., Dean
Associate Dean for Curriculum and Administration J. Kline Harrison

Associate Dean for Academic Programs and Resources Dale R. Martin
Assistant Dean for Student Professional Affairs Helen W. Akinc
Assistant Dean for Student Academic Affairs Katherine S. Hoppe
F.M. Kirby Chair of Business Excellence Roger L. Jenkins
Professors Umit Akinc (Thomas H. Davis Professor of Business), Stephen Ewing,
    J. Kline Harrison, Lee G. Knight, Dale R. Martin (Wayne Calloway Professor of
    Accountancy), Donald P. Robin (J. Tylee Wilson Professor of Business Ethics),
    Thomas C. Taylor (Hylton Professor of Accountancy), Ralph B. Tower
    (Wayne Calloway Professor of Taxation), Jack E. Wilkerson Jr.
Associate Professors George R. Aldhizer, S. Douglas Beets, James F. Cotter, Arun
    P. Dewasthali, Jonathan E. Duchac, Thomas S. Goho (Benson-Pruitt Associate
    Professor), Yvonne L. Hinson (PricewaterhouseCoopers Faculty Fellow),
    Paul E. Juras (PricewaterhouseCoopers Associate Professor of Accountancy),
    Gordon E. McCray (BellSouth Mobility Technology Associate Professor),
    G. Page West III
Assistant Professors Terry A. Baker (PricewaterhouseCoopers Faculty Fellow),
    Sheri A. Bridges, Debra R. Jessup, William M. Marcum (Citibank Faculty
    Fellow), Denise J. McManus, Amy E. Randel, Annette L. Ranft
    (Exxon-Wayne Calloway Faculty Fellow)
Visiting Professor K. Wayne Smith
Instructors Helen W. Akinc, Katherine A. Baker, John Campbell, Mary L. Kesel,
    Mary Martha McKinley, Karen E. Mishra, Karen D. Nard, Karen K. Rogalski
Senior Lecturer in Business E. Clayton Hipp Jr.
Lecturers in Business Tamara M. Greenwood, Katherine S. Hoppe, David K. Isbister

2003–2004
Jack E. Wilkerson Jr., Dean
Associate Dean J. Kline Harrison
Associate Dean Gordon E. McCray
Assistant Dean for Student Professional Affairs Helen W. Akinc
Assistant Dean for Student Academic Affairs Katherine S. Hoppe
Professors Umit Akinc (Thomas H. Davis Professor of Business),
    S. Douglas Beets, Stephen Ewing, J. Kline Harrison, Lee G. Knight,
    Dale R. Martin (Wayne Calloway Professor of Accountancy),
    Donald P. Robin (J. Tylee Wilson Professor of Business Ethics),
    Thomas C. Taylor (Hylton Professor of Accountancy), Ralph B. Tower
    (Wayne Calloway Professor of Taxation), Jack E. Wilkerson Jr.
Associate Professors George R. Aldhizer, Sheri A. Bridges, James F. Cotter,
    Arun P. Dewasthali, Jonathan E. Duchac (Merrill Lynch Associate Professor of
    Accountancy), Thomas S. Goho, Yvonne L. Hinson (PricewaterhouseCoopers
    Faculty Fellow), Paul E. Juras (PricewaterhouseCoopers Associate Professor of
    Accountancy), Gordon E. McCray (BellSouth Mobility Technology Associate
    Professor), G. Page West III (Benson-Pruitt Associate Professor)
Assistant Professors Terry A. Baker (PricewaterhouseCoopers Faculty Fellow and
    Assistant Professor), Debra R. Jessup, Bruce R. Lewis, William M. Marcum

(Citibank Faculty Fellow), Denise J. McManus (Exxon-Wayne Calloway
Faculty Fellow), Amy E. Randel (Coca-Cola Faculty Fellow), Annette L. Ranft
(Exxon-Wayne Calloway Faculty Fellow)
Visiting Professor K. Wayne Smith
Instructors Helen W. Akinc, Mary L. Kesel, Karen E. Mishra, Karen K. Rogalski
Senior Lecturer in Business E. Clayton Hipp Jr.
Lecturers in Business Tamara M. Greenwood, Katherine S. Hoppe, David K. Isbister

2004–2005
Jack E. Wilkerson Jr., Dean
Associate Dean J. Kline Harrison
Associate Dean Gordon E. McCray
Assistant Dean for Student Professional Affairs Helen W. Akinc
Assistant Dean for Student Academic Affairs Katherine S. Hoppe
Professors Umit Akinc (Thomas H. Davis Professor of Business), S. Douglas Beets,
    Stephen Ewing, J. Kline Harrison, Lee G. Knight (Hylton Professor of
    Accountancy), Dale R. Martin (Wayne Calloway Professor of Accountancy),
    Donald P. Robin (J. Tylee Wilson Professor of Business Ethics),
    Ralph B. Tower (Wayne Calloway Professor of Taxation), Jack E. Wilkerson Jr.
Associate Professors George R. Aldhizer, Sheri A. Bridges, James F. Cotter,
    Arun P. Dewasthali, Jonathan E. Duchac (Merrill Lynch Associate Professor
    of Accountancy), Thomas S. Goho, Yvonne L. Hinson (PricewaterhouseCoopers
    Faculty Fellow), Paul E. Juras (PricewaterhouseCoopers Associate Professor
    of Accountancy), William M. Marcum (Citibank Faculty Fellow), Gordon E.
    McCray (BellSouth Mobility Technology Associate Professor), G. Page West III
    (Benson-Pruitt Associate Professor)
Assistant Professors Terry A. Baker (PricewaterhouseCoopers Faculty Fellow),
    Debra R. Jessup, Bruce R. Lewis (Cooper Family Fellow in Information Systems),
    Denise J. McManus (Exxon-Wayne Calloway Faculty Fellow), Amy E. Randel
    (Coca-Cola Faculty Fellow), Annette L. Ranft (Exxon-Wayne Calloway Faculty
    Fellow)
Exchange Professor (Bordeaux) Christophe Estay
Visiting Assistant Professor Vinay K. Vasudev
Adjunct Assistant Professor Julie H. Wayne
Instructors Helen W. Akinc, Michaele M. Cook, Robert E. Fly, David A. Gilbert,
    Mary L. Kesel, Daniel J. Paul, Thomas H. Ramsey, Tina F. Rizzi, Cyndi Skaar
Senior Lecturer in Business E. Clayton Hipp Jr.
Lecturer in Business Katherine S. Hoppe

2005–2006
Jack E. Wilkerson Jr., Dean
Associate Dean J. Kline Harrison
Associate Dean Gordon E. McCray
Assistant Dean for Student Professional Affairs Helen W. Akinc
Assistant Dean for Student Academic Affairs Katherine S. Hoppe

Professors Umit Akinc (Thomas H. Davis Professor of Business), S. Douglas Beets, Robert R. Bliss (F.M. Kirby Professor of Business Excellence), Stephen Ewing, J. Kline Harrison, Lee G. Knight (Hylton Professor of Accountancy), Dale R. Martin (Wayne Calloway Professor of Accountancy), Donald P. Robin (J. Tylee Wilson Professor of Business Ethics), Ralph B. Tower (Wayne Calloway Professor of Taxation), Jack E. Wilkerson Jr.

Associate Professors George R. Aldhizer, Terry A. Baker (PricewaterhouseCoopers Faculty Fellow and Director of Graduate Studies), Sheri A. Bridges, James F. Cotter, Arun P. Dewasthali, Jonathan E. Duchac (Merrill Lynch Associate Professor of Accountancy), Thomas S. Goho, Yvonne L. Hinson (Pricewater-houseCoopers Faculty Fellow), Paul E. Juras, William M. Marcum (Citibank Faculty Fellow), Gordon E. McCray (BellSouth Mobility Technology Associate Professor), Annette L. Ranft (Exxon-Wayne Calloway Faculty Fellow), G. Page West III (Benson-Pruitt Associate Professor)

Assistant Professors Bruce R. Lewis (Cooper Family Fellow in Information Systems), Denise J. McManus (Exxon-Wayne Calloway Faculty Fellow), Amy E. Randel (Coca-Cola Faculty Fellow), Michelle Steward

Adjunct Assistant Professors Debra R. Jessup, Julie H. Wayne

Instructors Helen W. Akinc, Robert E. Fly, David A. Gilbert, R. Scott Keith, Mary L. Kesel, Benjamin Paz, Thomas H. Ramsey, Cyndi Skaar

Senior Lecturer in Business E. Clayton Hipp Jr.

Lecturer in Business Katherine S. Hoppe

CHEMISTRY (CHM)

1983–1984

Ronald E. Noftle, Chair

Professors Phillip J. Hamrick Jr., Roger A. Hegstrom, Harry B. Miller, Ronald E. Noftle, John W. Nowell

Associate Professors Paul M. Gross Jr., Willie L. Hinze

Assistant Professors Robert F. Ferrante, Charles F. Jackels, Susan C. Jackels, Richard R. M. Jones

Instructor Margaret F. Plemmons

1984–1985

Ronald E. Noftle, Chair

Professors Phillip J. Hamrick Jr., Roger A. Hegstrom, Ronald E. Noftle, John W. Nowell

Associate Professors Paul M. Gross Jr., Willie L. Hinze, Charles F. Jackels, Susan C. Jackels

Assistant Professors Huw M. L. Davies, Robert F. Ferrante, Richard R. M. Jones

1985–1986

Ronald E. Noftle, Chair

Professors Phillip J. Hamrick Jr., Roger A. Hegstrom, Willie L. Hinze, Ronald E. Noftle, John W. Nowell

Associate Professors Paul M. Gross Jr., Charles F. Jackels, Susan C. Jackels
Assistant Professors Huw M. L. Davies, Robert F. Ferrante, Richard R. M. Jones

1986–1987
Ronald E. Noftle, Chair
Professors Phillip J. Hamrick Jr., Roger A. Hegstrom, Willie L. Hinze,
    Ronald E. Noftle, John W. Nowell
Associate Professors Paul M. Gross Jr., Charles F. Jackels, Susan C. Jackels
Assistant Professors Huw M. L. Davies, Robert F. Ferrante

1987–1988
John W. Nowell, Chair
Professors Phillip J. Hamrick Jr., Roger A. Hegstrom, Willie L. Hinze,
    Ronald E. Noftle, John W. Nowell
Associate Professors Paul M. Gross Jr., Charles F. Jackels, Susan C. Jackels
Assistant Professors Huw M. L. Davies, Robert F. Ferrante,
    N. Ganapathisubramanian, Mark E. Welker
Instructor Jimmy Turner III

1988–1989
Phillip J. Hamrick Jr., Chair
Professors Paul M. Gross Jr., Phillip J. Hamrick Jr., Roger A. Hegstrom,
    Willie L. Hinze, Ronald E. Noftle
Associate Professors Huw M. L. Davies, Charles F. Jackels, Susan C. Jackels,
    Frank H. Quina
Assistant Professors N. Ganapathisubramanian, Dilip K. Kondepudi,
    Mark E. Welker
Instructor Jimmy Turner III

1989–1990
Phillip J. Hamrick Jr., Chair
Professors Phillip J. Hamrick Jr., Roger A. Hegstrom, Willie L. Hinze, Ronald E. Noftle
Associate Professors Huw M. L. Davies, Charles F. Jackels, Susan C. Jackels
Assistant Professors James C. Fishbein, N. Ganapathisubramanian,
    Dilip K. Kondepudi, Mark E. Welker
Instructor Jimmy Turner III

1990–1991
Phillip J. Hamrick Jr., Chair
Professors Phillip J. Hamrick Jr., Roger A. Hegstrom, Willie L. Hinze,
    Ronald E. Noftle
Associate Professors Huw M. L. Davies, Charles F. Jackels, Susan C. Jackels
Assistant Professors James C. Fishbein, N. Ganapathisubramanian,
    Bradley T. Jones, Dilip K. Kondepudi, Mark E. Welker
Instructor Jimmy Turner III

1991–1992
Willie L. Hinze, Chair
Professors Phillip J. Hamrick Jr., Roger A. Hegstrom, Willie L. Hinze,
    Charles F. Jackels, Susan C. Jackels, Ronald E. Noftle
Associate Professor Huw M. L. Davies
Assistant Professors James C. Fishbein, N. Ganapathisubramanian,
    Bradley T. Jones, Dilip K. Kondepudi, Mark E. Welker
Visiting Assistant Professor Philip S. Hammond

1992–1993
Willie L. Hinze, Chair
Professors Phillip J. Hamrick Jr., Roger A. Hegstrom, Willie L. Hinze,
    Charles F. Jackels, Susan C. Jackels, Gordon A. Melson, Ronald E. Noftle
Associate Professors Huw M. L. Davies, Dilip K. Kondepudi, Mark E. Welker
Assistant Professors James C. Fishbein, N. Ganapathisubramanian,
    Bradley T. Jones, Abdessadek Lachgar
Visiting Assistant Professor Philip S. Hammond
Adjunct Professor Robert A. Heckman

1993–1994
Willie L. Hinze, Chair
Wake Forest Professors Roger A. Hegstrom, Willie L. Hinze
Professors Phillip J. Hamrick Jr., Charles F. Jackels, Susan C. Jackels,
    Gordon A. Melson, Ronald E. Noftle
Associate Professors Huw M. L. Davies, Dilip K. Kondepudi, Mark E. Welker
Assistant Professors James C. Fishbein, N. Ganapathisubramanian,
    Bradley T. Jones, Abdessadek Lachgar
Visiting Assistant Professor Philip S. Hammond

1994–1995
Willie L. Hinze, Chair
Wake Forest Professors Roger A. Hegstrom, Willie L. Hinze
Professors Huw M. L. Davies, Phillip J. Hamrick Jr., Charles F. Jackels,
    Susan C. Jackels, Gordon A. Melson, Ronald E. Noftle, Robert L. Swofford
Associate Professors James C. Fishbein, Dilip K. Kondepudi, Mark E. Welker
Assistant Professors Bradley T. Jones, Abdessadek Lachgar
Visiting Assistant Professors Michelle M. Baillargeon, Neal E. Busch,
    Philip S. Hammond, Jane Joseph

1995–1996
Robert L. Swofford, Chair
Wake Forest Professors Roger A. Hegstrom, Willie L. Hinze
Professors Huw M. L. Davies, Phillip J. Hamrick Jr., Charles F. Jackels,
    Susan C. Jackels, Gordon A. Melson, Ronald E. Noftle, Robert L. Swofford

Associate Professors James C. Fishbein, Bradley T. Jones, Dilip K. Kondepudi,
   Mark E. Welker
Assistant Professor Abdessadek Lachgar
Visiting Associate Professor Jane Joseph
Visiting Assistant Professors Neal E. Busch, Philip S. Hammond

1996–1997
Robert L. Swofford, Chair
Wake Forest Professors Roger A. Hegstrom, Willie L. Hinze
Professors Charles F. Jackels, Susan C. Jackels, Gordon A. Melson,
   Ronald E. Noftle, Robert L. Swofford, Mark E. Welker
Associate Professors James C. Fishbein, Bradley T. Jones, Dilip K. Kondepudi
Assistant Professors S. Bruce King, Abdessadek Lachgar, Richard A. Manderville
Visiting Associate Professor Jane Joseph
Visiting Assistant Professors Neal E. Busch, P. Michelle Fitzsimmons,
   Angela Glisan King

1997–1998
Roger A. Hegstrom, Chair
Wake Forest Professors Roger A. Hegstrom, Willie L. Hinze
Professors Dilip K. Kondepudi, Gordon A. Melson, Ronald E. Noftle,
   Robert L. Swofford, Mark E. Welker
Associate Professors James C. Fishbein, Bradley T. Jones, Abdessadek Lachgar
Assistant Professors Steven C. Haefner, S. Bruce King, Richard A. Manderville
Visiting Assistant Professors Neal E. Busch, Angela Glisan King, Eugene P. Wagner

1998–1999
Roger A. Hegstrom, Chair
Wake Forest Professors Roger A. Hegstrom, Willie L. Hinze
Professors James C. Fishbein, Dilip K. Kondepudi, Gordon A. Melson,
   Ronald E. Noftle, Robert L. Swofford, Mark E. Welker
Associate Professors Bradley T. Jones, Abdessadek Lachgar
Assistant Professors Christa L. Colyer, Steven C. Haefner, Angela Glisan King,
   S. Bruce King, Richard A. Manderville
Visiting Professors Neal E. Busch, Herman J. Benezet

1999–2000
Bradley T. Jones, Chair
Wake Forest Professors Roger A. Hegstrom, Willie L. Hinze
Professors James C. Fishbein, Dilip K. Kondepudi, Gordon A. Melson,
   Ronald E. Noftle, Robert L. Swofford, Mark E. Welker
Associate Professors Bradley T. Jones, Abdessadek Lachgar
Assistant Professors Christa L. Colyer, Steven C. Haefner, Angela Glisan King,
   S. Bruce King, Richard A. Manderville
Visiting Professors Thomas Buhse, Alexandra MacDermott, Catherine Owens Welder

2000–2001
Bradley T. Jones, Chair
Wake Forest Professors Roger A. Hegstrom, Willie L. Hinze, Mark E. Welker
Professors Dilip K. Kondepudi, Gordon A. Melson, Ronald E. Noftle,
    Robert L. Swofford
Associate Professors Bradley T. Jones, Abdessadek Lachgar
Assistant Professors Ulrich Bierbach, Christa L. Colyer, Steven C. Haefner,
    S. Bruce King, Richard A. Manderville
Visiting Professors Nanette A. Stevens, Catherine Owens Welder
Senior Lecturer Angela Glisan King

2001–2002
Bradley T. Jones, Chair
Wake Forest Professors Roger A. Hegstrom, Willie L. Hinze, Mark E. Welker
Professors Bradley T. Jones, Dilip K. Kondepudi, Gordon A. Melson,
    Ronald E. Noftle, Robert L. Swofford
Associate Professors S. Bruce King, Abdessadek Lachgar, Richard A. Manderville
Assistant Professors Rebecca W. Alexander, Ulrich Bierbach, Christa L. Colyer,
    Paul B. Jones
Visiting Professors Nanette A. Stevens, Catherine Owens Welder
Senior Lecturer Angela Glisan King

2002–2003
Bradley T. Jones, Chair
Wake Forest Professors Willie L. Hinze, Mark E. Welker
Professors Bradley T. Jones, Dilip K. Kondepudi, Gordon A. Melson,
    Ronald E. Noftle, Robert L. Swofford
Associate Professors S. Bruce King (Z. Smith Reynolds Faculty Fellow),
    Abdessadek Lachgar, Richard A. Manderville
Assistant Professors Rebecca W. Alexander, Ulrich Bierbach, Christa L. Colyer,
    Paul B. Jones
Visiting Assistant Professors Nanette A. Stevens, Catherine Owens Welder
Senior Lecturer Angela Glisan King

2003–2004
Bradley T. Jones, Chair
Wake Forest Professors Willie L. Hinze, Dilip K. Kondepudi, Mark E. Welker
Professors Bradley T. Jones, Gordon A. Melson, Ronald E. Noftle, Robert L.
    Swofford
Associate Professors S. Bruce King (Z. Smith Reynolds Faculty Fellow),
    Abdessadek Lachgar, Richard A. Manderville
Assistant Professors Rebecca W. Alexander, Ulrich Bierbach, Bernard A. Brown,
    Christa L. Colyer (Dunn-Riley Jr. Professor), Paul B. Jones
Visiting Professor Harold Bell
Visiting Assistant Professors Nanette A. Stevens, Catherine Owens Welder
Senior Lecturer Angela Glisan King

2004–2005
Bradley T. Jones, Chair
Wake Forest Professors Willie L. Hinze, Dilip K. Kondepudi, Mark E. Welker
Professors Bradley T. Jones, Gordon A. Melson, Ronald E. Noftle,
    Robert L. Swofford
Associate Professors S. Bruce King (Z. Smith Reynolds Faculty Fellow),
    Abdessadek Lachgar, Richard A. Manderville (Junior Faculty Fellow)
Assistant Professors Rebecca W. Alexander, Ulrich Bierbach, Bernard A. Brown,
    Paul B. Jones, Akbar Salam
Visiting Assistant Professors Frank Quina, Albert Rivers, Catherine Owens Welder
Adjunct Associate Professor Ann Glenn
Senior Lecturer Angela Glisan King

2005–2006
Bradley T. Jones, Chair
Wake Forest Professors Willie L. Hinze, Dilip K. Kondepudi, Mark E. Welker
Professors Bradley T. Jones, Abdessadek Lachgar, Gordon A. Melson,
    Ronald E. Noftle, Robert L. Swofford
Associate Professors Christa L. Colyer, S. Bruce King (Z. Smith Reynolds Faculty
    Fellow), Richard A. Manderville (Junior Faculty Fellow)
Assistant Professors Rebecca W. Alexander, Ulrich Bierbach, Bernard A. Brown,
    Paul B. Jones, Akbar Salam
Visiting Assistant Professors Latifa Chahoua, Jian Dai, Frank Quina, Albert Rivers
Senior Lecturer Angela Glisan King

CLASSICAL LANGUAGES (CLA)
1983–1984
Robert W. Ulery Jr., Chair
Professor Carl V. Harris
Associate Professors John L. Andronica, Robert W. Ulery Jr.
Visiting Assistant Professor Christopher P. Frost
Instructor John E. Rowland

1984–1985
Robert W. Ulery Jr., Chair
Professor Carl V. Harris
Associate Professors John L. Andronica, Robert W. Ulery Jr.
Visiting Assistant Professors Christopher P. Frost, Mary L. B. Pendergraft
Instructor John E. Rowland

1985–1986
Robert W. Ulery Jr., Chair
Professor Carl V. Harris
Associate Professors John L. Andronica, Robert W. Ulery Jr.
Visiting Assistant Professors Christopher P. Frost, John E. Rowland

1986–1987
Robert W. Ulery Jr., Chair
Professor Carl V. Harris
Associate Professors John L. Andronica, Robert W. Ulery Jr.
Visiting Assistant Professors Teri E. Marsh, John E. Rowland

1987–1988
John L. Andronica, Chair
Professor Carl V. Harris
Associate Professors John L. Andronica, Robert W. Ulery Jr.
Visiting Assistant Professors Teri E. Marsh, John E. Rowland

1988–1989
John L. Andronica, Chair
Professors John L. Andronica, Carl V. Harris
Associate Professor Robert W. Ulery Jr.
Visiting Assistant Professors Teri E. Marsh, John E. Rowland

1989–1990
John L. Andronica, Chair
Professors John L. Andronica, Carl V. Harris
Associate Professor Robert W. Ulery Jr.
Assistant Professor Mary L. B. Pendergraft
Visiting Assistant Professors James G. DeVoto, Teri E. Marsh, James T. Powell

1990–1992
John L. Andronica, Chair
Professors John L. Andronica, Robert W. Ulery Jr.
Assistant Professors Mary L. B. Pendergraft, James T. Powell
Visiting Assistant Professor James G. DeVoto

1992–1993
John L. Andronica, Chair
Professors John L. Andronica, Robert W. Ulery Jr.
Assistant Professors Mary L. B. Pendergraft, James T. Powell
Visiting Assistant Professor David W. Frauenfelder

1993–1995
John L. Andronica, Chair
Professors John L. Andronica, Robert W. Ulery Jr.
Assistant Professors Mary L. B. Pendergraft, James T. Powell

1995–1996
John L. Andronica, Chair
Professors John L. Andronica, Robert W. Ulery Jr.

Associate Professor Mary L. B. Pendergraft
Assistant Professor James T. Powell

1996–1997
John L. Andronica, Chair
Professors John L. Andronica, Robert W. Ulery Jr.
Associate Professor Mary L. B. Pendergraft
Assistant Professor James T. Powell
Visiting Assistant Professor Laurie S. Cosgriff

1997–1998
John L. Andronica, Chair
Professors John L. Andronica, Robert W. Ulery Jr.
Associate Professor Mary L. B. Pendergraft
Assistant Professor James T. Powell

1998–2000
John L. Andronica, Chair
Professors John L. Andronica, Robert W. Ulery Jr.
Associate Professors Mary L. B. Pendergraft, James T. Powell

2000–2002
John L. Andronica, Chair
Professors John L. Andronica, Robert W. Ulery Jr.
Associate Professors Mary L. B. Pendergraft, James T. Powell
Adjunct Assistant Professor Patricia Marshall

2002–2003
John L. Andronica, Chair
Professors John L. Andronica, Robert W. Ulery Jr.
Associate Professors Mary L. B. Pendergraft, James T. Powell

2003–2004
John L. Andronica, Chair
Professors John L. Andronica, Robert W. Ulery Jr.
Associate Professors Mary L. B. Pendergraft, James T. Powell
Adjunct Instructor Dorothy M. Westmoreland

2004–2005
John L. Andronica, Chair
Professors John L. Andronica, Robert W. Ulery Jr.
Associate Professors Mary L. B. Pendergraft, James T. Powell
Visiting Assistant Professor Jill Chmielewski
Adjunct Instructor Dorothy M. Westmoreland

2005–2006
John L. Andronica, Chair
Professors John L. Andronica, Robert W. Ulery Jr.
Associate Professors Mary L. B. Pendergraft, James T. Powell
Adjunct Assistant Professor Darlene R. May
Adjunct Instructor Dorothy M. Westmoreland
Visiting Egyptian Fulbright Scholar Reda Bedeir

COMMUNICATION (COM)

(The Department of Communication was originally the Department of Speech Communication and Theatre Arts until 1991–1992, when it became the Department of Speech Communication. This change was first noted in the 1992–1993 *Bulletin*. In 1995–1996 it became the Department of Communication. The change was first noted in the 1996–1997 *Bulletin*.)

1992–1993
Michael D. Hazen, Chair
Professors Julian C. Burroughs Jr., Michael D. Hazen
Associate Professors Allan D. Louden, Jill Jordan McMillan
Assistant Professor John T. Llewellyn
Visiting Assistant Professor Randall G. Rogan
Adjunct Professor Jo Whitten May
Instructors Mary M. Dalton, Margaret D. Zulick
Adjunct Instructors Susan L. Faust, Melanie H. Louden, Karen L. Oxendine
Debate Coach Ross K. Smith

1993–1994
Michael D. Hazen, Chair
Professors Julian C. Burroughs Jr., Michael D. Hazen
Associate Professors Allan D. Louden, Jill Jordan McMillan
Assistant Professors John T. Llewellyn, Randall G. Rogan
Adjunct Professor Jo Whitten May
Instructors Mary M. Dalton, Margaret D. Zulick
Visiting Instructor Andrew W. Leslie
Adjunct Instructors Susan L. Faust, Mardene G. Morykwas, Karen L. Oxendine
Debate Coach Ross K. Smith

1994–1995
Michael D. Hazen, Chair
Professors Julian C. Burroughs Jr., Michael D. Hazen
Associate Professors Allan D. Louden, Jill Jordan McMillan
Assistant Professors John T. Llewellyn, Randall G. Rogan, Margaret D. Zulick
Adjunct Professor Jo Whitten May
Instructor Mary M. Dalton

Visiting Instructor Andrew W. Leslie
Adjunct Instructors Susan L. Faust, Mardene G. Morykwas, Karen L. Oxendine
Debate Coach Ross K. Smith

1995–1996
Michael D. Hazen, Chair
J. Tylee Wilson Professor of Business Ethics Michael J. Hyde
Professor Michael D. Hazen
Associate Professors Allan D. Louden, Jill Jordan McMillan
Assistant Professors John T. Llewellyn, Ananda Mitra, Randall G. Rogan,
    Margaret D. Zulick
Visiting Assistant Professor Kathleen Hoffman
Adjunct Professor Jo Whitten May
Instructor Mary M. Dalton
Adjunct Instructors Susan L. Faust, Denise Franklin, Mardene G. Morykwas,
    Karen L. Oxendine
Debate Coach Ross K. Smith

1996–1997
Michael D. Hazen, Chair
University Professor of Communication Ethics Michael J. Hyde
Professor Michael D. Hazen
Associate Professors Allan D. Louden, Jill Jordan McMillan
Assistant Professors John T. Llewellyn, Ananda Mitra, Randall G. Rogan,
    Margaret D. Zulick
Adjunct Professor Jo Whitten May
Instructor Mary M. Dalton
Adjunct Instructors Susan L. Faust, Denise Franklin, Mardene G. Morykwas,
    Dee Oseroff-Varnell, Karen L. Oxendine
Debate Coach Ross K. Smith

1997–1998
Michael D. Hazen, Chair
University Professor of Communication Ethics Michael J. Hyde
Professor Michael D. Hazen
Associate Professors Allan D. Louden, Jill Jordan McMillan, Randall G. Rogan
Assistant Professors John T. Llewellyn, Ananda Mitra, Eric K. Watts,
    Margaret D. Zulick
Visiting Assistant Professor Mary M. Dalton
Adjunct Professor Jo Whitten May
Adjunct Assistant Professors Andrew W. Leslie, Dee Oseroff-Varnell
Adjunct Instructors Susan L. Faust, Denise Franklin, Joanna F. Hudson,
    Ernest S. Jarrett, Mardene G. Morykwas, Karen L. Oxendine
Debate Coach Ross K. Smith

1998–1999
Michael D. Hazen, Chair
University Distinguished Chair in Communication Ethics and Professor of
    Communication Ethics Michael J. Hyde
Professors Michael D. Hazen, Jill Jordan McMillan
Associate Professors Allan D. Louden, Randall G. Rogan, Margaret D. Zulick
Assistant Professors John T. Llewellyn, Ananda Mitra, Eric K. Watts
Visiting Assistant Professor Mary M. Dalton
Adjunct Professor Jo Whitten May
Adjunct Assistant Professors Andrew W. Leslie, Dee Oseroff-Varnell
Visiting Instructor Theresa R. Castor
Adjunct Instructors Susan L. Faust, Denise Franklin, Ernest S. Jarrett,
    Mardene G. Morykwas, Karen L. Oxendine
Debate Coach Ross K. Smith

1999–2000
Michael D. Hazen, Chair
University Distinguished Chair in Communication Ethics and
    Professor of Communication Ethics Michael J. Hyde
Professors Michael D. Hazen, Jill Jordan McMillan
Associate Professors John T. Llewellyn, Allan D. Louden, Randall G. Rogan,
    Margaret D. Zulick
Assistant Professors Ananda Mitra, Eric K. Watts
Visiting Assistant Professors Mary M. Dalton, Betty LaFrance
Adjunct Professor Jo Whitten May
Adjunct Assistant Professors Steven M. Giles, Andrew W. Leslie, Dee
    Oseroff-Varnell
Adjunct Instructors Anne Boozell, Susan L. Faust, Denise Franklin, Ernest S. Jarrett,
    Mardene G. Morykwas, Karen L. Oxendine
Debate Coach Ross K. Smith

2000–2001
Michael D. Hazen, Chair
University Distinguished Chair in Communication Ethics and
    Professor of Communication Michael J. Hyde
Professors Michael D. Hazen, Jill Jordan McMillan
Associate Professors John T. Llewellyn, Allan D. Louden, Randall G. Rogan,
    Margaret D. Zulick
Assistant Professors Betty LaFrance, Ananda Mitra, Eric K. Watts
Visiting Assistant Professor Mary M. Dalton
Adjunct Professor Jo Whitten May
Adjunct Assistant Professors Steven M. Giles, Andrew W. Leslie, Dee
    Oseroff-Varnell
Adjunct Instructors Anne Boozell, Susan L. Faust, Denise Franklin,
    Ernest S. Jarrett, Mardene G. Morykwas, Karen L. Oxendine
Debate Coach Ross K. Smith

2001–2002
Randall G. Rogan, Chair
University Distinguished Chair in Communication Ethics and
   Professor of Communication Michael J. Hyde
Professors Michael D. Hazen, Jill Jordan McMillan
Associate Professors John T. Llewellyn, Allan D. Louden, Ananda Mitra,
   Randall G. Rogan, Margaret D. Zulick
Assistant Professors Mary M. Dalton, Betty LaFrance, Eric K. Watts
Visiting Assistant Professors Elizabeth M. Davis, Steven M. Giles
Adjunct Assistant Professor Dee Oseroff-Varnell
Visiting Instructor Deepa Kumar
Adjunct Instructors Anne Boozell, Susan L. Faust, Denise Franklin,
   Ernest S. Jarrett, Mardene G. Morykwas, Karen L. Oxendine
Debate Coach Ross K. Smith

2002–2003
Randall G. Rogan, Chair
University Distinguished Chair in Communication Ethics and
   Professor of Communication Michael J. Hyde
Professors Michael D. Hazen, Jill Jordan McMillan
Associate Professors John T. Llewellyn, Allan D. Louden, Ananda Mitra,
   Randall G. Rogan, Margaret D. Zulick
Assistant Professors Mary M. Dalton, Eric K. Watts
Visiting Assistant Professors Geoffrey Baym, Deepa Kumar, Claude Miller
Adjunct Assistant Professors Steven M. Giles, Dee Oseroff-Varnell
Instructor Ernest S. Jarrett
Adjunct Instructors Wayne R. Bills, Connie Chesner, Susan L. Faust,
   Denise Franklin, Karen L. Oxendine
Debate Coach Ross K. Smith

2003–2004
Randall G. Rogan, Chair
University Distinguished Chair in Communication Ethics and
   Professor of Communication Michael J. Hyde
Professors Michael D. Hazen, Jill Jordan McMillan
Associate Professors John T. Llewellyn, Allan D. Louden, Ananda Mitra,
   Randall G. Rogan, Eric K. Watts, Margaret D. Zulick
Assistant Professors Mary M. Dalton, Steven M. Giles
Visiting Assistant Professor Deepa Kumar
Adjunct Assistant Professor Dee Oseroff-Varnell
Instructor Ernest S. Jarrett
Adjunct Instructors Wayne R. Bills, Connie Chesner, Robert Costner,
   Susan L. Faust
Debate Coach Ross K. Smith

2004–2005
Randall G. Rogan, Chair
University Distinguished Chair in Communication Ethics and
    Professor of Communication Michael J. Hyde
Professors Michael D. Hazen, Jill Jordan McMillan
Associate Professors John T. Llewellyn, Allan D. Louden, Ananda Mitra,
    Randall G. Rogan, Eric K. Watts, Margaret D. Zulick
Assistant Professors Mary M. Dalton, Steven M. Giles, Don Helme
Visiting Assistant Professor Deepa Kumar
Adjunct Assistant Professor Dee Oseroff-Varnell
Instructor Ernest S. Jarrett
Adjunct Instructors Wayne R. Bills, Connie Chesner, Susan L. Faust
Lecturer Brett Ingram
Debate Coach Ross K. Smith

2005–2006
Randall G. Rogan, Chair
Reynolds Professor of Film Studies and Professor of Communication Peter Brunette
University Distinguished Chair in Communication Ethics and
    Professor of Communication Michael J. Hyde
Professors Michael D. Hazen, Jill Jordan McMillan
Associate Professors John T. Llewellyn, Allan D. Louden, Ananda Mitra,
    Randall G. Rogan, Eric K. Watts, Margaret D. Zulick
Assistant Professors Mary M. Dalton, Steven M. Giles, Don Helme
Visiting Associate Professor Marina Krcmar
Adjunct Assistant Professor Dee Oseroff-Varnell
Instructor Ernest S. Jarrett
Adjunct Instructors Wayne R. Bills, Connie Chesner, Susan L. Faust,
    Janel Leone, Danielle Powell
Lecturer Brett Ingram
Visiting Lecturer F. Curtis Gaston
Debate Coach Ross K. Smith

COMPUTER SCIENCE (CSC)

(The Department of Computer Science was originally the Department of Mathematics and Computer Science until 1999–2000. The change was first listed in the 2000–2001 *Bulletin*.)

2000–2001
Jennifer J. Burg, Chair
Reynolds Professor Robert J. Plemmons
Associate Professors Daniel Cañas, David J. John, Stan J. Thomas, Todd C.
    Torgensen
Assistant Professors Jennifer J. Burg, Yaorong Ge, Paul Hemler
Instructor Patricia Y. Underhill

2001–2002
Jennifer J. Burg, Chair
Reynolds Professor Robert J. Plemmons
Associate Professors Jennifer J. Burg, Daniel Cañas, David J. John,
    Stan J. Thomas, Todd C. Torgensen
Assistant Professors Errin W. Fulp, Yaorong Ge, Paul Hemler

2002–2003
Jennifer J. Burg, Chair
Reynolds Professor Robert J. Plemmons
Associate Professors Jennifer J. Burg, Daniel Cañas, David J. John,
    Stan J. Thomas, Todd C. Torgensen (Dana Faculty Fellow)
Assistant Professors Errin W. Fulp, Yaorong Ge, Paul Hemler
Visiting Associate Professor Donna J. Williams
Lecturer in Digital Media Yue-Ling Wong

2003–2004
Jennifer J. Burg, Chair
Reynolds Professor Robert J. Plemmons
Associate Professors Jennifer J. Burg, Daniel Cañas, David J. John,
    Stan J. Thomas, Todd C. Torgensen
Assistant Professors Errin W. Fulp, Paul Hemler, V. Paúl Pauca
Visiting Associate Professor Donna J. Williams
Lecturer in Digital Media Yue-Ling Wong

2004–2005
Jennifer J. Burg, Chair
Reynolds Professor Robert J. Plemmons
Reynolds Professor of Computational Biophysics Jacquelyn S. Fetrow
Associate Professors Jennifer J. Burg, Daniel Cañas, David J. John,
    Stan J. Thomas, Todd C. Torgensen
Assistant Professors Errin W. Fulp, Paul Hemler, V. Paúl Pauca
Adjunct Assistant Professor Timothy E. Miller
Lecturer in Digital Media Yue-Ling Wong

2005–2006
Stan J. Thomas, Chair
Reynolds Professor Robert J. Plemmons
Reynolds Professor of Computational Biophysics Jacquelyn S. Fetrow
Associate Professors Jennifer J. Burg, Daniel Cañas, David J. John,
    Stan J. Thomas, Todd C. Torgensen
Assistant Professors Errin W. Fulp, V. Paúl Pauca
Visiting Assistant Professor William H. Turkett Jr.
Adjunct Assistant Professor Timothy E. Miller
Lecturer in Digital Media Yue-Ling Wong

COUNSELING (CNS)

(The Department of Counseling began in 2003–2004. Until then the faculty were part of the Department of Education. The change first appears in the 2004–2005 *Bulletin*.)

2004–2005
Samuel T. Gladding, Chair
Professors John P. Anderson, Samuel T. Gladding
Associate Professor Donna A. Henderson
Assistant Professors Debbie W. Newsome, Laura J. Veach
Adjunct Assistant Professors Alan S. Cameron, Marianne A. Schubert,
    Elizabeth H. Taylor
Instructors Johnne W. Armentrout, Pamela R. Karr

2005–2006
Samuel T. Gladding, Chair
Professors John P. Anderson, Samuel T. Gladding
Associate Professor Donna A. Henderson
Assistant Professors Debbie W. Newsome, Laura J. Veach
Adjunct Assistant Professors Leslie Armeniox, Robert Daniel, Elizabeth H. Taylor
Instructors Johnne W. Armentrout, Pamela R. Karr

CULTURAL RESOURCE PRESERVATION (CRP)

Interdisciplinary Minor

1993–2004
Ned Woodall (Anthropology), Coordinator

2004–2006
Paul Thacker (Anthropology), Coordinator

EARLY CHRISTIAN STUDIES

Interdisciplinary Minor

1993–2006
Mary L. B. Pendergraft (Classical Languages) and **Kenneth G. Hoglund** (Religion),
    Coordinators

EAST ASIAN LANGUAGES AND CULTURES (EAL)

(The East Asian Languages and Literatures Program became the Department of East Asian Languages and Cultures in 2003–2004. The change was first listed in the 2004–2005 *Bulletin*.)

1992–1993
Patrick Moran, Coordinator
Assistant Professors Janice Bardsley and Patrick Moran

1993–1994
Janice Bardsley, Coordinator
Assistant Professors Janice Bardsley and Patrick Moran

1994–1995
Patrick Moran, Coordinator
Assistant Professors Janice Bardsley and Patrick Moran

1995–1997
Assistant Professor Patrick Moran, Coordinator
Instructor David P. Phillips

1997–1999
Assistant Professor Patrick Moran, Coordinator
Assistant Professor David P. Phillips
Visiting Assistant Professor Kyoko T. Wilkerson

1999–2002
Associate Professor Patrick Moran, Coordinator
Assistant Professor David P. Phillips
Visiting Assistant Professor Yasuko Takata

2002–2003
Patrick Moran, Coordinator
Associate Professors Patrick Moran, David P. Phillips
Assistant Professor Yaohua Shi
Lecturer Yasuko Takata

2003–2004
David P. Phillips, Coordinator
Associate Professors Patrick Moran, David P. Phillips
Assistant Professor Yaohua Shi
Lecturer Yasuko T. Rollings
Instructor Grace Ku

2004–2005
David P. Phillips, Chair
Associate Professors Patrick Moran, David P. Phillips
Assistant Professor Yaohua Shi
Lecturer Yasuko T. Rollings
Instructor Grace Ku

2005–2006
David P. Phillips, Chair
Associate Professors Patrick Moran, David P. Phillips
Assistant Professor Yaohua Shi

Senior Lecturer Yasuko T. Rollings
Instructor Grace Ku

EAST ASIAN STUDIES (EAS)

Interdisciplinary Minor
   (East Asian Studies was originally a Foreign Area Study until it became an
interdisciplinary minor in 2003–2004. The change was first listed in the 2004–2005
Bulletin.)

1993–1997
Win-chiat Lee (Philosophy), Coordinator

1998–2000
Wei-chin Lee (Politics), Coordinator

2000–2004
Charles H. Kennedy (Political Science), Coordinator

2004–2006
David P. Phillips (East Asian Languages and Cultures), Coordinator

ECONOMICS (ECN)

1983–1984
John C. Moorhouse, Chair
Professors William D. Grampp, John C. Moorhouse, J. Van Wagstaff
Associate Professor Donald E. Frey
Assistant Professors Diana L. Fuguitt, J. Daniel Hammond, Richard P. Hydell
Visiting Assistant Professor Claire Holton Hammond
Instructor Tony H. Elavia

1984–1985
John C. Moorhouse, Chair
Professors Walter Adams, Donald E. Frey, John C. Moorhouse, J. Van Wagstaff
Associate Professor J. Daniel Hammond
Assistant Professors Tony H. Elavia, Diana L. Fuguitt, Richard P. Hydell
Visiting Assistant Professor Claire Holton Hammond
Visiting Instructors J. Rody Borg, John Lodewijks

1985–1986
John C. Moorhouse, Chair
Professors Donald E. Frey, John C. Moorhouse, J. Van Wagstaff
Associate Professor J. Daniel Hammond
Assistant Professors Tony H. Elavia, Claire Holton Hammond, Richard P. Hydell
Visiting Instructors John Lodewijks, Steven H. Smith

1986–1987
Donald E. Frey, Chair
Reynolds Professor John H. Wood
Professors Donald E. Frey, John C. Moorhouse, J. Van Wagstaff
Associate Professor J. Daniel Hammond
Assistant Professors Tony H. Elavia, Claire Holton Hammond, Richard P. Hydell
Instructor John B. Crihfield
Visiting Instructor Kathleen Neal

1987–1988
Donald E. Frey, Chair
Reynolds Professor John H. Wood
Professors Donald E. Frey, John C. Moorhouse, J. Van Wagstaff
Associate Professor J. Daniel Hammond
Assistant Professors John B. Crihfield, Tony H. Elavia, Claire Holton Hammond,
    Michael S. Lawlor, Perry L. Patterson

1988–1989
Donald E. Frey, Chair
Reynolds Professor John H. Wood
Professors Donald E. Frey, John C. Moorhouse, J. Van Wagstaff
Associate Professors Claire Holton Hammond, J. Daniel Hammond
Assistant Professors John B. Crihfield, Michael S. Lawlor, Perry L. Patterson
Visiting Assistant Professor Gary R. Albrecht
Instructor Gregory A. Lilly

1989–1990
Donald E. Frey, Chair
Reynolds Professor John H. Wood
Professors Donald E. Frey, John C. Moorhouse, J. Van Wagstaff
Associate Professors Claire Holton Hammond, J. Daniel Hammond
Assistant Professors John B. Crihfield, Michael S. Lawlor, Perry L. Patterson
Visiting Assistant Professors Gary R. Albrecht, Art Goldsmith, Gregory A. Lilly

1990–1991
J. Daniel Hammond, Chair
Reynolds Professor John H. Wood
Professors Donald E. Frey, John C. Moorhouse, J. Van Wagstaff
Associate Professors Claire Holton Hammond, J. Daniel Hammond
Assistant Professors Allin F. Cottrell, Michael S. Lawlor, Perry L. Patterson
Visiting Assistant Professor Gregory A. Lilly
Instructors Paul F. Huck, Glenn M. Lail

1991–1992
J. Daniel Hammond, Chair
Reynolds Professor John H. Wood

Professors David G. Brown, Donald E. Frey, John C. Moorhouse, J. Van Wagstaff
Associate Professors Claire Holton Hammond, J. Daniel Hammond
Assistant Professors Allin F. Cottrell, Michael S. Lawlor, Perry L. Patterson
Visiting Assistant Professor Serguei Miassoedov
Adjunct Associate Professor Gary R. Albrecht
Instructors Paul F. Huck, Marios Karayannis, Glenn M. Lail

1992–1993
J. Daniel Hammond, Chair
Reynolds Professor John H. Wood
Professors David G. Brown, Donald E. Frey, J. Daniel Hammond,
    John C. Moorhouse, J. Van Wagstaff
Associate Professors Claire Holton Hammond, Michael S. Lawlor,
    Perry L. Patterson
Assistant Professors Allin F. Cottrell, Robert M. Whaples
Adjunct Associate Professor Gary R. Albrecht
Instructors Paul F. Huck

1993–1994
J. Daniel Hammond, Chair
Reynolds Professor John H. Wood
Professors David G. Brown, Donald E. Frey, J. Daniel Hammond,
    John C. Moorhouse
Associate Professors Claire Holton Hammond, Michael S. Lawlor,
    Perry L. Patterson
Assistant Professors Allin F. Cottrell, Paul F. Huck, Robert M. Whaples
Visiting Assistant Professor J. Farley Ordovensky
Adjunct Associate Professor Gary R. Albrecht

1994–1995
Claire Holton Hammond, Chair
Reynolds Professor John H. Wood
Professors David G. Brown, Donald E. Frey, J. Daniel Hammond,
    John C. Moorhouse
Associate Professors Allin F. Cottrell, Claire Holton Hammond,
    Michael S. Lawlor, Perry L. Patterson
Assistant Professors Paul F. Huck, Robert M. Whaples, Andrew J. Yates
Adjunct Associate Professor Gary R. Albrecht

1995–1996
Claire Holton Hammond, Chair
Reynolds Professor John H. Wood
Professors David G. Brown, Donald E. Frey, J. Daniel Hammond,
    John C. Moorhouse
Associate Professors Allin F. Cottrell, Claire Holton Hammond,
    Michael S. Lawlor, Perry L. Patterson

Assistant Professors Paul F. Huck, Robert M. Whaples, Andrew J. Yates
Visiting Assistant Professors Hakan Berument, Jac C. Heckelman
Adjunct Associate Professor Gary R. Albrecht

1996–1997
Claire Holton Hammond, Chair
Reynolds Professor John H. Wood
Professors David G. Brown, Donald E. Frey, J. Daniel Hammond,
    John C. Moorhouse
Associate Professors Allin F. Cottrell, Claire Holton Hammond,
    Michael S. Lawlor, Perry L. Patterson
Assistant Professors Paul F. Huck, Robert M. Whaples, Andrew J. Yates
Visiting Assistant Professor Michael H. Slotkin
Adjunct Associate Professor Gary R. Albrecht

1997–1998
Claire Holton Hammond, Chair
Archie Carroll Professor of Ethical Leadership John C. Moorhouse
Reynolds Professor John H. Wood
Professors David G. Brown, Donald E. Frey, J. Daniel Hammond
Associate Professors Allin F. Cottrell, Claire Holton Hammond,
    Michael S. Lawlor, Perry L. Patterson, Robert M. Whaples
Assistant Professors Jac C. Heckelman, Andrew J. Yates
Visiting Assistant Professor John W. Dawson
Adjunct Associate Professor Gary R. Albrecht

1998–1999
Claire Holton Hammond, Chair
Archie Carroll Professor of Ethical Leadership John C. Moorhouse
Reynolds Professor John H. Wood
Professors David G. Brown, Donald E. Frey, J. Daniel Hammond
Associate Professors Allin F. Cottrell, Claire Holton Hammond,
    Michael S. Lawlor, Perry L. Patterson, Robert M. Whaples
Assistant Professors Jac C. Heckelman, Andrew J. Yates
Visiting Assistant Professor John W. Dawson
Instructor Chiara Gratton

1999–2001
Allin F. Cottrell, Chair
Archie Carroll Professor of Ethical Leadership John C. Moorhouse
Reynolds Professor John H. Wood
Professors David G. Brown, Allin F. Cottrell, Donald E. Frey,
    Claire Holton Hammond, J. Daniel Hammond, Michael S. Lawlor,
    Perry L. Patterson
Associate Professor Robert M. Whaples

Assistant Professors Sylvain H. Boko, Jac C. Heckelman
Instructor Richard DePolt

2001–2002
Allin F. Cottrell, Chair
Archie Carroll Professor of Ethical Leadership John C. Moorhouse
Reynolds Professor John H. Wood
Professors David G. Brown, Allin F. Cottrell, Donald E. Frey,
    Claire Holton Hammond, J. Daniel Hammond, Michael S. Lawlor,
    Perry L. Patterson
Associate Professor Robert M. Whaples
Assistant Professors Sylvain H. Boko, Jac C. Heckelman
Instructors Frederick H. Chen, Richard DePolt

2002–2003
Allin F. Cottrell, Chair
Archie Carroll Professor of Ethical Leadership John C. Moorhouse
Reynolds Professor John H. Wood
Professors David G. Brown, Allin F. Cottrell, Donald E. Frey,
    Claire Holton Hammond, J. Daniel Hammond, Michael S. Lawlor,
    Perry L. Patterson
Associate Professors Jac C. Heckelman, Robert M. Whaples
Assistant Professor Sylvain H. Boko
Instructors Frederick H. Chen, Richard DePolt

2003–2004
Allin F. Cottrell, Chair
Archie Carroll Professor of Ethical Leadership John C. Moorhouse
Reynolds Professor John H. Wood
Professors David G. Brown, Allin F. Cottrell, Donald E. Frey,
    Claire Holton Hammond, J. Daniel Hammond, Michael S. Lawlor,
    Perry L. Patterson
Associate Professors Jac C. Heckelman (McCulloch Family Fellow),
    Robert M. Whaples
Assistant Professors Sylvain H. Boko, Frederick H. Chen
Instructor Richard DePolt

2004–2005
Allin F. Cottrell, Chair
Archie Carroll Professor of Ethical Leadership John C. Moorhouse
Reynolds Professor John H. Wood
Professors Allin F. Cottrell, Donald E. Frey, Claire Holton Hammond,
    J. Daniel Hammond, Michael S. Lawlor, Perry L. Patterson
Associate Professors Sylvain H. Boko, Jac C. Heckelman
    (McCulloch Family Fellow), Robert M. Whaples

Assistant Professor Frederick H. Chen
Instructor Richard DePolt

2005–2006
Allin F. Cottrell, Chair
Archie Carroll Professor of Ethical Leadership John C. Moorhouse
Reynolds Professor John H. Wood
Professors Allin F. Cottrell, Donald E. Frey, Claire Holton Hammond, J. Daniel
    Hammond, Michael S. Lawlor, Perry L. Patterson, Robert M. Whaples
Associate Professors Sylvain H. Boko, Jac C. Heckelman (McCulloch Family Fellow)
Assistant Professor Frederick H. Chen
Visiting Assistant Professor Rushad Faridi
Visiting Instructor Todd McFall

EDUCATION (EDU)

1983–1984
Joseph O. Milner, Chair
Professors Thomas M. Elmore, John E. Parker Jr., Herman J. Preseren,
    J. Don Reeves
Associate Professors John H. Litcher, Joseph O. Milner
Assistant Professors Patricia M. Cunningham, Linda N. Nielsen,
    Leonard P. Roberge
Instructor Ann C. Leonard
Lecturers Marianne A. Schubert, Stuart Wright
Visiting Lecturers Joseph Dodson, Nancy Dominick, Richard I. Tirrell

1984–1985
Joseph O. Milner, Chair
Professors Thomas M. Elmore, John E. Parker Jr., J. Don Reeves
Associate Professors Patricia M. Cunningham, John H. Litcher,
    Joseph O. Milner, Leonard P. Roberge
Assistant Professors Robert H. Evans, Linda N. Nielsen
Instructor Dorothy P. Hall
Lecturers Brian M. Austin, G. Dianne Mitchell, Marianne A. Schubert,
    Stuart Wright
Visiting Lecturer Richard I. Tirrell

1985–1986
Joseph O. Milner, Chair
Professors Thomas M. Elmore, John E. Parker Jr., J. Don Reeves
Associate Professors Patricia M. Cunningham, John H. Litcher,
    Joseph O. Milner, Linda N. Nielsen, Leonard P. Roberge
Assistant Professor Robert H. Evans
Instructor Dorothy P. Hall

Lecturers Brian M. Austin, G. Dianne Mitchell, Marianne A. Schubert,
　　Stuart Wright
Visiting Lecturer Richard I. Tirrell

1986–1987
Joseph O. Milner, Chair
Professors Thomas M. Elmore, John H. Litcher, John E. Parker Jr., J. Don Reeves
Associate Professors Patricia M. Cunningham, Joseph O. Milner, Linda N. Nielsen,
　　Leonard P. Roberge
Assistant Professor Robert H. Evans
Instructors Dorothy P. Hall, Katherine Mullett
Lecturers Brian M. Austin, G. Dianne Mitchell, Marianne A. Schubert,
　　Stuart Wright
Visiting Lecturer Richard I. Tirrell

1987–1988
Joseph O. Milner, Chair
Professors Thomas M. Elmore, John H. Litcher, Joseph O. Milner,
　　John E. Parker Jr., J. Don Reeves
Associate Professors Patricia M. Cunningham, Linda N. Nielsen,
　　Leonard P. Roberge
Assistant Professor Robert H. Evans
Instructor Katherine Mullett
Lecturers Brian M. Austin, G. Dianne Mitchell, Marianne A. Schubert,
　　Stuart Wright

1988–1989
Joseph O. Milner, Chair
Professors Thomas M. Elmore, John H. Litcher, Joseph O. Milner, J. Don Reeves
Associate Professors Patricia M. Cunningham, Robert H. Evans, Linda N. Nielsen,
　　Leonard P. Roberge
Instructor Nancy K. Solomon
Lecturers Brian M. Austin, G. Dianne Mitchell, Marianne A. Schubert,
　　Stuart Wright

1989–1990
Joseph O. Milner, Chair
Professors Thomas M. Elmore, John H. Litcher, Joseph O. Milner, J. Don Reeves
Associate Professors Patricia M. Cunningham, Robert H. Evans, Linda N. Nielsen,
　　Leonard P. Roberge
Instructor Nancy K. Solomon
Visiting Instructor H. Michael Britt
Lecturers G. Dianne Mitchell, Marianne A. Schubert
Visiting Lecturer Georgia S. Lawrence

1990–1991
Joseph O. Milner, Chair
Professors Patricia M. Cunningham, Thomas M. Elmore, John H. Litcher,
  Joseph O. Milner, J. Don Reeves
Associate Professors Robert H. Evans, Linda N. Nielsen, Leonard P. Roberge
Visiting Assistant Professor Mary Lynn B. Redmond
Instructors Patricia H. Campbell, Robert E. Nalley
Adjunct Instructor John C. Cheska
Lecturers G. Dianne Mitchell, Marianne A. Schubert

1991–1992
Joseph O. Milner, Chair
Professors Patricia M. Cunningham, Thomas M. Elmore, Samuel T. Gladding,
  John H. Litcher, Joseph O. Milner, Linda N. Nielsen, J. Don Reeves
Associate Professors Robert H. Evans, Leonard P. Roberge
Visiting Assistant Professor Mary Lynn B. Redmond
Instructor Patricia H. Reavis
Lecturers G. Dianne Mitchell, Marianne A. Schubert, Loraine M. Stewart

1992–1993
Joseph O. Milner, Chair
Professors Patricia M. Cunningham, Thomas M. Elmore, Samuel T. Gladding,
  John H. Litcher, Joseph O. Milner, Linda N. Nielsen, J. Don Reeves
Associate Professors Robert H. Evans, Leonard P. Roberge
Assistant Professors Leah P. McCoy, Mary Lynn B. Redmond, Loraine M. Stewart
Instructor Amanda C. Heinemann
Lecturers G. Dianne Mitchell, Marianne A. Schubert

1993–1994
Joseph O. Milner, Chair
Professors John P. Anderson, Patricia M. Cunningham, Thomas M. Elmore,
  Samuel T. Gladding, John H. Litcher, Joseph O. Milner,
  Linda N. Nielsen, J. Don Reeves
Associate Professors Robert H. Evans, Leonard P. Roberge
Assistant Professors Leah P. McCoy, Mary Lynn B. Redmond,
  Loraine M. Stewart
Visiting Instructor Marjorie Johnson
Lecturers G. Dianne Mitchell, Marianne A. Schubert
Research Associate Shelley L. Olson

1994–1995
Joseph O. Milner, Chair
Professors John P. Anderson, Patricia M. Cunningham, Thomas M. Elmore,
  Samuel T. Gladding, John H. Litcher, Joseph O. Milner, Linda N. Nielsen,
  J. Don Reeves, Leonard P. Roberge

Associate Professors Robert H. Evans, Leah P. McCoy
Assistant Professors Mary Lynn B. Redmond, Loraine M. Stewart
Visiting Assistant Professor G. Dianne Mitchell
Visiting Instructor Marjorie Johnson
Lecturer Marianne A. Schubert
Research Associate Shelley L. Olson

1995–1996
Joseph O. Milner, Chair
Professors John P. Anderson, Patricia M. Cunningham, Thomas M. Elmore,
    Samuel T. Gladding, John H. Litcher, Joseph O. Milner, Linda N. Nielsen,
    Leonard P. Roberge
Associate Professors Robert H. Evans, Leah P. McCoy
Assistant Professors R. Scott Baker, Mary Lynn B. Redmond, Loraine M. Stewart
Visiting Assistant Professor G. Dianne Mitchell
Visiting Instructor Marjorie Johnson
Lecturer Marianne A. Schubert
Research Associate Shelley L. Olson

1996–1997
Joseph O. Milner, Chair
Professors John P. Anderson, Patricia M. Cunningham, Thomas M. Elmore,
    Samuel T. Gladding, John H. Litcher, Joseph O. Milner, Linda N. Nielsen,
    Leonard P. Roberge
Associate Professors Robert H. Evans, Leah P. McCoy, Mary Lynn B. Redmond
Assistant Professors R. Scott Baker, Loraine M. Stewart
Visiting Assistant Professor G. Dianne Mitchell
Visiting Instructor Debbie Hill
Lecturer Marianne A. Schubert

1997–1998
Joseph O. Milner, Chair
Professors John P. Anderson, Patricia M. Cunningham, Samuel T. Gladding,
    John H. Litcher, Joseph O. Milner, Linda N. Nielsen, Leonard P. Roberge
Associate Professors Robert H. Evans, Leah P. McCoy, Mary Lynn B. Redmond
Assistant Professors R. Scott Baker, Donna A. Henderson, Loraine M. Stewart
Adjunct Assistant Professors Alan S. Cameron, G. Dianne Mitchell, Marianne A.
    Schubert, Elizabeth H. Taylor
Instructor Johnne W. Armentrout
Visiting Instructor Debbie Hill

1998–1999
Joseph O. Milner, Chair
Professors John P. Anderson, Patricia M. Cunningham, Samuel T. Gladding,
    John H. Litcher, Joseph O. Milner, Linda N. Nielsen, Leonard P. Roberge
Associate Professors Robert H. Evans, Leah P. McCoy, Mary Lynn B. Redmond
Assistant Professors R. Scott Baker, Donna A. Henderson, Loraine M. Stewart
Adjunct Assistant Professors Alan S. Cameron, G. Dianne Mitchell, Marianne A.
    Schubert, Elizabeth H. Taylor
Instructor Johnne W. Armentrout
Visiting Instructor Vanda D. Thomas

1999–2000
Joseph O. Milner, Chair
Professors John P. Anderson, Patricia M. Cunningham, Samuel T. Gladding,
    John H. Litcher, Joseph O. Milner, Linda N. Nielsen, Leonard P. Roberge
Associate Professors Robert H. Evans, Leah P. McCoy, Mary Lynn B. Redmond
Assistant Professors R. Scott Baker, Donna A. Henderson, Loraine M. Stewart
Adjunct Assistant Professors Alan S. Cameron, G. Dianne Mitchell, Marianne A.
    Schubert, Elizabeth H. Taylor
Instructor Johnne W. Armentrout

2000–2001
Joseph O. Milner, Chair
Professors John P. Anderson, Patricia M. Cunningham, Samuel T. Gladding,
    John H. Litcher, Joseph O. Milner, Linda N. Nielsen, Leonard P. Roberge
Associate Professors Robert H. Evans, Donna A. Henderson, Leah P. McCoy,
    Mary Lynn B. Redmond, Loraine M. Stewart
Assistant Professors Ann C. Cunningham, Laura J. Veach
Visiting Assistant Professors Dorothy Hall, Debbie W. Newsome
Adjunct Assistant Professors Alan S. Cameron, G. Dianne Mitchell,
    Marianne A. Schubert, Elizabeth H. Taylor
Instructor Johnne W. Armentrout

2001–2002
Joseph O. Milner, Chair
Professors John P. Anderson, Patricia M. Cunningham, Samuel T. Gladding,
    John H. Litcher, Joseph O. Milner, Linda N. Nielsen
Associate Professors Robert H. Evans, Donna A. Henderson, Leah P. McCoy,
    Mary Lynn B. Redmond, Loraine M. Stewart
Assistant Professors Ann C. Cunningham, Debbie W. Newsome, Laura J. Veach
Adjunct Assistant Professors Alan S. Cameron, Marianne A. Schubert,
    Elizabeth H. Taylor
Instructor Johnne W. Armentrout

2002–2003
Joseph O. Milner, Chair
Wake Forest Professor Patricia M. Cunningham

Professors John P. Anderson, Samuel T. Gladding, Joseph O. Milner,
   Linda N. Nielsen
Associate Professors Robert H. Evans, Donna A. Henderson, Leah P. McCoy,
   Mary Lynn B. Redmond, Loraine M. Stewart
Assistant Professors R. Scott Baker, Ann C. Cunningham, Raymond C. Jones,
   Debbie W. Newsome, Laura J. Veach
Adjunct Assistant Professors Alan S. Cameron, Marianne A. Schubert,
   Elizabeth H. Taylor
Instructors Johnne W. Armentrout, Pamela R. Karr

2003–2004
Joseph O. Milner, Chair
Wake Forest Professor Patricia M. Cunningham
Professors John P. Anderson, Samuel T. Gladding, Joseph O. Milner,
   Linda N. Nielsen
Associate Professors Robert H. Evans, Donna A. Henderson, Leah P. McCoy,
   Mary Lynn B. Redmond, Loraine M. Stewart
Assistant Professors R. Scott Baker, Ann C. Cunningham, Raymond C. Jones,
   Debbie W. Newsome, Laura J. Veach
Adjunct Assistant Professors Alan S. Cameron, Dorothy Hall, Andrew McKnight,
   Elizabeth H. Taylor
Instructor Johnne W. Armentrout, Pamela R. Karr, Shawn Weatherman
Lecturer Marianne A. Schubert

2004–2005
Joseph O. Milner, Chair
Wake Forest Professor Patricia M. Cunningham
Professors Robert H. Evans, Joseph O. Milner, Linda N. Nielsen
Associate Professors Leah P. McCoy, Mary Lynn B. Redmond, Loraine M. Stewart
Assistant Professors R. Scott Baker, Ann C. Cunningham, Raymond C. Jones
Adjunct Assistant Professors Dorothy Hall, Karen Hudson, Rebecca Shore
Instructors Jeanie Marklin, Tracy Wilson

2005–2006
Joseph O. Milner, Chair
Wake Forest Professor Patricia M. Cunningham
Professors Robert H. Evans, Joseph O. Milner, Linda N. Nielsen
Associate Professors Leah P. McCoy, Mary Lynn B. Redmond, Loraine M. Stewart
Assistant Professors R. Scott Baker, Ann C. Cunningham, Raymond C. Jones
Adjunct Assistant Professors Alan Cameron, Dorothy Hall, Rebecca Shore
Instructor Tracy Wilson

ENGLISH (ENG)

1983–1984
Robert N. Shorter, Chair
Professors John A. Carter Jr., Doyle R. Fosso, Thomas F. Gossett,
Alonzo W. Kenion, Elizabeth Phillips, Lee Harris Potter, Robert N. Shorter,
Edwin G. Wilson
Professor of Journalism Bynum Shaw
Associate Professors Nancy J. Cotton, Andrew V. Ettin, W. Dillon Johnston,
Robert W. Lovett, William M. Moss, Blanche C. Speer
Assistant Professor James S. Hans
Visiting Assistant Professors Mary K. DeShazer, Barry G. Maine, Gillian R. Overing,
Mark R. Reynolds
Instructors Cynthia L. Caywood, Robert E. Mielke
Lecturers Patricia A. Johansson, Dolly A. McPherson
Visiting Lecturer Robert A. Hedin

1984–1985
Robert N. Shorter, Chair
Professors John A. Carter Jr., Doyle R. Fosso, Thomas F. Gossett, Elizabeth Phillips,
Lee Harris Potter, Robert N. Shorter, Edwin G. Wilson
Professor of Journalism Bynum Shaw
Associate Professors Nancy J. Cotton, Andrew V. Ettin, W. Dillon Johnston,
Robert W. Lovett, William M. Moss
Assistant Professor James S. Hans
Visiting Assistant Professors Cynthia L. Caywood, Barry G. Maine,
Gillian R. Overing
Instructors Carol Gardner, William J. Hartley, Robert E. Mielke, Emily P. Miller
Lecturers Patricia A. Johansson, Dolly A. McPherson
Visiting Lecturer Robert A. Hedin

1985–1986
Robert N. Shorter, Chair
Professors John A. Carter Jr., Doyle R. Fosso, Thomas F. Gossett,
Elizabeth Phillips, Lee Harris Potter, Robert N. Shorter, Edwin G. Wilson
Professor of Journalism Bynum Shaw
Associate Professors Nancy J. Cotton, Andrew V. Ettin, W. Dillon Johnston,
Robert W. Lovett, William M. Moss
Assistant Professors James S. Hans, Barry G. Maine, Hugh Ormsby-Lennon,
Gillian R. Overing
Visiting Assistant Professor Emily P. Miller
Instructors Carol Gardner, Robert E. Mielke
Lecturers Patricia A. Johansson, Dolly A. McPherson
Visiting Lecturer Robert A. Hedin

1986–1987
Robert N. Shorter, Chair
Professors John A. Carter Jr., Doyle R. Fosso, Thomas F. Gossett,
    W. Dillon Johnston, Elizabeth Phillips, Lee Harris Potter, Robert N. Shorter,
    Edwin G. Wilson
Professor of Journalism Bynum Shaw
Associate Professors Nancy J. Cotton, Andrew V. Ettin, James S. Hans,
    Robert W. Lovett, William M. Moss, Gillian R. Overing
Assistant Professor Barry G. Maine
Visiting Assistant Professors Randy Brandes, Barbara Heusel, Emily Miller
Instructors Robert E. Mielke, Emily Seelbinder
Lecturers Patricia A. Johansson, Dolly A. McPherson
Visiting Lecturer Robert A. Hedin

1987–1988
Robert N. Shorter, Chair
Professors John A. Carter Jr., Nancy J. Cotton, Doyle R. Fosso,
    Thomas F. Gossett, W. Dillon Johnston, Elizabeth Phillips,
    Lee Harris Potter, Robert N. Shorter, Edwin G. Wilson
Professor of Journalism Bynum Shaw
Associate Professors Andrew V. Ettin, James S. Hans, Robert W. Lovett,
    Dolly A. McPherson, William M. Moss, Gillian R. Overing
Assistant Professors Barry G. Maine, Claudia N. Thomas
Visiting Assistant Professors Anne Boyle, Randy Brandes, Barbara Heusel
Instructors Kathleen Reuter, Helen Robbins, Emily Seelbinder
Lecturer Patricia A. Johansson
Visiting Lecturer Robert A. Hedin

1988–1989
Barry G. Maine, Chair
Professors John A. Carter Jr., Nancy J. Cotton, Doyle R. Fosso,
    W. Dillon Johnston, Robert W. Lovett, Elizabeth Phillips, Lee Harris Potter,
    Robert N. Shorter, Edwin G. Wilson
Professor of Journalism Bynum G. Shaw
Associate Professors Mary K. DeShazer, Andrew V. Ettin, James S. Hans,
    Barry G. Maine, Dolly A. McPherson, William M. Moss, Gillian R. Overing
Assistant Professors Timothy Bent, Gale Sigal, Claudia N. Thomas
Visiting Assistant Professors Anne Boyle, Randy Brandes, Barbara Heusel,
    Kathleen A. Reuter, Emily Seelbinder, Mark S. Sexton
Instructor Helen Robbins
Lecturers Linda C. Brinson, Patricia A. Johansson
Poet-in-Residence Robert A. Hedin

1989–1990

Barry G. Maine, Chair

Professors John A. Carter Jr., Nancy J. Cotton, Doyle R. Fosso,
   W. Dillon Johnston, Robert W. Lovett, Elizabeth Phillips, Lee Harris Potter,
   Robert N. Shorter, Edwin G. Wilson

Professor of Journalism Bynum G. Shaw

Associate Professors Mary K. DeShazer, Andrew V. Ettin, James S. Hans,
   Barry G. Maine, Dolly A. McPherson, William M. Moss, Gillian R. Overing

Assistant Professors Timothy Bent, Gale Sigal, Claudia N. Thomas

Visiting Professor George Watson

Visiting Assistant Professors Anne Boyle, Kathleen A. Reuter, Helen W. Robbins,
   William Rowland, Michael Selmon, Mark S. Sexton

Instructors Mark Lytal, Andrea Rowland

Lecturers Linda C. Brinson, Patricia A. Johansson

Poet-in-Residence Robert A. Hedin

1990–1991

Barry G. Maine, Chair

Professors John A. Carter Jr., Nancy J. Cotton, Doyle R. Fosso, James S. Hans, W.
   Dillon Johnston, Robert W. Lovett, Robert N. Shorter, Edwin G. Wilson

Professor of Journalism Bynum G. Shaw

Associate Professors Mary K. DeShazer, Andrew V. Ettin, Barry G. Maine,
   Dolly A. McPherson, William M. Moss, Gillian R. Overing

Assistant Professors Timothy Bent, Beth Giddens, Philip Kuberski, Gale Sigal,
   Claudia N. Thomas

Visiting Assistant Professors Anne Boyle, William Rowland, Michael Selmon,
   Mark S. Sexton

Instructors Ellen Kovner, Mark Lytal, Andrea Rowland, Henry Russell

Lecturers Linda C. Brinson, Patricia A. Johansson

Poet-in-Residence Robert A. Hedin

1991–1992

Barry G. Maine, Chair

Professors John A. Carter Jr., Nancy J. Cotton, Andrew V. Ettin, Doyle R. Fosso,
   James S. Hans, W. Dillon Johnston, Robert W. Lovett, William M. Moss,
   Robert N. Shorter, Edwin G. Wilson

Professor of Journalism Bynum G. Shaw

Associate Professors Mary K. DeShazer, Barry G. Maine, Dolly A. McPherson,
   Gillian R. Overing

Assistant Professors Anne Boyle, Bashir El-Beshti, Philip Kuberski, Gale Sigal,
   Claudia N. Thomas

Visiting Professor Declan Kiberd

Visiting Assistant Professors David Cody, Andrea Rowland, William Rowland,
   Michael Selmon, Mark S. Sexton

Instructors Ellen Kovner, Mark Lytal, Thomas McGohey, Christopher Metress,
   Lynette Rothe, Henry Russell

Lecturers Linda C. Brinson, Patricia A. Johansson
Poet-in-Residence Robert A. Hedin

1992–1993
Barry G. Maine, Chair
Professors John A. Carter Jr., Nancy J. Cotton, Andrew V. Ettin, Doyle R. Fosso,
    James S. Hans, W. Dillon Johnston, Robert W. Lovett, Dolly A. McPherson,
    William M. Moss, Robert N. Shorter, Edwin G. Wilson
Professor of Journalism Bynum G. Shaw
Associate Professors Mary K. DeShazer, Barry G. Maine, Gillian R. Overing
Assistant Professors Anne Boyle, Bashir El-Beshti, Scott W. Klein, Philip Kuberski,
    Elizabeth Petrino, Gale Sigal, Claudia N. Thomas
Visiting Assistant Professors David Cody, Helen Emmitt, Christopher Metress,
    Mary Anne Nunn, Ellen R. Rosenberg, Henry Russell, Mark S. Sexton
Instructor Thomas McGohey
Lecturers Linda C. Brinson, Patricia A. Johansson
Poet-in-Residence Robert A. Hedin

1993–1994
Barry G. Maine, Chair
Professors John A. Carter Jr., Nancy J. Cotton, Andrew V. Ettin, Doyle R. Fosso,
    James S. Hans, W. Dillon Johnston, Robert W. Lovett, Dolly A. McPherson,
    William M. Moss, Robert N. Shorter, Edwin G. Wilson
Professor of Journalism Bynum G. Shaw
Associate Professors Mary K. DeShazer, Philip Kuberski, Barry G. Maine,
    Gillian R. Overing, Gale Sigal, Claudia N. Thomas
Assistant Professors Anne Boyle, Bashir El-Beshti, Scott W. Klein, Elizabeth Petrino
Visiting Assistant Professors David Adams, Helen Emmitt, LeeAnna Lawrence,
    Christopher Metress, Mary Anne Nunn, Thomas Peyser, Mark S. Sexton
Instructor Thomas McGohey
Visiting Instructor Marianne Eismann
Lecturer Patricia A. Johansson
Poet-in-Residence Kate Daniels

1994–1995
Barry G. Maine, Chair
Professors John A. Carter Jr., Nancy J. Cotton, Andrew V. Ettin, Doyle R. Fosso,
    James S. Hans, W. Dillon Johnston, Robert W. Lovett, Dolly A. McPherson,
    William M. Moss, Gillian R. Overing, Robert N. Shorter, Edwin G. Wilson
Associate Professors Anne Boyle, Mary K. DeShazer, Philip Kuberski,
    Barry G. Maine, Gale Sigal, Claudia N. Thomas
Assistant Professors Bashir El-Beshti, Scott W. Klein, Elizabeth Petrino
Visiting Assistant Professors David Adams, Helen Emmitt, LeeAnna Lawrence, Julie
    Grossman, Thomas Peyser, Mark S. Sexton
Instructor Thomas McGohey

Visiting Instructors Andrea Atkin, Marianne Eismann, Teresa Michals
Lecturer Patricia A. Johansson
Lecturer in Journalism Wayne King
Visiting Lecturer Justin Catanoso
Poet-in-Residence Kate Daniels

1995–1996
Barry G. Maine, Chair
Professors John A. Carter Jr., Nancy J. Cotton, Andrew V. Ettin, Doyle R. Fosso,
    James S. Hans, W. Dillon Johnston, Robert W. Lovett, Dolly A. McPherson,
    William M. Moss, Gillian R. Overing, Robert N. Shorter, Edwin G. Wilson
Associate Professors Anne Boyle, Mary K. DeShazer, Philip Kuberski, Barry G.
    Maine, Gale Sigal, Claudia N. Thomas
Assistant Professors Julie B. Edelson, Bashir El-Beshti, Scott W. Klein, Elizabeth
    Petrino
Visiting Assistant Professors Helen Emmitt, Julie Grossman, Hope H. Hodgkins,
    Mark S. Sexton, Michele S. Ware
Instructor Thomas McGohey
Visiting Instructors Andrea Atkin, Carolyn L. Mathews, Teresa Michals, Phillip
    Novak, Jeryl J. Prescott
Lecturer Patricia A. Johansson
Lecturer in Journalism Wayne King
Visiting Lecturer in Journalism Justin Catanoso
Poet-in-Residence Irena Klepfisz

1996–1997
Barry G. Maine, Chair
Nancy J. Cotton, Chair-elect
Professors John A. Carter Jr., Nancy J. Cotton, Mary K. DeShazer,
    Andrew V. Ettin, James S. Hans, W. Dillon Johnston, Robert W. Lovett,
    Dolly A. McPherson, William M. Moss, Gillian R. Overing, Robert N. Shorter,
    Edwin G. Wilson
Associate Professors Anne Boyle, Philip Kuberski, Barry G. Maine, Gale Sigal,
    Claudia N. Thomas
Assistant Professors Julie B. Edelson, Bashir El-Beshti, Scott W. Klein,
    Elizabeth Petrino
Visiting Assistant Professors Andrea Atkin, Marsha Holmes, Mark S. Sexton,
    Michele S. Ware
Instructor Thomas McGohey
Visiting Instructors Carolyn L. Mathews, Phillip Novak, Jeryl J. Prescott
Lecturer Patricia A. Johansson
Lecturer in Journalism Wayne King
Visiting Lecturer in Journalism Justin Catanoso
Poets-in-Residence Carol Ann Duffy, Robert A. Hedin

1997–1998
Nancy J. Cotton, Chair
Visiting Distinguished Professor of Poetry A.R. Ammons
Professors John A. Carter Jr., Nancy J. Cotton, Mary K. DeShazer, Andrew V. Ettin,
   James S. Hans, W. Dillon Johnston, Robert W. Lovett, Barry G. Maine,
   Dolly A. McPherson, William M. Moss, Gillian R. Overing, Robert N. Shorter,
   Edwin G. Wilson
Associate Professors Anne Boyle, Bashir El-Beshti, Philip F. Kuberski,
   Gale Sigal (Zachary T. Smith Associate Professor), Claudia N. Thomas
Assistant Professors Scott W. Klein, Elizabeth A. Petrino, Olga Valbuena
Visiting Assistant Professors Andrea Atkin, E. Barnsley Brown, Marsha Holmes,
   Carolyn L. Mathews, Jeryl J. Prescott, Michele S. Ware, Karen Weyler,
   Eric G. Wilson
Instructor Thomas W. McGohey
Visiting Instructor Ralph Black
Lecturer Patricia A. Johansson
Lecturer in Journalism Wayne King
Visiting Lecturer in Journalism Justin Catanoso
Poet-in-Residence Jane Mead
Visiting Writer-in-Residence Peter Benson

1998–1999
Nancy J. Cotton, Chair
W. R. Kenan Jr. Professor of Humanities Allen Mandelbaum
Professors Nancy J. Cotton, Mary K. DeShazer, Andrew V. Ettin, James S. Hans,
   W. Dillon Johnston, Robert W. Lovett, Barry G. Maine, Dolly A. McPherson,
   William M. Moss, Gillian R. Overing, Robert N. Shorter, Edwin G. Wilson
Associate Professors Anne Boyle, Bashir El-Beshti, Scott W. Klein,
   Philip F. Kuberski, Gale Sigal (Zachary T. Smith Associate Professor),
   Claudia N. Thomas
Assistant Professors Janis Caldwell, Elizabeth A. Petrino, Lisa Sternlieb,
   Olga Valbuena
Visiting Assistant Professors E. Barnsley Brown, Caroline Levine,
   Carolyn L. Mathews, Jeryl J. Prescott, Shona Simpson, Michele S. Ware,
   Karen Weyler, Suzanne Young
Adjunct Assistant Professors Eileen Cahill, Julie Edelson
Instructor Thomas W. McGohey
Visiting Instructors Ralph Black, Michael Horn, Jeannine Johnson,
   Steven Shoemaker
Lecturer Patricia A. Johansson
Lecturer in Journalism Wayne King
Visiting Lecturer in Journalism Justin Catanoso
Poet-in-Residence Jane Mead

1999–2000
Nancy J. Cotton, Chair
W. R. Kenan Jr. Professor of Humanities Allen Mandelbaum

Professors Nancy J. Cotton, Mary K. DeShazer, Andrew V. Ettin, James S. Hans, W. Dillon Johnston, Philip F. Kuberski, Robert W. Lovett, Barry G. Maine, Dolly A. McPherson, William M. Moss, Gillian R. Overing, Robert N. Shorter, Gale Sigal (Zachary T. Smith Professor), Edwin G. Wilson

Associate Professors Anne Boyle, Bashir El-Beshti, Scott W. Klein, Claudia N. Thomas

Assistant Professors Janis Caldwell, Jeryl J. Prescott, Lisa Sternlieb, Olga Valbuena, Eric G. Wilson

Visiting Assistant Professors E. Barnsley Brown, Jeannine Johnson, Kristen Kennedy, Borislav Knezevic, David Lipscomb, Carolyn L. Mathews, Steven Shoemaker, Shona Simpson, Karen Weyler, Suzanne Young

Adjunct Assistant Professor Julie Edelson

Instructor Thomas W. McGohey

Visiting Instructors Ralph Black, James Ryan

Lecturer Patricia A. Johansson

Lecturer in Journalism Wayne King

Visiting Lecturer in Journalism Justin Catanoso

Adjunct Lecturer in Journalism Michael Horn

Poet-in-Residence Jane Mead

2000–2001

Nancy J. Cotton, Chair

W. R. Kenan Jr. Professor of Humanities Allen Mandelbaum

Wake Forest Professor James S. Hans

Professors Nancy J. Cotton, Mary K. DeShazer, Andrew V. Ettin, W. Dillon Johnston, Philip F. Kuberski, Robert W. Lovett, Barry G. Maine, Dolly A. McPherson, William M. Moss, Gillian R. Overing, Gale Sigal, Edwin G. Wilson

Associate Professors Anne Boyle, Bashir El-Beshti, Claudia N. Thomas Kairoff, Scott W. Klein

Associate Professor in Journalism Wayne King

Assistant Professors Janis Caldwell, Jeryl J. Prescott, Lisa Sternlieb, Olga Valbuena, Eric G. Wilson

Visiting Assistant Professors Barbara Bennett, Ralph Black, Loren Glass, Borislav Knezevic, Allen Michie, Madhuparna Mitra, Steven Shoemaker, Michael Strysick, Suzanne Young

Adjunct Assistant Professor Julie Edelson

Instructor Thomas W. McGohey

Visiting Instructors Alex Garganigo, Christopher Neumann

Adjunct Lecturers in Journalism Justin Catanoso, Michael Horn

Poet-in-Residence Jane Mead

2001–2002

Gale Sigal, Chair

W. R. Kenan Jr. Professor of Humanities Allen Mandelbaum

Wake Forest Professor James S. Hans

Professors Anne Boyle, Nancy J. Cotton, Mary K. DeShazer, Andrew V. Ettin, W.
　　Dillon Johnston, Claudia N. Thomas Kairoff, Philip F. Kuberski,
　　Robert W. Lovett, Barry G. Maine, Dolly A. McPherson, William M. Moss,
　　Gillian R. Overing, Gale Sigal, Edwin G. Wilson
Associate Professors Bashir El-Beshti, Scott W. Klein, Olga Valbuena
Associate Professor in Journalism Wayne King
Assistant Professors Janis Caldwell, Jeryl J. Prescott, Lisa Sternlieb, Eric G. Wilson
Visiting Assistant Professors Barbara Bennett, Lisa Eck, Alex Garganigo,
　　Allen Michie, Madhuparna Mitra, Farrell O'Gorman, Norbert Schürer,
　　Russell Schweller, Michael Strysick, Robert West
Adjunct Assistant Professors Julie Edelson, Patricia Marshall
Instructor Thomas W. McGohey, Nagesh Rao
Visiting Instructors LeAnne Howe, Christopher Neumann, Dennis Sampson
Adjunct Instructor Martin Arnold
Visiting Lecturer in Journalism Justin Catanoso
Adjunct Lecturer in Journalism Michael Horn
Poet-in-Residence Jane Mead

2002–2003
Gale Sigal, Chair
W. R. Kenan Jr. Professor of Humanities Allen Mandelbaum
Wake Forest Professor James S. Hans
Professors Anne Boyle, Nancy J. Cotton, Mary K. DeShazer, Andrew V. Ettin,
　　W. Dillon Johnston, Claudia N. Thomas Kairoff, Philip F. Kuberski,
　　Barry G. Maine, William M. Moss, Gillian R. Overing, Gale Sigal,
　　Edwin G. Wilson
Associate Professors Bashir El-Beshti, Scott W. Klein, Olga Valbuena
Associate Professor in Journalism Wayne King
Assistant Professors Janis Caldwell, Dean Franco, Nagesh Rao, Lisa Sternlieb,
　　Eric G. Wilson (Z. Smith Reynolds Faculty Fellow)
Visiting Assistant Professors Barbara Bennett, Lisa Eck, Alex Garganigo,
　　Madhuparna Mitra, Farrell O'Gorman, Norbert Schürer, Russell Schweller,
　　Michael Strysick, Robert West
Instructors Michael Hill, Evelyn Shockley
Visiting Instructors Christopher Neumann, Dennis Sampson
Lecturer Thomas W. McGohey
Visiting Lecturer in Journalism Justin Catanoso
Adjunct Lecturer in Journalism Michael Horn
Poet-in-Residence Jane Mead

2003–2004
Gale Sigal, Chair
W. R. Kenan Jr. Professor of Humanities Allen Mandelbaum
Wake Forest Professor James S. Hans

Professors Anne Boyle, Mary K. DeShazer, Andrew V. Ettin, Claudia N. Thomas
Kairoff, Philip F. Kuberski, Barry G. Maine, William M. Moss,
Gillian R. Overing, Gale Sigal
Associate Professors Bashir El-Beshti, Scott W. Klein, Olga Valbuena
Associate Professor in Journalism Wayne King
Assistant Professors Janis Caldwell, Dean Franco, John McNally, Nagesh Rao,
Lisa Sternlieb, Eric G. Wilson (Z. Smith Reynolds Faculty Fellow)
Visiting Assistant Professors Barbara Bennett, Lisa Eck, Alex Garganigo,
Madhuparna Mitra, Farrell O'Gorman, Norbert Schürer, Russell Schweller,
Robert West
Instructors Michael Hill, Victoria Schooler, Evelyn Shockley, Scott Walker
Visiting Instructors Christopher Neumann, Dennis Sampson
Lecturer Thomas W. McGohey
Lecturer in Journalism Justin Catanoso
Adjunct Lecturer in Journalism Michael Horn
Poet-in-Residence Jane Mead

2004–2005
Gale Sigal, Chair
W. R. Kenan Jr. Professor of Humanities Allen Mandelbaum
Wake Forest Professor James S. Hans
Professors Anne Boyle, Mary K. DeShazer, Andrew V. Ettin,
Claudia N. Thomas Kairoff, Philip F. Kuberski, Barry G. Maine,
William M. Moss, Gillian R. Overing, Gale Sigal
Associate Professors Bashir El-Beshti, Scott W. Klein, Lisa Sternlieb,
Olga Valbuena, Eric G. Wilson (Z. Smith Reynolds Faculty Fellow)
Associate Professor in Journalism Wayne King
Assistant Professors Janis Caldwell, Dean Franco, Jefferson Holdridge,
John McNally, Nagesh Rao, Jessica Richard, Evie Shockley
Visiting Assistant Professors Susan Bussey, Ian Finseth, Stephanie Hawkins,
Paul Hecht, Barislav Knezevic, Scott Walker
Instructor Michael Hill
Visiting Instructors Beth Bradburn, R. Temple Cone Jr., John Martin,
Dennis Sampson
Visiting Instructor in Journalism Mary Martin Niepold
Lecturer Thomas W. McGohey
Lecturer in Journalism Justin Catanoso
Adjunct Lecturer in Journalism Michael Horn
Poet-in-Residence Jane Mead

2005–2006
Eric G. Wilson, Chair
W. R. Kenan Jr. Professor of Humanities Allen Mandelbaum
Wake Forest Professor James S. Hans

Professors Anne Boyle, Mary K. DeShazer, Andrew V. Ettin,
   Claudia N. Thomas Kairoff, Philip F. Kuberski, Barry G. Maine,
   William M. Moss, Gillian R. Overing, Gale Sigal
Associate Professors Bashir El-Beshti, Scott W. Klein, Lisa Sternlieb, Olga Valbuena,
   Eric G. Wilson (Z. Smith Reynolds Faculty Fellow)
Associate Professor and Poet-in-Residence Jane Mead
Associate Professor in Journalism Wayne King
Assistant Professors Janis Caldwell, Dean Franco, Michael Hill, Jefferson Holdridge,
   John McNally, Nagesh Rao, Jessica Richard, Evie Shockley
Visiting Assistant Professors Susan Bussey, Bonnie Carr, William Hacker, Stepha-
   nie Hawkins, Paul Hecht, Andrew Leiter, Michael Malouf, Jason Powell, Kersti
   Powell, Chad Trevitte, Scott Walker
Visiting Instructors Marlon Kuzmick Jr., John Martin, Stéphane Robolin
Visiting Instructor in Journalism Mary Martin Niepold
Lecturer Thomas W. McGohey
Lecturers in Journalism Justin Catanoso, Michael Horn
Visiting Poet-in-Residence Dennis Sampson
Visiting Hebrew University Scholar Jon Whitman

ENVIRONMENTAL PROGRAM (ENV)

Interdisciplinary Minors offered in Environmental Science and Environmental Studies
   (The Environmental Program was originally Environmental Studies until 2002–
2003. The change was first listed in the 2003–2004 *Bulletin*.)

1996–1997
No coordinator listed

1997–2000
John Litcher (Education), Coordinator

2000–2005
Robert Browne (Biology), Coordinator

2005–2006
Robert Browne (Biology), Director

FILM STUDIES (FLM)

Interdisciplinary Minor

2004–2005
Mary Dalton (Communication), Interim Coordinator

2005–2006
Peter Brunette (Art and Communication), Director

GERMAN AND RUSSIAN

(The Department of German and Russian was originally the Department of German until 1986–1987 when it became the Department of German and Russian. This change was first listed in the 1987–1988 *Bulletin.*)

1983–1985
Wilmer D. Sanders, Chair
Professors Ralph S. Fraser, James C. O'Flaherty, Wilmer D. Sanders
Associate Professors Timothy F. Sellner, Larry E. West

1985–1986
Wilmer D. Sanders, Chair
Professors Ralph S. Fraser, Wilmer D. Sanders
Associate Professors Timothy F. Sellner, Larry E. West
Instructor Linda T. Frost

1986–1987
Larry E. West, Chair
Professors Ralph S. Fraser, Wilmer D. Sanders, Timothy F. Sellner, Larry E. West
Instructor Christa Carollo

1987–1988
Larry E. West, Chair
Professors Ralph S. Fraser, Wilmer D. Sanders, Timothy F. Sellner, Larry E. West
Associate Professor William S. Hamilton
Instructor Christa Carollo

1988–1989
Larry E. West, Chair
Professors Ralph S. Fraser, Wilmer D. Sanders, Timothy F. Sellner, Larry E. West
Associate Professor William S. Hamilton
Instructor Christa Carollo, Kurt C. Shaw

1989–1992
Larry E. West, Chair
Professors Wilmer D. Sanders, Timothy F. Sellner, Larry E. West
Associate Professor William S. Hamilton
Assistant Professors Michael Gilbert, Kurt C. Shaw
Instructor Christa G. Carollo

1992–1993
Timothy F. Sellner, Chair
Professors Wilmer D. Sanders, Timothy F. Sellner, Larry E. West

Associate Professor William S. Hamilton
Assistant Professors Michael Gilbert, Kurt C. Shaw
Lecturers Christa G. Carollo, Perry L. Patterson

1993–1994
Timothy F. Sellner, Chair
Professors Timothy F. Sellner, Larry E. West
Associate Professor William S. Hamilton
Assistant Professors Rebecca Duplantier, Kurt C. Shaw
Lecturers Christa G. Carollo, Perry L. Patterson

1994–1995
Timothy F. Sellner, Chair
Professors Timothy F. Sellner, Larry E. West
Associate Professor William S. Hamilton
Assistant Professors Rebecca Duplantier, Kurt C. Shaw
Lecturers Christa G. Carollo, Perry L. Patterson, Stefanie H. Tanis

1995–1996
Timothy F. Sellner, Chair
Professors Timothy F. Sellner, Larry E. West
Associate Professors William S. Hamilton, Kurt C. Shaw
Assistant Professor Rebecca Thomas
Instructor Wendy Pfeiffer-Quaile
Lecturers Christa G. Carollo, Perry L. Patterson, Stefanie H. Tanis

1996–2001
Timothy F. Sellner, Chair
Professors William S. Hamilton, Timothy F. Sellner, Larry E. West
Associate Professor Kurt C. Shaw
Assistant Professor Rebecca Thomas
Lecturers Christa G. Carollo, Perry L. Patterson, Stefanie H. Tanis

2001–2002
Kurt C. Shaw, Chair
Professors William S. Hamilton, Timothy F. Sellner, Larry E. West
Associate Professors Kurt C. Shaw, Rebecca Thomas
Lecturers Christa G. Carollo, Perry L. Patterson, Stefanie H. Tanis

2002–2004
Kurt C. Shaw, Chair
Professors William S. Hamilton, Timothy F. Sellner, Larry E. West
Associate Professors Kurt C. Shaw, Rebecca Thomas
Assistant Professor Grant P. McAllister
Lecturers Christa G. Carollo, Perry L. Patterson, Stefanie H. Tanis

2004–2006
Kurt C. Shaw, Chair
Professors William S. Hamilton, Larry E. West
Associate Professors Kurt C. Shaw, Rebecca Thomas
Assistant Professors Alyssa Lonner, Grant P. McAllister
Lecturers Christa G. Carollo, Perry L. Patterson

GERMAN STUDIES

Foreign Area Study

1993–2004
Timothy F. Sellner (German/Russian), Coordinator

2004–2006
Rebecca Thomas (German), Coordinator

GLOBAL TRADE & COMMERCE STUDIES (GTCS)

Interdisciplinary Minor

2002–2006
Pia Christina Wood (Political Science), Coordinator

HEALTH AND EXERCISE SCIENCE (HES)

(The Department of Health and Exercise Science was originally the Department of
Physical Education until 1985–1986, when it became the Department of Health and
Sport Science. This change was first noted in the 1986–1987 *Bulletin.* The current
name was adopted in 1995–1996 and first noted in the 1996–1997 *Bulletin.*)

1983–1984
William L. Hottinger, Chair
Professors William L. Hottinger, Paul M. Ribisl
Assistant Professors Dorothy Casey, Leo Ellison Jr., Stephen P. Messier,
    W. Jack Rejeski
Visiting Assistant Professor Sarah D. Hutslar
Instructors Susan E. Balinsky, Donald Bergey, Gary Hall, Rebecca Myers

1984–1985
William L. Hottinger, Chair
Professors William L. Hottinger, Paul M. Ribisl
Associate Professor W. Jack Rejeski
Assistant Professors Dorothy Casey, Leo Ellison Jr., Stephen P. Messier
Visiting Assistant Professor Sarah D. Hutslar
Instructors Susan E. Balinsky, Donald Bergey, Gary Hall, Rebecca Myers

1985–1986
William L. Hottinger, Chair
Professors William L. Hottinger, Paul M. Ribisl
Associate Professor W. Jack Rejeski
Assistant Professors Dorothy Casey, Leo Ellison Jr., Stephen P. Messier
Visiting Assistant Professor Sarah D. Hutslar
Instructors Donald Bergey, Rebecca Myers, David H. Stroupe, Janice Hall Weiss

1986–1987
William L. Hottinger, Chair
Professors William L. Hottinger, Paul M. Ribisl
Associate Professors Dorothy Casey, Leo Ellison Jr., W. Jack Rejeski
Assistant Professors Michael J. Berry, Stephen P. Messier
Instructors Donald Bergey, Rebecca Myers, David H. Stroupe, Janice Hall Weiss

1987–1988
William L. Hottinger, Chair
Professors William L. Hottinger, Paul M. Ribisl
Associate Professors Dorothy Casey, Leo Ellison Jr., Stephen P. Messier, W. Jack
    Rejeski
Assistant Professor Michael J. Berry
Instructors Donald Bergey, Rebecca Myers, David H. Stroupe, Janice Hall Weiss

1988–1989
William L. Hottinger, Chair
Professors William L. Hottinger, Paul M. Ribisl
Associate Professors Dorothy Casey, Leo Ellison Jr., Stephen P. Messier, W. Jack
    Rejeski
Assistant Professor Michael J. Berry
Instructors Donald Bergey, Susan Fisher, Bobbie Goodnough, Rebecca Myers

1989–1990
William L. Hottinger, Chair
Professors William L. Hottinger, Paul M. Ribisl
Associate Professors Leo Ellison Jr., Stephen P. Messier, W. Jack Rejeski
Assistant Professors Michael J. Berry, June K. Nutter
Instructors Donald Bergey, Susan Fisher, Bobbie Goodnough, Rebecca Myers

1990–1991
William L. Hottinger, Chair
Professors William L. Hottinger, Paul M. Ribisl
Associate Professors Leo Ellison Jr., Stephen P. Messier, W. Jack Rejeski
Assistant Professors Michael J. Berry, Barbee C. Myers
Instructors Donald Bergey, Susan Fisher, Bobbie Goodnough, Rebecca Myers

1991–1992
William L. Hottinger, Chair
Professors William L. Hottinger, W. Jack Rejeski, Paul M. Ribisl
Associate Professors Michael J. Berry, Leo Ellison Jr., Stephen P. Messier
Assistant Professor Barbee C. Myers
Instructors Donald Bergey, Bobbie Goodnough, Rebecca Myers, David H. Stroupe

1992–1993
Paul M. Ribisl, Chair
Professors William L. Hottinger, W. Jack Rejeski, Paul M. Ribisl
Associate Professors Michael J. Berry, Leo Ellison Jr., Stephen P. Messier
Assistant Professor Barbee Myers Oakes
Instructors Donald Bergey, Bobbie Goodnough, David H. Stroupe

1993–1995
Paul M. Ribisl, Chair
Professors William L. Hottinger, Stephen P. Messier, W. Jack Rejeski, Paul M. Ribisl
Associate Professors Michael J. Berry, Leo Ellison Jr.
Assistant Professor Barbee Myers Oakes
Instructors Donald Bergey, Bobbie Goodnough, David H. Stroupe

1995–1996
Paul M. Ribisl, Chair
Professors William L. Hottinger, Stephen P. Messier, W. Jack Rejeski, Paul M. Ribisl
Associate Professors Michael J. Berry, Leo Ellison Jr.
Assistant Professors Peter H. Brubaker, Barbee Myers Oakes
Visiting Adjunct Professor Lawrence R. Brawley
Instructors Donald Bergey, Bobbie Goodnough, David H. Stroupe

1996–1997
Paul M. Ribisl, Chair
Professors William L. Hottinger, Stephen P. Messier, W. Jack Rejeski, Paul M. Ribisl
Associate Professors Michael J. Berry, Leo Ellison Jr.
Assistant Professors Peter H. Brubaker, Jennifer L. Etnier, Barbee Myers Oakes
Visiting Assistant Professor Robert W. Brooks
Adjunct Assistant Professor Timothy J. Zehnder
Instructors Donald Bergey, Johnnie O. Foye, David H. Stroupe

1997–1998
Paul M. Ribisl, Chair
Professors Stephen P. Messier, W. Jack Rejeski, Paul M. Ribisl
Associate Professors Michael J. Berry, Leo Ellison Jr.

Assistant Professors Peter H. Brubaker, Jennifer L. Etnier,
    Anthony P. Marsh, Gary D. Miller
Instructors Donald Bergey, Johnnie O. Foye, Sara E. Kelling, David H. Stroupe

1998–1999
Paul M. Ribisl, Chair
Wake Forest Professor W. Jack Rejeski
Professors Stephen P. Messier, Paul M. Ribisl
Associate Professors Michael J. Berry, Leo Ellison Jr.
Assistant Professors Peter H. Brubaker, Jennifer L. Etnier,
    Anthony P. Marsh, Gary D. Miller
Instructors Donald Bergey, Johnnie O. Foye, Michele Pitbladdo, David H. Stroupe

1999–2000
Paul M. Ribisl, Chair
Wake Forest Professor W. Jack Rejeski
Professors Michael J. Berry, Stephen P. Messier, Paul M. Ribisl
Associate Professors Peter H. Brubaker, Leo Ellison Jr.
Assistant Professors Anthony P. Marsh, Gary D. Miller
Visiting Assistant Professor John C. Simonsen
Instructors Donald Bergey, Johnnie O. Foye, David H. Stroupe
Visiting Instructor Capri G. Foy

2000–2002
Paul M. Ribisl, Chair
Wake Forest Professor W. Jack Rejeski
Professors Michael J. Berry, Stephen P. Messier, Paul M. Ribisl
Associate Professors Peter H. Brubaker, Patricia A. Nixon
Assistant Professors Anthony P. Marsh, Shannon L. Mihalko, Gary D. Miller
Instructors Donald Bergey, Johnnie O. Foye, David H. Stroupe, Sharon K. Woodard

2002–2003
Paul M. Ribisl, Chair
Wake Forest Professor W. Jack Rejeski
Professors Michael J. Berry, Stephen P. Messier, Paul M. Ribisl
Associate Professors Peter H. Brubaker, Anthony P. Marsh, Gary D. Miller,
    Patricia A. Nixon
Assistant Professor Shannon L. Mihalko
Instructors Donald Bergey, Johnnie O. Foye, David H. Stroupe, Sharon K. Woodard

2003–2004
Paul M. Ribisl, Chair
Wake Forest Professors W. Jack Rejeski, Paul M. Ribisl
Professors Michael J. Berry, Stephen P. Messier

Associate Professors Peter H. Brubaker, Anthony P. Marsh, Gary D. Miller,
  Patricia A. Nixon
Assistant Professor Shannon L. Mihalko
Instructors Donald Bergey, Johnnie O. Foye, David H. Stroupe, Sharon K. Woodard

2004–2005
Paul M. Ribisl, Chair
Wake Forest Professors W. Jack Rejeski, Paul M. Ribisl
Professors Michael J. Berry, Stephen P. Messier
Associate Professors Peter H. Brubaker, Anthony P. Marsh, Gary D. Miller,
  Patricia A. Nixon
Assistant Professor Shannon L. Mihalko (Dunn-Riley Jr. Professor)
Instructors Donald Bergey, Richard Bloomer, Johnnie O. Foye, David H. Stroupe,
  Sharon K. Woodard

2005–2006
Paul M. Ribisl, Chair
Wake Forest Professors W. Jack Rejeski, Paul M. Ribisl
Professors Michael J. Berry, Stephen P. Messier
Associate Professors Peter H. Brubaker, Anthony P. Marsh, Shannon L. Mihalko
  (Dunn-Riley Jr. Professor), Gary D. Miller, Patricia A. Nixon
Instructors Donald Bergey, Johnnie O. Foye, David H. Stroupe, Sharon K. Woodard

HEALTH POLICY AND ADMINISTRATION (HPA)

Interdisciplinary Minor

2000–2006
Michael S. Lawlor (Economics), Director

HISTORY

(HST)

1983–1984
Richard L. Zuber, Chair
Professors Richard C. Barnett, Cyclone Covey, Balkrishna Govind Gokhale,
  J. Edwin Hendricks, Thomas E. Mullen, Percival Perry, David L. Smiley,
  Henry Smith Stroupe, Lowell R. Tillett, W. Buck Yearns, Richard L. Zuber
Associate Professors James P. Barefield, Merrill G. Berthrong, David W. Hadley,
  Michael L. Sinclair, J. Howell Smith, Alan J. Williams
Visiting Assistant Professors Victor Kamendrowsky, Anne Parrella
Lecturer Negley Boyd Harte (London)

1984–1985
Richard C. Barnett, Chair
Worrell Professor of Anglo-American Studies James Ralph Scales

Professors Richard C. Barnett, Cyclone Covey, Balkrishna Govind Gokhale, J.
Edwin Hendricks, Thomas E. Mullen, Percival Perry, David L. Smiley,
Henry Smith Stroupe, Lowell R. Tillett, W. Buck Yearns, Richard L. Zuber
Associate Professors James P. Barefield, Merrill G. Berthrong, David W. Hadley,
Michael L. Sinclair, J. Howell Smith, Alan J. Williams
Visiting Assistant Professors Victor Kamendrowsky, Anne Parrella
Lecturer Negley Boyd Harte (London)

1985–1986
Richard C. Barnett, Chair
Worrell Professor of Anglo-American Studies James Ralph Scales
Professors Richard C. Barnett, Cyclone Covey, Balkrishna Govind Gokhale, J.
Edwin Hendricks, Thomas E. Mullen, Percival Perry, David L. Smiley,
Lowell R. Tillett, W. Buck Yearns, Richard L. Zuber
Associate Professors James P. Barefield, Merrill G. Berthrong, David W. Hadley,
Michael L. Sinclair, J. Howell Smith, Alan J. Williams
Assistant Professors Michael L. Hughes, Victor Kamendrowsky
Visiting Associate Professor Reinhold Mueller (Venice)
Lecturer Negley Boyd Harte (London)

1986–1987
Richard C. Barnett, Chair
Worrell Professor of Anglo-American Studies James Ralph Scales
Professors Richard C. Barnett, Cyclone Covey, Balkrishna Govind Gokhale, J.
Edwin Hendricks, Thomas E. Mullen, Percival Perry, David L. Smiley,
Lowell R. Tillett, W. Buck Yearns, Richard L. Zuber
Associate Professors James P. Barefield, Merrill G. Berthrong, David W. Hadley,
Michael L. Sinclair, J. Howell Smith, Alan J. Williams
Assistant Professors Michael L. Hughes, Susan P. McCaffray
Visiting Associate Professor Reinhold Mueller (Venice)
Lecturer Negley Boyd Harte (London)

1987–1988
Richard C. Barnett, Chair
Worrell Professor of Anglo-American Studies James Ralph Scales
Professors James P. Barefield, Richard C. Barnett, Cyclone Covey,
Balkrishna Govind Gokhale, J. Edwin Hendricks, Thomas E. Mullen,
Percival Perry, David L. Smiley, J. Howell Smith, Lowell R. Tillett, W. Buck
Yearns, Richard L. Zuber
Associate Professors Merrill G. Berthrong, David W. Hadley,
Michael L. Sinclair, Alan J. Williams
Assistant Professors Michael L. Hughes, Susan P. McCaffray
Visiting Associate Professor Reinhold Mueller (Venice)
Lecturer Negley Boyd Harte (London)

1988–1989
J. Howell Smith, Chair
Worrell Professor of Anglo-American Studies James Ralph Scales
Professors James P. Barefield, Richard C. Barnett, Cyclone Covey,
  Balkrishna Govind Gokhale, J. Edwin Hendricks, Thomas E. Mullen, David L.
  Smiley, J. Howell Smith, Lowell R. Tillett, W. Buck Yearns, Richard L. Zuber
Associate Professors Merrill G. Berthrong, David W. Hadley, Michael L. Sinclair, J.
  Howell Smith, Alan J. Williams
Assistant Professors Michael L. Hughes, Susan P. McCaffray, Sarah L. Watts
Lecturer Negley Boyd Harte (London)

1989–1990
J. Howell Smith, Chair
Worrell Professor of Anglo-American Studies James Ralph Scales
Professors James P. Barefield, Richard C. Barnett, Balkrishna Govind Gokhale, J.
  Edwin Hendricks, Thomas E. Mullen, David L. Smiley, J. Howell Smith,
  Lowell R. Tillett, Richard L. Zuber
Associate Professors Merrill G. Berthrong, David W. Hadley, Michael L. Sinclair,
  Alan J. Williams
Assistant Professors Michael L. Hughes, William K. Meyers, Sarah L. Watts
Visiting Instructor Bruce C. Vandervort
Lecturer Negley Boyd Harte (London)
Visiting Lecturer Alonzo T. Stephens
Visiting Scholar Liu Ning

1990–1991
J. Howell Smith, Chair
Worrell Professor of Anglo-American Studies James Ralph Scales
Professors James P. Barefield, Richard C. Barnett, Paul D. Escott, Balkrishna Govind
  Gokhale, David W. Hadley, J. Edwin Hendricks, Thomas E. Mullen, Michael L.
  Sinclair, David L. Smiley, J. Howell Smith, Alan J. Williams, Richard L. Zuber
Assistant Professors Kevin M. Doak, Michael L. Hughes, William K. Meyers,
  Anthony S. Parent Jr., Yuri Slezkine, Sarah L. Watts
Visiting Assistant Professor Gloria J. Fitzgibbon
Adjunct Professor William T. Alderson
Lecturer Negley Boyd Harte (London)

1991–1992
J. Howell Smith, Chair
Reynolds Professor Paul D. Escott
Worrell Professor of Anglo-American Studies James Ralph Scales
Professors James P. Barefield, Richard C. Barnett, David W. Hadley, J. Edwin
  Hendricks, Thomas E. Mullen, Michael L. Sinclair, David L. Smiley, J. Howell
  Smith, Alan J. Williams, Richard L. Zuber
Associate Professor Michael L. Hughes

Assistant Professors Kevin M. Doak, William K. Meyers, Anthony S. Parent Jr., Yuri
   Slezkine, Sarah L. Watts
Visiting Assistant Professor Gloria J. Fitzgibbon
Adjunct Professor William T. Alderson
Lecturer Negley Boyd Harte (London)

1992–1993
J. Howell Smith, Chair
Reynolds Professor Paul D. Escott
Worrell Professor of Anglo-American Studies James Ralph Scales
Professors James P. Barefield, Richard C. Barnett, David W. Hadley, J. Edwin Hen-
   dricks, Thomas E. Mullen, Michael L. Sinclair, J. Howell Smith, Alan J. Williams,
   Richard L. Zuber
Associate Professors Michael L. Hughes, Sarah L. Watts
Assistant Professors Simone M. Caron, Kevin M. Doak, William K. Meyers,
   Anthony S. Parent Jr., Yuri Slezkine
Visiting Assistant Professor Christopher H. Owen
Adjunct Professor William T. Alderson
Lecturer Negley Boyd Harte (London)

1993–1994
J. Howell Smith, Chair
Reynolds Professor Paul D. Escott
Professors James P. Barefield, Richard C. Barnett, David W. Hadley, J. Edwin
   Hendricks, Thomas E. Mullen, Michael L. Sinclair, J. Howell Smith, Alan J.
   Williams, Richard L. Zuber
Associate Professors Michael L. Hughes, Sarah L. Watts
Assistant Professors Simone M. Caron, Kevin M. Doak, William K. Meyers,
   Anthony S. Parent Jr.
Visiting Assistant Professor Christopher Melchert
Adjunct Professor William T. Alderson
Instructor James J. Kennelly
Lecturer Negley Boyd Harte (London)

1994–1995
J. Howell Smith, Chair
Reynolds Professor Paul D. Escott
Professors James P. Barefield, Richard C. Barnett, David W. Hadley, J. Edwin
   Hendricks, Thomas E. Mullen, Michael L. Sinclair, J. Howell Smith, Alan J.
   Williams, Richard L. Zuber
Associate Professors Michael L. Hughes, William K. Meyers, Anthony S. Parent Jr.,
   Sarah L. Watts
Assistant Professors Simone M. Caron, Kevin M. Doak, Susan Z. Rupp
Lecturer Negley Boyd Harte (London)

1995–1996
J. Howell Smith, Chair
Reynolds Professor Paul D. Escott
Professors James P. Barefield, David W. Hadley, J. Edwin Hendricks, Thomas E. Mullen, Michael L. Sinclair, J. Howell Smith, Alan J. Williams, Richard L. Zuber
Associate Professors Michael L. Hughes, William K. Meyers, Anthony S. Parent Jr., Sarah L. Watts
Assistant Professors Simone M. Caron, Susan Z. Rupp
Visiting Assistant Professor Jeffrey D. Lerner
Instructor Joshua M. Landis
Visiting Instructor Wade Kit
Lecturer Negley Boyd Harte (London)

1996–1997
J. Edwin Hendricks, Chair
Reynolds Professor Paul D. Escott
Wake Forest Professor James P. Barefield
Professors J. Edwin Hendricks, Thomas E. Mullen, Michael L. Sinclair, J. Howell Smith, Alan J. Williams, Richard L. Zuber
Associate Professors Michael L. Hughes, William K. Meyers, Anthony S. Parent Jr., Sarah L. Watts
Assistant Professors Simone M. Caron, Susan Z. Rupp
Visiting Assistant Professor Jeffrey D. Lerner
Instructors Joanne Izbicki, Joshua M. Landis
Visiting Instructor Wade Kit
Lecturer Negley Boyd Harte (London)

1997–1998
J. Edwin Hendricks, Chair
Reynolds Professor Paul D. Escott
Wake Forest Professor James P. Barefield
Professors J. Edwin Hendricks, Thomas E. Mullen, Michael L. Sinclair, J. Howell Smith, Alan J. Williams, Richard L. Zuber
Associate Professors Michael L. Hughes, William K. Meyers, Anthony S. Parent Jr., Sarah L. Watts
Assistant Professors Simone M. Caron, Joanne Izbicki, Susan Z. Rupp
Visiting Assistant Professor Jeffrey D. Lerner
Instructor Joshua M. Landis

1998–1999
J. Edwin Hendricks, Chair
Reynolds Professor Paul D. Escott
Wake Forest Professor James P. Barefield
Professors J. Edwin Hendricks, Thomas E. Mullen, Michael L. Sinclair, J. Howell Smith, Alan J. Williams, Richard L. Zuber

Associate Professors Michael L. Hughes, William K. Meyers, Anthony S. Parent Jr.,
    Sarah L. Watts
Assistant Professors Simone M. Caron, Paul M. Cobb, Joanne Izbicki, Susan Z.
    Rupp, Claire S. Schen
Visiting Assistant Professors Gloria J. Fitzgibbon, Terence Kehoe, Jeffrey D. Lerner,
    David Libby
Visiting Adjunct Lecturer M. Beth Hopkins

1999–2000
J. Edwin Hendricks, Chair
Reynolds Professor Paul D. Escott
Wake Forest Professor James P. Barefield
Professors J. Edwin Hendricks, Michael L. Hughes, Thomas E. Mullen,
    Michael L. Sinclair, J. Howell Smith, Alan J. Williams, Richard L. Zuber
Associate Professors Simone M. Caron, William K. Meyers, Anthony S. Parent Jr.,
    Sarah L. Watts
Assistant Professors Paul M. Cobb, Joanne Izbicki, Jeffrey D. Lerner,
    Susan Z. Rupp, Claire S. Schen
Visiting Assistant Professors Robert Beachy, Terence Kehoe, Jama Mohamed
Visiting Adjunct Lecturer M. Beth Hopkins

2000–2001
Michael L. Hughes, Chair
Reynolds Professor Paul D. Escott
Wake Forest Professor James P. Barefield
Professors J. Edwin Hendricks, Michael L. Hughes, Thomas E. Mullen,
    Michael L. Sinclair, J. Howell Smith, Alan J. Williams, Richard L. Zuber
Associate Professors Simone M. Caron, Michele K. Gillespie, William K. Meyers,
    Anthony S. Parent Jr., Sarah L. Watts
Assistant Professors Joanne Izbicki, Jeffrey D. Lerner, Susan Z. Rupp,
    Claire S. Schen
Visiting Assistant Professors Robert Beachy, Jama Mohamed

2001–2002
Michael L. Hughes, Chair
Reynolds Professor Paul D. Escott
Wake Forest Professor James P. Barefield
Professors J. Edwin Hendricks, Michael L. Hughes, Michael L. Sinclair,
    J. Howell Smith, Alan J. Williams
Associate Professors Simone M. Caron, Michele K. Gillespie,
    Jeffrey D. Lerner, William K. Meyers, Anthony S. Parent Jr., Susan Z. Rupp,
    Sarah L. Watts
Assistant Professor Claire S. Schen
Visiting Assistant Professors Robert Beachy, Paul Burton, Jama Mohamed

2002–2003
Michael L. Hughes, Chair
Reynolds Professor Paul D. Escott
Wake Forest Professor James P. Barefield
Professors J. Edwin Hendricks, Michael L. Hughes, Michael L. Sinclair, J. Howell
Smith, Alan J. Williams
Associate Professors Simone M. Caron, Michele K. Gillespie, Jeffrey D. Lerner
(Z. Smith Reynolds Faculty Fellow), William K. Meyers, Anthony S. Parent Jr.,
Susan Z. Rupp, Sarah L. Watts
Assistant Professor Claire S. Schen
Visiting Assistant Professors Robert Beachy, Eliza Ferguson, Gloria J. Fitzgibbon
Instructor Ronald Bobroff

2003–2004
Michael L. Hughes, Chair
Reynolds Professor Paul D. Escott
Wake Forest Professor James P. Barefield
Professors J. Edwin Hendricks, Michael L. Hughes, Michael L. Sinclair, J. Howell
Smith, Alan J. Williams
Associate Professors Simone M. Caron, Michele K. Gillespie, Jeffrey D. Lerner
(Z. Smith Reynolds Faculty Fellow), William K. Meyers, Anthony S. Parent Jr.,
Susan Z. Rupp, Claire S. Schen, Sarah L. Watts
Assistant Professors Angus Lockyer, Cynthia Villagomez, James Wilson
Visiting Assistant Professors Robert Beachy, Ronald Bobroff, Gloria J.
Fitzgibbon, James Hastings

2004–2005
Susan Z. Rupp, Chair
Reynolds Professor Paul D. Escott
Wake Forest Professor James P. Barefield
Professors J. Edwin Hendricks, Michael L. Hughes, Michael L. Sinclair, J. Howell
Smith, Sarah L. Watts, Alan J. Williams
Associate Professors Simone M. Caron, Michele K. Gillespie (Kahle Associate
Professor), Jeffrey D. Lerner (Z. Smith Reynolds Faculty Fellow), William K.
Meyers, Anthony S. Parent Jr., Susan Z. Rupp, Claire S. Schen
Assistant Professors Angus Lockyer, Cynthia Villagomez, James Wilson
Visiting Assistant Professors Ronald Bobroff, Gloria J. Fitzgibbon, James Hastings
Instructor William Connell

2005–2006
Susan Z. Rupp, Chair
Reynolds Professor Paul D. Escott
Professors J. Edwin Hendricks, Michael L. Hughes, Michael L. Sinclair, J. Howell
Smith, Sarah L. Watts, Alan J. Williams

Associate Professors Simone M. Caron, Michele K. Gillespie (Kahle Associate
    Professor), Jeffrey D. Lerner, William K. Meyers, Anthony S. Parent Jr., Susan Z.
    Rupp
Assistant Professors Monique O'Connell, Cynthia Villagomez, James Wilson
Visiting Assistant Professors Ronald Bobroff, Gloria J. Fitzgibbon, James Hastings
Adjunct Professor Felicitas Opwis
Visiting Instructor Kent McConnell

HUMANITIES (HMN)

Interdisciplinary Minor
    (Humanities became an interdisciplinary minor in 1997–1998. The change was
first listed in the 1998–1999 *Bulletin.*)

1983–1985
N. Rick Heatley, Coordinator

1985–1986
William S. Hamilton, Coordinator
Reynolds Professor of American Studies Maya Angelou
Sam J. Ervin University Lecturer Wallace Carroll
Associate Professor Robert L. Utley Jr.

1986–1990
William S. Hamilton, Coordinator
Reynolds Professor of American Studies Maya Angelou
Associate Professor Robert L. Utley Jr.

1990–1991
William S. Hamilton, Coordinator
W. R. Kenan Jr. Professor of Humanities Allen Mandelbaum
Reynolds Professor of American Studies Maya Angelou
Associate Professor Robert L. Utley Jr.

1991–1996
Robert N. Shorter, Coordinator
Reynolds Professor of American Studies Maya Angelou
W. R. Kenan Jr. Professor of Humanities Allen Mandelbaum
Associate Professor Robert L. Utley Jr.

1996–1997
William S. Hamilton, Coordinator
W. R. Kenan Jr. Professor of Humanities Allen Mandelbaum
Reynolds Professor of American Studies Maya Angelou
Associate Professors Robert L. Utley Jr., Ulrike Wiethaus

1997–2001
William S. Hamilton, Coordinator
W. R. Kenan Jr. Professor of Humanities Allen Mandelbaum
Reynolds Professor of American Studies Maya Angelou
Associate Professors Robert L. Utley Jr., Ulrike Wiethaus
Assistant Professor Candyce Leonard

2001–2003
William S. Hamilton, Coordinator
W. R. Kenan Jr. Professor of Humanities Allen Mandelbaum
Reynolds Professor of American Studies Maya Angelou
Associate Professors Candyce Leonard, Robert L. Utley Jr., Ulrike Wiethaus

2003–2006
William S. Hamilton, Coordinator
W. R. Kenan Jr. Professor of Humanities Allen Mandelbaum
Reynolds Professor of American Studies Maya Angelou
Professor Ulrike Wiethaus
Associate Professors Candyce Leonard, Robert L. Utley Jr.

INTERDISCIPLINARY HONORS (HON)

1983–1988
Paul M. Gross Jr. (Chemistry), Coordinator

1988–2005
James P. Barefield (History), Coordinator

2005–2006
Barry Maine (English), Coordinator

INTERNATIONAL STUDIES (INS)

Interdisciplinary Minor

1993–1994
Richard Sears (International Studies), Coordinator

1994–1999
Richard Sears (Political Science), Coordinator

1999–2000
Richard Sears (Politics), Coordinator
Associate Professor Ian M. Taplin (Sociology)

2000–2002
Pia Christina Wood (Politics), Coordinator
Associate Professor Ian M. Taplin (Sociology)

2002–2003
Pia Christina Wood (Political Science), Coordinator
Professor Ian M. Taplin (Sociology)

2003–2006
Pia Christina Wood (Political Science), Coordinator

ITALIAN STUDIES
Foreign Area Study

1993–2006
Antonio Vitti (Romance Languages), Coordinator

JOURNALISM (JOU)
Minor

1995–2000
Wayne King, Coordinator
Visiting Lecturer Justin Catanoso

2000–2003
Wayne King, Coordinator
Adjunct Lecturers Justin Catanoso, Michael Horn

2003–2004
Wayne King, Coordinator
Lecturer Justin Catanoso
Adjunct Lecturer Michael Horn

2004–2005
Wayne King, Coordinator
Instructor Mary Martin Niepold
Lecturer Justin Catanoso
Adjunct Lecturer Michael Horn

2005–2006
Wayne King, Coordinator
Visiting Instructor Mary Martin Niepold
Lecturers Justin Catanoso, Michael Horn

LANGUAGES ACROSS THE CURRICULUM (LAC)

2003–2006
Candelas S. Gala (Romance Languages), Coordinator

LATIN-AMERICAN STUDIES (LAS)

Interdisciplinary Minor
   (The Foreign Area Study in Latin-American Studies became an interdisciplinary minor in 1995–1996. The change was first listed in the 1996–1997 *Bulletin.*)

1993–1994
Mary Friedman and Linda Maier (Romance Languages), Coordinators

1994–1995
Mary Friedman (Romance Languages), Coordinator

1995–2000
Mary Friedman (Romance Languages) and **William K. Meyers** (History), Coordinators

2000–2002
Mary Friedman (Romance Languages), Coordinator

2002–2004
Linda Howe (Spanish), Director

2004–2005
Linda Howe (Spanish), Director
Luis Roniger (Political Science)

2005–2006
Luis Roniger (Political Science), Director
Linda Howe (Spanish)

LINGUISTICS (LIN)

Interdisciplinary Minor

1994–2006
M. Stanley Whitley (Romance Languages), Coordinator

MATHEMATICS AND COMPUTER SCIENCE (MCS)

(The Department of Mathematics and Computer Science was originally the Department of Mathematics until 1983–1984. This change was first listed in the 1984–1985 *Bulletin*. In 1999–2000 the Department of Mathematics and Computer Science became separate departments: the Department of Mathematics and the Department of Computer Science. This change was first listed in the 2000–2001 *Bulletin*.)

1983–1984
Marcellus E. Waddill, Chair
Professors John V. Baxley, Richard D. Carmichael, Ivey C. Gentry, Frederic T.
    Howard, J. Gaylord May, W. Graham May, John W. Sawyer Sr., Ben M.
    Seelbinder, Marcellus E. Waddill
Associate Professors Elmer K. Hayashi, Ellen E. Kirkman, James Kuzmanovich
Assistant Professor David J. John
Instructors Deborah L. Harrell, Joanne M. Sulek, Ann R. Taylor

1984–1985
Marcellus E. Waddill, Chair
Professors John V. Baxley, Richard D. Carmichael, Ivey C. Gentry, Frederic T. Howard, James Kuzmanovich, J. Gaylord May, W. Graham May, John W. Sawyer Sr.,
    Ben M. Seelbinder, Marcellus E. Waddill
Associate Professors Elmer K. Hayashi, Ellen E. Kirkman
Assistant Professors David J. John, Stan J. Thomas
Visiting Professor S. Wilfred Hahn
Instructor Deborah L. Harrell

1985–1986
Marcellus E. Waddill, Chair
Professors John V. Baxley, Richard D. Carmichael, Ivey C. Gentry, Frederic T. Howard, James Kuzmanovich, J. Gaylord May, W. Graham May, John W. Sawyer Sr.,
    Ben M. Seelbinder, Marcellus E. Waddill
Associate Professors Elmer K. Hayashi, David J. John, Ellen E. Kirkman
Assistant Professor Stan J. Thomas
Visiting Assistant Professor John W. Sawyer Jr.
Instructor David C. Wilson

1986–1987
Marcellus E. Waddill, Chair
Professors John V. Baxley, Richard D. Carmichael, Ivey C. Gentry,
    Frederic T. Howard, James Kuzmanovich, J. Gaylord May, W. Graham May,
    John W. Sawyer Sr., Ben M. Seelbinder, Marcellus E. Waddill
Associate Professors Elmer K. Hayashi, David J. John, Ellen E. Kirkman
Assistant Professors James D. Kiper, Stan J. Thomas
Instructor Jule M. Connolly

1987–1988
Marcellus E. Waddill, Chair
Professors John V. Baxley, Richard D. Carmichael, Ivey C. Gentry,
　Frederic T. Howard, James Kuzmanovich, J. Gaylord May, W. Graham May,
　John W. Sawyer Sr., Ben M. Seelbinder, Marcellus E. Waddill
Associate Professors Elmer K. Hayashi, David J. John, Ellen E. Kirkman
Assistant Professor Stan J. Thomas
Instructors Jule M. Connolly, Eric E. Fink
Lecturer Gene T. Lucas

1988–1989
Marcellus E. Waddill, Chair
Professors John V. Baxley, Richard D. Carmichael, Ivey C. Gentry,
　Frederic T. Howard, James Kuzmanovich, J. Gaylord May, W. Graham May,
　John W. Sawyer Sr., Ben M. Seelbinder, Marcellus E. Waddill
Associate Professors Elmer K. Hayashi, David J. John, Ellen E. Kirkman
Assistant Professors Daniel Cañas, Stan J. Thomas
Instructors Jule M. Connolly, David C. Wilson
Lecturer Gene T. Lucas

1989–1990
Richard D. Carmichael, Chair
Professors John V. Baxley, Richard D. Carmichael, Ivey C. Gentry,
　Elmer K. Hayashi, Frederic T. Howard, James Kuzmanovich, J. Gaylord May,
　W. Graham May, Ben M. Seelbinder, Marcellus E. Waddill
Associate Professors David J. John, Ellen E. Kirkman, Stan J. Thomas
Assistant Professors Daniel Cañas, Charles R. Grissom Jr., Betty M. Tang
Instructors Jule M. Connolly, Eric E. Fink, David C. Wilson
Lecturer Gene T. Lucas

1990–1991
Richard D. Carmichael, Chair
Professors John V. Baxley, Richard D. Carmichael, Elmer K. Hayashi, Frederic T.
　Howard, Ellen E. Kirkman, James Kuzmanovich, J. Gaylord May, W. Graham
　May, Marcellus E. Waddill
Associate Professors David J. John, Stan J. Thomas
Assistant Professors Daniel Cañas, Charles R. Grissom Jr., Betty M. Tang,
　Todd C. Torgersen
Instructors Salman Azhar, Jule M. Connolly, Eric E. Fink, Graham S. Gersdorff,
　James L. Norris III, Dale T. Smith, David C. Wilson
Lecturer Gene T. Lucas

1991–1992
Richard D. Carmichael, Chair
Reynolds Professor Robert J. Plemmons

Professors John V. Baxley, Richard D. Carmichael, Elmer K. Hayashi,
    Frederic T. Howard, Ellen E. Kirkman, James Kuzmanovich, J. Gaylord May,
    W. Graham May, Wesley E. Snyder, Marcellus E. Waddill
Associate Professors David J. John, Stan J. Thomas
Assistant Professors Daniel Cañas, James L. Norris III, Todd C. Torgersen
Instructors Eva M. Allen, Jule M. Connolly, Graham S. Gersdorff,
    Karen A. Henderson, David C. Wilson
Lecturer Gene T. Lucas

1992–1994
Richard D. Carmichael, Chair
Reynolds Professor Robert J. Plemmons
Professors John V. Baxley, Richard D. Carmichael, Elmer K. Hayashi,
    Frederic T. Howard, Ellen E. Kirkman, James Kuzmanovich, J. Gaylord May,
    W. Graham May, Wesley E. Snyder, Marcellus E. Waddill
Associate Professors Daniel Cañas, David J. John, Stan J. Thomas
Assistant Professors Edward E. Allen, James L. Norris III, Stephen B. Robinson,
    Todd C. Torgersen
Instructors Eva M. Allen, Jule M. Connolly, David C. Wilson
Lecturer Gene T. Lucas

1994–1995
Richard D. Carmichael, Chair
Reynolds Professor Robert J. Plemmons
Professors John V. Baxley, Richard D. Carmichael, Elmer K. Hayashi,
    Frederic T. Howard, Ellen E. Kirkman, James Kuzmanovich, J. Gaylord May,
    W. Graham May, Wesley E. Snyder, Marcellus E. Waddill
Associate Professors Daniel Cañas, David J. John, Stan J. Thomas
Assistant Professors Edward E. Allen, James L. Norris III, Stephen B. Robinson,
    Todd C. Torgersen
Visiting Assistant Professor Jennifer J. Burg
Instructors Eva M. Allen, Jule M. Connolly, David C. Wilson
Lecturer Gene T. Lucas

1995–1996
Richard D. Carmichael, Chair
Reynolds Professor Robert J. Plemmons
Professors John V. Baxley, Richard D. Carmichael, Elmer K. Hayashi,
    Frederic T. Howard, Ellen E. Kirkman, James Kuzmanovich, J. Gaylord May,
    W. Graham May, Marcellus E. Waddill
Associate Professors Daniel Cañas, David J. John, Stan J. Thomas
Assistant Professors Edward E. Allen, James L. Norris III, Stephen B. Robinson,
    Todd C. Torgersen
Visiting Assistant Professors F. Glenn Acree, Jennifer J. Burg, Jeffrey K. Lawson
Instructors Jule M. Connolly, David C. Wilson

1996–1997
Richard D. Carmichael, Chair
Reynolds Professor Robert J. Plemmons
Professors John V. Baxley, Richard D. Carmichael, Elmer K. Hayashi,
    Frederic T. Howard, Ellen E. Kirkman, James Kuzmanovich, J. Gaylord May,
    W. Graham May, Marcellus E. Waddill
Associate Professors Daniel Cañas, David J. John, Stan J. Thomas,
    Todd C. Torgersen
Assistant Professors Edward E. Allen, Yaorong Ge, Paul F. Hemler,
    James L. Norris III, Stephen B. Robinson
Visiting Assistant Professors F. Glenn Acree, Jennifer J. Burg, Jeffrey K. Lawson
Instructors Jule M. Connolly, David C. Wilson

1997–1998
Richard D. Carmichael, Chair
Reynolds Professor Robert J. Plemmons
Professors John V. Baxley, Richard D. Carmichael, Elmer K. Hayashi,
    Frederic T. Howard, Ellen E. Kirkman, James Kuzmanovich, J. Gaylord May,
    Marcellus E. Waddill
Associate Professors Daniel Cañas, David J. John, Stan J. Thomas,
    Todd C. Torgersen
Assistant Professors Edward E. Allen, Jennifer J. Burg, Yaorong Ge,
    Paul F. Hemler, Stephen B. Robinson
Visiting Associate Professor Margaret A. Francel
Visiting Assistant Professors F. Glenn Acree, Jeffrey K. Lawson
Instructors Christa Beck, Janice Blackburn, Jule M. Connolly, Marc Renault,
    David C. Wilson

1998–1999
Richard D. Carmichael, Chair
Reynolds Professor Robert J. Plemmons
Wake Forest Professor John V. Baxley
Professors Richard D. Carmichael, Elmer K. Hayashi, Frederic T. Howard, Ellen E.
    Kirkman, James Kuzmanovich, J. Gaylord May
Associate Professors Edward E. Allen, Daniel Cañas, David J. John,
    James L. Norris III, Stephen B. Robinson, Stan J. Thomas, Todd C. Torgersen
Assistant Professors Jennifer J. Burg, Yaorong Ge, Paul F. Hemler,
    Hugh N. Howards
Visiting Assistant Professors Richard H. Hammack, Jeffrey K. Lawson,
    David W. Lyons
Instructors Christa Beck, Janice Blackburn, Jule M. Connolly, Patricia Y. Underhill,
    David C. Wilson

1999–2000
Richard D. Carmichael, Chair
Reynolds Professor Robert J. Plemmons

Wake Forest Professor John V. Baxley
Professors Richard D. Carmichael, Elmer K. Hayashi, Frederic T. Howard, Ellen E.
    Kirkman, James Kuzmanovich, J. Gaylord May
Associate Professors Edward E. Allen, Daniel Cañas, David J. John, James L. Norris
    III, Stephen B. Robinson, Stan J. Thomas, Todd C. Torgersen
Assistant Professors Jennifer J. Burg, Yaorong Ge, Paul F. Hemler, Hugh N. How-
    ards, Miaohua Jiang
Visiting Assistant Professors Richard H. Hammack, David W. Lyons
Instructors Janice Blackburn, Jule M. Connolly, Patricia Y. Underhill, David C.
    Wilson

MATHEMATICS (MTH)

(The Department of Mathematics was originally the Department of Mathematics
and Computer Science until 1999–2000. The change was first listed in the 2000–2001
Bulletin.)

2000–2001
Richard D. Carmichael, Chair
Reynolds Professor Robert J. Plemmons
Wake Forest Professor John V. Baxley
Professors Richard D. Carmichael, Elmer K. Hayashi, Frederic T. Howard,
    Ellen E. Kirkman, James Kuzmanovich, J. Gaylord May
Associate Professors Edward E. Allen, James L. Norris III, Stephen B. Robinson
Assistant Professors Hugh N. Howards, Miaohua Jiang
Visiting Assistant Professors Richard H. Hammack, David W. Lyons
Instructors Janice Blackburn, Jule M. Connolly, David C. Wilson

2001–2002
Richard D. Carmichael, Chair
Reynolds Professor Robert J. Plemmons
Wake Forest Professor John V. Baxley
Professors Richard D. Carmichael, Elmer K. Hayashi, Frederic T. Howard,
    Ellen E. Kirkman, James Kuzmanovich, J. Gaylord May
Associate Professors Edward E. Allen, James L. Norris III, Stephen B. Robinson
Assistant Professors Kenneth S. Berenhaut, Hugh N. Howards, Miaohua Jiang
Visiting Assistant Professors R. Douglas Chatham, Douglas S. Daniel
Instructors Janice Blackburn, Jule M. Connolly, David C. Wilson

2002–2003
Richard D. Carmichael, Chair
Reynolds Professor Robert J. Plemmons
Wake Forest Professor John V. Baxley
Professors Richard D. Carmichael, Elmer K. Hayashi, Frederic T. Howard,
    Ellen E. Kirkman, James Kuzmanovich, J. Gaylord May

Associate Professors Edward E. Allen (Sterge Faculty Fellow), James L. Norris III,
Stephen B. Robinson (Sterge Faculty Fellow)
Assistant Professors Kenneth S. Berenhaut, Hugh N. Howards, Miaohua Jiang,
Marielba Rojas
Visiting Assistant Professor Douglas S. Daniel
Instructors Janice Blackburn, Jule M. Connolly, David C. Wilson

2003–2004
Richard D. Carmichael, Chair
Reynolds Professor Robert J. Plemmons
Wake Forest Professor John V. Baxley
Professors Richard D. Carmichael, Elmer K. Hayashi, Frederic T. Howard,
Ellen E. Kirkman, James Kuzmanovich, J. Gaylord May, James L. Norris III
Associate Professors Edward E. Allen (Sterge Faculty Fellow), Stephen B. Robinson
(Sterge Faculty Fellow)
Assistant Professors Kenneth S. Berenhaut, Hugh N. Howards, Miaohua Jiang,
Marielba Rojas
Visiting Assistant Professor Douglas S. Daniel
Instructors Janice Blackburn, Jule M. Connolly, David C. Wilson

2004–2005
Richard D. Carmichael, Chair
Reynolds Professor Robert J. Plemmons
Wake Forest Professor John V. Baxley
Professors Richard D. Carmichael, Elmer K. Hayashi, Frederic T. Howard,
Ellen E. Kirkman, James Kuzmanovich, J. Gaylord May, James L. Norris III
Associate Professors Edward E. Allen, Hugh N. Howards (Sterge Faculty Fellow),
Stephen B. Robinson
Assistant Professor Kenneth S. Berenhaut (Sterge Faculty Fellow), Miaohua Jiang,
Sarah Raynor, Marielba Rojas, Gregory Warrington
Visiting Assistant Professor Christopher E. Dometrius
Instructors Janice Blackburn, Jule M. Connolly, Mary Kathryn McKinnon,
David C. Wilson

2005–2006
Stephen B. Robinson, Chair
Reynolds Professor Robert J. Plemmons
Professors Richard D. Carmichael, Frederic T. Howard, Ellen E. Kirkman, James
Kuzmanovich, J. Gaylord May, James L. Norris III
Associate Professors Edward E. Allen, Hugh N. Howards (Sterge Faculty Fellow),
Miaohua Jiang, Stephen B. Robinson
Assistant Professor Kenneth S. Berenhaut (Sterge Faculty Fellow), Sarah Raynor,
Marielba Rojas, Gregory Warrington
Visiting Assistant Professor Christopher E. Dometrius
Instructors Janice Blackburn, Jule M. Connolly, David C. Wilson

MEDIEVAL STUDIES
Interdisciplinary Minor

1994–2006
Gillian Overing (English) and **Gale Sigal** (English), Coordinators

MIDDLE EAST AND SOUTH ASIA STUDIES
Minor

2004–2006
Charles H. Kennedy (Political Science), Coordinator

MILITARY SCIENCE (MIL)

1983–1984
Lieutenant Colonel Matthew P. Murray Jr., Professor
Assistant Professors: Major Robert H. Lewis, Major Daniel F. Smith, Captain Max E. Brewer, Captain Gregg L. Hill, Captain David E. Janney, Captain Jasper L. McBride, Captain Curtis L. Shelton
Instructors: Sergeant Major Ezequiel B. Evaro, Master Sergeant Arlanza L. Cook, Sergeant First Class Donald F. Pope, Staff Sergeant Albert E. Folds

1984–1985
Lieutenant Colonel Matthew P. Murray Jr., Professor
Assistant Professors: Major Peter J. Adolf, Major Daniel F. Smith, Captain Max E. Brewer, Captain Richard H. Crocker, Captain Scott A. Fernald, Captain Gregg L. Hill, Captain Henry C. Newell
Instructors: Sergeant Major Ezequiel B. Evaro, Master Sergeant Arlanza L. Cook, Sergeant First Class Calvin Barnes, Staff Sergeant Albert E. Folds

1985–1986
Lieutenant Colonel Daniel F. Smith, Professor
Assistant Professors: Major Peter J. Adolf, Major Max E. Brewer, Captain Scott A. Fernald, Captain Henry C. Newell
Instructors: Sergeant Major Charles F. Richardson, Sergeant First Class Calvin Barnes, Staff Sergeant Albert E. Folds

1986–1987
Lieutenant Colonel Daniel F. Smith, Professor
Assistant Professors: Major Peter J. Adolf, Major Heyward G. Brown, Major Richard H. Crocker, Captain Scott A. Fernald, Captain Henry C. Newell

Instructors: Sergeant Major Charles F. Richardson, Sergeant First Class Calvin Barnes, Staff Sergeant Johnny Ferguson

1987–1988
Lieutenant Colonel Thomas A. Glenn, Professor
Assistant Professors: Major Heyward G. Brown, Major James W. DeVocht, Captain Scott A. Fernald, Captain Horace S. Tucker, Captain Scott A. Marquardt
Instructors: Sergeant Major Charles F. Richardson, Sergeant First Class James R. Degenkolb, Staff Sergeant Johnny Ferguson

1988–1989
Lieutenant Colonel Thomas A. Glenn, Professor
Assistant Professors: Major James W. DeVocht, Captain Scott A. Fernald, Major Stanley R. Lawson, Captain Scott A. Marquardt
Instructors: Sergeant Major Lincoln C. Mitchell, Sergeant First Class James R. Degenkolb

1989–1990
Lieutenant Colonel Thomas A. Glenn, Professor
Assistant Professors: Major Stanley R. Lawson, Captain Charles Hands, Captain Scott A. Marquardt
Instructors: Sergeant Major Lincoln C. Mitchell, Sergeant First Class James R. Degenkolb

1990–1991
Lieutenant Colonel John P. Modica, Professor
Assistant Professors: Major Stanley R. Lawson, Captain Charles Hands, Captain Scott A. Marquardt, Captain Frank M. Williamson
Instructors: Captain Stephen J. Huebner, Sergeant Major Lincoln C. Mitchell Jr., Sergeant First Class James R. Degenkolb

1991–1992
Lieutenant Colonel John P. Modica, Professor
Assistant Professors: Captain David P. Bumgarner, Captain Thomas B. Dalton III, Captain Charles Hands, Captain Frank M. Williamson
Instructors: Major Stephen J. Huebner, Sergeant Major Lincoln C. Mitchell Jr., Sergeant First Class Clifton Lowery

1992–1993
Lieutenant Colonel John P. Modica, Professor
Assistant Professors: Captain David P. Bumgarner, Captain Thomas B. Dalton III, Captain Charles Hands, Captain Frank M. Williamson

Instructors: Major Stephen J. Huebner, Sergeant Major Lewis L. Green, Master
  Sergeant Clifton Lowery

1993–1994
Lieutenant Colonel Kenneth M. Walker, Professor
Assistant Professors: Captain David P. Bumgarner, Captain Rufus S. Gatlin Jr.,
  Captain William M. Pedersen, Captain Frank M. Williamson
Instructors: Major Stephen J. Huebner, Sergeant Major Lewis L. Green, Master
  Sergeant Clifton Lowery

1994–1995
Lieutenant Colonel Kenneth M. Walker, Professor
Assistant Professors: Major William M. Pedersen, Major Frank M. Williamson,
  Captain Rugus S. Gatlin Jr., Captain Jeffrey A. Marquez
Instructors: Major Stephen J. Huebner, Sergeant Major Gregory A. Duhon,
  Master Sergeant George T. Loebe Jr.

1995–1996
Lieutenant Colonel Kenneth M. Walker, Professor
Assistant Professors: Major William M. Pedersen, Major Frank M. Williamson,
  Captain Jeffrey A. Marquez, Captain Kathy A. Underwood
Instructors: Sergeant Major Gregory A. Duhon, Master Sergeant James H. Barrett,
  Master Sergeant George T. Loebe Jr.
Adjunct Instructor: Major Stephen J. Huebner

1996–1997
Lieutenant Colonel Donald J. Moser, Professor
Adjunct Professor: Lieutenant Colonel Kenneth M. Walker
Assistant Professors: Major James C. Brand, Captain Patrick L. Rimron, Captain
  Kathy A. Underwood
Instructor: Sergeant First Class Anthony Pardella
Adjunct Instructor: Major Stephen J. Huebner

1997–1998
Lieutenant Colonel Donald J. Moser, Professor
Adjunct Professor: Lieutenant Colonel Kenneth M. Walker
Assistant Professors: Major James C. Brand, Captain Christian J. Abell,
  Captain Patrick L. Rimron, Captain Kathy A. Underwood
Instructors: Sergeant First Class Anthony Pardella, Sergeant First Class Elton L.
  Richards Jr.
Adjunct Instructor: Major Stephen J. Huebner

1998–1999
Lieutenant Colonel Donald J. Moser, Professor
Adjunct Professor: Lieutenant Colonel Kenneth M. Walker

Assistant Professors: Major James C. Brand, Captain Christian J. Abell, Captain Patrick L. Rimron
Instructors: Master Sergeant Elton L. Richards Jr., Sergeant First Class Anthony Pardella
Adjunct Instructor: Lieutenant Colonel Stephen J. Huebner

1999–2000
Lieutenant Colonel James R. Page II, Professor
Adjunct Professor: Lieutenant Colonel Kenneth M. Walker
Assistant Professors Captain Joseph P. Colebaugh, Captain Brian K. Coppersmith, Captain Jimmy E. Hall, Major Dennis J. Scheuermann
Instructor Sergeant First Class Anthony L. Pardella

2000–2001
Lieutenant Colonel James R. Page II, Professor
Assistant Professors: Major Joseph P. Colebaugh, Major Brian K. Coppersmith, Major Jimmy E. Hall, Major Dennis J. Scheuermann
Instructor: Master Sergeant Gregory Campbell

2001–2002
Lieutenant Colonel James R. Page II, Professor
Assistant Professors: Tina M. Colston, Major Brian K. Coppersmith, Captain Edward C. Jackman
Instructor: Master Sergeant Gregory Campbell
Training NCO: Sergeant First Class Matthew C. Pickett

2002–2003
Lieutenant Colonel James R. Page II, Professor
Assistant Professors: Tina M. Colston, Captain Edward C. Jackman, William J. Ryan
Instructor: Master Sergeant Gregory Campbell

2003–2004
Lieutenant Colonel James R. Page II, Professor
Assistant Professors: Tina M. Colston, William J. Ryan, Robert D. Seals

2004–2005
Lieutenant Colonel James R. Page II, Professor
Assistant Professors: William J. Ryan, Robert D. Seals, Walter Todd, Rodney Wallace
Adjunct Instructor: Donald J. Moser

2005–2006
Lieutenant Colonel M. Keith Callahan, Professor
Assistant Professors: James F. Baker III, Brian P. Steele, Walter Todd, Rodney Wallace
Adjunct Instructor: Donald J. Moser

MUSIC (MUS)

1983–1984
Susan Harden Borwick, Chair
Associate Professor Susan Harden Borwick
Assistant Professors Stewart Carter, Christopher Giles, Louis Goldstein,
    David B. Levy, Dan Locklair, John V. Mochnick
Assistant Director of Instrumental Ensembles Martin Province
Instructors Lucille S. Harris, Teresa Radomski

1984–1985
Susan Harden Borwick, Chair
Associate Professor Susan Harden Borwick
Assistant Professors Stewart Carter, Christopher Giles, Louis Goldstein,
    David B. Levy, Dan Locklair, John V. Mochnick
Director of Instrumental Ensembles George W. Trautwein
Assistant Director of Instrumental Ensembles Martin Province
Instructors Lucille S. Harris, Teresa Radomski

1985–1986
Susan Harden Borwick, Chair
Associate Professor Susan Harden Borwick
Assistant Professors Stewart Carter, Christopher Giles, Louis Goldstein,
    David B. Levy, Dan Locklair, Teresa Radomski
Visiting Assistant Professor Patti B. Peterson
Director of Choral Ensembles Brian Gorelick
Director of Instrumental Ensembles George W. Trautwein
Assistant Director of Instrumental Ensembles Martin Province
Instructor Lucille S. Harris

1986–1987
Susan Harden Borwick, Chair
Associate Professors Susan Harden Borwick, Christopher Giles, Louis Goldstein
Assistant Professors Stewart Carter, David B. Levy, Dan Locklair, Teresa Radomski
Director of Choral Ensembles Brian Gorelick
Director of Instrumental Ensembles George W. Trautwein
Assistant Director of Instrumental Ensembles Martin Province
Visiting Assistant Director of Instrumental Ensembles Barbara Trautwein
Instructor Lucille S. Harris

1987–1989
Susan Harden Borwick, Chair
Associate Professors Susan Harden Borwick, Stewart Carter, Christopher Giles,
    Louis Goldstein

Assistant Professors David B. Levy, Dan Locklair, Teresa Radomski
Director of Choral Ensembles Brian Gorelick
Director of Instrumental Ensembles George W. Trautwein
Assistant Director of Instrumental Ensembles Martin Province
Instructors Patricia Dixon, Lucille S. Harris

1989–1990
Susan Harden Borwick, Chair
Professor Susan Harden Borwick
Associate Professors Stewart Carter, Louis Goldstein, David B. Levy, Dan Locklair
Assistant Professors Peter Kairoff, Teresa Radomski
Director of Choral Ensembles Brian Gorelick
Director of Instrumental Ensembles George W. Trautwein
Assistant Director of Instrumental Ensembles Martin Province
Instructors Patricia Dixon, Lucille S. Harris, Kathryn Levy

1990–1991
Susan Harden Borwick, Chair
Professor Susan Harden Borwick
Associate Professors Stewart Carter, Louis Goldstein, David B. Levy, Dan Locklair
Assistant Professors Peter Kairoff, Teresa Radomski
Visiting Assistant Professor Pamela Howland
Director of Choral Ensembles Brian Gorelick
Director of Instrumental Ensembles George W. Trautwein
Assistant Director of Instrumental Ensembles Martin Province
Instructors Patricia Dixon, Lucille S. Harris, Kathryn Levy

1991–1992
Susan Harden Borwick, Chair
Professor Susan Harden Borwick
Associate Professors Stewart Carter, Louis Goldstein, David B. Levy, Dan Locklair
Assistant Professors Peter Kairoff, Teresa Radomski
Visiting Assistant Professor Pamela Howland
Director of Choral Ensembles Brian Gorelick
Director of Instrumental Ensembles George W. Trautwein
Visiting Director of Choral Ensembles Robert Cowles
Assistant Director of Instrumental Ensembles Martin Province
Instructors Patricia Dixon, Lucille S. Harris, Kathryn Levy

1992–1993
Susan Harden Borwick, Chair
Professor Susan Harden Borwick
Associate Professors Stewart Carter, Louis Goldstein, David B. Levy, Dan Locklair
Assistant Professors Pamela Howland, Peter Kairoff, Teresa Radomski
Director of Choral Ensembles Brian Gorelick

Director of Instrumental Ensembles George W. Trautwein
Assistant Director of Instrumental Ensembles Martin Province
Instructors Patricia Dixon, Kathryn Levy

1993–1994
Susan Harden Borwick, Chair
Professor Susan Harden Borwick
Associate Professors Stewart Carter, Louis Goldstein, Peter Kairoff, David B. Levy,
    Dan Locklair
Assistant Professors Pamela Howland, Teresa Radomski
Director of Choral Ensembles Brian Gorelick
Director of Instrumental Ensembles George W. Trautwein
Assistant Director of Instrumental Ensembles Martin Province
Instructors Patricia Dixon, Kathryn Levy

1994–1995
Susan Harden Borwick, Chair
Professors Susan Harden Borwick, Louis Goldstein
Associate Professors Stewart Carter, Peter Kairoff, David B. Levy, Dan Locklair,
    Teresa Radomski
Assistant Professor Pamela Howland
Director of Choral Ensembles Brian Gorelick
Director of Instrumental Ensembles George W. Trautwein
Assistant Director of Instrumental Ensembles Martin Province
Instructors Patricia Dixon, Kathryn Levy

1995–1997
David B. Levy, Chair
Professors Susan Harden Borwick, Louis Goldstein
Associate Professors Stewart Carter, Peter Kairoff, David B. Levy, Dan Locklair
    (Composer-in-Residence), Teresa Radomski
Assistant Professor Pamela Howland
Director of Choral Ensembles Brian Gorelick
Director of Instrumental Ensembles George W. Trautwein
Assistant Director of Instrumental Ensembles C. Kevin Bowen
Instructors Patricia Dixon, Kathryn Levy

1997–1998
David B. Levy, Chair
Professors Susan Harden Borwick, Stewart Carter, Louis Goldstein,
    Dan Locklair (Composer-in-Residence)
Associate Professors Peter Kairoff, David B. Levy, Teresa Radomski
Assistant Professors Brian Gorelick (Director of Choral Ensembles),
    Pamela Howland
Director of Bands C. Kevin Bowen

Director of Orchestra David Hagy
Instructors Patricia Dixon, Richard E. Heard, Kathryn Levy

1998–1999
David B. Levy, Chair
Professors Susan Harden Borwick, Stewart Carter, Louis Goldstein,
    David B. Levy, Dan Locklair (Composer-in-Residence)
Associate Professors Peter Kairoff, Teresa Radomski
Assistant Professors Brian Gorelick (Director of Choral Ensembles),
    Pamela Howland
Director of Bands C. Kevin Bowen
Director of Orchestra David Hagy
Instructors Patricia Dixon, Richard E. Heard, Kathryn Levy

1999–2000
David B. Levy, Chair
Professors Susan Harden Borwick, Stewart Carter, Louis Goldstein,
    David B. Levy, Dan Locklair (Composer-in-Residence)
Associate Professors Peter Kairoff, Teresa Radomski
Assistant Professors Brian Gorelick (Director of Choral Ensembles),
    Richard E. Heard
Director of Bands C. Kevin Bowen
Director of Orchestra David Hagy
Instructors Patricia Dixon, Kathryn Levy

2000–2001
David B. Levy, Chair
Professors Susan Harden Borwick, Stewart Carter, Louis Goldstein,
    David B. Levy, Dan Locklair (Composer-in-Residence)
Associate Professors Peter Kairoff, Teresa Radomski
Assistant Professors Jacqui Carrasco, Brian Gorelick
    (Director of Choral Ensembles), Richard E. Heard
Director of Bands C. Kevin Bowen
Director of Orchestra David Hagy
Instructors Patricia Dixon, Kathryn Levy

2001–2002
David B. Levy, Chair
Professors Susan Harden Borwick, Stewart Carter, Louis Goldstein,
    David B. Levy, Dan Locklair (Composer-in-Residence)
Associate Professors Brian Gorelick (Director of Choral Ensembles),
    Peter Kairoff, Teresa Radomski
Assistant Professors Jacqui Carrasco, Richard E. Heard
Director of Bands C. Kevin Bowen

Director of Orchestra David Hagy
Instructors Patricia Dixon, Kathryn Levy
Lecturer Morten Solvik (Vienna)

2002–2003
David B. Levy, Chair
Professors Susan Harden Borwick, Stewart Carter, Louis Goldstein, Peter Kairoff,
    David B. Levy, Dan Locklair (Composer-in-Residence), Teresa Radomski
Associate Professor Brian Gorelick (Director of Choral Ensembles)
Assistant Professors Jacqui Carrasco, Richard E. Heard
Director of Bands C. Kevin Bowen
Director of Orchestra David Hagy
Lecturers Patricia Dixon, Kathryn Levy, Morten Solvik (Vienna)

2003–2004
David B. Levy, Chair
Professors Susan Harden Borwick, Stewart Carter, Louis Goldstein, Peter Kairoff,
    David B. Levy, Dan Locklair (Composer-in-Residence), Teresa Radomski
Associate Professors Brian Gorelick (Director of Choral Ensembles),
    Richard E. Heard
Assistant Professor Jacqui Carrasco
Director of Bands C. Kevin Bowen
Director of Orchestra David Hagy
Adjunct Instructors Bama Lutes Deal, Charles Stein
Lecturers Patricia Dixon, Kathryn Levy, Morten Solvik (Vienna)
Visiting Lecturer in Music Lorraine DiSimone

2004–2005
David B. Levy, Chair
Professors Susan Harden Borwick, Stewart Carter, Louis Goldstein, Peter Kairoff,
    David B. Levy, Dan Locklair (Composer-in-Residence), Teresa Radomski
Associate Professors Brian Gorelick (Director of Choral Ensembles),
    Richard E. Heard
Assistant Professor Jacqui Carrasco
Director of Bands C. Kevin Bowen
Director of Orchestra David Hagy
Adjunct Instructor Bama Lutes Deal
Lecturers Patricia Dixon, Kathryn Levy, Morten Solvik (Vienna)
Visiting Lecturers Lorraine DiSimone, Janet Orenstein

2005–2006
David B. Levy, Chair
Professors Susan Harden Borwick, Stewart Carter, Louis Goldstein,
    Peter Kairoff, David B. Levy, Dan Locklair (Composer-in-Residence),
    Teresa Radomski

Associate Professors Brian Gorelick (Director of Choral Ensembles),
    Richard E. Heard
Assistant Professor Jacqui Carrasco
Director of Bands C. Kevin Bowen
Director of Orchestra David Hagy
Adjunct Instructor Bama Lutes Deal
Lecturers Patricia Dixon, Kathryn Levy, Morten Solvik (Vienna)
Visiting Lecturer Janet Orenstein

NATURAL SCIENCES (NAS)

1985–2002
Dudley Shapere, Reynolds Professor of Philosophy and History of Science

NEUROSCIENCE (NEU)

Interdisciplinary Minor

2000–2006
Wayne L. Silver (Biology), Coordinator

PHILOSOPHY (PHI)

1983–1984
Gregory D. Pritchard, Chair
Professors Robert M. Helm, Marcus B. Hester, Gregory D. Pritchard
Associate Professors Ralph C. Kennedy III, Charles M. Lewis

1984–1985
Gregory D. Pritchard, Chair
Worrell Professor Robert M. Helm
Professors Marcus B. Hester, Gregory D. Pritchard
Associate Professors Ralph C. Kennedy III, Charles M. Lewis
Instructor Win-chiat Lee

1985–1987
Gregory D. Pritchard, Chair
Worrell Professor Robert M. Helm
Professors Marcus B. Hester, Gregory D. Pritchard
Associate Professors Ralph C. Kennedy III, Charles M. Lewis
Instructor Win-chiat Lee
Lecturer Hannah M. Hardgrave

1987–1988
Gregory D. Pritchard, Chair
Worrell Professor Robert M. Helm
Professors Thomas K. Hearn Jr., Marcus B. Hester, Gregory D. Pritchard
Associate Professors Ralph C. Kennedy III, Charles M. Lewis
Visiting Assistant Professor Win-chiat Lee
Instructor Charles J. Kinlaw
Lecturer Hannah M. Hardgrave

1988–1989
Gregory D. Pritchard, Chair
Worrell Professor Robert M. Helm
Professors Thomas K. Hearn Jr., Marcus B. Hester, Charles M. Lewis,
    Gregory D. Pritchard
Associate Professor Ralph C. Kennedy III
Assistant Professor Win-chiat Lee
Instructors Charles M. Gass, Charles J. Kinlaw
Lecturer Hannah M. Hardgrave

1989–1991
Gregory D. Pritchard, Chair
Worrell Professor Robert M. Helm
Professors Thomas K. Hearn Jr., Marcus B. Hester, Charles M. Lewis,
    Gregory D. Pritchard
Associate Professor Ralph C. Kennedy III
Assistant Professor Win-chiat Lee
Instructor Charles J. Kinlaw
Lecturer Hannah M. Hardgrave

1991–1994
Gregory D. Pritchard, Chair
Worrell Professor Robert M. Helm
Professors Thomas K. Hearn Jr., Marcus B. Hester, Charles M. Lewis,
    Gregory D. Pritchard
Associate Professors Ralph C. Kennedy III, Win-chiat Lee
Instructor Charles J. Kinlaw
Lecturer Hannah M. Hardgrave

1994–1995
Win-chiat Lee, Chair
Gregory D. Pritchard, Acting Chair
Worrell Professor Robert M. Helm
Professors Thomas K. Hearn Jr., Marcus B. Hester, Charles M. Lewis,
    Gregory D. Pritchard

Associate Professors Ralph C. Kennedy III, Win-chiat Lee
Instructor Charles J. Kinlaw
Visiting Instructor Andrew Cross
Lecturer Hannah M. Hardgrave

1995–1996
Win-chiat Lee, Chair
Worrell Professor Robert M. Helm
Professors Thomas K. Hearn Jr., Marcus B. Hester, Charles M. Lewis
Associate Professors Ralph C. Kennedy III, Win-chiat Lee
Assistant Professor Josefine C. Nauckhoff
Instructor Charles J. Kinlaw
Lecturer Hannah M. Hardgrave

1996–1997
Win-chiat Lee, Chair
A.C. Reid Visiting Professor J. Martin Hollis
Worrell Professor Robert M. Helm
Professors Thomas K. Hearn Jr., Marcus B. Hester, Charles M. Lewis
Associate Professors Ralph C. Kennedy III, Win-chiat Lee
Assistant Professor Josefine C. Nauckhoff
Visiting Assistant Professor H. Lee Overton
Instructor N. Dane Scott
Lecturer Hannah M. Hardgrave

1997–1999
Win-chiat Lee, Chair
Worrell Professor Robert M. Helm
Professors Thomas K. Hearn Jr., Marcus B. Hester, Charles M. Lewis
Associate Professors Ralph C. Kennedy III, Win-chiat Lee
Assistant Professor Josefine C. Nauckhoff
Visiting Assistant Professor H. Lee Overton
Instructors Charles J. Kinlaw, N. Dane Scott
Lecturer Hannah M. Hardgrave

1999–2000
Win-chiat Lee, Chair
Worrell Professor Robert M. Helm
Professors Thomas K. Hearn Jr., Marcus B. Hester, Charles M. Lewis
Associate Professors Ralph C. Kennedy III, Win-chiat Lee
Assistant Professors Andrew A. Cross, Josefine C. Nauckhoff
Visiting Assistant Professor H. Lee Overton
Instructor N. Dane Scott
Lecturer Hannah M. Hardgrave

2000–2001
Win-chiat Lee, Chair
Worrell Professor Robert M. Helm
Professors Thomas K. Hearn Jr., Marcus B. Hester, Charles M. Lewis
Associate Professors Ralph C. Kennedy III, Win-chiat Lee
Assistant Professors Andrew A. Cross, Josefine C. Nauckhoff
Visiting Assistant Professors Michael V. Griffin, H. Lee Overton, N. Dane Scott
Instructor Eric E. Brandon
Lecturer Hannah M. Hardgrave

2001–2002
Win-chiat Lee, Chair
A.C. Reid Visiting Professor Robert Audi
Worrell Professor Robert M. Helm
Professors Thomas K. Hearn Jr., Marcus B. Hester, Charles M. Lewis
Associate Professors Ralph C. Kennedy III, Win-chiat Lee
Assistant Professors Andrew A. Cross, Josefine C. Nauckhoff
Visiting Assistant Professors Amy Lara Cross, Michael V. Griffin, H. Lee Overton
Instructor Eric E. Brandon
Lecturer Hannah M. Hardgrave

2002–2003
Ralph C. Kennedy III, Chair
Worrell Professor Robert M. Helm
Professors Thomas K. Hearn Jr., Marcus B. Hester, Charles M. Lewis
Associate Professors Ralph C. Kennedy III, Win-chiat Lee
Assistant Professor Andrew A. Cross
Visiting Assistant Professors Michael V. Griffin, Dorthea Lotter, Clark Thompson
Instructor Eric E. Brandon
Lecturer Hannah M. Hardgrave

2003–2004
Ralph C. Kennedy III, Chair
A.C. Reid Professor George Graham
Professors Thomas K. Hearn Jr., Marcus B. Hester, Charles M. Lewis
Associate Professors Ralph C. Kennedy III, Win-chiat Lee
Assistant Professors Adrian Bardon, Andrew A. Cross
Visiting Assistant Professors Eric E. Brandon, Dorthea Lotter, Clark Thompson
Lecturer Hannah M. Hardgrave

2004–2005
Ralph C. Kennedy III, Chair
A.C. Reid Professor George Graham
Professors Thomas K. Hearn Jr., Marcus B. Hester, Charles M. Lewis

Associate Professors Ralph C. Kennedy III, Win-chiat Lee
Assistant Professor Adrian Bardon
Visiting Assistant Professors Dorthea Lotter, Clark Thompson
Instructor Avram Hiller
Lecturer Hannah M. Hardgrave

2005–2006
Ralph C. Kennedy III, Chair
A.C. Reid Professor George Graham
Professors Thomas K. Hearn Jr., Marcus B. Hester, Charles M. Lewis
Associate Professors Ralph C. Kennedy III, Win-chiat Lee
Assistant Professors Adrian Bardon, Stavroula Glezakos, Christian Miller
Visiting Assistant Professor Clark Thompson
Adjunct Assistant Professor Dorthea Lotter
Lecturer Hannah M. Hardgrave

PHYSICS (PHY)

1983–1984
George P. Williams Jr., Chair
Professors Robert W. Brehme, Ysbrand Haven, Howard W. Shields,
    George P. Williams Jr.
Associate Professor William C. Kerr
Assistant Professor George Eric Matthews

1984–1985
George P. Williams Jr., Chair
Professors Robert W. Brehme, William C. Kerr, Howard W. Shields,
    George P. Williams Jr.
Associate Professor George Eric Matthews
Assistant Professor Natalie A.W. Holzwarth
Lecturer George M. Holzwarth

1985–1988
George P. Williams Jr., Chair
Reynolds Professor Richard T. Williams
Professors Robert W. Brehme, William C. Kerr, Howard W. Shields,
    George P. Williams Jr.
Associate Professor George Eric Matthews
Assistant Professor Natalie A.W. Holzwarth
Lecturer George M. Holzwarth

1988–1991
George P. Williams Jr., Chair
Reynolds Professor Richard T. Williams

Professors Robert W. Brehme, William C. Kerr, Howard W. Shields,
   George P. Williams Jr.
Associate Professors George M. Holzwarth, George Eric Matthews
Assistant Professor Natalie A.W. Holzwarth

1991–1993
Howard W. Shields, Chair
Reynolds Professor Richard T. Williams
Professors Robert W. Brehme, George M. Holzwarth, William C. Kerr,
   George Eric Matthews, Howard W. Shields, George P. Williams Jr.
Associate Professor Natalie A.W. Holzwarth
Assistant Professor Paul R. Anderson
Adjunct Professor George B. Cvijanovich
Adjunct Associate Professor C. Anne Wallen
Adjunct Assistant Professor Peter Santago

1993–1995
Howard W. Shields, Chair
Reynolds Professor Richard T. Williams
Professors Robert W. Brehme, George M. Holzwarth, William C. Kerr,
   George Eric Matthews, Howard W. Shields, George P. Williams Jr.
Associate Professors Keith D. Bonin, Natalie A.W. Holzwarth
Assistant Professor Paul R. Anderson
Adjunct Professor George B. Cvijanovich
Adjunct Associate Professor C. Anne Wallen
Adjunct Assistant Professor Peter Santago

1995–1996
Howard W. Shields, Chair
Reynolds Professor Richard T. Williams
Professors Robert W. Brehme, George M. Holzwarth, William C. Kerr,
   George Eric Matthews, Howard W. Shields, George P. Williams Jr.
Associate Professors Keith D. Bonin, Natalie A.W. Holzwarth
Assistant Professor Paul R. Anderson
Adjunct Professors Monroe J. Cowan, George B. Cvijanovich
Adjunct Assistant Professor Peter Santago

1996–1997
Howard W. Shields, Chair
Reynolds Professor Richard T. Williams
Professors George M. Holzwarth, Natalie A.W. Holzwarth, William C. Kerr, George
   Eric Matthews, Howard W. Shields, George P. Williams Jr.
Associate Professor Keith D. Bonin
Assistant Professors Paul R. Anderson, Eric D. Carlson

Adjunct Professors Monroe J. Cowan, George B. Cvijanovich
Adjunct Assistant Professor Peter Santago

1997–1999
Howard W. Shields, Chair
Reynolds Professor Richard T. Williams
Professors George M. Holzwarth, Natalie A.W. Holzwarth, William C. Kerr, George
  Eric Matthews, Howard W. Shields, George P. Williams Jr.
Associate Professors Paul R. Anderson, Keith D. Bonin
Assistant Professors Eric D. Carlson, Daniel B. Kim-Shapiro
Adjunct Professors Monroe J. Cowan, George B. Cvijanovich
Adjunct Associate Professor Frederic H. Fahey
Adjunct Assistant Professors John D. Bourland, Peter Santago

1999–2000
Howard W. Shields, Chair
Reynolds Professor Richard T. Williams
Professors Keith Bonin, George M. Holzwarth, Natalie A.W. Holzwarth, William C.
  Kerr, George Eric Matthews, Howard W. Shields, George P. Williams Jr.
Associate Professors Paul R. Anderson, Eric D. Carlson
Assistant Professor Daniel B. Kim-Shapiro
Adjunct Professors Monroe J. Cowan, George B. Cvijanovich
Adjunct Associate Professors Frederic H. Fahey, Peter Santago
Adjunct Assistant Professor John D. Bourland

2000–2001
George Eric Matthews, Chair
Reynolds Professor Richard T. Williams
Professors Keith Bonin, George M. Holzwarth, Natalie A.W. Holzwarth, William C.
  Kerr, George Eric Matthews, Howard W. Shields
Associate Professors Paul R. Anderson, Eric D. Carlson
Assistant Professors Gregory B. Cook, Daniel B. Kim-Shapiro
Adjunct Professors Monroe J. Cowan, George B. Cvijanovich
Adjunct Associate Professors Frederic H. Fahey, Peter Santago
Adjunct Assistant Professor John D. Bourland

2001–2002
George Eric Matthews, Chair
Reynolds Professor Richard T. Williams
Professors Keith Bonin, George M. Holzwarth, Natalie A.W. Holzwarth,
  William C. Kerr, George Eric Matthews, Howard W. Shields
Associate Professors Paul R. Anderson, Eric D. Carlson
Assistant Professors Gregory B. Cook, Daniel B. Kim-Shapiro, Jeremy S. Qualls
Adjunct Professor George B. Cvijanovich

Adjunct Associate Professors Frederic H. Fahey, Peter Santago
Adjunct Assistant Professor John D. Bourland

2002–2003
George Eric Matthews, Chair
Reynolds Professor Richard T. Williams
Professors Keith Bonin, George M. Holzwarth, Natalie A.W. Holzwarth,
    William C. Kerr, George Eric Matthews
Associate Professors Paul R. Anderson, Eric D. Carlson
Assistant Professors Gregory B. Cook, Daniel B. Kim-Shapiro (Z. Smith Reynolds
    Faculty Fellow), Jeremy S. Qualls
Adjunct Professor George B. Cvijanovich
Adjunct Associate Professors Frederic H. Fahey, Peter Santago
Adjunct Assistant Professor John D. Bourland

2003–2004
George Eric Matthews, Chair
Reynolds Professor Richard T. Williams
Professors Keith Bonin, George M. Holzwarth, Natalie A.W. Holzwarth,
    William C. Kerr, George Eric Matthews
Associate Professors Paul R. Anderson, Eric D. Carlson, Daniel B. Kim-Shapiro
    (Z. Smith Reynolds Faculty Fellow)
Assistant Professors Gregory B. Cook, Martin Guthold, Fred Salsbury
Adjunct Professors Monroe J. Cowan, George B. Cvijanovich
Adjunct Associate Professors Frederic H. Fahey, Peter Santago
Adjunct Assistant Professor John D. Bourland

2004–2005
George Eric Matthews, Chair
Reynolds Professors Jacquelyn S. Fetrow, Richard T. Williams
Professors Paul R. Anderson, Keith Bonin, George M. Holzwarth,
    Natalie A.W. Holzwarth, William C. Kerr, George Eric Matthews
Associate Professors Eric D. Carlson, David L. Carroll, Daniel B. Kim-Shapiro
    (Z. Smith Reynolds Faculty Fellow)
Assistant Professors Gregory B. Cook, Martin Guthold, Fred Salsbury
Adjunct Professor Monroe J. Cowan
Adjunct Associate Professors Frederic H. Fahey, Peter Santago
Adjunct Assistant Professors John D. Bourland, Timothy E. Miller

2005–2006
George Eric Matthews, Chair
Reynolds Professor of Computational Biophysics Jacquelyn S. Fetrow
Reynolds Professor Richard T. Williams

Professors Paul R. Anderson, Keith Bonin, Natalie A.W. Holzwarth,
William C. Kerr, George Eric Matthews
Associate Professors Eric D. Carlson, David L. Carroll, Daniel B. Kim-Shapiro
(Z. Smith Reynolds Faculty Fellow), Kamil Burak Üçer (Research Associate
Professor)
Assistant Professors Gregory B. Cook, Martin Guthold, Jed Macosko, Fred Salsbury
Visiting Professor of Physics Lukasz Turski
Adjunct Associate Professor Peter Santago
Adjunct Assistant Professors John D. Bourland, Timothy E. Miller

POLITICAL SCIENCE (POL)

(The Department of Political Science was originally the Department of Politics until
2000–2001 when it became the Department of Political Science. This change was first
noted in the 2001–2002 *Bulletin*.)

1983–1984
Richard D. Sears, Chair
Professors Jack D. Fleer, Carl C. Moses, Jon M. Reinhardt, C.H. Richards Jr.,
Donald O. Schoonmaker
Professor of History and Asian Studies Balkrishna Govind Gokhale
Associate Professors David B. Broyles, Richard D. Sears
Assistant Professors Gerald F. Gaus, Kathy B. Smith, Robert L. Utley
Instructor Mark A. Cichock

1984–1985
Richard D. Sears, Chair
Professors Jack D. Fleer, Carl C. Moses, Jon M. Reinhardt, C.H. Richards Jr.,
Donald O. Schoonmaker
Professor of History and Asian Studies Balkrishna Govind Gokhale
Associate Professors David B. Broyles, Richard D. Sears
Assistant Professors Mark A. Cichock, Saguiv A. Hadari, Kathy B. Smith
Visiting Assistant Professor Robert L. Utley

1985–1986
Richard D. Sears, Chair
Professors Jack D. Fleer, Carl C. Moses, C.H. Richards Jr., Donald O. Schoonmaker
Professor of History and Asian Studies Balkrishna Govind Gokhale
Associate Professors David B. Broyles, Richard D. Sears
Assistant Professors Mark A. Cichock, Saguiv A. Hadari, Kathy B. Smith

1986–1987
Jack D. Fleer, Chair
Professors Jack D. Fleer, Carl C. Moses, Donald O. Schoonmaker, Richard D. Sears
Professor of History and Asian Studies Balkrishna Govind Gokhale

Associate Professors David B. Broyles, Kathy B. Smith
Assistant Professors Saguiv A. Hadari, Charles H. Kennedy
Instructor Katy J. Harriger

1987–1988

Jack D. Fleer, Chair
Professors Jack D. Fleer, Carl C. Moses, Donald O. Schoonmaker, Richard D. Sears
Professor of History and Asian Studies Balkrishna Govind Gokhale
Associate Professors David B. Broyles, Kathy B. Smith
Assistant Professors Saguiv A. Hadari, Katy J. Harriger, Charles H. Kennedy

1988–1989

Jack D. Fleer, Chair
Professors Jack D. Fleer, Carl C. Moses, Donald O. Schoonmaker, Richard D. Sears
Professor of History and Asian Studies Balkrishna Govind Gokhale
Associate Professors David B. Broyles, Kathy B. Smith
Assistant Professors Katy J. Harriger, Charles H. Kennedy, Wei-chin Lee

1989–1990

Jack D. Fleer, Chair
Professors Jack D. Fleer, Carl C. Moses, Donald O. Schoonmaker, Richard D. Sears
Professor of History and Asian Studies Balkrishna Govind Gokhale
Associate Professors David B. Broyles, Kathy B. Smith
Assistant Professors Katy J. Harriger, Charles H. Kennedy, John Christian Laursen,
    Wei-chin Lee
Visiting Assistant Professors Robert J. Griffiths, William E. Schmickle, Martha
    Swann

1990–1991

Jack D. Fleer, Chair
Professors David B. Broyles, Jack D. Fleer, Carl C. Moses, Donald O. Schoonmaker,
    Richard D. Sears
Professor of History and Asian Studies Balkrishna Govind Gokhale
Associate Professors Charles H. Kennedy, Kathy B. Smith
Assistant Professors Katy J. Harriger, Wei-chin Lee
Visiting Professor Jerry Pubantz
Visiting Assistant Professors Yomi Durotoye, Martha Swann, David P. Weinstein

1991–1992

Jack D. Fleer, Chair
Professors David B. Broyles, Jack D. Fleer, Carl C. Moses, Donald O. Schoonmaker,
    Richard D. Sears
Associate Professors Charles H. Kennedy, Kathy B. Smith
Assistant Professors Katy J. Harriger, Wei-chin Lee, David P. Weinstein

Visiting Associate Professor William E. Schmickle
Visiting Assistant Professor Yomi Durotoye
Instructor Melissa Haussman

1992–1993
Jack D. Fleer, Chair
Professors David B. Broyles, Jack D. Fleer, Donald O. Schoonmaker,
    Richard D. Sears
Associate Professors Katy J. Harriger, Charles H. Kennedy, Kathy B. Smith
Assistant Professors Brian F. Crisp, Wei-chin Lee, David P. Weinstein
Visiting Professor Jerry Pubantz
Visiting Assistant Professor James Willson-Quayle

1993–1994
Jack D. Fleer, Chair
Professors David B. Broyles, Jack D. Fleer, Donald O. Schoonmaker,
    Richard D. Sears
Associate Professors Katy J. Harriger, Charles H. Kennedy, Kathy B. Smith
Assistant Professors Brian F. Crisp, Wei-chin Lee, David P. Weinstein
Visiting Professors Carl C. Moses, Jerry Pubantz
Visiting Assistant Professor Bradley Macdonald

1994–1995
Jack D. Fleer, Chair
Professors David B. Broyles, Jack D. Fleer, Richard D. Sears
Associate Professors Katy J. Harriger (Zachary T. Smith Associate Professor),
    Charles H. Kennedy, Wei-chin Lee, Kathy B. Smith
Assistant Professors Brian F. Crisp, David P. Weinstein, Helga A. Welsh
Visiting Professor Jerry Pubantz
Instructors Joe Cole, Xiaobo Hu

1995–1996
Jack D. Fleer, Chair
Professors David B. Broyles, Jack D. Fleer, Charles H. Kennedy, Richard D. Sears
Associate Professors Katy J. Harriger (Zachary T. Smith Associate Professor),
    Wei-chin Lee, Kathy B. Smith
Assistant Professors Brian F. Crisp, David P. Weinstein, Helga A. Welsh
Visiting Professor Jerry Pubantz
Instructor James H. Cox

1996–1997
Jack D. Fleer, Chair
Professors David B. Broyles, Jack D. Fleer, Charles H. Kennedy,
    Richard D. Sears, Kathy B. Smith

Associate Professors Katy J. Harriger (Zachary T. Smith Associate Professor),
    Wei-chin Lee, David P. Weinstein
Assistant Professor Helga A. Welsh
Visiting Professor Jerry Pubantz
Visiting Associate Professor Yomi Durotoye
Instructors Tomoaki Nomi, Thomas W. Smith

1997–1998
Jack D. Fleer, Chair
Professors David B. Broyles, Jack D. Fleer, Charles H. Kennedy,
    Richard D. Sears, Kathy B. Smith
Associate Professors Katy J. Harriger, Wei-chin Lee, David P. Weinstein
Assistant Professors Peter M. Siavelis, Helga A. Welsh
Visiting Professor Jerry Pubantz
Visiting Associate Professor Yomi Durotoye
Visiting Assistant Professor John J. Dinan

1998–1999
Kathy B. Smith, Chair
Professors David B. Broyles, Jack D. Fleer, Charles H. Kennedy,
    Richard D. Sears, Kathy B. Smith
Associate Professors Katy J. Harriger, Wei-chin Lee, David P. Weinstein,
    Helga A. Welsh
Assistant Professor Peter M. Siavelis
Visiting Professor Jerry Pubantz
Visiting Associate Professor Yomi Durotoye
Visiting Assistant Professor John J. Dinan

1999–2000
Kathy B. Smith, Chair
Professors David B. Broyles, Jack D. Fleer, Charles H. Kennedy,
    Richard D. Sears, Kathy B. Smith
Associate Professors Katy J. Harriger, Wei-chin Lee,
    David P. Weinstein, Helga A. Welsh
Assistant Professor Peter M. Siavelis
Visiting Associate Professors Yomi Durotoye, Michael A. Gorkin
Visiting Assistant Professor John J. Dinan

2000–2001
Kathy B. Smith, Chair
Worrell Professor of Anglo-American Studies David Coates
Professors David B. Broyles, Jack D. Fleer, Charles H. Kennedy,
    Richard D. Sears, Kathy B. Smith

Associate Professors Katy J. Harriger, Wei-chin Lee, David P. Weinstein,
　　Helga A. Welsh
Assistant Professors Andrew O. Rich, Peter M. Siavelis
Visiting Professors Michael A. Gorkin, Jerry Pubantz
Visiting Associate Professor Yomi Durotoye
Visiting Assistant Professor John J. Dinan

2001–2002
Kathy B. Smith, Chair
Worrell Professor of Anglo-American Studies David Coates
Professors Jack D. Fleer, Charles H. Kennedy, Richard D. Sears, Kathy B. Smith
Associate Professors Katy J. Harriger, Wei-chin Lee, David P. Weinstein,
　　Helga A. Welsh
Assistant Professors Andrew O. Rich, Peter M. Siavelis
Visiting Professors Michael A. Gorkin, Jerry Pubantz
Visiting Associate Professor Yomi Durotoye
Instructor Michaelle L. Browers
Senior Lecturer and Fellow of Political Science Baruch Knei-Paz

2002–2003
Kathy B. Smith, Chair
Worrell Professor of Anglo-American Studies David Coates
Professors Jack D. Fleer, Charles H. Kennedy, Richard D. Sears, Kathy B. Smith
Associate Professors Katy J. Harriger, Wei-chin Lee, David P. Weinstein,
　　Helga A. Welsh (Zachary T. Smith Associate Professor)
Assistant Professors Michaelle L. Browers, John J. Dinan, Andrew O. Rich,
　　Peter M. Siavelis
Visiting Professor Jerry Pubantz
Adjunct Instructor Johnny Goldfinger
Senior Lecturer Yomi Durotoye

2003–2004
Kathy B. Smith, Chair
Worrell Professor of Anglo-American Studies David Coates
Professors Katy J. Harriger, Charles H. Kennedy, Wei-chin Lee, Kathy B. Smith
Associate Professors Peter M. Siavelis (Hultquist Junior Faculty Fellow),
　　David P. Weinstein, Helga A. Welsh (Zachary T. Smith Associate Professor),
　　Pia Wood
Assistant Professors Michaelle L. Browers, John J. Dinan, Peter Furia,
　　Andrew O. Rich,
Visiting Assistant Professor Russell L. Lucas
Adjunct Professor Richard D. Sears
Adjunct Instructors Doug Casson, Ari Kohen, Jonathan Marks
Senior Lecturer Yomi Durotoye

2004–2005
Kathy B. Smith, Chair
Worrell Professor of Anglo-American Studies David Coates
Professors Katy J. Harriger, Charles H. Kennedy, Wei-chin Lee, Kathy B. Smith
Associate Professors John J. Dinan (Zachary T. Smith Associate Professor),
    Peter M. Siavelis (Hultquist Junior Faculty Fellow), David P. Weinstein,
    Helga A. Welsh, Pia Wood
Assistant Professors Michaelle L. Browers, Peter Furia, Ellie Schemenauer
Visiting Professor Yehuda Blum
Visiting Assistant Professor Adam Newmark
Adjunct Professor Richard D. Sears
Visiting Instructor Doug Casson
Senior Lecturer Yomi Durotoye

2005–2006
Kathy B. Smith, Chair
Reynolds Professor of Political Science and Latin-American Studies Luis Roniger
Worrell Professor of Anglo-American Studies David Coates
Professors Katy J. Harriger, Charles H. Kennedy, Wei-chin Lee, Kathy B. Smith
Associate Professors John J. Dinan (Zachary T. Smith Associate Professor),
    Peter M. Siavelis (Hultquist Junior Faculty Fellow), David P. Weinstein,
    Helga A. Welsh, Pia Wood
Assistant Professors Michaelle L. Browers, Peter Furia
Visiting Assistant Professors Doug Casson, Bonnie Field, Mahendra Lawoti,
    Krista Weigand
Adjunct Professor Richard D. Sears
Senior Lecturer Yomi Durotoye

PSYCHOLOGY (PSY)

1983–1984
John E. Williams, Chair
Professors Robert C. Beck, Robert H. Dufort, Charles L. Richman, John E. Williams
Associate Professors David W. Catron, Philippe R. Falkenberg, David A. Hills
Assistant Professors Deborah L. Best, Jerry M. Burger, Maxine L. Clark,
    Cecilia H. Solano
Visiting Assistant Professors C. Drew Edwards, Jean C. Seeman
Adjunct Associate Professor Frank B. Wood
Adjunct Instructors Catherine A. Jourdan, David S. Stump
Lecturer Brian M. Austin

1984–1985
John E. Williams, Chair
Professors Robert C. Beck, Robert H. Dufort, Charles L. Richman, John E. Williams

Associate Professors Deborah L. Best, David W. Catron, Philippe R. Falkenberg,
David A. Hills, Cecilia H. Solano
Assistant Professors Jerry M. Burger, Maxine L. Clark
Visiting Assistant Professor Nur Gryskiewicz
Adjunct Associate Professor Frank B. Wood
Adjunct Assistant Professor C. Drew Edwards
Adjunct Instructors Susan R. Leonard, Marianne A. Schubert
Lecturer Brian M. Austin

1985–1986
John E. Williams, Chair
Professors Robert C. Beck, Robert H. Dufort, Charles L. Richman, John E. Williams
Associate Professors Deborah L. Best, David W. Catron, Philippe R. Falkenberg,
David A. Hills, Cecilia H. Solano
Assistant Professor Maxine L. Clark
Visiting Professor James G. McCormick
Adjunct Associate Professor Frank B. Wood
Adjunct Assistant Professor C. Drew Edwards
Instructor Susan R. Leonard
Adjunct Instructors Catherine A. Jourdan, Marianne A. Schubert
Lecturer Brian M. Austin

1986–1987
John E. Williams, Chair
Professors Robert C. Beck, Robert H. Dufort, Charles L. Richman, John E. Williams
Associate Professors Deborah L. Best, David W. Catron, Maxine L. Clark,
Philippe R. Falkenberg, David A. Hills, Cecilia H. Solano
Assistant Professor Mark R. Leary
Visiting Assistant Professor Susan R. Leonard
Adjunct Associate Professor Frank B. Wood
Adjunct Assistant Professor C. Drew Edwards
Adjunct Instructors Catherine A. Jourdan, Marianne A. Schubert
Lecturer Brian M. Austin

1987–1988
John E. Williams, Chair
Professors Robert C. Beck, Robert H. Dufort, Charles L. Richman, John E. Williams
Associate Professors Deborah L. Best, David W. Catron, Maxine L. Clark, Philippe
R. Falkenberg, David A. Hills, Cecilia H. Solano
Assistant Professor Mark R. Leary
Visiting Professor Janak Pandey
Visiting Assistant Professor Susan B. Wallace
Adjunct Associate Professor Frank B. Wood
Adjunct Assistant Professors C. Drew Edwards, Susan R. Leonard,
Marianne A. Schubert

1988–1989
John E. Williams, Chair
Professors Robert C. Beck, Robert H. Dufort, Charles L. Richman, John E. Williams
Associate Professors Deborah L. Best, David W. Catron, Maxine L. Clark, Philippe
    R. Falkenberg, David A. Hills, Cecilia H. Solano
Assistant Professors Terry D. Blumenthal, Mark R. Leary
Visiting Assistant Professors Janet S. Moore, Catherine E. Seta, Susan B. Wallace
Adjunct Associate Professor Frank B. Wood
Adjunct Assistant Professors C. Drew Edwards, Susan R. Leonard, Marianne A.
    Schubert
Instructor Timothy P. Foley

1989–1990
John E. Williams, Chair
Professors Robert C. Beck, Robert H. Dufort, Charles L. Richman, John E. Williams
Associate Professors Deborah L. Best, David W. Catron, Maxine L. Clark, Philippe
    R. Falkenberg, David A. Hills, Mark R. Leary, Cecilia H. Solano
Assistant Professor Terry D. Blumenthal
Visiting Assistant Professors Catherine E. Seta, Susan B. Wallace
Adjunct Associate Professors C. Drew Edwards, Jay R. Kaplan, Frank B. Wood
Adjunct Assistant Professors Susan R. Leonard, Marianne A. Schubert, Carol A.
    Shively

1990–1991
John E. Williams, Chair
Professors Robert C. Beck, Deborah L. Best, Robert H. Dufort, Charles L. Richman,
    John E. Williams
Associate Professors David W. Catron, Maxine L. Clark, Philippe R. Falkenberg,
    David A. Hills, Mark R. Leary, Cecilia H. Solano
Assistant Professor Terry D. Blumenthal
Visiting Assistant Professors Sarah S. Catron, Kelly B. Kyes, Catherine E. Seta, Susan
    B. Wallace
Adjunct Associate Professors C. Drew Edwards, Jay R. Kaplan, Frank B. Wood
Adjunct Assistant Professors Marianne A. Schubert, Carol A. Shively
Instructor Robin M. Kowalski

1991–1992
John E. Williams, Chair
Professors Robert C. Beck, Deborah L. Best, Robert H. Dufort, Charles L. Richman,
    John E. Williams
Associate Professors David W. Catron, Philippe R. Falkenberg, David A. Hills, Mark
    R. Leary, Cecilia H. Solano
Assistant Professors Terry D. Blumenthal, Dale Dagenbach
Visiting Assistant Professors Sarah S. Catron, Kelly B. Kyes, Catherine E. Seta
Adjunct Associate Professors C. Drew Edwards, Jay R. Kaplan, Frank B. Wood

Adjunct Assistant Professors Marianne A. Schubert, Carol A. Shively, Susan B. Wallace

Adjunct Instructor Randall C. Kyes

1992–1993

John E. Williams, Chair

Professors Robert C. Beck, Deborah L. Best, Robert H. Dufort, Mark R. Leary, Charles L. Richman, John E. Williams

Associate Professors David W. Catron, Philippe R. Falkenberg, David A. Hills, Cecilia H. Solano

Assistant Professors Terry D. Blumenthal, Dale Dagenbach

Visiting Assistant Professors Sarah S. Catron, Kelly B. Kyes, Catherine E. Seta

Adjunct Professor W. Jack Rejeski Jr.

Adjunct Associate Professors C. Drew Edwards, Jay R. Kaplan, Frank B. Wood

Adjunct Assistant Professors Phillip G. Batten, Marianne A. Schubert, Carol A. Shively

Adjunct Instructor Randall C. Kyes

1993–1994

John E. Williams, Chair

Wake Forest Professor John E. Williams

Professors Robert C. Beck, Deborah L. Best, David W. Catron, Robert H. Dufort, Mark R. Leary, Charles L. Richman

Associate Professors Terry D. Blumenthal, Dale Dagenbach, Philippe R. Falkenberg, David A. Hills, Cecilia H. Solano

Assistant Professor Christy M. Buchanan

Visiting Assistant Professors Sarah S. Catron, Kelly B. Kyes, Catherine E. Seta

Adjunct Professor W. Jack Rejeski Jr.

Adjunct Associate Professors C. Drew Edwards, Jay R. Kaplan, Frank B. Wood

Adjunct Assistant Professors Phillip G. Batten, Marianne A. Schubert, Carol A. Shively

Adjunct Instructor Randall C. Kyes

1994–1995

John E. Williams, Chair

Wake Forest Professor John E. Williams

Professors Robert C. Beck, Deborah L. Best, David W. Catron, Robert H. Dufort, Mark R. Leary, Charles L. Richman

Associate Professors Terry D. Blumenthal, Dale Dagenbach, Philippe R. Falkenberg, David A. Hills, Cecilia H. Solano

Assistant Professors Christy M. Buchanan, Catherine E. Seta

Adjunct Professor W. Jack Rejeski Jr.

Adjunct Associate Professors C. Drew Edwards, Jay R. Kaplan, Frank B. Wood

Adjunct Assistant Professors Phillip G. Batten, Marianne A. Schubert, William W. Sloan Jr.

1995–1996
Deborah L. Best, Chair
Wake Forest Professor John E. Williams
Professors Robert C. Beck, Deborah L. Best, Robert H. Dufort, Mark R. Leary,
    Charles L. Richman
Associate Professors Terry D. Blumenthal, Dale Dagenbach, Philippe R. Falkenberg,
    David A. Hills, Catherine E. Seta, Cecilia H. Solano
Assistant Professors Christy M. Buchanan, Eric R. Stone
Adjunct Professor W. Jack Rejeski Jr.
Adjunct Associate Professors C. Drew Edwards, Jay R. Kaplan, Frank B. Wood
Adjunct Assistant Professors Phillip G. Batten, Sandra C. Chadwick, Jerry W.
    Noble, Marianne A. Schubert, William W. Sloan Jr.
Adjunct Instructor Stephen W. Davis

1996–1997
Deborah L. Best, Chair
Wake Forest Professor John E. Williams
Professors Robert C. Beck, Deborah L. Best, Robert H. Dufort, Philippe R. Falken-
    berg, David A. Hills, Mark R. Leary, Charles L. Richman
Associate Professors Terry D. Blumenthal, Dale Dagenbach, Catherine E. Seta,
    Cecilia H. Solano
Assistant Professors Christy M. Buchanan, Eric R. Stone
Adjunct Professor W. Jack Rejeski Jr.
Adjunct Associate Professors C. Drew Edwards, Jay R. Kaplan, Frank B. Wood
Adjunct Assistant Professors Phillip G. Batten, Jerry W. Noble, Marianne A.
    Schubert, William W. Sloan Jr.
Visiting Instructor Mark V. Pezzo
Adjunct Instructor Stephen W. Davis

1997–1998
Deborah L. Best, Chair
Wake Forest Professor Mark R. Leary
Professors Robert C. Beck, Deborah L. Best, Robert H. Dufort,
    Philippe R. Falkenberg, Charles L. Richman
Associate Professors Terry D. Blumenthal, Dale Dagenbach, Catherine E. Seta,
    Cecilia H. Solano
Assistant Professors Christy M. Buchanan, Eric R. Stone, William W. Fleeson,
    James A. Schirillo
Visiting Assistant Professor Mark V. Pezzo
Adjunct Professors Jay R. Kaplan, W. Jack Rejeski Jr., Frank B. Wood
Adjunct Associate Professors C. Drew Edwards, Carol A. Shively
Adjunct Assistant Professors Phillip G. Batten, Jerry W. Noble, Marianne A.
    Schubert, William W. Sloan Jr., Elizabeth H. Taylor
Adjunct Instructor Stephen W. Davis

1998–1999

Deborah L. Best, Chair

Wake Forest Professors Deborah L. Best, Mark R. Leary

Professors Robert C. Beck, Robert H. Dufort, Charles L. Richman

Associate Professors Terry D. Blumenthal, Dale Dagenbach, Catherine E. Seta, Cecilia H. Solano

Assistant Professors Christy M. Buchanan, William W. Fleeson, Batja Mesquita, James A. Schirillo, Eric R. Stone

Visiting Assistant Professors H. Janey B. Barnes, Marie M. O'Hara, Mark V. Pezzo, Mary M. Roufail

Adjunct Professors Jay R. Kaplan, W. Jack Rejeski Jr., Frank B. Wood

Adjunct Associate Professors C. Drew Edwards, Carol A. Shively

Adjunct Assistant Professors Phillip G. Batten, Jerry W. Noble, Marianne A. Schubert, William W. Sloan Jr., Elizabeth H. Taylor

Adjunct Instructor Stephen W. Davis

1999–2000

Deborah L. Best, Chair

Wake Forest Professors Deborah L. Best, Mark R. Leary

Professors Robert C. Beck, Robert H. Dufort, Charles L. Richman

Associate Professors Terry D. Blumenthal, Dale Dagenbach, Catherine E. Seta, Cecilia H. Solano

Assistant Professors Christy M. Buchanan, William W. Fleeson, Batja Mesquita, James A. Schirillo, Eric R. Stone

Visiting Assistant Professors Marie M. O'Hara, Mark V. Pezzo

Adjunct Professors Jay R. Kaplan, W. Jack Rejeski Jr., Frank B. Wood

Adjunct Associate Professors C. Drew Edwards, Carol A. Shively

Adjunct Assistant Professors Phillip G. Batten, Jerry W. Noble, Marianne A. Schubert, William W. Sloan Jr., Elizabeth H. Taylor

Adjunct Instructor Stephen W. Davis

2000–2001

Deborah L. Best, Chair

Wake Forest Professors Deborah L. Best, Mark R. Leary

Professors Robert C. Beck, Charles L. Richman

Associate Professors Terry D. Blumenthal, Christy M. Buchanan, Dale Dagenbach, Catherine E. Seta, Cecilia H. Solano

Assistant Professors William W. Fleeson, Batja Mesquita, Karen L. Roper, James A. Schirillo, Eric R. Stone

Visiting Assistant Professors Marie M. O'Hara, Mark V. Pezzo, Mary M. Roufail

Adjunct Professors Jay R. Kaplan, W. Jack Rejeski Jr., Frank B. Wood

Adjunct Associate Professors C. Drew Edwards, Carol A. Shively

Adjunct Assistant Professors Phillip G. Batten, Jerry W. Noble, Marianne A. Schubert, William W. Sloan Jr., Elizabeth H. Taylor

Adjunct Instructor Stephen W. Davis

2001–2002
Deborah L. Best, Chair
Wake Forest Professors Deborah L. Best, Mark R. Leary
Professors Robert C. Beck, Charles L. Richman, Carol A. Shively
Associate Professors Terry D. Blumenthal, Christy M. Buchanan, Dale Dagenbach,
    James A. Schirillo, Catherine E. Seta, Cecilia H. Solano
Assistant Professors William W. Fleeson, Janine M. Jennings, Batja Mesquita,
    Karen L. Roper, Eric R. Stone, Julie H. Wayne
Visiting Assistant Professors Julia Jackson-Newsom, Marie M. O'Hara
Adjunct Professors Jay R. Kaplan, W. Jack Rejeski Jr., Frank B. Wood
Adjunct Associate Professor C. Drew Edwards
Adjunct Assistant Professors Phillip G. Batten, Jerry W. Noble, William W. Sloan Jr.
Visiting Instructor Donna R. Carroll
Adjunct Instructor Stephen W. Davis

2002–2003
Deborah L. Best, Chair
Wake Forest Professors Deborah L. Best, Mark R. Leary
Professors Robert C. Beck, Charles L. Richman, Carol A. Shively
Associate Professors Terry D. Blumenthal, Christy M. Buchanan
    (Junior Faculty Fellow), Dale Dagenbach, James A. Schirillo,
    Catherine E. Seta, Cecilia H. Solano, Eric R. Stone
Assistant Professors William W. Fleeson, Janine M. Jennings, Batja Mesquita,
    Karen L. Roper, Julie H. Wayne
Adjunct Professors Jay R. Kaplan, W. Jack Rejeski Jr., Frank B. Wood
Adjunct Associate Professor C. Drew Edwards
Adjunct Assistant Professors Phillip G. Batten, Julia Jackson-Newsom, William W.
    Sloan Jr.
Visiting Instructor Donna R. Carroll
Adjunct Instructor Stephen W. Davis

2003–2004
Mark R. Leary, Chair
Wake Forest Professors Deborah L. Best, Mark R. Leary
Professors Robert C. Beck, Terry D. Blumenthal, Dale Dagenbach,
    Charles L. Richman, Carol A. Shively
Associate Professors Christy M. Buchanan (Junior Faculty Fellow), William W.
    Fleeson, Batja Mesquita, James A. Schirillo, Catherine E. Seta,
    Cecilia H. Solano, Eric R. Stone
Assistant Professors Janine M. Jennings, Karen L. Roper, Julie H. Wayne
Adjunct Professors Jay R. Kaplan, W. Jack Rejeski Jr., Frank B. Wood
Adjunct Associate Professor C. Drew Edwards
Adjunct Assistant Professors Phillip G. Batten, Julia Jackson-Newsom,
    William W. Sloan Jr.
Adjunct Instructor Stephen W. Davis

2004–2005
Mark R. Leary, Chair
Wake Forest Professors Deborah L. Best, Mark R. Leary
Professors Robert C. Beck, Terry D. Blumenthal, Dale Dagenbach,
    Charles L. Richman, Carol A. Shively
Associate Professors Christy M. Buchanan, William W. Fleeson
    (Ollen R. Nalley Associate Professor), Batja Mesquita, James A. Schirillo,
    Catherine E. Seta, Cecilia H. Solano, Eric R. Stone
Assistant Professors Janine M. Jennings, Karen L. Roper
Adjunct Professors Jay R. Kaplan, W. Jack Rejeski Jr., Frank B. Wood
Adjunct Associate Professor C. Drew Edwards
Adjunct Assistant Professors Phillip G. Batten, Julia Jackson-Newsom,
    Max E. Levine, G. Todd McElroy, Lori A. Sheppard, William W. Sloan Jr.
Adjunct Instructor Stephen W. Davis

2005–2006
Mark R. Leary, Chair
Wake Forest Professors Deborah L. Best, Mark R. Leary
Professors Robert C. Beck, Terry D. Blumenthal, Dale Dagenbach,
    Charles L. Richman, Carol A. Shively
Associate Professors Christy M. Buchanan, William W. Fleeson
    (Ollen R. Nalley Associate Professor), Batja Mesquita, James A. Schirillo,
    Catherine E. Seta, Cecilia H. Solano, Eric R. Stone
Assistant Professors R. Michael Furr, Janine M. Jennings, Karen L. Roper
Visiting Assistant Professors Janet Boseovski, Lori A. Sheppard, Alycia K. Silman
Adjunct Professors Jay R. Kaplan, W. Jack Rejeski Jr., Frank B. Wood
Adjunct Associate Professor C. Drew Edwards
Adjunct Assistant Professors Phillip G. Batten, Max E. Levine, William W. Sloan Jr.
Adjunct Instructor Stephen W. Davis

RELIGION (REL)

1983–1984
Carlton T. Mitchell, Chair
Professors John William Angell, George McLeod Bryan, Robert Allen Dyer, Emmett
    Willard Hamrick, E. Glenn Hinson, Carlton T. Mitchell, Charles H. Talbert
Associate Professors John E. Collins, Fred L. Horton Jr., Ralph C. Wood Jr.
Adjunct Professor Jerome R. Dollard
Instructor John D. Sykes Jr.
Visiting Lecturer Thomas E. Dougherty Jr.

1984–1985
Carlton T. Mitchell, Chair

Professors John William Angell, George McLeod Bryan, Emmett Willard Hamrick,
   E. Glenn Hinson, Carlton T. Mitchell, Charles H. Talbert
Associate Professors John E. Collins, Fred L. Horton Jr., Ralph C. Wood Jr.
Adjunct Associate Professor Thomas E. Dougherty Jr.
Instructor John D. Sykes Jr.

1985–1986
Carlton T. Mitchell, Chair
Professors John William Angell, George McLeod Bryan, Emmett Willard Hamrick,
   James A. Martin Jr., Carlton T. Mitchell, Charles H. Talbert
Associate Professors John E. Collins, Fred L. Horton Jr., Ralph C. Wood Jr.
Adjunct Associate Professor Thomas E. Dougherty Jr.
Instructors Sharyn E. Dowd, John D. Sykes Jr.

1986–1987
Carlton T. Mitchell, Chair
Professors John William Angell, George McLeod Bryan, Emmett Willard Hamrick,
   James A. Martin Jr., Carlton T. Mitchell, Charles H. Talbert
Associate Professors John E. Collins, Fred L. Horton Jr., Ralph C. Wood Jr.
Assistant Professor Stephen B. Boyd
Adjunct Associate Professor Thomas E. Dougherty Jr.
Instructors Sharyn E. Dowd, John D. Sykes Jr.

1987–1988
Carlton T. Mitchell, Chair
Professors John William Angell, George McLeod Bryan, Emmett Willard Hamrick,
   Fred L. Horton Jr., James A. Martin Jr., Carlton T. Mitchell, Charles H. Talbert
Associate Professors John E. Collins, Ralph C. Wood Jr.
Assistant Professor Stephen B. Boyd
Adjunct Associate Professor Thomas E. Dougherty Jr.
Instructor Sharyn E. Dowd

1988–1989
Carlton T. Mitchell, Chair
Albritton Professor Emmett Willard Hamrick
John Easley Professor of Religion John William Angell
University Professor James A. Martin Jr.
Professors Fred L. Horton Jr., Carlton T. Mitchell, Charles H. Talbert, Ralph C.
   Wood Jr.
Associate Professor John E. Collins
Assistant Professors Stephen B. Boyd, Louke Van Wensveen
Adjunct Associate Professor Thomas E. Dougherty Jr.
Instructor Charles J. Kinlaw
Visiting Lecturers Francis T. Cancro, Thomas P. Liebschutz

1989–1990
Carlton T. Mitchell, Chair
John Easley Professor of Religion John William Angell
University Professor James A. Martin Jr.
Professors John E. Collins, Fred L. Horton Jr., Carlton T. Mitchell,
    Charles H. Talbert, Ralph C. Wood Jr.
Assistant Professors Stephen B. Boyd, Judith W. Kay, Alton B. Pollard III
Adjunct Associate Professor Thomas E. Dougherty Jr.
Instructors Charles J. Kinlaw, Carol Zinn
Visiting Lecturer Thomas P. Liebschutz

1990–1991
Carlton T. Mitchell, Chair
John Easley Professor of Religion John William Angell
University Professor James A. Martin Jr.
Wake Forest Professor Charles H. Talbert
Professors John E. Collins, Fred L. Horton Jr., Carlton T. Mitchell,
    Ralph C. Wood Jr.
Assistant Professors Stephen B. Boyd, Judith W. Kay, Alton B. Pollard III
Adjunct Associate Professor Thomas E. Dougherty Jr.
Instructor Carol Zinn
Visiting Lecturer Thomas P. Liebschutz

1991–1992
Carlton T. Mitchell, Chair
Albritton Professor Fred L. Horton Jr.
John Easley Professor of Religion Ralph C. Wood Jr.
University Professor James A. Martin Jr.
Wake Forest Professor Charles H. Talbert
Professors John E. Collins, Carlton T. Mitchell
Associate Professor Stephen B. Boyd
Assistant Professors Kenneth G. Hoglund, Judith W. Kay, Alton B. Pollard III
Visiting Assistant Professor Wilton O. Seal Jr.
Adjunct Associate Professor Thomas E. Dougherty Jr.
Instructor Carol Zinn
Visiting Lecturer Thomas P. Liebschutz

1992–1993
Fred L. Horton Jr., Chair
Albritton Professor Fred L. Horton Jr.
John Easley Professor of Religion Ralph C. Wood Jr.
University Professor James A. Martin Jr.
Wake Forest Professor Charles H. Talbert
Professor John E. Collins
Associate Professor Stephen B. Boyd

Assistant Professors Kenneth G. Hoglund, Judith W. Kay, Alton B. Pollard III,
    Ulrike Wiethaus
Visiting Assistant Professor Philip LeMasters
Adjunct Associate Professor Thomas E. Dougherty Jr.
Visiting Lecturer Thomas P. Liebschutz

1993–1994
Fred L. Horton Jr., Chair
 Albritton Professor of the Bible Fred L. Horton Jr.
Easley Professor of Religion Ralph C. Wood Jr.
University Professor James A. Martin Jr.
Wake Forest Professor Charles H. Talbert
Professor John E. Collins
Associate Professors Stephen B. Boyd, Alton B. Pollard III
Assistant Professors Kenneth G. Hoglund, Ulrike Wiethaus
Visiting Assistant Professor Philip LeMasters
Adjunct Associate Professor Thomas E. Dougherty Jr.
Visiting Lecturer Thomas P. Liebschutz

1994–1995
Fred L. Horton Jr., Chair
Albritton Professor of the Bible Fred L. Horton Jr.
Easley Professor of Religion Ralph C. Wood Jr.
University Professor James A. Martin Jr.
Wake Forest Professor Charles H. Talbert
Professor John E. Collins
Associate Professors Stephen B. Boyd, Alton B. Pollard III
Assistant Professors Kenneth G. Hoglund, Simeon Ilesanmi, Ulrike Wiethaus
Visiting Assistant Professor Stephen C. Goranson
Adjunct Associate Professor Mark Jensen
Visiting Lecturer Thomas P. Liebschutz

1995–1996
Ralph C. Wood Jr., Chair
Albritton Professor of the Bible Fred L. Horton Jr.
John Easley Professor of Religion Ralph C. Wood Jr.
University Professor James A. Martin Jr.
Wake Forest Professor Charles H. Talbert
Professor John E. Collins
Associate Professors Stephen B. Boyd, Kenneth G. Hoglund, Alton B. Pollard III
Assistant Professors Simeon Ilesanmi, Ulrike Wiethaus
Adjunct Associate Professor Mark Jensen

1996–1997
Samuel T. Gladding, Interim Chair
Charles A. Kimball, Chair-elect
Albritton Professor of the Bible Fred L. Horton Jr.
John Easley Professor of Religion Ralph C. Wood Jr.
University Professor James A. Martin Jr.
Wake Forest Professor Charles H. Talbert
Professor John E. Collins
Associate Professors Stephen B. Boyd, Kenneth G. Hoglund, Alton B. Pollard III
Assistant Professor Simeon Ilesanmi
Adjunct Associate Professor Mark Jensen

1997–1998
Charles A. Kimball, Chair
Albritton Professor of the Bible Fred L. Horton Jr.
John Easley Professor of Religion Ralph C. Wood Jr.
University Professor James A. Martin Jr.
Professors John E. Collins, Charles A. Kimball
Associate Professors Stephen B. Boyd, Kenneth G. Hoglund, Alton B. Pollard III
Assistant Professor Simeon Ilesanmi
Adjunct Professor Bill J. Leonard
Adjunct Associate Professor Mark Jensen

1998–1999
Charles A. Kimball, Chair
Albritton Professor of the Bible Fred L. Horton Jr.
University Professor James A. Martin Jr.
Professors Stephen B. Boyd, John E. Collins, Charles A. Kimball
Associate Professors Kenneth G. Hoglund, Alton B. Pollard III
Assistant Professors Simeon Ilesanmi, Mary F. Foskett
Visiting Professor E. Frank Tupper
Adjunct Professor Bill J. Leonard
Adjunct Associate Professor Mark Jensen

1999–2000
Charles A. Kimball, Chair
Albritton Professor of the Bible Fred L. Horton Jr.
University Professor James A. Martin Jr.
Professors Stephen B. Boyd, John E. Collins, Charles A. Kimball
Associate Professors Kenneth G. Hoglund, Alton B. Pollard III
Assistant Professors Simeon Ilesanmi, James Ford, Mary F. Foskett
Visiting Professor E. Frank Tupper
Visiting Associate Professor Phyllis R. Pleasants
Adjunct Professor Bill J. Leonard
Adjunct Associate Professor Mark Jensen

2000–2001
Charles A. Kimball, Chair
Albritton Professor of the Bible Fred L. Horton Jr.
John Easley Professor of Religion Stephen B. Boyd
University Professor James A. Martin Jr.
Professors John E. Collins, Charles A. Kimball
Associate Professors Kenneth G. Hoglund, Simeon Ilesanmi
Assistant Professors James Ford, Mary F. Foskett
Visiting Associate Professor Phyllis R. Pleasants
Visiting Assistant Professor Elaine Swartzentruber
Adjunct Professor Bill J. Leonard
Adjunct Associate Professor Mark Jensen

2001–2002
Charles A. Kimball, Chair
Albritton Professor of the Bible Fred L. Horton Jr.
John Easley Professor of Religion Stephen B. Boyd
University Professor James A. Martin Jr.
Professors John E. Collins, Kenneth G. Hoglund, Charles A. Kimball
Associate Professor Simeon Ilesanmi (Zachary T. Smith Associate Professor)
Assistant Professors James Ford, Mary F. Foskett
Visiting Associate Professor Carol LaHurd
Visiting Assistant Professor Elaine Swartzentruber
Adjunct Professor Bill J. Leonard
Adjunct Associate Professor Mark Jensen

2002–2003
Charles A. Kimball, Chair
Albritton Professor of the Bible Fred L. Horton Jr.
John Easley Professor of Religion Stephen B. Boyd
University Professor James A. Martin Jr.
Professors John E. Collins, Kenneth G. Hoglund, Charles A. Kimball
Associate Professor Simeon Ilesanmi (Zachary T. Smith Associate Professor)
Assistant Professors James Ford, Mary F. Foskett, Elaine Swartzentruber
Visiting Associate Professor Carol LaHurd
Adjunct Professor Bill J. Leonard
Adjunct Associate Professor Mark Jensen
Instructor Valerie C. Cooper

2003–2004
Charles A. Kimball, Chair
Albritton Professor of the Bible Fred L. Horton Jr.
John Easley Professor of Religion Stephen B. Boyd
University Professor James A. Martin Jr.

Professors John E. Collins, Kenneth G. Hoglund, Charles A. Kimball
Associate Professor Simeon Ilesanmi (Zachary T. Smith Associate Professor)
Assistant Professors James Ford, Mary F. Foskett, Elaine Swartzentruber
Visiting Assistant Professor Susan R. Bales
Adjunct Professor Bill J. Leonard
Adjunct Associate Professor Mark Jensen
Adjunct Assistant Professor Anne Carter Shelley
Instructor Valerie C. Cooper

2004–2005
Charles A. Kimball, Chair
Albritton Professor of the Bible Fred L. Horton Jr.
John Easley Professor of Religion Stephen B. Boyd
Professors John E. Collins, Kenneth G. Hoglund, Charles A. Kimball
Associate Professors Mary F. Foskett (Zachary T. Smith Associate Professor),
    Simeon Ilesanmi
Assistant Professors James Ford, Elaine Swartzentruber
Visiting Assistant Professor Lynn Neal
Adjunct Professors Bill J. Leonard, Felicitas Opwis
Adjunct Associate Professor Mark Jensen
Instructor Valerie C. Cooper
Visiting Fulbright Scholar of Religion and Humanities Reda Bedeir

2005–2006
Stephen B. Boyd, Chair
Albritton Professor of the Bible Fred L. Horton Jr.
John Easley Professor of Religion Stephen B. Boyd
Professors John E. Collins, Kenneth G. Hoglund, Charles A. Kimball
Associate Professors James Ford, Mary F. Foskett
    (Zachary T. Smith Associate Professor), Simeon Ilesanmi
Assistant Professors Valerie C. Cooper, Elaine Swartzentruber
Visiting Assistant Professor Lynn Neal
Adjunct Professor Bill J. Leonard
Adjunct Associate Professor Mark Jensen

ROMANCE LANGUAGES
1983–1984
Kathleen M. Glenn, Chair
Professor of Humanities Germaine Brée
Professors Shasta M. Bryant, Kathleen M. Glenn, John E. Parker Jr., Mary Frances
    Robinson, Anne S. Tillett
Associate Professors Doranne Fenoaltea, Milorad R. Margitić, Gregorio C. Martić,
    Blanche C. Speer
Assistant Professor Candelas M. Newton

Visiting Assistant Professors Julián Bueno, Candide Carrasco
Instructors Catherine Anne Beaudry, Charles V. Ganelin, Rubén L. Gómez,
    David A. Petreman, Anna-Vera Sullam (Venice), Sylvia Trelles, Byron R. Wells
Lecturers Bianca Artom, Eva Marie Rodtwitt

1984–1985

Kathleen M. Glenn, Chair
Professor of Humanities Germaine Brée
Professors Shasta M. Bryant, Kathleen M. Glenn, John E. Parker Jr., Mary Frances
    Robinson, Anne S. Tillett
Associate Professors Doranne Fenoaltea, Milorad R. Margitić, Gregorio C. Martić
Assistant Professor Candelas M. Newton
Visiting Assistant Professors Candide Carrasco, Susan M. Linker
Instructors Rubén L. Gómez, Edward Miller, David A. Petreman,
    Anna-Vera Sullam (Venice), Sylvia Trelles, Barbara Welch, Byron R. Wells
Visiting Instructors Joyce Loland, Jennifer Sault
Lecturers Bianca Artom, Eva Marie Rodtwitt

1985–1986

Kathleen M. Glenn, Chair
Professor of Humanities Germaine Brée
Professors Shasta M. Bryant, Kathleen M. Glenn, John E. Parker Jr., Mary Frances
    Robinson, Anne S. Tillett
Associate Professors Doranne Fenoaltea, Milorad R. Margitić,
    Gregorio C. Martić, Candelas M. Newton
Assistant Professors Margaret Snook, Byron R. Wells
Visiting Assistant Professors Susan M. Linker, David A. Petreman, Barbara Welch
Instructors Barbara Clark, Mary C. Frye, Joyce Loland, Susan Mraz,
    Sheryl Postman, Anna-Vera Sullam (Venice)
Visiting Instructor Jennifer Sault
Lecturers Bianca Artom, Eva Marie Rodtwitt

1986–1987

Kathleen M. Glenn, Chair
Professors Shasta M. Bryant, Kathleen M. Glenn, John E. Parker Jr., Mary Frances
    Robinson, Anne S. Tillett
Associate Professors Doranne Fenoaltea, Milorad R. Margitić,
    Gregorio C. Martić, Candelas M. Newton
Assistant Professors Margaret Snook, Byron R. Wells
Visiting Assistant Professors Sarah E. Barbour, Susan M. Linker,
    David A. Petreman, Kari Weil
Instructors Barbara Clark, Mary C. Frye, Joyce Loland, Susan Mraz,
    Sheryl Postman, Jennifer Sault, Anna-Vera Sullam (Venice)
Lecturers Bianca Artom, Kikuko T. Imamura, Matthew P. Murray, Eva Marie
    Rodtwitt

1987–1988

Shasta M. Bryant, Chair

Professors Shasta M. Bryant, Kathleen M. Glenn, John E. Parker Jr., Mary Frances
  Robinson
Associate Professors Doranne Fenoaltea, Milorad R. Margitić, Candelas M. Newton
Assistant Professors Margaret Snook, Antonio C. Vitti, Kari Weil, Byron R. Wells
Visiting Assistant Professors Sarah E. Barbour, Michèle Drouart, Gilberto Gómez,
  Kenneth Hall, Susan M. Linker
Instructors Whangbai Bahk, Barbara Clark, Mary C. Frye, Anna Krauth,
  Gail McNeill, Susan Mraz, Sheryl Postman, Bianca Rivera, Jennifer Sault,
  Anna-Vera Sullam (Venice)
Lecturers Bianca Artom, Kikuko T. Imamura, Matthew P. Murray,
  Eva Marie Rodtwitt

1988–1989

Shasta M. Bryant, Chair

Professors Shasta M. Bryant, Kathleen M. Glenn, Milorad R. Margitić,
  Mary Frances Robinson
Associate Professors Candelas M. Newton, Byron R. Wells
Assistant Professors Jane W. Albrecht, Victoria Bridges, Ramiro Fernández,
  Mary L. Friedman, Judy K. Kem, Linda S. Maier, Stephen Murphy, Juan Orbe,
  Margaret Snook, Antonio C. Vitti, Kari Weil
Visiting Assistant Professors Whangbai Bahk, Sarah E. Barbour, Kenneth Hall,
  Susan M. Linker
Instructors Mary C. Frye, Anna Krauth, Jennifer Sault, Walter W. Shaw,
  Anna-Vera Sullam (Venice)
Lecturers Bianca Artom, C. Lee Dubs, Kikuko T. Imamura, Eva Marie Rodtwitt

1989–1990

Byron R. Wells, Chair

Professors Kathleen M. Glenn, Milorad R. Margitić, Mary Frances Robinson
Associate Professors Candelas M. Newton, Byron R. Wells
Assistant Professors Jane W. Albrecht, Sarah E. Barbour, Victoria Bridges, Ramiro
  Fernández, Mary L. Friedman, Judy K. Kem, Linda S. Maier,
  Ana Menendez-Collera, Stephen Murphy, Juan Orbe, Margaret Snook,
  Antonio C. Vitti, Kari Weil
Visiting Assistant Professors Whangbai Bahk, Susan M. Linker
Instructors Anna Krauth, Jennifer Sault, Walter W. Shaw,
  Anna-Vera Sullam (Venice), Florence M. Toy
Lecturers Bianca Artom, Kikuko T. Imamura, Eva Marie Rodtwitt

1990–1991

Byron R. Wells, Chair

Professors Kathleen M. Glenn, Milorad R. Margitić
Associate Professors Mary L. Friedman, Candelas M. Newton, Byron R. Wells

Assistant Professors Jane W. Albrecht, Sarah E. Barbour, Jan Bardsley,
   Debra Boyd-Buggs, Victoria Bridges, Ramiro Fernández, Judy K. Kem,
   Linda S. Maier, Pat Moran, Stephen Murphy, Juan Orbe,
   Antonio C. Vitti, Kari Weil
Instructors Guy M. Arcuri, Cheryl Block, David M. Glass, Anna Krauth, Kathleen
   O'Quinn, Jennifer Sault, Walter W. Shaw, Alison T. Smith, Anna-Vera Sullam
   (Venice), Florence M. Toy
Lecturers Kikuko T. Imamura, Eva Marie Rodtwitt

1991–1992
Byron R. Wells, Chair
Professors Kathleen M. Glenn, Milorad R. Margitić
Associate Professors Mary L. Friedman, Candelas M. Newton,
   Byron R. Wells, M. Stanley Whitley
Assistant Professors Jane W. Albrecht, Gunnar Anderson, Sarah E. Barbour,
   Jan Bardsley, Debra Boyd-Buggs, Ramiro Fernández, Judy K. Kem, Linda S.
   Maier, Pat Moran, Stephen Murphy, Juan Orbe, Antonio C. Vitti, Kari Weil
Instructors Guy M. Arcuri, David M. Glass, Anna Krauth, Bill B. Raines,
   Jennifer Sault, Walter W. Shaw, Alison T. Smith, Anna-Vera Sullam (Venice),
   Florence M. Toy
Lecturer Eva Marie Rodtwitt

1992–1993
Byron R. Wells, Chair
Professors Kathleen M. Glenn, Milorad R. Margitić, Candelas M. Newton
Associate Professors Mary L. Friedman, Antonio C. Vitti, Byron R. Wells,
   M. Stanley Whitley
Assistant Professors Jane W. Albrecht, Gunnar Anderson, Sarah E. Barbour,
   Debra Boyd-Buggs, Constance L. Dickey, Ramiro Fernández, Judy K. Kem,
   Linda S. Maier, Stephen Murphy, Juan Orbe, Kari Weil
Instructors Guy M. Arcuri, David M. Glass, Anna Krauth, Bill B. Raines,
   Jennifer Sault, Walter W. Shaw, Alison T. Smith, Anna-Vera Sullam (Venice),
   Florence M. Toy
Lecturer Eva Marie Rodtwitt

1993–1994
Byron R. Wells, Chair
Wake Forest Professor Kathleen M. Glenn
Professors Milorad R. Margitić, Candelas M. Newton
Associate Professors Sarah E. Barbour, Mary L. Friedman, Antonio C. Vitti, Kari
   Weil, Byron R. Wells, M. Stanley Whitley
Assistant Professors Jane W. Albrecht, Gunnar Anderson, Debra Boyd-Buggs,
   Constance L. Dickey, Ramiro Fernández, Judy K. Kem, Linda S. Maier, Stephen
   Murphy, Juan Orbe

Instructors Guy M. Arcuri, Martha Golden, Sabine Loucif, Bill B. Raines, Jennifer
    Sault, Walter W. Shaw, Alison T. Smith, Anna-Vera Sullam (Venice), Florence
    M. Toy
Lecturer Eva Marie Rodtwitt

1994–1995
Byron R. Wells, Chair
Wake Forest Professor Kathleen M. Glenn
Professors Milorad R. Margitić, Candelas M. Newton, Byron R. Wells
Associate Professors Jane W. Albrecht, Sarah E. Barbour, Mary L. Friedman, Judy K.
    Kem, Antonio C. Vitti, Kari Weil, M. Stanley Whitley
Assistant Professors Debra Boyd-Buggs, Constance L. Dickey, Ramiro Fernández,
    Soledad Miguel-Prendes, Stephen Murphy, Juan Orbe
Visiting Professor Giovanni Cecchetti
Visiting Assistant Professor Guy M. Arcuri
Instructors David M. Glass, Linda S. Howe, Sabine Loucif, Pilar McMichael, Bill B.
    Raines, Catherine Rodgers, Jennifer Sault, Anna-Vera Sullam (Venice)
Lecturer Eva Marie Rodtwitt

1995–1996
Byron R. Wells, Chair
Wake Forest Professor Kathleen M. Glenn
Professors Milorad R. Margitić, Candelas M. Newton, Byron R. Wells
Associate Professors Jane W. Albrecht, Sarah E. Barbour, Mary L. Friedman, Judy K.
    Kem, Stephen Murphy, Antonio C. Vitti, Kari Weil, M. Stanley Whitley
Assistant Professors Debra Boyd-Buggs, Constance L. Dickey, Ramiro Fernández,
    Linda S. Howe, Soledad Miguel-Prendes, Juan Orbe
Visiting Assistant Professors Guy M. Arcuri, Shelley Olson, Alison T. Smith
Instructors Sabine Loucif, Bill B. Raines, Catherine Rodgers, Jennifer Sault, Anna-
    Vera Sullam (Venice), Florence M. Toy
Lecturer Eva Marie Rodtwitt

1996–1997
Byron R. Wells, Chair
Candelas M. Newton, Chair-elect
Wake Forest Professor Kathleen M. Glenn
Professors Milorad R. Margitić, Candelas M. Newton, Byron R. Wells
Associate Professors Jane W. Albrecht, Sarah E. Barbour, Mary L. Friedman,
    Judy K. Kem, Stephen Murphy, Antonio C. Vitti, Kari Weil, M. Stanley Whitley
Assistant Professors Debra Boyd, Constance L. Dickey, Ramiro Fernández, Linda S.
    Howe, Soledad Miguel-Prendes, Juan Orbe
Visiting Assistant Professors Melissa Lockhart, Patricia McEachern
Instructors Alexandra Iruela, Anne W. Gilfoil, Sabine Loucif, Jenny Puckett, Cath-
    erine Rodgers, Nelson J. Sanchez, Jennifer Sault, Anna-Vera Sullam (Venice)
Lecturer Eva Marie Rodtwitt

1997–1998
Candelas M. Newton, Chair
Wake Forest Professor Kathleen M. Glenn
Professors Milorad R. Margitić, Candelas M. Newton, Byron R. Wells
Associate Professors Jane W. Albrecht, Sarah E. Barbour, Mary L. Friedman, Judy K.
    Kem, Stephen Murphy, Antonio C. Vitti, Kari Weil, M. Stanley Whitley
Assistant Professors Debra S. Boyd, Constance L. Dickey, Linda S. Howe, Soledad
    Miguel-Prendes, María Teresa Sanhueza
Visiting Associate Professor Peter S. Roger, S. J.
Visiting Assistant Professors Marlyse E. Bach, Anne W. Gilfoil, Sandra L. Kingery
Instructors Alexandra Iruela, Sabine Loucif, Kristen H. Nickel, Jenny Puckett,
    Catherine Rodgers, Nelson J. Sanchez, Christine E. Swain, Anna-Vera Sullam
    (Venice), Kendall B. Tarte, Alicia M. Vitti
Lecturer Eva Marie Rodtwitt

1998–1999
Candelas S. Gala, Chair
Wake Forest Professor Kathleen M. Glenn
Professors Candelas S. Gala, Milorad R. Margitić, Antonio C. Vitti, Byron R. Wells
Associate Professors Jane W. Albrecht, Sarah E. Barbour, Mary L. Friedman, Judy K.
    Kem, Stephen Murphy, M. Stanley Whitley
Assistant Professors Victoria E. Campos, Constance L. Dickey, Luis González, Linda
    S. Howe, Soledad Miguel-Prendes, María Teresa Sanhueza
Visiting Assistant Professors Geneviève J. Brock, Enrico Cesaretti, François
    Dragacci-Paulsen, Anne W. Gilfoil, Kendall B. Tarte
Instructors Rebekah L. Morris, Kristen H. Nickel, Salvador Antón Pujol, Catherine
    Rodgers, Nelson J. Sanchez, Jennifer Sault (Spring), Christine E. Swain, Anna-
    Vera Sullam (Venice), Alicia M. Vitti (Fall)
Adjunct Instructor Jenny Puckett

1999–2000
Candelas S. Gala, Chair
Professors Candelas S. Gala, Milorad R. Margitić, Antonio C. Vitti, Byron R. Wells
Associate Professors Jane W. Albrecht, Sarah E. Barbour, Mary L. Friedman, Judy K.
    Kem, Stephen Murphy, M. Stanley Whitley
Assistant Professors Victoria E. Campos, Luis González, Linda S. Howe,
    Soledad Miguel-Prendes, Salvador Antón Pujol, María Teresa Sanhueza
Visiting Assistant Professors Elizabeth Mazza Anthony, Shaul Bassi (Venice),
    Geneviève J. Brock, Enrico Cesaretti, Kendall B. Tarte
Adjunct Assistant Professor Christina Ball
Adjunct Instructors Jenny Puckett, Florence M. Toy, Alicia M. Vitti
Instructors Corrado Corradini, Lisa M. Merschel, Rebekah L. Morris,
    Violeta Padrón-Bermejo, Justin R. Peterson, Catherine Rodgers,
    María Rodríguez, Leticia I. Romo, Nelson J. Sanchez, Christine E. Swain

2000–2001
Candelas S. Gala, Chair
Professors Candelas S. Gala, Milorad R. Margitić, Antonio C. Vitti, Byron R. Wells,
  M. Stanley Whitley
Associate Professors Jane W. Albrecht, Sarah E. Barbour, Mary L. Friedman,
  Judy K. Kem, Soledad Miguel-Prendes, Stephen Murphy
Assistant Professors Victoria E. Campos, Ola Furmanek, Luis González,
  Patricia Heid, Linda S. Howe, Salvador Antón Pujol, María Teresa Sanhueza,
  Kendall B. Tarte
Visiting Assistant Professors Elizabeth Mazza Anthony, Christina Ball, Shaul Bassi
  (Venice)
Adjunct Assistant Professor Janet Joyner
Adjunct Instructors Michel Bourquin, Jenny Puckett, Florence M. Toy,
  Maria-Encarna Moreno Turner, Alicia M. Vitti
Instructors Elizabeth Barron, Corrado Corradini, Elisabeth d'Empaire,
  Rebekah L. Morris, Violeta Padrón-Bermejo, Justin R. Peterson,
  Jesús Pico-Argel, María Rodríguez, Leticia I. Romo, Christine E. Swain,
  Carlos Valencia

2001–2002
Candelas S. Gala, Chair
 Wake Forest Professor Candelas S. Gala
Professors Milorad R. Margitić, Antonio C. Vitti, Byron R. Wells, M. Stanley
  Whitley
Associate Professors Jane W. Albrecht, Sarah E. Barbour, Mary L. Friedman, Linda
  S. Howe, Judy K. Kem, Soledad Miguel-Prendes, Stephen Murphy
Assistant Professors Ola Furmanek, Luis González, Patricia Heid, Salvador Antón
  Pujol, María Teresa Sanhueza, Kendall B. Tarte
Visiting Professor Roch C. Smith
Visiting Assistant Professor Elizabeth Mazza Anthony
Adjunct Assistant Professor Janet Joyner
Instructors Elizabeth Barron, Corrado Corradini, Elisabeth d'Empaire, Rebekah
  L. Morris, Violeta Padrón-Bermejo, Justin R. Peterson, Jesús Pico-Argel, María
  Rodríguez, Leticia I. Romo, Christine E. Swain, Carlos Valencia
Adjunct Instructors Jenny Puckett, Maria-Encarna Moreno Turner, Alicia M. Vitti

2002–2003
Candelas S. Gala, Chair
Wake Forest Professor Candelas S. Gala
Professors Milorad R. Margitić, Antonio C. Vitti (Dana Faculty Fellow), Byron R.
  Wells, M. Stanley Whitley
Associate Professors Jane W. Albrecht, Sarah E. Barbour, Mary L. Friedman, Linda
  S. Howe, Judy K. Kem, Soledad Miguel-Prendes, Stephen Murphy

Assistant Professors Margaret Ewalt, Ola Furmanek, Luis González, Patricia Heid,
   Roberta Morosini, Salvador Antón Pujol, María Teresa Sanhueza, Kendall B.
   Tarte
Visiting Assistant Professors Elizabeth Mazza Anthony, Elizabeth Barron,
   Paul Kelley, Keith Richards, Leticia Romo
Instructors Corrado Corradini, Elisabeth d'Empaire, Rebekah L. Morris, Justin R.
   Peterson, Jesús Pico-Argel, Christine E. Swain, Maria-Encarna Moreno Turner,
   Tricia Walter, Jennifer Wooten
Adjunct Instructor Jenny Puckett

2003–2004
Candelas S. Gala, Chair
Wake Forest Professor Candelas S. Gala
Professors Milorad R. Margitić, Antonio C. Vitti, Byron R. Wells, M. Stanley
   Whitley
Associate Professors Jane W. Albrecht, Sarah E. Barbour, Mary L. Friedman, Linda
   S. Howe, Judy K. Kem, Soledad Miguel-Prendes, Stephen Murphy, María Teresa
   Sanhueza
Assistant Professors Margaret Ewalt, Ola Furmanek, Luis González, Anne E. Hard-
   castle, Roberta Morosini, Salvador Antón Pujol, Kendall B. Tarte
Visiting Assistant Professors Elizabeth Mazza Anthony, María E. González-
   Robayna, Paul Kelley, Hosun Kim, Ana León-Távora, Valérie Pruvost, Keith
   Richards, Leticia Romo
Instructors Corrado Corradini, Elisabeth d'Empaire, Alicia Lorenzo García, Véro-
   nique M. McNelly, Rebekah L. Morris, Justin R. Peterson, Jesús Pico-Argel,
   Jenny Puckett, Maria-Encarna Moreno Turner, Tricia Walter, Jennifer Wooten

2004–2005
Candelas S. Gala, Chair
Wake Forest Professor Candelas S. Gala
Professors Milorad R. Margitić, Antonio C. Vitti, Byron R. Wells, M. Stanley
   Whitley
Associate Professors Jane W. Albrecht, Sarah E. Barbour, Mary L. Friedman, Linda
   S. Howe, Judy K. Kem, Soledad Miguel-Prendes, Stephen Murphy, María Teresa
   Sanhueza
Assistant Professors Margaret Ewalt, Ola Furmanek, Luis González, Anne E. Hard-
   castle, Kathryn Mayers, Roberta Morosini, Kendall B. Tarte
Visiting Assistant Professors Elizabeth Mazza Anthony, Simona Bondavalli,
   Gabriela Cerghedean, María E. González-Robayna, Janet Joyner, Hosun Kim,
   Ana León-Távora, Keith Richards
Instructors Corrado Corradini, Renée Gutiérrez, Melvin Hinton, Véronique M.
   McNelly, Justin R. Peterson, Jesús Pico-Argel, Jenny Puckett, Maria-Encarna
   Moreno Turner, Elisabeth d'Empaire Wilbert, Jennifer Wooten

2005–2006
Candelas S. Gala, Chair
Wake Forest Professor Candelas S. Gala
Professors Milorad R. Margitić, Antonio C. Vitti, Byron R. Wells, M. Stanley
Whitley
Associate Professors Jane W. Albrecht, Sarah E. Barbour, Mary L. Friedman, Linda
S. Howe, Judy K. Kem, Soledad Miguel-Prendes, Stephen Murphy, María Teresa
Sanhueza
Assistant Professors Margaret Ewalt, J. Michael Fulton, Ola Furmanek, Luis
González, Anne E. Hardcastle, Kathryn Mayers, Roberta Morosini, Kendall B.
Tarte
Visiting Assistant Professor Ana León-Távora
Instructors Jorge Avilés-Diz, Justin Bennett, Celia Garzón-Arrabal, Renée Gutiér-
rez, Véronique M. McNelly, Jenny Puckett, Maria Dolores Santamaria, Maria-
Encarna Moreno Turner, Elisabeth d'Empaire Wilbert, Jennifer Wooten, Itzá
Zavala Garrett
Lecturers Elizabeth Mazza Anthony, Corrado Corradini, Jesús Pico-Argel

RUSSIAN AND EAST EUROPEAN STUDIES (REE)

Interdisciplinary Minor
   (The Foreign Area Study in East European Studies became an interdisciplinary
minor in Russian and East European Studies in 1997–1998. The change was first
listed in the 1998–1999 *Bulletin*.)

1993–1996
Perry Patterson (Economics), Coordinator

1996–1998
Susan Z. Rupp (History), Coordinator

1998–2006
Susan Z. Rupp (History), Coordinator

SCHOOL OF BUSINESS AND ACCOUNTANCY (BUS & ACC)

The School of Business and Accountancy was established in 1980 as a separate
"School," no longer a "Department" in Wake Forest College. Thus, bulletins from
that time on had a separate section towards the back under the heading "School of
Business and Accountancy" to differentiate the School from the College. Here the
various policies and courses of the School were disclosed. Previously the BUS and
ACC courses had been listed under the Department of Business and Accountancy as
part of Wake Forest College along with the other departments and various courses in
the arts, humanities, mathematic, sciences, etc.

From 1983–1984 through 1994–1995, the School of Business and Accountancy prefixed its courses with the codes BUS (for business courses) and ACC (for accountancy courses). The school changed its name to Wayne Calloway School of Business and Accountancy in 1995–1996.

The School of Business and Accountancy is also listed under "Business and Accountancy" with this same information.

1983–1984
Thomas C. Taylor, Dean
Professors Delmer P. Hylton, F. Jeanne Owen, Thomas C. Taylor
Associate Professors Umit Akinc, Leon P. Cook Jr., A. Sayeste Daser, Arun P. Dewasthali, Carol Elbing, Stephen Ewing, Thomas S. Goho, Dale R. Martin, Ralph B. Tower
Assistant Professor Michael Roberts
Instructors Olive S. Thomas, Robin Tower, Julie Yu
Lecturer Lee Stokes

1984–1985
Thomas C. Taylor, Dean
Professors Delmer P. Hylton, F. Jeanne Owen, Thomas C. Taylor
Associate Professors Umit Akinc, Leon P. Cook Jr., A. Sayeste Daser, Arun P. Dewasthali, Carol Elbing, Stephen Ewing, Thomas S. Goho, Dale R. Martin, Ralph B. Tower
Assistant Professors John S. Dunkelberg, Michael Roberts, Julie Yu
Instructor Olive S. Thomas
Lecturer Lee Stokes

1985–1986
Thomas C. Taylor, Dean
Professors Delmer P. Hylton, F. Jeanne Owen, Thomas C. Taylor
Associate Professors Umit Akinc, Leon P. Cook Jr., A. Sayeste Daser, Arun P. Dewasthali, Carol Elbing, Stephen Ewing, Thomas S. Goho, Dale R. Martin, Ralph B. Tower
Assistant Professor John S. Dunkelberg
Visiting Professor Eddie V. Easley
Instructor Olive S. Thomas
Lecturer Lee Stokes

1986–1987
Thomas C. Taylor, Dean
Professors Eddie V. Easley, Delmer P. Hylton, F. Jeanne Owen, Thomas C. Taylor
Associate Professors Umit Akinc, Leon P. Cook Jr., A. Sayeste Daser, Arun P. Dewasthali, Stephen Ewing, Thomas S. Goho, Dale R. Martin, Ralph B. Tower
Assistant Professor John S. Dunkelberg

Adjunct Associate Professor Carol Elbing
Instructors Kim W. Driesbach, Timothy P. Summers
Lecturers Lee Stokes, Olive S. Thomas

1987–1988
Thomas C. Taylor, Dean
Professors Eddie V. Easley, Delmer P. Hylton, F. Jeanne Owen, Thomas C. Taylor
Associate Professors Umit Akinc, Leon P. Cook Jr., A. Sayeste Daser, Arun P. Dewasthali, Stephen Ewing, Thomas S. Goho, Dale R. Martin, Ralph B. Tower
Assistant Professors John S. Dunkelberg, Timothy P. Summers
Adjunct Associate Professor Carol Elbing
Instructors S. Douglas Beets, Kim W. Driesbach
Lecturers Lee Stokes, Olive S. Thomas

1988–1989
Thomas C. Taylor, Dean
University Professor K. Wayne Smith
Professors Eddie V. Easley, Delmer P. Hylton, F. Jeanne Owen, Thomas C. Taylor
Associate Professors Umit Akinc, Leon P. Cook Jr., A. Sayeste Daser, Arun P. Dewasthali, John S. Dunkelberg, Stephen Ewing, Thomas S. Goho, Dale R. Martin, Ralph B. Tower
Assistant Professor S. Douglas Beets
Adjunct Instructor Helen Akinc
Lecturers DeLeon E. Stokes, Olive S. Thomas
Adjunct Lecturer Horace O. Kelly Jr.

1989–1990
Thomas C. Taylor, Dean
University Professor K. Wayne Smith
Professors Eddie V. Easley, Delmer P. Hylton, F. Jeanne Owen, Thomas C. Taylor
Associate Professors Umit Akinc, Leon P. Cook Jr., A. Sayeste Daser, Arun P. Dewasthali, John S. Dunkelberg, Stephen Ewing, Thomas S. Goho, Dale R. Martin, Ralph B. Tower
Assistant Professor S. Douglas Beets
Adjunct Instructors Helen Akinc, Jules Laskey, Kaye Nifong, Robin Tower
Lecturers DeLeon E. Stokes, Olive S. Thomas
Adjunct Lecturer Horace O. Kelly Jr.

1990–1991
Thomas C. Taylor, Dean
Professors Eddie V. Easley, Delmer P. Hylton, F. Jeanne Owen, Thomas C. Taylor
Associate Professors Umit Akinc, Leon P. Cook Jr., A. Sayeste Daser, Arun P. Dewasthali, John S. Dunkelberg, Stephen Ewing, Thomas S. Goho, Dale R. Martin, Ralph B. Tower, Jack E. Wilkerson Jr.

Assistant Professors S. Douglas Beets, P. Candace Deans
Adjunct Instructor Helen Akinc
Lecturers Horace O. Kelly Jr., DeLeon E. Stokes, Olive S. Thomas

1991–1992
Thomas C. Taylor, Dean
Professors Eddie V. Easley, Delmer P. Hylton, F. Jeanne Owen, Thomas C. Taylor
Associate Professors Umit Akinc, Leon P. Cook Jr., A. Sayeste Daser, Arun P. Dew-
asthali, John S. Dunkelberg, Stephen Ewing, Thomas S. Goho, Dale R. Martin,
Ralph B. Tower, Jack E. Wilkerson Jr.
Assistant Professors S. Douglas Beets, P. Candace Deans, J. Kline Harrison
Adjunct Instructor Helen Akinc
Lecturers Horace O. Kelly Jr., DeLeon E. Stokes, Olive S. Thomas, C. Michael
Thompson

1992–1993
Thomas C. Taylor, Dean
Professors Eddie V. Easley, Thomas C. Taylor
Associate Professors Umit Akinc, Leon P. Cook Jr., A. Sayeste Daser, Arun P. Dew-
asthali, John S. Dunkelberg, Stephen Ewing, Thomas S. Goho, E. Clayton Hipp
Jr., Dale R. Martin, Ralph B. Tower, Jack E. Wilkerson Jr.
Assistant Professors S. Douglas Beets, P. Candace Deans, J. Kline Harrison
Instructor Paul E. Juras
Adjunct Instructors Helen Akinc, Emily G. Neese
Lecturers Horace O. Kelly Jr., DeLeon E. Stokes, Olive S. Thomas, C. Michael
Thompson

1993–1994
Dana J. Johnson, Dean
C. Michael Thompson, Assistant Dean
Professors Umit Akinc, Eddie V. Easley, Stephen Ewing, Dale R. Martin, Thomas C.
Taylor (Hylton Professor of Accountancy), Ralph B. Tower
Associate Professors S. Douglas Beets, Leon P. Cook Jr., A. Sayeste Daser, Arun P.
Dewasthali, John S. Dunkelberg, Thomas S. Goho, E. Clayton Hipp Jr., Jack E.
Wilkerson Jr.
Assistant Professors P. Candace Deans, J. Kline Harrison, Paul E. Juras
Adjunct Instructors Helen Akinc, Emily G. Neese
Lecturers Horace O. Kelly Jr., DeLeon E. Stokes, Olive S. Thomas, C. Michael
Thompson

1994–1995
Dana J. Johnson, Dean
C. Michael Thompson, Assistant Dean

Professors Umit Akinc (Thomas H. Davis Professor of Business), A. Sayeste Daser, Eddie V. Easley, Stephen Ewing, Dale R. Martin, Thomas C. Taylor (Hylton Professor of Accountancy), Ralph B. Tower
Associate Professors S. Douglas Beets, Arun P. Dewasthali, John S. Dunkelberg (Benson-Pruitt Professor of Business), Thomas S. Goho, E. Clayton Hipp Jr., Jack E. Wilkerson Jr.
Assistant Professors P. Candace Deans, Jonathan E. Duchac, J. Kline Harrison, Paul E. Juras
Instructors Helen Akinc, Katherine S. Hoppe
Adjunct Instructors Suzanne S. Buchanan, Cynthia R. Sutton
Lecturers Horace O. Kelly Jr., DeLeon E. Stokes, Olive S. Thomas, C. Michael Thompson
Visiting Lecturer Locke M. Newlin

1995–1996
Dana J. Johnson, Dean
Assistant Deans Horace O. Kelly Jr., C. Michael Thompson
Professors Umit Akinc (Thomas H. Davis Professor of Business), John S. Dunkelberg (Benson-Pruitt Professor of Business), Eddie V. Easley, Stephen Ewing, Dale R. Martin, Thomas C. Taylor (Hylton Professor of Accountancy), Ralph B. Tower
Associate Professors S. Douglas Beets, Helen M. Bowers (Kemper Faculty Fellow), Arun P. Dewasthali, Thomas S. Goho, J. Kline Harrison, E. Clayton Hipp Jr., Jack E. Wilkerson Jr.
Assistant Professors Jonathan E. Duchac, Paul E. Juras, Gordon E. McCray
Visiting Assistant Professors Dennis Cole, Steven J. Crowell
Instructors Helen Akinc, Katherine S. Hoppe
Lecturers Horace O. Kelly Jr., C. Michael Thompson
Visiting Lecturers David K. Isbister, Locke M. Newlin

1996–1997
Dana J. Johnson, Dean
Assistant Dean Katherine S. Hoppe
Professors Umit Akinc (Thomas H. Davis Professor of Business), John S. Dunkelberg (Benson-Pruitt Professor of Business), Eddie V. Easley, Stephen Ewing, Dale R. Martin, Thomas C. Taylor (Hylton Professor of Accountancy), Ralph B. Tower
Associate Professors S. Douglas Beets, Helen M. Bowers (Kemper Faculty Fellow), Arun P. Dewasthali, Thomas S. Goho, J. Kline Harrison, Jack E. Wilkerson Jr.
Assistant Professors Jonathan E. Duchac, Patricia A. Graybeal, Paul E. Juras, Gordon E. McCray, C. Michael Thompson, G. Page West III
Instructors Helen Akinc (Director of Student Services), Katherine S. Hoppe
Visiting Assistant Professors Dennis Cole, Kathryn R. Nickles
Visiting Lecturers E. Clayton Hipp Jr., David K. Isbister, Emily Neese, Thomas Ogburn

1997–1998
Jack E. Wilkerson Jr., Acting Dean
Assistant Dean Katherine S. Hoppe
Professors Umit Akinc (Thomas H. Davis Professor of Business),
    John S. Dunkelberg, Eddie V. Easley, Stephen Ewing, Dale R. Martin
    (Price Waterhouse Professor of Accountancy), Thomas C. Taylor
    (Hylton Professor of Accountancy), Ralph B. Tower, Jack E. Wilkerson Jr.
Associate Professors S. Douglas Beets, Helen M. Bowers (Kemper Faculty Fellow),
    Arun P. Dewasthali, Thomas S. Goho, J. Kline Harrison (Benson-Pruitt Associ-
    ate Professor), Paul E. Juras
Assistant Professors Sheri A. Bridges, Jonathan E. Duchac, Patricia A. Lobingier,
    Gordon E. McCray, G. Page West III
Visiting Assistant Professors Mark W. Huber, William M. Marcum,
    Margaret C. Smith
Instructors Helen Akinc, Tamara M. Greenwood, Katherine S. Hoppe
Lecturers E. Clayton Hipp Jr., David K. Isbister, Debra R. Jessup, Thomas Ogburn
Adjunct Lecturers Robyn Earthman, Emily Neese
Executives-in-Residence Hunter Cook, John F. Ward

1998–1999
Jack E. Wilkerson Jr., Dean
Assistant Dean Katherine S. Hoppe
Professors Umit Akinc (Thomas H. Davis Professor of Business),
    John S. Dunkelberg, Eddie V. Easley, Stephen Ewing, Dale R. Martin
    (Price Waterhouse Professor of Accountancy), Donald P. Robin
    (J. Tylee Wilson Professor of Business Ethics), Thomas C. Taylor
    (Hylton Professor of Accountancy), Ralph B. Tower, Jack E. Wilkerson Jr.
Associate Professors S. Douglas Beets, Arun P. Dewasthali, Thomas S. Goho, J.
    Kline Harrison (Benson-Pruitt Associate Professor), Paul E. Juras
Assistant Professors Sheri A. Bridges, Jonathan E. Duchac, Debra R. Jessup,
    William M. Marcum, Patricia A. Lobingier, Gordon E. McCray, Yvonne H.
    Stewart (Coopers & Lybrand Faculty Fellow), G. Page West III
Visiting Professor Donald H. Taylor
Visiting Assistant Professor Mark W. Huber
Instructors Helen Akinc, Anna M. Cianci, Tamara M. Greenwood, Katherine S.
    Hoppe
Lecturers James L. Dominick, E. Clayton Hipp Jr., David K. Isbister, Thomas
    Ogburn
Executives-in-Residence James H. Clippard Jr., Peter C. Valenti

1999–2000
Jack E. Wilkerson Jr., Dean
Assistant Dean Katherine S. Hoppe
F.M. Kirby Chair of Business Excellence Roger L. Jenkins

Professors Umit Akinc (Thomas H. Davis Professor of Business),
John S. Dunkelberg (Kemper Professor), Eddie V. Easley, Stephen Ewing,
Dale R. Martin (PricewaterhouseCoopers Professor of Accountancy),
Donald P. Robin (J. Tylee Wilson Professor of Business Ethics),
Thomas C. Taylor (Hylton Professor of Accountancy), Ralph B. Tower,
Jack E. Wilkerson Jr.
Associate Professors S. Douglas Beets, Arun P. Dewasthali, Jonathan E. Duchac,
Thomas S. Goho, J. Kline Harrison (Benson-Pruitt Associate Professor),
Paul E. Juras
Assistant Professors Terry A. Baker, Sheri A. Bridges, Audrey A. Gramling
(PricewaterhouseCoopers Faculty Fellow), Debra R. Jessup, Patricia A. Lob-
ingier, William M. Marcum, Gordon E. McCray (BellSouth Mobility Technology
Faculty Fellow), Yvonne H. Stewart (PricewaterhouseCoopers Faculty Fellow),
G. Page West III
Instructors Helen Akinc, Anna M. Cianci, Tamara M. Greenwood,
Katherine S. Hoppe
Visiting Instructor of Information Systems James W. Enyon
Lecturer in Accounting Maureen L. Carpenter
Lecturers in Business Andrew C. Ellis, E. Clayton Hipp Jr., David K. Isbister, Karen
E. Mishra, Daniel Paul, Tracy D. Rishel
Executive-in-Residence Peter C. Valenti

2000–2001
Jack E. Wilkerson Jr., Dean
Associate Dean for Curriculum and Administration J. Kline Harrison
Associate Dean for Academic Programs and Resources Dale R. Martin
Assistant Dean for Student Professional Affairs Helen W. Akinc
Assistant Dean for Student Academic Affairs Katherine S. Hoppe
F.M. Kirby Chair of Business Excellence Roger L. Jenkins
Professors Umit Akinc (Thomas H. Davis Professor of Business), John S. Dunkel-
berg (Kemper Professor), Stephen Ewing, Dale R. Martin (Wayne Calloway Pro-
fessor of Accountancy), Donald P. Robin (J. Tylee Wilson Professor of Business
Ethics), Thomas C. Taylor (Hylton Professor of Accountancy), Ralph B. Tower
(Wayne Calloway Professor of Taxation), Jack E. Wilkerson Jr.
Associate Professors S. Douglas Beets, Arun P. Dewasthali, Jonathan E. Duchac,
Thomas S. Goho (Benson-Pruitt Associate Professor), J. Kline Harrison, Paul E.
Juras
Assistant Professors Terry A. Baker, Sheri A. Bridges, Audrey A. Gramling
(PricewaterhouseCoopers Faculty Fellow), Debra R. Jessup, Patricia A. Lob-
ingier, William M. Marcum (Director of the Risk Management Faculty Fellow
Program), Gordon E. McCray (BellSouth Mobility Technology Faculty Fellow),
Amy E. Randel, Annette L. Ranft (Exxon-Wayne Calloway Faculty Fellow),
Yvonne H. Stewart (PricewaterhouseCoopers Faculty Fellow and Director of the
Arthur Andersen Center), G. Page West III

Instructors Helen Akinc, Katherine A. Baker, John Bennett, Tamara M. Greenwood,
   Katherine S. Hoppe, Mary Martha McKinley
Visiting Instructors James W. Enyon, Karen E. Mishra
Senior Lecturer in Business E. Clayton Hipp Jr.
Lecturer in Business David K. Isbister

2001–2002
Jack E. Wilkerson Jr., Dean
Associate Dean for Curriculum and Administration J. Kline Harrison
Associate Dean for Academic Programs and Resources Dale R. Martin
Assistant Dean for Student Professional Affairs Helen W. Akinc
Assistant Dean for Student Academic Affairs Katherine S. Hoppe
F.M. Kirby Chair of Business Excellence Roger L. Jenkins
Professors Umit Akinc (Thomas H. Davis Professor of Business),
   John S. Dunkelberg (Kemper Professor), Stephen Ewing, J. Kline Harrison,
   Dale R. Martin (Wayne Calloway Professor of Accountancy), Donald P. Robin
   (J. Tylee Wilson Professor of Business Ethics), Thomas C. Taylor (Hylton Profes-
   sor of Accountancy), Ralph B. Tower (Wayne Calloway Professor of Taxation),
   Jack E. Wilkerson Jr.
Associate Professors S. Douglas Beets, Arun P. Dewasthali, Jonathan E. Duchac,
   Thomas S. Goho (Benson-Pruitt Associate Professor), Gordon E. McCray (Bell-
   South Mobility Technology Faculty Fellow), G. Page West III
Assistant Professors Terry A. Baker (PricewaterhouseCoopers Faculty Fellow),
   Robert M. Ballenger (Cooper Family Fellow in Information Systems), Sheri
   A. Bridges, Yvonne L. Hinson (PricewaterhouseCoopers Faculty Fellow and
   Director of the Arthur Andersen Center), Debra R. Jessup, Paul E. Juras (Price-
   waterhouseCoopers Faculty Fellow), Patricia A. Lobingier, William M. Marcum
   (Citibank Faculty Fellow, Director of the Risk Management Faculty Fellow
   Program), Amy E. Randel, Annette L. Ranft (Exxon-Wayne Calloway Faculty
   Fellow)
Visiting Professors Lee G. Knight, K. Wayne Smith
Instructors Helen W. Akinc, Katherine A. Baker, Katherine S. Hoppe, Mary L.
   Kesel, Mary Martha McKinley, Karen E. Mishra, Karen D. Nard, Karen K.
   Rogalski
Senior Lecturer in Business E. Clayton Hipp Jr.
Lecturers in Business Tamara M. Greenwood, David K. Isbister, Wayne Forrest
   Morgan

2002–2003
Jack E. Wilkerson Jr., Dean
Associate Dean for Curriculum and Administration J. Kline Harrison
Associate Dean for Academic Programs and Resources Dale R. Martin
Assistant Dean for Student Professional Affairs Helen W. Akinc
Assistant Dean for Student Academic Affairs Katherine S. Hoppe
F.M. Kirby Chair of Business Excellence Roger L. Jenkins

Professors Umit Akinc (Thomas H. Davis Professor of Business), Stephen Ewing, J. Kline Harrison, Lee G. Knight, Dale R. Martin (Wayne Calloway Professor of Accountancy), Donald P. Robin (J. Tylee Wilson Professor of Business Ethics), Thomas C. Taylor (Hylton Professor of Accountancy), Ralph B. Tower (Wayne Calloway Professor of Taxation), Jack E. Wilkerson Jr.

Associate Professors George R. Aldhizer, S. Douglas Beets, James F. Cotter, Arun P. Dewasthali, Jonathan E. Duchac, Thomas S. Goho (Benson-Pruitt Associate Professor), Yvonne L. Hinson (PricewaterhouseCoopers Faculty Fellow), Paul E. Juras (PricewaterhouseCoopers Associate Professor of Accountancy), Gordon E. McCray (BellSouth Mobility Technology Associate Professor), G. Page West III

Assistant Professors Terry A. Baker (PricewaterhouseCoopers Faculty Fellow), Sheri A. Bridges, Debra R. Jessup, William M. Marcum (Citibank Faculty Fellow), Denise J. McManus, Amy E. Randel, Annette L. Ranft (Exxon-Wayne Calloway Faculty Fellow)

Visiting Professor K. Wayne Smith

Instructors Helen W. Akinc, Katherine A. Baker, John Campbell, Mary L. Kesel, Mary Martha McKinley, Karen E. Mishra, Karen D. Nard, Karen K. Rogalski

Senior Lecturer in Business E. Clayton Hipp Jr.

Lecturers in Business Tamara M. Greenwood, Katherine S. Hoppe, David K. Isbister

2003–2004

Jack E. Wilkerson Jr., Dean

Associate Dean J. Kline Harrison

Associate Dean Gordon E. McCray

Assistant Dean for Student Professional Affairs Helen W. Akinc

Assistant Dean for Student Academic Affairs Katherine S. Hoppe

Professors Umit Akinc (Thomas H. Davis Professor of Business), S. Douglas Beets, Stephen Ewing, J. Kline Harrison, Lee G. Knight, Dale R. Martin (Wayne Calloway Professor of Accountancy), Donald P. Robin (J. Tylee Wilson Professor of Business Ethics), Thomas C. Taylor (Hylton Professor of Accountancy), Ralph B. Tower (Wayne Calloway Professor of Taxation), Jack E. Wilkerson Jr.

Associate Professors George R. Aldhizer, Sheri A. Bridges, James F. Cotter, Arun P. Dewasthali, Jonathan E. Duchac (Merrill Lynch Associate Professor of Accountancy), Thomas S. Goho, Yvonne L. Hinson (PricewaterhouseCoopers Faculty Fellow), Paul E. Juras (PricewaterhouseCoopers Associate Professor of Accountancy), Gordon E. McCray (BellSouth Mobility Technology Associate Professor), G. Page West III (Benson-Pruitt Associate Professor)

Assistant Professors Terry A. Baker (PricewaterhouseCoopers Faculty Fellow and Assistant Professor), Debra R. Jessup, Bruce R. Lewis, William M. Marcum (Citibank Faculty Fellow), Denise J. McManus (Exxon-Wayne Calloway Faculty Fellow), Amy E. Randel (Coca-Cola Faculty Fellow), Annette L. Ranft (Exxon-Wayne Calloway Faculty Fellow)

Visiting Professor K. Wayne Smith

Instructors Helen W. Akinc, Mary L. Kesel, Karen E. Mishra, Karen K. Rogalski

Senior Lecturer in Business E. Clayton Hipp Jr.

Lecturers in Business Tamara M. Greenwood, Katherine S. Hoppe, David K. Isbister

2004–2005
Jack E. Wilkerson Jr., Dean
Associate Dean J. Kline Harrison
Associate Dean Gordon E. McCray
Assistant Dean for Student Professional Affairs Helen W. Akinc
Assistant Dean for Student Academic Affairs Katherine S. Hoppe
Professors Umit Akinc (Thomas H. Davis Professor of Business), S. Douglas Beets,
　　Stephen Ewing, J. Kline Harrison, Lee G. Knight (Hylton Professor of Accoun-
　　tancy), Dale R. Martin (Wayne Calloway Professor of Accountancy), Donald P.
　　Robin (J. Tylee Wilson Professor of Business Ethics), Ralph B. Tower (Wayne
　　Calloway Professor of Taxation), Jack E. Wilkerson Jr.
Associate Professors George R. Aldhizer, Sheri A. Bridges, James F. Cotter, Arun P.
　　Dewasthali, Jonathan E. Duchac (Merrill Lynch Associate Professor of Accoun-
　　tancy), Thomas S. Goho, Yvonne L. Hinson (PricewaterhouseCoopers Faculty
　　Fellow), Paul E. Juras (PricewaterhouseCoopers Associate Professor of Accoun-
　　tancy), William M. Marcum (Citibank Faculty Fellow), Gordon E. McCray
　　(BellSouth Mobility Technology Associate Professor), G. Page West III (Benson-
　　Pruitt Associate Professor)
Assistant Professors Terry A. Baker (PricewaterhouseCoopers Faculty Fellow),
　　Debra R. Jessup, Bruce R. Lewis (Cooper Family Fellow in Information Systems),
　　Denise J. McManus (Exxon-Wayne Calloway Faculty Fellow), Amy E. Randel
　　(Coca-Cola Faculty Fellow), Annette L. Ranft (Exxon-Wayne Calloway Faculty
　　Fellow)
Exchange Professor (Bordeaux) Christophe Estay
Visiting Assistant Professor Vinay K. Vasudev
Adjunct Assistant Professor Julie H. Wayne
Instructors Helen W. Akinc, Michaele M. Cook, Robert E. Fly, David A. Gilbert,
　　Mary L. Kesel, Daniel J. Paul, Thomas H. Ramsey, Tina F. Rizzi, Cyndi Skaar
Senior Lecturer in Business E. Clayton Hipp Jr.
Lecturer in Business Katherine S. Hoppe

2005–2006
Jack E. Wilkerson Jr., Dean
Associate Dean J. Kline Harrison
Associate Dean Gordon E. McCray
Assistant Dean for Student Professional Affairs Helen W. Akinc
Assistant Dean for Student Academic Affairs Katherine S. Hoppe
Professors Umit Akinc (Thomas H. Davis Professor of Business),
　　S. Douglas Beets, Robert R. Bliss (F.M. Kirby Professor of Business
　　Excellence), Stephen Ewing, J. Kline Harrison, Lee G. Knight (Hylton Professor
　　of Accountancy), Dale R. Martin (Wayne Calloway Professor of Accountancy),
　　Donald P. Robin (J. Tylee Wilson Professor of Business Ethics), Ralph B. Tower
　　(Wayne Calloway Professor of Taxation), Jack E. Wilkerson Jr.
Associate Professors George R. Aldhizer, Terry A. Baker (PricewaterhouseCoopers
　　Faculty Fellow and Director of Graduate Studies), Sheri A. Bridges, James F.

Cotter, Arun P. Dewasthali, Jonathan E. Duchac (Merrill Lynch Associate Professor of Accountancy), Thomas S. Goho, Yvonne L. Hinson (PricewaterhouseCoopers Faculty Fellow), Paul E. Juras, William M. Marcum (Citibank Faculty Fellow), Gordon E. McCray (BellSouth Mobility Technology Associate Professor), Annette L. Ranft (Exxon-Wayne Calloway Faculty Fellow), G. Page West III (Benson-Pruitt Associate Professor)

Assistant Professors Bruce R. Lewis (Cooper Family Fellow in Information Systems), Denise J. McManus (Exxon-Wayne Calloway Faculty Fellow), Amy E. Randel (Coca-Cola Faculty Fellow), Michelle Steward

Adjunct Assistant Professors Debra R. Jessup, Julie H. Wayne

Instructors Helen W. Akinc, Robert E. Fly, David A. Gilbert, R. Scott Keith, Mary L. Kesel, Benjamin Paz, Thomas H. Ramsey, Cyndi Skaar

Senior Lecturer in Business E. Clayton Hipp Jr.

Lecturer in Business Katherine S. Hoppe

SOCIOLOGY (SOC)

1983–1985
Philip J. Perricone, Chair
Professor John R. Earle
Associate Professors William H. Gulley, Philip J. Perricone
Assistant Professors Catherine T. Harris, Willie Pearson Jr.
Visiting Assistant Professor H. Kenneth Bechtel

1985–1986
Philip J. Perricone, Chair
Professor John R. Earle
Associate Professors William H. Gulley, Philip J. Perricone
Assistant Professors Catherine T. Harris, Willie Pearson Jr.
Visiting Assistant Professor H. Kenneth Bechtel
Visiting Instructor Shelley L. Pendleton

1986–1988
Philip J. Perricone, Chair
Professor John R. Earle
Associate Professors William H. Gulley, Catherine T. Harris, Willie Pearson Jr., Philip J. Perricone
Assistant Professor Ian M. Taplin
Visiting Assistant Professor H. Kenneth Bechtel

1988–1989
Philip J. Perricone, Chair
Professors John R. Earle, Philip J. Perricone
Associate Professors Catherine T. Harris, Willie Pearson Jr.

Assistant Professors H. Kenneth Bechtel, Ian M. Taplin
Visiting Assistant Professor Nancy Elizabeth Rushing

1989–1990
Philip J. Perricone, Chair
Professors John R. Earle, Philip J. Perricone
Associate Professors Catherine T. Harris, Willie Pearson Jr., Beverly Wright
Assistant Professors H. Kenneth Bechtel, Ian M. Taplin
Visiting Assistant Professor Cynthia Gentry

1990–1991
Philip J. Perricone, Chair
Professors John R. Earle, Catherine T. Harris, Willie Pearson Jr., Philip J. Perricone
Associate Professor Beverly Wright
Assistant Professors H. Kenneth Bechtel, Ian M. Taplin
Visiting Assistant Professor Cynthia Gentry

1991–1992
Philip J. Perricone, Chair
Professors John R. Earle, Catherine T. Harris, Willie Pearson Jr., Philip J. Perricone
Associate Professors H. Kenneth Bechtel, Beverly Wright
Assistant Professor Ian M. Taplin
Visiting Assistant Professor Cynthia Gentry
Instructor Vicky M. MacLean

1992–1993
Philip J. Perricone, Chair
Wake Forest Professor Charles F. Longino
Professors John R. Earle, Catherine T. Harris, Willie Pearson Jr., Philip J. Perricone
Associate Professors H. Kenneth Bechtel, Beverly Wright
Assistant Professor Ian M. Taplin
Visiting Assistant Professors Cynthia Gentry, Vicky M. MacLean

1993–1994
Philip J. Perricone, Chair
Wake Forest Professor Charles F. Longino
Professors John R. Earle, Catherine T. Harris, Willie Pearson Jr., Philip J. Perricone
Associate Professors H. Kenneth Bechtel, Beverly Wright
Assistant Professor Ian M. Taplin
Visiting Instructors Kevin D. Everett, Doug Pryor

1994–1995
Philip J. Perricone, Chair
Wake Forest Professor Charles F. Longino

Professors John R. Earle, Catherine T. Harris, Willie Pearson Jr., Philip J. Perricone
Associate Professors H. Kenneth Bechtel, Cheryl B. Leggon
Assistant Professor Ian M. Taplin
Visiting Instructors Ralph B. McNeal Jr., Doug Pryor, Teresa R. Smith

1995–1996
Philip J. Perricone, Chair
Wake Forest Professor Charles F. Longino
Professors John R. Earle, Catherine T. Harris, Willie Pearson Jr., Philip J. Perricone
Associate Professors H. Kenneth Bechtel, Cheryl B. Leggon, Ian M. Taplin
Visiting Assistant Professor Doug Pryor
Visiting Instructors Ralph B. McNeal Jr., Teresa R. Smith

1996–1997
Philip J. Perricone, Chair
Wake Forest Professor Charles F. Longino
Professors John R. Earle, Catherine T. Harris, Willie Pearson Jr., Philip J. Perricone
Associate Professors H. Kenneth Bechtel, Cheryl B. Leggon, Ian M. Taplin
Instructor Jonathon S. Epstein
Visiting Instructor Teresa R. Smith

1997–1998
Philip J. Perricone, Chair
Rubin Professor of American Ethnic Studies Earl Smith
Wake Forest Professor Charles F. Longino
Professors John R. Earle, Catherine T. Harris, Willie Pearson Jr., Philip J. Perricone
Associate Professors H. Kenneth Bechtel, Cheryl B. Leggon, Ian M. Taplin
Assistant Professor Jeffery S. Mullis
Visiting Assistant Professor Timothy McGettigan
Visiting Instructor Teresa R. Smith

1998–1999
Earl Smith, Chair
Rubin Professor of American Ethnic Studies Earl Smith
Wake Forest Professors Charles F. Longino, Willie Pearson Jr.
Professors John R. Earle, Catherine T. Harris, Philip J. Perricone
Associate Professors H. Kenneth Bechtel, Cheryl B. Leggon, Ian M. Taplin
Assistant Professors Angela Hattery, Jeffery S. Mullis
Visiting Assistant Professor Timothy McGettigan
Visiting Instructor Teresa R. Smith

1999–2000
Earl Smith, Chair
Rubin Professor of American Ethnic Studies Earl Smith

Wake Forest Professors Charles F. Longino, Willie Pearson Jr.
Professors John R. Earle, Catherine T. Harris, Philip J. Perricone
Associate Professors H. Kenneth Bechtel, Cheryl B. Leggon, Ian M. Taplin
Assistant Professor Angela Hattery
Visiting Assistant Professor Timothy McGettigan
Visiting Instructor Teresa R. Smith

2000–2001
Earl Smith, Chair
Rubin Professor of American Ethnic Studies Earl Smith
Wake Forest Professors Charles F. Longino, Willie Pearson Jr.
Professors John R. Earle, Catherine T. Harris, Philip J. Perricone
Associate Professors H. Kenneth Bechtel, Cheryl B. Leggon, Ian M. Taplin
Assistant Professor Angela Hattery

2001–2002
Earl Smith, Chair
Rubin Professor of American Ethnic Studies Earl Smith
Wake Forest Professors Charles F. Longino, Willie Pearson Jr.
Professors Catherine T. Harris, Philip J. Perricone, Ian M. Taplin
Associate Professors H. Kenneth Bechtel, Cheryl B. Leggon
Assistant Professors R. Saylor Breckenridge, Teresa Ciabattari, Angela Hattery

2002–2003
Earl Smith, Chair
Rubin Professor of American Ethnic Studies Earl Smith
Wake Forest Professor Charles F. Longino
Professors Catherine T. Harris, Philip J. Perricone, Ian M. Taplin
Associate Professors H. Kenneth Bechtel, Cheryl B. Leggon
Assistant Professors Teresa Ciabattari, Angela Hattery
Visiting Assistant Professor Don Bradley
Instructor R. Saylor Breckenridge

2003–2004
Earl Smith, Chair
Rubin Professor of American Ethnic Studies Earl Smith
Wake Forest Professor Charles F. Longino
Professors Catherine T. Harris, Philip J. Perricone, Ian M. Taplin
Associate Professor H. Kenneth Bechtel
Assistant Professors R. Saylor Breckenridge, Teresa Ciabattari, Angela Hattery, Ana
   M. Wahl
Visiting Assistant Professor Dana M. Greene

2004–2005
Earl Smith, Chair
Rubin Professor of American Ethnic Studies Earl Smith

Wake Forest Professor Charles F. Longino
Professors Catherine T. Harris, Ian M. Taplin
Associate Professors H. Kenneth Bechtel, Angela Hattery, Joseph Soares
Assistant Professors R. Saylor Breckenridge, Teresa Ciabattari, Ana M. Wahl
Visiting Assistant Professor Dana M. Greene

2005–2006
Earl Smith, Chair
Rubin Professor of American Ethnic Studies Earl Smith
Wake Forest Professor Charles F. Longino
Professors Catherine T. Harris, Ian M. Taplin
Associate Professors H. Kenneth Bechtel, Angela Hattery (Z. Smith Reynolds Foundation Fellow), Joseph Soares
Assistant Professors R. Saylor Breckenridge, Teresa Ciabattari, Ana M. Wahl, David Yamane
Adjunct Assistant Professor Steve Gunkel

SPANISH STUDIES

Foreign Area Study

1993–1999
Kathleen M. Glenn (Romance Languages), Coordinator

1999–2006
Candelas S. Gala (Romance Languages), Coordinator

SPEECH COMMUNICATION AND THEATRE ARTS (SCT)

(In 1991–1992, the Department of Speech Communication and Theatre Arts became separate departments: the Department of Speech Communication and the Department of Theater. This change was first listed in the 1992–1993 *Bulletin.*)

1983–1984
Donald H. Wolfe, Chair
Professors Julian C. Burroughs Jr., Franklin R. Shirley, Harold C. Tedford
Associate Professors Michael D. Hazen, Donald H. Wolfe
Assistant Professor Mae Jean Go
Visiting Assistant Professor Jo Whitten May
Instructor David C. Williams
Lecturers Caroline S. Fullerton, John Steele, Mary R. Wayne
Visiting Lecturers James H. Dodding, Todd A. Wronski

1984–1985
Donald H. Wolfe, Chair
Professors Julian C. Burroughs Jr., Franklin R. Shirley, Harold C. Tedford

Associate Professors Michael D. Hazen, Donald H. Wolfe
Assistant Professor Jill Jordan McMillan
Visiting Assistant Professor Jo Whitten May
Instructor David C. Williams
Lecturers Jonathan H. Christman, Caroline S. Fullerton, Mary R. Wayne
Visiting Lecturer James H. Dodding

1985–1986
Donald H. Wolfe, Chair
Professors Julian C. Burroughs Jr., Harold C. Tedford, Donald H. Wolfe
Associate Professor Michael D. Hazen
Assistant Professors Kathy L. Harbert, Jill Jordan McMillan
Visiting Assistant Professor Jo Whitten May
Adjunct Professor Darwin R. Payne
Instructors Helen B. Warren, David C. Williams
Lecturers Jonathan H. Christman, Caroline S. Fullerton, Mary R. Wayne
Visiting Lecturer James H. Dodding
Debate Coach Ross K. Smith

1986–1988
Donald H. Wolfe, Chair
Professors Julian C. Burroughs Jr., Harold C. Tedford, Donald H. Wolfe
Associate Professor Michael D. Hazen
Assistant Professor Jill Jordan McMillan
Visiting Assistant Professor Jo Whitten May
Adjunct Professor Darwin R. Payne
Instructors Allan D. Louden, Helen B. Warren, David C. Williams
Lecturers Jonathan H. Christman, Caroline S. Fullerton, Mary R. Wayne
Visiting Lecturer James H. Dodding
Debate Coach Ross K. Smith

1988–1989
Donald H. Wolfe, Chair
Professors Julian C. Burroughs Jr., Harold C. Tedford, Donald H. Wolfe
Associate Professor Michael D. Hazen
Assistant Professors Jill Jordan McMillan, Susan Schultz Huxman
Visiting Assistant Professors Nancy A. Burrell, Jo Whitten May
Adjunct Professor Darwin R. Payne
Instructor Allan D. Louden
Visiting Instructor Karen Robinson
Adjunct Instructors Mike Allen, Mary Lucy Bivins, Mary M. Dalton, Karen L.
    Oxendine, Linda Ellen Sloan
Lecturers Jonathan H. Christman, Caroline S. Fullerton, Mary R. Wayne
Visiting Lecturer James H. Dodding
Debate Coach Ross K. Smith

1989–1990

Donald H. Wolfe, Chair
Professors Julian C. Burroughs Jr., Harold C. Tedford, Donald H. Wolfe
Associate Professor Michael D. Hazen
Assistant Professors Jill Jordan McMillan, Susan Schultz Huxman
Adjunct Professors Jo Whitten May, Darwin R. Payne
Instructors Mary M. Dalton, Allan D. Louden
Adjunct Instructors Mary Lucy Bivins, Karen L. Oxendine, Taishen Siao, Linda
	Ellen Sloan, Julie Tomberlin
Lecturers Jonathan H. Christman, Caroline S. Fullerton, Mary R. Wayne
Visiting Lecturer James H. Dodding
Debate Coach Ross K. Smith

1990–1991

Donald H. Wolfe, Chair
Professors Julian C. Burroughs Jr., Harold C. Tedford, Donald H. Wolfe
Associate Professors Michael D. Hazen, Jill Jordan McMillan
Assistant Professor Susan Schultz Huxman
Visiting Assistant Professor Hyun Lee
Adjunct Professors Jo Whitten May, Darwin R. Payne
Instructors Mary M. Dalton, Allan D. Louden
Adjunct Instructors Mary Lucy Bivins, Paige Pettyjohn Edley, Karen L. Oxendine,
	Taishen Siao
Lecturers Jonathan H. Christman, Caroline S. Fullerton, Mary R. Wayne
Visiting Lecturer James H. Dodding
Debate Coach Ross K. Smith

1991–1992

Donald H. Wolfe, Chair
Professors Julian C. Burroughs Jr., Harold C. Tedford, Donald H. Wolfe
Associate Professors Michael D. Hazen, Jill Jordan McMillan
Assistant Professor Allan D. Louden
Visiting Associate Professor Carol J. Jablonski
Visiting Assistant Professors John M. Gulley, Hyun Lee, Randall G. Rogan
Adjunct Professors Jo Whitten May, Darwin R. Payne
Adjunct Assistant Professor John T. Llewellyn
Instructor Mary M. Dalton
Adjunct Instructors Mary Lucy Bivins, Paige Pettyjohn Edley, Karen L. Oxendine
Lecturers Jonathan H. Christman, John E.R. Friedenberg, Patricia W. Toole, Mary
	R. Wayne
Visiting Lecturer James H. Dodding
Debate Coach Ross K. Smith

THEATRE AND DANCE (THE)

(The Department of Theatre and Dance was originally the Department of Speech Communication and Theatre Arts until 1991–1992, when it became the Department of Theater. The change was first noted in the 1992–1993 *Bulletin*. In 1999–2000 it became the Department of Theatre. The change was first noted in the 2000–2001 *Bulletin*. In 2001–2002 the Department of Theatre became the Department of Theatre and Dance. The change was first noted in the 2002–2003 *Bulletin*.)

1992–1993
Donald H. Wolfe, Chair
Professors Harold C. Tedford, Donald H. Wolfe
Adjunct Professor Darwin R. Payne
Adjunct Instructor Mary Lucy Bivins
Lecturers Zanna Beswick (London), Jonathan H. Christman, John E.R. Friedenberg,
    Patricia W. Toole, Mary R. Wayne
Visiting Lecturer James H. Dodding

1993–1994
Donald H. Wolfe, Chair
Professors James H. Dodding, Harold C. Tedford, Donald H. Wolfe
Adjunct Professor Darwin R. Payne
Adjunct Instructor Mary Lucy Bivins
Lecturers Zanna Beswick (London), Jonathan H. Christman, John E.R. Friedenberg,
    Patricia W. Toole, Mary R. Wayne

1994–1995
Donald H. Wolfe, Chair
Professors James H. Dodding, Harold C. Tedford, Donald H. Wolfe
Adjunct Professor Darwin R. Payne
Adjunct Assistant Professor R. Craig Hamilton
Instructor and Director of Dance Rebecca Myers
Adjunct Instructor Mary Lucy Bivins
Lecturers Zanna Beswick (London), Jonathan H. Christman, John E.R. Friedenberg,
    Patricia W. Toole, Mary R. Wayne

1995–1996
Donald H. Wolfe, Chair
Professors James H. Dodding, Harold C. Tedford, Donald H. Wolfe
Adjunct Professor Darwin R. Payne
Adjunct Assistant Professor R. Craig Hamilton
Instructor Rebecca Myers (Director of Dance)
Adjunct Instructor Sharon Andrews
Lecturers Zanna Beswick (London), Jonathan H. Christman, John E.R. Friedenberg,
    Patricia W. Toole, Mary R. Wayne

1996–1997
Donald H. Wolfe, Chair
Professors James H. Dodding, Harold C. Tedford, Donald H. Wolfe
Adjunct Professor Darwin R. Payne
Adjunct Assistant Professor R. Craig Hamilton
Instructors Lisa L. Blanton (Director of Dance, Fall 1995), Kimberly L. Klose
  (Interim Director of Dance, Spring 1996)
Lecturers Sharon Andrews, Zanna Beswick (London), Jonathan H. Christman, John
  E.R. Friedenberg, Patricia W. Toole, Mary R. Wayne-Thomas

1997–1998
Donald H. Wolfe, Chair
Professors James H. Dodding, Harold C. Tedford, Donald H. Wolfe
Assistant Professor Mary R. Wayne-Thomas
Adjunct Professor Darwin R. Payne
Adjunct Assistant Professor R. Craig Hamilton
Lecturers Sharon Andrews, Zanna Beswick (London), Jonathan H. Christman, John
  E.R. Friedenberg, Director of Dance Nina M. Lucas, Patricia W. Toole

1998–1999
Donald H. Wolfe, Chair
Professors James H. Dodding, Harold C. Tedford, Donald H. Wolfe
Assistant Professors Nina M. Lucas (Director of Dance), Mary R. Wayne-Thomas
Adjunct Professor Darwin R. Payne
Adjunct Assistant Professor R. Craig Hamilton
Lecturers Sharon Andrews, Zanna Beswick (London), Jonathan H. Christman,
  Brook M. Davis, John E.R. Friedenberg

1999–2001
Donald H. Wolfe, Chair
Professors James H. Dodding, Donald H. Wolfe
Assistant Professors Sharon Andrews, Jane Kathleen Curry, Cynthia M. Gendrich,
  Nina M. Lucas (Director of Dance), Mary R. Wayne-Thomas
Visiting Assistant Professor Brook M. Davis
Adjunct Professor Darwin R. Payne
Lecturers Zanna Beswick (London), Jonathan H. Christman, John E.R. Friedenberg

2001–2002
Claudia Thomas Kairoff, Interim Chair
Associate Professor Mary R. Wayne-Thomas
Assistant Professors Sharon Andrews, Jonathan H. Christman, Jane Kathleen Curry,
  Brook M. Davis, Cynthia M. Gendrich, Nina M. Lucas (Director of Dance),
  Francis P. Ludwig
Visiting Assistant Professor Helen Huff

Adjunct Instructors Fanchon Cordell, Brantley Shapiro, Robert Simpson
Lecturers Zanna Beswick (London), John E.R. Friedenberg (Director of Theatre)

2002–2003
Mary Wayne-Thomas, Chair
Associate Professors Nina Lucas (Director of Dance), Mary Wayne-Thomas
Assistant Professors Sharon Andrews, Jonathan H. Christman, Jane Kathleen Curry,
    Brook M. Davis, Cynthia M. Gendrich, Francis P. Ludwig
Visiting Assistant Professor Mark Cohen
Adjunct Instructors Fanchon Cordell, Brantley Shapiro, Robert Simpson
Lecturers Zanna Beswick (London), John E.R. Friedenberg (Director of Theatre)

2003–2004
Mary Wayne-Thomas, Chair
Professor James H. Dodding
Associate Professors Sharon Andrews, Jane Kathleen Curry, Nina Lucas (Director of
    Dance), Mary Wayne-Thomas
Assistant Professors Jonathan H. Christman, Brook M. Davis, Cynthia M. Gendrich,
    Francis P. Ludwig
Visiting Assistant Professor Leah Roy
Adjunct Instructors Fanchon Cordell, Brantley Shapiro, Robert Simpson
Lecturers Zanna Beswick (London), John E.R. Friedenberg (Director of Theatre)

2004–2005
Mary Wayne-Thomas, Chair
Professor James H. Dodding
Associate Professors Sharon Andrews, Jane Kathleen Curry, Nina Lucas (Director of
    Dance), Mary Wayne-Thomas
Assistant Professors Jonathan H. Christman, Brook M. Davis, Cynthia M. Gendrich,
    Francis P. Ludwig, Diann Sichel
Visiting Assistant Professor Leah Roy
Adjunct Instructors Fanchon Cordell, Brantley Shapiro, Robert Simpson
Lecturers Zanna Beswick (London), John E.R. Friedenberg (Director of Theatre)

2005–2006
Mary Wayne-Thomas, Chair
Professor James H. Dodding
Associate Professors Sharon Andrews, Jonathan H. Christman, Jane Kathleen
    Curry, Cynthia M. Gendrich (Junior Faculty Fellow), Nina Lucas (Director of
    Dance), Francis P. Ludwig, Mary Wayne-Thomas
Assistant Professors Brook M. Davis, Diann Sichel
Visiting Assistant Professor Leah Roy

Adjunct Instructors Ray Collins, Fanchon Cordell, Kimberly Moore, Robert Simpson, Deborah Spencer
Lecturers Zanna Beswick (London), John E.R. Friedenberg (Director of Theatre), Brantley Shapiro

URBAN STUDIES (URB)

Interdisciplinary Minor

1994–2006
Donald E. Frey (Economics), Coordinator

WOMEN'S AND GENDER STUDIES (WGS)

Interdisciplinary Minor
(Women's and Gender Studies was originally Women's Studies until 2003–2004. The change was first listed in the 2004–2005 *Bulletin*.)

1993–1994
Mary K. DeShazer (Women's Studies), Coordinator

1994–1996
Mary K. DeShazer (English), Coordinator

1996–1997
Mary K. DeShazer (English), Coordinator; Susan Harden Borwick (Music), Coordinator-elect

1997–1998
Mary K. DeShazer (English), Coordinator, Fall 1996
Susan Harden Borwick (Music), Director, Spring 1997

1998–2001
Susan Harden Borwick (Music), Director

2001–2003
Cheryl B. Leggon (Sociology), Director

2003–2004
Anne M. Boyle (English), Director
Adjunct Assistant Professor Rose Sackeyfio

2004–2005
Anne M. Boyle (English), Director

2005–2006
Anne M. Boyle (English), Director
Professors Mary K. DeShazer, Linda Nielsen
Visiting Assistant Professor Wanda Balzano
Adjunct Professors Gary Ljungquist, Michelle J. Naughton, Teresa Smith

APPENDIX B

Deaths of Faculty, Staff, Trustees, and Close Friends of Wake Forest

1984

Jon M. Reinhardt, Professor of Politics, died on May 24. He was forty-eight.

Nelle Louise Futch Tribble, wife of Wake Forest's tenth President, died March 19. She was eighty-five.

Madge Hedrick Easley, wife of Professor Emeritus of Religion J. Allen Easley, died July 31. She was eighty-two.

E. McGruder Faris Jr., a former law professor, died on December 5.

Robert T. Bartholomew ('57), Executive Director of the Deacon Club and a member of the athletic hall of fame, died on April 19 after an automobile accident.

1985

Franklin R. Shirley, Professor Emeritus of Speech Communication and founder of the Department of Speech Communication and Theatre Arts and its first chairman, died on February 27. He was seventy. Shirley joined the Wake Forest Department of English in 1948. He retired from the faculty in 1983. He was a city alderman from 1963 until 1970 and was mayor from 1970–1977.

Nancy Susan Reynolds, last surviving child of Richard J. and Mary Katherine Reynolds, died January 11. The December 1983 issue of *Town and Country* magazine listed Reynolds as one of the ten most generous living Americans, the only woman in the top ten. She was seventy-four.

Colin Stokes (LittD '77), University Trustee, Chair of the Board of Trustees (1980, 1981) and retired chair and CEO of R.J. Reynolds Industries, died on December 14.

David H. Walker, retired Professor of Theatre Arts, died May 12. He was sixty-eight.

Judson Boyce Allen, Assistant Professor of English at the University from 1962 to 1969, died July 23. He was fifty-three.

Emily Crandall Shaw ('45), wife of Professor of Journalism Bynum G. Shaw ('51), died May 10. She was sixty-one.

Emily Lincoln, secretary in the Politics Department, died July 18.

1986

Robert L. Sullivan, Professor of Biology, died November 5. He was fifty-eight.

1987

K.A.N. Luther, Associate Professor at the Babcock Graduate School of Management, died on December 27 at the age of forty-one. He had recently been named Director of the Flow Institute for Pacific Rim Management.

James C. McDonald, a member of the Biology Department since 1960, and its chair from 1971 to 1975, died July 1.

Owen F. Herring ('13, MA '14), Professor Emeritus of Religion, died January 23. He was ninety-four. He was a recipient of the Medallion of Merit Award in 1981. The Religion Department also dedicated the Owen F. Herring Seminar Room in Wingate Hall to Owen on his 92nd birthday.

1988

A.C. Reid, Chairman of the Department of Philosophy at Wake Forest University for forty-six years, died on March 19. He was ninety-three years old. He received the University Medallion of Merit (1979), and in 1960 friends and former students established the A.C. Reid Philosophy Fund.

Saguiv A. Hadari, a former Assistant Professor of Politics from 1983 to 1987, died on June 27 at the age of thirty-two. He was the 1986 recipient of the Reid-Doyle Prize for Excellence in Teaching.

Jim Leighton, the Men's Tennis Coach for more than twenty years, died September 10. He had retired in 1984. His record at Wake Forest was 267–169–2.

1989

Harold Hayes ('48), former editor of Esquire magazine, died on April 5. He was sixty-two. During commencement in May, the University awarded posthumously an honorary doctor of letters degree to Hayes.

1990

Graham Martin ('32) died on March 23. He helped Wake Forest acquire the Artom House on the Grand Canal in Venice, Italy, which established the basis for the International Studies Program.

1991

Lowell Tillett, Professor of History and a Soviet Union specialist, died on December 31. He taught at Wake Forest from 1956 to 1978.

Joseph Branch ('38), five-term Trustee, two-time Chair of the Board of Trustees (1970–1971, 1986–1987), and recipient of numerous Wake Forest honors including an honorary degree (1983) and the Medallion of Merit (1987), died on February 18 in Raleigh. Branch was also Chief Justice of the North Carolina Supreme Court.

Jasper Memory ('21), a retired Professor Emeritus of Education, died March 21 at the age of ninety in Durham. Memory served Wake Forest for forty-two years as a teacher and as an administrator, operating the school's news bureau, editing the alumni magazine, and running the placement office.

1992

D.A. Brown, Professor of English from 1941 to 1973, died on May 17. He received the Medallion of Merit, the University's highest honor, in 1982.

J. Allen Easley, former Chair of the Department of Religion, died at the age of ninety-nine on June 30. He was a faculty member for fifty-five years. In 1988 a chair in the Religion Department was established in his name. He was a recipient of the Medallion of Merit, the University's highest honor, in 1972.

Elizabeth R. Scales, the wife of Wake Forest President James Ralph Scales, died on August 11.

1993

Donald Schoonmaker ('60), Professor of Politics, died on May 19. The Community Service Award for faculty was named in his honor.

1994

Lois Johnson, Wake Forest's first Dean of Women, died on October 22 in Pinehurst. She was ninety-eight. She became Dean of Women in 1942 and retired in 1962. She was a recipient of the Medallion of Merit, the University's highest honor, in 1973.

Bianca Artom, who taught in the Department of Romance Languages for sixteen years and received the Excellence in Teaching Award in 1982, died on February 5.

1995

E. Pendleton Banks, who developed the Department of Anthropology, founded the Museum of Anthroplogy, and taught at Wake Forest for forty years, died July 12 at the age of seventy-one.

David Hadley, Professor of History who taught at Wake Forest for thirty years and was Director of the Worrell House in London, died June 15 at the age of fifty-seven.

Leon H. Hollingsworth, the first full-time Chaplain at Wake Forest (1959–1970), died on February 24 at the age of seventy-seven. For thirty years, he prayed before every home football game at Wake Forest. A collection of his prayers was published in a book, *God Goes to Football Games: A Book of Uncommon Prayer.*

William E. "Bill" Cage, Associate Professor of Economics from 1967 to 1978, died
    on February 6. He was the founder and adviser to the chapter of Omicron Delta
    Epsilon, the international economics honor society.

Lucile Hasselvander Aycock, Director of the Information Desk in Reynolda Hall from
    1956 to 1971 and widow of A. Lewis Aycock, Professor of English, died June 15
    at the age of ninety-four.

George Washington Paschal Jr. died at age eighty-six on February 15. Paschal was
    a life Trustee and son of George W. Paschal, who was a Wake Forest professor
    and author of the three-volume history of the College. Paschal Jr. established the
    Paschal Collection of American History in the Z. Smith Reynolds Library.

1996

James Ralph Scales (President of Wake Forest University from 1967 to 1983) died
    March 12 at the age of seventy-six. During the Scales era, Wake Forest increased
    its enrollment, started the Babcock School of Management, built the Scales Fine
    Arts Center, and inaugurated study-abroad programs at Casa Artom in Venice
    and Worrell House in London. He was a recipient of the Medallion of Merit, the
    University's highest honor, in 1984.

W. Graham May, Professor of Mathematics at Wake Forest for thirty-five years,
    died on March 1.

Christopher Giles, Associate Professor of Music, who taught piano at Wake Forest
    from 1951 to 1988, died on December 23. Winston-Salem attorney Paul Sinal set
    up a competition in the name of Giles and a fellow piano teacher, Lucille Harris,
    in 1977.

Patricia Alwine, a secretary in the Department of Athletics since 1987, died of cancer
    on October 24 at the age of thirty-six.

1997

Martin Henry "Hank" Garrity III ('48) died on May 17. He was the Director of
    Development and Alumni Affairs at Wake Forest from 1964 to 1969. During that
    time he was also Editor of Wake Forest Magazine and headed the Capital Cam-
    paign, which raised the funds for the construction of Groves Stadium.

Mark Reece ('49) died May 12 at the age of seventy-one. He joined the Wake Forest
    staff in 1956, serving first as Associate Director of Alumni Affairs. In 1963 he was
    named Dean of Men, and in 1984 he was promoted to Dean of Students after the
    offices of the Dean of Men and Dean of Women were combined. He was instru-
    mental in starting the Student Union Collection of Contemporary Art, which
    began in 1963, when Reece started taking students to New York to purchase new
    works for the collection. This collection was later renamed in his honor. Reece
    received the Medallion of Merit, the University's highest honor, in 1996.

Horace Albert, "Bones" McKinney, Head Basketball Coach at Wake Forest from
    1957 to 1965, died on May 16, at the age of seventy-eight. He joined Wake
    Forest in 1952 while attending Southeastern Baptist Seminary. His eight-year
    record as a basketball coach was 122–94. He won ACC conference championships
    in 1961 and 1962 and took the 1962 team to the NCAA Final Four.

Robert E. Lee, an Emeritus Law Professor and Dean of the Law School, died August 21. Lee taught at the law school for over thirty years.

Horace O. Kelly Jr., an Assistant Dean of the Calloway School of Business and Accountancy, died on February 6. He was fifty-seven years old.

Chris Reed, an Assistant Strength Coach in the Athletic Department, died after a sudden illness on February 25. He was twenty-eight years old.

Grace O'Neil, manager of the Magnolia Room and for Wake Forest banquets, died unexpectedly of a heart attack on March 16 at age sixty-one. A memorial service for her was held in Davis Chapel on March 20, with President Hearn as one of the chief participants. The Chapel was filled to capacity with friends and staff. On December 2, a tree was planted and dedicated in her honor to the left front of Tribble Hall.

1998

Ivey C. Gentry ('40) died on February 14 in Winston-Salem. He was Professor (1949–1989) and former Department Chair of the Department of Mathematics for twenty-five years. He was a recipient of the Medallion of Merit, the University's highest honor, in 1997.

Jane Cottle Joyner, wife of G. William Joyner Jr. ('66), former Vice President for University Relations, died unexpectedly on October 22.

Phillippe Falkenberg, a Professor Emeritus of Psychology, died June 6. He retired in 1997 after twenty-eight years of service to Wake Forest.

Walter Flory, Professor Emeritus of Biology, died on June 8th. Flory was the Babcock Professor of Botany before retiring in 1980. He also was Director of Reynolda Gardens from 1964 to 1976.

J. Glen Blackburn, the Chaplain at the College from 1948 to 1958 and pastor of the Wake Forest Baptist Church on both the old and new campuses, died at age eighty-five on October 4.

Wayne Calloway, Chair of the WFU Board of Trustees from 1986 to 1996 and CEO of PepsiCo, Inc., died at age sixty-two. Hearn called him "one of the pivotal leaders in the modern history of Wake Forest." He served as tri-chair of the Heritage and Promise Campaign that raised more than $177 million and received the University's highest honor, the Medallion of Merit, in 1986. The University's undergraduate business and accountancy school was named the Wayne Calloway School of Business and Accountancy in his honor in 1995.

1999

Clarence H. Patrick, who started Wake Forest's Sociology Department in 1948 and later became a well-known authority on criminology, died March 17.

Dana Johnson, former Dean of the Calloway School from 1992 to 1996, died of cancer February 18. She was forty-nine years old.

Stacy Cox, a former Assistant Coach with the women's basketball team, was killed in a car accident on November 8.

2000

Royce Raymond Weatherly, Superintendent of Buildings at Wake Forest from 1947
   to 1981, died on February 23. Weatherly and his family lived for twenty-five
   years in the original farm house that was given to the University in the 1940s,
   which was later remodeled to house the WFDD radio station. The house became
   known as the "Weatherly House."
John F. Dimmick, who taught for more than nineteen years in the Department of
   Biology, died on September 26.
Thomas Olive, Professor Emeritus of Biology, died September 14.
David Broyles, a retired Professor of Politics, died August 22, 2000.
W. Boyd Owen ('38, MD '40), a Trustee since 1954, a Life Trustee since 1991. Owen
   died August 20, at the age of eighty-two.

2001

William Gray Starling ('57), Dean of Admission and Financial Aid, died on June
   18, at age sixty-five. Starling had served Wake Forest for forty-three years since
   being appointed to his first position in the Office of Admissions in 1958. Under
   Starling, more than 30,000 students were admitted to the University.
Bynum Shaw ('48) long-time Professor of Journalism (1965–1993) and author of the
   fourth volume of the University's history, died on August 27 at age seventy-eight.
Archie R. Ammons ('49), a former visiting Assistant Professor of English and a
   renowned poet, died February 25.
Robert S. Carlson, first Dean of the Babcock Graduate School of Management, died
   October 6 following a traffic accident in Hin Hua, Thialand. He was sixty-eight.
Germaine Brée, Kenan Professor Emerita of Humanities, died September 22 at the
   age of ninety-three. Brée was an international authority on 20th-century French
   literature, taught at Wake Forest from 1973 to 1984, and received the University's
   Medallion of Merit in 1994.
James Taylor Jr., a former Associate Dean and Professor at the School of Law, died
   December 16. He was seventy-four.
Quen Taylor ('70), the public address announcer for Wake Forest football and
   basketball games for twenty years, died December 23. He was fifty-three.
Claud H. Richards Jr., Professor Emeritus of Politics and the founding Chairman of
   the Political Science Department, died December 20. He was eighty-four.
John W. "Jack" Nowell, retired Chemistry Professor, died November 21. He was a
   member of the faculty from 1945 to 1987 and chaired the Department of Chemistry from 1962 to 1972. Nowell also served as an Assistant Dean of the College
   (with Ed Wilson) for a few years.
Robert Allen Dyer, Religion Professor and Associate Dean of the College, died on
   April 14 at the age of eighty-eight. He had retired in 1983 and was a recipient of
   the Medallion of Merit award.

2002

James C. O'Flaherty, Professor Emeritus of German, Chair of the Department from
   1961 to 1969 and a renowned scholar of 18th-century German literature and

philosophy, died July 27 at age eighty-eight. O'Flaherty spent his entire career at Wake Forest, from 1947 until retiring in 1984. He established a student exchange program between Wake Forest and the Free University of Berlin.

John Williams, the first Chair of the Department of Psychology, died May 28 at age seventy-three. Williams came to Wake Forest in 1959 and was named a Wake Forest University Professor in 1992. He retired in 1995. Williams studied and wrote extensively on cross-cultural sex, age, race stereotypes, and the racial attitudes of pre-school children.

James W. Mason, a former Chair of the Board of Trustees six times between 1968 and 1989 who played a key role in establishing the University's self-governance, died in Southern Pines December 2 at the age of eighty-six. He received the Medallion of Merit in 1980 and an honorary doctorate of laws degree in 1996.

2003

Merrill G. Berthrong, Director of Libraries at Wake Forest and an Associate Professor of History from 1964 to 1989, died January 14. He was third Head Librarian of Z. Smith Reynolds Library. He implemented open-stacks, the Library of Congress book-classification system to the library, and saw the collection grow from 200,000 volumes to over a million.

Jeanne Owen, who taught in the Calloway School of Business and Accountancy for thirty-five years and was the University's first female full professor (earning the distinction in 1967), died July 27. She was eighty-two. She began her career at Wake Forest in 1956 as one of only six women on the faculty. She served as Acting Dean of Women from 1962 to 1964. She was awarded the Jon Reinhardt Award for Excellence in Teaching in 1987 and retired in 1991.

Rhoda K. Channing, Director of Z. Smith Reynolds Library since 1989, died on July 25. She was sixty-one. Channing led Wake Forest to digitize its most unique resources and developed an online public access catalog that linked Z. Smith Reynolds Library with the libraries at the School of Medicine and the Worrell Professional Center.

Hubert B. Humphry Jr. ('48), former Chair (1999–2001) of the Wake Forest Board of Trustees, died March 18 at the age of seventy-four. He served three terms on the Board between 1989 and 2001.

Nancy Priddy, a housing operations coordinator for Residence Life and Housing for fourteen years, died on April 8 at forty years old.

2004

Mary E. Tiejen (MA '02), a core curriculum provider for the Biology Department, died on March 22 at age thirty.

Percival Perry ('37), Professor Emeritus of History and Dean of the Summer School, died August 15. He was eighty-seven. He served the University as a Professor of American history for over forty years.

David Smiley, Professor Emeritus of History died December 27 at the age of eighty-three. Smiley focused on Southern history and had a forty-one-year tenure at Wake Forest from 1950 to 1991. In addition to teaching history, Smiley taught the Reid-Stanton Sunday School class at the Wake Forest Baptist Church. It was broadcast over WFDD until 2002. He was known also for his eccentricities, such as picking up litter or wearing a French beret.

Terisio Pignatti, Reynolds Professor Emeritus of Art, died on December 31 at the age of eighty-four. Pignatti was renowned as a scholar of Venetian art and a museum director. He helped the University acquire Casa Artom and taught art history there for three decades.

Ralph Fraser, Chair of the German Department from 1969 to 1977, died on October 19 at eighty-two. Fraser collected more than one thousand rare books and donated them to the Ralph S. Fraser Holocaust Collection at Z. Smith Reynolds Library.

2005

Russell Brantley ('45), Director of Communications for thirty-four years (1953–1987), died February 13 at the age of eighty. Brantley received the Medallion of Merit in 1987.

Mary Ann Hampton Taylor ('56, MD '60), Director of Student Health Services, died on October 1 at age seventy. She was a recipient of the Medallion of Merit in 1999.

Balkrishna "B.G." Gokhale, Professor of History from 1960 to 1990, died at age eighty-five on August 11. Gokhale had started the Universtiy's Asian Studies program.

Charles M. Allen Jr. ('39, MA '41), Professor of Biology (1941–1989), Director of the Artists Series (1958–1976), died at age eighty-seven on August 30.

Marjorie Crisp, who pioneered the development of women's athletics at Wake Forest University, died February 13 at the age of ninety-two. She became the first full-time female faculty member at Wake Forest when she joined the Physical Education Department in 1947. Crisp was named to the Wake Forest Sports Hall of Fame in 1993 for her role in shaping women's athletics.

Thomas F. Gossett, author of a landmark book exploring the roots of racism in American society, died December 11 at the age of eighty-nine. He was Professor Emeritus of English.

Bashir El-Beshti, Associate Professor of English, died on March 18. He was fifty-one and had taught at Wake Forest since 1990.

APPENDIX C

Faculty Retirees, 1983–2005

1983

Reynolda Campus

Robert A. Dyer (Religion)

Ysbrand Haven (Physics)

Alonzo W. Kenion (English)

Harry B. Miller (Chemistry)

Herman J. Preseren (Education)

Medical School

C. Nash Herndon (Medical Genetics)

Carolyn C. Huntley (Pediatrics)

Charles McCreight (Anatomy)

Manson Meads (V.P. for Health Affairs & Director of the Medical Center)

Robert P. Morehead (Pathology)

1984

Reynolda Campus

James C. O'Flaherty (German)

Franklin R. Shirley (Speech Communication)

Henry S. Stroupe (History)

Medical School

Eben Alexander Jr. (Neurosurgery)

Charles M. Howell Jr. (Dermatology)

Julius A. Howell (Plastic Surgery)

Isadore Meschan (Radiology)

Ernest H. Yount (Medicine)

1985

Reynolda Campus

Germaine Brée (Humanities)

Claud H. Richards Jr. (Politics)

Medical School

Ruth O'Neal (Pediatrics)

James T. McRae (Surgery)

Richard C. Proctor (Psychiatry)

Angus C. Randolph (Psychiatry)

Louis deS. Shaffner (Surgery)

Horatio P. Van Cleve (Family
     Medicine)

1986

Reynolda Campus

Anne S. Tillett (Romance Languages)

Medical School

Alanson Hinman (Pediatrics)

Frank R. Johnston
     (Surgery–Cardiothoracic)

Ross L. McLean
     (Medicine–Pulmonary)

1987

Reynolda Campus

George McLeod Bryan (Religion)

Robert S. Carlson (Management)

Thomas F. Gossett (English)

William H. Gulley (Sociology)

John W. Nowell (Chemistry)

John E. Parker Jr. (Education & Romance
     Lang.)

Percival Perry (History)

Medical School

Damon D. Blake (Radiology)

Frederick A. Blount (Pediatrics)

Charles L. Spurr (Hematology/
     Oncology)

1988

Reynolda Campus

Shasta M. Bryant (Romance Languages)

Dorothy Casey (Health & Sport Science)

Cyclone Covey (History)

Medical School

William H. Davis Jr. (Pediatrics)

Richard T. Myers (Surgery)

M. Frank Sohmer Jr.
     (Gastroenterology)

Ralph S. Fraser (German)

Christopher Giles (Music)
Paul M. Gross Jr. (Chemistry)
Emmett Willard Hamrick (Religion)
Thomas Olive (Biology)
John W. Sawyer (Mathematics)
W. Buck Yearns Jr. (History)

Henry S.M. Uhl (Gen. Medicine/
Geriatrics)

1989

Reynolda Campus

Charles M. Allen (Biology)
Merrill G. Berthrong (History)
Ivey C. Gentry (Mathematics)

Carl V. Harris (Classical Languages)
Elizabeth Phillips (English)

Lee H. Potter (English)
Mary Frances Robinson (Romance Lang.)

Ben M. Seelbinder (Mathematics)
Lowell R. Tillett (History)

Medical School

Jean N. Angelo (Pathology)
William H. Boyce (Surgery–Urology)
Frederick W. Glass (Surgery–
Emergency Medicine)
Joseph G. Gordon (Radiology)
Frank C. Greiss (Obstetrics &
Gynecology)
Robert C. McKone (Pediatrics)
Emery C. Miller Jr. (Endocrinology &
Metabolism)
William S. Pearson (Psychiatry)
C. Glenn Sawyer (Cardiology)
Nat E. Smith (Medicine)

1990

Reynolda Campus

John W. Angell (Religion)

Bianca Artom (Romance Languages)

Caroline S. Fullerton (Theatre Arts)
Balkrishna G. Gokhale (History & Asian
Studies)

Medical School

John P. Gusdon Jr. (Obstetrics &
Gynecology)
Quentin N. Myrvik (Microbiology &
Immunology)
Modesto Scharyj (Pathology)
N. Sheldon Skinner Jr. (Internal
Medicine–Cardiology)
Cornelius F. Strittmatter IV
(Biochemistry)
Henry L. Valk (Internal Medicine &
Gerontology)

1991

Reynolda Campus

Lucille S. Harris (Music)

D. Paul Hylton (Accounting)

Carlton T. Mitchell (Religion)

Carl C. Moses (Politics)

F. Jeanne Owen (Business Law)

David L. Smiley (History)

Medical School

Alvin Brodish (Physiology & Pharmacology)

Henry Drexler (Microbiology & Immunology)

Harold O. Goodman (Pediatrics–Medical Genetics)

George C. Lynch (Biomedical Communications)

William J. May (Ob/Gyn and Family & Community Medicine)

Richard B. Patterson (Pediatrics)

1992

Reynolda Campus

Wilmer D. Sanders (German)

James E. Sizemore (Law)

J. Van Wagstaff (Economics)

Raymond L. Wyatt (Biology)

Medical School

Augustin G. Formanek (Radiology)

1993

Reynolda Campus

Ralph D. Amen (Biology)

Leon P. Cook Jr. (Accounting)

Henry C. Lauerman (Law)

Bynum G. Shaw (English-Journalism)

Medical School

Philip R. Aronson (Internal Medicine/ Gerontology)

John H. Felts (Internal Medicine–Nephrology)

Jesse H. Meredith (Surgical Sciences– Gen. Surgery)

W. Keith O'Steen (Neurobiology & Anatomy)

Jack M. Rogers (Psychiatry & Behavioral Medicine)

1994

Reynolda Campus

E. Pendleton Banks (Anthropology)

Richard C. Barnett (History)

Julian C. Burroughs Jr. (Speech Communication)

David W. Catron (Psychology)

Gregory D. Pritchard (Philosophy)

J. Don Reeves (Education)

John D. Scarlett (Law)

Medical School

Robert N. Headley (Internal Medicine–Cardiology)

Charles N. Remy (Biochemistry)

1995

Reynolda Campus

Robert W. Brehme (Physics)

Doyle R. Fosso (English)

Phillip J. Hamrick Jr. (Chemistry)

Medical School

A. Robert Cordell (Surgical Sciences–Cardiothoracic Surgery

Henry C. Turner (Anesthesia)

1996

Reynolda Campus

Thomas M. Elmore (Education)

David A. Hills (Psychology)

William L. Hottinger (Health & Sport Science)

George W. Trautwein (Music)

John E. Williams (Psychology)

Medical School

Ivan L. Holleman Jr. (Pathology)

Howard D. Homesley (Obstetrics & Gynecology)

John R. Jacoway (Pathology)

Laurence B. Leinbach (Radiology)

Eugene B. Linton (Obstetrics & Gynecology)

Milton Raben (Radiation Oncology)

1997

Reynolda Campus

Marion W. Benfield Jr. (Law)

John A. Carter Jr. (English)

Philippe R. Falkenberg
(Psychology)

Eva Marie Rodtwitt (Romance
Languages)

David Riffe, Methodist campus
minister

Medical School

Stanley P. Bohrer (Radiology)

Richard W. Brunstetter (Psychiatry & Behavioral Medicine)

Marcus M. Gulley (Psychiatry & Behavioral Medicine)

Howard D. Homesley (Obstetrics & Gynecology)

Phillip M. Hutchins (Physiology & Pharmacology)

Abdel-Mohsen Nomeir (Internal Medicine–Cardiology)

John D. Tolmie (Anesthesia)

1998

Reynolda Campus

Kathleen M. Glenn (Romance
Languages)

Mordecai J. Jaffe (Biology)

Patricia A. Johansson (English)

Robert W. Shively (Management)

Harold C. Tedford (Theatre)

James Dodding (Theatre)

Medical School

Edgar T. Chandler (Internal Medicine)

Robert J. Cowan (Radiology)

Robert M. Kerr (Internal
Medicine–Gastroenterology)

Jon C. Lewis (Pathology)

William M. McKinney (Neurology)

J. Michael Sterchi (Surgical Sciences)

Richard L. Witcofski (Radiology)

1999

Reynolda Campus

Robert H. Dufort (Psychology)

Eddie V. Easley (Business)

Leo Ellison Jr. (Health & Exercise
Sc.)

David K. Evans (Anthropology)

Medical School

David M. Biddulph (Neurobiology &
Anatomy)

Ronald B. Mack (Pediatrics)

Inglis J. Miller (Neurobiology & Anatomy)

John W. Reed (Surgical
Sciences–Opthalmology)

Robert N. Shorter (English)

George P. Williams Jr. (Physics)

Alfred J. Rufty (Internal
Medicine–Cardiology)

2000

Reynolda Campus

David B. Broyles (Politics)

Thomas E. Mullen (History)

Peter R. Peacock (Marketing)

James Taylor Jr. (Law)

Stanton K. Tefft (Anthropology)

Medical School

Ralph W. Barnes (Neurology)

George J. Doellgast (Biochemistry)

William R. Hazzard (Internal
Medicine–Gerontology)

Clara M. Heise (Radiology) posthumously

Allen S. Hudspeth (Surgical
Sciences–Cardiothoracic)

Robert I. Kohut (Surgical
Sciences–Otolaryngology)

Henry S. Miller Jr. (Internal
Medicine–Cardiology)

Paul R. Moran (Radiology)

Frederick Richards II (Internal
Medicine–Hematology/Oncology)

Stephen H. Richardson (Microbiology &
Immunology)

Jai H. Ryu (Surgical
Sciences–Otolaryngology)

B. Moseley Waite (Biochemistry)

Velma Watts (Medical Education)

Duke B. Weeks (Anesthesiology)

Neil T. Wolfman (Radiology)

2001

Reynolda Campus

Paul A. Dierks
  (Accounting-Babcock Sch)

John S. Dunkelberg
  (Business-Calloway Sch)

John R. Earle (Sociology)

Roger A. Hegstrom (Chemistry)

Robert W. Lovett (English)

Dolly A. McPherson (English)

Howard W. Shields (Physics)

Medical School

Bill C. Bullock (Pathology-Comparative
  Medicine)

Thomas E. Clark
  (Psychiatry & Behavioral Medicine)

Roy C. Haberkern III
  (Psychiatry & Behavioral Medicine)

Lloyd H. Harrison (Surgical
  Sciences–Urology)

Eugene Heise (Microbiology &
  Immunology)

Francis M. James III (Anesthesiology)

R. Lawrence Kroovand (Surgical
  Sciences–Urology)

Alfredo L. Pauca (Anesthesiology)

Michael D. Sprinkle (Library Science)

Wallace C. Wu (Internal
  Medicine–Gastroenterology)

2002

Reynolda Campus

Nancy J. Cotton (English)

Jack D. Fleer (Political Science)

Richard D. Sears (Political
  Science)

Dudley A. Shapere
  (Philosophy & History of Sc.)

David S. Weaver (Anthropology)

Medical School

Eugene W. Adcock III (Pediatrics)

M. Robert Cooper (Internal Medicine–
  Hematology & Oncology)

Robert L. Michielutte (Family & Community
  Medicine)

Pentti M. Rautaharju (Public Health
  Sciences)

Thomas E. Sumner (Radiology & Pediatrics)

James N. Thompson (Surgical
  Sciences–Otolaryngology)

Ivo van de Rijn (Microbiology &
  Immunology)

Nat E. Watson Jr. (Radiology)

2003

Reynolda Campus

Rhoda B. Billings (Law)

I. Bruce Covington (Law)

Robert M. Helm Jr. (Philosophy)

James A. Martin Jr. (University Professor)

Timothy F. Sellner (German)

Thomas C. Taylor (Accountancy)

J. Ned Woodall (Anthropology)

Medical School

David A. Albertson (Surgical Sciences– Gen. Surgery)

David M. Dewan (Anesthesiology)

Richard Janeway (Neurology, Medicine & Mgmt.)

C. Douglas Maynard (Radiology)

Thomas E. Nelson (Anesthesiology)

Earl Schwartz (Surgical Sciences–Emergency Medicine)

Penny C. Sharp (Family & Community Med.)

Benedict L. Wasilauskas (Pathology)

Lester E. Watts (Internal Medicine–Cardiology)

Richard G. Weaver Sr. (Surgical Sciences–Opthalmology)

Richard L. Webber (Dentistry)

Kenneth T. Wheeler Jr. (Radiology)

2004

Reynolda Campus

James P. Barefield (History)

John V. Baxley (Mathematics)

Elmer K. Hayashi (Mathematics)

Buddy O.H. Herring (Law)

George M. Holzwarth (Physics)

John H. Litcher (Education)

Phil J. Perricone (Sociology)

Medical School

M. Gene Bond (Neurobiology & Anatomy)

David W. Gelfand (Radiology)

Christine A. Johnson (Pediatrics)

Timothy C. Pennell (Surgical Sciences–Gen. Surgery)

Lee F. Rogers (Radiology)

2005

Reynolda Campus

James H. Dodding (Theatre)

Milorad R. Margitic (Romance Languages)

James C. Makens (Management)

Christa E. Carollo (German)

Medical School

Louis S. Kucera (Microbiology & Immunology)

Herman H. Samson III (Physiology & Pharmacology)

B. Todd Troost (Neurology)

APPENDIX D

Board of Trustees

(Trustees serving at least one term during Dr. Hearn's tenure as President, 11/4/1983 through 6/30/2005)

Marvin D. Gentry, King, NC

Gloria F. Graham, M.D., Wilson, NC

Constance F. Gray, Winston-Salem, NC

Murray C. Greason Jr., Winston-Salem, NC

William B. Greene Jr., Gray, TN

O. Bruce Gupton, Gordonsville, VA

Deborah S. Harris, Charlotte, NC

Weston P. Hatfield, Winston-Salem, NC

Joy Vermillion Heinsohn, Winston-Salem, NC

James R. Helvey, III, Winston-Salem, NC

Harvey R. Holding, Jacksonville Beach, FL

C. C. Hope Jr., Charlotte, NC

Lawrence D. Hopkins, M.D., Winston-Salem, NC

Edward A. Horrigan Jr., Winston-Salem, NC

Alice Kirby Horton, Durham, NC

Dr. Joseph C. Hough Jr., New York, NY

E. Michael Howlette, OD, Richmond, VA

Hubert B. Humphrey Jr., Greensboro, NC

Albert R. Hunt Jr., Washington, DC

James B. Hunt Jr., Lucama, NC

Roberto J. Hunter, Scarsdale, NY

Jeanette Wallace Hyde, Raleigh, NC

James E. Johnson Jr., Charlotte, NC

James L. Johnson, Rowland, NC

James W. Johnston, Mooresville, NC

James W. Judson, Roswell, GA

Sandra R. Kahle, Vero Beach, FL

Jonathan L. Kelly, Greensboro, NC

Lauren Hunt Krauss, Frisco, TX

Petro Kulynych, Wilkesboro, NC

Deborah D. Lambert, Raleigh, NC

William W. Leathers, III, Rockingham, NC

Dee Hughes LeRoy, Winston-Salem, NC

John M. Lewis, Raleigh, NC

Pete Lovette, Wilkesboro, NC

John R. Lowden, Greenwich, CT

Joseph W. Luter, III, Smithfield, VA

Douglas F. Manchester, San Diego, CA

William L. Marks, New Orleans, LA

James G. Martin Jr., Charlotte, NC

James W. Mason, Southern Pines, NC

George B. Mast, Clayton, NC

Alton H. McEachern, Greensboro, NC

Claude A. McNeill Jr., M.D., Elkin, NC

John G. Medlin Jr., Winston-Salem, NC

Theodore R. Meredith, Vero Beach, FL

Louis B. Meyer Jr., Wilson, NC

Russell W. Meyer Jr., Wichita, KS

Kenneth D. Miller, Greensboro, NC

Sheereen Miller-Russell, Charlotte, NC

Barbara B. Millhouse, New York, NY

W. Harold Mitchell, Valdese, NC

Mary Lide Morris, M.D., Durham, NC

Katharine B. Mountcastle, New Canaan, CT

Elwyn G. Murray, III, Rose Hill, NC

Stephen L. Neal, McLean, VA

J. Donald Nichols, Nashville, TN

L. Glenn Orr Jr., Winston-Salem, NC

W. Boyd Owen, M.D., Waynesville, NC

Arnold D. Palmer, Orlando, FL

George W. Paschal Jr., M.D., Raleigh, NC

Steven L. Perricone, Winston-Salem, NC

J. Robert Philpott, Lexington, NC

Celeste Mason Pittman, Rocky Mount, NC

Sean M. Prince, Norfolk, VA

Frances P. Pugh, Raleigh, NC

Michael G. Queen, Wilmington, NC

J. Guy Revelle Jr., Murfreesboro, NC

Leon L. Rice Jr., Winston-Salem, NC

Harold O. Rosser, New Canaan, CT

William B. Sansom, Knoxville, TN

Andrew J. Schindler, Winston-Salem, NC

Charles M. Shelton, Charlotte, NC

Bob D. Shepherd, Morganton, NC

R. Jay Sigel, Berwyn, PA

Dr. M. Mahan Siler Jr., Asheville, NC

J. Dale Simmons, M.D., Lake Wales, FL

Duncan J. Sinclair Jr., Laurinburg, NC

Adelaide A. Sink, Thonotosassa, FL

K. Wayne Smith, Newton, NC

Board Chairs and Vice Chairs 1983–2005

Year	Chair	Vice Chair
1983	C. C. Hope Jr.	Charles W. Cheek (Fall 1983)
1984	Weston P. Hatfield	J. Robert Philpott
1985	Weston P. Hatfield	J. Robert Philpott
1986	Joseph Branch	L. Glenn Orr Jr.
1987	Joseph Branch	D. Wayne Calloway
1988	Weston P. Hatfield	Albert L. Butler Jr.
1989	Weston P. Hatfield	Albert L. Butler Jr.
1990	Weston P. Hatfield	D. Wayne Calloway
1991	D. Wayne Calloway	C. C. Hope Jr.
1992	D. Wayne Calloway	C. C. Hope Jr.
1993	D. Wayne Calloway	C. C. Hope Jr.
		Vice Chair 2: John G. Medlin Jr. (Replaced Hope April 1993)
1994	D. Wayne Calloway	John G. Medlin, Jr
1994–1995*	John G. Medlin Jr.	Harvey R. Holding
1995–1996	D. Wayne Calloway	Adelaide A. Sink
1996–1997	D. Wayne Calloway	John G. Medlin, Jr
1997–1998	D. Wayne Calloway	Murray C. Greason Jr.
		Vice Chair 2: John G. Medlin Jr.
		Vice Chair 3: Adelaide A. Sink
1998–1999	D. Wayne Calloway	Murray C. Greason Jr.
		Vice Chair 2: John G. Medlin Jr.
		Vice Chair 3: Adelaide A. Sink (Partial year in 1998)
1998–1999	John G. Medlin Jr.	Murray C. Greason Jr.
		Vice Chair 2: Adelaide A. Sink (Partial year in 1998)
1999–2000	Hubert B. Humphrey	Murray C. Greason Jr.
		Vice Chair 2: Adelaide A. Sink
2000–2001	Hubert B. Humphrey	Murray C. Greason Jr.
		Vice Chair 2: Adelaide A. Sink
2001–2002	William B. Greene Jr.	Murray C. Greason Jr.
		Vice Chair 2: Adelaide A. Sink
2002–2003	William B. Greene Jr.	Murray C. Greason Jr.

2002–2003	William B. Greene Jr.	Murray C. Greason Jr.
2003–2004	Murray C. Greason Jr.	L. Glenn Orr Jr.
2004–2005	Murray C. Greason Jr.	L. Glenn Orr Jr. (June 2005)

*Switch from calendar year to fiscal year.

APPENDIX E

Medallion of Merit, 1984–2005

1984	Harold W. Tribble, *Tenth President, 1950–1967*
	James Ralph Scales, *Eleventh President, 1967–1983*
1985	Robert A. Dyer, *Professor of Religion, 1956–1983*
1986	D. Wayne Calloway ('59), *Chairman, Board of Trustees*
1987	Russell H. Brantley Jr. ('45), *Director of Communications, 1953–1987*
1988	Richard T. Myers, *Chair, Department of Surgery, School of Medicine, 1950–2000*
1989	Harold M. Barrow, *Chair of Physical Education, 1948–1977*
1990	Eben Alexander, *Professor of Neurosurgery, School of Medicine, 1949–2004*
1991	Weston P. Hatfield ('41), *Chairman, Board of Trustees*
1992	Elizabeth Phillips, *Professor of English, 1957–1989*
1993	Eugene Hooks ('50), *Director of Athletics, 1956–1992*
1994	Germaine Brée, *Kenan Professor of Humanities, 1973–1985*
1995	Thomas E. Mullen, *Dean of the College and Professor of History, 1957–2000*
1996	Lula M. Leake, *Associate Vice President and Dean of Women, 1964–1997*
	Mark H. Reece ('49), *Dean of Students and Dean of Men, 1956–1988*
1997	Ivey C. Gentry ('40), *Professor of Mathematics, 1949–1989*
1998	Henry S. Stroupe ('35, MA '37), *Dean of the Graduate School and Professor of History, 1937–1984*
1999	Mary Ann Taylor ('56, MD '60), *Director, Student Health Service, 1961–1991*
2000	Richard Janeway, *Executive Vice President for Health Affairs, 1966–1997*
2001	Victor I. Flow Jr. ('52), *Trustee and Benefactor*
2002	C. Douglas Maynard ('55, MD '59), *Chair, Department of Radiology, School of Medicine, 1966–2003*

2003   Leon H. Corbett Jr. ('59, JD '61), *Vice President and Counsel, 1968–2002*

2004   Edwin G. Wilson ('43), *Provost and Professor of English, 1951–2002*

2005   Timothy Pennell ('55, '60), *Professor of Surgery, School of Medicine, 1966–2002*

            Willis E. "Doc" Murphrey ('52, JD '57), *Old Campus Personality*

APPENDIX F

Distinguished Alumni Awards, 1983–2005

1983
Dr. Billy F. Andrews ('53)
*Byron Lee Davis ('40)
Timothy S. Y. Lam ('60)
Jo DeYoung Thomas ('65)

1984
William Raymond Cowan ('54, MD '57)
*James E. Peters ('33)
*Arthur D. Gore ('48)

1985
Weston P. Hatfield ('41)
*Glenn M. Tucker ('33)

1986
Jan McQuere McDonough ('64)
H. Dean Propst ('56)

1987
Brig. Gen. E. Patricia Foote ('52)
Lawrence David Hopkins ('72, MD '77)
*Bert Lee Shore ('37)

1988
Earle A. Connelly ('48)
Ernest W. Accorsi ('63)
*W. Boyd Owen ('38, MD '42)
Helen Bryan Owen ('37) and family

1989
J. Lanston Wadkins Jr. ('72)
Victor I. Flow Jr. ('52)

1990
*Page W. Acree ('40)
Virginia N. Britt ('70, MA '73)
William B. Greene Jr. ('59)

1991
Clifton L. Benson Jr. ('64)
Willis C. Maddrey ('60)

1992
*J. Elliot Galloway ('42)
Jesse I. Haddock ('52)
Dee Hughes LeRoy ('57)

1993
Edwin G. Wilson ('43)
Nicholas B. Bragg ('58)
Adelaide A. Sink ('70)

1994
Edward Reynolds ('64)
Murray C. Greason Jr. ('59, JD '62)

1995
Jeanette Hyde ('58)
*J. William Disher Sr. ('59)

1996
Jane F. Crosthwaite ('59)
William L. Marks ('66)

1997
George M. Stamps ('47)

1998
J. Fred Young ('56)

1999
G. Eugene Boyce ('54, JD '56)

2000
Susan Powell Brinkley ('62)

2001
Douglass M. Bailey III ('60)
*William Gray Starling ('57)

2002
Howard Fabing Twiggs ('54, JD' 57)
Frank B. Holding ('52)

2003
Edgar Douglas Christman ('50, JD '53)
Curtis N. Strange ('77)

2004
Charles Duckett ('54, MD '57)
David Zacks ('64, JD '67)

2005
D.E. Ward ('43, MD '45)

* Deceased; awarded posthumously

APPENDIX G

Sports Hall of Fame, 1983/1984–2004/2005

1983–1984
Bob Bartholomew, football
Charlie Davis, basketball
Jay Sigel, golf

1984–1985
Jim Duncan, football
Dave Harris, football player/HS administrator
Linwood Holt, baseball
Jack Lewis, golf

1985–1986
Carl Tacy, basketball coach

1987–1988
Ed Bradley, football
Jay Haas, golf
Bill Scripture, baseball
Curtis Strange, golf

1988–1989
Larry Hopkins, football
Gene Overby, radio announcer
Larry Russell, football

1989–1990
Moe Bauer, baseball
Dave Budd, basketball
Pat Williams, pro basketball executive

1990–1991
Jim Clack, football
Herb Cline Sr., football/basketball
Scott Hoch, golf
Jack Stallings, baseball

1991–1992
Skip Brown, basketball
Frank Christie, basketball
Bill Hull, basketball/football
James McDougald, football

1992–1993
Bill Ard, football
Dot Casey, women's athletic director/coach
Marge Crisp, women's golf coach/administrator
Harry Nicholas, baseball

1993–1994
Jim Flick, basketball/golf
Gene Hooks, athletic director
Win Headley, football

1994–1995
Marvin "Skeeter" Francis, publicist
Gary Hallberg, golf
Jane Jackson, basketball
John Mackovic, football coach/player
John Polanski, football

1995–1996
Bill Armstrong, football
Jim Simons, golf
Brick Smith, baseball

1996–1997
Rod Griffin, basketball
Bill Merrifield, baseball
Nick Ognovich, football

James Parker, football
Leonard Thompson, golf

1997–1998
Bob Gaona, football
Bill George, football
Frank Johnson, basketball
Dick Tiddy, golf

1998–1999
Brenda Corrie Keuhn, golf
Harry Dowda, football
Jack Sawyer, administrator

1999–2000
Tommy Gregg, baseball
Amy Privette Perko, basketball
Jay Venuto, football

2000–2001
Gary Baldinger, football
Tyrone "Muggsy" Bogues, basketball
Jack Williams, basketball

2001–2002
Joe Inman, golf
Tony Mayberry, football
Ricky Proehl, football

2002–2003
Elmer Barbour, football
Dickie Davis, football
Vic Sorrell, baseball

2003–2004
Billy Andrade, golf
Jake Austin, baseball
Bob Leonard, basketball
Jennifer Rioux Straub, CC/track & field

2004–2005
Rodney Rogers, basketball
Ed Stetz, football

APPENDIX H

Commencement Speakers, 1984–2005

1984—Bill Moyers, CBS News, Senior News Analyst
1985—Reynolds Professor and Poet Maya Angelou
1986—Doonesbury cartoonist Garry Trudeau
1987—North Carolina Governor James G. Martin
1988—PepsiCo CEO Wayne Calloway ('59)
1989—Benjamin Bradlee, Executive Editor, The Washington Post
1990—Millard Fuller, Founder, Habitat for Humanity International
1991—Virginia Governor Doug Wilder
1992—Novelist Tom Clancy
1993—Notre Dame President Emeritus Theodore Hesburgh
1994—Former Congressman Jack Kemp
1995—CNN News Anchor Judy Woodruff
1996—US Senator Sam Nunn
1997—IBM CEO Lou Gerstner
1998—White House Chief of Staff Erskine Bowles
1999—Cardinal Francis Arinze
2000—Cisco CEO John Chambers
2001—Former First Lady Barbara Bush
2002—US Senator John McCain
2003—New York City Mayor Michael Bloomberg
2004—Secretary of State Colin Powell
2005—Professional golfer Arnold Palmer ('51)

APPENDIX I

Baccalaureate Speakers, 1984–2005

Will D. Campbell	Committee of Southern Churchmen, Nashville, Tennessee	Preacher-at-large 1984
Warren T. Carr	Wake Forest Baptist Church	Minister 1985
Robert T. Handy	Union Theological Seminary, New York City	Professor 1986
Richard E. Groves	Wake Forest Baptist Church, Winston-Salem	Minister 1987
R. Eugene Owen	Myers Park Baptist Church, Charlotte	Minister 1988
Joseph Dewey Hobbs Jr.	School of Pastoral Care	Director 1989
Richard Gene Puckett	The Biblical Recorder	Executive Editor 1990
Joseph C. Hough Jr.	Divinity School, Vanderbilt University	Dean 1991
Frances Sue Fitzgerald	Center for Christian Education Ministries, Mars Hill College	Director 1992
Jane F. Crosthwaite	Mt. Holyoke College, South Hadley, Massachusetts	Professor 1993
J. Taylor Field	East 7th Baptist Ministry, New York City	Pastor & Director 1994
Roy J. Smith	Baptist State Convention	Executive Director and Treasurer 1995

Edward Reynolds	University of California–San Diego	Professor 1996
Phyllis Trible	Union Theological Seminary, New York City	Professor 1997
Joan Brown Campbell	National Council of Churches	General Secretary 1998
Bill Leonard	Wake Forest University Divinity School	Dean 1999
Frederick Buechner	Author and novelist	Minister 2000
Brad Braxton	Wake Forest University Divinity School	Professor 2001
Marian Wright Edelman	Founder and President of the Children's Defense Fund	President 2002
Douglass Bailey	Wake Forest Divinity School and Director of Center for Urban Ministry	Professor 2003
John R. Claypool	McAfee School of Theology at Mercer University	Professor 2004
Jane R. Crosthwaite	Mount Holyoke College	Professor 2005

APPENDIX J

Residential Professors for Overseas Houses

Flow Haus Residential Professors

Fall 1999	Larry West	German
Spring 2000	David Levy	Music
Fall 2000	Michael Hughes	History
Spring 2001	Christy Buchanan	Psychology
Fall 2001	Timothy Sellner	German
Spring 2002	Susan Rupp	History
Fall 2002	Rebecca Thomas	German
Spring 2003	Fred Horton	Religion
Fall 2003	Larry West	German
Spring 2004	Clay Hipp	Business
Fall 2004	David Levy	Music
Spring 2005	Robert Evans	Education

Casa Artom Residential Professors

Fall 1983	Charles Talbert	Religion
Spring 1984	Patricia Johansson	English
Fall 1984	Paul Kaplan	Art
Spring 1985	James Barefield	History
Fall 1985	Ralph Kennedy	Philosophy
Spring 1986	Stewart Carter	Music
Fall 1986	Harry Titus	Art
Spring 1987	Robert Ulery	Classical Languages
Fall 1987	Byron Wells	Romance Languages
Spring 1988	Jack Fleer	Politics
Fall 1988	Lee Potter	English
Spring 1989	Donald Schoonmaker	Politics
Fall 1989	James Barefield	History
Spring 1990	Ralph Kennedy	Philosophy
Fall 1990	Patricia Johansson	English
Spring 1991	Louis Goldstein	Music
Fall 1991	Thomas Phillips	Scholarships
Spring 1992	David Broyles	Politics
Fall 1992	John Andronica	Classical Languages
Spring 1993	Deborah Best	Psychology
Fall 1993	Charles Kennedy	Politics
Spring 1994	Jennifer Sault	Romance Languages
Fall 1994	James Barefield	History
Spring 1995	Peter Kairoff	Music
Fall 1995	Steve Messier	Health and Exercise Science
Spring 1996	Robert Ulery	Classical Languages
Fall 1996	Ralph Kennedy	Philosophy
Spring 1997	Carole Browne	Biology
Fall 1997	Tom Phillips	Admissions/ Scholarships
Spring 1998	Antonio Vitti	Romance Languages
Fall 1998	Alan Williams	History
Spring 1999	Bernadine Barnes	Art

Fall 1999	Peter Kairoff	Music
Spring 2000	Olga Valbuena	English
Fall 2000	Helga Welsh	Politics
Spring 2001	Candelas Gala	Romance Languages
Fall 2001	Daniel Hammond	Economics
Spring 2002	Randall Rogan	Communication
Fall 2002	Robert Knott	Art
Spring 2003	Peter Siavelis	Political Science
Fall 2003	Peter Brubaker	Health and Exercise Science
Spring 2004	Antonio Vitti	Romance Languages
Fall 2004	David Hagy	Music
Spring 2005	James Hans	English

London Residential Professors

Fall 1983	Carl Moses	Politics
Spring 1984	Tom Gossett	English
Fall 1984	Buck Yearns	History
Spring 1985	Bynum Shaw	English
Fall 1985	Peggy Smith	Art
Spring 1986	B.G. Gokhale	History
Fall 1986	Dillon Johnston	English
Spring 1987	David Levy	Music
Fall 1987	Ralph Wood	Religion
Spring 1988	Susan Borwick	Music
Fall 1988	Harold Tedford	Theatre
Fall 1989	Richard Barnett	History
Fall 1990	Barry Maine	English
Spring 1991	Donald Wolfe	SCTA
Fall 1991	David Hadley	History
Spring 1992	Claire Hammond	Economics
Fall 1992	Howell Smith	History
Spring 1993	Richard Sears	Politics
Fall 1993	Robert Knott	Art
Spring 1994	Edwin Wilson	English

Fall 1994	Jack Fleer	Politics
Spring 1995	Claudia Thomas	English
Fall 1995	Thomas Mullen	History
Spring 1996	Ian Taplin	Sociology
Fall 1996	Dillon Johnston	English
Spring 1997	Kathy Smith	Politics
Fall 1997	Mary DeShazer	Women's Studies
Spring 1998	John Dunkelberg	Business and Accountancy
	Tom Goho	
Fall 1998	Charles Longino	Sociology
Spring 1999	Anne Boyle	English
Fall 1999	Joseph Milner	Education
Spring 2000	Katy Harriger	Politics
Fall 2000	Ronald Dimock	Biology
Spring 2001	Nancy Cotton	English
Fall 2001	James Barefield	History
Spring 2002	Doug Beets	Calloway School
Fall 2002	Philip Perricone	Sociology
Spring 2003	Page West	Calloway School
Fall 2003	John Llewellyn	Communication
Spring 2004	Michael Lawlor	Economics
Fall 2004	Alan Williams	History
Spring 2005	Mary DeShazer	English/Women's Studies

Salamanca Residential Professors

Spring 2000	Violeta Padrón Bermejo	Romance Languages
Spring 2001	Jane Albrecht	Romance Languages
Spring 2002	Leticia Romo	Romance Languages
Fall 2002	Justin Peterson	Romance Languages
Spring 2003	Justin Peterson	Romance Languages
Fall 2003	Tania González-Robayna	Romance Languages
Spring 2004	Tania González-Robayna	Romance Languages
Fall 2004	Justin Peterson	Romance Languages
Spring 2005	Manuel Gonzalez De La Aleja	University of Salamanca

Dijon Residential Professors

Fall 1992	Sally Barbour	Romance Languages
Fall 1993	Byron Wells	Romance Languages
Fall 1994	Kari Weil	Romance Languages
Fall 1995	Miki Margitic	Romance Languages
Fall 1996	Sally Barbour	Romance Languages
Fall 1997	Stephen Murphy	Romance Languages
Fall 1998	Sally Barbour	Romance Languages
Fall 1999	Byron Wells	Romance Languages
Fall 2000	Judy Kem	Romance Languages
Fall 2001	Miki Margitic	Romance Languages
Fall 2002	Stephen Murphy	Romance Languages
Fall 2003	Byron Wells	Romance Languages
Fall 2004	Miki Margitic	Romance Languages

Japan Residential Professors

Fall 1991	(Tokai) Mike Hazen	Communication
Fall 1992	(Tokai) Kevin Doak	History
Fall 1993	(Tokai) David Catron	Psychology
Fall 1994	(Tokai) Jan Bardsley	East Asian Languages
Fall 1995	(Tokai) George Trautwein	Music
Fall 1996	(Tokai) Byron Wells	Romance Languages
Fall 1997	(Tokai) Wayne Silver	Biology
Fall 1998	(Tokai) Joanne Izbicki	History
Fall 1999	(Tokai) Kurt Shaw	German & Russian
Fall 2000	(Tokai) Ulrike Wiethaus	Humanities
Fall 2001	(Nagoya) Bill Moss	English
Fall 2002	(Kansai Gaidai) Jay Ford	Religion
Fall 2003	(Kansai Gaidai) Phil Kuberski	English
Fall 2004	(Kansai Gaidai) David Phillips	EAL&L

Reynolds Research Leaves, 1983–2005

1983–1984
David B. Broyles — Politics
G. McLeod Bryan — Religion
Gary A. Cook — Art
Ronald V. Dimock Jr. — Biology
Ellen E. Kirkman — Mathematics
David B. Levy — Music
John C. Moorhouse — Economics
Mary Francis Robinson — Romance Languages
Robert W. Ulery — Classical Languages
Richard L. Zuber — History

1984–1985
Richard D. Carmichael — Mathematics
Philippe R. Falkenberg — Psychology
B. G. Gokhale — History
Fred L. Horton — Religion
D. Paul Hylton — Accountancy
William C. Kerr — Physics
Willie Pearson Jr. — Sociology
Teresa Radomski — Music
J. Van Wagstaff — Economics
Peter D. Weigl — Biology

1985–1986
Susan H. Borwick — Music
Patricia M. Cunningham — Education

Thomas M. Elmore	Education
Thomas F. Gossett	English
Charles F. Jackels	Chemistry
Susan C. Jackels	Chemistry
Paul H.D. Kaplan	Art
Raymond E. Kuhn	Biology
Percival Perry	History
Lee H. Potter	English
Charles H. Talbert	Religion
Anne S. Tillet	Romance Languages
George P. Williams Jr.	Physics

1986–1987

J. William Angell	Religion
Robert A. Browne	Biology
Maxine L. Clark	Psychology
John E. Collins	Religion
Doyle R. Fosso	English
Kathleen M. Glenn	Romance Languages
J. Edwin Hendricks	History
Candelas S. Newton (Gala)	Romance Languages
Ronald E. Noftle	Chemistry
Gillian R. Overing	English
Timothy F. Sellner	German
Cecilia H. Solano	Psychology
W. Buck Yearns	History

1987–1988

James P. Barefield	History
David W. Catron	Psychology
Herman E. Eure	Biology
J. Daniel Hammond	Economics
James S. Hans	English
Michael D. Hazen	SCTA
Robert W. Lovett	English
J. Don Reeves	Education
Harry B. Titus	Art
Byron R. Wells	Romance Languages
Ralph C. Wood	Religion
J. Ned Woodall	Anthropology

1988–1989

John V. Baxley	Mathematics
Stewart Carter	Music
Gerald W. Esch	Biology

Andrew V. Ettin	English
Louis R. Goldstein	Music
Michael L. Hughes	History
W. Dillon Johnston	English
Robert Knott	Art
Dan S. Locklair	Music
Milorad R. Margitic	Romance Languages
Joseph O. Milner	Education
Linda L. Nielsen	Education
W. Jack Rejeski	Health & Sport Science

1989–1990

E. Pendleton Banks	Anthropology
Sarah Barbour	Romance Lang. (ZSR)
Deborah L. Best	Psychology
David Faber	Art (ZSR)
B.G. Gokhale	Asian Studies
Katy J. Harriger	Politics (ZSR–Hadari)
Ellen E. Kirkman	Math/Comp. Sc.
Perry Patterson	Economics (ZSR)
Charles L. Richman	Psychology
Donald Schoonmaker	Politics
Michael L. Sinclair	History
Margaret S. Smith	Art
Ian M. Taplin	Sociology
Ralph B. Tower	Business & Accountancy
Marcellus E. Waddill	Math/Comp. Sc.
Sarah Watts	History (ZSR)

1990–1991

Nina S. Allen	Biology
Mary K. DeShazer	Women's Studies
Jack D. Fleer	Politics
Donald E. Frey	Economics
Brian Gorelick	Music (ZSR)
Catherine T. Harris	Sociology
Roger A. Hegstrom	Chemistry
Fredric T. Howard	Math/Comp.Sc.
Michael Lawlor	Economics (ZSR–Hadari)
David Levy	Music
Barry G. Maine	English
Jill J. McMillan	SCTA
Paul M. Ribisl	Health & Sp. Science
Gale Sigal	English (ZSR)
Charles Talbert	Religion

| Claudia Thomas | English (ZSR) |
| Antonio Vitti | Romance Lang. (ZSR) |

1991–1992
Jane Albrecht	Romance Lang. (ZSR)
Kenneth Bechtel	Sociology
Terry Blumenthal	Psychology (ZSR)
Stephen Boyd	Religion
Anne Boyle	English
Carole Browne	Biology
Robert Browne	Biology
Pat Cunningham	Education
Paul Escott	History
Judith Kay	Religion (ZSR–Hadari)
Judy Kem	Romance Lang. (ZSR)
Gillian Overing	English
Len Roberge	Education
Robert Ulery	Class. Lang.
Mark Welker	Chemistry (ZSR)
Beverly Wright	Sociology

1992–1993
Kevin Doak	History (ZSR)
Mary Friedman	Romance Lang.
James Hans	English
Willie Hinze	Chemistry
Dilip Kondepudi	Chemistry
Philip Kuberski	English (ZSR)
Page Laughlin	Art (ZSR)
Mark Leary	Psychology
Allan Louden	SCTA
Linda Maier	Romance Lang. (ZSR–Hadari)
Anthony Parent	History (ZSR)
Teresa Radomski	Music
Wayne Silver	Biology
Kathy Smith	Politics
Tom Taylor	Business & Accountancy

1993–1994
Robert Beck	Psychology
Huw Davies	Chemistry
John Earle	Sociology
Eddie Easley	Business & Accountancy
Bashir El-Beshti	English (ZSR–Hadari)
Kathleen Glenn	Romance Languages

Fred Horton — Religion
Charles & Sue Jackels — Chemistry
Raymond Kuhn — Biology
Ralph Kennedy — Philosophy
Win-chiat Lee — Philosophy
Dolly McPherson — English
Candelas Newton — Romance Languages
Harold Tedford — Theatre
David Weinstein — Politics (ZSR)
Ralph Wood — Religion

1994–1995
Simone Caron — History (ZSR)
Constance Dickey — Romance Languages (ZSR)
Gerald Esch — Biology
Andrew Ettin — English
Dillon Johnston — English
Dale Martin — Business & Accountancy
G. Eric Matthews — Physics
Leah McCoy — Education
William Meyers — History
William Moss — English
Gloria Muday — Biology (ZSR)
Ron Noftle — Chemistry
Philip Perricone — Sociology
Elizabeth Petrino — English (ZSR–Hadari)
Eva Rodtwitt — Romance Lang.
Larry West — German & Russian
Richard Williams — Physics

1995–1996
Umit Akinc — SBA
Allin Cottrell — Economics
Brian Crisp — Politics (ZSR)
Michael Hughes — History
William Kerr — Physics
Kathleen Kron — Biology (ZSR–Hadari)
James Kuzmanovich — Math/Comp. Science
Wei-chin Lee — Politics
John Llewellyn — Speech Communication (ZSR)
Stephen Messier — Health/Sport Science
Stephen Murphy — Romance Languages
Alton Pollard — Religion
Loraine Stewart — Education (ZSR)
Stanton Tefft — Anthropology

Stan Thomas   Math/Comp. Science
Peter Weigl   Biology

1996–1997
David Anderson   Biology (ZSR–Hadari)
John Baxley   Math & Computer Science
Susan Borwick   Music
Robert Browne   Biology
William Conner   Biology
Mary DeShazer   Women's Studies/English
John Dunkelberg   Business & Accountancy
Thomas Goho   Business & Accountancy
Katy Harriger   Politics
Simeon Ilesanmi   Religion (ZSR)
David John   Math & Computer Science
Bradley Jones   Chemistry
Soledad Miguel-Prendes   Romance Languages (ZSR)
Joseph Milner   Education
John Moorhouse   Economics
Kari Weil   Romance Languages
Mark Welker   Chemistry
Byron Wells   Romance Languages

1997–1998
Scott Baker   Education (ZSR)
Terry Blumenthal   Psychology
Stephen Ewing   Calloway School
Jack Fleer   Politics
Catherine Harris   Sociology
Kenneth Hoglund   Religion
Fredric Howard   Math & Computer Science
Linda Howe   Romance Languages (ZSR–Hadari)
Peter Kairoff   Music
Judy Kem   Romance Languages
Robert Knott   Art
Michael Lawlor   Economics
Barry Maine   English
Milorad Margitic   Romance Languages
Jill McMillan   Communication
Willie Pearson Jr.   Sociology
Gale Sigal   English
Howell Smith   History
Todd Torgersen   Math & Computer Science
Sarah Watts   History
Ulrike Wiethaus   Humanities

1998–1999

Jane Albrecht	Romance Languages
Paul Anderson	Physics
Michael Berry	Health & Exer. Science
Stephen Boyd	Religion
Dale Dagenbach	Psychology
Ronald Dimock	Biology
Mary Friedman	Romance Languages
Roger Hegstrom	Chemistry
Charles Kennedy	Politics (postponed until 1999)
Daniel Kim-Shapiro	Physics (ZSR–Hadari)
Scott Klein	English
Daniel Locklair	Music
Patrick Moran	East Asian Lang. & Lit.
Gillian Overing	English
Anthony Parent	History
Robert Plemmons	Math & Computer Science
Alton Pollard	Religion
Randall Rogan	Communication
Claire Schen	History (ZSR)
Catherine Seta	Psychology
Peter Siavelis	Politics (ZSR)
Brian Tague	Biology (ZSR)
Olga Valbuena	English (ZSR)
Mary Wayne-Thomas	Theatre (ZSR)

1999–2000

Mary Jane Berman	Anthropology (Jr.)
Janis Caldwell	English (Jr.)
Victoria Campos	Romance Languages (Jr.)
Paul Cobb	History (Jr.–Hadari)
Patricia Cunningham	Education
James Hans	English
Jac Heckelman	Economics (Jr.)
Willie Hinze	Chemistry
Hugh Howards	Math & Computer Science (Jr.)
Michael Hyde	Communication
Dillon Johnston	English
Charles Kimball	Religion
Ellen Kirkman	Math & Computer Science
Page Laughlin	Art
William Meyers	History
Gloria Muday	Biology
Stephen Robinson	Math & Computer Science
Maria Sanhueza	Romance Languages (Jr.)

Richard Sears	Politics
Ian Taplin	Sociology
Helga Welsh	Politics
Stanley Whitley	Romance Languages

2000–2001

Edward Allen	Math & Computer Science
Sylvain Boko	Economics (Jr.)
J.K. Curry	Theatre (Jr.)
Gerald Esch	Biology
Robert Evans	Education
David Faber	Art
Michael Hazen	Communication
Fred Horton	Religion
Dilip Kondepudi	Chemistry
Philip Kuberski	English
Mark Leary	Psychology
Jeffrey Lerner	History
Jack Rejeski	Health & Exercise Science
Eric Wilson	English (Jr.–Hadari)
Clifford Zeyl	Biology (Jr.)

2001–2002

David Anderson	Biology
Miriam Ashley-Ross	Biology (Jr.–Hadari)
Bernadine Barnes	Art
Christy Buchanan	Psychology
Mary Dalton	Communication (Jr.)
Mary Foskett	Religion (Jr.)
Olgierda Furmanek	Romance Languages (Jr.)
Edwin Hendricks	History
Kathleen Kron	Biology
Linda Nielsen	Education
Timothy Sellner	German & Russian
Miles Silman	Biology (Jr.)
Jeanne Simonelli	Anthropology
David Weinstein	Political Science
Mark Welker	Chemistry
Page West	Calloway School

2002–2003

Simone Caron	History
Mary DeShazer	English
Jonathan Duchac	Calloway School
James Ford	Religion (Jr.)

Cynthia Gendrich	Theatre (Jr.)
Michele Gillespie	History
Luis Gonzalez	Romance Languages (Jr.)
Angela Hattery	Sociology (Jr.)
Patricia Heid	Romance Languages (Jr.)
Bruce King	Chemistry
Win-chiat Lee	Philosophy
David Levy	Music
Angus Lockyer	History (Jr.)
Richard Manderville	Chemistry
Soledad Miguel-Prendes	Romance Languages
Ronald Noftle	Chemistry
James Norris	Mathematics
Teresa Radomski	Music
Mary Lynn Redmond	Education
Andrew Rich	Political Science (Jr.–Hadari)
James Schirillo	Psychology
Margaret Smith	Art
Kendall Tarte	Romance Languages (Jr.)
Todd Torgersen	Computer Science
Ned Woodall	Anthropology

2003–2004

Sarah Barbour	Romance Languages
Margaret Bender	Anthropology (Jr.)
Kenneth Berenhaut	Math (Jr.)
Deborah Best	Psychology
Terry Blumenthal	Psychology
Susan Borwick	Music
Michaelle Browers	Political Science (Jr.–Hadari)
Peter Brubaker	Health & Exer. Science
Jacqueline Carrasco	Music (Jr.)
Ann Cunningham	Education (Jr.)
Richard Heard	Music
Robert Knott	Art
Abdessadek Lachgar	Chemistry
William Meyers	History
Roberta Morosini	Romance Languages (Jr.)
Gillian Overing	English
Charles Richman	Psychology
Earl Smith	Sociology
William Smith	Biology
Loraine Stewart	Education
Stan Thomas	Computer Science
Robert Ulery	Classical Languages

Sarah Watts	History
2004–2005	
Robert Browne	Biology
Jennifer Burg	Computer Science
Stewart Carter	Music
Frederick Chen	Economics (Jr.)
David Coates	Political Science
William Conner	Biology
Allin Cottrell	Economics
Brook Davis	Theatre & Dance (Jr.)
William Fleeson	Psychology
Donald Frey	Economics
Errin Fulp	Computer Science (Jr.)
Katy Harriger	Political Science
Linda Howe	Romance Languages
Paul Juras	Calloway School
Claudia Kairoff	English
Peter Kairoff	Music
William Kerr	Physics
Nina Lucas	Theatre & Dance
Batja Mesquita	Psychology
John Pickel	Art
Nagesh Rao	English (Jr.)
Peter Siavelis	Political Science
Gale Sigal	English
Cynthia Villagomez	History (Jr.)
Eric Watts	Communication
Peter Weigl	Biology
Ulrike Wiethaus	Humanities

APPENDIX L

Average Full-Time Faculty Salaries during Hearn Years

Reynolda Campus

Fall 2003		Fall 1983	
Prof	$ 102,400	Prof	$ 38,000
Assoc	$ 76,400	Assoc	$ 30,100
Assist	$ 55,400	Assist	$ 23,900
Instr	$ 39,500	Instr	$ 16,900
All Ranks	$ 77,500	All Ranks	$ 30,400

APPENDIX M

Award for Excellence in Advising

1988	Carl V. Harris, Classical Languages
1989	Peter Weigl, Biology
1990	Carl C. Moses, Politics
1991	Edgar D. Christman, University Chaplain
1992	Lula M. Leake, Assistant Vice President, and Herman E. Eure, Biology
1993	John L. Andronica, Classical Languages
1994	Catherine T. Harris, Sociology
1995	Larry E. West, German/Russian, and Phil Falkenberg, Psychology
1996	James P. Barefield, History, and Harry B. Titus Jr., Art
1997	Jean Kimmer, Registrar's Office, and Robert W. Ulery, Classical Languages
1998	Leo Ellison Jr., Health and Exercise Science
1999	Mary Lynn Redmond, Education
2000	Hugo C. Lane, Biology
2001	Helen W. Akinc, Calloway School of Business and Accountancy
2002	Elmer K. Hayashi, Mathematics, and Anne Boyle, English
2003	James T. Powell, Classical Languages, and Kathy B. Smith, Political Science
2004	Helga A. Welsh, Political Science, and Leah P. McCoy, Education

APPENDIX N

The Alumni Association/Schoonmaker Faculty Prize for Community Service

1989   Ivey Gentry
1990   J. Edwin Hendricks
1991   Marcellus Waddill
1992   John Earle
1993   The Alumni Association Faculty Prize for Community Service was
       renamed in 1993 in honor of Donald O. Schoonmaker, a professor of
       politics, who died the previous spring. The first Schoonmaker Award was
       given posthumously to Donald O. Schoonmaker in 1993.
1994   Deborah L. Best
1995   Richard Barnett
1996   Donald Frey
1997   Howell Smith
1998   John Litcher
1999   Peter Weigl
2000   Willie Pearson
2001   Richard Sears
2002   Andrew Ettin
2003   Thomas Taylor
2004   Charlie Richman
2005   Stephen Boyd

APPENDIX O

Award for Excellence in Research

1985–1986	W. Jack Rejeski, Health & Sport Science; Deborah L. Best, Psychology
1986–1987	Paul H.D. Kaplan, Art
1987–1988	Willie Pearson Jr., Sociology; Robert A. Browne, Biology; James S. Hans, English
1988–1989	Huw M.L. Davies, Chemistry; Gillian R. Overing, English
1989–1990	Mark R. Leary, Psychology
1990–1991	Mark E. Welker, Chemistry; Byron R. Wells, Romance Languages
1991–1992	Dilip K. Kondepudi, Chemistry
1991–1992	Philip F. Kuberski, English
1992–1993	James C. Fishbein, Chemistry
1993–1994	Allin F. Cottrell, Economics
1994–1995	Dale Dagenbach, Psychology
1995–1996	Terry Blumenthal, Psychology
1996–1997	Gloria Muday, Biology
1997–1998	Paul Anderson, Physics; David J. Anderson, Biology
1998–1999	Peter Brubaker, Health and Exercise Science
1999–2000	S. Bruce King, Chemistry
2000–2001	Kathleen Kron, Biology; James Schirillo, Psychology
2001–2002	Eric Wilson, English; Daniel Kim-Shapiro, Physics
2002–2003	Richard Manderville, Chemistry
2003–2004	Clifford Zeyl, Biology
2004–2005	Ulrich Bierbach, Chemistry

Founders Day Speakers, 1984–2005

1984 John Chandler ('45)
1985 Elie Wiesel
1986 Betty Ford
1987 Thomas K. Hearn
1988 Joseph Branch ('38)
1989 Horace A. "Bones" McKinney
1990 John H. Sununu
1991 Paul Escott
1992 Edwin G. Wilson ('43)
1993 Charlayne Hunter-Gault
1994 Clifton R. Wharton Jr.
1995 Dale Bumpers
1996 Jim Hunt
1997 James Earl Jones
1998 Tony Campolo
1999 Wole Soyinka
2000 David Suzuki
2001 Mary Ann Glendon
2002 Doris Kearns
2003 Bill Bradley
2004 Ann Quidlen
2005 James Carville

APPENDIX Q

Honorary Degrees, 1984–2005

Year	Recipient	Degree	Hooder
1984	Eleanor Clark	DLitt	Germaine Brée
1984	Eudora Welty	LLD	Thomas Gossett
1984	J. Tylee Wilson*	LLD	
1984	Paul Volcker*	LLD	
1984	Robert Penn Warren	DLitt	Stuart Wright
1984	Sherman Mellinkoff	LHD	Joseph Johnson III
1984	Thomas H. Davis	LLD	Peter Peacock
1984	Will Davis Campbell (1948)	LHD	G. McLeod Bryan
1985	Elie Wiesel	DLitt	
1985	Harold Clark Bennett (1949)	DD	Edgar Christman (Religion)
1985	Helen Hill Miller	LHD	Germaine Brée (Humanities)
1985	John Allen Dicks Cooper	DSc	Fairfield Goodale (Medical)
1985	Roy Hampton Park	LLD	Robert Shivley (Babcock)
1985	Vernon E. Jordan Jr.	LLD	Lee Potter (English)
1986	Bill Bradley	LLD	
1986	Garret B. Trudeau	DLitt	Margaret Supplee Smith (Art)
1986	Jack Kemp	LLD	
1986	John Hope Franklin	LHD	David Smiley (History)
1986	Robert G. Petersdorf	DSc	Fairfield Goodale (Medical)
1986	Robert T. Handy	DD	James Martin (Religion)
1986	Ruth Patrick	DSc	Walter Flory (Biology)
1987	Bert L. Bennett	LLD	Thomas Goho (Business)
1987	Bruce Ezell Whitaker (1944)	LLD	Carl Harris (Classical Languages)

1987	Eloise Rallings Lewis	LHD	James Leist (Medical)
1987	Gardner Taylor	D.D.	
1987	James Grubb Martin	LLD	Tim Pennell (Medical)
1987	Selma Hortense Burke	DFA	Dolly McPherson (English)
1988	Barbara Babcock Millhouse	LHD	Margaret Supplee Smith (Art)
1988	David Wayne Calloway (1959)	LLD	Paul Hylton (Business)
1988	Gordan Alexander Craig	LHD	Michael Sinclair (History)
1988	Joan Brown Campbell	DD	
1988	Raymond Eugene Owens (1952)	DD	Edgar Christman (Religion)
1988	Roone Arledge	LLD	
1988	Shigeyoshi Matsumae	LLD	
1989	Alan Greenspan	LLD	
1989	Arthur R. Ashe	LLD	
1989	Benjamin C. Bradlee	LHD	Wallace Carroll/Sam Ervin Jr.
1989	Elie Maynard Adams	LHD	Gregory Pritchard (Philosophy)
1989	Evelyn Patricia Foote	LLD	Deborah Best (Psychology)
1989	Harold T.P. Hayes	LHD	Bynum Shaw (Journalism)
1989	Joseph Dewey Hobbs Jr.	DD	Thomas Dougherty Jr. (Religion)
1989	Zachary Taylor Smith II	LLD	James Barnard (History)
1990	David R. Bryant	DSc	Phillip Hamrick Jr. (Medical)
1990	Eleanor Holmes Norton	LLD	Suzanne Reynolds (Law)
1990	John G. Medlin	LLD	
1990	John H. Sununu	LLD	
1990	Millard Dean Fuller	LHD	Marcus Hester (Philosophy)
1990	R. Philip Hanes Jr.	LHD	Robert Lovett (English)
1990	Richard Gene Puckett	DD	John William Angell (Religion)
1991	Albert Reinhold Hunt Jr.	DLitt	Paul Escott (History)
1991	Joseph Carl Hough Jr.	DD	Carlton Mitchell (Religion)
1991	Lawrence Douglas Wilder	LLD	Beth Hopkins
1991	Stephen Lybrook Neal	LLD	Katy Harriger (Political Science)
1992	Frances Sue Fitzgerald	DD	Fred Horton Jr. (Religion)
1992	James Calvin Hunt	DSc	Richard Janeway (Medical)
1992	James Gordon Hanes	LLD	E. Pendleton Banks (Anthropology)
1992	Penelope Ellen Niven	DLitt	Elizabeth Phillips (English)
1992	Thomas Leo Clancy	LLD	George Walker (Law)
1993	Charlayne Hunter-Gault	DLitt	
1993	James Kirk Glenn	LLD	Tim Pennell (Medical)
1993	LeRoy Tashreau Walker	LLD	Harold Barrow
1993	Paule Marshall	DLitt	Dolly McPherson (English)
1993	Sandra Day O'Connor	LLD	

1993	Shogo Sasaki	DSc	Steve Mizell (Medical)
1993	Theodore M. Hesburgh	LHD	Bob Walsh (Law)
1994	Clarence E. "Bighouse" Gaines	DLitt	William Hottinger
1994	Gertrude B. Elion	DSc	Mariana Morris (Medical)
1994	Herbert Brenner	LHD	Jimmy Simon (Medical)
1994	Robert Reynold Merhige	LLD	David Logan (Law)
1994	William H. Rehnquist	LLD	
1995	Frank Liipfert Horton	LLD	Charles Rose
1995	Jacob Lawrence	DFA	William Hazzard (Medical)
1995	Joseph Paul Sticht	LLD	William Hazzard (Medical)
1995	Judy Carline Woodruff	DLitt	Nancy Cotton
1995	Roy Jordan Smith	DD	Michael Hazen (Commun.)
1995	Sidney Verba	LLD	Jack Fleer (Politics)
1996	Christian Frederick Beyers Naude	DD	George McLeod Bryan
1996	Hiram Hamilton Ward (JD 1950)	LLD	Ed Wilson
1996	James Walter Mason (1938)	LLD	Ken Zick
1996	Louis Wade Sullivan MD	DSc	Jay Moskowitz (Medical)
1996	Samuel Augustus Nunn	LLD	Lu Leake
1996	Virginia Niblock Britt (1970, '73 MAEd)	DD	Alton Pollard
1996	Werner Platzer	DSc	Ned Woodall (Anthropology)
1996	Weston Poole Hatfield (1941)	LLD	Leon Corbett (Counsel)
1997	Chloe Anthony Morrison	DLitt	Alton Pollard
1997	Cora Bagley Marrett	LHD	Cheryl Leggon
1997	James Earl Jones	DFA	
1997	Jordan Jay Cohen	DSc	Jim Thompson (Medical)
1997	Louis Vincent Gerstner	LLD	Charlier Moyer (Babcock)
1997	Petro Kulynych	LLD	Leon Corbett (Counsel)
1997	Phyllis Tribble	DD	Lu Leake
1998	Anthony Stephen Fauci	DSc	Jay Moskowitz (Medical)
1998	Erskine Boyce Bowles	LLD	Jack Fleer (Politics)
1998	Francis Eugene Corrigan	LLD	Jack Sawyer (Athletics)
1998	Henlee Hulix Barnett (1940)	DD	Bill Leonard (Divinity)
1998	Romulus Linney	DLitt	Harold Tedford (Theater)
1999	Andrew Jackson Young	LLD	Maya Angelou
1999	Betty Ray McCain	LHD	Peggy Smith (Art)
1999	Francis Cardinal Arnize	DD	Simon Ilesanni (Religion)
1999	Michael Elllis DeBakey	DSc	Glenn Purrington (Medical)
1999	Richard Darman	LLD	Frederick Harris (Babcock)
2000	A.E. Dick Howard	LLD	George K. Walker (Law)
2000	Claude Lenfant	DSc	Jay Moskowitz (Medical)
2000	Frederick Buechner	LHD	Maya Angelou
2000	Helen Matthews Lewis	DD	Bill Leonard (Divinity)

2000	John Chambers	LLD	Ajay Patel (Babcock)
2000	Thomas Willlis Lambeth	LLD	Jim Barefield (History)
2001	Barbara Pierce Bush	LHD	Charles Branch (Medical)
2001	Martin Johannes Sebastian Isepp	DFA	Teresa Radmonski (Music)
2001	William Percy Hytche	LLD	Herman Eure (Biology)
2002	David Satcher	DSc	Sharon Jackson (Medical)
2002	Floyd Abrams	LLD	Michael Curtis (Law)
2002	Fred Morgan Kirby	LLD	John Dunkelberg (Calloway)
2002	Marian Wright Edelman	LHD	James Dunn (Divinity)
2002	Senator John McCain	LLD	Katy Harriger (Pol. Science)
2003	Eric N. Olsen	DSc	Larry Daniel (Biochemistry)
2003	Martha W. Barnett	LLD	Tom Roberts (Law)
2003	Martin E. Marty	DD	Bill Leonard (Divinity)
2003	Michael R. Bloomberg	LLD	Bruce Resnick (Babcock)
2003	Richard H. Carmona	DSc	Wayne Meredith (Surgical Sciences)
2004	Colin L. Powell	LLD	Herman Eure (Biology)
2004	Geneva B. Brown	LHD	Ed Hendricks (History)
2004	John R. Claypool	DD	Carl Harris (Professor Emeritus of Classical Languages)
2004	Lewis Lockwood	DFA	David Levy (Music)
2004	M. Jocelyn Elders	DSc	Dr. Kristy Woods
2005	Bernard Lown	DSc	Steven Block (Faculty Services)
2005	Michael D. Piscal	LHD	Charles Richman (Psychology)
2005	Oliver W. Hill Sr.	LLD	Simone Rose (Law)

DD = Doctor of Divinity
DFA = Doctor of Fine Arts
DLitt = Doctor of Letters
DSc = Doctor of Science
LHD = Doctor of Humanitites
LLD = Doctor of Laws

*Conferred March 23, 1984

Honorary Degrees in 1984

Given at University Convocation on March 23, 1984
J. Tylee Wilson, President and CEO of R.J. Reynolds Industries—Doctor of Law
Paul A. Volcker, Chairman, Board of Governors Federal Reserve System—Doctor of Law

Jon Reinhart Award for Excellence in Teaching

1985	Catherine Harris
1986	Bynum G. Shaw
1987	Jeanne Owen
1988	David L. Smiley
1989	Anne Tillett
1990	Carl V. Harris
1991	Ralph C. Wood Jr.
1992	Fred L. Horton Jr.
1993	Elmer K. Hayashi
1994	Robert W. Brehme
1995	Ralph S. Fraser
1996	James P. Barefield
1997	Marcellus Waddill
1998	Charles M. Allen
1999	Kathleen M. Glenn
2000	Doyle R. Fosso
2001	Herman E. Eure
2002	Katy Harriger
2003	Peter D. Weigl
2004	Sarah Watts
2005	Edwin G. Wilson

APPENDIX S

Reid-Doyle Excellence in Teaching Award

1983–1984	Deborah L. Best, Psychology
1984–1985	Catherine T. Harris, Sociology
1985–1986	Saguiv Hadari, Politics; Carole L. Browne, Biology
1986–1987	Susan P. McCaffray History; Barry G. Maine, English
1987–1988	Katy Harriger, Politics
1988–1989	Ann Boyle, English
1989–1990	Stephen B. Boyd, Religion
1990–1991	Antonio Vitti, Romance Languages
1991–1992	Alton B. Pollard, Religion
1992–1993	Claudia N. Thomas, English
1993–1994	Page Laughlin, Art
1994–1995	Simone Caron, History
1995–1996	James T. Powell, Classical Languages
1996–1997	Helga Welsh, Politics
1997–1998	Michele S. Ware, English
1998–1999	Jeffrey D. Lerner, History
1999–2000	Gordon E. McCray, Calloway
2000–2001	Nina M. Lucas, Theatre (Dance)
2001–2002	Christa L. Colyer, Chemistry
2002–2003	Peter Siavelis, Political Science
2003–2004	Hugh Howards, Mathematics
2004–2005	Martin Guthold, Physics

APPENDIX T

The Kulynych Family Omicron Delta Kappa Award Recipients, 1987–2005

1987	Don Schoonmaker
1988	Marcellus Waddill
1989	Howell Smith
1990	Ed Wilson
1991	James Barefield
1992	Alton Pollard
1993	Jack Wilkerson
1994	Simone Caron
1995	Anne Boyle
1996	William Meyers
1997	Kline Harrison
1998	Katy Harriger
1999	Bob Evans
2000	Mary Dalton
2001	Angela Hattery
2002	Helga Welsh
2003	Sylvain Boko
2004	James Cotter
2005	James Powell

APPENDIX U

Wake Forest University Graduation and Student Percentages, 1983 and 2005

Graduation Rate (Undergraduates)
1983: 74%
2005: 88%

Non-Baptists (Undergraduates)
1982: 74%
2005: 86%

APPENDIX V

Alumni Council Presidents 1983–2005

1983   Howard G. Dawkins Jr. ('63)
1984   William H. Flowe Sr. ('41)
1985   George E. Brooks ('71) and Adelaide Alexander Sink ('70)
1986   Earle Allen Connelly ('48)
1987   W. Prentiss Baker III ('65)
1988   James Ronald Gadd ('71)
1989   Abram Doyle Early Jr. ('65, JD '67)
1990   Abram Doyle Early Jr. ('65, JD '67)
1991   Gary B. Lambert ('77)
1992   W. Louis Bissette Jr. ('65)
1993   Celeste Mason Pittman ('67)
1994   Stephen W. Coles ('77, JD '80)
1995   David J. Stefany ('80)
1996   J. Lloyd Nault II ('76, JD '78)
1997   Graham W. Denton Jr. ('67)
1998   Diana Moon Adams ('78)
1999   Samuel P. Rothrock ('73)
2000   Bobby R. Burchfield ('76)
2001   Susan Yates Stephenson ('69)
2002   Frederick W. Eubank II ('86)
2003   Alfred G. Adams ('68, JD '73)
2004   James T. Stone ('70)
2005   Nancy Rich Kuhn ('73)

APPENDIX W

College Board of Visitors Chairs, 1983–2005

1983–1984: James Alfred Martin Jr.
1984–1985: J. Tylee Wilson
1985–1986: J. Tylee Wilson
1986–1987: Hubert Humphrey
1987–1988: F. Hudnall Christopher Jr.
1988–1989: F. Hudnall Christopher Jr.
1989–1990: James B. Hunt Jr.
1990–1991: Adelaide A. Sink
1991–1992: Adelaide A. Sink
1992–1993: Bruce M. Babcock
1993–1994: Bruce M. Babcock
1994–1995: L.M. Baker Jr.
1995–1996: L.M. Baker Jr.
1996–1997: Gillian Lindt
1997–1998: Thomas W. Lambeth
1998–1999: Thomas W. Lambeth
1999–2000: Thomas W. Lambeth
2000–2001: Dale R. Walker
2001–2002: Dale R. Walker
2002–2003: Evelyn P. Foote
2003–2004: Donna Boswell
2004–2005: Donna Boswell

APPENDIX X

Administrative Personnel, Schools on the Reynolda Campus, 1983–2005

BABCOCK GRADUATE SCHOOL OF MANAGEMENT

1983–1984
Robert W. Shively, Dean
James M. Clapper, Associate Dean
Jean B. Hopson, Assistant Dean

1984–1986
Robert W. Shively, Dean
James M. Clapper, Associate Dean
Jean B. Hopson, Assistant Dean

1986–1987
Robert W. Shively, Dean
James M. Clapper, Associate Dean and Director of the Institute for Executive Education
Jean B. Hopson, Assistant Dean and Librarian
M. Willisia Holbrook, Assistant Dean for External Affairs and Director of Career Planning and Placement

1987–1989
Robert W. Shively, Dean
Jean B. Hopson, Assistant Dean and Librarian
M. Willisia Holbrook, Assistant Dean for External Affairs and Director of Career Planning and Placement

1989–1990
Paul A. Kierks, Acting Dean
Jean B. Hopson, Assistant Dean and Librarian

1990–1991
John B. McKinnon, Dean
Paul A. Dierks, Associate Dean
Jean B. Hopson, Assistant Dean

1991–1992
John B. McKinnon, Dean
James G. Ptaszynski, Associate Dean
Jean B. Hopson, Assistant Dean

1992–1993
John B. McKinnon, Dean
James M. Clapper, Associate Dean
James G. Ptaszynski, Associate Dean
Jean B. Hopson, Assistant Dean

1993–1995
John B. McKinnon, Dean
James M. Clapper, Associate Dean
James G. Ptaszynski, Associate Dean

1995–1996
Gary E. Costley, Dean
James M. Clapper, Associate Dean
James G. Ptaszynski, Associate Dean

1996–1997
Gary E. Costley, Dean
James M. Clapper, Associate Dean
Frederick H. DeB Harris, Associate Dean for Faculty Affairs
Charles R. Kennedy Jr., Associate Dean for Academic Affairs
Mary C. Goss, Assistant Dean of Admissions

1997–1998
R. Charles Moyer, Dean
Charles R. Kennedy Jr., Associate Dean for Academic Affairs
Mary C. Goss, Assistant Dean of Admissions
Marianne M. Hill, Assistant Dean of Management and Executive Program
James A. Narus, Assistant Dean, Charlotte MBA Program

1998–1999
R. Charles Moyer, Dean
Charles R. Kennedy Jr., Associate Dean for Academic Affairs
Robin Roy Ganzert, Assistant Dean of Administration
Mary C. Goss, Assistant Dean of Admissions

1999–2000
R. Charles Moyer, Dean
Charles R. Kennedy Jr., Associate Dean for Academic Affairs
Robin Roy Ganzert, Assistant Dean of Administration
Mary C. Goss, Assistant Dean of Admissions
Patricia B. Divine, Assistant Dean of External Relations and Program Development
James A. Narus, Assistant Dean of the Evening Program, Charlotte
Steve Price, Assistant Dean of Management Education

2000–2002
R. Charles Moyer, Dean
Charles R. Kennedy Jr., Associate Dean for Academic Affairs
J. Kendall Middaugh II, Associate Dean for Management Education
Robin Roy Ganzert, Assistant Dean of Administration
Mary C. Goss, Assistant Dean of Admissions
Patricia B. Divine, Assistant Dean of External Relations and Program Development
Steve Price, Assistant Dean of Management Education

2002–2003
R. Charles Moyer, Dean
Ajay Patel, Associate Dean of Academic Affairs
J. Kendall Middaugh II, Associate Dean for Management Education
Robin Roy Ganzert, Assistant Dean of Finance and Administration
Mary C. Goss, Assistant Dean of Full–Time Program Admissions and Student
Services
Patricia B. Divine, Assistant Dean of External Relations and Program Development

2003–2004
R. Charles Moyer, Dean
Ajay Patel, Associate Dean of Academic Affairs
J. Kendall Middaugh II, Associate Dean for Management Education
Patricia B. Divine, Assistant Dean of External Relations and Program Development
Kim Westmoreland, Assistant Dean for Career Management and Full–Time Program Admissions

2004–2005
Ajay Patel, Interim Dean
J. Kendall Middaugh II, Associate Dean for Management Education

Patricia B. Divine, Assistant Dean of External Relations and Program Development
Daniel S. Fogel, Assistant Dean and Dean of Charlotte Program
Kim Westmoreland, Assistant Dean for Full–Time Admissions and Career
Management

COLLEGE OF ARTS AND SCIENCES

1983–1984
Thomas E. Mullen, Dean
Robert A. Dyer, Associate Dean
Toby A. Hale, Assistant Dean

1984–1988
Thomas E. Mullen, Dean
Toby A. Hale, Associate Dean
William S. Hamilton, Assistant Dean
Patricia Adams Johansson, Assistant Dean

1988–1994
Thomas E. Mullen, Dean
Toby A. Hale, Associate Dean
William S. Hamilton, Associate Dean
Patricia Adams Johansson, Associate Dean

1994–1995
Thomas E. Mullen, Dean
Toby A. Hale, Associate Dean
William S. Hamilton, Associate Dean
Patricia Adams Johansson, Associate Dean
Paul N. Orser, Associate Dean and Dean of Freshmen

1995–1996
Thomas E. Mullen, Dean
Laura Christian Ford, Associate Provost*
Toby A. Hale, Associate Dean
William S. Hamilton, Associate Dean
Patricia Adams Johansson, Associate Dean
Paul N. Orser, Associate Dean and Dean of Freshmen
*Assigned for 1994–1995 to the Office of the Dean of the College

1996–1997
Paul D. Escott, Dean
Toby A. Hale, Associate Dean
William S. Hamilton, Associate Dean

Patricia Adams Johansson, Associate Dean
Paul N. Orser, Associate Dean and Dean of Freshmen
Claudia Newell Thomas, Associate Dean

1997–2002
Paul D. Escott, Dean
Toby A. Hale, Associate Dean
William S. Hamilton, Associate Dean
Patricia Adams Johansson, Associate Dean
Paul N. Orser, Associate Dean and Dean of Freshmen
Claudia Newell Thomas, Associate Dean
Jeryl Prescott, Assistant Dean
Jeryl Prescott, Associate Dean

2002–2005
Paul D. Escott, Dean
Linda McKinnish Bridges, Associate Dean
Toby A. Hale, Associate Dean
William S. Hamilton, Associate Dean
Claudia Thomas Kairoff, Associate Dean
Paul N. Orser, Associate Dean and Dean of Freshmen

GRADUATE SCHOOL OF ARTS AND SCIENCES

1983–1984
Henry S. Stroupe, Dean
Harold O. Goodman, Associate Dean for Biomedical Graduate Studies

1984–1985
Gerald W. Esch, Dean
Harold O. Goodman, Associate Dean for Biomedical Graduate Studies

1985–1987
Gerald W. Esch, Dean

1987–1990
Gerald W. Esch, Dean
Nancy J. Cotton, Director of Master of Arts in Liberal Studies Program

1990–1991
Gerald W. Esch, Dean
Nancy J. Cotton, Assistant Dean and Director of Master of Arts in Liberal Studies
Program

1991–1992
Nancy J. Cotton, Acting Dean

1992–1993
Gordon A. Melson, Dean

1993–1994
Gordon A. Melson, Dean
Nancy Cotton, Director of Master of Arts in Liberal Studies Program

1994–1996
Gordon A. Melson, Dean

1996–1999
Gordon A. Melson, Dean
Robert N. Shorter, Associate Dean

1999–2003
Gordon A. Melson, Dean

2003–2005
Gordon A. Melson, Dean
Cecilia H. Solano, Associate Dean

SCHOOL OF DIVINITY

1999–2000
Bill J. Leonard, Dean
Phyllis Trible, Associate Dean

2000–2002
Bill J. Leonard, Dean

2002–2003
Bill J. Leonard, Dean
Jill Crainshaw, Associate Dean for Vocational Formation

2003–2005
Bill J. Leonard, Dean
Katherine E. Amos, Associate Dean of Academic Affairs
Jill Crainshaw, Associate Dean for Vocational Formation

SCHOOL OF LAW

1983–1984
John D. Scarlett, Dean
Leon H. Corbett Jr., Associate Dean
Robert F. Clodfelter, Associate Dean for Academic Affairs

1984–1985
John D. Scarlett, Dean
Robert F. Clodfelter, Associate Dean for Academic Affairs

1985–1989
John D. Scarlett, Dean
Kenneth A. Zick II, Associate Dean, Academic Affairs
James Taylor Jr., Associate Dean, External Affairs

1989–1991
John D. Scarlett, Dean
Arthur R. Gaudio, Associate Dean, Academic Affairs
James Taylor Jr., Associate Dean, External Affairs

1991–1996
Robert K. Walsh, Dean
H. Miles Foy III, Associate Dean, Academic Affairs
James Taylor Jr., Associate Dean, External Affairs

1996–2001
Robert K. Walsh, Dean
Ralph A. Peeples, Associate Dean, Academic Affairs
James Taylor Jr., Associate Dean, External Affairs

2001–2002
Robert K. Walsh, Dean
H. Miles Foy III, Associate Dean, Academic Affairs
Ann Setien Gibbs, Associate Dean, External Affairs and Administration
Deborah L. Parker, Assistant Dean for Students

2002–2005
Robert K. Walsh, Dean
H. Miles Foy III, Executive Associate Dean, Academic Affairs
Ann Setien Gibbs, Associate Dean, External Affairs and Administration
Deborah L. Parker, Associate Dean for Students
Marian F. Parker, Associate Dean for Information Services

APPENDIX Y

Personal Interviews Conducted for the Book

Martha Allman
John Anderson
Debbie Best
Leon Corbett
Sandra Boyettee
David Brown
Paul Escott
Ross Griffith
Weston Hatfield
Thomas K. Hearn Jr.
Thomas K. Hearn III
Laura Hearn
Bill Joyner
Reid Morgan
Tom Mullen
Tom Phillips
Tom Taylor
Bill Wells
Jack Wilkerson
Ed Wilson
Tylee Wilson
Ken Zick

REFERENCES

1983–1984

Baggett, Julie. 1984. Club hosts first intercollegiate horse show. *Old Gold and Black* 66 (19, March 2): 1.

Baggett, Julie. 1984. Wake Forest hosts Constitutional colloquium. *Old Gold and Black* 66 (22, April 6): 1.

Bevan, Elizabeth. 1983. Scholarships prove beneficial. *Old Gold and Black* 66 (1, September 9): 2.

Bilich, Ted. 1984. N.C. Political Science Association convenes. *Old Gold and Black* 66 (22, April 6): 1.

Board of Trustees approve building of new dorm. 1984. *Old Gold and Black* 66 (20, March 23): 1.

Hearn, Thomas. K. 1976. General rules and moral sentiments in Hume's *Treatise. Review of Metaphysics* 30 (1): 57–72.

Lentz, M. 1984. John Anderson: A do-er's profile. *Wake Forest: The University Magazine* 31(1, September): 18–20.

Miller, Marjorie. 1983a. Hearn plans to preserve established strengths. *Old Gold and Black* 66 (6, September 30): 1.

Miller, Marjorie. 1983b. Outgoing president criticizes search. *Old Gold and Black,* 66 (6, September 30): 1.

Miller, Majorie. 1983c. Changes enhance entrance. *Old Gold and Black* 66 (7, October 7): 1.

Miller, Majorie., & Taylor, J. 1983. News leak disrupts selection process. *Old Gold and Black* 66 (3, September 9): 1, 6.

Ormand, Lisa. 1983. Women's Studies program plans to explore female achievements. *Old Gold and Black* 66 (3, September 9): 1.

Paschal, George. Washington. 1935. *History of Wake Forest College, volume 1.* Wake Forest, NC: Wake Forest College.

Paschal, George. Washington. 1943. *History of Wake Forest College, volumes 2–3.* Wake Forest, NC: Wake Forest College.

Pettyjohn, Paige. 1984. Hearn approves visitation and party-hour proposal. *Old Gold and Black* 66 (17, February 17): 1.

Purdy, Daniel. 1983. Law school's reputation concerns dean, students. *Old Gold and Black* 66 (4, September 16): 1.

Purdy, Daniel. 1983. Debaters honor retiring coach. *Old Gold and Black* 66 (13, December 2): 7.

Rauch, J. 1983. Candidates for WFU post narrowed to 2. *Winston-Salem Journal* (June 22): 1–2.

Rinehart, Jennifer. 1984. WAKE rides the air waves. *Old Gold and Black* 66 (20, March 23): 1–2.

Shaw, Bynum. 1988. *The History of Wake Forest College, volume IV (1943–1967)*. Winston-Salem, NC: Wake Forest University.

Schoonmaker, Donald. 1983. Improve presidential search. *Old Gold and Black* 66 (6, September 30): 4.

Sorrell, Jeannette. 1984. Concert thanks community. *Old Gold and Black* 66 (14, January 27): 2.

Sutton, Marybeth. 1983. Room inspection reinstated. *Old Gold and Black* 66 (10, November 4): 1.

Sutton, Marybeth & Davis, Donald. 1984. Troop encampment brings 18th century to life. *Old Gold and Black* 66 (25, April 13): 6.

Wake Forest inaugurates 12th president. 1983. *Old Gold and Black* 66 (10): 1.

Wilson, Edwin. Graves. 2010. *The History of Wake Forest University, volume V (1967–1983)*. Winston-Salem, NC: Wake Forest University.

1984–1985

Ashley, Elizabeth A. 1985. New Deacon network started. *Old Gold and Black* 68 (24, March 22): 1.

Atkinson, Carla. 1984. Faculty apartments offer alternative lifestyle. *Old Gold and Black* 68 (13, November 16): 6.

Baker, Daniel R. 1985. Haddock enters his silver year. *Old Gold and Black* 68 (23, March 7): 7.

Bargaining power. 1984. *Old Gold and Black* 68 (8, October 12): 4.

Cameron, Alan. 1984. Wellness programs begin. *Old Gold and Black* 68 (8, October 12): 2.

Carpenter, Scott. 1984. Preachers stir students' emotions. *Old Gold and Black* 68 (13, November 16): 1.

Davis, Daryl. 1984. The pros and cons of humanitate. *Old Gold and Black* 68 (7, October 5): 4.

Dibiase, Tad. 1984. Women harriers capture first place. *Old Gold and Black* 68 (10, October 26): 11.

Hart, Ronald Hastings Jr. 1984. Hearn considers tuition hike to change image. *Old Gold and Black* 68 (8, October 12): 1.

Hart, Ronald Hastings Jr. 1984. Hearn explains purpose of his letter. *Old Gold and Black* 68 (9, October 18): 1.

Hunsley, Eric. 1985. Drop-out rate approaches 12 percent. *Old Gold and Black* 68 (22, February 22): 1.

King, Kerry K. 1985. Law school plans to decrease student body size. *Old Gold and Black* 68 (23, March 1): 1.

Miller, Majorie. 1984. Sound and light recreates history. *Old Gold and Black* 66 (22, April 6): 2.

Ormand, Lisa. 1985. Experimental college resurfaces. *Old Gold and Black* 68 (19, February 1): 2.

Parks, Susan. 1984. Computer center opens. *Old Gold and Black* 68 (15, November 30): 1.

Purdy, Daniel, & Bonahue, Edward. 1985. Students upset over changes. *Old Gold and Black* 68 (28 April 12): 1.

Report card. 1984. *Old Gold and Black* 68 (11, November 2): 4.

Sinclair, Jeannie. 1984. Deacon's appearance angers Democrats. *Old Gold and Black* 68 (5, September 21): 1.

Smiley, David L. 1984. The seal. *Old Gold and Black* 68 (6, September 28): 4.

Varholy, Cristine. 1984. Faculty mourn loss of University seal. *Old Gold and Black* 68 (6, September 28): 1.

Varholy, Cristine. 1985. University purchases new language houses. *Old Gold and Black* 68 (31, May 3): 1.

1985–1986

Ashley, Elizabeth A. 1985. Group considers honor code changes. *Old Gold and Black* 69 (11, November 8): 1, 8.

Bowman Gray School of Medicine receives $1 million gift. 1986. *Wake Forest Magazine* 32 (4, February): 1.

Coliseum bond issues passes by 4 to 1 margin. 1985. *Wake Forest University Magazine* 32 (1, August): 2.

Foote, Robert. 1986. University increases faculty salaries significantly. *Old Gold and Black* 69 (29, April 25): 1.

Griffith, Tony. 1985. Faculty condos near completion. *Old Gold and Black* 69 (3, September 13): 2.

Hart, Robert. H., Jr. 1985. Memo says buildings possible. *Old Gold and Black* 69 (11, November 8): 1, 8.

Hunsley, Eric. 1985. Placement office welcomes Tenhagen as new assistant. *Old Gold and Black* 69 (1, September 20): 1.

Jenkins, Maria. 1985. 'Macbeth' opens. *Old Gold and Black* 69 (11, November 15): 7.

Kersh, Rogan. 1985. Faculty approves divestment move. *Old Gold and Black* 69 (3, September 13): 1.

King, Kerry M. 2002. Faith and reason. *Wake Forest Magazine* 49 (3): 18–25.

Law School announces 440 plan. 1985. *Wake Forest University Magazine* 31 (6, June): 20–21.

Pretorius, Scott. 1986. Admissions office receives over 5,000 applications. *Old Gold and Black* 69 (23, March 21): 1.

Phillips, Tom. 1986. Rhodes Scholar Chapman: One member of a talented class. *Wake Forest Magazine* 32 (4, February): 8.

Quad in danger of losing trees. 1985. *Old Gold and Black* 69 (2, September 6): 1, 9.

Residence life approves visitation policy change. 1986. *Old Gold and Black* 69 (15, January 24): 1.

Reynolds Foundation awards $2 million to Wake Forest. 1986. *Wake Forest University Magazine* 32 (4, February): 3.

Reynolds Foundation grants additional funds. 1986. *Old Gold and Black* 69 (14, January 17): 1.

Snyder, James C. 1986. Trustees want greater control over selection. *Old Gold and Black* 69 (14, January 17): 1, 3.

Toney, Steve. 1986. Faculty refuses to approve SFA charter. *Old Gold and Black* 69 (26, April 11): 1, 7.

Trustees to elect successors with Convention approval. 1986. *Wake Forest University Magazine* 32 (3, January): 2.

Watts, Kathy. 1985. Alcohol restricted. *Old Gold and Black* 69 (7, October 10): 1.

1986–1987

Becht, Karen. 1986. Alcohol policy affects campus. *Old Gold and Black* 70 (1, August 29): 1.

Brantley, Russell. 1987. Wake Forest, Baptist Convention begin new relationship. *Wake Forest University Magazine* 33 (3, January): 2–3.

Chapman, Harriet. 1987. Snow interrupts classes, disrupts food services. *Old Gold and Black* 70 (16, January 30): 1.

Chapman, Harriet. 1987. Board examines drop in black WFU applications. *Old Gold and Black* 70 (18, February 13): 1.

Daughtry, Bill. 1986. Number of tenured professors is higher than national average. *Old Gold and Black* 70 (8, 16 October): 1.

Farley, Shawn. 1987. Proposed extension may reduce traffic. *Old Gold and Black* 70 (16, January 30): 1.

Howe, J. 1987. Pro Humanitate Society initiates members. *Wake Forest Magazine* 33 (6, June): 8. Reprinted from the March 31, 1987, issue of the *Winston-Salem Journal*.

Hunsley, Eric. 1986. Administration removes telephones from dorms. *Old Gold and Black* 70 (1, August 29): 1.

James, Joni. 1986. Extended visitation goes into effect this semester. *Old Gold and Black* 70 (1, August 29): 1.

James, Joni. 1987. Dekes reject IFC proposal, will not seek WFU recognition. *Old Gold and Black* 70 (24, April 3): 1.

Joyner, G. William. 1986. Giving to Wake Forest up $8.6 million. *Wake Forest University Magazine* 33 (2, October): 30.

Killebrew, Chad. 1987. Athletic council approves volleyball termination. *Old Gold and Black* 70 (22, March 20): 1.

Koontz, Colleen. 1986. Wake watchers weigh in as hit. *Old Gold and Black* 70 (1, August 29): 11.

Legan, Tom. 1986. Business tops list of popular majors. *Old Gold and Black* 70 (8, October 16): 1.

Liberal encores. 1986. *Old Gold and Black* 70 (12, November 14): 4.

Pretorius, Scott. 1986. SG gains more lower seating for students. *Old Gold and Black* 70 (2, September 5): 1.

Pretorius, Scott. 1987. Undergraduate tuition increases by 9.9 percent. *Old Gold and Black* 70 (16, January 30): 1.

Pretorius, Scott. 1987. Legislature condemns harassment. *Old Gold and Black* 70 (17, February 6): 1.

Robinson, B. S. 1987. Wake Forest team wins national competition. *Winston-Salem Journal* (March 23). Reprinted by permission in the *Wake Forest University Magazine* 33(6, June 1987): 7.

Rose, C. P. Jr. 1987. Moot Court team brings home the silver. *Wake Forest Magazine* 33 (6, June): 6.

Sampsell, Dave. 1986. Baptist change role at WFU. *Old Gold and Black* 70 (12, November 14): 1.

Sampsell, Dave. 1987. Museum of Man moves to new location; open Monday. *Old Gold and Black* 70 (15, January 16): 2.

Varholy, Cristine. M. 1986. People magazine cites WFU on value school list. *Old Gold and Black* 70 (14, December 5): 1.

Woodard, B. 1986. Deacon golfers come from behind to win NCAA tournament. *Wake Forest University Magazine* 33 (1, August): 16–17.

Yarger, Lisa. 1987. Registration. *Old Gold and Black* 70 (15, January 16): 1.

1987–1988

Chapman, Harriet. 1988. Wingate computer lab opens. *Old Gold and Black* 71 (17, January 29): 3.

Chapman, Harriet. 1988. Trustees vote to raise tuition. *Old Gold and Black* 71 (19, February 12): 1, 10.

Dean, Brian. 1988. Faculty passes resolutions. *Old Gold and Black* 71 (23, March 18): 1, 8.

Dopke, Kevin. 1987. Policy allows painting in dorms. *Old Gold and Black* 71 (1, August 28): 3.

Faculty salaries show increase over 5-year period. 1988. *Window on Wake Forest II* (2, March): 4.

Greene, Kelly. 1988. Women's issues group supports WFU gay and lesbian students. *Old Gold and Black* 71 (21, February 26): 1, 8.

Hollowell, Lin. 1988. Faculty, staff want day care for Wake Forest community, *Old Gold and Black* 71 (21, February 26): 1, 8.

Hunsley, Eric. 1987. Campus begins 5-year beautification plan. *Old Gold and Black* 71 (6, October 3): 1.

Hunsley, Eric. 1987. Capital planning committee creates long-range plans. *Old Gold and Black,* 71 (9, October 26): 1.

Huthwaite, Lance. 1987. Decision-making program offered to upperclass leaders. *Old Gold and Black* 71 (13, November 20): 3.

Killebrew, Anita. 1988. Wake Forest senior named best collegiate debater in nation. *Old Gold and Black* 71 (26, April 8): 1, 3.

McKinley, Michael. 1988. WFU adopts minority recruitment plan. *Old Gold and Black* 71 (29, April 29): 1, 8.

Morton, Elizabeth. 1988. Hearn develops program to build communication. *Old Gold and Black* 71 (25, April 1): 1, 8.

Perritt, H. Franklin. III. 1988. Board approves capital plan. *Old Gold and Black* 71 (26, April 8): 1, 3.

Poovey, Cherin. 1988. Student activists: They make things happen. *Wake Forest University Magazine* 34 (3, April): 19–21.

Poovey, Cherin. 1988. After 39 years, she's calling time out. *Wake Forest University Magazine* 34 (3, April): 26–28.

Pretorius, Scott. 1987. Reynolds will lease building from WFU. *Old Gold and Black* 71 (1, August 28): 1.

$2 Million grant will support faculty salaries, research. (1988, October/November). *Window on Wake Forest* 2 (8): 8.

Walker, Sam. 2008. Saying goodbye. *Gold Rush* 17 (15, May 24): 6–7.

Whitman, Jeanne. 1988. Evening MBA has a home of its own. *Wake Forest University Magazine* 34 (3, April): 23–25.

Whitman, Jeanne. 1988. The admissions office has its hands full these days. *Wake Forest University Magazine* 34 (5, June): 12.

Yarger, Lisa. 1987. Video craze hits the admissions office. *Old Gold and Black* 71 (5, September 25): 1.

Yarger, Lisa. 1987. New fight song celebrates Deacon victories. *Old Gold and Black* 71 (5, October 16): 2.

Yarger, Lisa. 1987. Report questions WFU student values. *Old Gold and Black* 71 (8, October 16): 1, 9.

Yarger, Lisa. 1988. Library halts acquisitions. *Old Gold and Black* 71 (15, January 15): 1, 3.

Yarger, Lisa. 1988. WFU Library resumes book purchases. *Old Gold and Black* 71 (16, January 22): 1, 5.

1988–1989

Budget boosts faculty salaries, financial aid. 1989. *Window on Wake Forest* 3 (5, May): 3.

Chapman, Harriet. 1989. Trustees pass tuition increase. *Old Gold and Black* 72 (19, February 10): 1, 5.

Dean, Brian. 1988. Wake Forest succeeds in efforts to increase minority student enrollment. *Old Gold and Black* 72 (2, September 9): 1.

Drayer, Dan. 1988. Pit converted into successful press filing center. *Old Gold and Black* 7 2 (5, September 30): 2.

Eller, Amanda. 1988. Long awaited security system finally implemented in campus dormitories. *Old Gold and Black* 72 (8, October 21): 1.

Fugate, J. D. 1988. Undergraduates manage to attend debate despite original ticket scarcity. *Old Gold and Black* 72 (5, September 30): 1, 5.

Greene, Kelly, Dean, Brian, & Tescoine, Lynne. 1988. New visitation policy takes effect this fall. *Old Gold and Black* 71 (Tabloid 1 August 25A): 1.

Greene, Kelly, Dean, Brian, & Tescoine, Lynne. 1988. Registration offers chance to apply for debate tickets. *Old Gold and Black* 71 (Tabloid 1, August 25B): 1.

Greene, Kelly., Dean, Brian & Tescoine, Lynne. 1988. Campus mourns tragic losses. *Old Gold and Black* 72 (1, September 2): 2.

Hale, Shelley. 1988. Students Against Apartheid hold rally for diverstiture. *Old Gold and Black* 72 (13, December 2): 1, 4.

Hale, Shelley. 1989. Group rallies for divestment. *Old Gold and Black* 72 (29, April 28): 1, 6.

Killebrew, Anita. 1988. Housing brings student disappointment. *Old Gold and Black* 72 (1, September 2): 1, 9.

Koontz, Colleen. 1988. Deacons make personal attack on substance abuse problem. *Old Gold and Black* 72 (6, October 7): 9.

Koontz, Colleen. 1988. Deacon Spirits reorganize for basketball season. *Old Gold and Black* 72 (13, December 2): 8.

McKinley, Michael. 1988. Hearn administration has enhanced Wake Forest. *Old Gold and Black* 72 (7, October 13): 1, 5.

McKinley, Michael. 1989. Hearn names new WFU law school dean. *Old Gold and Black* 72 (26, April 7): 1, 4.

Pinyan, Clint. 1988. McGregor joins Hornets radio, leaves WFU. *Old Gold and Black* 72 (5, September 30): 9, 11.

Pinyan, Clint. 1988. Men runners receive bid to the NCAA tourney. *Old Gold and Black* 72 (12, November 18): 9, 11.

Nardo, John. 1989. Landscaper advises transplanting of quad trees. *Old Gold and Black* 72 (19, February 10): 2.

Those medals sure can add some weight. 1988. *Window on Wake Forest* 2 (9, December): 4.

Vaughn, Jennie. 1989. Blaze blackens Pika suite. *Old Gold and Black* 72 (20, February 17): 1, 4.

Vaughn, Jennie. 1989. Presidential aides receive excellent reviews. *Old Gold and Black* 72 (20, February 17): 2.

1989–1990

Blake, Russ. 1990. Hearn appears on ABC news show, talks about education of athletes. *Old Gold and Black* 73 (23, March 23): 1.

Chapman, Harriet. 1989. Campus pub to open this month. *Old Gold and Black* 73 (1, September 1): 1, 5.

Chapman, Harriet. 1990. Trustees raise tuition to $9,700 for 1990–1991. *Old Gold and Black* 73 (17, February 2): 1, 5.

Dixon, Brad. 1989. President Hearn receives doctorate degree from Tokai University. *Old Gold and Black* 73 (11, November 10): 2.

Drayer, Dan. 1989. Students see Chinese unrest. *Old Gold and Black* 73 (1, September 1): 1, 5.

Forum to Focus on Civil Rights Acts of 1964. 1989. *Window on Wake Forest* 3 (10, November): 1–2.

Gaver, Vince. 1989. University clubroom fails to draw large crowds. *Old Gold and Black* 73 (10, November 3): 1.

Greene, Kelly. 1990. A decade with the Deacons. *Old Gold and Black* 73 (15, January 19): 8.

Group promotes interests of women faculty, adminstrators. 1990. *Window on Wake Forest* 4 (3, May): 1.

Horton, Bill. 1989. Volunteer corps starts 'Helping you to help others.' *Old Gold and Black* 73 (9, October 27): 3.

Lantz, Rocky. 1990. Report finds guard's action discriminatory. *Old Gold and Black* 73 (17, February 2): 1.

Listeners heed call; WFDD prepares for new home. 1990. *Wake Forest University Magazine* 36 (4, April): 25.

Martin, Bo. 1990. WFU restores Graylyn's Mews. *Old Gold and Black* 73 (16, January 26): 3, 4.

Martin, Bo. 1990. WFU collects $151,791 for parking tickets. *Old Gold and Black* 73 (18, February 9): 1, 4.

Martin, Bo. 1990. University installs new systems of signs. *Old Gold and Black* 73 (21, March 2): 2.

McKinley, Michael. 1989. Student I.D.s now required at gym entrance. *Old Gold and Black* 73 (13, December 1): 1, 4.

McKinley, Michael. 1990. Graduate student represents WFU in Playboy's 'Girls of the ACC.' *Old Gold and Black* 73 (21, March 2): 1, 4.

McQueeny, Ryan. 1989. Playboy interviews; police disband protest. *Old Gold and Black* 73 (11, November 10): 1, 4.

Mohl, Steph. 1990. Apartheid rally awaits trustees. *Old Gold and Black* 73 (16, January 26): 1, 5.

Mohl, Steph. 1990. 200 students participate in volunteer corps. *Old Gold and Black* 73 (25, April 6): 2.

Parking management. 1989. *Window on Wake Forest* 3 (9, October): 2.

Pringle, Alan. 1990. Hearn moves into 10,000 square-foot home. *Old Gold and Black* 73 (15, January 19): 2.

Ramey, Janet. 1989. New campus group will provide 'safe rides.' *Old Gold and Black* 72 (16, January 20): 3.

Rodman, Stephen. 1990. *USA Today* recognizes WFU students. *Old Gold and Black* 73 (16, January 26): 1, 5.

Seana Arnold wins All-American Recognition. 1990. *Wake Forest University Magazine* 36 (3, February): 17.

Signage system changing face of Reynolda Campus. 1989. *Window on Wake Forest* 4 (4, April): 1.

Sherwood, Nancy. 1989. Music professor earns Fulbright scholar grant. *Old Gold and Black* 73 (9, October 27): 13.

Spellers, Stephanie. 1990. Wake Forest doubles number of black faculty members within two years. *Old Gold and Black* 73 (20, February): 1, 5.

Vaughn, Jennie. 1989. WFU begins investigation of racial incident. *Old Gold and Black* 73 (11, November 10): 1, 4.

Vaughn, Jennie. 1990. Salem Hall closed until at least April 6 because of discovery of asbestos. *Old Gold and Black* 73 (23, March 23): 1, 5.

Vaughn, Jennie., & Chapman, Harriet. 1989. Honor council finds Tim Bell guilty. *Old Gold and Black* 73 (13, December 1): 1, 5.

Z. Smith Reynolds Grant will extend minority scholarship program. 1990. *Wake Forest University Magazine* 36 (3, February): 25.

1990–1991

Cotton Named acting dean of graduate school. 1990. *Window on Wake Forest* 4 (8, September): 4.

Faculty, staff pledge $1.5 million. 1991. *Window on Wake Forest* 5 (3, April): 1–2.

Mohl, Steph. 1990. New environmental committee to implement recycling program. *Old Gold and Black* 74 (1, August 31): 1, 5.

People, programs are focus of campaign. 1990. *Wake Forest University Magazine* 36 (5, July): 29.

University Center is dedicated. 1990. *Wake Forest University Magazine* 37 (2, November): 3–5.

Vaughn, Jennie. 1990. Cable TV installed during summer. *Old Gold and Black* 74 (1, August 31): 2.

Whitman, Jeanne. 1990. David G. Brown. *Wake Forest University Magazine* 37 (1, September): 12–15.

Worrells pledge $5 million to Professional Center. 1990. *Wake Forest University Magazine* 37 (2, November): 6–7.

ZSR announces gift; faculty are honored. 1991. *Window on Wake Forest* 5 (2, March): 1.

1991–1992

Aging is advanced. 1991. *Wake Forest University Magazine* 38 (2, September): 3–4.

Bargeron, Kristen. 1991. 'My door is open.' *Old Gold and Black* 75 (2, September 5): 8.

Blue, Kelly. 1991. SG begins campus newspaper recycling program this week. *Old Gold and Black* 75 (13, November 21): 1, 3.

Blue, Kelly. 1992. University community to travel to old campus. *Old Gold and Black* 75 (19, February 13): 2.

Boutwell, Julie. 1991. Five new theme houses in existence this year for a wide variety of groups. *Old Gold and Black* 75 (2, September 5): 3.

Broadcast News. 1991. *Wake Forest University Magazine* 38 (2, September): 2–3.

Chevy, Cherry. 1991. 300 Freshmen choose new 'substance-free' housing. *Old Gold and Black* 75 (Tabloid 1, August 22): 1, 3.

Chevy, Cherry. 1991. 'New' fraternity obtains charter after 22 years. *Old Gold and Black* 75 (2, September 5): 1.

David, Laurence. 1992. A different world. *Old Gold and Black* 75 (23, March 19): 5.

Dixon, Brad. 1992. University theatre celebrates 50 years of excellence. *Old Gold and Black* 75 (20, February 20): 11.

Dixon, Brad. 1992. Board approves small budget. *Old Gold and Black* 75 (26, April 9): 1, 5.

Dunlop, Julie. 1991. ASA forms to give help to Asians. *Old Gold and Black* 75 (13, November 21): 4.

Dunlop, Julie. 1992. Wake Forest featured as one of 35 most beautiful campuses in the US. *Old Gold and Black* 75 (16, January 23): 5.

Dunlop, Julie. 1992. Registration in spring will become a reality. *Old Gold and Black* 75 (23, March 19): 1, 3.

Eller, Amanda. 1991. Sunday starts school year. *Old Gold and Black* 75 (Tabloid 1, August 22): 10.

Fitzgerald, Mike. 1991. Faculty committee proposes recommendations for student-athletes. *Old Gold and Black* 75 (8, October 17): 1.

Galloway, Eli. 1992. The ground of our being. *Wake Forest University Magazine* 39 (3, March): 32–33.

Grant, Scott. 1992. Americans need to turn to each other, pastor says. *Old Gold and Black* 75 (16, January 23): 1, 5.

Hudson, Chris. 1991. Soccer loses in NCAA first round. *Old Gold and Black* 73 (13, November 21): 11.

King, Kerry. 2011. Celebrating the Wilson Wing's 20th Anniversary. *Wake Forest Magazine* (October 18). http://magazine.wfu.edu/2011/10/18/celebrating-the-wilson-wings-20th-anniversary/

Lantz, Rocky. 1991. Faculty Drive permanently closed to through traffic. *Old Gold and Black* 75 (6, October 3): 2.

Mack, Terese. 1992. Project *Pro Humanitate* reaches goal. *Old Gold and Black* 75 (23, March 19): 1.

Mohl, Steph. 1991. Ch-Ch-Ch-Ch-Change. *Old Gold and Black* 75 (Tabloid 1, August 22): 9.

Mohl, Steph. 1991. Wake Forest community to build Habitat house. *Old Gold and Black* 75 (2, September 5): 2.

Mohl, Steph. 1991. ARA manager attacked in fourth assault Tuesday. *Old Gold and Black* 75 (3, September 12): 1, 3.

Mohl, Steph. 1991. Library extends hours due to student demand. *Old Gold and Black* 75 (11, November 7): 2.

Mohl, Steph. 1991. ACC student leaders meet to discuss concerns. *Old Gold and Black* 75 (14, December 5): 1, 5.

Mohl, Steph. 1992. Wilson to be honored during today's festivities. *Old Gold and Black* 75 (18, February 6): 1, 5.

Reddick, Jay. 1992. Sanchez steps down as women's basketball coach. *Old Gold and Black* 75 (25, April 2): 11.

Seeman, Rob. 1991. Black Student Alliance begins newspaper. *Old Gold and Black* 75 (13, November 21): 2.

Shaw, Bynum. 1992. The year the curtain went up. *Wake Forest University Magazine* 39 (3, March): 34–35.

Southern, Eddie. 1991. Administration size doubles in 10 years. *Old Gold and Black* 75 (8, October 17): 1, 3.

Southern, Eddie. 1991. Day students receive lounge. *Old Gold and Black* 75 (10, October 24): 5.

Southern, Eddie. 1992. Administrators make strange bedfellows as part of Dorm Storm. *Old Gold and Black* 75 (17, January 30): 1, 5.

Southern, Eddie. 1992. Journalists to honor *Esquire* editor. *Old Gold and Black* 75 (25, April 2): 1.

Southern, Eddie. 1993. North Carolina students become minority at Wake Forest. *Old Gold and Black* 76 (18, February 4): 8.

Spellers, Stephanie. 1992. Historical trek to old campus preserves heritage, renews hopes. *Old Gold and Black* 75 (24, March 26): 11.

Spiraling excellence. 1992. *Wake Forest University Magazine* 39 (3, March): 6–7.

The cost of quality. 1992. *Wake Forest University Magazine* 39 (3, March): 5.

The end of the road. 1991. *Window on Wake Forest* 5 (6, August): 1.

The wings of a man. 1992. *Wake Forest University Magazine.* 39 (3, March): 2–4.

The roar of the winner's circle. 1992. *Wake Forest University Magazine* 39 (4, June): 33.

Williams, Eric. 1992. Blacks blessed with leadership, King says. *Old Gold and Black* 75 (24, March 26): 1.

Woodruff, Jay. 1991. Student shuttle bus to begin operation on Sunday. *Old Gold and Black* 75 (9, October 24): 2.

1992–1993

Agnoli, Benedetta. 1993. First female black student shares life experiences. *Old Gold and Black* 76 (20, February 18): 2.

Agnoli, Benedetta. 1993. PREPAR promotes awareness of rape. *Old Gold and Black* 76 (21, February 25): 1, 6.

Almanac. 1993. *Wake Forest University Magazine* 41 (1, September): 8.

Blue, Kelly. 1993. New hall to help housing problem. *Old Gold and Black* 76 (22, March 4): 4.

Book buoyers. 1995. *Wake Forest University Press* 42 (3, March): 13.

Boyette, Sandra C. 1993. Goodbye, sweet house. *Window on Wake Forest* (January): 16.

Burford, Valencia. 1992. Library adds computer, media, video services. *Old Gold and Black* 75 (3, September 10): 2.

Chevy, Cherry. 1992. Scholarships eliminated. *Old Gold and Black* 76 (6, October 1): 1, 5.

Coffer, Natalie. 1992. Campus-wide power outage causes flooding in lower parking lot. *Old Gold and Black* 76 (14, December 3): 1.

Dixon, Brad. 1992. Substance-free housing option expanded for freshman students. *Old Gold and Black* 76 (Tabloid 1, August 20): 2.

Dixon, Brad. 1992. Committee enacts new alcohol policy. *Old Gold and Black* 76 (2, September 3): 1, 5.

Donath, Lori. 1992. Workers renovate chapel after 40 years. *Old Gold and Black* 76 (9, October 22): 3.

Dreaming with an open eye. 1992. *Wake Forest University Magazine* 40 (2, December): 3.

Dunlop, Julie. 1992. Five decades of women discuss changes at WFU. *Old Gold and Black* 76 (1, August 27): 2.

First things first. 1993. *Wake Forest University Magazine* 40 (3, March): 6.

Fitzergerald, Mick. 1992. Women's cross-country wins first district title; men also qualify for NCAAs. *Old Gold and Black* 76 (13, November 19): 13.

Fyten, David. 1992. Women at 50. *Wake Forest University Magazine* 40 (1, September): 11–14, 17, 20.

Fyten, David. 1992. Dreaming with an open eye. *Window on Wake Forest* (November): 1–2.

Fyten, David. 1993. A leaner machine. *Window on Wake Forest* (January): 2.

Gidwani, Rahul. 1993. Board of trustees increases tuition to $12,996. *Old Gold and Black* 76 (19, February 11): 1, 5.

Gidwani, Rahul. 1993. Greek organizations accept 329 pledges after spring rush. *Old Gold and Black* 76 (19, February 11): 3.

Gidwani, Rahul. 1993. Administrators, faculty to spend night with students as part of 'Dorm Storm 2.' *Old Gold and Black* 76 (20, February 18): 1.

Goodman, Joy. 1993. Reynolda Campus endowment keeps pace with University budget increase. *Old Gold and Black* 76 (21, February 25): 1.

Its day in the sun. 1993. *Wake Forest University Magazine* 40 (4, June): 3.

King, Kerry M. 1993. Jewel on the crown. *Wake Forest University Magazine* 40 (4, June): 32.

Lerman, Jay. 1993. 'Storm of the Century' slams campus. *Old Gold and Black* 76 (23, March 18): 1, 5.

Mack, Terese. 1992. Service core. *Window on Wake Forest* (October): 3.

Mack, Terese. 1992. Men to women ratio nears 50 percent for freshman students. *Old Gold and Black* 76 (Tabloid 1, August 20): 1, 3.

Mack, Terese. 1992. ARA takes over Sundry Shop, debuts Dunkin' Donuts products. *Old Gold and Black* 76 (1, August 27): 4.

Mack, Terese. 1992. Students appear on nationwide news program. *Old Gold and Black* 76 (6, October 1): 1, 6.

Mack, Terese. 1992. WFU students discuss election on MacNeil/Lehrer New Hour. *Old Gold and Black* 76 (8, October 15): 1, 5.

Mack, Terese. 1993. 435 men, women join Rush to find new brothers, sisters. *Old Gold and Black* 76 (16, January 21): 1, 5.

Martin, Lisa. 1992. SG beings pilot glass recycling program in four residence halls. *Old Gold and Black* 76 (11, November 3): 3.

Mohl, Steph. 1992. Volunteer coordinator leaves post. *Old Gold and Black* 76 (1, August 27): 1, 3.

Mohl, Steph. 1992. Prize-winning journalist speaks at convocation. *Old Gold and Black* 76 (1, August 27): 1, 5.

Moore, Rusty. 1992. Sweet Honey unites through its brilliant music. *Old Gold and Black* 76 (5, September 24): 12.

Quigley, Bernie. 1993. The TQM Journey. *Window on Wake Forest* (January): 1, 3.

Quigley, Bernie. 1993. Awake in wonderment. *Wake Forest University Magazine* 41 (1, September): 26–27.

Reece, Tiffany. 1993. Students plan trip to inauguration. *Old Gold and Black* 76 (15, January 14): 1.

Reddick, Jay. 1992. For Wake Forest fans, win over Clemson 'unbelievable.' *Old Gold and Black* 76 (11, November 5): 12.

Rinker, John. 1993. WAKE Radio plans future, explores past decade on campus. *Old Gold and Black* 76 (21, February 25): 3.

The Campus Plan. 1992. *Window on Wake Forest* (September): 5.

The pulse of morning. 1993. *Wake Forest University Magazine* 40 (3, March): 4.

The end of an era. 1992. *Wake Forest University Magazine* 40 (1, September): 4–5.

Uzwiak, Brian J. 1993. The rise and rise of tuition. *Old Gold and Black* 76 (19, February 11): 8.

Uzwiak, Brian J. 1993. Women Greeks to get lounges in '94. *Old Gold and Black* 76 (22, March 4): 1, 3.

Woodruff, Jay. 1992. Administration changes practices of student judiciary. *Old Gold and Black* 76 (1, August 27): 1, 3.

Woodruff, Jay. 1993. Hanes donates Winston estate, American art to Wake Forest. *Old Gold and Black* 76 (15, January 14): 1, 6.

Woodruff, Jay. 1993. University protest Critic's use of name. *Old Gold and Black* 76 (23, March 18): 1, 3.

Wright, Richard. 1992. Rush ends with 178 pledges. *Old Gold and Black* 76 (5, September 24): 3.

1993–1994

Almanac. 1993. *Wake Forest University Magazine* 41 (1, September): 8.

Almanac. 1994. *Wake Forest University Magazine* 41 (3, March): 6.

Fyten, David. 1993. With a song in their hearts. *Wake Forest University Magazine* 41 (2, December): 14–18.

Fyten, David. 1994. At a milestone and a crossroads. *Wake Forest University Magazine* 41 (3, March): 12–21.

Good grades. 1993. *Wake Forest University Magazine* 41 (2, December): 12.

Hendrick, J. Edwin. 1994. *Wake Forest University School of Law: 100 years of legal education 1894–1994.* Winston-Salem, NC: Wake Forest University.

King, Kerry. 1995. Its promise fulfilled. *Wake Forest University Magazine* 42 (4, June): 10–13.

On with the game. 1994. *Wake Forest University Magazine* 42 (1, September): 3.

Pillars of an institution. 1993. *Wake Forest University Magazine* 41 (1, September): 3.

Son honors father with teaching excellence awards. 1994. *Wake Forest University Magazine* 41 (3, March): 44.

'The work of many hands.' 1993. *Wake Forest University Magazine* 41 (2, December): 2.

1994–1995

A lost inspiration. 1994. *Wake Forest University Magazine* 42 (2, December): 7.

Almanac. 1994. *Wake Forest University Magazine* 42 (1, September): 4.

Almanac. 1994, December. *Wake Forest University Magazine* 42 (2, December): 7.

Almanac. 1995. *Wake Forest Magazine* 42 (3, March): 9.

Almanac. 1995. *Wake Forest University Magazine* 43 (2, December): 5.

Bold new blueprint. 1995. *Wake Forest University Magazine* 42 (4, June): 3.

Debate squad. 1995. *Wake Forest University Magazine* 42 (4, June): 3.

First tier. 1994. *Wake Forest University Magazine* 42 (2, September): 3.

Fyten, David. 1995. Back to the future. *Wake Forest University Magazine* 43 (1, September): 8–14.

Italian Olympic Team to train at WFU. 1995. *Wake Forest University Magazine* 42 (3, March): 34.

Last hand at cards. 1995. *Window on Wake Forest* (March): 12.

Major science. 1994. *Wake Forest University Magazine* 42 (2, December): 8.

Profound. 1995. *Wake Forest Magazine* 42 (3, March): 9.

Regeneration. 1995. *Wake Forest University Magazine* 42 (3, March): 35.

Riding a crest. 1994. *Wake Forest University Magazine* 42 (2, December): 4–5.

1995–1996

Almanac. 1995. *Wake Forest University Magazine* 43 (1, September): 4.

Almanac. 1995. *Wake Forest University Magazine* 43 (2, December): 5.

Almanac. 1996. *Wake Forest University Magazine* 43 (4, June): 5.

Almanac. 1996. *Wake Forest University Magazine* 44 (1, September): 4.

Boyette, Sandra C. 1995. Upon this rock. *Wake Forest University Magazine* 43 (2, December): 23–25.

Capshaw. Teri. 1996. *MBA team finishes second in national competition.* News release (May 9).

Cox, Kevin. 1996. *Trustees approve budget, elect new members.* News release (April 19).

Cox, Kevin. 1996. *Bryan gift benefits men's, women's golf programs.* News release (April 22).

Cox, Kevin. 1996. *Leonard named dean of new divinity school.* News release (May 21).

Cox, Kevin. 1996. *Renovation, construction projects fill summer.* Press release (June 6).

Dimmick, Brian. 1996. Faculty abolishes divisional rule. *Old Gold and Black* 79 (23, March 21): 1, 3.

Fyten, David. 1996. The most liberal arts. *Wake Forest University Magazine* 44 (1, September): 20–22, 25–26.

Good chemistry. 1996. *Wake Forest University Magazine* 44 (1, September): 8.

Griffing, Kimberly. 1996. *Stroupe wins national chemistry awards.* Press release (May 10).

Griffing, Kimberly. 1996. *Johnson accepts new post at University of Delaware.* Press release (May 28).

Griffing, Kimberly. 1996. *Rodwell family establishes scholarship at WFU.* Press release (June 11).

Growth pains. 1996. *Wake Forest University Magazine* 43 (4, June): 10.

Milestones. 1996. *Window on Wake Forest* (January): 12.

One more year. 1996. *Wake Forest University Magazine* 43 (4, June): 3.

Saying 'when.' 1995. *Wake Forest University Magazine* 43 (2, December): 15.

Seminal seminars. 1996. *Window on Wake Forest* (January): 1, 3.

Signs of the times. 1996. *Wake Forest University Magazine* 43 (4, June): 11.

The dean of deans departs. 1996. *Wake Forest University Magazine* 44 (1, September): 3.

Triple threat. 1995. *Wake Forest University Magazine* 43 (2, December): 32–33.

Unwired. 1995. *Window on Wake Forest* (October): 12.

Walker, Cheryl. 1996. *WFU Hires Two Media Relations Officers.* News release (June 4).

Whitehead, Lloyd. 1996. Birds of a feather. *Wake Forest University Magazine* 43 (4, June): 26–31.

1996–1997

A loyal son departs. 1996. *Wake Forest University Magazine* 44 (2, December): 2–3.

Almanac. 1996. *Wake Forest University Magazine* 44 (2, December): 9.

Almanac. 1997. *Wake Forest University Magazine* 44 (4, June): 9.

Cox, Kevin. 1996. *Class of 2000 first to benefit from new plan.* News release (August 13).

Cox, Kevin. 1997. *NBC spotlights law school, expert in broadcast.* Press release (February 5).

Cox, Kevin. 1997. *ABC's "Nightline" to broadcast live from wait chapel.* Press release (February 6).

Cox, Kevin. 1997. *WFU switches to 758 telephone prefix.* Press release (July 1).

First-class treatment. 1996. *Window on Wake Forest* (August/September); 1, 4.

Fyten, David. 1996. The most liberal arts. *Wake Forest University Magazine* 44 (1, September): 20–22, 25–26).

Fyten, David. 1997. Advancement. *Wake Forest University Magazine* 44 (4, June): 11.

Griffing, Kimberly. 1996. *Wilkerson named Acting Dean of Calloway School.* News release (August 12).

Griffing, Kimberly. 1996. *Professor Contributes to Surgeon General's Report.* News release (July 12).

Griffing, Kimberly. 1997. *Wilkerson Named Dean of Calloway School.* News release (May 20).

King, Kerry. 1997. We meet again. *Wake Forest University Magazine* 44 (3, March): 8.

King, Kerry. 1997. Leadership's name. *Wake Forest University Magazine* 44 (4, June): 11.

Loss of innocents. 1996. *Wake Forest University Magazine* 44 (2, December): 3.

McCollum, Stephen. 1997. Moyer named dean of Babcock School. Press release (March 20).

Thompson, Wayne. 1996. Support center expands hours. News release (September 11).

Thompson, Wayne. 1996. *WFU begins new construction program.* News release (November 13).

Thompson, Wayne. 1996. *Biologist finds seabird kills in order to thrive.* News release (December 6).

Thompson, Wayne. 1997. *Public affairs takes top honors for communications.* Press release (February 4).

Thompson, Wayne. 1997. *Stroupe wins National Science Foundation award.* Press release (May 6).

Thompson, Wayne. 1997. *WFDD news director wins award for report.* Press release (May 1).

Walker, Cheryl. 1996. *WFU to celebrate year of the arts for 1996–97.* News release (August 7).

Walker, Cheryl. 1996. *Freshman to arrive from 41 states.* News release (August 15).

Walker, Cheryl. 1996. *Charlotte Opal becomes WFU's latest Rhodes Scholar.* News release (December 9).

Walker, Cheryl. 1997. *WFU helps women surf for science/math careers.* News release (January 7).

Walker, Cheryl. 1997. *Annual music competitions to be held.* Press release (February 12).

Walker, Cheryl. 1997. Alec Baldwin to star in "Love Letters." Press release (February 27).

1997–1998

Andrews, Amy A.. 1988. Golden days of radio. *Window on Wake Forest* (May): 1, 3.

Dockham, Ellen. 1997. Rage to justice. *Wake Forest University Magazine* 45 (2, December): 2–4.

Dockham, Ellen. 1998. A gateway to the glorious. *Wake Forest University Magazine* 45 (4, June): 10–13.

Dockham, Ellen. 1997. Women's agenda. *Window on Wake Forest* (October): 1, 3.

Dockham, Ellen. 1997. Women's agenda. *Wake Forest Magazine* 45 (2, December): 4–5.

Fyten, David. 1997. A department under scrutiny. *Wake Forest University Magazine* 45 (1, September): 2–3.

Leading class. 1997. *Window on Wake Forest* (November/December): 1–2.

McCollum, Steve. 1998. In the interest of justice. *Window on Wake Forest* (March): 1, 4.

Morrison, Doug. 1998. No small change. *Window on Wake Forest* (May): 5.

Poovey, Cherin. 1998. Open swimming. *Window on Wake Forest* (March): 3, 12.

Spreading the news. 1998. *Wake Forest University Magazine* 45 (3, March): 4–5.

Two for one. 1998. *Window on Wake Forest* (March): 3–4.

Waters, Andrew. 1997. Comeback of a classic. *Wake Forest University Magazine* 45 (1, September): 4.

Waters, Andrew. 1997. Leading class. *Window on Wake Forest* (November/December): 3, 12.

What's in a name. 1997. *Window on Wake Forest* (November/December): 1–2.

Whitehead, Lloyd. 1997. Class leader. *Wake Forest Magazine* 45 (2, December): 10–11.

Woestendiek, Kathryn. 1998. Souls' journey. *Window on Wake Forest* (August/September): 15.

1998–1999

Andrews, Amy. A 1988. Work in progress. *Window on Wake Forest* (August/September): 4.

Boyette, Sandra. C. 1999. The last word. *Wake Forest Magazine* 46 (3, March): 64.

Brewer, Emily. 1999. As a matter of course. *Window on Wake Forest* (February): 2.

Elliott, Frank. 1999. Millennial mission. *Window on Wake Forest* (January): 1, 3.

End of an era. 1998. *Window on Wake Forest* (August/September): 7.

John Templeton Foundation (Eds.). (1999). *Colleges that encourage character development*. Philadelphia, PA: Author.

Poovey, Cherin. C. 1999. Fit as can be. *Wake Forest Magazine* 46 (3, March): 4.

Trinity. 1998. *Window on Wake Forest* (August/September): 13.

Waters, Andrew. 1999. A year old and growing. *Window on Wake Forest* (January): 3.

1999–2000

Carr, Genie. 1999. Its way. *Window on Wake Forest* 11 (2, October): 1, 3.

Closing the gap. 2000. *Wake Forest Magazine* 47 (3, March): 5.

Dockham, Ellen. 1999. A world-class leader. *Window on Wake Forest* 11 (2, December): 4.

Elliott, Frank. 2000. No news was good news. *Window on Wake Forest* 11 (5, February): 2, 4.

Elliott, Frank. 2000. A super computer. *Wake Forest Magazine* 47 (4, June): 10–11.

Fyten, David. 1999. Housing for the homeless. *Window on Wake Forest* 11 (1 August/September): 1–2.

Fyten, David. 2000. Closing the gap. *Window on Wake Forest* 11 (5, February): 1–2.

Fyten, David. 2000. Closing the gap. *Wake Forest Magazine* 47 (3, March): 5.

Fyten, David. 2000. *Wake Forest Magazine* 47 (3, March): 2–3.

Fyten, David. 2000. Aired news on WFDD. *Window on Wake Forest* 11 (6, March): 11.

Fyten, David. 2000. Which first? *Window on Wake Forest* 11 (8, May): 1–2.

Hoogervorst, Amy Andrews. 2001. Hard work, hard play. *Window on Wake Forest* 13 (1, August/September): 1, 4.

King, Kerry. 2000. Campaign promise. *Wake Forest Magazine* 47 (3, March): 7.

King, Kerry. 2013. The rise of *Pro Humanitate* in students' lives. *Wake Forest Magazine* 61 (1, Fall): 61–65.

Poe, Patricia. 1999. Scientific advancement. *Window on Wake Forest* 11 (1, August/September): 6.

Poovey, Cherin. 1999. East with West. *Window on Wake Forest* 11 (1, August/September): 5.

Underwood, Christine. 2000. One of a kind. *Window on Wake Forest* 13 (1, October): 1–2.

Underwood, Christine. 2001. Mouth of the South. *Wake Forest Magazine* 48 (3, March): 8.

2000–2001

Barrett, Brian. 2001. 30-hour famine raises awareness of world hunger. *Old Gold and Black* 84 (24, March 29): A2.

Bays, Jennifer. & Fyten, David. 2000. A grand old party. *Window on Wake Forest* 12 (3, November/December): 1, 3–4.

Campus Chronicle. 2000. ZSR gift is the largest ever pledged to the University. *Wake Forest Magazine* (December): 2.

Changing station. 2000. *Window on Wake Forest* 12 (1 August/September): 2.

Clark, Tom. 2002. First ever *Pro Humanitate* grant recipients announced. *Old Gold and Black* 85 (16, January 24): A5.

Collins, Dan. 2001. Slow track, fast lane. *Wake Forest Magazine* 48 (4, June): 2–3.

Deacon sports ranked 33rd overall nationally in 2000–2001. 2001. *Wake Forest Magazine* 49 (1, September): 33.

Deacons on parade. 2001. *Wake Forest Magazine* 48 (4, June): 42–45.

Dockham, Ellen. 2000. Second party. *Window on Wake Forest* 12 (1, August/September): 1, 3–4.

Dockham, Ellen. 2001. Giving credit to hours. *Window on Wake Forest* 12 (5, February): 1, 3.

Dockham, Ellen. 2001. Campaign on parade. *Window on Wake Forest* 12 (7, April): 1, 3.

Hill, Sheridan. 2000. Bridge-builder. *Window on Wake Forest* 12 (3, November/December): 3.

Hill, Sheridan. 2001. A model of math education. *Wake Forest Magazine* 48 (4, June): 6–7.

McPherson, Dolly. 1994. *Order out of chaos: The autobiographical works of Maya Angelou.* Boston: Little, Brown.

Underwood, Christine. 2001. Passing friend. *Wake Forest Magazine* 48 (4, June): 8.

Walters, Brandon. 2001. University proposes undergraduate tuition hike in 2001–2002. *Old Gold and Black* 84 (24, March 29): 1, 6.

Webster, Jordan. 2001. South Carolina lures Odom from Deacons. *Old Gold and Black* 84 (26, April 12): 1, 3.

2001–2002

A center for soul-search. 2002. *Window on Wake Forest* 13 (4, January): 1.

Angelou Center to focus on minority health. 2002. *Wake Forest Magazine* 49 (3, March): 5.

Coming home. 2002. *Wake Forest Magazine* 49 (4, June): 7–9.

Fyten, David. 2001. Looking up. *Window on Wake Forest* 13 (3, November/December), 2.

Fyten, David. 2002. Brick and mortarboard. *Window on Wake Forest* 13 (8, May): 1, 12.

Fyten, David. 2002. Hallowed ground. *Wake Forest Magazine* (4, June): 6.

Hoogervorst, Amy Andrews. 2001. All-purpose enhancement. *Wake Forest Magazine* 49 (1, September): 4.

King, Kerry. M. 2002. End of an era. *Wake Forest Magazine* 49 (4, June): 4–5.

Mathemagians. 2002. *Wake Forest Magazine* 49 (4, June): 11.

Moretz, Laura. 2001. The man behind the mikes. *Window on Wake Forest* 13 (1, August/September): 1, 3.

P-art-nership. 2002. *Window on Wake Forest* 13 (5, February): 1–2.

Under one. 2002. *Window on Wake Forest* 13 (4, January): 2.

2002–2003

Debate coach of the year. 2003. *Wake Forest Magazine* 50 (4, June): 9.

Dixon Symposium: Confrontation and catharsis. 2003. *Wake Forest Magazine* 50 (4, June): 3.

Dockham, Ellen. 2003. Christ Man. *Wake Forest Magazine* 50 (4, June): 12–19.

2003–2004

Poovey, Cherin. C. 2003. O Sing a new song. *Wake Forest Magazine* 51 (2, December): 19.

Signature facility. 2003. *Wake Forest Magazine* 51 (1, September): 3.

2004–2005

Home, technologically advanced home. 2004. *Wake Forest Magazine* 52 (1, September): 4.

King, Kerry 2005. Servant of ambition. *Wake Forest Magazine* 52 (3, March): 12–32.

Presidential search. 2004. *Wake Forest Magazine* 52 (1, September): 2–3.

2011–2012

Hsu, Angel. 2012. Shorty's a mainstay after five years of controversy. *OGB.online* (accessed May 20, 2012). https://www.google.com/search?q=Old+Gold+and+Black+online&ie=utf-8&oe=utf-8

INDEX

The index covers pages 1 through 406, and is limited to the names of individuals who are mentioned on those pages. The index does not include topics, organizations, performing groups, or special visitors.

A

Acord, Bobbi Jo, 388
Acton, Laura, 232, 258–259
Adamson, Leah, 203
Adkins, Michelle, 395
Agard, Gloria Cooper, 216
Akinc, Helen, 291
Akinc, Umit, 178, 236, 302
Aldhizer, George, 331, 380, 393
Alexander, Matthew, 232
Alimohammadi, Nazlia, 362, 364
Allen, Charles M., 271, 323
Allen, Dede, 80
Allen, Edward F., 223, 320, 368
Allen, Nina, 48, 67
Allen, Sean, 240
Allman, Martha, 187, 200, 315, 380
Almon, Rebecca May, 34
Almond, Eric, 361
Ammons, A. R., 75, 199, 200, 236, 313, 358, 393
Amos, Katherine (Kitty) E., 351

Anders, Shirley, 47
Anderson, Carol, 253, 311
Anderson, David J., 196, 235, 253, 254
Anderson, John P.
    AT&T's Reynolda Road facility conversion, 85
    Athletic Oversight Committee, 114
    athletic policy review, 46
    Baptist State Convention negotiations, 55
    "Birmingham Mafia," 129
    bi-weekly meetings with Leon Corbett, 216
    budget reductions, 85
    Campus Landscape Committee, 103
    Capital Planning Committee, 85
    committee to examine race relations, 65–66
    cost efficiency studies, 146
    Crisis Response Team, 130
    day-care center project, 301
    divinity school committee, 74, 96

    election to Board of Directors of MCNC, 335
    Graylyn restoration, 16
    landscaping plans, 108
    Management Oversight Committee on Admissions, 77
    oversight of substance abuse programs, 65
    program planning committee, 178
    renovations of Amos Cottage, 57
    R.J. Reynolds Tobacco Company lease, 85
    RJR Nabisco headquarters donation, 56
    search committee for Vice President of Academic Affairs, 94
    supervision of construction project, 67
    temporary director of Reynolda House Museum of American Art, 329
    Total Quality Management, 162

tuition increases, 155,
189, 206
Vice President for
Administration and
Budget, 77, 95
Vice President of Planning
and Administration, 9,
10, 107
visitation agreement, 33
WAKE Radio, 262
Anderson, Paul, 253
Andrade, Billy, 42, 43
Andrews, Sharon, 396
Andronica, John, 143
Angell, John William, 76,
127
Angelou, Maya, 76, 158
criticism of, 214
Freshman Evenings, 200
Gardner Calvin Taylor
speech, 74
Maya Angelou Day, 351
National Medal of Arts,
312
North Carolina Award, 75
participation in literary
benefit, 178
reading of Martin Luther
King's "Letter from
Birmingham Jail," 271
recital at United Nations'
fiftieth anniversary
celebration, 196
recital of 1992 presidential
inauguration poem,
158, 159, 174, 230
Reynolds Professor, 44
Sara Lee Corporation
Forerunner Award, 180
And Still I Rise musical,
168
visit of Coretta Scott King,
143, 155
Z. Smith Reynolds
professor, 215–216
Applegate, William B., 334,
335
Archer, Phil, 185–186, 202
Arey, Craig, 118
Armentrout, Kyle, 131

Armistead, Russell, 112
Armstrong, Bill, 218
Arnett, Kathy, 400
Arnold, Seana, 113, 114
Artom, Bianca, 204
Atchison, Jarrod, 352
Atkins, Ross, 219
Auld, Patrick, 117
Auman, Timothy L., 315,
370, 374
Aust, Mark, 272
Austin, Brian M., 30
Averill, Jennifer, 147, 292,
347–348, 365, 368, 386
Avila, Cristopher, 394

B

Babcock, Bill, 98
Backus, Dale, 132, 357
Bader, Jill, 328, 329
Bailey, Allen A., 188
Bailey, Douglass M., 331,
332, 351, 388, 389, 411
Bain, David, 111
Baker, L. M., Jr., 16
Baker, Robert T., 58–59, 77,
95, 129, 135
Baker, Terry, 393
Baker, W. Prentiss, III, 86
Baliga, Ram, 372
Ballbach, Jane, 149
Balzer, Brenda, 395
Banks, E. Pendleton, 111,
161, 253
Banks, Jay, 314, 335, 336
Bannister, Tricia, 103
Barefield, James P., 41, 213,
215, 373
Bargeron, Kristin, 151
Barksdale, David, 354
Barnes, Bernadine, 283
Barnes, Meda, 217
Barnes, Paul W., 272
Barnett, Richard C., 214
Barras, Jamie, 354
Barrow, Harold M., 93, 143,
214
Bartholomew, Bob, 31
Bartholomew, Rebecca, 244

Bartlett, Thomas, 3
Bason, Katie, 357
Basset, Amy, 261
Baugher, Chris, 152
Bavinger, Brooke, 321
Baxley, John, 236
Bayliff, Buck, 255
Beatty, Bethany, 223
Bechtel, Brett, 338, 362
Beck, Robert C., 125, 136,
271
Becker, Liz, 98
Beil, Mary T., 45, 84, 116,
151
Bell, Sylvia, 261
Bell, Tim, 116
Bender, Margaret, 350, 372
Benfield, Marion, 128
Bennett, Annie Schweitzer,
293, 355
Bennett, William, 8
Benson, Cliff, 67, 135
Berg, Jennifer, 312
Bergasel, Anne, 355–356
Bergman, Janet, 336
Berthrong, Merrill, 112–113
Best, Deborah L., 28, 368
1994 Schoonmaker
Faculty Prize for
Community Service,
179
23rd International
Congress of Psychology,
27
Bowman Gray School
of Medicine Venture
Grant, 44
Dean of the College, 368
forum to discuss
undergraduate
education questions,
212
Heritage and Promise
Campaign, 124, 194
Provost Search
Committee, 314
Psychology department
space problem, 225
Wake Forest Professor,
236

Bhattacharya, Ritu, 402
Biedrzycki, Lisa, 338
Bielik, Bea, 336, 337, 345, 357, 376
Bierbach, Ulrich, 390
Bilich, Edward K. (Ted), 15
Billings, Rhoda Bryan, 43, 44, 58, 110, 179
Billue, Sylva, 365
Bindel, Trina, 218, 219, 227
Birnbach, Lisa, 15
Bishop, Anne, 272, 314
Bishop, John E. "Jack," 405
Bissette, Lou, 155
Black, Ralph W., 259
Blackburn, Shelmer Doyle, 388
Blackford, Jenny, 274, 298
Bland, Doug, 114, 133
Bland, Elizabeth, 378
Blank, Thomas Rannels, 388
Bloom, Andy, 182, 198, 199, 218, 227, 316
Blucas, Marc, 193
Blumenthal, Terry, 214
Bogues, Tyrone "Muggsy," 32, 61, 62
Bohrer, Stanley, 394
Boko, Sylvain, 338, 351–352
Booe, Lillian, 101
Borchert, Karen Stephan, 299
Borwick, Douglas, 4
Borwick, Susan, 236
Bourn, Sonya, 102
Bowen, C. David, 196
Bowman, Donna, 50
Bowman, John, 340
Boyce, G. Eugene, 362
Boyd, Beth, 235
Boyd, Renee, 314
Boyd, Steve, 110, 403
Boyette, Sandra C.
    Crisis Response Team, 130
    enrollment decreases, 274
    Grand Award in CASE competition, 198
    media coverage of same-sex union, 283
    NCAA certification steering committee, 182
    planning duties, 216
    research on Tom Jeffries, 379
    study of athletics program, 396
    theme years, 222
    Vice President for University Advancement, 254
    Vice President for University Relations, 237
Boyle, Anne, 93, 196, 354, 368
Bradley, Barbara, 114, 147
Brady, Kelly, 256
Bragg, Nicholas, 190
Brakefield, Betsy, 149
Branch, Joseph, 40, 54, 74
Branson, Brian, 319
Brantley, Russell, 10, 55, 58, 60, 315
Braskamp, Steve, 169
Braswell, Jerry, 211
Braxton, Brad R., 287, 349
Braxton, David, 97
Breckenridge, Saylor, 391
Brée, Germaine, 4, 179
Brehme, Robert, 196
Brehove, Jordan, 339
Brennan, Patrick, 400
Brenner, Herbert, 86
Bridges, Linda McKinnish, 335, 354
Bridges, Sheri, 373
Briggs, Paul, 332
Brinkley, Susan, 226, 243
Britton, Hannah, 133
Brooks, Aja, 402
Brooks, David, 275
Brooks, George E., 36, 51
Brooks, James Taylor, 51
Brooks, Jean Bailey, 51
Brooks, Steve, 250
Brovero, Adrienne, 203
Browers, Michaelle, 328, 368
Browne, Carole L., 44, 94, 126, 187, 234, 289
Brown, David G.
    Always in Touch: A Practical Guide to Ubiquitous Computing, 291
    faculty hiring form reintroduction, 143
    first-year seminars, 229
    interdepartmental scholars' breakfasts, 178–179
    Provost appointment, 125
    Spires of Excellence program, 129, 145–146
    technology consortium, 351
    University priority planning retreat, 178
    Vice President and Dean of the International Center for Computer-Enhanced Learning, 250
    Vice President for Special Programs, 254
    Ways of Thinking about Presidential Campaigns seminar, 307
Brown, David W., 3
Brown, Drew, 272
Brown, Edward, 150
Brown, Paul, 239, 254, 272, 283
Brown, Ricky, 96
Brown, Simpson O. (Skip), 256, 388
Brown, Steve, 96–98, 316
Browne, Robert A., 58, 74, 186
Broyhill, Paul H., 57
Broyles, David, 202
Brubaker, Peter H., 127
Brunso-Bechtold, Judy, 388, 389
Bryan, G. McLeod, 43, 101
Bryan, Joseph M., 205
Buchanan, Christy, 235, 236
Buczek, Mary, 292
Buff, Majorie, 64
Bullock, James R., 59, 95, 181, 254, 342
Bullock, Steven, 98
Bumgarner, Jennifer, 262, 276, 280

Bumgarner, Joseph, 400
Bumgarner, Steve, 200, 201, 205
Bunn, Davis, 365
Bunn, Kevin, 11
Burg, Jennifer, 235
Burgos, Tanya, 186
Burnham, Stuart, 131, 183
Burns, Rachel, 336
Burr, Richard, 206, 405
Burroughs, Julian, 154, 265
Bush, Dave, 317
Butler, Albert, 10
Butler, Jerome, 234
Butts, Mary Claire, 339, 340
Byrum, Porter B., 226

C

Cabada, Gloria, 81, 82
Caldwell, Jim, 165, 166, 182, 201, 255, 273, 292, 316, 325
Caldwell, Robert, 8
Callison, Cleve, 148, 238
Calloway, D. Wayne, 68, 195
    Baptist State Convention negotiations, 54
    donations, 67
    Heritage and Promise campaign, 124
    nomination to Chair the Board of Trustees, 206
    President and CEO of PepsiCo, 37
    Sesquicentennial Campaign, 21
    Vice Chair of University Board of Trustees, 113
    Wayne Calloway School of Business and Accountancy, 195
Cameron, Alan S., 30, 150
Campbell, Will, 323, 324
Cardwell, Charlita, 158
Carl, William F., 49
Carlson, Amanda, 310, 320, 321
Carmichael, Richard D., 27, 312, 368, 375

Caron, Simone M., 179, 196
Carpenter, Coy C., 17, 246
Carpenter, Maureen, 238
Carr, Warren, 3
Carriker, Doug, 194
Carson, Connie, 220, 380
Carter, Stewart, 92, 233, 311, 313, 314
Carville, James, 390
Casey, Dot, 79–80, 98, 166
Cash, W. J., 126
Casstevens, Randy S., 353
Cawood, Hobie, 394
Chalk, Richard E. (Trip), III, 399
Chandler, John W., 7
Channing, Rhoda K., 112
    cybercafé plans, 361
    death of, 375
    Director of Z. Smith Reynolds Library, 112
    implementation of President's Commission on Race Relations report, 146
    Information Management Award, 235
    introduction of technological services, 160
    lay-offs during construction project, 132
    pilot ThinkPad program, 220
    Power Up! program, 184
    review of undergraduate curriculum, 233–234
Chapman, Betsy J., 291
Chapman, Richard, 41, 64
Chappel, John, 32
Chappell, Heather, 275
Chee, Manlin, 184
Childress, Randolph, 147, 166, 192, 193, 210, 316
Chinlund, Cathy, 272
Chorley, Susan, 142
Christensen, Aaron, 117, 119
Christman, Edgar D.
    The Book of Days, 249–250

Divinity School
    Distinguished Service Award, 392
    Freshman Evenings, 200
    Gray Matters program, 84
    "O Sing to the Lord a New Song," 348
    quadruple bypass surgery, 217
    retirement, 353
    scholarship in honor of, 279
Christman, Jean Sholar, 279
Chyzowych, Walter S., 46, 97, 114, 166, 198
Clabo, Tyson, 375
Clark, Anna, 362, 364
Clark, Desmond, 273, 280
Clark, Ed, 117
Clark, Mary Dawne, 395
Clark, Tom, 399
Clarke, Carey, 99
Clarke, Clifford H., 188
Clau, Nuria, 356
Clay, Richard (Dick), 11, 30
Clendenin, Kathryn Ann (KC), 297
Click, Karen, 261
Coates, David, 287, 328, 372
Cobb, Bill, 343
Cobb, Rhoda, 343
Coffey, Jim, 103, 108, 181, 186, 204, 399
Cogdill, Jim, 205
Coghill, George, 167
Cohen, Joel, 379
Cole, Julie B., 95, 130, 178, 205, 213
Cole, Sean, 244
Coleman, Ben, 167
Coleman, Jill, 336
Coles, Stephen, 206
Collins, Ann Marie, 299–300
Collins, Brad, 202
Collins, Michael, 335
Collins, Sue, 189
Collins, William A., 189
Colwell, Linda, 47
Combes, Melissa N., 238, 395

Comito, Irene A., 217
Conley, Jason, 162
Connelly, Earle A., 57, 69
Conner, Tracy, 166, 167
Conner, William E., 296, 379
Connor, Sandra
  Athletic Oversight
    Committee, 114
  budget reductions, 86
  Director of Public
    Information and
    Assistant to the
    President, 58
  Hearn inauguration
    preparations, 4
  Management Oversight
    Committee on
    Admissions, 77
  presidential debate, 90
  search committee for Vice
    President of Academic
    Affairs, 92
  Vice President for Public
    Affairs, 94
  Vice President for
    University Relations,
    107
Cook, Ben, 336
Cook, Rebecca E., 402, 403,
  404
Cooper, Chris, 185, 222
Cooper, Gloria,100, 145,
  178, 180, 197
Cooper, Henry, 101–102, 171
Cooper, Jean, 106
Corbett, Leon
  AT&T's Reynolda Road
    facility conversion, 85
  athletic policy review, 46
  Baptist State Convention
    negotiations, 54–55
  bi-weekly meetings with
    John Anderson, 216
  budget reductions, 85
  Crisis Response Team, 130
  divinity school
    committee, 96
  Executive Secretary/Office
    of the President, 95
  Inauguration Committee, 3

  retirement, 290, 354
  RJR Nabisco headquarter
    space allocation, 56
  Senior Counsel, 314
  University Counsel and
    Secretary to the Board
    of Trustees, 30
  University Legal Counsel,
    116
  University Secretary, 10
  Vice President for Legal
    Affairs, 58
Corkey, Allison, 290
Corpening, Julius H., 8, 45,
  77, 95, 172, 383
Corpening, Wayne, 4, 12, 67
Corrie, Brenda, 11, 42
Corts, Becky, 12
Costley, Gary E., 197,
  237–238
Cott, Paulette, 289
Cotter, James, 350, 372, 373
Cotton, Nancy, 57, 94, 128,
  209
Cotton, Stan, 239
Cottrell, Allin F., 179
Couch, Carolyn, 290
Coverstone, Alan, 81
Covey, Cyclone, 75
Covone, Neil, 131
Cowan, William Raymond,
  37
Cox, Anna, 335
Cox, Kevin, 145, 254, 272,
  308, 319
Cox, Tyler, 394
Craigwell-Graham, Jeanetta,
  402
Crainshaw, Jill, 331
Crater, Marvin, 80
Creech, Zeke, 169, 170
Creel, Colin, 405
Crenshaw, Jill, 282
Cridlin, Jay, 327
Crisp, Marge, 12, 166
Crookenden, Ian, 239
Crouch, Nancy, 314
Crow, William, 358
Crowe, David, 12
Crowell, Alexander, 170–171

Crumpler, Fred Guthrie, 388
Cummins, Emily, 186
Cunningham, Patricia, 215,
  351
Cunnings, Ed, 59
Currin, William C., 95
Curtis, Charlene, 239, 376
Curtis, Michael Kent, 331

D

Dagenbach, Dale, 196–197
Daggy, Kimberlea, 290
Dailey, Dianne, 98, 99, 147,
  182, 198, 317, 336
Daisley, Tricia, 64
Dalton, Mary
  Civil Rights Symposium,
    297
  documentaries, 312, 350,
    392
  Presidential Debate of
    1988, 91
  reading of *Breath: Life in
    the Rhythm of an Iron
    Lung* (Mason), 356
  video yearbooks, 150
  visit with Martha Mason,
    358–359
da Luz, Tony, 239
Daniels, Kate, 160, 196
D'Antona, James, 356
Davey, Jessica, 184, 200, 202,
  203
Davidson, Margaret, 336
Davies, Huw M. L., 93, 178
Davis, Annie Pearl Shore,
  226, 320
Davis, Brook, 396
Davis, Charles M., 24, 147,
  166
Davis, David, 272
Davis, Egbert L., Jr., 49, 120,
  226, 278–279
Davis, Jim, 294
Davis, Julie, 31
Davis, Mike, 50
Davis, Nancy, 51
Davis, Pete, 51
Davis, Stan, 380

Davis, Thomas H., 226, 278–279
Davis, Timothy, 314
Dawson, Beth, 72, 89
Day, Sara, 316, 355
Dean, James A., 388
Dean, Jamie, 339, 389
Dean, Richard, 238, 255, 330
Deaver, Danielle, 261
Dellinger, Bill, 294
DeShazer, Mary, 75, 110, 159, 195, 236, 314
DeVries, David, 198
Dickens, Alan, 46
Dickey, Adam, 320, 340
Dierks, Paul, 77, 94, 127
Dimock, Jeff, 133
Dimock, Ronald V., 9, 331
Dinkins, Kriss, 254, 354
Dinkleberg, John S., 178
Dishman, Lori, 291
Dixon, David, 50
Dixon, Patricia, 159
Dodding, Jim, 22, 115, 131, 148, 219, 222, 230, 257, 387, 398
Dodson, Barry, 247
Doggett, Leane, 81
Doggett, Robert, 193
Dombro, Barry L., 182
Dominick, James (Jay) L., 238, 269, 271, 290, 402
Dooley, Bill, 60, 69, 78, 113, 130, 146, 164
Dopke, Kevin, 102
Doton, Kelly, 348, 368, 376, 386
Dotson, Amy, 261
Dow, Carolyn, 14, 101, 129
Dow, Ramsey, 151
Doyle, Wilbur S., 43–44
Drake, Roxanna, 380
Draughn, Anna, 33
DuBois, Scott, 72, 89
Duchac, Jonathan, 311, 373–374
Dumar, Leah, 199
Duncan, Tim, 192, 210, 211, 217, 240, 309, 316, 376
Dunlop, Laird, 11

Dunn, James M., 282, 405
Dunn, Karen, 12, 46, 61, 113
Dunn, Marilyn, 405
DuPre, Virginia, 100
Dupree, David Wright, 388
Durand, Dan, 262, 299
Durham, Lynn, 323
Durotoye, Yomi, 392, 394
Dyer, David, 193
Dyer, Mary, 265
Dyer, Robert, 265

E

Earle, John R., 125, 161
Early, Doyle, 104, 136, 155
Early, Jim, 357
Easley, Allen, 76, 91
Easley, Edward, 65–66, 201
Easley, Mary, 345
Eckenroth, Gary L., 272
Eckert, Brian, 113, 154
Edelson, Julie, 336
Edgeton, Doug, 314
Edmonson, Ashley, 234
Edwards, Amanda Lee, 262
Edwards, C. Drew, 271
Edwards, Todd, 354
Eggers, Susan, 274
Egleston, Robert, 62
Ehrlich, Bob, 365
Elbertse, Polly, 402
Elkins, Mike, 97
Ellis, Andrea, 299
Ellis, Elizabeth, 380
Else, Joshua, 238, 255
English, Alan, 362, 378–379
Enrico, Roger A., 342
Esch, Gerald W., 30, 128, 143, 215, 286
Escott, Paul D., 210
    administration of Lilly Endowment, 332
    ceremony for fall semester graduates, 233
    Dean of the College, 209–210, 368
    Founders' Day speech, 134
    program planning committee, 178

questions about undergraduate education, 212
    recruitment of female and minority faculty, 197
    Reynolds Professor, 109
    The Minds of the South Symposium, 126
    Z. Smith Reynolds professor, 215
Estelrich, Marisa, 394
Esther, Robert, 117, 128, 136
Estwanik, Chris, 336
Etters, Helen, 130
Ettin, Andrew, 28, 195–196, 352
Eure, Herman, 15, 30, 125, 179, 331, 368, 379
Evans, David, 390–391
Evans, Robert H., 179
Evans, Stephen, 399
Everest, Carl, 127
Everett, Willie, 394
Everman, David, 50
Ewing, Steve, 116

F

Faber, David, 81, 231, 285, 350
Fabyan, Barry, 42
Faircloth, Barry, 357
Faircloth, Bill, 31, 377
Falkenberg, Phil, 214
Fanelli, Deborah, 27
Fansler, Craig, 368
Fansler, Kathy, 278
Farley, Ryan, 381
Farmer, Nathan, 151
Farrow, Raymond Benjamin, III, 105
Faude, Dirk, 145
Faust, Susan, 41, 159, 297, 339
Felders, Theresa, 298
Fenton, Jonathan, 380
Ferrell, James (Jim) L., 45, 120, 129, 180, 204, 278, 291
Finch, Bobby, 255

Finger, Nikki, 203
Finn, David, 362, 372, 373, 402
Fishbein, James, 161
Fitzpatrick, Jim, 381
Fledderman, Rick, 159, 231
Fleer, Jack, 8, 160, 333
Fleeson, William, 349, 352
Fleishman, Brian, 355
Fletcher, Drew, 300
Flick, Jim, 182
Flow, Don, 102
Flow, Roddy, 263, 283, 284, 303
Flow, Vic, 104, 263, 283, 284, 303, 312
Flowe, William H., Sr., 3, 4
Floyd, Max, 198, 294
Folmar, Steven, 310–311
Foote, Evelyn Patricia, 86
Ford, Jay, 349
Ford, Laura C., 30, 45, 178, 198
Ford, Mike, 34, 45, 83, 84, 187, 262, 400
Forrow, Brian D., 323
Forrow, Eleanor Reid, 323
Foskett, Mary, 310
Fosso, Doyle, 43, 312
Foy, Miles, 112, 128, 283
Franklin, Denise, 335, 363
Frantz, Carolyn, 184
Fraser, Ralph S., 3, 214
Freeman, Karen, 239
Frey, Andrew, 202, 203, 223, 262
Frey, Don, 197
Friday, William, 3, 4
Friedenberg, John E.R., 115, 271
Fugate, John David, 50
Fuller, Loraine V., 184
Furgurson, Lauren, 261
Fyten, David, 181, 334

G

Gadd, James R., 86
Gagnon, Joseph, 223
Gala, Candelas, 285

Galaida, Greg, 134
Gallant, Wade M., Jr., 135
Gallo, Larry, 130
Ganzert, Robin Roy, 162
Garber, Mary, 3
Garg, Anjali, 381
Garin, Will, 224
Garrison, Paul S., 279
Gartenstein-Ross, Daveed, 222, 231, 244, 245, 277
Gatesy, Steve, 196
Gatewood, Elizabeth J., 370
Gaudio, Arthur R., 112
Gedicks, Alexander, 259
Geitner, Amy, 12
Gendrich, Cynthia, 317, 372, 373, 374
Gentry, Ivey, 104, 235
Gentry, Rebecca, 185
George, Jennifer, 339, 378
Gerardy, Mary
    advisory committee for annual student activities fee allocation, 379
    Assistant Vice President of the Division of Student Life, 180
    The Book of Days, 249–250
    Coordinator of Gay and Lesbian Students, 314
    Division of Student Life leadership course, 187
    help with transition from societies into sororities, 177–178
    University Traffic Commission, 264
Gerrard, Lew, 199
Geyer, Granice, 34, 36
Gilbert, Michael, 150
Gill, David N., 405
Gill, Diane P., 405
Gillespie, Michele, 353, 388, 389
Gillikin, Cynthia, 339
Gilsenan, Thomas, 45, 129, 181, 238
Ginchereau, Albert P., 16, 45

Givens, Dana, 378
Gladding, Sam
    Assistant to the President for Special Projects, 129
    Associate Provost, 250, 251
    Executive Committee of the North Carolina Association of Independent Colleges and Universities, 162
    first-year seminars, 229
    graduate counseling program, 374
    in Hall of Fame of the University of Alabama at Birmingham's counselor education program, 391
    interim chair of the Department of Religion, 214
    President of the American Counseling Association, 351
    psychological first aid work after September 11, 327, 328
    Race Relations Committee, 201
    supervision of WFDD, 289
    Year of Ethics and Honor, 310
Glenn, Kathleen, 215
Godsey, R. Kirby, 6
Goff, Maeve, 378
Gokhale, Balkrishna, 92
Goldstein, Louis, 6, 32, 242, 287, 317
Goodale, Fairfield, 45
Goodridge, Francie, 61, 80, 199, 293
Goodridge, John, 98, 114, 131, 182, 199, 294
Goodwin, Joy, 185–186, 202
Gordon, Joseph G., 134
Gordon, William (Bill) C., 334, 347, 365, 367, 368, 369, 374

Gore, Arthur D., 37
Gould, Graham, 232
Graham, George, 349, 368, 373
Graham, Sarah, 277
Grant, Mark, 159
Gray, Connie (Mrs. Gordon), 17
Gray, Gordon, 16
Gray, Nick, 381
Gray, Patricia, 27
Greason, Murray, 143, 206, 354, 387–388, 394, 395
Green, Justin, 244
Green, Michael, 372
Green, Nikeya, 376
Greene, A. J., 61, 97
Greene, William B., Jr., 146, 303, 324, 330, 388
Greer, Betsy, 171, 200
Greer, George, 80, 199, 272, 317, 396
Gregg, Lauren, 357
Gregory, Dennis, 59, 85, 100, 169
Griffin, Cook, 31
Griffin, Julie, 258, 259
Griffing, Kimberly S., 217
Griffith, Ross, 11, 45, 95, 145, 212
Griffiths, Robert, 101
Grobe, Jim, 316, 317, 325, 335, 355, 375, 377
Groh, Al, 59
Gross, Brian, 319
Groves, Richard, 42, 74
Gurysh, Steve, 404
Guthold, Martin, 390

H

Haas, Bill, 356, 376–377
Haas, Jerry, 256
Hadari, Saguiv A., 44
Haddock, Jesse, 31, 42, 99, 147
Hadley, David, 161, 187
Haglan, Dennis, 13
Hagy, David, 221, 230, 310, 387

Haining, Robert, 360
Hairston, Kamieka, 389
Hairston, Levar, 340
Hale, Toby, 9, 35, 216, 234, 397
Hall, Dorothy, 351
Hall, Mark, 47, 116, 187
Hall, Randal, 325, 353–354
Hamilton, Donna, 95
Hamilton, Robert, 261
Hamilton, William (Billy), 58, 59, 160, 216, 340
Hammond, Claire, 27–28, 75, 368
Hammond, Dan, 312
Han, James, 74
Hand, Samantha, 255, 284
Hanes, Charlotte, 173, 341
Hanes, R. Philip, Jr., 173, 341
Hans, Heather, 402
Hans, James, 196
Hansen, Julie, 231, 248, 277, 321, 359
Hardgrave, Hannah M., 28
Hardy, Harriet Smith, 157
Harrelson, Walter, 197, 209
Harriger, Katy
  Academic and Community Engagement (ACE) Fellowship program, 270
  Democracy Fellows, 361, 394
  faculty advisory committee, 388
  Harriger Report, 258
  interim advisory committee on editorial concerns, 283
  Jon Reinhardt Award for Excellence in Teaching, 352
  Kulynych Family Omicron Delta Kappa Award, 253
  presidential transition committee, 389
  prominent scholarship honors for students, 41

  Reid-Doyle Prize for Excellence in Teaching, 74
  Teaching and Learning Center, 252–253
  testifying before Senate Subcommittee on Oversight of Government Management, 160
  William C. Friday Fellow for Human Relations, 213
  Zachary T. Smith Professorship, 179
Harris, Carl, 93
Harris, Catherine T., 28, 126, 181, 196, 311
Harris, Erika, 403
Harris, Frederick, 178, 314
Harris, Jamie, 61
Harris, Jennifer, 362, 368, 381
Harrison, J. Kline, 235, 236, 291
Hart, Ronald H., II, 64
Hartzog, Rebecca (Becky) Glen, 290
Hass, Bill, 356, 376–377
Hass, Jerry, 11, 256
Hatch, Julie, 390
Hatch, Nathan O., 389, 405
Hatfield, Weston P., 30, 40, 54, 113, 135, 141, 411
Hattery, Angela, 311, 312, 372, 401
Haus, Maren, 336
Hayashi, Elmer K., 127, 179
Hayes, Harold T. P., 142
Hazen, Michael, 94, 125, 144, 283
Headley, Win, 182
Heard, Richard E., 388
Hearn, Barbara, 3, 4, 32, 35, 37, 47
Hearn, Laura W., 140, 141, 394, 396
Hearn, Lindsay, 3
Hearn, Thomas, 3
Hearn, Thomas K., Jr.

academic requirements
for athletic
scholarships, 46
ACC expansion, 130
accolades, 112, 130
administrative
planning,94
advisory committee for
elm trees, 48
annual commitment to
athletics department,
356
appointment, 1–3
appointment of Richard
Dean, 255
assurance to parents after
September 11, 327
Athletic Oversight
Committee, 114
Baptist governance, 25
Baptist State Convention
negotiations, 40–41,
54–56
Benson University Center
opening ceremony, 134
"Birmingham Mafia," 129
brain cancer treatment,
367
budget guidelines,
277–278, 344, 364
Campaign for Wake
Forest University:
Honoring the Promise,
302, 389
cardiac surgery, 192, 207
Chair of the Knight
Commission, 396
Chair of the Piedmont
Triad Development
Corporation, 146
christening of Thomas K.
Hearn shell, 397
commencement speeches,
1, 21, 39, 53, 71, 73, 89,
107, 123, 139, 157, 175,
191, 209, 229, 249, 267,
281, 305, 325, 327, 347,
367, 387
Committee to Implement
the Report on the

Status of Women,
313–314
communication
between faculty
and administration,
288–289
compensation package,
206
concerns about AT&T's
Reynolda Road facility,
85
concern with eating
disorders among
students, 201
concern with referee
manipulation, 335
concern with student
alcohol consumption,
14–15, 75, 220,
255–256
construction projects, 67
criticism of presidential
search, 5–6
denial of tenure for
Michael Gilbert, 150
description of
institutional strengths,
163
diversity concerns, 24
Divinity School, 96
electrical substation
project, 263–264
exchange programs, 111,
313
faculty compensation,
146, 334
financial campaigns,
23–24, 50, 51, 68, 136,
308–310, 387, 389
first Student Government
State of the University
address, 243
first-year seminars, 229
focus on administrative
planning, 59
founding of Leadership
Winston-Salem, 10
Freshman Evenings, 200
Gilbert and Sullivan Gala
in honor of, 387

goal for Wake Forest to
remain in upper tier
of private institutions,
268–269
Graylyn restoration, 16–17
Heritage and Promise
Campaign, 136
Honoring the Promise
Campaign, 306–307,
389
inauguration, 3–5
intentions to renovate and
rebuild, 48–49
interest in student
opinions, 139–140
intolerance for foul
language in sports, 166
on investment in School
of Law, 8
J. Paul Sticht Center on
Aging, 96
landscaping plans,108
letters to Nancy Susan
Reynolds, 23
library renovation, 135
lunch-counter sit-in
anniversary, 338–339
maintenance of Calvin
Jones House, 226
market value of
endowment in 2000,
324
member of North
Carolina Standards
and Accountability
Commission, 181
minority enrollment, 169
Moby Dick Marathon,
259
name change for Bowman
Gray School of
Medicine, 251–252
negotiations for new
coliseum, 61
North Carolina Presidents'
Summit on Alcohol Use
& Abuse, 379
North Carolina public
transportation
commission, 217

personal life, 140–141
Piedmont Research Park expansion, 363
planning subcommittee for NCAA Committee on Integrity and Intercollegiate Athletics, 182
portrait of James Ralph Scales, 59
praise of Catherine T. Harris for Orientation Committee participation, 126
praise of James Ralph Scales , "Scales Improved University," 227
praise of Joseph Milner for Writing Project participation, 126
Presidential Aides program, 101
Presidential Debate of 1988, 89, 91
Presidential Debate of 2000, 306
Presidents' Leadership Conference, 81
promoting diversity, 75
Proposition 42, 97
Race Relations Committee, 65–66, 201
reaction to anti-Semitic brochure, 298
recycling initiatives, 154
resignation of Charles Talbert, 214
respect for sexual orientation in community, 159
response to criticism of athletics, 62
retirement, 290, 387
review of faculty member performance, 161
review of judicial system, 118
Reynolda Campus development, 322

RJR Nabisco donation of corporate headquarters building, 55–56
role in bringing PepsiCo facility to Winston-Salem, 162
ROTC program, 215–216
Safe Roads Act ceremony, 258–259
sale of Wake Forest merchandise at airport, 343
sesquicentennial experiences, 7
setup of Academic Council, 44–45
setup of athletic policy review, 46
signing Reynolda House agreement, 330
six-week study leave in 1995, 197
substance abuse programs, 65
Thomas K. Hearn Jr. Fund for Civic Responsibility, 176
To Dream with One Eye Open report, 175
Tree of Life Award, 130
tuition increases, 86
visits to faculty, 140
Wake Forest Health Sciences (WFHS), 330
Winston-Salem Business, Inc., 77, 96
work with student leaders, 14
Worrell Professional Center dedication, 172
Hearn, Will, 3
Heatley, Rick, 9, 77
Hedin, Robert, 143
Heflin, Howell, 3
Hegstrom, Roger, 215
Heim, Mary Elizabeth, 51
Helm, David, 171
Helm, Robert M., 3, 9, 43, 312
Helms, Allen, 182

Helms, Kristen, 223
Hemphill, Joshua, 380
Henderson, Donna, 351
Hendricks, Ed, 144, 149, 180, 372
Hendrix, Phil, 334
Henson, Larry, 128
Henson, Maria, 157, 158
Herbert, Robert A., 182
Herman, Stephen, 322
Herring, Emily, 22, 188
Herring, Owen F., 27
Hesmer, William, 375
Hester, Marcus, 1
Hight, Anna, 339
Hill, Alton M., 33, 77
Hill, S. Richardson, 3, 9
Hillman, Phoebe, 171
Hinshaw, Billy, 64
Hinson, Matt, 340, 362
Hinson, Yvonne, 319, 350, 3808, 393
Hinze, Willie, 215
Hipp, Clay, 216, 261, 286
Hoak, James M., Jr., 388
Hobbs, Dewey, 96
Holder, Carlos, 135, 140, 181
Holding, Frank, 365
Holland, Jennifer, 402
Holland, Rob, 321
Hollingsworth, Riley, 360
Holmes, Harold R., 78
    Dean of Student Services, 95
    Director of Career Placement and Planning, 77
    Kappa Alpha fraternity ruling, 321
    Provost search committee, 94
    Race Relations Committee, 129, 201
    subcommittee on equity, welfare, and sportsmanship, 397
    United Way Campaign, 120
Holzwarth, George M., 44

Holzwarth, Natalie, 44, 234
Honeycutt, Lori, 186
Hooks, Gene, 10, 45, 46, 114, 146, 147, 163–164, 182
Hoover, Jen, 294
Hope, C.C., 3, 5, 69, 162
Hopkins, Beth Norbrey, 3, 33, 65–66, 129
Hopkins, Lawrence David, 86
Hoppe, Betsy, 214, 291, 314
Horton, Alice K., 303, 383
Horton, Fred, 127, 161
Hottinger, Bill, 99
Houmand, Corey, 320, 340
House, Marian J., 149, 170
Houser, Stephanie, 14
Howard, Fred, 127, 196, 286
Howard, Josh, 355, 356, 375
Howards, Hugh, 360, 372
Hsu, Angel, 399
Hubbard, Russ, 202
Hubbard, Sarah, 361–362
Hubbard, Shari, 15
Hudgins, Scott, 255
Hudson, Margaret Elizabeth (Meg), 381
Hughes, John, 203, 231
Hughes, Michael, 328
Hughes, Willie, 255
Hull, William E., 6
Hume, Jon, 114, 117
Humphrey, Hubert B., Jr., 385
Hunt, Cashin, 83, 102, 128
Hunt, James B., 4
Hunt, Lauren, 261
Hunt, Mimi, 98
Hunter, Susan, 145
Hyde, Jeanette, 387
Hyde, Michael J., 195, 234, 329, 390

I

Imamura, Kikuko, 394
Ingram, Brett, 372, 392
Ireland, Ginny Bridges, 395
Irwin, Winston, 321
Iwata, Joanna, 198, 275, 320

J

Jackels, Charles F., 44
Jackman, John, 81
Jackson, Jen, 202
Jackson, Jessica, 338
Jackson, Sedrick, 272
Jackson, Tommy, 271, 354
Jaffe, Mordecai, 44
James, Joni L, 81
Janeway, Richard
  Chair of the Association of American Medical Colleges, 30
  clinical sciences building named in honor of, 246
  compensation package, 206
  discussions on health care with William F. Buckley, 180
  Distinguished Professor of Healthcare Management, 216
  Executive Dean and Chief Executive Officer, 45
  Executive Vice President for Health Affairs, 112
  Inauguration Committee, 3
  Medallion of Merit, 291
  Shigeyoshi Matsumae memorial service, 143
  Vice President for Health Affairs and Dean of the Bowman Gray School of Medicine, 9
Jarrett, Steve, 392
Jasper, Kevin, 291
Jeffries, Tom, 379
Jiang, Miaohua, 320
Johansson, Patricia, 9, 216, 238
Johns, David J., 27
Johnson, Brian, 96
Johnson, Dana, 145, 216, 237
Johnson, Dillon, 43
Johnson, Eve, 118
Johnson, Frank, 79–80
Johnson, F. Ross, 55–56

Johnson, Gerald, 2
Johnson, Jeannette, 50
Johnson, Michelle, 262, 283
Johnston, Ann A., 388
Johnston, Dillon, 42
Jones, Bradley, 314
Jones, Deidra, 142
Jones, Jennifer, 203
Jones, Joseph A., 332
Jones, Khalid, 298
Jones, Mary, 218
Jones, Paul, 362
Jordan, John, 118
Jordan, Jonathan, 117–118
Joseph, Craig, 183
Joyner, Bill
  administrative planning, 59
  Athletic Oversight Committee, 114
  athletic policy review, 46
  Baptist State Convention negotiations, 55
  budget reductions, 86
  divinity school committee, 96
  General Baptist Foundation's annual award for excellence, 45
  Inauguration Committee, 3
  Management Oversight Committee on Admissions, 77
  retirement and accomplishments, 236–237
  Vice President for University Relations, 9
Juras, Paul, 234, 311, 350, 373
Justice, John, 294

K

Kairoff, Claudia Thomas, 300
Kairoff, Peter, 92, 214, 257, 317, 337, 357
Kelley, Steve, 21
Kelly, Jonathan, 321, 338, 362

Kemp, Danny, 3735
Kemper, Hunter, 316
Kendall, David, 388
Kendall, Donald M., 342
Kennedy, Charles H. (Hank),
    127, 328
Kennedy, Charles R.
    (Chuck), Jr., 127, 141,
    145
Kennedy, George, 46
Kent, Jessica, 261
Kentner, Jeffrey W., 240
Kerlin, Sam O., 224
Kerr, William, 127
Kersh, Rogan, 15, 50
Kidd, Craig, 186
Kilebrew, Chad, 103
Kimball, Charles, 214–215,
    250, 253, 328, 349, 354
Kimball, Judd, 81
Kim-Shapiro, Daniel B., 349,
    391
Kincaid, Ingrid, 102
Kincaid, Tess Malis, 241
Kindel, A. J., 102
King, Eric, 375
King, Kerry M., 33, 113,
    181,335, 395
King, Llew Ann, 389
King, S. Bruce, 223, 286
King, Stan, 193
King, Wayne, 178, 283
Kirkman, Ellen, 212
Kiser, Paul, 61
Kite, Chris, 42, 43
Klein, Marjorie Sharon, 100
Klein, Scott, 195
Kletzin, Jenny A., 47, 64
Kline, Jacob, 299
Knetch, Will, 81
Knight, John Ruffin, 51
Knight, Lee, 350, 373
Knott, Lisa, 50
Knox, Ann M., 120
Kokulis, Christy, 64
Kondepudi, Dilip K., 141, 331
Kornegay, Horace, 190
Kralovich, Wendel, 319
Kraus, Janelle, 256, 273–274,
    293

Krishnan, Lakshmi, 398
Kron, Kathleen, 196, 312
Kuberski, Phillip, 195
Kuhn, Nancy, 389
Kuhn, Raymond, 44, 58, 215
Kuklick, Brian, 273
Kuretich, J.K., 316
Kuzmanovich, James, 124
Kyles, Scott, 119, 152

L

Lai, Mary Piette, 217
LaMastra, Steve, 64, 65, 68
Lambert, Charles, 149
Lambert, Deborah Dixon,
    389
Lambeth, Donna I., 4
Lamy, Robert E., 161
Lanane, Kim, 12
Laney, Elizabeth, 232
Langford, Jim, 54
Langwell, Kristin, 222
Lantz, Rocky, 149
LaRue, Rusty, 210, 218–219,
    227, 273
Latimer, Cameron, 403
Laughlin, Page, 179, 234
Lautemann, George, 16
Lawing, Barry, 316, 357
Lawler, Michael, 234
Lawrence, Ashleigh, 402
Lawson, Connie, 255
Lawson, Regina, 145, 265,
    385
Layman, Kyle, 402
Layton, Melvin, 301
Leach, John, 182
Leak, C. J., 273
Leake, Lu, 11
    Assistant Vice President
        for Administration and
        Planning, 10
    Award for Excellence in
        Advising, 179
    Campus Landscape
        Committee, 103
    Commission on the Status
        of Women at Wake
        Forest, 212–213

Dean of Summer School,
    77, 111
Divinity School
    committee, 74
interim registrar, 271
Medallion of Merit, 214
placement of educational
    markers on campus,
    119
retirement, 237
Leaman, Stacey, 186
Leary, Mark R., 110, 163,
    179, 215, 349, 390
LeCrone, Jon, 13
Lee, Dave, 223
Lee, Win-Chiat, 388, 389
Leggon, Cheryl, 178
Leighton, Jim, 31, 46
Lentz, Marty, 4
Leonard, Bill J.
    administration of Lilly
        Endowment, 332
    Baptist Ways: A History,
        372–373
    *Christianity in Appalachia:
        Profiles in Regional
        Pluralism*, 270
    Dean of Divinity School,
        209–210
    definition of school, 282
    fundraising, 283
    Provost Search
        Committee, 314
    symposium on life and
        legacy of Thomas
        Dixon Jr., 353
Leonard, Candyce, 267
Leonard, Julie, 272
LeRoy, Garnette "Dee"
    Hughes, 157
Levy, David, 14, 230–231,
    285, 311, 314
Levy, Kathryn, 6, 257
Lewis, Amanda, 198
Lewis, Bruce, 350, 373
Lewis, DeAnna, 261
Lewis, Jack, 114, 256
Lewis, Kayamma, 274
Lindemann, Dana, 360
Lineberry, Harvey L., 217

Link, Bryan, 272
Lisher, Erik, 202
Listokin, Ann, 233
Litcher, John, 116, 234, 271
Littlefield, Lindsay J., 339
Llewellyn, John, 331
Lloyd, Mary Ellen, 47
Locklair, Dan
    American Society of
        Composers, Authors,
        and Publishers award,
        254, 372
    Chamber Music CD, 391
    Christmas anthems, 295
    concerts, 254
    The *Fabric of Creation*
        inauguration anthem, 4
    Hinda Hongiman
        Composer's Cup, 43
    1996 American Guild of
        Organists Composer of
        the Year, 214
    1996 Centennial
        Convention of the
        American Guild of
        Organists (AGO), 236
    North Carolina Arts
        Council Artist
        Fellowship, 287
    "O Sing to the Lord a New
        Song", 350
    "Phoenix and Again," 6
    "Pilgrim's Lot," 317–318
    Since Dawn, 230
    Symphony of Seasons, 350
    "The Peace May Be
        Exchanged," 372
Logan, David, 234
Logan, Michael, 322
Long, L. Donald, Jr., 16
Longino, Charles F., Jr., 144,
    215, 235, 311, 391
Lord, Frank, 21
Lord, Kay, 21, 95, 118, 237
Lord, Michael, 372
Lorenz, Brianna, 275
LoRusso, Paul, 269, 290
Louden, Allan, 81, 92, 244,
    286, 307
Loughrey, Jennifer, 223

Lovejoy, Scott, 64–65
Lovett, Robert, 196, 258
Lubin, David M., 285, 350,
    390
Lucas, Nina, 312, 368
Lucy, Chris, 150
Ludwick, Karen, 380
Luter, Joseph W., III, 67, 85
Luther, K.A.N., 44
Lutz, Erin, 261
Lynch, Thomas Jack, 278

M

MacDougal, Mike, 272
Mackie, George C., 279
Maine, Barry G., 92, 187,
    234, 373, 388, 389
Manchester, Doug, 336, 342
Manchester, Elizabeth, 336,
    342
Mandel, Stanley W., 271
Mandelbaum, Allen, 109,
    127, 180, 270
Mann, Sam, 142
Manning, Elton, 226, 247
Manning, Mary Alice,
    244–245
Marcum, William, 373
Marks, Connie, 200
Martin, Bo, 119
Martin, Dale, 118, 144, 178,
    236, 271, 291, 373
Martin, Deborah, 10
Martin, James A., Jr., 214
Martin, Robert Lewis "Doc,"
    113
Martin, Zeno, Sr., 383
Maso de Moya, Trina, 289,
    293, 336
Mason, Martha, 358, 359,
    385
Mass, Aaron, 402
Masse, Billy, 98
Massey, Elaine, 12
Matthews, Eric "Rick," 388,
    389
Mattiace, Len, 42
Maynard, C. Douglas, 94,
    334, 388

McBride, George, 395
McCaffrey, Susan, 65–66
McConnell, David, 272
McCoy, Leah, 235
McCrary, Mike, 167
McCray, Gordon E., 271,
    275, 350, 388, 389
McDaniel, Jerome, 186, 205
McDonagh, Jan McQuere,
    68
McDonald, Mac, 167, 218,
    239
McGee, Sam, 194
McGhie, Melissa, 328
McGill, Darryl, 61
McGirr, Mary Beth, 42, 98
McGregor, Gilbert, 31, 62, 97
McHenry, Kathryn, 337
McKeon, Diane, 147
McKinley, Michael, 93–94,
    117, 133
McKinna, Jonathan Steven,
    265
McKinney, Horace A.
    "Bones," 92, 93
McKinnon, John, 95, 105,
    197
McKoy, Nick, 223
McLemore, John, 116
McManus, Denise, 374
McMillan, Jill, 361, 394
McMillan, Lewis, 34
McNally, Minta Aycock, 237,
    254, 314, 368, 384
McPherson, Dolly A., 127,
    144, 196, 312
McQueen, Derrick, 147
Mead, Jane, 241, 294, 328,
    331
Meador, Ann, 111
Meadows, Sarah, 102
Meads, Manson, 246
Medlin, John G., Jr., 10, 124,
    127, 272, 283
Melito, Mark, 219
Melson, Gordon, 144–145,
    146, 214, 315, 368
Memory, Jasper D., Jr., 6
Mendez, John, 101
Meroney, John, 170

Merritt, Carol, 316
Merritt, Maria, 12, 63–64, 69
Messer, Lori, 354
Messick, Chi-Chi, 254
Messick, Kendall, 358
Messier, Stephen, 271, 392
Meyer, Ray, 11
Meyers, Hiram A. "Bif," III, 51
Meyers, William K., 159, 196, 213
Michael, Geoffrey, 186, 223
Middaugh, Ken, 110, 352
Mihalko, Shannon, 312
Miller, Ashlee, 378
Miller, Chester "Chet," 388, 389
Miller, Henry S., Jr., 288
Miller, Kenneth D., 341
Miller, Marjorie, 5
Miller, Maurice, 167
Miller, Sheereen, 298
Millhouse, Barbara, 329
Mills, John Henry, 130, 167
Mills, Robert D., 45, 86, 95, 181, 205, 254
Milner, Joseph, 44, 126
Mitchell, Carlton, 74, 96
Mitchell, Lynda, 354
Mitchell, Marvin, 96, 146
Mitchell, Tucker, 46
Mitra, Ananda, 373, 391, 392
Moore, Harold Sims "Pete," 35, 103, 128, 129
Moore, Richard, 232
Moore, Sean, 376
Moorhouse, John C., 161, 215, 314
Moranda, Bobby, 272
Morgan, Bill, 34
Morgan, Reid, 67, 94, 95, 130, 290, 314, 354
Moricle, C. Hunter, 114
Morrell, Louis R., 217, 265, 278, 302
Morris, Leslie M., 273
Morris, Mariana, 110
Morrison, Tim, 61
Mory, Paul S., IV, 224
Moser, Donald "Buz," 290, 291, 377, 381

Moses, Carl C., 127
Moyer, Charles, 146, 238, 332, 352
Mozon, Almena Lowe, 157
Muday, Gloria K., 196, 234, 235, 363, 388, 389
Mukombe, Hattie, 370
Mullen, Thomas E., 50, 58, 94, 161, 181, 187, 190, 197
Mullins, Rodney, 96
Munn, Jordan, 338
Murphy, Charles, 275
Murphy, William, 402
Murray, Jessica, 261
Murray, Sonja H., 120, 155
Myers, Becky, 75
Myers, Richard, 74
Myers-Oakes, Barbee, 215

N

Najmi, Rosita, 338, 362, 381
Napier, Martha, 403
Ndiaye, Makhtar, 183
Neff, John, 329
Neill, Stephanie, 167–168, 182, 183, 226
Nesbitt, Ernie, 275
Newton, Isabel, 262
Nichols, J. Donald, 303
Nicholson, Terrell, 402
Nickles, Steve, 311
Nielsen, Linda, 8, 311, 351
Niven, Penelope, 155, 157, 230, 273
Nolan, Deborah A., 393
Norris, Lee, 354, 381
Northrup, Marjorie, 394
Novatny, Laura, 15
Numbers, Robert, II, 298, 320

O

Oakes, Barbee, 394
O'Brien, Joanne, 4, 14, 113, 177–178
O'Brien, Julie Myers, 157
Odom, David, 98, 105, 131, 147, 183, 192, 210, 217, 315, 325, 405

O'Flaherty, James C., 43
Ogle, Daniel, 272
O'Neil, Grace, 263
Opal, Charlotte Anne, 244
Orr, L. Glenn, 3, 25, 354, 365, 388, 395
Orser, Paul, 180, 190, 200, 201, 216
Overby, Gene, 37, 99
Overholt, Kenneth W., 181, 375
Overing, Gillian R., 93, 195
Overstreet, Tyler, 340, 362
Owens, Trelonnie, 193
Ownby, Scott, 153

P

Pace, Calvin, 356, 375
Page, Kimberly, 34
Palmer, Arnold, 124, 194, 406
Palmer, Mike, 12
Palmiter, Alan R., 179
Parent, Anthony, 234
Parker, Wilson, 178
Parkhurst, Michael, 375
Patel, Ajay, 312, 374
Patrick, Adele, 75
Patrick, Clarence H., 75
Patterson, Allen H. (Chip), 59
Patterson, Angie, 33
Patterson, Charlie, 13
Patterson, Perry, 159, 196, 260
Paul, Chris, 375, 376
Pawson, Katharine R., 22–23
Peacock, Peter R., 57, 127
Pearman, Roger, 84
Pearson, Willie, Jr., 74, 236, 312
Pecina, Adam, 376
Pecorella, Anthony, 340
Pedersen, Ralph D., 291
Peeples, Ralph, 179
Peil, Michael, 150, 185
Penney, Fiona, 232
Peral, Ricky, 211, 240
Perez, Elizabeth, 340
Perricone, Steve, 103

Perritt, Henry Franklin, III, 100–101, 225
Perry, Margaret, 11, 45, 65, 94, 152, 180, 271
Perry, Pauline Davis, 226, 278–279
Perry, Percival, 77
Perry, Stan, 101
Peters, James E., 37
Petersen, Mark, 376
Peverley, Evan, 220
Phillips, David, 374
Phillips, Elizabeth, 92, 141
Phillips, Thomas O., 34, 41, 250, 374–375
Philo, Laura, 198
Philpott, J. Robert, 40, 54
Pickel, John, 236
Pignatti, Terisio, 43, 109, 215
Pinder, Jonathan, 390
Pinyan, Clark, 152
Piscetille, Mike, 397
Plackemeier, Ryan, 375
Player, Roddey, 243
Plemmons, Robert J., 109, 215, 218–219
Plumridge, Scott, 261
Poe, Bill, 54
Poe, Melissa, 277, 328, 329
Poe-Kennedy, Shannon, 262
Pollard, Alton, III, 133, 142, 184
Poole, Thomas, 286
Poovey, Cherin, 96, 334, 354
Posner, Jessica, 299, 321
Poteat, William Louis, 39, 56
Potter, Lee, 144
Poulson, Zoe, 203
Powell, Amy, 277
Powell, James T., 214, 258, 368, 390
Powell, Mary, 131
Pratapus, Mike, 357
Prescott, Jeryl, 238
Presseren, Herman, 99
Pressley, Dolly Lynn, 203
Prestes, Brian, 231, 244, 245
Pretorius, Scott, 92
Price, Cecil D., 145, 203, 261, 355, 379
Price, Martin, 275

Prince, Brian, 98
Prince, Jeff, 98
Prince, Robert G., 77, 130, 145
Prince, Sean, 339
Pringle, Alan, 117
Proehl, Ricky, 113
Propst, H. Dean, 68
Prosser, Skip, 316, 317, 325, 355
Proulx, Maura, 339
Province, Martin, 79
Pruett, Andy, 320
Pruitt, Mark C., 62
Ptaszynski, James G., 127, 161
Pugh, Frances, 135
Pugh, Watson, 135
Purnsley, Ernie, 96

Q

Queen, Michael G., 283

R

Rackley, Sarah Holland, 262
Radomski, Teresa, 6, 57, 178, 187, 287, 317, 337, 387, 398
Ramsey, Allen, 162
Ramsey, Ryan, 362
Ranft, Annette Lytle, 286, 373
Rao, Nagesh, 328
Ray, Cecil, 3
Redmond, Mary Lynn, 391
Reece, Mark H., 10, 11, 33, 94, 101, 105, 214
Reid, A.C., 4, 43
Reif, Megan E., 203
Reinemund, Steven S., 342
Reinisch, Paul, 131
Rejeski, W. Jack, Jr., 44, 92, 235, 236, 368, 373
Rembielek, Rick, 396
Respess, Nancy, 271
Revels, Ruth, 394
Reyes, Alexandria J., 395
Reynolds, Edward, 134, 206
Reynolds, Nancy Susan, 23
Reynolds, Suzanne, 110, 196

Rhodes, Milton, 16
Ribisl, Paul, 94, 178, 312, 331
Rice, Leon, 3
Richards, C.H., 27
Richardson, Liz, 405
Richardson, Neal, 360
Richey, Evan, 335
Richman, Charles, 201, 390
Richwine, Jennifer, 309
Rimmer, Ron, 271
Rioux, Jennifer, 46, 61
Rives, Chip, 62, 63, 64, 78, 184
Roberts, Higdon C., Jr., 3
Roberts, Patricia J., 312
Roberts, Tom, 94
Robertson, Linda B., 44
Robin, Don, 311–312
Robinson, E. O'Neal, 238
Robinson, Mary Francis, 75
Robinson, Stephen B., 223, 320
Rodgers, Bobby, 219
Rodriguez, Daisy, 394
Rodwell, Nancy, 226
Rodwell, Rebecca, 226
Rodwell, Roy O., Jr., 226
Roebuck, Vivian, 103
Roehm, Michelle, 372
Rogan, Randy, 235
Rogers, Guy C., 15
Rogers, Rodney, 131, 132, 147, 166, 193
Rollfinke, Brian, 15
Romeo, Natascha, 128, 180
Rose, Charles P., Jr., 110, 244, 388, 389
Rose, Simone, 390
Roser, Harold "Hal," 343
Roser, Rita, 343
Roy, Leah, 374
Ruebel, Noel, 336
Ruiz, Christine, 149
Runyan, Nicole, 222
Rush, Matthews, 178

S

Sanchez, Joseph C., 80, 111, 145
Sanford, Terry, 3

Sawkiw, Warren, 131
Sawyer, Jack, 97
Scales, Betty, 37
Scales, James Ralph
 death of, 227
 Ecumenical Institute's
  Cuthbert E. Allen
  Award, 28
 inauguration of Hearn,
  4–5
 similarities between
  Hearn and, 1–2
 Worrell Professor of
  Anglo-American
  studies, 9
 Year of the Arts dedicated
  to memory of, 230
Scarlett, John D., 8, 10, 76,
 96
Schafer, Marianna, 12
Schiller, Brian, 320
Schippers, Tina, 243
Schirillo, James, 312
Schneider, Scott, 47
Schooler, Larry, 314
Schoonmaker, Donald O.
 concern over focus of
  Wake Forest, 140
 criticism of presidential
  search, 5
 death of, 143
 English Romanticism:
  Preludes and Postulates
  project, 161
 posthumous Faculty
  Award for Community
  Service, 179
 Race Relations
  Committee, 65–66
 support of Hearn's reform
  efforts, 130
Schoonover, Ben, 114, 131
Schumacher, Sally J., 43
Schurmeier, Mark, 327
Schweitzer-Bennett, Annie,
 355
Sears, Richard, 30, 290–291,
 328, 333
Secrest, Marion, 63
Seelbinder, Ben M., 95

Seely, Heather, 320
Sekhon, Joti, 394
Sellner, Timothy E., 43
Shah, Mitesh Bharat, 388
Shapere, Dudley, 28, 44, 160,
 215
Shapiro, Sidney A., 373
Shaw, Bynum, 58, 74, 144,
 147, 161, 178, 226
Shaw, Charlotte, 161
Shaw, Kurt, 234
Shearin, Kaye, 12
Shelton, Lillian, 255
Shepard, Bobby, 244
Shepherd, Noel, 395, 397
Sherman, Marie, 335
Sherman, Warren, 199
Shirley, Franklin R., 8
Shively, Robert W., 10, 76
Shlikas, Ed, 260
Shock, Jackie, 339
Shoesmith, Gary L., 161, 235
Shore, Bert L., 2, 86
Shores, David, 161
Shores, Lori, 220
Shortall, Jessica Jackson, 299
Shumaker, Sally, 312, 314,
 391
Sides, Bill, 198, 201, 363
Sidone, Paul B., 117, 132
Sievers, Gary, 336
Sigal, Gail, 196
Silman, Miles, 372, 373
Silver, Wayne, 44, 313
Silversten, Matt, 310
Simmons, Evabelle, 158
Simonelli, Jeanne, 287
Simons, Jim, 218
Sink, A. Alex, 51, 190, 303
Sisco, Nathan, 336
Sisson, Donna, 64–65
Slater, Thomas, 298
Sleeth, Kyle, 373
Smiley, David, 29, 30, 111,
 144
Smith, Brick, 218
Smith, Carolyn, 14
Smith, Chris, 96
Smith, Earl, 234, 236, 311, 401
Smith, Jessie Lee, 400

Smith, J. Howell, 9, 93
Smith, J. Matthew, 149, 150,
 171
Smith, Kathy, 298, 307
Smith, K. Wayne, 75, 323,
 388, 389
Smith, Margaret Supplee, 8,
 65–66, 74, 75, 179–180,
 209, 285
Smith, Michael, 72, 87, 91,
 94, 103
Smith, Ross, 81, 127, 159,
 222, 244, 254, 352, 353
Smith, Scott, 171
Smith, Wayne, 101,
Smith, Wayne, Jr., 253
Smith-Deering, Patricia, 158
Smunt, Timothy, 390
Snyder, Jim, 47
Snyder, Tim, 272
Somerville, Monica, 370
Songaila, Darius, 316, 318
Sonnenfeld, Kirk, 319
Sorensen, Robin M., 314
Sorrell, Jeanette, 15
Spargur, John, 244
Spellers, Stephanie, 116, 136,
 150
Spence, Shannan, 64
Spinks, W. Robert, 113, 154,
 181
Squires, J. Drew, 186
Staak, Robert, 45, 61, 98
Stamey, William Keith, 342
Starling,William G. (Bill),
 24, 100, 272, 315, 316,
 325, 343, 344
Steinberg, Jennifer, 232
Stevens, William, 339
Stewart, Loraine, 201
Stewart, Yvonne, 291
Stokes, Henry B., 113
Stokes, L. Wade, 255, 283
Stoltz, Ed, 48
Stone, James Thomas, 388
Straub, Tim, 42, 98
Stroupe, Margaret Elizabeth
 (Beth), 223–224, 233,
 244
Stroupe, Henry S., 10, 30, 253

Stubbs, Scott, 133
Stuckey, J. Ken, 185
Sugden, Dorothy A. "Dot," 271
Sullivan, Patrick, 290
Surface, Eric, 150
Sutton, Lynn, 375
Sutton, Mary Elizabeth, 47
Swann, Amos, 279
Swanson, Nolan, 257
Swicegood, Judy, 395
Swofford, Robert, 271

T

Tacy, Carl, 11, 45, 46, 61
Talbert, Charles, 74, 214, 215
Taplin, Ian, 178, 391
Tarrant, Wayne, 186
Tart, Hunter, 223
Taylor, Betsy, 354
Taylor, Crystal, 340
Taylor, Gardner Calvin, 74
Taylor, Gerald, 350
Taylor, James, 26
Taylor, Mary Ann Hampton,
    83, 128–129, 145, 279,
    350, 388
Taylor, Thomas C., 76–77,
    92, 94, 127, 145, 370
Tedford, Harold, 22, 127, 148
Tedford, Rosalind, 133
Telfer, Janice, 50
Thacker, Paul, 394
Thomas, Claudia N.
    Associate Dean of the
        College, 216
    Committee to Implement
        the Report on the
        Status of Women,
        238–239, 313
    program planning
        committee, 178
    published books, 195
    Reid-Doyle Prize for
        Excellence in Teaching,
        161
    undergraduate
        curriculum review,
        233–234, 270
Thomas, Jack, 265

Thomas, Ramsay, 12
Thomas, Stan, 58
Thompson, Derrick, 320
Thompson, Emerson (Em),
    III, 47
Thompson, James N., 180,
    238, 334
Thompson, Wayne, 217, 255
Thrower, Shelia, 335
Tillett, Anne S., 110
Timanus, Eddie, 303
Titus, Harry, 283, 389
Toler, Maria, 320
Tower, Ralph, 271
Trammell, Alan, 321
Trautwein, Barbara, 79
Trautwein, George, 99, 111
Tribble, Harold, 52, 123
Trible, Phyllis, 270, 282
Tripp, Wykesha, 203
Tucker, Anthony, 99
Tupper, Frank, 270
Turner, Chris, 198, 239
Turner, George Todd, 169,
    185, 388
Twiggs, Howard, 365
Tyson, Ted, 81

U

Upchurch, Beth Perry, 157
Upchurch, David, 149, 152
Upchurch, Robert, 178
Utley, Robert L., Jr., 27, 44
Uzwiak, Brian J., 200, 202,
    220

V

Van Camp, James R., 188
Van Der Sluys, Cherie, 187
Van Pelt, David, 12
Van Veen, Ricky, 321, 362
Vaz, Rosalind M., 44
Vermillion, Joy, 220, 243
Vesely, Alex, 371
Vidovich, Jay, 198
Von Herbulis, Jessica, 320
Voorhees, Kyle, 340
Vredenburg, Mike, 362

W

Waddill, David, 196
Waddill, Marcellus, 74, 127,
    196
Waddill, Shirley, 196
Wade, Emily, 275
Wade, Ernest, 30, 65–66,
    100, 133–134, 146
Wagner, Kyle, 219
Wagster, John W., 388
Walker, Allie, 402
Walker, Barbara, 294, 389
Walker, Cheryl V., 254, 272
Walker, Douglas Clyde
    "Peahead," 113
Walker, George K., 328
Walker, Laura, 14
Waller, Doug, 328
Walls, Neal, 351
Walsh, Robert K., 95, 96,
    105, 136, 195, 279, 396
Ward, Linda, 238, 314
Ware, Michele S., 253
Warshauer, Phil, 12
Washam, Liz, 316
Watts, Sarah, 110, 159, 288,
    372, 390
Wayne, Julie, 373
Wayne-Thomas, Mary, 287
Weatherly, Royce R., 104
Weathers, Carroll, 279
Weaver, David, 209, 234
Webb, Rod, 1520
Webb, Ty, 322
Weber, Charlotte C., 285
Weber, Sam, 270
Weigl, Peter D., 161, 370
Weiskopf, Jill, 152, 179, 185
Welker, Mark E., 178, 179,
    331, 349, 374, 395
Wellman, Ron, 164–165,
    356
Wells, William, 251, 252,
    315
Welsh, Helga, 196, 235
Welsh, James G. (Jim), Jr.,
    59, 95
West, Ken, 31
West, Larry, 214, 283

West, G. Page III, 236, 321, 350, 373

Weston, Joel A., 51

Whalen, Dave, 272

Whaples, Robert, 244

White, Jeremiah, 375, 376

White, Michael, 362

Whitehead, Lloyd, 254

Whitman, Jeanne P., 96

Whitmire, John, 194

Whitt, Monroe C., 128, 181

Whittington, Stephen L., 354

Wiethaus, Ulrike, 333, 371, 394

Wilbanks, Paige, 270

Wiles, Tammy, 272

Wilkerson, Jack E., Jr., 161, 237, 238, 382

Willard, John G., 9, 10, 24, 77, 85, 95, 120, 173, 181, 190

Willhoit, David, 340

Williams, Alan, 405

Williams, Anthony, 130

Williams, Christy, 357

Williams, George (Jack), Jr., 127

Williams, John, 143, 215

Williams, Karen, 64–65

Williams, Richard T., 27, 28, 44, 215

Williams, Tycely, 245

Williamson, D. Brent, 169, 185

Williamson, Janet, 355

Williamson, Kelly, 402

Williamson, Sam, 336

Willingham, Jonathan, 327

Wilson, Ed, 10
  administrative planning, 59
  Athletic Oversight Committee, 114
  athletic policy review, 46
  change of administrative role, 94
  decision to stay on with Hearn, 9

Distinguished Alumni Award, 190

Divinity School committee, 74, 96

faculty representative, 97

Freshman Evenings, 200

Heritage and Promise Campaign, 195

Inauguration Committee, 4

Management Oversight Committee on Admissions, 77

Medallion of Merit, 372

NCAA certification steering committee, 182

North Carolina Award, 351

Office of International Studies, 30

Omicron Delta Kappa Award for Contributions to Student Life, 110

Philomathesian Society, 186

presidential search committee, 388

presidential transition committee, 389

provost search committee, 314

race relations committee, 65

reading of *Breath: Life in the Rhythm of an Iron Lung*, 358

retirement, 105, 181

Senior Vice President, 250, 251

"Unrivaled by Any" address, 297

Vice President for Special Projects, 124

Visions and Dreams, 22

Wilson Wing of Z. Smith Reynolds Library dedication, 108, 141

Wilson, Ed, Jr., 303

Wilson, Emily Herring, 188, 285

Wilson, Gregory, 259

Wilson, James, 352

Wilson, J. Tylee, 3, 10, 21, 30, 84, 104, 161

Wilson, Marian, 335

Wingfield, Will, 339, 362

Wininger, Stephan, 182

Witzl, Maia, 231–232, 248, 277, 321, 359

Wolfe, Donald H., 22, 287

Womack, Hu, 395

Wood, Brent, 33

Wood, John, 44, 215

Wood, Martha Swain, 157

Wood, Pia, 290, 379

Wood, Ralph C., 29, 92, 127, 143, 234

Woodall, Emily, 275

Woodall, J. Ned, 44

Woodard, John R., 335

Woodruff, Jay, 169

Woods, Kevin, 298

Word, Emily, 339

Workmon, Bob, 289

Worrell, Anne, 135–136

Worrell, Eugene, 135–136

Wright, Ron, 214

Y

Yandell, Anne, 238

Young, C. Jeffrey, 303

Young, Jennifer, 48

Young, J. Smith, 73, 383–384

Yu, Cristina, 297

Z

Zabel, Amanda, 118

Zeyl, Clifford, 372

Zick, Kenneth A.
  Associate Dean of Internal Affairs, 26
  creation of Shorty's café, 132
  Crisis Response Team, 130

divinity school committee, 74
Philomathesian Society, 202
review of judicial system, 118
study of athletics program, 396
study of campus climate for gay students, 260, 288
transition of Wake Forest societies into national sororities, 177–178
University Security, 181
Vice President for Student Life and Instructional Resources, 77, 93, 107
Wake Forest Emergency Response Team, 261
Zinn, Jeff, 239
Zipple, Kristin, 339
Zuber, Isabel, 188

Made in United States
Cleveland, OH
16 December 2024

11904826R20380